Classical Myths and Legends in the Middle Ages and Renaissance

Classical Myths and Legends in the Middle Ages and Renaissance

A Dictionary of Allegorical Meanings

H. David Brumble

Greenwood Press
Westport, Connecticut

Library of Congress Cataloging-in-Publication Data

Brumble, H. David.
   Classical myths and legends in the Middle Ages and Renaissance : a
dictionary of allegorical meanings / H. David Brumble.
      p.   cm.
   Includes bibliographical references and index.
   ISBN 0–313–29451–8 (alk. paper)
      1. Literature, Medieval—Dictionaries.   2. European literature—
Renaissance, 1450–1600, —Dictionaries.   3. Myth in literature—
Dictionaries.   4. Legends in literature—Dictionaries.   I. Title.
PN669.B78   1998
809′.02′03—DC21   96–53527

British Library Cataloguing in Publication Data is available.

Library of Congress Catalog Card Number: 96–53527
ISBN: 0–313–29451–8

First published in 1998

Greenwood Press, 88 Post Road West, Westport, CT 06881
An imprint of Greenwood Publishing Group, Inc.

Printed in the United States of America

The paper used in this book complies with the
Permanent Paper Standard issued by the National
Information Standards Organization (Z39.48–1984).

10 9 8 7 6 5 4 3 2 1

Copyright Acknowledgments

For my father, Herbert D. Brumble,
and
Lizzie and Jonathan

Contents

Photo essay appears following page 203.

Illustrations

Fig. 1. *The Fray of Cupid and Apollo, with All the Gods Present*, engraving after Baccio Bandinelli (1545), Paris, Louvre (*Cabinet des Estampes*).

Fig. 2. Title page for Alexander Ross, *Mystagogus Poeticus, or The Muses Interpreter* (London, 1648). Beinecke Library, Yale Univ.

Fig. 3. *Aristotle and Phyllis*, Master of the Amsterdam Cabinet (c. 1488), drypoint, Coburg, Veste Coburg.

Fig. 4. *Aristotle and Phyllis*, Aquamanile (c. 1400), bronze, New York, Metropolitan Museum of Art, Robert Lehman, 1975 (1975.1.1416).

Fig. 5. *The Fair at Hoboken*, Peter Bruegel the Elder (c. 1559), engraving, Brussels, Bibliothèque royale Albert Ier (Cabinet des Estampes).

Fig. 6. *Pallas and the Centaur* (c. 1482), Sandro Botticelli, Florence, Galleria degli Uffizi.

Fig. 7. Book 2, Emblem 4, in Frances Quarles, *Emblemes* (Cambridge, 1643). Beinecke Library, Yale Univ.

Fig. 8. Title page for Jacob Cats, *Proteus, ofte Minne-beelden Verandert in Sinne-beelden* (Rotterdam, 1627). Newberry Library.

Fig. 9. *Cupid Unblindfolding Himself* (c. 1525-1530), Lucas Cranach the Elder, Philadelphia, Philadelphia Museum of Art.

Fig. 10. *St. Luke Portraying the Virgin* (1532), Maerten van Heemskerck, Haarlem, Frans Hals Museum.

Fig. 11. Title page for Sir Walter Raleigh, *The History of the World* (London, 1614). Beinecke Library, Yale Univ.

Fig. 12. *Wild Family* (1480), anonymous Netherlandish artist, engraving, Paris, Louvre (*Cabinet des Estampes*), E. de Rothschild collection (inventory number 288 LR).

Fig. 13. *Primavera* (c. 1484), Sandro Botticelli, Florence, Galleria degli Uffizi.

Preface

The classics bestowed upon Medieval and Renaissance Christians a rich legacy of myth and legend. This *Dictionary* brings together in convenient form the varied allegorical meanings these figures accrued over the centuries.

WHAT YOU'LL FIND IN THIS DICTIONARY

1. This *Dictionary* concentrates on material from the early Middle Ages to Milton; however, most entries cite classical sources as well, for necessary background.

Since the allegorical traditions traced here were widespread, quotations are taken from material in English, Latin, Greek, Italian, French, Dutch, German, and Spanish. Since I hope to encourage nonspecialists to interest themselves in mythic allegory, every quotation appears in English. Translations are mine unless otherwise noted.

2. For the most part, this *Dictionary* confines itself to the gods, goddesses, heroes, heroines, and places of classical myth. But I do occasionally include such figures of legend as Roman Lucretia—and even the legendary aspects of such persons as Virgil and Aristotle.

3. This is a dictionary, and so, like most dictionaries, it tries to avoid idiosyncratic meanings. Alexander Ross, for example, writes in his *Mystagogus Poeticus* (1648) that Danae, to whom lusty Jupiter came in a shower of gold, is a figure for "Learning; which by Acrisius the Scholar, or Learned man, is hid and shut up in the Tower of his Brain till Jupiter, or some rich and potent man, by gifts and rewards court her, aid, cherish and excite her" (90). Ross's yearning is nearly

palpable; he wants a Jupiter, a rich man, a patron to shower gold upon *him*. Ross feels this interpretation keenly. But deeply as I sympathize with Ross in his scholarly poverty, I do not cite this bit of allegory, because it is idiosyncratic. It is not a part of any particular interpretive tradition. Ross's allegory is unlikely to help us to understand anyone else's figurative use of Danae.

The same principle guided my selection of mythic figures. In general, I include only those for whom I can identify specific allegorical *traditions* of meaning. I include Orpheus, for example, not just because church fathers, poets, mythographers, and artists all made figurative use of him—but because it is possible to discern traditions of allegorical interpretation.

I have little to say about Philoctetes, for example. Philoctetes was heir to Hercules' bow and arrows, and he shot Paris with one of these arrows in the late stages of the Trojan War. Philoctetes was important to the ancients. Aeschylus, Sophocles, and Euripides all wrote plays about him[1]—but Medieval and Renaissance Christians seldom mentioned Philoctetes. The *Ovide Moralisé* (12.1495-1506, 13.1336-1441) retells the story, as does Thomas Cooper's *Dictionary* (under *Philoctetes*), very briefly. The mythographer George Sandys (*Ovid*: 604) mentions him in passing. Neither Cooper nor Sandys refers to any figurative meaning for Philoctetes. Spenser refers indirectly to him (see **AESCULAPIUS**). Chaucer, Botticelli, Titian, Shakespeare—none of them refer to Philoctetes at all. I might, of course, have missed some references to Philoctetes, but I am confident modern readers of Medieval and Renaissance literature will only rarely have occasion to look up Philoctetes.[2] And so I do not include Philoctetes.

For another example, Laocoön, caught as he was in the toils of a serpent while striving against the will of Minerva, would seem a perfect platform for Christian allegory. But in fact Christian writers paid him little attention. The interest of painters, on the other hand, was quickened by the discovery in 1506 of the famous late-Hellenistic statue of Laocoön and his sons beset by the serpents: El Greco's only mythological painting was of Laocoön, and we see a recollection of the statue's Laocoön in Titian's painting of *Bacchus and Ariadne* (Saxl 1970: 75, 125). Doubtless there is meaning in these images. But the meanings are not sufficiently certain, I think, to make for useful citations in a dictionary. And so I neglect Laocoön.

Another example: I neglect Priam. Priam was well known; everyone who knew the story of Troy knew about Priam, but Priam did not acquire allegorical habiliments, as did Helen and Paris. As we read Petrarch or Spenser, what we need to know about Priam is the *stories* in which he appears, and these stories we can find in a classical dictionary. In general, I do not include figures who did not generate at least one fairly well known allegorical tradition.

This *Dictionary* does not pretend to be comprehensive. One glance at the number of sources in the Bibliography should suggest the remarkable number and the range of authors who participated in these traditions—and this Bibliography could easily have been doubled. There is, quite simply, more myth allegory than a single volume can comprehend.

I do, however, try to suggest just which traditions were current at what time. I want readers who come upon Actaeon while reading Shakespeare to be able to find out what range of meanings were current for *Actaeon* in the time of Shakespeare, in the same way that one might go to the *Oxford English Dictionary* to find out whether the word *nice* had its modern meaning in the time of Jane Austen. I sometimes suggest who influenced whom and where certain stories and allegories originate, but the main purpose of this *Dictionary* is to provide a guide to conventional meanings, not literary genetics.

THE ORGANIZATION OF THE DICTIONARY

Often mythic figures generated more than one allegorical meaning. In general, this *Dictionary* presents these meanings—each allegorical tradition—in chronological order. I do, however, sometimes deviate from chronological order for the sake of clarity. In any case, dates for each author are given in the Bibliography, and the list of illustrations dates each work of art.

Many figures who have not been treated in a separate article are easily accessible through the Index. The fratricidal Theban princes Eteocles and Polynices, for example, are discussed under **THEBES**; Cacus is treated under **HERCULES**; and so forth.

NAMES

In general, the names I use for gods, goddesses, and the rest are the names that were most commonly used during the Middle Ages and the Renaissance. Usually, this means that the Roman names are used rather than the Greek: Venus rather than Aphrodite, then, and Juno rather than Hera. There are exceptions, however. Uranus (Greek), for example, was better known than Caelus (Latin). Medieval and Renaissance writers made no fetish of consistency in these matters. And neither do I. It is sometimes awkward to speak of Jupiter, for example, immediately after a quotation that refers to Zeus. I leave it to the Index to sort out the inevitable problems.

ACKNOWLEDGMENTS

I feel a particular debt to those who have taken such pains to make mythographic texts available. Thomas Munckerus put together a collection of Latin mythographies in 1681; G. H. Bode gave the world the three "Vatican Mythographers" in 1834. Stephen Orgel's modern series of facsimile reprints with Garland Press has been an on-going wonder. And then there are all the scholars who have taken the trouble to produce illuminating translations of difficult books:

Wetherbee's Bernardus, Whitbread's Fulgentius, Michael J.B. Allen's Ficino, Jones' *Chess of Love* commentary, Schreiber and Maresca's Bernardus, and many others. These scholars have increased the audience and the appetite for mythic allegory well beyond what I had thought was possible.

More personal thanks go to colleagues who have helped me with this study: Lynette Black, Robert Evans, Bob Gale, Melinda Hegarty, Dennis Looney, Frances Malpezzi, James Nohrnberg, Paul Olson, Michael West, Les Whipp, Ann Wilkins, and David Wilkins.

I have been aided by grants from Pitt's College of Arts and Sciences and a Pitt Faculty Grant. I wish to express gratitude as well to the libraries and librarians who make such work possible. I am particularly grateful to the University of Pittsburgh libraries, the Yale University libraries, and the Newberry Library.

Finally, let me thank Connie Way, who has patiently labored to convert all of this into camera-ready copy.

Abbreviations

AH	*Art History*
AnA	*Antike und Abenland*
BM	*Burlington Magazine*
ChauR	*Chaucer Review*
ClasQ	*Classical Quarterly*
CLS	*Comparative Literature Studies*
CQ	*Critical Quarterly*
CR	*Cambridge Review*
ELH	*English Literary History*
ELR	*English Literary Renaissance*
Emblematica	*Emblematica: An Interdisciplinary Journal of Emblem Studies*
FrF	*French Forum*
Florilegium	*Florilegium: Carleton University Annual Papers on Late Antiquity and the Middle Ages*
Hispania	*Hispania*
HLQ	*Huntington Library Quarterly*
ICNLS	*International Congress of Neo-Latin Studies*
Italianist	*Italianist*
JEGP	*Journal of English and Germanic Philology*
JHP	*Journal of Hispanic Philology*
JMRS	*Journal of Medieval and Renaissance Studies*
JWCI	*Journal of the Warburg and Courtauld Institutes*
LD	*Lectura Dantis*
Mediaevalia	*Mediaevalia: A Journal of Mediaeval Studies*
MH	*Medievalia et Humanistica*
MiltonS	*Milton Studies*
MLN	*Modern Language Notes*

MLQ	*Modern Language Quarterly*
MP	*Modern Philology*
MRTS	*Medieval and Renaissance Texts and Studies*
MS	*Medieval Studies*
Neophil	*Neophilologus*
NQ	*Notes and Queries*
NYRB	*New York Review of Books*
PL	*Patrologia Latina*
RB	*Revue biblique*
RES	*Review of English Studies*
RQ	*Renaissance Quarterly*
RS	*Renaissance Studies*
SAC	*Studies in the Age of Chaucer*
SAR	*South Atlantic Review*
SCJ	*Sixteenth Century Journal*
SEL	*Studies in English Literature*
ShakS	*Shakespeare Studies*
SI	*Studies in Iconography*
Simiolus	*Simiolus*
SL	*Spiegel der Letteren*
SP	*Studies in Philology*
Speculum	*Speculum*
SQ	*Shakespeare Quarterly*
SRen	*Studies in the Renaissance*
SSF	*Studies in Short Fiction*
SSt	*Spenser Studies*
Traditio	*Traditio*
TSLL	*Texas Studies in Language and Literature*
UCrow	*Upstart Crow: A Shakespeare Journal*

Introduction

THE NATURE OF ALLEGORY

George Puttenham, writing in 1589, defined allegory as that form of expression in which "we speake one thing and thinke another, and that our wordes and our meanings meete not" (*Art of English Poesy*). Puttenham's example is Plato's *Republic*, which "speakes" of a cave, and a fire, and people looking at shadows cast upon the wall of the cave—but according to Puttenham, these are merely the "wordes," the literal surface. Plato's "meanings" have to do with human reluctance to turn from what only *seems* to be real (the shadows) to what is really real (the fire).

It is difficult to say when Western poets and artists began to work allegorically. Homer is probably thinking allegorically as he describes the gathering battle:

> And Terror drove them, and Fear, and Hate whose wrath is relentless,
> she the sister and companion of murderous Ares,
> she who is only a little thing at the first, but thereafter
> grows until she strides on the earth with her head striking heaven.
> (*Iliad*: 4.440-443)

There are other passages, too, which Homer might have intended allegorically. But whatever Homer's intentions may have been, allegorical *interpretation* of Homer predominated from Heraclitus in the first century A.D. down to the seventeenth century. Virgil, Ovid, and other ancient writers were also interpreted allegorically. Servius (c. 400), Fulgentius[3] (sixth century), Bernardus Silvestris[4] (twelfth century), and Cristoforo Landino (fifteenth century) were among the most important allegorizing interpreters of Virgil's *Aeneid*. Allegorical interpreters of Ovid's *Metamorphoses* were legion[5]: Lactantius Placidus (sixth century), Arnolphe of Orléans (eleventh century), the *Ovide Moralisé* (fourteenth century), Berchorius (fourteenth century), George Sandys (1632), and Thomas Hall's *Wisdoms Conquest. or, An explanation and...Translation of the thirteenth Book of Ovids Metamorphoses* (1651)—to mention just a few.

We must remember that, if we want to understand Medieval and Renaissance art and literature in something like the way Medieval and Renaissance Christians themselves did, we must never wander far from allegory. Consider this passage from Erasmus (1466-1536), where he explains how a good Christian should look not just at art, but at the *world*:

it behooves us never to be idle, but by means of some appropriate analogy, to refer whatever assaults our senses either to the spiritual world or—a more serviceable procedure—to ethical values and that part of man which corresponds to the spiritual world....So it will come about that anything presenting itself to the senses at any time will become for you an occasion of righteousness. When this visible sun daily refreshes your physical eyes as it bathes the earth with new light, think immediately of...that joy of a pure mind illuminated by the radiance of God....Recollect...places in the Holy Scriptures where here and there the grace of the Holy Spirit is compared to light. If night seems dark and foreboding to you, imagine a soul deprived of divine radiance and darkened by sin....If physical beauty is pleasing to the eye, think how splendid is beauty of soul. If an ugly face seems disagreeable, remember how odious is a mind steeped in vice. (*Enchiridion*: 101-103)

Erasmus was the most popular writer of his day—and he is encouraging his readers to make a habit of looking at *everything* allegorically.

MYTH ALLEGORY: EGYPTIAN GOLD

Augustine's *On Christian Doctrine* is an important early document in the tradition that formed Erasmus's ideas. According to this book, allegory is a part of Christian doctrine. Augustine tells Christians how they ought to read the Bible, how they ought to "read" the world—and how they ought to read the pagans. When the pagans write things that can be read by the light of Christ, these pagans "should not be feared," Augustine writes:

rather, what they have said should be taken from them as from unjust possessors and converted to our use. Just as the Egyptians...had vases and ornaments of gold and silver and clothing which the Israelites took with them secretly when they fled, as if to put them to a better use. They did not do this on their own authority but at God's commandment, while the Egyptians unwittingly supplied them with things which they themselves did not use well. (2.40, referring to Exodus 3:22, 11:2, 12:35)

Poets, preachers, painters, cosmologists, mythographers, theologians—they all took Augustine at his word; they all took what they could from the pagans. And they came away with a staggering freight. To cite a single example, Chaucer used some 282 personal names derived from the Greek and Roman classics, everything from Achilles and Ariadne to Venus and Zephyr. In order to see this number in perspective, we might remember that Chaucer took only 84 names from the Bible, not a third so many.

We can understand many of Chaucer's, Botticelli's, Spenser's, and Milton's mythic figures simply by referring to a classical dictionary: Arion was a singer upon a lyre; he was on a ship when the sailors decided to throw him overboard to get his gold. Arion begged lèave to sing one last song and then threw himself into the sea, trusting to Apollo, the god of singers. A dolphin came and bore Arion on his back to Corinth. This is the sort of thing that one could find in any dictionary of classical mythology; and this is enough to make sense, for example, of these lines from *Twelfth Night*. The good captain tells Viola of the wreck at sea:

> I saw your brother,
> Most provident in peril, bind himself,
> Courage and hope both teaching him the practice,
> To a strong mast that lived upon the sea;
> Where, like Arion on the dolphin's back,
> I saw him hold acquaintance with the waves
> So long as I could see. (1.2.11-17)

But some of those in Shakespeare's audience who would have known more than the mere story of Arion; some would have remembered Arion and his spellbinding music as an allegorical figure for the ordering principle of the universe, the divinely instituted harmony. They might have remembered this as they watched Orsino, Olivia, Toby Belch, Viola, and the rest tumbling into their little temporary slice of chaos. Allegory works this way. For another example, early in *The Faerie Queene* the Red Cross Knight loses his way in the Wood of Error. Spenser calls this wood a "labyrinth" (1.1.11). Now, this describes well the kind of thick, dark forest in which one could be hopelessly lost. But some of Spenser's readers would have been aware of the thousand-year-old tradition in which the labyrinth was an allegorical figure for the world in the theological sense—that place of temptations and dark turnings where Christians can so easily lose their way.

This *Dictionary* is designed to make a wide range of such meanings available to the modern reader. For as Panofsky, Seznec, Wind, Robertson, Don C. Allen, Nohrnberg, and others have shown us, even a very good classical dictionary will be inadequate—sometimes even misleading—for Medieval and Renaissance literature and art, because Achilles, Adonis, Bacchus, and Zephyr continued to lead active lives after the deaths of Virgil and Ovid. Achilles, Adonis, and the rest continued to accrue connotations, and allegorical and typological associations; sometimes they even found their way into new stories. Spenser read Medieval and Renaissance mythographers closely, closely enough sometimes to derive whole episodes from such allegorizing mythographies as Boccaccio's *Genealogia Deorum Gentillium* or from Natale Conti's *Mythologie*. To read Chaucer, Lydgate, Gower, Shakespeare, Milton, de Meun, to look at the paintings of Botticelli, Titian, and Cranach, without a sense of the meanings the myths accumulated is like reading *The Divine Comedy* or *Paradise Lost* without knowing what Christian tradition had added to the meaning of such words as *cross*, *fall*, *faith*, *dark*, and *light*.

What of Chaucer's 282 classical names? According to my count, close to half of them would not be adequately glossed by a good dictionary of classical antiquities. Such a dictionary would not tell us that Theseus was interpreted as a wisdom figure; as an example of perfect friendship, of the ideal ruler, of the unfaithful lover; as a type for God or Christ; as an allegorical figure for the balance of the active and contemplative lives. A dictionary of classical antiquities will not tell us that the Minotaur, the monster whose image we see on Theseus's standard ("Knight's Tale": 978-980), was interpreted as a figure for human bestiality; nor would a classical dictionary tell us that Medieval Christians could understand Theseus's killing of the Minotaur as a victory over the flesh or the devil. Most of Chaucer's readers would have known some of these traditions; the better read would have known them all.

THE KINDS OF MYTH ALLEGORY

I am using this old, old word *allegory* in its most inclusive sense,[6] and so I include allegory of all the following kinds:

Moral allegory: Mythic figures could stand for, personify, virtues, vices, states of mind, desires, inclinations. Venus, for example, could serve as a figure for libidinous desire, Minerva for reason, Diana for chastity.

Examples: Mythic and legendary figures were often used as examples (*exempla*) of one or another virtue or moral failing, as when Arachne was treated as an example of presumption, or Pyramus and Thisbe as examples of the dangers of unbridled passion.[7]   Very often the examples were *de casibus exempla*—examples of falls from good fortune. Boccaccio's *De Casibus virorum illustrium* was a whole book full of such examples; Chaucer's "Monk's Tale" is another such collection, the *Mirror for Magistrates* another.

Physical allegory, or nature, or cosmic allegory: Beginning with the Stoic philosophers, the gods were interpreted as representing elements of the natural universe.[8] Jupiter, for example, could be a figure for the fiery ether, Apollo the sun, or Venus the (morally neutral) generative impulse. Sometimes this allegory ascended beyond physical nature, as when Minerva was interpreted as the Mind of God.

Astrology: Venus, Mars, Jupiter, and others exerted powers and meant certain things in astrological terms. I do skimp on astrological meanings, because of the dauntingly good treatments of Medieval astrology by Kay (1994) and Wood (1970) and of Renaissance astrology by Richardson (1989); see also Gombrich (1993: 109-118).

Emblems: Properly speaking, an emblem should combine a picture, a motto, and a poem, to invite profound meditations on a single subject.[9] The gods are frequent inhabitants of the emblem books assembled by Wither, Alciati, Whitney, Peacham, van Veen, Quarles, and others.

Typology: Mythic figures could serve as types for Old or New Testament figures; Deucalion was a type of Noah, Hippolytus of Joseph; Theseus, Hercules, Orpheus, and many others served as types of Christ.

On the other hand, I seldom refer to the following interpretations of the myths:

Euhemerism: following Euhemerus, the Greek mythographer (c. 300 B.C.), the Medieval and Renaissance mythographers frequently explained the gods in terms of supposed human origins.[10] In this tradition Atlas, for example, was explained as having been originally a man named Atlas; this man was the discoverer of astrology—and so he came to be considered a god, specifically the god who holds the earth upon his shoulders. Saturn could be explained as a famous early king who reigned during the Golden Age, who then came to be remembered as a god.

I do not often mention Euhemerist interpretations, because the poets and artists very seldom made figurative use of Euhemerist traditions—popular though these traditions certainly were with the mythographers.

Historical (or topical) allegory: Here a mythic figure would personify a real person, usually a contemporary. Botticelli's mythic paintings refer (at one level of allegory) to members of the Medici family (Wind 1968: 112). From 1578 to 1582, for another example, the Duc d'Alençon courted Queen Elizabeth—a courtship that Lyly's *Sapho and Phao* treats allegorically: we are supposed to recognize Alençon in Phaon and Elizabeth in Sappho.[11] Endymion, in Lyly's *Endimion*, seems to have been the Earl of Leicester, hopelessly in love with chaste Cynthia-Elizabeth.[12] Spenser's *Shepheardes Calender* is full of intricate historical allegory.[13]

This kind of allegory was popular during the late Middle Ages and the Renaissance; but I seldom cite examples of such allegory, because we seldom find such allegory developing into a tradition.

MULTIPLE INTERPRETATION

In the introduction to his book of moral-allegorical commentary on Ovid's *Metamorphoses*, Berchorius lists the authorities he has consulted—Fulgentius, Rabanus, and Petrarch, among others—and then he assures us that he "separated the chaff from the wheat." that he "gathered the wheat into the storehouse for the praise and glory of the true God" (*Ovidius Moralizatus.* 36). This separation of the chaff from the wheat was not an easy matter. For Berchorius, the main criterion had to do with how well a certain allegorization might teach lessons of Christian morality and theology. Berchorius can thus allow himself allegorical flights that are idiosyncratic indeed—as in his comment on the story of Io, the beautiful maid whom Jupiter changed into a heifer to hide her from jealous Juno. According to Ovid, Io was eventually changed from a heifer back into a woman. Berchorius quotes these lines from Ovid's *Metamorphoses* (1.738-743): "The rough hair falls away from her body, her horns disappear, her great round eyes grow smaller....Though she has gained back her form she did not dare speak lest she moo like a heifer, and she was timid in trying her abandoned speech again." Then Berchorius provides the following interpretation: "It is useful for those who are newly converted to be silent lest they speak as heifers—that is carnal and indiscreet people" (147).

Now, the idea that Io's metamorphosis into a heifer suggested something about the carnality of her desires was quite common; but the notion that in not mooing, the de-metamorphosed Io represents bashful Christian converts—this is pure Berchorius. Berchorius felt himself free to invent such allegories with gusto. I, alas, must eschew such quirky inventions. But it is important for readers of this *Dictionary* to realize that Medieval and Renaissance Christians did not always feel themselves bound by interpretive traditions, however well these were known.

This hearty acceptance of idiosyncratic interpretation went hand in hand with Medieval and Renaissance readers' tendency to concentrate on detail. Berchorius's disquisition on Io's failure to moo may be idiosyncratic as an interpretation, but it is quite typical in its willingness to dwell upon the significance of what a modern reader might be forgiven for considering an insignificant detail. And this is a concentration on detail that can cheerfully disregard Ovid's *Metamorphoses* as a whole, the story of Io as a whole—even others of Berchorius's own comments on the story. And the commentary was not always allegorical: The mention of Io might call forth a little disquisition on cows. Io, we read, ended up in Egypt—and this might be the commentator's occasion for a geography lesson.

Many Medieval and Renaissance readers assumed a fluid sense of meaning. Medieval and Renaissance commentators often provided alternative interpretations both of details and of whole stories.[14] Fulgentius (*Mythologies*: 1.2), for example, first explains Saturn Euhemeristically, as a tyrant king of ancient Italy; then he explains Saturn in terms of nature allegory: Saturn "is reported as having devoured his own sons because every season devours what it produces." Then Fulgentius tells us that Saturn is a figure for "the divine intelligence as it creates all things." Then Saturn, father of four sons, is "the father of the four elements"—and all of this within some three hundred words! Elsewhere Fulgentius interprets Saturn as a planet (*Mythologies*: 1.18) and as a figure for time (2.1).

Bernardus provided a rationale for this kind of reading early in his commentary on Virgil's *Aeneid*:

One must remember in this book as well as in other allegorical works that there are equivocations and multiple significations, and therefore one must interpret poetic fictions in diverse ways. For example, in Martianus's book one should interpret Jove sometimes as the superior fire, sometimes as a star, and even sometimes as the Creator himself....Hence, one must pay attention to the diverse aspects of the poetic fictions and the multiple interpretations in all allegorical matters if in fact the truth cannot be established by a single interpretation. (on book 1)

It is interesting to consider the method of fourfold allegory in this connection.[15] Dante's formulation in his Letter to Can Grande is well known[16]; it may be summarized as follows:

First, there is the literal or historical level of understanding.
Second, the typological level, where we search for typological connections between what
    we read and the events of the New Testament; Dante calls this the level of
    allegory.
Third, the moral, or tropological level, where we search for moral analogies as we read.
Fourth: the anagogical level, where we search for analogies between what we read and final
    things—the final things according to the Christian conception of the last days.

Fourfold allegory exercised the ingenuity of poets and commentators alike. Sometimes poets worked at two levels, sometimes one, sometimes, in a *tour de force*, all four. And of course, it was easier for commentators to discover three or four levels than it was for poets to produce them. As late as 1591, Harington structured his commentary on Ariosto's *Orlando Furioso* with a version of fourfold allegory in mind: at the end of each canto we find commentary labeled *Moral*, *Historie*, *Allegorie*, and *Allusion*. Much more could be said about fourfold allegory.[17] But here it is worthwhile simply to point out that, whatever else it might be, fourfold allegory is just one expression of the Medieval and Renaissance inclination to multiple interpretation.

This inclination seems to have been pervasive, especially from the late Middle Ages to 1650. It is as much a guiding principle for the *Ovidé Moralisé* and Berchorius in the fourteenth century as it is for Sandys' commentary on Ovid and for Ross's mythography, *Mystagogus Poeticus*, in the seventeenth century. Ross on Arachne provides a nice example of the wandering-eclectic reader:

1. The cause of Arachnes overthrow was the rejecting of the old womans counsel, into whose shape Pallas had transformed her self: Then are young people ready for ruine, when they follow their own heads; and despise the counsel of the aged, whose experience and gravity, should temper their temerity.... 2. This Arachne did learn of the spider to spin and weave, for the Beasts are in many things our Schoolmasters. 3. It is not good to be proud and insolent of any art or knowledge. 4. Subtil and trifling Sophisters...are no better then Spiders, whose captious fallacies are no less hateful to the Wise, than Arachnes web was to Minerva. 5. Partial Judges use their laws, as Spiders do their webs, to catch little flies and let the great ones pass through. 6. Covetous men are like Spiders....Envy and slandering tongue is like a Spider.... 8. We should be Spiders in Providence; they hang their nets in windows, where they know flies most resort...and like Mice, they fortel the ruin of a house, by falling and running away, as Pliny sheweth. (29-30)

There is no concern for consistency here, let alone for anything like Coleridge's "organic unity." Peacham wrote that a metaphor is "like a starre in respect of beautie, brightnesse and direction"—while allegory is like a "signe compounded of many stars, ...a constellation" (*Garden of Eloquence*: 27).

What I am suggesting needs considerable qualification, of course. It is clear—to cite two examples among many—that Fulgentius and Bernardus do each articulate an overall interpretation of the *Aeneid* (see **AENEAS**). And Sidney, Spenser, and others were aware of the Aristotelian unities. Still, it seems clear that careful Medieval and Renaissance readers were much more likely to interpret, and delight in, individual lines and details out of context than careful modern readers are likely to do. For we are Coleridge's children: even the Deconstructionists among us tend to assume organic unity in the things we read.

But if we want to understand Medieval and Renaissance texts historically, if we want to try to imagine ourselves into the minds of Medieval and Renaissance readers, then we probably ought to devote more attention to multiple meanings, less to organic unity. And we certainly should pay very close attention to individual lines, passages, and details.

Those who use this *Dictionary*, then, should perhaps look beyond *the* meaning that Shakespeare or Dante or Chaucer had in mind to the whole range of meanings that the mention of Venus or Actaeon or Diana might have brought to an active reader's mind.

FOR FURTHER READING

The scholarship on allegory is vast. But I might suggest the following as having been particularly helpful to me: Augustine's *On Christian Doctrine*, Erasmus's *Enchiridion*, and Harington's *Apologie of Poetrie* provide clear and moving explanations of the importance of allegorical understanding; they also explain methods of allegorical interpretation.

And the moderns: Chance (1985) and Whitman (1987) describe the history of allegory from classical times to the end of the Middle Ages. Lamberton (1989) provides an introduction to the early history of allegorical reading in the course of his treatment of early Neo-Platonist allegorical responses to Homer. Rahner (1971) describes the early Christian allegorical uses of the Greek myths, especially the Homeric material. Chance (1994) provides an extensive account of Medieval mythographers. Nees (1991) gives an exemplary extended account of the allegorical uses of one figure, Hercules, in Carolingian times in particular. Stock (1972: 31-62) and Dronke (1974) concentrate on the important twelfth century. Seznec (1953) and Don C. Allen (1968, 1970) and Chance (1990: 3-44) provide broad-based accounts of the allegorical impulse, especially in relation to the mythographers; Wetherbee (1972) is also important for those who are interested in allegory in this period. For the importance of Ovid and the pervasiveness of allegorical reading of Ovid, from the fifteenth to the seventeenth century, see

Harding (1946: 1-26). Although she is not concerned with allegory, Reid (1993) is much the most comprehensive guide to the ancient sources of individual classical myths—and to the works of art, music, and literature where those figures have appeared, from 1300 to the 1990s. Bush (1960) is a standard account of classical mythology in Renaissance literature, but again, very little attention is paid to allegory. For myth allegory in some important poets, see, for example, on Dante: Dozon (1991), Hollander (1969), Pépin (1970), Sowell (1991), and Jacoff and Schnapp (1991); on Boccaccio: Hollander (1977); on Chaucer: Robertson (1962), McCall (1955, 1962, 1979), and Hoffman (1966); on Spenser: Nohrnberg (1976), Haskins (1971), and Watkins (1995); on Milton: Harding (1946). For myth allegory among the painters, see, for example, Panofsky (especially 1930, 1962, 1972), Wind (1968), Barkan (1986), and Hope (1985).

NOTES TO THE PREFACE AND INTRODUCTION

[1] Only a few fragments remain of Aeschylus's and Euripides' Philoctetes plays; Sophocles actually wrote two, one of which survives.

[2] Reid (1993: 892-895) finds just three appearances of Philoctetes in European art and literature before 1650: in the *Ovide Moralizé*, and in two obscure paintings.

[3] For Fulgentius's influence, see, e.g., Edwards (1990).

[4] For Bernardus's influence during the Middle Ages, see, e.g., Desmond (1990).

[5] See, e.g., Moss (1982).

[6] For a history of the term *allegory*, see Whitman (1987: 263-268).

[7] For treatments of the tradition of the literary *exemplum*, see, e.g., Welter (1927) and Aerts and Gosman (1988).

[8] See Buffiere (1956: 136-154).

[9] For more on the emblem, see, e.g., Daly (1979, 1988, 1989), Höltgen (1986), Russell (1985), Donker and Muldrow (1982: 86-89), Porteman (1977), and Henkel and Schöne (1967); for a book-length bibliography of emblem-book editions and scholarship, see Daly and Silcox (1990).

[10] For Euhemerus and Euhemerism see Seznec (1953: 11-15) and Chance (1994: 25-26).

[11] See Bond's introduction to his edition of Lyly's *Works*: 366-367.

[12] See Bond's introduction to his edition of Lyly's *Works*: 9-14.

[13] See McLane (1968); for more on historical allegory in Spenser, see, e.g., Haskins (1971: 200-227). See also, e.g., Orgel (1975: 70-77) for an account of the projected performance of Jonson's *Neptune's Triumph for the Return of Albion* (1615), wherein King James was represented by Neptune.

[14] This is at least in some measure a carrying on of the Greco-Roman understanding of the gods. There were many gods. And many of the gods—most notoriously, perhaps, Diana and Apollo—were understood in many sometimes contradictory ways.

[15] The fourfold method was first applied to the Bible; see de Lubac (1964).

[16] The attribution to Dante is uncertain; see Minnis and Scott (1988: 440-441) for a brief summary of the related scholarship.

[17] See Hollander (1969: 15-56) for a wide-ranging discussion of fourfold allegory, particularly in relation to Dante's statements in the Letter to Can Grande and in the *Convivio*.

The Dictionary

A

ACHILLES was the son of Peleus and the sea goddess Thetis. He was the greatest of the Greek warriors, according to Homer's *Iliad* (see also Ovid, *Metamorphoses*: 12, 13; Statius, *Achilleid*, and this poem's medieval commentaries listed in Clogan 1968; Hyginus, *Fabulae*: 96, 101, 106, 107, 112). Sometimes Medieval and Renaissance poets also remembered him as an *exemplum* of valor. Here is Sidney, for example: "See whether wisdom and temperance in Ulisses and Diomedes, valure in Achilles...even to an ignorant man carry not an apparant shining" (*Defense of Poesy*: 15; see also Tritonio, *Mythologia*: 22).

With the rise of Renaissance Neo-Platonism, Achilles sometimes served as an example of Platonic love/friendship because of his devotion to Patroclus. Ficino (*Commentary on Plato's Symposium*: 1.4) mentions him in this sense, as do Brant (*Ship of Fools*: 10) and Spenser ("Hymne of Love": 232); and in a masque staged for Elizabeth in 1594 there was "erected an altar to the Goddess of Amity....Then issued forth...the first pair of friends, which were Theseus and Perithous; they came arm in arm....Then likewise came Achilles and Patroclus" (in Nichols 1823, vol. 3: 281).

But more commonly Achilles was interpreted in one way or another as a negative example (for more on Renaissance ambivalence toward Achilles, see Briggs 1981). Sometimes he was an example of wrath. Thus Erasmus wrote that Achilles was "shamefully overcome by anger" (*Enchiridion*: 44). And here is Ross: "a Souldier...must be heated by Choler as Achilles was by Fire, but too much Choler is naught, as it was in Achilles, who by it did undo his Country" (*Mystagogus Poeticus*: 1). But Achilles was also known to have had his troubles with the venerian passions. He was often interpreted as a figure for lust during the Middle Ages (King 1987: 171-217). His sojourn in the court of Lycomedes (where his mother disguised him as a girl to prevent his going to war at Troy) was seen as a perversion of nature: manly virtue succumbing to womanly passions (for male/female allegory, see **AMAZONS**). The court of Lycomedes was "the kingdom of lust," according to Fulgentius (*Mythologies*: 3.7; see also Alanus, *Complaint of Nature*: mt. 1; *Anticlaudian*: 9.5). Achilles was consequently often mentioned as a *de casibus* love figure; he was a great hero who fell because of his love or lust for Priam's daughter Polyxena, for whom he was lured inside the walls of Troy, where he was shot in the heel by Paris (e.g., Petrarch, *Rime*: 391-392). In another version of the story, he suffers because of his love for the Amazon Pentheseleia. Dante thus places Achilles among the lustful in the *Inferno* (5.65), and Chaucer includes Achilles among the profane lovers pictured on the walls of the Temple of Brass (*Parliament of Fowls*: 290). Ross also mentions Achilles as a *de casibus* love figure (*Mystagogus Poeticus*: 3).

Spenser has a related tradition in mind when he has Cupid shoot an arrow into Thomalin's heel (*Shepheardes Calender*: March, 95-100; see Nohrnberg 1976: 587-588). Spenser's poem was published with glosses by a certain "E. K.," whose gloss on these lines summarizes the main lines of the interpretative tradition:

in Homer it is sayd of Thetis, that shee tooke her young babe Achilles being newely borne, and holding him by the heele, dipped him in the River of Styx. The vertue whereof is, to defend and keepe the bodyes washed therein from any mortall wound. So Achilles being washed all over, save onely his hele, by which his mother held, was in the rest invulnerable: therefore by Paris was feyned to be shotte with a poysoned arrowe in the heele, whiles he was busie about the marying of Polyxena in the temple of Apollo. Which mystical fable Eustathius vnfolding, sayth: that by wounding in the hele, is meant lustfull love. For from the heele...to the privie partes there passe certaine veines and slender synnewes, as also the lyke come from the head...so that...yf those veynes there be cut a sonder, the partie straighte becommeth cold and unfruitful.

E. K. cites Eustathius's twelfth-century commentary on Homer, but he could have found the same interpretation in Fulgentius (*Mythologies*: 3.7), Vatican Mythographer II (208), Vatican Mythographer III (11.24), Boccaccio (*Genealogie Deorum*: 12.52), Conti (*Mythologie*: 9.12), and others. Later, Fraunce (*Countesse of Pembrokes Yvychurch*: 47v), Valeriano (*Hieroglyphica*: 367), and Sandys (*Ovid*: 567-568) wrote in the same vein.

Shakespeare suspected something sexual (and thus unseemly) in Achilles' love for Patroclus: thus in *Troilus and Cressida* Patroclus is Achilles' "masculine whore" (5.1.17; see also 2.1.114).

Bernardus understood Achilles to be a figure for mankind, because, according to Bernardus's etymology, Achilles meant "joyless hardship" (*On Martianus Capella*: 6.668).

For the education of Achilles, see **CHIRON**.

Bibliography: John C. Briggs, "Chapman's *Seaven Bookes of the Iliades*: Mirror for Essex," *SEL*, 21 (1981): 59-73; Paul M. Clogan, *The Medieval Achilleid* of Statius (1968); Katherine C. King, *Achilles: Paradigms of the War Hero from Homer to the Middle Ages* (1987); John Nichols, *The Progresses and Public...*

Processions of Queen Elizabeth, 3 vols. (1823); James Nohrnberg, *The Analogy of The Faerie Queene* (1976).

ACTAEON, son of Aristaeus and Autonoe and grandson of Cadmus, was out hunting when he happened upon Diana bathing in a stream (Ovid, *Metamorphoses*: 3.173-252; Apollodorus, *Library*: 3.4.4; Hyginus, *Fabulae*: 180-181). Angry at being so discovered, Diana changed Actaeon into a stag. He was then set upon and killed by his own hounds. Fraunce suggests two allegorical interpretations, first that

> we ought not to be over curious and inquisitive in spying and prying into those matters, which be above our reache....Or lastly, thus, a wiseman ought to refraine his eyes, from beholding sensible and corporall bewty, figured by Diana: least, as Actaeon was devoured of his owne doggs, so he be distracted and torne in peeces with his own affections, and perturbations. (*Countesse of Pembrokes Yvychurch*: 43r)

The first interpretation, that the story is a warning against curiosity as to the mysteries, was not unusual (see, e.g, Fulgentius, *Mythologies*: 3.3; Conti, *Mythologie*: 6.25; Dinet, *Hieroglyphiques*: 389; Viana, *Ovidio*: 2.8; Sandys, *Ovid*: 151; and Ross, *Mystagogus Poeticus*: 7). But more common was the second allegorization: Actaeon exemplified the self-destructive consequences of the loss of rational control over the passions. We find this interpretation, with some variations, in Vatican Mythographer III (7.3), the *Ovide Moralisé* (3.571-603), Conti (*Mythologie*: 6.25), Golding ("Epistle": 96-102), Dinet (*Hieroglyphiques*: 390), and Ross (*Mystagogus Poeticus*: 7). Elizabethan painters also made use of this allegory (Evett 1989), as did Dutch painters from the same period (Blankert et al.: 58-59). Whitney makes explicit the idea of bestiality, which is often at least implicit in other versions of this interpretation (see Appendix B, "Bestialization"). According to Whitney, the story means

> That those whoe do pursue
> Their fancies fonde, and things unlawfull crave,
> Like brutishe beastes appeare unto the viewe,
> And shall at lengthe, Actaeons guerdon have:
> And as his houndes, soe theire affections base,
> Shall them devoure, and all their deedes deface.
> (*Choice Book of Emblemes*: 15)

Shakespeare refers to this allegory when Duke Orsino recalls the first time he saw the lovely Olivia:

> That instant was I turn'd into a hart,
> And my desires, like fell and cruel hounds,
> E'er since pursue me.
> (*Twelfth Night*: 1.1.20-22)

Boccaccio's *Diana's Hunt* is a self-conscious reversal of this allegory: The lover begins as a stag and is then hunted by the virtuous Diana and her votaries, in something like the way Dante was hunted and spiritually transformed by Beatrice (e.g., Barkan 1986: 153). Thus Boccaccio is "changed beyond doubt from a stag into a human being and a rational creature" (*Diana's Hunt*: 18.11-12).

Petrarch likens himself to Actaeon, transformed as he has been by his love for his insistently chaste Laura (*Rime sparse*: 23.147-160). This became a staple of Petrarchan love poetry (Murphey 1991).

Occasionally Actaeon was a figure for the persecuted Christ. Berchorius (following the *Ovide Moralisé*: 3.604-669) offers this as one of his interpretations: Actaeon, killed by his own dogs, "signifies the son of God who with his companions—that is the patriarchs and prophets—ruled many dogs—that is the Jewish people who were especially able to be called dogs because of their raging cruelty" (*Ovidius Moralizatus*: 185).

For more on the moral allegory of hunting, see **ADONIS**.

Bibliography: Leonard Barkan, "Diana and Actaeon: The Myth as Synthesis," *ELR*, 10 (1980): 317-359; Barkan, *The Gods Made Flesh: Metamorphosis and the Pursuit of Paganism* (1986); Albert Blankert et al., *Gods, Saints, and Heroes: Dutch Painting in the Age of Rembrandt* (1980); Walter R. Davis, "Actaeon in Arcadia," *SEL*, 2 (1962): 95-110; David Evett, "Some Elizabethan Allegorical Paintings: A Preliminary Inquiry," *JWCI*, 52 (1989): 140-166; Stephen Murphey, "The Death of Actaeon as Petrarchist Topos," *CLS*, 28 (1991): 137-153; Peggy Muñoz Simonds, *Myth, Emblem, and Music in Shakespeare's Cymbeline* (1992): 103-108.

ADMETUS AND ALCESTE. Admetus was the king of Pherae in Thessaly and one of the Argonauts. Apollo served as his shepherd for a time; the reasons for this vary from version to version, but in some versions Apollo serves because of Admetus's remarkable piety. Certainly he was a favorite of Apollo: Apollo helped him win his wife Alceste and even promised to release Admetus from death, if someone could be found who would be willing to die in his place. When eventually Admetus did fall deathly ill, Alceste volunteered to die for him. She was in turn rescued forth from Hades, by Proserpina in some versions of the story, by Hercules in others (following Euripides, *Alcestis*, and Fulgentius, *Mythologies*: 1.22). Plato mentions Alceste as an example of the power of love (*Symposium*: 179b-c). Jerome included her in his short list of virtuous wives (*Dialogue against Jovinianus*: 1.45). And here is Berchorius:

because Alceste...loved her husband, she subjected herself to death for him and descended to hell in his place. Afterwards, when Hercules went down to hell to bring back the dog Cerberus, he found her and moved by her virtue took her out and led her back to life.

Allegorize this about the affection of good women who love their husbands so much that for love of them they want to expose themselves to death if it be necessary. They are worthy to have Hercules—that is Christ—draw them out of hell—that is purgatory—and lead them with Him to glory. (*Ovidius Moralizatus*: 118)

Lydgate also refers to her as a self-sacrificing wife (*Reson and Sensuallyte*: 6828-6836); and we find her listed in catalogues of good wives: in Chaucer (*Legend of Good Women*: 203-223; "Franklin's Tale": 1442), for example, and Gower (*Confessio Amantis*: 7.1917-1949; 8.2640-2646); see also Pettie (*Petite Pallace*: 146). Shakespeare probably has the rescue of Alceste in mind in the "resurrection" scene of *The Winter's Tale* (Simonds 1992: 56). And Milton speaks of his own deceased wife, his "late espoused Saint," as an Alceste ("Sonnet 23").

In another story, in order to win Alceste to wife, Admetus was required to yoke to his chariot "two different and incompatible wild beasts." He managed this with the help of Apollo and Hercules, who brought him a wild boar and a lion to join under the yoke (Philostratus, *Images*: 710). According to Philostratus (and his source, Fulgentius, *Mythologies*: 1.22), the two beasts may be interpreted as the strength of mind and body. Clearly, these beasts had to be controlled, and so the story could be interpreted as an allegory for self-control. Thus it was that Admetus driving his yoked beasts was carved in stone over the seventeenth-century gateway of the Amsterdam House of Corrections (Langley 1990: 184).

Bibliography: T. R. Langley, "All Steened Up," *CR*, 19 (1990): 183-197; Peggy Muñoz Simonds, *Myth, Emblem, and Music in Shakespeare's Cymbeline* (1992); DeWitt T. Starnes and E. W. Talbert, *Classical Myth and Legend in Renaissance Dictionaries* (1955): 40-41.

ADONIS was the son of Myrrha's incestuous union with her father Cinyras. He grew to be a boy of such surpassing beauty that Venus fell in love with him (Ovid, *Metamorphoses*: 10.519-559, 708-739; Apollodorus, *Library*: 3.14.3-4; Hyginus, *Fabulae*: 58, 248, 251). Fraunce provides two interpretations, the first nature allegory, the second moral allegory:

Now, for Venus, her love to Adonis, and lamentation for his death: by Adonis, is meant the sunne, by Venus, the upper hemisphere of the earth (as by Proserpina the lower) by the boare, winter: by the death of Adonis, the absence of the sunne for the sixe wintrie monethts; all which time, the earth lamenteth: Adonis is wounded in those parts, which are the instruments of propagation: for, in winter the son seemeth impotent, and the earth barren...and therefore Venus sits, lamentably hanging downe her head....

Adonis was turned into a fading flowre; bewty decayeth, and lust leaveth the lustfull, if they leave not it....Adonis was borne of Myrrha; Myrrhe [i.e., the gum of the Myrrh tree] provoketh lust: Adonis was kilde by a boare, that is he was spent and weakened by old age: Venus lamenteth, lust decayeth. (*Countesse of Pembrokes Yvychurch*: 45v)

Fraunce's idea that the story of Adonis might be understood as an allegory of the alteration of the seasons goes back at least to Theocritus, who composed a song to celebrate Adonis's return:

O Lady Aphrodite with the face that beams like gold,
Twelve months are sped and soft-footed Heav'ns pretty laggards see,
Bring o'er the never-tarrying stream Adonis back to thee.
The Seasons, the Seasons, full slow they go and come....
Thy lad doth dight with all delight upon this holyday;
For there's not a fruit the orchard bears but is here for his hand to take,
And cresses trim all kept for him in many a silver tray....

> Adonis sweet, Adonis dear,
> Be gracious for another year.
> (*Idyls*: 15.101-142)

Boccaccio (*Genealogie Deorum*: 2.53) and Ross (*Mystagogus Poeticus*: 8) develop the same nature allegory, both citing Macrobius (*Saturnalia*: 1.21.1) as their authority (see also Christine de Pizan, *L'Epitre*: 65; Giraldi, *De deis gentium*: 565; van Mander, *Wtlegginghe op den Metamorphosis*: 79r). Conti does much the same thing, but he also builds on Theocritus's brief description of Adonis in the fruitful garden: In Conti's "garden of Adonis" seeds are sown, and there are "many fruit-bearing trees" (*Mythologie*: 5.16). Spenser seems to have Conti in mind when he describes the Garden of Adonis, where Adonis becomes a Neo-Platonic "Father of all Formes" (*Faerie Queene*: 3.6.47; see Lotspeich 1932: 32; Nohrnberg 1976: 520-521). For Reynolds (*Mythomystes*: 176), the Garden of Adonis was the Garden of Eden.

The story of Venus and Adonis was more often interpreted in terms of moral allegory. Here, for example, is Caxton's comment on the Ovid's account of Adonis in the *Metamorphoses*:

Venus loved Adonyn. She had made of Mirrie a pygment of hote nature gyvynge appetyte of lecherye. Adonyn sygnyfyeth suavyte or swetnes. He was fayre and delyted hym in hys beaute. Venus was hys love. For luxurye delyteth in a fayre body. He was a hunter and hunted and soughte after luxurye. Venus charged hym moch and prayd that he shold not chace ne assaylle no prowde ne fyres bestis, as beres, Lyons, Lupaerds, Tygres, or wylde boores. That is to understonde that Luxurye wolde be ydle, and recheth not of travayll. The swynne slew Adonyn. That is thardure of luxurye. Whyche he ledde all hys lyf in. (*Metamorphoses*: on book 2)

This is close to Lydgate's sense of the story. In Lydgate, Adonis hunts specifically in the Garden of Deduit, in Venus's garden, where "Ther is ful many wilde bore" (*Reson and Sensuallyte*: 3678). (See **HERMAPHRODITUS AND SALMACIS** for closely related allegory: A young man resists the first, essentially female, promptings of sexuality.) For Lydgate, Adonis's encounter with the boar is a figure for the dangers of loving in the garden of the fallen Venus; and so Adonis is a *de casibus* lover for Lydgate. Thus Erasmus talks of "the voluptuous charms of Adonis" (*Enchiridion*: 39), for example; and in what Sheidley calls "the conventional moral gloss on Ovid's tale" (1975: 4), Greene wrote,

> The Syren Venus nourist in hir lap
> Faire Adon, swearing whiles he was a youth
> He might be wanton: Note his after-hap
> The guerdon that such lawlesse lust ensueth,
> So long he followed flattering Venus lore,
> Till seely Lad, he perisht by a bore.
>
> ("Perymedes": 89; see also Spenser, *Faerie Queene*: 3.1.38; van Mander, *Wtlegginghe*: 88v)

This allegory was also frequent in Dutch paintings in the age of Rembrandt (Blankert et al.: 58-59, 61, 94-95).

Such ideas are related to the traditional allegory of the hunt. Already in ancient times a distinction was drawn between the "virtuous" hunt and the kind of hunt that could allegorize the pursuit of pleasure or lust. The pursuit of the boar was manly in the allegorical sense; it required courage. Caxton's Venus (above) urges Adonis to avoid "fyres bestis" such as "beres, Lyons, Lupaerds"—just as Shakespeare's Venus urges her Adonis to hunt the "timorous flying hare" (*Venus and Adonis*: 674). Such prey required no courage of the hunter, and the rabbit was traditionally associated with Venus and "venery" (Robertson 1962: 263-264; Bowers 1979; Cassell and Kirkham's introduction to Boccaccio's *Diana's Hunt*, 1991: 19-21, 39-51; Chance 1994: 480-481; see also **VENUS**). By the end of the sixteenth century a number of books were published in order to instruct gentlemen as to the nobility and the virtue of hunting. George Turberville's *The Noble Arte of Venerie or Hunting* was such a book; George Gascoigne wrote these dedicatory verses:

> It occupies the mynde, which else must chaunce to muse
> On mischiefe, malice, filth, and fraudes, that mortal men do use....
> It exercyseth strength, it exercyseth wit,
> And all the poars and sprites of Man, are exercisede by it.
> It shaketh off all slouth, it presseth downe all pryde,
> It cheres the hart, it glads the eye, and through the ears doth glyde.
> I might at large expresse how earely huntsmen ryse,
> And leave the sluggish sleepe for such as leachers lust devyse.

Peacham applies this allegory of the hunt specifically to the story of Venus and Adonis:

> I much did muse, why Venus could not brooke,
> The savadge Baore, and Lion cruell feirce,
> Since Kings and Princes, have such pleasure tooke
> In hunting: haply cause a Boare did pierce
>   Her Adon faire, who better lik't the sport,
>   Then spend his daies, in wanton pleasures court.

> Which fiction though devisd by Poets braine,
> It signifies unto the Reader this;

Such exercise Love will not entertaine,
Who liketh best, to live in Idlenes:
    The foe to vertue, Cancker of the wit,
    That bringes a thousand miseries with it.
               (*Minerva Britanna*: 169)

The Garden of Adonis did, however, have other, homelier, meanings as well. Plato mentioned gardens of Adonis, pleasure gardens where things grew quickly, as distinct from a garden for "serious purposes" (*Phaedrus*: 276b; Ficino, *Commentum cum summis capitulorum*: 51, comments on this passage from Plato; see also Isaiah 17:10). Here is Erasmus's explanation of this tradition:

Gardens of Adonis, used to be applied to trivial things, which served no useful purpose and were suitable only for giving a brief passing pleasure. Pausanius [second c. A.D.] tells how people used to be very fond of "Adonis-gardens, well stocked particularly with lettuce and fennel; they would plant seeds in them just as one does in pots. Thus the thing became a proverb directed against worthless, trifling men," born for silly pleasures....These gardens were sacred to Venus, on account of her darling Adonis. (*Adages*: 1.1.4)

For the birth of Adonis, see **MYRRHA**; for the allegory of manly *vir*tue (*L. vir*, "man"), see **AMAZONS**; for more on the moral allegory of hunting, see **ATALANTA, DIANA**.

Bibliography: Don C. Allen, *Image and Meaning* (1968): 42-57; Albert Blankert et al., *Gods, Saints, and Heroes: Dutch Painting in the Age of Rembrandt* (1980); Robin Bowers, "'Hard Armours' and 'Delicate Amours' in Shakespeare's 'Venus and Adonis'," *ShakS*, 12 (1979): 1-24; Anthony Cassell and Victoria Kirkham, "Introduction" to Boccaccio's *Diana's Hunt* (1991); Jane Chance, *Medieval Mythography* (1994); A. C. Hamilton, *The Spenser Encyclopedia* (1990): under *Adonis, gardens of*; H. G. Lotspeich, *Classical Mythology in the Poetry of Edmund Spenser* (1932); Richard Neuse, "Planting Words in the Soul: Spenser's Socratic Garden of Adonis," *SSt*, 8 (1987): 79-100; James Nohrnberg, *The Analogy of The Faerie Queene* (1976); Nicholas Orme, "Medieval Hunting: Fact and Fancy," in Barbara Hanawalt, ed., *Chaucer's England: Literature in Historical Context* (1992): 133-153; D. W. Robertson, Jr., *Preface to Chaucer* (1962); William F. Sheidley, "'Unless It Be a Boar': Love and Wisdom in Shakespeare's *Venus and Adonis*," *MLQ*, 35 (1974): 3-15.

AEGISTHUS was remembered mainly for his seduction of Clytemnestra while her husband Agamemnon was leading the Greeks against the Trojans. He was thus an example of lust, as much for Cicero (*Nature of the Gods*: 3.91) as for Boccaccio (*Concerning Famous Women*: 1.35).

AENEAS. According to Virgil's *Aeneid*, when the Greeks sacked Troy, the Trojan prince Aeneas was instructed by the gods to take some of the survivors away from Troy in ships (see also Ovid, *Metamorphoses*: 13.623-724, 14.72-157, 445-608). It was their great destiny to found the city that was to become Rome. Since Virgil was conforming to the epic conventions (see **EPIC**), he makes it clear that the gods are largely in control of these great events. Juno, for example, took every opportunity to do Aeneas harm. It thus occurred to the anti-Roman Augustine that Aeneas could be understood as a type of the Christian hero because, like the Christian martyrs, Aeneas had struggled against the "demons or powers of the air, and among them Juno herself"—and because Juno was commonly represented by the poets as "hostile to virtue, and jealous of men of mark aspiring to the heavens" (*City of God*: 10.21). In this interpretative tradition, Aeneas fell short only because he did whatever he could to propitiate rather than oppose this goddess (Lamberton 1989: 259).

But the three major Christian interpretative commentaries on Virgil's *Aeneid*—Fulgentius (*On the Content of Virgil*) in the sixth century, Bernardus (*On Virgil's Aeneid*) in the twelfth, and Landino (*Disputationes Camuldenses*) in the fifteenth—agree to a surprising extent as to the meaning of the poem in general and the meaning of Aeneas in particular. According to these commentators, Aeneas matures over the course of the poem, moving from heedlessness and sin to spiritual insight and grace. For all three commentators the journey to the underworld in book 6 is central: this journey provides Aeneas with the key elements of his understanding. (Dante's brief commentary on the *Aeneid* in the *Convivio* (4.26.8-9) is in this same tradition; for Dante's interpretation of Aeneas, see Chance 1985: 56-64.)

Fulgentius may be taken as typical: "'This is a tale of arms and man' [Virgil, *Aeneid*: 1.1], indicating manliness [L. *virtutem*: virtue or manliness] by 'arms' and wisdom by 'man,' for all perfection depends on manliness of body and wisdom of mind" (*On the Content of Virgil*: 6). For Fulgentius, Aeneas's shipwreck is "an allegory of the dangers of birth" (12); the death of Aeneas's father shows that "youth as it grows up casts off the burden of parental control" (15); and so the dalliance with Dido suggests "the spirit of adolescence, on holiday from paternal control." Thus it is that Aeneas "is inflamed by passion and, driven on by storm and cloud, that is, by confusion of mind, commits adultery....Mercury is introduced as the god of the intellect; it is by the urgings of the intellect that youth quits the straits of passion" (16). Influenced by Mercury/intellect, Aeneas will now investigate "the secrets of knowledge." This is why "Aeneas goes down into the lower world and there, looking on as an eyewitness, he sees both the punishments for the evil, the rewards for the good, and the sad wanderings of those given over to passion. Then piloted by Charon he crosses the Acheron" (22). Finally, Aeneas enters Elysium, "where, the labor of learning now over, he celebrates the perfecting of memory." When eventually Aeneas comes to Italy, his marriage to Lavinia is (rather unflatteringly) the good and proper "road of toil" (24).

Many other commentators provided variations on this basic theme. John of Salisbury, for example:

Under the cloak of poetic imagination in his Eneid [Virgil] subtly represents the six periods of life by the division of the work into six [sic] books. In these, in imitation of the Odyssey, he appears to have represented the origin and progress of a man. The character he sets forth and develops he leads on and conducts down into the nether world. For Eneas who therein represents the soul, is so named for the reason it is a dweller in the body, for *ennos*, according to the Greeks, is "dweller", and *demas* "body." The name Eneas is formed of these two elements to signify life dwelling, as it were, in a hut of flesh. (*Policraticus*: 8.24)

Aeneas was also understood to be a man with a divine mission. Here is Dante: "in the Empyrean heaven he was chosen as father of glorious Rome and of her empire, and both, to say the truth, were established as the holy place where the successor of great Peter has his seat" (*Inferno*: 2.19-24).

The Medieval appreciation of Aeneas could go further. The *Ovide Moralisé* interprets Aeneas as the "holy church"; Aeneas was persecuted, then, as the church was persecuted by Jews and other pagans (14.527-535). Gawain Douglas understood Aeneas to exemplify "every vertew, belanging [to] a Nobyllman" ("Preface": vi). For Spenser, too, Virgil's Aeneas "ensampled a good governour and a vertuous man" ("Letter to Raleigh"; see, e.g., Nohrnberg 1976: 63); see also Ross (*Mystagogus Poeticus*: 15).

For individual episodes of the Aeneas story, see **AEOLUS, DIDO, SIBYL**.

Bibliography: Don C. Allen, *Mysteriously Meant* (1970); Jane Chance, "The Origins and Development of Medieval Mythography: From Homer to Dante," in Chance and R. O. Wells, *Mapping the Cosmos* (1985); Henri de Lubac, *Exégèse Médiévale: Les Quarte Sense de L'Ecriture* (1964): 233-262; Robert Lamberton, *Homer the Theologian* (1989); Henry Lotspeich, *Classical Mythology in the Poetry of Edmund Spenser* (1932): 33-34; James Nohrnberg, *The Analogy of The Faerie Queene* (1976); Earl G. Schreiber and Thomas E. Maresca, "Introduction" to Bernardus, *On Virgil's Aeneid* (1979); Sharon Stevenson, "Aeneas in Fourteenth-Century England," in A. S. Bernardo and S. Levin, *The Classics in the Middle Ages* (1990): 371-378.

AEOLUS was the god of the winds. Thus in Homer's *Odyssey* (10.1-77) it was Aeolus who gave Ulysses the oxhide bottle containing all the winds except that wind which was blowing him and his ship back to his home in Ithaca. But, alas, while Ulysses slept, his men opened the bottle, and so the winds escaped to blow Ulysses' ship off to perilous places. In Virgil's *Aeneid* (1.51-141) this same Aeolus whips up the storm that drives Aeneas off course and eventually to Dido's Carthage. In Bernardus's interpretation, Aeneas allegorizes the development of the good man, from the indiscretions typical of youth to the wisdom of maturity. Consequently, Bernardus asserts that *Aeolus* is etymologically *childbirth*, and so Aeolus's storm is the destruction of the real world, since when a man is born, the world (that is, the life of the spirit) dies, as long as it is oppressed by the heaviness of the flesh, descends from its divinity, and assents to the passions of the flesh....Thus, Aeolus (that is birth) brings forth winds (that is, the excitement of vice). With these he attacks the sea, the human body which is a deep whirlpool of ebbing and flowing humors. (*On Virgil's Aeneid*: on book 1)

Bernardus's association of Aeolus with childbirth and destruction derives from a more than usually obscure passage in Fulgentius (*On the Content of Virgil*: 11-12) and from the Neo-Platonic notion that birth is a kind of death for the soul (see **UNDERWORLD**). The association of Aeolus's winds with vices or the passions, however, was quite common. Landino, for example, interprets Aeolus, and storm winds in general, as "the appetites" or "the lower reason" (*Disputationes Camuldenses*: 165). And Spenser wrote that Orgoglio—the Satanic, vice-ridden giant of the first book of *The Faerie Queene*—was the ill-begotten son of Earth and Aeolus:

> The greatest Earth his uncouth Mother was,
> And blustring Aeolus his boasted sire,
> Who with his breath, which through the world doth pas,
> Her hollow womb did secretly inspire,
> And fild her hidden caves with stormie yre,
> That she conceiv'd.
>
> (*Faerie Queene*: 1.7.9)

Sandys wrote that the winds of Aeolus are the "tempests" of the "affections" (*Ovid*: 651; see also Ross, *Mystagogus Poeticus*: 16).

Another tradition associated Aeolus with Fame, or made Aeolus, with a trumpet, Fame's herald. This probably came about because both Aeolus and Fame were often represented with trumpets (de Weever 1987: 128; Panofsky 1962: 45-46; for Fame's trumpet, see **FAME**). Both Gower (*Miroir de l'homme*: 22129-22152) and Chaucer (*House of Fame*: 1570-1688) give Aeolus two trumpets, one for good fame, one for bad. In Chaucer's phrase, one is "Sklaundre...a blake trumpe of bras, / That fouler than the devel was"; the other, "Laude," is a "trumpe of golde."

Aeolus could also represent winter, as in a design by Maerten de Vos (1532-1603) for a tapestry of *The Seasons* (see Reid 1993: 1.68).

The winds could also be associated with Fortune; see **FORTUNE**. For other wind dieties, see **BOREAS, ZEPHYR**.

Bibliography: Don C. Allen, *Mysteriously Meant* (1970): 156, 214; Jacqueline de Weever, *Chaucer Name Dictionary* (1987); Erwin Panofsky, *Studies in Iconology* (1962); Jane Davidson Reid, *The Oxford Guide to Classical Mythology in the Arts, 1300-1990s* (1993); Rosemond Tuve, *Allegorical Imagery* (1966): 25.

AESCULAPIUS (Asclepius or Epidaurius, after the city of Epidaurus, where tradition had it that he was first worshipped). Aesculapius was the physician god, the mortal son of Apollo and Coronis. The followers of Pythagoras, who worshipped Apollo as the god of light and music, held this son in special regard. Pythagorean doctors developed a cult around Aesculapius, claiming that he had cured madness and deafness with Apollo-inspired music (Hoeniger 1984: 57). According to Pindar (*Pythian Odes*: 3) and Ovid (*Metamorphoses*: 2.630; see also *Fasti*: 6.746-754), Aesculapius was raised by Chiron, from whom he learned so well the art of medicine that he was "said to have restored life either to Glaucus, son of Minos, or to [Theseus's son] Hippolytus" (Hyginus, *Fabulae*: 49; see also Virgil, *Aeneid*: 7.760-783; Apollodorus, *Library*: 3.10.3-4; Lucian, *Dialogues of the Gods*: 15). Jupiter regarded this as an act of presumption, and so he struck Aesculapius with a thunderbolt. Macrobius wrote of Aesculapius as follows:

> The association of a serpent with the statues of Aesculapius and Salus points to the relation of these deities with the nature of the sun and the moon, for Aesculapius is the healthful power which comes from the essence of the sun to give help to mortal minds and bodies, and Salus is the activity proper to the nature of the moon, which aids the bodies of living creatures and strengthens them by its health-giving disposition.
>
> Statues of Aesculapius and Salus, then, have figures of serpents in attendance because these two deities enable human bodies, as it were, to slough off the skin of weakness and to recover the bloom of their former strength, just as serpents each year shed the skin of old age and renew their youth....
>
> The identity of Aesculapius with Apollo is proved not only by the fact that he is believed to be Apollo's son, but also by reason of the power of prophecy which too is attributed to him....Aesculapius presides over divination and augury. And there is nothing surprising here, since the skills of medicine and divination are closely allied. (*Saturnalia*: 1.20.1-4)

On the whole, these ideas remained quite constant: Aesculapius was either the god of medicine or the personification of it (e.g., Bernardus, *On Martianus Capella*: 5.760). The following account by Sandys is not far from Macrobius:

> Aesculapius is snatcht by Apollo from the womb of his slaughtred mother: taken for the son of Apollo and Coronis; in that Coronis is the moderate moist aire, which by the impression of the Sun conceaves Aesculapius, or the Giver of health. For if the aire be not rarified by the Sun, or if contrarily overdryed by his fervor, there is no salubrity: and therefore Coronis is said to be shot to death by Apollo, when his over-violent rayes...do wound the aire with a mortall pestilence. (*Ovid*: 118)

Because he was a great physician, one who could even bring the dead to life, Aesculapius was understood as a type of *the* physician, Christ. We find this as early as Justin Martyr (*Apologies*: 1.22); and the *Ovide Moralisé* (2.3145-3181) makes the same connection, as does Berchorius: "The sun can signify God the Father whose son is Jesus" (*Ovidius Moralizatus*: 172); and thus "Aesculapius who was the greatest doctor and the son of the sun is...Christ" (426). "Christ is the true

Aesculapius," wrote Ross (*Mystagogus Poeticus*: 18). In the same way, Ficino refers to St. Paul, "that doctor of souls from Tarsus," as Aesculapius (*Letters*, vol. 3: 10).

Very occasionally, during the Renaissance, Aesculapius was the false healer, the idol through whom Satan worked miracles to deceive the faithful (see Nohrnberg 1976: 175). More commonly, Aesculapius was contrasted with Plato, the former a healer of the body, the later of the spirit. This allegory was formulated in classical times (e.g., Diogenes Laertius, *Lives of the Eminent Philosophers*: 3.45) and was revived during the Renaissance (e.g., Ferrand, *Treatise on Lovesickness*: 1).

Aesculapius could also serve as an example of the effects of envy. Here is the *Chess of Love* commentary: "It is also true, according to the ancient histories, that Jupiter, moved by extreme envy of the great fame and name Asclapius had, killed him in fact. For he couldn't bear that anyone should be reputed a god except himself....And so it was pretended that Asclapius was blasted finally by the gods" (522; see also Giraldi, *De deis gentium*: 346-354).

Aesculapius had two sons, Podalirius and Machaon (see Homer, *Iliad*: 2.728-733). Both were physicians like their father (see **PODALIRIUS**).

From ancient times the serpent—capable of shedding its skin, and so a sign of physical renewal—was associated with Aesculapius (see, e.g., Aristophanes, *Plutus*: 3.2; Ovid, *Metamorphoses*: 15.715).

Bibliography: A. C. Hamilton, *The Spenser Encyclopedia* (1990): under *Aesculapius*; F. D. Hoeniger, "Musical Cures of Melancholy and Mania in Shakespeare," in J. C. Gray, *Mirror up to Shakespeare* (1984): 54-67; Howard C. Kee, "Asklepius the Healer," in *Miracle in the Early Christian World* (1983): 78-104; Charles Lemmi, *The Classical Deities in Bacon* (1933): 118-122; James Nohrnberg, *The Analogy of The Faerie Queene* (1976).

AGAMEMNON, brother of Menelaus, was king of Mycenae (or of Argos) and the leader of the Greek forces at Troy (Homer, *Iliad*; Ovid, *Metamorphoses*: 12.25-38; Hyginus, *Fabulae*: 98, 117, 122). It was Agamemnon who sacrificed his daughter Iphigenia to appease the wrath of Diana, and so assure the safe passage of the Greek ships to Troy. And it was Agamemnon whose quarrel with Achilles precipitated the events of Homer's *Iliad*. Modern readers tend to be hard on Agamemnon (e.g., Willcock 1976: 9). But Medieval and Renaissance readers usually interpreted Agamemnon quite favorably. Boethius cites him along with Ulysses and Hercules as an example of a man impervious to Fortune:

You can make of your fortune what you will; for any fortune which seems difficult either tests virtue or corrects or punishes vice....[For example,] Agamemnon, the avenging son of Atreus, waged war for ten years until, by devastating Troy, he purged the dishonor done his brother's marriage. When he wished to fill the sails of the Greek fleet, and bring back the winds by a bloody sacrifice, he put off the role of father and, as a sorrowing priest, cut the throat of his daughter....

Go now, strong men! Follow the high road of great example. Why slack off and turn your backs? When you overcome the earth, the stars will be yours. (*Consolation of Philosophy*: 4.pr 7-mt 7)

A thousand years later, Spenser's interpretation is much the same: "Homere...in the Persons of Agamemnon and Ulysses hath ensampled a good governour and a vertuous man, the one in his *Ilias*, the other in his *Odysseis*" ("Letter to Raleigh"). According to Bernardus, "He is called Agamemnon as if *agonis mene*, that is, *certaminis claritas*, 'clarity of argument.' Reason illumines the virtues oppressing the vices" (*On Virgil's Aeneid*: 6.489-493). Shakespeare's Fluellen praises the Duke of Exeter as being "as magnanimous as Agamemnon" (*Henry V*: 3.6.7; probably Shakespeare picked up this epithet for Agamemnon from the Renaissance dictionaries; see Starnes 1955: 113).

Agamemnon was, of course, also recognized as a tragic figure. His army sacked Troy and carried off much booty, but almost all of the Greeks were drowned in a great storm on their way home from Troy. Agamemnon managed to return home only to be killed by his wife's lover, Aegisthus, or by his wife, in another version. Boccaccio tells Agamemnon's story in his book of *The Fates of Famous Men*: "Agamemnon...as a result of the fall of Priam, wished for himself a magnificent and glittering triumph....Agamemnon's army was enriched by the booty of Asia, and he achieved an almost immortal reputation. Ilium was destroyed, the outrage of Paris avenged." But, Boccaccio continues, upon returning home, Agamemnon "was killed at Clytemnestra's pleading, and his murderer seized the palace and all the kingdom....The man who ruled kings was not able to bridle the passion of his own wife. Agamemnon felled Troy, but the Aegisthus, the adulterer, felled him. Thus perfidy vanquished virtue" (33-36). Even when he was understood as a tragic figure, then, Agamemnon could be seen as an example of virtue.

Bibliography: James Nohrnberg, *The Analogy of The Faerie Queene* (1976): 58-62; DeWitt Starnes and E. W. Talbert, *Classical Myth and Legend in Renaissance Dictionaries* (1955); M. M. Willcock, *A Companion to the Iliad* (1976).

AGLAURUS AND HERSE were sisters, in Ovid's version of the story (*Metamorphoses*: 2.708-832). When Mercury fell in love with the beautiful Herse, jealous Aglaurus demanded gold from him before she would allow access to her sister. Offended by this covetousness, Minerva then intervened. She called upon the hag Envy to curse Aglaurus; with this curse she becames bitterly envious of her sister, and then Mercury turned her to stone. Aglaurus was thus an example of envy, as we find in Dante (*Purgatorio*: 14.139). The *Chess of Love* commentary is typical:

We can also say that this signifies to us that those who...defame the wise and the good, whom Pallas signifies, as the envious are accustomed to do, whom Aglaurus signifies, should be cast out and hated by everyone, reputed as viler than stones. And as reason also, and human prudence, which can be understood by Pallas, request and desire that the envious be punished, so one could also certainly say that envy itself pays and punishes them in their bodies and souls....It blinds all of them and takes away their sense and reason, so that they are made insensate, as are stones. (739; see also 468; see also Sandys, *Ovid*: 121-122)

AJAX, son of Telamon, was a huge and fearless man. Among the Greeks Ajax was second only to Achilles as a warrior. Homer's *Iliad* (e.g., 7.181-312) provides instances of his greatness upon the plains of Troy. But Ovid wrote a vivid account of Ajax's unseemly contest with Ulysses for the arms of dead Achilles and of Ajax's mad fury when the arms and the attendant honor went to Ulysses (*Metamorphoses*: 13.1-398; see also Sophocles, *Ajax*, and Apollodorus, *Epitome*: 5.6-7). And so Christians remembered Ajax more for his envious anger than for his valor. Alanus, for example: "Ajax exceeds the discipline of the warrior, out-soldiering the soldier, and runs beyond the manner of military service in his rage" (*Anticlaudian*: 1.5). And Sidney writes about the power of poetry to provide moral examples; he offers Ajax as an example of Anger: "Anger the stoikes said, was a sort madnesse: let but Sophocles bring you Ajax upon a stage, killing and whipping sheepe and oxen, thinking them the Army of Greekes, with their Chieftaines Agamemnon, and Menelaus: and tell me if you have not a more familiar insight into Anger, then finding in the schoolemen his Genus and Difference" (*Defense of Poesy*: 14-15). Thus Tritonio lists Ajax as one of his examples of "The Furious" (*Mythologia*: 22); Tritonio also includes Ajax in his list of "The Envious," because of his lust for Achilles' arms (27).

There is a long-standing tradition that associates bigness of body with smallness of mind; Chaucer's Miller and college football players come most immediately to mind. Ajax is a prototype instance of such allegory. Golding wrote that Ajax "doth represent a man / Stout, headie, ireful, hault of mynd, and such a one as can / Abyde to suffer no repulse." Golding concludes that Ajax is an example of human covetousness for "glorie and reward" ("Epistle": 250-253).

The contest for the arms was itself understood allegorically, as we find in Sandys: "In this contention for the Armor, that difference is arbitrated, how the courage of the mind, and strength of the body, is of lesse use in affaires of warre, then councell and pollicy: the one personated in Ajax, and the other in Ulysses" (*Ovid*: 602).

Ajax could also serve in scatological puns. From about 1530 until the mid-eighteenth century, an English privy could be called a jakes (Partridge 1972: under *jakes*), as in Shakespeare's *King Lear*: "I will tread this unbolted villain into mortar, and daub the walls of a jakes with him" (2.2.67). This allowed puns on *a jakes* and *Ajax*. Harington's remarkable book, *The Metamorphosis of Ajax*, relies on this pun throughout, since the book treats of Harington's own invention, the flush toilet (Leland 1982). Shakespeare also makes the pun: "Your lion, that holds his poll-ax sitting on a close-stool, will be given to Ajax" (*Love's Labor's Lost*: 5.2.576-578).

Bibliography: John Leland, "A Joyful Noise: *The Metamorphosis of Ajax* as Spiritual Tract," *SAR*, 47 (1982): 53-62; Eric Partridge, *A Dictionary of Historical Slang* (1972).

ALCMAEON, AMPHIARAUS, AND ERIPHYLE. Alcmaeon killed his mother Eriphyle for betraying his father Amphiaraus. This unfortunate family appears in the story of the War of the Seven against Thebes, as this was told, for example, by Statius (*Thebaid*: 4.187-213) and the *Roman de Thèbes* (4711-4918). Ross retails the story in this way:

> Eriphyle...was the wife of Amphiaraus [a seer], who, understanding, that if he went to the Theban war, he should be killed, hid himself, till he was betrayed by his wife Eriphyle; who to that end received a golden chain from Polynices. Being forced therefore to go to war, left in charge with his son Alcmeon, that as soon as he should hear of his death, he should kill his Mother: Amphiarus was killed by Pyrrhus...: Upon the report of which news, Eriphyle was murthered by her son. (*Mystagogus Poeticus*: 111)

As de Weever (1987: 131) has suggested, Eriphyle thus became an example of a bad wife. De Weever cites Jerome (*Against Jovinianus*: 1.48) and Chaucer ("Wife of Bath's Tale": 740-746). See also Bernardus, who wrote that Eriphyle is to be counted among the "greedy lovers" (*On Virgil's Aeneid*: 6.445-447), and Sandys (*Ovid*: 444).

According to Statius, Alcmaeon was pursued by the avenging Furies. But his torments were thought to have continued after death as well: He was sometimes included in lists of those who suffer the torments of the damned in Hades (e.g., Propertius, *Elegies*: 3.5.31). Because he rose up against his mother, Alcmaeon could serve as an example of pride; Dante, for instance, makes Alcmaeon one of the examples of pride graven into the walkway on the terrace of pride in the *Purgatorio* (12.49-51)—those who were puffed up with pride are now trodden under foot. Ross writes that "In Alcmaeon we see the unnaturalness of a Son" (*Mystagogus Poeticus*: 111).

Bibliography: Jacqueline de Weever, *Chaucer Name Dictionary* (1987).

ALCYONE AND CEYX. In the ancient stories there were three women named Alcyone. One of the Pleiades—the seven daughters of Atlas—was named Alcyone (Apollodorus, *Library*: 3.10.1); one of Medusa's sisters was named Alcyone (Apollodorus, *Library*: 2.4.5); and there was Alcyone, daughter of Aeolus. Christians largely neglected the first two; but the daughter of Aeolus lived on. Christians remembered her as Ovid described her, as the loving wife of Ceyx (*Metamorphoses*: 11.383-749). When Ceyx set off on a sea journey, Alcyone offered up constant prayers for his safety; but he was drowned in a storm. Morpheus (god of sleep) came to her in the shape of her husband, to tell her of his fate. So distraught was she that the gods took pity on the pair and changed them into Halcyons, "flying in loving harmony over the broad waters" (11.749). Thus she was almost always interpreted as an example of the loving, faithful wife (Martin 1983). In Chaucer's version of the story, for example, we read that Ceyx "had a wife, / The beste that mighte bere lyfe" (*Book of the Duchess*: 63-64; see also Gower, *Confessio Amantis*: 4.2927-3123); she is one of Chaucer's virtuous pagans, an examplar of natural virtue (McCall 1979: 112-113). And Golding wrote that "In Ceyx and Alcyone appeeres most constant love, / Such as betweene the man and the wyfe too be it doth behove" (Epistle: 232-233).

Bibliography: Ellen Martin, "The Interpretation of Chaucer's Alcyone," *ChauR*, 18 (1983): 18-21; John P. McCall, *Chaucer among the Gods: The Poetics of Classical Myth* (1979).

ALPHEUS AND ARETHUSA. The Alpheus was a river of the Peloponnesus that flowed into the Ionian Sea. There were places along its course where it flowed underground, and legend had it that it flowed under the sea to issue forth again from the fountain of Arethusa at Syracuse. (This was still understood as fact as late as Sandys, *Ovid*: 261, and Ross, *Mystagogus Poeticus*: 19.) The explanatory fable told of the river god Alpheus, who was so much in love with the nymph Arethusa that he pursued her under the sea to Syracuse, where he mingled his waters with hers. Ovid tells the story in the *Metamorphoses* (5.572-641).

Fulgentius wrote that Alpheus was the "light of truth" seeking Arethusa, "the excellence of equity." (Whitbread translates this as "the equality of excellence," but "excellence of equity," or justice, makes better sense—this is how Sandys, *Ovid*: 262, for example, understands Fulgentius.) Fulgentius goes on to gloss Alpheus's going down under the earth as a descent "down to the lower world, that is into the hidden knowledge of good and evil"; Alpheus emerges, Fulgentius notes, without being tainted (*Mythologies*: 3.12; see also Ross, *Mystagogus Poeticus*: 19; for the allegory of the descent for knowledge, see **EPIC**). As Whitbread suggests in his note on this passage, Fulgentius further develops this notion of a descent for knowledge in his commentary on Virgil's *Aeneid*. Milton probably has Fulgentius's allegory in mind when he prays, in *Lycidas*, "Return, Alpheus" (132); the poet hopes perhaps that Lycidas's death/descent might remind us that is possible to travel through this fallen world without taint—and perhaps with some increase of wisdom (Allen 1956: 173).

For Berchorius, Arethusa "seems to be the soul which is loved by Alpheus—that is, by God; but sometimes she flees from him because of sin and scorns his company." God/Alpheus pursues her because he desires her, desires to join "her to himself in grace" (*Ovidius Moralizatus*: 244). Ross (*Mystagogus Poeticus*: 19) turns this about: Alpheus's pursuit of Arethusa is the human pursuit of virtue.

Bibliography: Don C. Allen, "Milton's Alpheus," *MLN*, 71 (1956): 172-173.

THE AMAZONS were a nation of warrior women, "men's equals" (Homer, *Iliad*: 3.189; see also Herodotus, *History*: 4.110-117; Plutarch, *Lives*: "Theseus"). These were troubling figures in ancient times: Warriors without a city, living apart from men, Amazons were often symbols of the world stood on its head, symbols of "otherness" and of the menace to civilized life (see, e.g., Larson 1995: 110-116). In ancient Greek paintings they were often portrayed in combat with such civilizing heroes as Hercules and Theseus (Pantel 1992: 226-229). In Batman's translation of Bartholomaeus we read that the Amazons' country was "parte in Asia, and parte in Europa, and is nigh Albania." But Batman himself was aware of the New World, and so he added the common contemporary opinion that Amazons were to be found in the Americas, where they "are most commonly assayled of their Enemies the barbarous Indians" (*Batman uppon Bartholomae*: 15.12). Raleigh, who had actually been to the New World, was also convinced that there were Amazons on those shores (*History of the World*: 431). But though opinion differed as to where the Amazons might be found, there was no question that they were fierce. Batman's Bartholomaeus had it that the Amazons "suffred no male live neither abide in no manner wise. But of nations that were nigh to them they chose husbandes because of children, and went to them in times that were ordeined, and conceived children, and...then they would compell theyr lovers to go from them...& would slay their sons, or send them to their fathers in certain times" (*Batman uppon Bartholomae*: 15.12).

As we consider the allegorical interpretations of Amazons, it is important to remember that manlike women were usually understood, figuratively, in one of two ways. Both interpretations grew out of the traditional Christian sense of the meaning of the relationship of man and woman. Augustine's statement is typical:

> our state is bad...when we adhere to fleshly pleasures. Let us conquer the blandishments and troubles of desire. If we are men let us subdue this woman, *Cupiditas*. With our guidance she will herself become better and no longer be called Cupidity but Temperance. When she leads and we follow she is called Lust....Let us follow Christ our Head, that she whose head we are may follow us....Women too have some virile quality whereby they can subdue feminine pleasures, and serve Christ and govern desire. (*Of True Religion*: 41)

According to the divinely instituted order of things, the wife was to be subservient to the husband. And so, as the spirit ought to control the flesh, so ought the husband to control his wife. The analogy was a commonplace. Erasmus: "Keep in mind that 'woman' is man's sensual part: she is our Eve...through whom that wiliest of serpents lures our passions into deadly pleasures" (*Enchiridion*: 39). The story of Aristotle ridden by Phyllis is a satiric inversion of this proper relationship (figs. 3, 4): the lovely Phyllis so beguiled sage Aristotle, that she could ride him, goading him with her little whip and controlling him with a bridle (see **ARISTOTLE**). It should be remembered that such ideas of controlling, bridling, and chastising of women were often realized in fact; for example, in sixteenth-century England female scolds were curbed with "the barbaric 'scold's bridle', or brank—an iron collar with a bit to prevent the victim from talking" (Underdown 1985: 123; see also Fletcher 1995: 273-274).

Indeed, the word "virtue" and the Latin *virtus* from which it derives have *vir*, "man," as their root—a fact frequently remarked upon during the Middle Ages and the Renaissance (see, e.g., Hoffman 1966: 41-42). In Jerome's Latin translation of the Bible, Eve is a *virago* before the fall (Gen 2:23), because before the fall she is *vir*tuous; in this sense she is manlike. After the fall Jerome calls her *mulier*, woman (Gen 3:12-13). Isidore makes Jerome's implied distinction explicit: A virago is a woman who "ignores the feminine passions. She is called a virago who acts like a man" (*Etymologiarum*: 11.2). *Vir*tuous, rational women, then, behave like men in Augustine's sense: They are subduing "feminine pleasures" by "some virile quality" (for more on male/female allegory see **ATTIS, CAENEUS, HERCULES: Hercules in General**, and **HERMAPHRODITUS AND SALMACIS**; for a history of such ideas in England, see Fletcher 1995: 83-98). This was accepted even by the feminist Christine de Pizan, who praised Dido for her strength and courage: "Because of her prudent government, they...called her Dido, which is the equivalent of saying *virago* in Latin, which means, "the woman who has the strength and force of a man" (*City of Ladies*: 1.46.3).

In the late Middle Ages, a few writers interpret the Amazons as being *vir*tuous in these terms. Christine de Pizan, for instance, wrote that the Amazon kingdom survived "For a long time...under the rule of several queens, very noble ladies whom they elected themselves, who governed them well and maintained their dominion with great strength" (*City of Ladies*: 1.4.3).

But there was another, more common, pejorative sense in which women acted like men—as we have seen, for example, in the story of Aristotle ridden by Phyllis (fig. 3 & 4), where the proper allegorical relationship of man and woman is inverted: Woman controls man; the passions control the reason. Such breaches of the natural order were taken seriously. During the Middle Ages women who dominated their husbands could be shamed, along with their husbands, in the *charivari*—festive processions organized to shame couples who were not conforming to the community's sexual mores (Underdown 1985: 121; see also Davis 1975: 124-151 on unruly women). Theseus's conquest of the Amazons and his marriage with Hippolyta in Chaucer's "Knight's Tale" could thus have been understood as a reestablishment of the proper natural order (Olson 1957: 101-103; Green 1960: 131). This idea goes back at least to Ovid's *Art of Love*, where the poet tells us that his purpose is to teach men how to subdue Amazons (2.743-744). Hercules, too, conquered the Amazons; he did so, according to Giovanni del Virgilio, "*a virtuoso*," by his *vir*tue ("Espositore delle *Metamorfosi*": 85).

Spenser's Britomart, for example, is a female Knight, representing warlike Elizabeth in book 3 of the *Faerie Queene*—but Britomart is *not* an Amazon. Spenser's cruel Radigund *is* an Amazon. Radigund enthralls Sir Artegall:

Thus there long while continu'd Artegall,
Serving proud Radigund with true subjection;

How ever it his noble heart did gall,
T'obay a womans tyrannous direction....
During which time, the warlike Amazon,
Whose wandring fancie after lust did raunge,
Gan cast a secret liking to this captive straunge.

Spenser explains:

Such is the crueltie of womenkynd,
When they have shaken off the shamefast band,
With which wise Nature did them strongly bynd,
T'obay the heasts of mans well ruling hand,
That then all rule and reason they withstand,
To purchase a licentious libertie.
But vertuous women wisely understand,
That they were borne to base humilitie,
Unlesse the heavens them lift to lawfull soveraintie.
(*Faerie Queene*: 5.5.25-26)

Spenser is careful to remember that the heavens can lift such a one as Elizabeth "to lawfull soveraintie," but for the rest Spenser is quite close to Augustine. And he would not call his Queen an Amazon.

Amazons were known for their cruelty: Webster makes Leonora exclaim,

Ha my sonne!
Ile be a fury to him—like an Amazon lady,
Ide cut off this right pap, that gave him sucke,
To shoot him dead.
(*Devil's Lawcase*: 3.3.288-91)

This notion that Amazons cut off their breasts had etymological roots. The Greeks characteristically understood the etymology of *Amazon* to be "no breasts"; but Isidore is typical of Medieval and Renaissance writers in assuming that Amazons cut off the right breast, so that it would not get in the way of their archery. Thus Amazons "were called unimammians" (*Etymologiarum*: 9.2.5; see also Batman, *Batman uppon Bartholomae*: 15.12).

With all of this, it is small wonder that, when John Knox wrote his *Regiment of Women* to decry the reign of Mary, Queen of Scots, he called Mary an Amazon. And he provides this marginal gloss: "Amazones were monstruous women, that coulde not abide the regiment of men, and therefore killed their husbandes" (*Monstrous Regiment of Women*: 13).

This conception of Amazons seems to have held even during the reign of Elizabeth—until, with England's defeat of the Armada, comparisons of puissant Elizabeth with Amazons became nearly irresistible (Schleiner 1978). By 1609 Ben Jonson (*Masque of Queens*) collaborated with Inigo Jones on a masque in which noble ladies played the parts of Amazons, as suggesting female virtue (Orgel 1975: 60-65). Ripa also made the Amazon an emblem of Virtue (*Iconologie*: 1.167).

Amazons seem to have been particularly important in sixteenth-century Spain, during a period when explorers were bringing back reports of actual tribes of Amazons in the New World across the sea. These Amazonian tribes were described as uncivilized, as barbarians—much in need of civilizing and Christianizing by the Spaniards. Talking about Amazons, then, was one way of talking about Indians (Taufer 1991).

For another example of woman rule, see **DIDO**.

Bibliography: N. Z. Davis, *Society and Culture in Early Modern France* (1975); A. Fletcher, *Gender, Sex and Subordination in England 1500-1800* (1995); R. H. Green, "Classical Fable and English Poetry," in D. Bethurum, *Critical Approaches to Medieval Literature* (1960): 110-133; R. L. Hoffman, *Ovid and The Canterbury Tales* (1966); G. B. Jackson, "Witches, Amazons, and Shakespeare's Joan of Arc," *ELR*, 18 (1988): 40-65; J. Larson, *Greek Heroine Cults* (1995); J. C. McLucas, "Amazon...Women and War in the Aristocratic Literature of 16th-Century Italy," *Italianist*, 8 (1988): 33-55; L. Montrose, "The Work of Gender in the Discourse of Discovery," in S. Greenblatt, *New World Encounters* (1993).

Paul A. Olson, "*A Midsummer Night's Dream* and the Meaning of Court Marriage," *ELH*, 24 (1957): 95-119; Stephen Orgel, *The Illusion of Power: Political Theater in the English Renaissance* (1975); Pauline Schmitt Pantel, *From Ancient Goddesses to Christian Saints* (1992); Winfried Schleiner, "*Divina virago*: Queen Elizabeth as an Amazon," *SP*, 75 (1978): 163-80; Simon Shepherd, *Amazons and Warrior Women: Varieties of Feminism in Seventeenth-Century Drama* (1981); Alison Taufer, "The Only Good Amazon Is a Converted Amazon: The Woman Warrior and Christianity in the *Amadís Cycle*," in Jean Brink et al., *Playing with Gender: A Renaissance Pursuit* (1991): 35-51; D. E. Underdown, "The Taming of the Scold," in Anthony Fletcher and John Stevenson, *Order and Disorder in Early Modern England* (1985): 116-136; Celeste Turner Wright, "The Amazons in Elizabethan Literature," *SP*, 37 (1940): 433-456.

AMPHION and Zethus were the twin sons of Antiope and Jupiter. In classical times, the twins were often contrasted, with Zethus relying on his strength, Amphion on his music (see Appendix A, "Music"). Thus when they built the walls for their city, Thebes, Zethus carried rocks, while Amphion moved rocks by the power of his playing upon the lyre. Amphion was the gentle, contemplative singer; Zethus the active man, the hunter.

But little was made of this contrast during the Middle Ages and the Renaissance. Indeed, since Pliny (*Natural History*: 7.204) had made Amphion the inventor of the music in the Lydian mode, Isidore has Zethus share the honors with Amphion for inventing music among the Thebans (*Etymologiarum*: 3.16.1; see also Rabanus, *De Universo*: 495; Boccaccio, *Genealogie Deorum*: 5.30,32; and Conti, *Mythologie*: 8.15).

For the most part, Christians remembered Amphion for his music, and here the allegory is closely related to that of Orpheus; indeed, Orpheus and Amphion are often linked, as they are in Martianus' chapter on Harmony (*Marriage of Philology and Mercury*: 907-908, quoted below under **ARION**), where their power to charm with music is a figure for Harmony, the divinely instituted ordering force in the universe. In Macrobius, Orpheus and Amphion were "the first to attract in their song men lacking any refinement and stolid as rocks" (*On the Dream of Scipio*: 2.3.8). Petrarch implores the unnamed recipient of one of his poems to let his "noble mind" and his "eloquence now show their power"; he will then be like "Orpheus and Amphion"; he will be able to awake "Italy with her sons...so that she takes up her lance for Jesus" (*Rime sparse*: 28.61-75). This is to say that Petrarch hopes the man will, by his eloquence, be able to unite the Italians in a determination to go on crusade. The *Chess of Love* commentary paraphrases these ideas:

> Therefore we should know that Orpheus and Amphion were two very wise ancient musicians, not only of harmonic music...but also of great discretion, intelligence, and the beautiful speech corresponding to these qualities....Because then Orpheus and Amphion by their pleasant music and their melodious eloquence often led the proud, the avaricious, and the madmen who live like animals, hardened in soul and vices and long stubborn in them, back to the path of reason and of good and virtuous life, the ancient poets pretended that mountains and stones followed these musicians. (281; see also Landino, *Disputationes Camuldenses*: 120)

Sandys' comment is also Euhemeristic and also typical of the moral commentary on Amphion: he was the "King of Thebes, who first incompassed that citty with a wall, to defend it against the assaults of Plegyas. But fained here to have drawne the stones together, and built it with the musick of his harpe: in that by his wisdome and eloquence he brought the salvage people to civility, and caused them to cohabit" (*Ovid*: 292). Bredero had this allegory in mind when he urged the young people of the Netherlands to forget self and think of the common weal: "This was Amphion's art," he wrote, "wherewith he wisely led the Barbarians to oneness of will and order" ("Apollo Speaks to the Netherlandish Youth": 158-160).

Ficino (*Letters*, vol. 1: 143) makes Amphion one of his exemplary musicians and so associates him with the kind of music that can harmonize the soul and even heal the body, as David's playing upon the lyre had healed Saul (1 Sam 16:16-23).

Amphion was also occasionally remembered as the husband of Niobe: all of their children were killed by Apollo and Diana as a punishment for presumption. In relation to this story, Amphion could be seen as an example of the punishment of "Contempt for the gods" (Reynolds, *Mythomystes*: 169)—but Niobe was much more often interpreted in this way (see **NIOBE**).

For related music allegory, see **ARION, ORPHEUS**, and Appendix A, "Music."

Bibliography: Richard L. Hoffman, *Ovid and the Canterbury Tales* (1966): 151-154.

AMYCLAS was Caesar's steersman. Lucan tells his story. In the course of his battle with Pompey at Epirus, Caesar decided to take a small boat across a dangerous stretch of water to call up reinforcements. Amyclas was not afraid to cross the wind-tossed waters, because he was so poor that he had nothing to lose. This provided a occasion for Lucan to moralize upon the advantages of poverty: "No thought of the war had he: he knew that poor men's huts are not plundered in time of civil war. How safe and easy the poor man's life and his humble dwelling!" (*Civil War*: 5.526-528; see also Plutarch, *Lives*: 877).

Thus it was that Amyclas became in the Middle Ages an example of virtuous poverty (Curtius 1963: 60-61). Petrarch, for example, gives the name Amyclas to a poor shepherd who will tend his sheep and make his music in virtuous poverty, while his interlocutor, "though rich, will yet find burning cares to trouble [his] leisure" (*Bucolicum Carmen*: 8). Dante also makes use of Amyclas in this way (*Paradiso*: 11.65-69).

Bibliography: Ernst Curtius, *European Literature and the Latin Middle Ages* (1963).

ANDROMEDA was the daughter of Cepheus, king of Ethiopia, and Cassiopia (for Andromeda as black, see McGrath 1992). Cassiopia was so vain of her own beauty as to vie with the Nereids, boasting that she was more beautiful than any of them. The Nereids, being sea-goddesses, demanded that Jupiter punish this presumption, and so Andromeda was chained to a rock, for her mother's sin, to be devoured by a terrible sea monster (see Ovid, *Metamorphoses*: 4.663-764; Apollodorus, *Library*: 2.4.3-4; Hyginus, *Fabulae*: 64). Perseus arrived upon the scene bearing the head of the Gorgon he had so recently slain. He fell in love with Andromeda the moment he saw her; and so he saved her, holding up the head of the Gorgon before the monster and so changing him into stone. Andromeda was later changed into a constellation (e.g., Hyginus, *Poetica Astronomica*: 2.11). The story was understood as a moral example at least as early as Hyginus, who wrote that Cassiopia "boasted that she excelled the Nereids in beauty. For this she was put among the constellations, seated in a chair. On account of her impiety, as the sky turns, she seems to be carried along lying on her back" (2.10).

Christians continued this tradition, but they also recognized in the story a parallel with the story of Christian salvation: humanity saved from the sin of their parents, Adam and Eve. This interpretation goes back at least as far as the *Ovide Moralisé* (5.1035-1078) and this passage from Berchorius:

Say that Perseus signifies the Son of God....At last from the air in which he flew [on Pegasus]—that is from the height of paradise—he saw the noble girl Andromeda—that is the human soul which was heir of the heavenly kingdom—who was condemned to be given over to a sea monster—that is the devil—and to be devoured because of the sin of her mother who wanted to compare herself to goddesses; for, at the devil's urging, she desired divinity....Bound by the chains of sin she was waiting for the devouring beast on the shore of this world. Perseus—that is Christ—pitied her and descended to her by his incarnation and...fought against the beast—that is the Devil—to free her and freed her by means of the wood of the cross. (*Ovidius Moralizatus*: 226-227)

Sandys' interpretation combines all the elements of the earlier allegorization:

By this the ancient reproved their pride and ambition, who would be thought more then mortall; when all humane beauty is worse then deformity, and all glory despicable, compared with the coelestiall: declaring besides that the offences of Princes are not seldome punished in their subjects and posterity. Yet Andromeda, innocent Virtue, shall never misse of that sacred succour, which will not only deliver her from the present danger, but match her to Perseus, that is, unto Honour and Felicitie: both after converted into glorious constellations. So...Cassiope...with her heeles upward, to deterre from the like preposterous arrogancy. (*Ovid*: 219-220)

Cassiopia could also serve as an example of the punishment of presumption or "Contempt of the gods," as Reynolds put it (*Mythomystes*: 169).

Bibliography: Elizabeth McGrath, "The Black Andromeda," *JWCI*, 55 (1992): 1-18; DeWitt T. Starnes and E. W. Talbert, *Classical Myth and Legend in Renaissance Dictionaries* (1955): 218; Rosemond Tuve, *Allegorical Imagery* (1966): 35-36, 320.

ANTAEUS was a giant, the son of Neptune and Gaia, the Earth. He was remembered as one of Hercules' mighty foes. Antaeus was said to grow stronger every time he touched his mother Earth (e.g., Lucan, *Civil War*: 4.593-660; Ovid, *Metamorphoses*: 9.184). According to Fulgentius,

Antaeus is explained as a form of lust...; he was born of the earth because lust is conceived of the flesh. Also he emerged the more agile by keeping touch with the earth, for lust rises the more evilly as it shares the flesh. Also he is overcome by Hercules...for he perishes when contact with the earth is denied him....For when virtue bears aloft the whole mind and denies it the sight of the flesh, it at once emerges victorious. (*Mythologies*: 2.4; see also Vatican Mythographer III: 13.2).

Boccaccio, mentioning Fulgentius as his authority, interprets Antaeus as "earthly desires, which are born of the flesh alone" (*Genealogie Deorum*: 1.13).

Many others wrote in the same tradition. Guido da Pisa, for example, has it that Hercules' victory is that of "the spirit" over "the flesh" (*Super Comediam Dantis*: 651). For Landino Antaeus signifies "the appetites" (*De Vera Nobilitate*: 108; see also Salutati, *De Laboribus Herculis*: 3.27.8). Ficino wrote that "reason within us is called Hercules: he destroys Antaeus, that is the monstrous images of fantasy." When Hercules lifts Antaeus off the ground, "he removes himself from the senses and physical images" (*Letters*, vol. 3: 27). And in Fraunce we find that Hercules wrestled with Antaeus, who ever throwne downe to the earth, receaved new strength from the earth, till at last, hee lifted him up, and strangled him in the ayre: so the spirit still striveth with the body, but can never overcome it, till he lift it up so high from the ground, that with his feete, to weete his affections, he receave no new assistance from his mother the earth. (*Countesse of Pembrokes Yvychurch*: 46v)

In Spenser's *Faerie Queen* one of Arthur's most difficult adversaries is an Antaeus-figure named Maleger; no sooner does Arthur strike him down,

> When suddein up the villein overthrowne,
> Out of his swowne arose, fresh to contend,
> And gan himself to second battell wend. (2.11.35)

After several iterations of this, Arthur remembers that Earth was Maleger's mother, so that every time Arthur casts him down, she "raysd him up much stronger than before" (45). Finally, Arthur holds Maleger aloft and squeezes the life out of him. We are not surprised to find that Spenser's Maleger/Antaeus is the leader of the personifications of the temptations of the senses. Sandys explained Antaeus in this same tradition (*Ovid*: 428); see also Ross, who interpreted Antaeus as the "earthly affections" (*Mystagogus Poeticus*: 171).

This is one of a number of stories in which Hercules was understood as a type of Christ. Guido da Pisa, for example, tells us that "Allegorically, truly by Hercules we understand Christ, by Antaeus truly the devil, with whom Christ fought on the mountain and on the cross, and finally defeated him" (*Super Comediam Dantis*: 652). Milton is writing in this tradition when he likens Satan to Antaeus at the end of *Paradise Regained* (4.563-568).

Bibliography: James Nohrnberg, *The Analogy of The Faerie Queene* (1976): 368-369; DeWitt T. Starnes and E. W. Talbert, *Classical Myth and Legend in Renaissance Dictionaries* (1955): 238.

ANTIGONE. The Antigone best known to moderns is Sophocles' Antigone, the bold daughter of Oedipus and Jocasta. Against the counsel of her more timid sister, Ismene, Antigone defied cruel King Creon's ban and scattered the dust of burial over her brother Polynices' corpse. But this Antigone attracted little attention during the Middle Ages and the Renaissance. Another Antigone, the daughter of Laomedon and sister of King Priam of Troy, excited more comment. She was vain of her hair, claiming that it was more beautiful even than Juno's. The goddess punished her by turning her hair into snakes. Eventually she was turned into a stork. Ovid places this Antigone among the figures proud Arachne weaves into her tapestry (*Metamorphoses*: 6.93-97; see **ARACHNE**). Berchorius thus interprets her as a figure for rebellious presumption (*Ovidius Moralizatus*: 251), as does Sandys (*Ovid*: 288-289). Tritonio (*Mythologia*) includes her in his list of "The Presumptuous."

Chaucer names one of Criseyde's nieces Antigone in *Troylus and Criseyde*. This is the niece who sings the love song in the garden (2.827-875). Her name—whether Chaucer had the Theban or the Trojan Antigone in mind—would have added to the freight of irony in this scene: a naive girl with a *de casibus* name singing of love without end in a city about to fall because of the misordered love of Paris and Helen (see **TROY**; see Wood 1984: 138-140).

Bibliography: Chauncey Wood, *The Elements of Chaucer's Troilus* (1984).

APOLLO (the Clarian, Cynthius, the Delphian, the Delian, Phoebus, Sol, Thymbraeus). Apollo was one of the Olympian gods. He and his sister Diana were born on Mount Cynthius, the children of Zeus and Leto. Apollo spawned an unusually wide range of meanings. Cicero wrote that Apollo "is identified with the sun....Sol (the sun) may have been so named from 'solus' (alone), either because he is 'alone' in his great size among the stars, or because he blots out all the others when he rises so that he 'alone' is visible" (*Nature of the Gods*: 2.68). But Apollo was also early associated with healing. "The sun also gives saving health to all," wrote Macrobius, "for its kindly warmth is believed to bring health to everything that has breath." And thus Apollo, "as having charge of all that brings health, is called 'Source of Healing'" (*Saturnalia*: 1.17.13,21). Rabanus (*De Universo*: 500) and Hugh of St. Victor (*Didascalicon*: 3.2) wrote of Apollo as the author of all medicine. Such ideas were still current during the Renaissance: In 1575 Robert Laneham wrote a detailed description of a pageant staged for Queen Elizabeth at Killingworth Castle in that year. At one point Apollo appears: "Phoebus, besides his continual and most delicious muzik...appointed the Princes too adourn her Highnes' Coourt, Counselerz, Herauds, and sanguine youth..., learned Phizicianz, and no need of them" (in Nichols 1823, vol. 1: 469). For Spenser, too, Apollo was the "King of Leaches" (*Faerie Queene*: 4.12.25; see also Fraunce, *Countesse of Pembrokes Yvychurch*: 33r; Seznec 1961: 28-29).

But the heat of the sun—and thus Apollo—could also bring about disease. It was Apollo, we remember, who brought the plague upon the Greeks in the book 1 of the *Iliad*, and the Greek word *apollyon* meant "destroyer" (see Revelation 9:11). Macrobius explains this:

Others hold that the sun is called Apollo as destructive (*apollunta*) of life; for it kills and destroys living creatures when it sends a pestilence among them in time of immoderate heat....[M]en consumed by a fever are said to be "smitten by Apollo" and "smitten by the sun"....This is why statues of Apollo are equipped with a bow and arrows, the arrows being understood to represent the force of the sun's rays—as Homer says of Apollo: "But then he launched his sharp arrow at the men, and smote." (*Saturnalia*: 1.17.9-12, quoting *Iliad*: 1.51; see also Heraclitus, *Allégories d'Homère*: 8.1-4; Fulgentius, *Mythologies*: 1.12; Fraunce, *Countesse of Pembrokes Yvychurch*: 33r)

Macrobius explains the contradiction in this way:

> It is not surprising that men pay honor to the god's twofold activities under different names, for we find other gods, too, with double powers and double names, contrary in meaning but relating to the same object....Thus it is that we worship Apollo, the sun, sometimes under names which signify health and sometimes under names which signify pestilence, although, nevertheless, the pestilence which he sends on the wicked indicates clearly that the god is the defender of the righteous. (*Saturnalia*: 1.17.22-23)

As the god of the sun, Apollo was also the god of light, and thus of wisdom, divination, and omens. Fulgentius wrote that the ancients "chose him as the god of omens, either because the sun turns into clear light everything obscure, or because in its rising and setting the orb gives effect to interpretations of many kinds....They also associate Apollo with the tripod because the sun has had knowledge of the past, sees the present, and will see the future" (*Mythologies*: 1.12, 17).

Bernardus refers to Apollo as "*Sapientia*," Wisdom (*On Martianus Capella*: 9.412); the *Ovide Moralisé* glosses Apollo as "divine wisdom" (2.2550); and in the *Chess of Love* commentary, the sun, among its several meanings, "also signifies prudence, sapience, and even the domination of occult things....And because of this, the ancient poems referred to the sun under the name of Phoebus, the god of sapience; as others, under the name of Apollo, the god of divination" (76; see also Landino, *Disputationes Camuldenses*: 138).

Apollo was also the god of music. In the first century A.D., Heraclitus (*Allégories d'Homère*: 12.3) had associated Apollo (as the Sun) with the music of the spheres. Fifteen hundred years later Sandys gives Apollo a lyre with seven strings, "in refference to the seven planets" (*Ovid*: 73; see also Lynche, *Fountaine of Ancient Fiction*: Eiii). Often Apollo's music was associated with his healing (see Appendix A, "Music"), as we find, for example, in Bernardus's euhemeristic explanation of Apollo: "historically, Apollo was a wise man who greatly prospered in medicine and discovered a medicinal method (that is, the musical method) and cured the sick with his songs. Therefore, he is said to have the Muses as companions" (*On Virgil's Aeneid*: 6.9). Here is Boccaccio on Apollo's healing and music:

> Apollo was the first to discover the virtues of herbs, and the first to adapt these virtues to the needs of mankind. And because of this, he was called not only the inventor but the god of medicine....And because he discovered the harmony of the human pulse, Mercury, the prince of number and measure, is said to have given him the lyre. This meant that just as the various strings of the lyre may be skillfully played to produce a melody, so the body's various pulses may be composed by a good physician into a bodily harmony. (*Genealogie Deorum*: 5.3)

Bacon writes in the same tradition: "This variable composition of man's body hath made it an instrument easy to distemper; and therefore the poets did well to conjoin

Music and Medicine in Apollo; because the office of medicine is but to tune this curious harp of man's body and to reduce it to harmony" (as found in Lemmi 1933: 118; for Apollo, music, and the Muses among the Renaissance Neo-Platonists, see Cheney 1993).

Apollo was also the god of the closely related art of poetry. Fulgentius again: "They also assign to Apollo the nine Muses and add him to the Muses as a tenth one, for the reason that there are ten organs of articulation for the human voice, whence Apollo is also depicted with a lyre of ten strings" (*Mythologies*: 1.15; see also Ausonius, *Appendix to Ausonius*: 3; Fraunce, *Countesse of Pembrokes Yvychurch*: 33v). The title page of Alexander Ross's *Mystagogus Poeticus, or the Muses Interpreter* (fig. 2) shows Apollo as the musician-poet—or rather, with the nine Muses who surround him, as the fountainhead of all music and poetry. The mythographer, Ross himself, stands with his key, ready to unlock the secret allegories of the poetry Apollo and the Muses inspire. Apollo is at work in the same way on the title page (fig. 16) of Sandys' *Ovid's Metamorphosis, Englished, Mythologized, and Represented in Figures* (for more on this title page, see **JUPITER, MINERVA, NEPTUNE**). Sandys explains this allegory in the last lines of the poem that follows the title page:

> Phoebus Apollo (sacred Poesy)
> Thus taught: for in these ancient Fables lie
> The mysteries of all Philosophie.
> Some Natures secrets shew; in some appeare
> Distempers staines; some teach us how to beare
> Both Fortunes, bridling Joy, Griefe, Hope, and Feare...
> All fitly mingling Profit with Delight.

Associated with light and sun as he was, Apollo could also be the god of learning (e.g., Fulgentius, *On Virgil*: 18). Lynche provides a typical explanation of this aspect of Apollo's meaning:

The auncients when they intended to set down how the liberall arts, and all other sciences, depended one upon the other, and were as it were knit and coheared together, depictured the Muses, holding one another by the hand and heedfully dauncing (as it were in a round) lead and guided by Apollo: which meaneth that superiour light and understanding, which illuminateth and enknowledgeth the intellectuall parts of man. The heavens (according to the opinion of the Platonickes) have every one their severall Muse, called by them oftentimes Syrens, as most harmoniously and sweetly singing, alluded unto the celestial orbes, which in number are likewise nine, and have their motions as the receive their severall powers from the son, which commandeth absolutely both above him, here with us, and in the lower center: by reason whereof he is called *Dio del Cielo, della terra, e dell'inferno* [God of the heaven, of the earth, and of hell]: and the ancients attribute unto him powerful commands over all the three. The Harpe which (as I have said before) he holdeth in his hand, denotateth the celestiall and incomparable musicke of the heavenly orbes: his shield or target by his side, represents the circular composition and rotunditie of our hemysphere. (*Fountaine of Ancient Fiction*: Eiii)

When all of this is added together, it is not surprising that some came to regard Apollo as a type of Christ. A fifth-century hymn praised Christ as the true Apollo (Ohly 1978: 133). At the beginning of the *Paradiso* Dante invokes Apollo: "O good Apollo, for this last labor make me such a vessel of your worth as you require for granting your beloved laurel" (1.13-15). Here the typology is complex: Apollo is the sun, "the planet that leads men aright by every path" (*Inferno*: 1.17-18); Christ is the source of grace and divine illumination. Apollo, the god who bestows poetic inspiration, is the grantor of the poet's laurel; Christ, the source of spiritual inspiration, is the grantor of the heavenly crown of glory.

Berchorius writes in the same tradition: "Or say that Apollo is the sun of justice Christ who through purity is ever-young. He had a golden tripod—that is the unity of a triple nature, soul, body, and divinity....With the arrow of the cross he laid low the python—that is Lucifer" (*Ovidius Moralizatus*: 60-61).

Apollo could also stand in general opposition to Venus and Bacchus, with Apollo figuring forth control, reason, and temperance; Venus and Bacchus figuring forth license and the passions. This is the meaning of a Neo-Platonic engraving after Baccio Bandinelli, *The Fray of Cupid and Apollo* (fig. 1)—Bandinelli's depiction of the war between the gods from book 21 of Homer's *Iliad*, where Mars and Venus lead one side into battle, Juno and Minerva the other. Heraclitus interprets this theomachia as a battle between "the virtues and the vices" (*Allégories d'Homère*: 54.1). He goes on to suggest that the theomachia can also be understood as the opposition of the elements—and he interprets the story as well in astrological terms (e.g., Buffière 1956: 593-594). In strictly Ficinian terms, Bandinelli's engraving illustrates the eternal conflict between Lust and Reason (Panofsky 1972: 190). We see two squadrons of gods on either side of a chasm. The Neo-Platonic Mind rides her cloud above the strife. On her left hand (the hand sinister) we see a Satyr-like Cupid (aiming his arrow), Venus (directing Cupid and handing him his arrows), and Vulcan (making weapons). The temple of Venus burns with the fires of lust. Apollo leads the group on Mind's right hand, the forces of reason and control: Apollo has just released his arrow; Saturn (deep thought) reclines just below Jupiter, Diana (chastity), Hercules (manly virtue; he leans upon his club), and Mercury (eloquence, acuteness).

For those observers who might have forgotten their Ficino, the Latin distichs at the bottom make all clear:

> Behold, divine Reason and calamitous human lust
> Do battle, with thee, noble Mind, as umpire.

> Here you cast your light on honourable deeds
> And there obscure profane deeds with clouds....

> Learn, O mortals, that the stars surpass the clouds
> As sacred reason does the idle appetites.

It was in this same tradition that Bredero entitled a poem of moral instruction "Apollo...Speaks to the Netherlandish Youth."

For other myths having to do with Apollo, see **MARSYAS, MUSES, PYTHON**.

Bibliography: Félix Buffière, *Les Mythes d'Homère* (1956); Girolami Cheney, "The Chamber of Apollo of the Casa Vasari," *SI*, 15 (1993): 135-176; Charles W. Lemmi, *The Classical Deities in Bacon* (1933); Henry Lotspeich, *Classical Mythology in the Poetry of Edmund Spenser* (1932): 37-38; John Nichols, *The Progresses and Public Processions of Queen Elizabeth*, 3 vols. (1823); Friedrich Ohly, "Typologische Figuren aus Natur und Mythus," in Walter Haug, *Formen und Functionen der Allegorie* (1978); Erwin Panofsky, *Renaissance and Renascences in Western Art* (1972); Jean Seznec, *The Survival of the Pagan Gods* (1961).

APULEIUS was a Roman poet. His best-known work was *The Metamorphoses* or *The Golden Ass*. The fiction of *The Metamorphoses* is that one Lucius, dabbling carelessly with magic, is turned into an ass; and in this form he hears many stories. Eventually, Isis transforms him into a man again. At the end of the book, the narrator is identified with Apuleius himself. *The Metamorphoses* was sometimes interpreted as being about the bestialization of human beings by the passions (see Appendix B, "Bestialization"). Here is Burton, for example:

> The major part of lovers are carried headlong like so many brute beasts; reason counsels one way...yet this furious lust precipitates, counterpoiseth, weighs down on the other; though it be their utter undoing, perpetual infamy, loss, yet will they do it, and become at last...void of sense; degenerate into dogs, hogs, asses, brutes; as Jupiter into a bull, Apuleius into an ass, Lycaon a wolf, Tereus a lapwing, Callisto a bear, Elpenor and Gryllus into swine by Circe. (*Anatomy of Melancholy*: 3.2.3)

The real Apuleius was brought to trial for using magic to get Pudentilla, a rich widow, to marry him. He responds to these charges in his *Apologia*; he argues, in effect, that those who accuse him of magic are so foolish that they fail to see his religious seriousness and the scientific merits of his research. Still, Apuleius was known as a magus during the Middle Ages (see Schlam 1990); indeed, some editions of the *Apologia* were entitled *On Magic*. Apuleius's *Metamorphoses* also has a good deal to say about magic.

Bibliography: Carl C. Schlam, "Apuleius in the Middle Ages," in A. S. Bernardo and S. Levin, *The Classics in the Middle Ages* (1990): 363-369.

ARACHNE presumed to contest Athena's skill in weaving. Arachne was consequently most commonly understood as an example of pride, or "insolent boasting," in the phrase of Vatican Mythographer I (91). She is, for instance, one of the examples of pride graven into the walkway on the Terrace of Pride in Dante's *Purgatorio* (12.43; see Macfie 1991). For Fraunce, Arachne was like Niobe, "worthily plagued" because of "her excessive pride and contempt of God" (*Countesse of Pembrokes Yvychurch*: 14r; see also Dolce, *Transformationi*: 135;

Viana, *Ovid*: 6.1; Ross, *Mystagogus Poeticus*: 30; Reynolds, *Mythomystes*: 169). But Arachne could also be understood as a profane artist. In the course of his commentary on Ovid's (*Metamorphoses*: 6.1-145) version of the story, Sandys explains both interpretations: "Arachne...durst compare, and challenge her in that art, which she her selfe had taught her....[Arachne and Athena] put their skill to the triall....Pallas weaves the ancient contention betweene her and Neptune about the naming of Athens." In the course of this contest, Athena brings an olive tree to Athens. Sandys assures us that this story which Athena weaves has a moral meaning:

Morally it preferres the excellency of peace and publique tranquillitie, expressed by the Olive; before the trouble and distemper of a state, deciphered by the Ocean: the one being the symbol of Peace, and the other of Turbulency; the first appropriated to Minerva, and the latter to Neptune. Moreover, this fable decides, and by the sentence of the Gods, that a Citty is not so much renowned for riches and empire, purchased by naval victories; as by civill arts and a peaceable government.

Athena adds to the picture, Sandys continues, four moral fables having to do with the punishment of pride: the stories of Haemus and Rhodope, the Pygmies, Laomedon's daughter Antigone, and Cinyras's daughters. All the stories Athena weaves, then, "serve for instruction."

But profane Arachne sets forth the rapes and adulteries of the Gods. She makes Jupiter in the likenesse of a Bull to steale away Europa....Neptune defiling Arne in the forme of a Bull....Bacchus to deceive Erigone in the likenesse of a grape....Lastly she produceth Saturne to beget the Centaure Chiron on Philyra in the likenesse of a Horse....
    These personages, with the places, being woven to the life by Arachne, she incloseth the web with a traile of Ivy; well suting with the wanton argument and her owne ambition....Minerva teares in peeces what envy could not but commend, because it published the vices of great ones; and beats her with the shuttle to chastise her presumption.

Finally, Athena changes her "into a Spider: that she might still retaine the art which she had taught her, but toile without profit. For uselesse and worthlesse labors are expressed by the spiders web: by which the Psalmist presents the infirmity of man, and vanity of his actions" (*Ovid*: 285-291; Sandys probably has Isaiah 59:5-6 in mind, rather than one of the Psalms). Sandys might have found much the same interpretation in Berchorius (*Ovidius Moralizatus*: 248-249) and a number of others. For Renouard, Arachne's web figures forth the sophistries of men whose doctrine lacks real substance (*Ovid*: 153).
    Bibliography: Pamela Royston Macfie, "Ovid, Arachne, and the Poetics of Paradise," in Rachel Jacoff and Jeffrey Schnapp, *The Poetry of Allusion: Virgil and Ovid in Dante's Commedia* (1991): 159-172.

ARCADIA. The historical Arcadia was a mountainous region in the midst of the Peloponnesus. The Arcadians were said to be a very ancient people, descendants of Arcas, one of the sons of Callisto (see, e.g., Isidore, *Etymologiarum*: 14.4.15). Their land was cut off from the sea; and so the Arcadians, shut up in their mountain valleys, lived famously primitive, simple lives. Hermes was said to have been born in Arcadia, and Pan made Arcadia his realm. But as Panofsky has explained, already in antiquity there were two sharply contrasting attitudes toward the Arcadians. Panofsky cites a wide range of Greek and Latin authors who disparaged Arcadian simplicity (1955: 297-303; see also Panofsky 1936: 223-224). Philostratus was typical in calling them "acorn-eating swine" (*Life of Apollonius*: 8.7). Thus it was that, though Arcadia was at Theocritus's doorstep, his pastoral poetry takes us not to Arcadia, but to far-off Sicily for scented air and bounding lambs. Some Latin poets agreed with this dim assessment of Arcadia. Ovid, for example, wrote that "The Arcadians are said to have possessed their land before the birth of Jove, and that folk is older than the moon. Their life was like that of beasts, unprofitably spent; artless as yet and raw was the common herd. Leaves did they use for houses...no land was under the dominion of the husbandman....Under the open sky they lived and went about naked" (*Fasti*: 2.290-300). According to some traditions, the Arcadians at least had music, a gift from Pan; Ovid neglects to mention even this.

But all this changed with Virgil. Virgil's *Eclogues* idealize Arcadia, forgetting the regions's chills and damp in favor of "mossy springs, and grass softer than sleep," where "the buds swell on the gladsome tendril" (*Eclogues*: 7.45-48). Arcadia is the Golden Age—distant in space rather than time. In Virgil's Arcadia there is ample time for shepherds to think of love and tootle on Pan pipes, while their sheep and goats nibble tender shoots. Graver matters do occasionally intrude—but they arise always against the Arcadian backdrop of primitive innocence.

Virgil's *Eclogues* were of course known to the Middle Ages, but his version of Arcadia was neglected. Lydgate, for example, refers to Arcadia simply as "the myghty londe" where "Lychaon was, lord and kyng" (*Reson and Sensuallyte*: 4722-4723). But during the Renaissance Virgil's Arcadia flourished remarkably, providing the leafy setting for Sannazaro's *Arcadia*, Montemayor's *Diana*, and Sidney's *Arcadia*, among many others. Arcadian shepherds, wrote Sidney, are "a happie people, wanting litle, because they desire not much" (*Arcadia*: 1.2.4). This conception of an idealized Arcadia exercised the imaginations particularly of the Elizabethans. The court of Elizabeth recreated Arcadian simplicty with inventive (and paradoxical) richness (Strong 1977: 129-162).

For more on Golden Age allegory, see **THE FOUR AGES**.

Bibliography: Petra Maisak, *Arcadien: Genese und Typologie einer idyllishcen Wunschwelt* (1981); Erwin Panofsky, "*Et in Arcadia Ego*; on the Conception of Transience in Poussin and Watteau," in R. Klibansky and H. Paton, *Philosophy and History: Essays Presented to Ernst Cassirer* (1936); Panofsky, *Meaning in the Visual Arts* (1955); Renato Poggioli, *The Oaten Flute: Essays on Pastoral Poetry and the Pastoral Ideal* (1975); Bruno Snell, "Arcadia: the Discovery of a Spiritual Landscape," in *Discovery of the Mind: The Greek Origins of European Thought* (1953): 281-309; Roy Strong, *The Cult of Elizabeth* (1977).

ARGUS was a giant with eyes all over his body. When Jupiter transformed his mistress Io into a heifer to avoid discovery of his adultery, jealous Juno set the hundred-eyed Argus to watch Io. Jupiter then sent Mercury to slay Argus. Argus was said ever to be watchful; some of his eyes were always open. But Mercury played his pipes so skillfully as to charm all Argus's eyes to sleep; then Mercury cut off his head. Juno took dead Argus's eyes and set them on the feathers of her bird, the peacock (Ovid, *Metamorphoses*: 1.622-722).

Usually Argus was understood pejoratively (McCall 1955: 253-254): Neckam, for example, explains that Argus is "worldly wisdom, which is foolishness before God" (*De Naturis Rerum*: 1.29); Giovanni del Virgilio wrote that "By Argus may be understood the vanities of this world" ("Espositore delle *Metamorfosi*": 47); and Chaucer calls Criseyde's scheming father, Calchas, "Argus eyed" (*Troylus and Criseyde*: 4.1459). The *Chess of Love* commentary interprets Argus in the same vein, as "the subtle man, malicious and wise, who is very circumspect"; or he may be understood as "the estate of the world, where there are so many deceits" (377). Fraunce's comment, paraphrasing Conti, is also pejorative:

Natalis Comes [*Mythologie*: 5.5] maketh this ethicall moralization of it. The celestiall and heavenly power in Man, called reason or understanding, figured by Mercurius, doth moderate, pacifie, and temper all those inordinate motions and affections proceeding from that other facultie of the minde, provoking to wrath and anger. This cholerike and angry parte of mans minde as long as it resteth, may bee called Argus, sith... *argus* signifieth heavie and slowe: but being provoked and incensed it hath an hundred eyes looking to every corner for revenge, and cannot be quiet, till Mercury dispatch him; that is, till Reason suppresse and keepe him under. (*Countesse of Pembrokes Yvychurch*: 13v-14r)

Favorable interpretations of Argus were less common but not unknown. Fulgentius, for example: "*Argeos* in Greek is *providentia* in Latin, whereby the Greeks are called Argi, that is, the foreseeing ones; from this the herdsman of Jove is called Argus, that is, foreseeing, as the poet implied when he declares, 'Argus had a head set round with a hundred eyes' [Ovid, *Metamorphoses*: 1.625], head standing for the mind as the highest part of a man just as the real head does for its body" (*Super Thebaiden*).

Bibliography: John P. McCall, *Classical Myth in Chaucer's Troilus and Criseyde* (1955).

ARIADNE (Adriane, Libera). Ariadne was the daughter of the Cretan king Minos and Pasiphae. When Theseus came to Crete to kill the monstrous Minotaur in the Labyrinth, Ariadne fell in love with him. And so (in some versions acting on the advice of Daedalus) she taught him how to find his way back out of the Labyrinth: Theseus had only to unroll a ball of yarn as he went into the Labyrinth and then follow the yarn to return. When Theseus had accomplished this labor, Ariadne fled Crete with him; but they got no farther than the island of Naxos (or Dia) when Theseus abandoned her, while she slept upon the shore. Waking, she despaired to find her love gone; but then Bacchus came to her and married her himself. Jupiter then gave her immortality and set her bridal crown among the stars (Ovid, *Metamorphoses*: 8.172-182; see also Homer, *Odyssey*: 11.321-325; Ovid, *Fasti*: 3.459-516; *Art of Love*: 1.525-564; Plutarch, *Lives*: "Theseus").

Boccaccio (*Fiammetta*: 19) understood her to have abandoned herself to love, and so he includes her in a list of guilty *de casibus* lovers: Paris, Clytemnestra, Achilles, Scylla, Ariadne, Leander, and Dido. But more often it is Theseus who is blamed, while Ariadne is interpreted as an example of faithful love. Chaucer, for example, tells her story in such a way as to make it clear that Theseus "as a traitour stal his way" (*Legend of Good Women*: 2174), and that "The goddes have hir holpen, for pitee" (2222). It is impossible, Sandys wrote, to escape "out of that intricate Labyrinth of Vice, without the counsell and wisdom of Dedalus, imparted by Ariadne, or sincere affection" (*Ovid*: 383).

She could also be understood as a figure for patient piety (e.g., Berchorius, *Ovidius Moralizatus*: 304-305). Ross provides a typical expression of this allegorical tradition, writing of the crown which was "bestowed upon Ariadne, and afterward it was placed among the stars: the way to prove ourselves to be the sons of God, is by patient enduring of our afflictions...and withal we shall obtain the Crown of Righteousness, which is laid up for us in Heaven" (*Mystagogus Poeticus*: 400).

Bibliography: Peggy Muñoz Simonds, *Myth, Emblem, and Music in Shakespeare's Cymbeline* (1992): 119-129; Melvin Storm, "From Knossos to Knight's Tale: The Changing Face of Chaucer's Theseus," in Jane Chance, *The Mythographic Art* (1990): 215-223.

ARION was a singer from Lesbos; he sang in the service of the tyrant of Corinth, Periander. Tradition had it that he was the inventor of the dithyramb, the cyclic chorus of the Greek tragedy (see, e.g., Yeager 1990: 238). While on a ship, returning home, the ship's crew determined to throw him overboard and take his gold. Arion begged leave to sing one more time before his death; and then, trusting to Apollo, the god of singers, Arion leaped into the sea. A dolphin caught him on his back and carried him to safety. When the sailors later came to harbor in Corinth, Periander had them executed. Apollo later changed the dolphin and Arion's lyre into constellations. Ovid's was probably the ancient version of the story best known to Christians (*Fasti*: 2.79-108; see also Herodotus, *History*: 1.23-24; Hyginus, *Fabulae*: 194).

Martianus comments on this story in the last chapter of his allegorical treatise on *The Marriage of Philology and Mercury*. This chapter is about Harmony, the divinely instituted ordering principle of the universe (see Appendix A, "Music"). Arion, Orpheus, and Amphion are at once figures for and examples of Harmony so conceived, says Martianus, because their music could charm. Just as the music of Orpheus could subdue wild beasts, so Amphion's music "brought life again to bodies stiff with cold, made mountains animate, and gave to hard rocks sensibilities....And the billows were not deaf to Arion's lyre, when he in desperate straits cried out for help....O Harmony...you have been able with your song to subdue Erebus, the seas, the stones, the wild beasts, and to bring sensation to rocks" (907-908). Arion could also figure forth harmony in social relations. Gower, for example, was much concerned about social discord in England, and in mankind in general. In the Prologue to the *Confessio Amantis*, Gower hopes for another Arion:

> Bot wolde god that now were on
> An other such as Arion,
> Which hadde an harpe of such temprure,
> And therto of so good mesure
> He song, that he the bestes wilde
> Made of his note tame and milde...
> And every man upon this ground
> Which Arion that time herde,
> Als well the lord as the schepherde,
> He broghte hem alle in good acord;
> So that the comun with the lord...
> He sette in love bothe tuo....
> That was a lusti melodie....
> And if ther were such on now,
> Which cowthe harpe as he tho dede,
> He myhte availe in many a stede
> To make pes wher now is hate. (1053-1075)

Clearly, Gower hopes that he himself might sing with Arion's effect: The *Confessio Amantis* is a book about love, written at a time when *love* was as much a way of talking about social harmony as sexual love (see **VENUS**; for Gower's use of Arion, see Yeager 1990: 238-244). For these same reasons, Spenser has Arion play his music, "a most celestiall sound" (*Faerie Queene*: 4.11.23) at the marriage of the Thames and the Medway; Arion's music is appropriate to—and in an allegorical sense explains—the spirit of concord that the marriage consecrates (see Nohrnberg 1976: 643-644).

Arion, like Orpheus and Amphion, could also serve as a figure for eloquence. Ross: "Here also we may see the force of eloquence, by which wild men are charmed" (*Mystagogus Poeticus*: 31).

It should be mentioned that the notion that music could charm animals was usually taken quite seriously, at least as late as Burton (*Anatomy of Melancholy*: 2.2.6.3), who talks about this phenomenon in relation to the story of Arion. Van Mander, in the course of his comment on Adonis's hunting, mentions how easily "the deer is fooled and caught because it listens to the flute" (*Wtlegginghe op den Metamorphosis*: 79r; see also *Wtbeeldinghen der Figuren*: 115r). Gamekeepers at this time did, in fact, use flutes in their efforts to lure deer.

For related music allegory, see **AMPHION, ORPHEUS**; for Arion as a figure for the life contemplative, see **ORPHEUS**.

Bibliography: James Nohrnberg, *The Analogy of The Faerie Queene* (1976); Elizabeth B. Welles, "Orpheus and Arion as Symbols of Music in Mantegna's *Camera degli Sposi*," *SI*, 14 (1990): 113-144; R. F. Yeager, *John Gower's Poetic: The Search for a New Arion* (1990).

ARISTOTLE was, of course, best known as a great philosopher and wise man, one of the greatest of the ancient authorities. An account of his influence would be outside the scope in these pages. But Aristotle also did allegorical service—as an example of the dangers of lust, particularly lust in old age. As the story went, Aristotle was devoted to reason; and so when his pupil, Alexander, fell in love with the beautiful Phyllis (Campaspe, in some tellings), Aristotle endeavored strenuously and repeatedly to convince his pupil to resist the demands of the passions. But then one morning Aristotle himself saw Phyllis—and immediately fell in love. He went to her to declare his passion, but Phyllis told him that he could only prove his love by putting on a saddle and bridle, and allowing her to ride on his back, as we see in the late fifteenth-century Dutch *Aristotle Being Ridden by Phyllis* (fig. 3), by the Master of the Amsterdam Cabinet. Here Alexander looks on—and so (as the Medieval preachers drew the moral) he learned the power of love: Love can ensnare even such a one as Aristotle (see also fig. 4, a French bronze, c. 1400, and Henri d'Andeli, *Le lai d'Aristotle*). Without Venus, wrote Brant, "As horse the wise man [i.e., Aristotle] would not fare" (*Ship of Fools*: 13). The story is also represented in a capital at the beginning of one of Poliziano's treatises on Aristotle (*Opera Omnia*, vol. 1: 451).

Because of a mistranslation by Ficino, Aristotle, until the beginning of the eighteenth century, was widely thought to have been a Jew (Allen 1970: 46).

Aristotle was not the only sage who had allegorized woman trouble: see **VIRGIL**, and for Socrates' troubles, see **XANTIPPE**.

Bibliography: Don C. Allen, *Mysteriously Meant* (1970); J. P. Filedt Kok, *Livelier Than Life: The Master of the Amsterdam Cabinet..., ca. 1470-1500* (1985).

ASTRAEA (Virgo), the daughter of Jupiter and Themis, was the goddess of justice. According to Ovid, she was "the last of the immortals" to abandon the earth with the passing of the Golden Age (*Metamorphoses*: 1.150; Juvenal, *Satires*: 6.19); Hyginus tells how she was changed into the constellation Virgo (Hyginus, *Poetica Astronomica*: 2.25). There was little mention of Astraea in Medieval times. During the Renaissance, however—doubtless due in part to the rediscovery of Hyginus in the early sixteenth century—there was a renewal of interest in the goddess. Her flight from the earth usually served as a figure for the Fall (Nohrnberg 1976: 353-354). Conti provides an extended account of her, telling us that in the Golden Age human beings acted justly because of inward promptings; when Astraea was forced to quit the earth, she left behind a "testament" of laws to take the place of the promptings that had earlier been a part of human nature (*Mythologie*: 2.2). Shakespeare's Titus Andronicus refers to Astraea's departure to account for all the injustices he has suffered (*Titus Andronicus*: 4.3.4). And Sandys wrote that mankind's "insolencie and outrage...affrighted Astraea or Justice from the earth (perhaps alluding to the righteous Henocks miraculous and early assumption [i.e., the Biblical Enoch's ascension: Gen 5:24]) producing this Iron Age" (*Ovid*: 60; see also Spenser, *Faerie Queene*: 7.7.37).

Queen Elizabeth was frequently referred to as Astraea (King 1989: 241-242). Dryden praised Charles II and the Restoration of monarchy in England in a poem entitled *Astraea Redux*. Astraea allegory served other monarchs as well (see, e.g., De Armas 1986).

For Venus as Virgo, see Di Matteo 1989.

Bibliography: Alberto Cacicedo, "Seeing the King: Biblical and Classical Texts in *Astraea Redux*," *SEL*, 32 (1992): 407-428; Frederick De Armas, *The Return of Astraea: An Astral-Imperial Myth in Calderón* (1986); Anthony Di Matteo, "Spenser's Venus-Virgo: The Poetics and Interpretive History of a Dissembling Figure," *SSt*, 10 (1989): 37-70; George Economou, *The Goddess Natura in Medieval Literature* (1972): 194; John King, *Tudor Royal Iconography* (1989); James Nohrnberg, *The Analogy of The Faerie Queene* (1976).

ATALANTA. In ancient times there were two main versions of Atalanta's story. In the Arcadian version, she was the daughter of Zeus and Clymene, suckled first by a bear, then raised by hunters. She grew up to be a skilled hunter. She took part in the Calydonian boar hunt (e.g., Apollodorus, *Library*: 1.8.2), and she participated, too, in the voyage of the Argonauts. Devoted as she was to such manly pursuits, she rejected many lovers, but eventually she did marry Milanion, who was devoted to her.

The Boeotian version of Atalanta's story, however, was much the best known to Christians. Here Atalanta was the daughter of mortals, famous for her beauty and her speed afoot. She was warned by an oracle never to marry, and so she tells her suitors that they must beat her in a foot race to win her; if they lose the race, they die. Eventually, Venus aids one of these suitors, Hippomenes. She gives him golden apples to throw in Atalanta's path. When the maiden stooped to retrieve them, Hippomenes ran on to win the race. Later the couple wander into the temple of Cybele, where they are changed to lions. Ovid wrote that the golden apples came from Venus's garden on the isle of Cyprus (*Metamorphoses*: 10.644-648; see also Lactantius Placidus, *Ovid*: 10.11). But according to most versions, the golden apples come from the Garden of the Hesperides (e.g., Servius, *In Virgilii Aeneidos*: 3.113). (In the *Metamorphoses* Ovid makes two different women of the two versions: there is this Atalanta who marries Hippomenes [10.560-680], and there is an Arcadian Atalanta who was the first hunter to wound the Calidonian Boar [8.380-444].)

Christians usually understood Atalanta to have been a virtuous woman who succumbed to temptation. Thus Chaucer places the virtuous Atalanta—Atalanta hunting the boar—in the temple of Diana ("Knight's Tale": 2070-2072; see **ADONIS** for the moral allegory of hunting; see **AMAZONS** and **HERCULES: Hercules in General** for *virtus* and manly virtue). The *Chess of Love* commentary says that it is important for a woman "to protect her chastity carefully," because in the case of chastity, "there is no safety or remedy whatever, except flight." And Atalanta is an example of a woman who, "for neglecting to run quickly...was caught up with" (1078-1079). Sidney saw Atalanta-overtaken as an example of lust; he puts her, together with Omphale, Helen, and Iole, in Kalander's house of pleasure (*Arcadia*: 1.3.1; see also Lactantius Placidus, *Ovid*: 10.11; Ferrand, *Treatise on Lovesickness*: 6; Sandys, *Ovid*: 491). Tritonio includes Hippomenes in his list of the "libidinous" (*Mythologia*: 28). Fraunce's commentary is also in this vein: Hippomenes' love was

> turnd to a lewd lust,
> So lewd; that Cybeles temple was fowly defiled,
> And themselves to Lyons, for a just plague, speedily changed.
> (*Countesse of Pembrokes Yvychurch*: 44v)

Ross extends this kind of allegory: Venus made Hippomenes "so mad and eager" for Atalanta, "that he was not ashamed to deflowr her in Cybeles temple." Ross adds that the story also shows us

what danger there is in idleness: whilest Atalanta was imployed with Diana in hunting, she kept her Virginity, and did help, yea, was the first that wounded the Chalidonian Boar; but when she gave her self to idleness, she fell into lust and prophaneness. Here we see how irreverence to God is punishable, when such a fearful punishment was laid upon this couple, as to be turned into Beasts....Here we see the picture of a Whore...; and as Atalanta defiled Cybeles Temple, so doth a whore pollute her Body, which is the Temple of the Holy Ghost: So doth the Whoremaster make his body, all one with the body of an Harlot; and so both degenerate from Humanity, and participate of the cruelty and lasciviousness of Lions; and by this means become miserable slaves and drudges to Cybele, Mother Earth, that is, to all earthly affections and lusts....Let us with Atalanta run the race that is set before us, and wound the Boar of our wanton lusts, and draw water from our Rocky hearts. Let us take heed that the Golden Apples of worldly pleasure and profit, which Hippomenes, the Devil, flings in our way, may not hinder our course. (*Mystagogus Poeticus*: 35-36; see Appendix B, "Bestialization")

Bacon mentions that Hippomenes threw "one of his golden balles before her...to make her linger, and also to draw her out of the right course." And so the story can suggest that she is tempted by "womanish desire" (*Wisedome of the Ancients*: 25). But Bacon's allegorization of the story as a whole made it an allegory for the contest between art (Atalanta) and nature (Hippomenes). Sandys' commentary is a close paraphrase of Bacon:

This fable is said to signifie the contention betweene Art and Nature. Art expressed by Atalanta; which in her owne virtue, if not interrupted, is swifter by far then Nature, or Hippomenes; and sooner arrives at the proposed end, as almost is evident in all things. Fruits are long in growing from kernells, but quickly produced by grafting....So in morality, continuance of time procures an oblivion of sorrow, and comforts as it were by the benefit of Nature: but Philosophy, which may be called the Art of living, expects not time but prevents it. Yet these Golden Apples give impediment to this prerogative and vigor of Art, to the infinite detriment of humane affaires. Neither is there any of the Arts and sciences which constantly proceed in a true and legitimate course to the end prefixed; but interrupt their undertakings...like Atalanta diverted by inticing lucre. (*Ovid*: 490)

For more on the allegory of the golden apples, see **THE HESPERIDES**.

Bibliography: Deborah Rubin, "Sandys, Ovid, and Female Chastity," in Jane Chance, *The Mythographic Art* (1990): 266-268.

ATE (Discord, Eris, Strife). In classical times Ate was the personification of delusion, the goddess of guilty infatuation and rash acts. Homer's Agamemnon, for example, refers to Ate to explain his foolish decision to take Briseis from Achilles:

Yet what could I do? It is the god who accomplishes all things.
Delusion is the elder daughter of Zeus, the accursed
who deludes all; her feet are delicate and they step not
on the firm earth, but she walks the air above men's heads
and leads them astray.
(*Iliad*: 19.90-94)

According to Hesiod (*Theogony*: 226-230), Ate was the daughter not of Zeus, but of Eris—Strife or Discord. During the Renaissance, however, Ate was conflated with Eris/Discord (e.g., Peele, *Arraignment of Paris*: pr; Cooper, *Thesaurus*; Spenser, *Faerie Queene*: 2.7.55; 4.1.22).

Whether she was called Discord, Ate, or Eris, she was credited with causing wars and civil shocks. Christians continued, allegorically of course, to ascribe especially civil wars to her. Shakespeare's Antony, for example, speaks of "Caesar's spirit, raning for vengeance, / With Ate by his side come hot from hell" (*Julius Caesar*: 3.1.270-271); and Shakespeare's Benedick, swearing that he will never marry her, likens the sharp-tongued, confounding Beatrice to Ate (*Much Ado about Nothing*: 2.1.253). She was probably best known to Christians, however, for her golden apple. Alone among the gods, she was not invited to the nuptials of Peleus and Thetis. Angry, she went to the wedding and presented a golden apple, inscribed "For the fairest." For Peele, this apple came from the tree from which Proserpina plucked her fatal fruit in the Underworld:

> Condemned soule Ate, from lowest hell....
> Beholde I come in place, and bring beside
> The bane of Troie: beholde the fatall frute
> Raught from the golden tree of Proserpine.
> *(Arraignment of Paris*: 1-7)

According to all accounts, Venus, Minerva, and Juno contested the prize—and the enmities that grew out of the contest eventually exploded into the Trojan war (see **PARIS**). Here is Augustine's account: "Being indignant that she was not invited with the other gods, she created dissension among the three goddesses by sending in the golden apple, which occasioned strife in heaven, victory to Venus, the rape of Helen, and the destruction of Troy" (*City of God*: 3.25). And here is Fulgentius: "So too discord is said to have rolled the golden apple, that is, greed, for the reason that there is in a golden apple what you look upon, not what you eat, just as greed can possess but not enjoy" (*Mythologies*: 3.7; see also Spenser, *Faerie Queene*: 2.7.55; van Mander, *Wtlegginghe op den Metamorphosis*: 90r-92r; Nohrnberg 1976: 414-415, 629-631).

But Ate figured in other ways as well. For Reynolds, as for many others, Ate was a type of Eve: "What can Homers Ate, whom he calls the first daughter of Jupiter, and a woman pernicious and harmefull to all us mortalls...; what can he, I say, meane...but Eve?" (*Mythomystes*: 175). Giraldi notes that "Our religious authors interpret her as Lucifer" (*De deis gentium*: 82). Spenser places her dwelling "Hard by the gates of hell" (*Faerie Queene*: 4.1.20).

Bibliography: E. R. Dodds, *The Greeks and the Irrational* (1964): 2-8; James Nohrnberg, *The Analogy of The Faerie Queene* (1976).

ATHENS was the city of Athena, the goddess of wisdom (see **MINERVA**). Augustine recounts the myth of Athena's conflict with Poseidon for the name and ownership of the city (*City of God*: 18.9). This struggle seemed to suggest something about the human condition, the constant struggle between rational control (Athena, the goddess of wisdom) and the passions (Neptune's realm, the sea, was associated with the passions; see **NEPTUNE, PROTEUS**). Athens thus sometimes stood in allegorical contrast with other cities. As early as the second century A.D., Numenius, one of the precursors of the Neo-Platonists, seems to have interpreted the war between Athens and Atlantis as pitting a superior group of souls, the Athenians, against another group, one concerned with mere generation (Lamberton 1989: 65). Statius's *Thebaid* tells the story of the war at Thebes; in book 12 the Argive women go weeping to Athens, to the statue of the goddess Clemency, there to beg king Theseus to march on Thebes, to force Creon to allow their husbands, slain in the war, to be given proper burial. Statius describes Athens in such a way as to contrast it with nasty, fratricidal, fleshly Thebes. He writes that to the gods "Athens was ever a welcoming land, as once [the gods] gave laws and a new man and sacred ceremonies and the seeds that here descended upon the empty earth, so now sanctified in this spot a common refuge for travailing souls, whence the wrath and threatenings of monarchs might be far removed, and Fortune depart from a shrine of righteousness" (*Thebaid*: 12.499-505).

Boccaccio's *Book of Theseus* and Chaucer's "Knight's Tale" both build on this same scene—and both make use of the same contrast: fleshly, chaotic Thebes and the well-ordered Athens of virtuous, wise Theseus (e.g., McCall 1979: 64-65, 91-93). Lydgate understood Athens in the same way:

> Athenes whilom, whan it was in his floures,
> Was callid norice of philisophres wise,
> Princesse off poetis & expert oratoures,
> Sonne off all sciences, as clerkis can devise....
> This cite was sacrid to Mynerve,
> For ther wisdam and ther sapience;
> Off Mercurie the feestis thei observe,
> For rethorik and for eloquence;
> And myhti Mars gaff hem influence
> With glad aspectis, ther parti to a-mende,
> Noblesse off knyhthod ther clergie to diffende.
> (*Falls of Princes*: 1.4244-4270)

Shakespeare had this tradition in mind when he contrasted Athens (where law and reason rule) and the woods (where the passions reign) in *Midsummer Night's Dream* (see, e.g., Olson 1957). Such connotations were doubtless in the minds of the people of Medieval Florence when they referred to their city as the New Athens (e.g., Boccaccio, *L'Ameto*: 18). In this same tradition Milton writes that Athens is "Mother of Arts and Eloquence,"

> The schools of ancient Sages...
> There thou shalt hear and learn the secret power
> Of harmony in tones and numbers hit
> By voice or hand, and various-measur'd verse.
> (*Paradise Regained*: 4.240-256)

Since modern readers are likely to think of Athens in connection with the ideals of democracy, it should be pointed out that Chaucer, Lydgate, Shakespeare, and the rest are ignoring Athenian democracy. Their Athens was ruled by a firm-handed duke, Theseus—no democrat he! In fact, Medieval and Renaissance Christians sometimes compared later, disorderly Athenian democracy unfavorably with the good, stern control exercised by the rulers of Sparta (Rawson 1969).

Bibliography: Robert Lamberton, *Homer the Theologian* (1989); John P. McCall, *Chaucer among the Gods: The Poetics of Classical Myth* (1979); Paul A. Olson, "*A Midsummer Night's Dream* and the Meaning of Court Marriage," *ELH*, 24 (1957): 95-119; Elizabeth Rawson, *The Spartan Tradition in European Literature* (1969).

ATLAS was one of the Giants who rebelled against Jupiter. His punishment was to hold forever the firmament of the sky upon his shoulders (e.g., Hesiod, *Theogony*: 517-520; Hyginus, *Fabulae*: 150, 192); the story of Atlas thus explained why the sky stays aloft, above the earth. But after Pliny (*Natural History*: 7.203), Atlas was best known in euhemeristic terms, as the inventor of astrology (e.g., Starnes and Talbert 1955: 46; Seznec 1961: 15, 22). As Isidore put it, "Atlas, the brother of Prometheus, was king of Africa, and was the first to invent the art of astrology; this is why he was said to support the heavens" (*Etymologiarum*: 14.8.10; see also 3.25.1). We find this same notion in Augustine (*City of God*: 18.8), Servius (*In Virgilii Aeneidos*: 1.741), Hugh of St. Victor (*Didascalicon*: 3.2), Vatican Mythographer III (13.4), Albricus (*De Deorum*: 22), Guido da Pisa (*Super Comediam Dantis*: 653), the *Ovide Moralisé* (4.6302-6310), Boccaccio (*Genealogie Deorum*: 4.31), the *Chess of Love* commentary (578), Lydgate (*Falls of Princes*: 1.5391-5397), Fraunce (*Countesse of Pembrokes Yvychurch*: 47r), E. K.'s comment on Spenser (*Shepheardes Calender*: May, 142; E. K.'s glosses appear in the original and all subsequent editions), Sandys (*Ovid*: 219), and others. Petrarch had this tradition in mind when he referred to "star-gazing Atlas" (*Africa*: 1.389).

Bibliography: Jean Seznec, *The Survival of the Pagan Gods* (1961); DeWitt Starnes and E. W. Talbert, *Classical Myth and Legend in Renaissance Dictionaries* (1955).

ATTIS. In the version of the story that would have been best known to Christians (Ovid, *Fasti*: 4.215-246), Attis was a beautiful youth who lived in the Phrygian woods near Cybele's temple. Cybele fell in love with Attis and made him priest of her temple, upon condition that Attis remain forever chaste. But Attis, alas, lost his virginity to the nymph Sagaritis. Cybele punished Attis with madness. Then in a fit of guilt inspired by the Furies, Attis emasculated himself. Hereafter Attis returned to Cybele's service; eventually he was transformed into a pine tree.

The fourth-century Neo-Platonist Sallustius worked out an elaborate allegorical interpretation of the story:

The Mother of the gods [i.e., Cybele] is a life-giving goddess, and therefore she is called mother, while Attis is creator of things that come into being and perish....So, as the first gods perfect the second, the Mother loves Attis, and gives him heavenly powers....Attis, however, loves the nymph, and the nymphs preside over coming into being, since whatever comes into being is in flux. But since it was necessary that the process of coming into being should stop and what was worse not sink to the worst, the creator who was making these things cast away generative powers into the world of becoming and was again united with the gods. (*Concerning the Gods*: 4)

In nature allegory Attis could represent the sun (e.g., Macrobius, *Saturnalia*: 1.21.9). And Augustine mentions "the doctrine of the Greek sages" that "Atys signifies the flowers of spring, which is the most beautiful season, and therefore was mutilated because the flower falls before the fruit appears" (*City of God*: 7.25; for more, see Nohrnberg 1976: 519-520).

But Augustine himself—like most Christians after him—was inclined to understand Attis in moral terms. Augustine has nothing but scorn for Cybele, this pagan "Great Mother" who forces her priests, like her lover, to be "effeminate" (*City of God*: 7.25-26). For Fulgentius the story is about lust. And Christians in general interpreted Attis as an example of love's dangerous thraldom. For example, when Ariosto's Ruggiero falls under the spell of the evil temptress Alcina, virtuous Mellisa rebukes him for being Alcina's "Atis or Adonis" (*Orlando Furioso*: 7.49). And here is Sandys: "A beautifull boy, beloved of Cybil the mother of the Gods,...who, for affecting the Nymph Sangritis was castrated by her jealousy; as all her [i.e., Cybele's] Priests ever after; whom they called Galli, of Gallus a River of Phrygia, whose waters made the drinker franticke. Atis is said to have his members cutt off, and to be transformed into a Pine, in regard of that trees infertility" (*Ovid*: 478).

Emasculation was often associated with lechery, as we find again in the allegorization of **HERMAPHRODITUS AND SALMACIS**. And see, for another example, Bruegel's engraving of *Lechery* (fig. 20), where we find in the right foreground a lecherous grotesque who has just cut off his own considerable member. In his comment on Attis Berchorius mentions those "who castrate themselves spiritually by breaking the vow of chastity" (*Ovidius Moralizatus*: 352).

Bibliography: Don C. Allen, *Mysteriously Meant* (1970): 15; James Nohrnberg, *The Analogy of The Faerie Queene* (1976); Maarten Vermaseren, *Cybele and Attis: The Myth and the Cult* (1977).

AURORA (Dawn, Eos). Aurora was the personification of the dawn. Following Homer (*Iliad*: 1.477), she was often referred to as "rosy fingered." She was remembered for her sexual intrigues: To punish her for bedding Mars, Venus had made her sexually insatiable. Aurora abducted Orion, Cephalus, and Tithonus, among others. But Christians—in the rare instances where they made allegorical use of Aurora at all—associate the dawn with the morn of resurrection, with the risen Son. Dante, for example, calls Aurora "the brightest handmaid of the sun" (*Paradiso*: 30.6-7). And so she could be a figure for Christ. Here is Ross, with a reference to Aurora's getting eternal life for her lover Tithonus: "our Saviour is the true Aurora, who was in love with mankind, whom he hath healed from all infirmities, and hath bestowed on them a lasting life, which knoweth not old age" (*Mystagogus Poeticus*: 39).

B

BACCHAE (Bacchantes, Bacchides, Maenads). The Bacchae were the frenetic votaries of Bacchus (*Gk. maenad*, "raving woman"). They roamed the countryside in their ecstasies, sometimes riding panthers and fondling wolf cubs; they lived like animals; and they were so strong that they could uproot trees. They formed a contingent of Bacchus's army in his campaign in India. In classical times they were also sometimes depicted in calmer moments, gathering grapes and making wine. But they were usually associated with animals and animalistic behavior (Pantel 1992: 222-223).

According to Euripides' *Bacchae*—which Ovid made use of in writing his own account of the Bacchae (*Metamorphoses*: 11.1-43)—certain Theban women followed Bacchus and so became Bacchae. Fulgentius names four Theban sisters as Bacchae: Ino, Autonoe, Semele (the mother of Bacchus), and Agave. For Fulgentius these four sisters are allegorical figures for the "four stages of intoxication—that is, first, excess of wine; second, forgetting things; third, lust; fourth, madness—whereby these four received the name of Bacchae: the Bacchae are so called for their raging (*baccantes*) with wine" (*Mythologies*: 2.12).

Semele was probably the best known of the four Bacchae. She was an apt figure for lust: She lay with Jupiter and conceived the child Bacchus by him—but she insisted on seeing her lover in his full glory; Jupiter granted her wish, only to see her killed by his flashing lightning. Semele could thus exemplify the self-destructiveness of lust. As Spenser wrote of her: "dearely she with death bought her desire" (*Faerie Queene*: 3.11.33). Agave was an apt figure for the madness that can ensue from intoxication: She killed her own son, Pentheus, when the Bacchae caught him spying on one of their Bacchic orgies. Tritonio includes her in his list of "The Mad" (*Mythologia*: 22); for Spenser, too, she was an example of the madness of excess: "that madding mother, mongst the rout / Of Bacchus Priests her owne deare flesh did teare" (*Faerie Queene*: 5.8.47).

Ovid tells the story of the Maenads killing Orpheus. Orpheus was holding "the beasts enthralled" with his playing upon the lyre (see Appendix A, "Music"), when "the crazed women of the Cicones, with skins flung over their breasts" attacked Orpheus for scorning them. Their weapons were powerless against Orpheus's music—until they drowned him out with their "flutes, mixed with discordant horns, the drums, and the breast beatings and howlings of the Bacchanals." Then they killed him (*Metamorphoses*: 11.1-19). In his comment on this story Berchorius wrote that "Orpheus signifies a preacher, a singer of the songs of the divine word"—a man who must avoid sexual allurements; but "it often happens that sinful women hate such men and [allegorically] kill them through infamy" (*Ovidius Moralizatus*: 349). Sandys wrote in something like the same vein. Orpheus avoided women "as a hinderance to the study of philosophy, & administration of civill affairs: he esteeming the propagation of wisdome & virtuous endeavours, more noble and immortall then that of posterity...; nothing more endangers the harmony of government then the distemperature of Bacchus, which by inflaming the spirits, make them deafe to perswasion, and intractable to Authority" (*Ovid*: 519).

In general, Medieval and Renaissance Christians remembered the Bacchae for their unnatural, unrestrained, unwomanly fury (e.g., Augustine, *City of God*: 18.13; Boccaccio, *Genealogie Deorum*: 5.25; Tritonio, *Mythologia*: 24; Spenser, *Faerie Queene*: 5.8.47). And so unruly women could be referred to as Bacchae, as in Nashe, where some women "gadded uppe and downe the streetes, like Bacchus Froes [women], franticke for the time" (*Return of Cavaliero*: 95). More generally, according to Erasmus, to live "Like a Bacchant" was an adage suggesting "habitually sullen silent people" or a "life of intemperance" (*Adages*: 1.6.45).

For the Bacchae killing Pentheus, see **PENTHEUS**.

Bibliography: Pauline Schmitt Pantel, *From Ancient Goddesses to Christian Saints* (1992); Thomas H. Carpenter and Christopher A. Faraone, *Masks of Dionysus* (1993).

BACCHUS (Dionysus, Iacchus, Liber, Lyaeus, Zagreus). Bacchus, the wine god, was one of the Olympian gods, the son of Jupiter and Semele (or of Jupiter and Demeter). In classical times he was regarded as a fertility god, a god of the flowing juices—semen, sap, and especially wine. As the god of intoxication, he was also associated with mystic ecstasy. He was worshipped with boisterous processions, wherein the spirits of the fecund earth appeared, as represented by masked figures. It was out of these celebrations that the Greek theater developed.

Because of his association with harvest and the wine press, Bacchus could serve as an allegorical figure for autumn (for a list of paintings that work in this way, see Reid 1993: 468-469). But as a god of fertility, he could also be remembered—like Proserpina—in connection with the renewal of life in the spring. Several of the Dionysus myths have, then, to do with his death and rebirth. In one such myth Hera, jealous that Zeus should have a child by Demeter, orders the Titans to tear Dionysus to pieces. (One of Dionysus's names was *Zagreus*, "torn to pieces.") But every three years he emerges reborn from the darkness of the underworld.

All of this was irresistible fodder for Christian allegorists, and very early on Bacchus came to be regarded as a type of Christ, who was also torn (not quite to pieces) and reborn after three days (rather than years). As early as the second century, Justin Martyr likened Christ to Bacchus in this connection (*Apologies*: 1.22). And we find Bacchus appearing on Christian funerary monuments as early as the second and third centuries (Panofsky n.d.: 33; see also Schiller 1971, vol. 1: 64, 95). Bacchus's signature grape vines and ivy also were appropriated to Christ. The sarcophagus of the Emperor Constantine (337 A.D.) was graven with *putti* gathering grapes (Allen 1990: 16). And Bacchus's (evergreen) ivy or grape vines sometimes sprout from Medieval representations of the cross as Tree of Life (several of these are included in Schiller 1971, vol. 2: fig. 444 [c. 1240], fig. 448 [c. 1365], fig. 489 [c. 1450], fig. 539 [1548]; see also Schiller's fig. 450, a manuscript illumination [c. 1275] with a grape-vine border around a crucifixion; for other Medieval connections between the iconography of Christ and Dionysus, see Allen 1990).

Bacchus was regarded as the pagan Noah (also a type of Christ), because Genesis 9:20-21 was understood to mean that Noah was the first to plant vineyards and make wine. Sandys is typical: "Noah was he who immediatly after the flood first planted a vineyard, and shewed the use of wine unto men. Therefore some write that of *Noachus* he was called *Boachus*, and after *Bacchus*" (*Ovid*: 165-166; see also 197; van Mander, *Wtlegginghe op den Metamorphosis*: 101r; and Reynolds, *Mythomystes*: 175).

Medieval and Renaissance artists and writers could sometimes mention even Bacchus's revels with approval. Berchorius, for example, wrote that "Bacchus is Christ," and "Through Bacchus who is drunk is perceived the true faith which makes the servants of Christ drunk with the fervor of devotion" (*Ovidius Moralizatus*: 189; see also the *Ovide Moralisé*: 3.2818). Peacham's emblem for Bacchus shows the god seated on a wine barrel, with wings on his head; in the background there is winged Pegasus: Bacchus "addest vigor to our wits" and to "the dullard spright / Quick invention" (*Minerva Britanna*: 191). Because of the pun on his name, Liber, Bacchus was sometimes said to liberate (e.g., Conti, *Mythologie*: 5.14; Cartari, *Le Imagini*, 1571: 425). The Neo-Platonists wrote seriously about Bacchus as a force of inspiration (e.g., Pico, *Conclusiones*: 58.6). Ficino wrote that Socrates was inspired by Bacchus to praise temperate love: "Finally, since he has become ecstatic through Bacchus, perhaps the Apollonian demon immediately enraptures him (for Apollo is closest to Bacchus) with the result that he even exceeds the bounds of human behavior and thereafter treats of the divine love that excites us through some frenzy" (*Commentum cum summis capitulorum*: 10).

Titian's painting of the *Bacchanal of the Andrians* represents the inhabitants of the Island of Andros, which was so entirely dominated by Bacchus that its river ran with wine. According to Panofsky (1969: 101-102), this painting is a celebration of the joys of life, which are enhanced by Bacchus and Venus. It is for this reason that nearly all the participants in the scene are young adults. For youth is the age best suited to these pleasures.

But Bacchus was dangerous, too. Hesiod wrote of "the crude grapes which Dionysus gave to men—a joy and a sorrow both" ("Shield of Heracles": 398-399). Christians certainly associated Bacchus more often with the dangers of drink than with the joys. Fraunce's account is typical:

I have heard, that Bacchus, a mightie warriour, overcame Lycurgus, Pentheus, and divers others, and subdued India, riding thence in triumphant manner, on an Elephant. Yet his greatest fame was procured by his invention of wine, which hath made him painted and described accordingly, a yong and mery youth, naked, crowned with an yvy garland, having a branch of a vine in his hand, riding in a chariot drawne by Tygers and Panthers: First, Bacchus is mery, Wine moderately taken, maketh men joyfull; he is also naked; for, *in vino veritas*: drunkards tell all, and sometimes more then all. Tygers draw his chariot; druncken men are fierce and outragious. Of Venus and Bacchus, Priapus was borne: lust comes from wine and delicacie....He is a companion to the Muses: wine quickeneth the wit. Women be his priests: women are sooner overcome with wine, then men....He hath sometimes hornes, then is he intolerable, and fierce, like a Bull, being drunke immoderately. Satyres, and such wantons be his folowers; and among the rest, Silenus is his Tutor, a fat, grosse, stammering drunckard, balde...with great eares, short neck...riding on an asse, as not able, for swelling, to stand on his feete; all effects of beastly carowsing....He is called Bacchus, of raging. Lyaeus, of freeing: and thereof *liber* in latine, for wine freeth men from care and thought. (*Countesse of Pembrokes Yvychurch*: 51r-51v)

And Whitney writes,

See heere, in time howe monsterous he grewe:
With drinkinge muche, and dailie bellie cheare....
For like a beaste, this doth transforme a man.
                    (*Emblemes*: 187)

Bacchus thus came to stand—often with Venus, Priapus, the Satyres, or Silenus (see, e.g., fig. 25)—as an allegorical figure for worldly desires in general. Alanus associated Bacchus with "the darkness of brutish sensuality" (*Complaint of Nature*: pr. 6; see Appendix B, "Bestialization"); and Bacon wrote that "Under the person of Bacchus is depicted the nature of Desire, or the passions and perturbations of the mind" (*De Augmentis*: 333; see also *Wisedome of the Ancients*: 24). We see much the same allegory in a Neo-Platonic engraving after Baccio Bandinelli, *The Fray of Cupid and Apollo* (fig. 1), where Bacchus and Venus oppose Apollo and Diana: the forces of excess and the passions in opposition to control, reason, and temperance. (See **APOLLO** for an account of this picture and a translation of the accompanying Latin distichs.) Ficino writes about such ideas in the following passage:

Therefore, stay away from...heavenly feasts, stay away, I say, you profane people, who are covered with earthly filth, who are completely enslaved to Bacchus and Priapus, and who trample the heavenly gift of love in the dirt and mud, like swine. But you virtuous guests, and all others dedicated to Diana and Pallas, who rejoice in the freedom of a guiltless soul, and in the endless pleasures of the intellect, you are welcome. (*On Plato's Symposium*: 6.1; for more on this conflict between the gods, see Ficino, *Three Books on Life*: 1.7)

In *The Wisedome of the Ancients* Bacon entitles one of his chapters "Dionysus, or Passions":

He was the inventor and institutor of Sacrifices, and Ceremonies, and full of corruption and cruelty. Hee had power to strike men with fury or madnes; for it is reported, that at the celebration of his Orgies, two famous worthies, Pentheus and Orpheus were torne in pieces by certaine franticke women, the one because he got upon a tree to behold their ceremonies...the other for making melodie with his harpe....

There is such excellent morality coucht in this Fable...for under the person of Bacchus is described the nature of affection, passion, or perturbation....

The invention of wine is wittily ascribed unto him, every affection being ingenious and skilfull in finding out that which brings nourishment unto it; And indeed of all things knowen to men, Wine is most powerfull and efficacious to excite and kindle passions of what kind soever....

Concerning the rending and dismembring of Pentheus and Orpheus, the parable is plaine, for every prevalent affection is outragious and severe against curious inquiry, and wholesome and free admonition. (24)

Milton had such allegory in mind when he made Bacchus and Circe the father of Comus, who is Milton's own allegorical figure for sensuality (*Comus*: 46-53; see Harding 1946: 58-60).

Bacchus was thought to be particularly apt to excite the venerian passions. Aristotle's opinion was widely quoted, that "wine excites sexual desire, and Dionysus and Aphrodite are rightly coupled together" (*Problemata*: 953b). This became a commonplace; see Terence (*Eunuch*: 732), the *Chess of Love* commentary (345, 510), Erasmus (*Adages*: 2.3.97), Landino (*Disputationes Camuldenses*: 122), Sandys (*Ovid*: 199), and many others. Henkel and Schöne (1967: 1733) reprint a French emblem from 1539 which shows Minerva (goddess of wisdom) caught in a net by Bacchus and Venus; the accompanying verse explains that "Wine and woman can bring the wisest man to a fall." Sometimes Bacchus was said to be the son of Venus (e.g., the *Chess of Love* commentary, 854-855). Ceres, as the goddess of food in plenty, was sometimes included with Venus and Bacchus in such proverbs (see **CERES**).

Bacchus's attributes in themselves could also suggest sin and passionate excess. The rod of Bacchus, wrote Catullus, drove men mad (*Carmina*: 64.256).

Bacchus was depicted as crowned or garlanded with ivy (e.g., Macrobius, *Saturnalia*: 1.18.2), and so it came to be that a garland of ivy, hung upon a pole, could serve as the sign of an inn. Bruegel often designates inns in this way; see, for example, the inn along the left margin of *The Fair at Hoboken* (fig. 5). The legend at the bottom of *The Fair at Hoboken* makes it clear that such a sign could play a part in the moral allegory of the engraving: "At such festivities, the bumpkins must enjoy themselves by dancing, jumping, and drinking themselves drunk as beasts. They must have their holidays, at peril of starving and dying from the cold." The engraving contrasts the pigs and the peasants with those who are filing into the church—it contrasts holy day and holiday (for more on this engraving's moral allegory, see Brumble, "Introduction" to Bredero, *Spanish Brabanter*).

For Bacchus's marriage, see **ARIADNE**; for his wild attendants, see **BACCHAE**; for Bacchus's aged, bibulous companion, see **SILENUS**.

Bibliography: Susan H. Allen, "Dionysiac Imagery in Coptic Texts and Later Medieval Art," in A. S. Bernardo and S. Levin, *The Classics in the Middle Ages* (1990): 11-24; H. David Brumble, "Introduction" to G. A. Bredero, *Spanish Brabanter* (1981); Malcolm Bull, "Poussin's Bacchanals for Cardinal Richelieu," *BM*, 137 (1995): 5-11; Thomas H. Carpenter and Christopher A. Faraone, *Masks of Dionysus* (1993); A.C. Hamilton, *The Spenser Encyclopedia* (1990): under *Bacchus*; Davis P. Harding, *Milton and the Renaissance Ovid* (1946); Arthur Henkel and Albrecht Schöne, *Emblemata: Handbuch zur Sinnbildkunst des XVI. und XVII. Jahrhunderts* (1967); Charles Lemmi, *The Classical Deities in Bacon* (1933): 202-207; Erwin Panofsky, *Tomb Sculpture* (n.d.), *Problems in Titian, Mostly Iconographic* (1969); Jane Davidson Reid, *The Oxford Guide to Classical Mythology in the Arts, 1300-1990s* (1993); Gertrud Schiller, *Iconography of Christian Art* (1971).

BATTUS. In Ovid's version of the story (*Metamorphoses*: 2.676-707), Mercury had stolen some cattle and hidden them in a certain wood. The only witness was a rustic named Battus. Mercury bribed him to remain silent. Then, mistrusting the man, Mercury changed his own appearance, came again to Battus, asked him to point out the cattle, and again offered a bribe. Battus promptly betrayed the secret—and Mercury punished him by turning him into flint. The hardness of his heart thus found its outward manifestation. "A very good example is described in Battus tale," wrote Golding, "For covetous people which for gayne doo set theyr toongs too sale" ("Epistle": 95-96).

Bibliography: Leonard Barkan, *The Gods Made Flesh: Metamorphoses and the Pursuit of Paganism* (1986): 211-213.

THE BELIDES (Danaides) were the fifty daughters of king Danaus, son of Belus. They were married to their cousins, the fifty sons of Aegyptus. Danaus, seeking revenge upon his brother for an old quarrel, made his daughters promise to cut off their husbands' heads on their wedding night. The Belides' punishment in Hades was forever to fill a leaking cistern with sieves. The Belides were thus sometimes included with Sisyphus, Tantalus, and Ixion in conventional accounts of those suffering in hell (e.g., Ovid, *Metamorphoses*: 10.40-44). The Belides became figures for covetousness, avarice, or gluttony, as in this passage from the *Chess of Love* commentary:

They want to fill a bottomless cask, and always strive to do it, and always labor in vain, for the cask always shows itself empty. And this is the pain the covetous suffer, who always desire to assemble riches and fill their hearts with them if they can, but they can't. The more they get, the more they always want.

One could also say that this pain is properly suffered by gluttons, who always want to fill a bottomless cask, their bellies. (486)

And here is Berchorius: "Avaricious men are like these Belides because they believe they will fill and satisfy the jar of their heart with the waters of wealth....Nor is the water of riches which they pour in ever sufficient. Proverbs 13:25: 'The belly of the wicked is never to be filled'" (*Ovidius Moralizatus*: 113). But the allegory could be extended to refer to all striving for things in this world. Berchorius continues:

Or say morally that these two brothers signify the spirit and the body between which there is always a war since they have contrary desires....

Therefore, Danaus—that is the body—allures his brother—that is the spirit—into agreeing; and the spirit sometimes consents to him and obeys the pleasures of the flesh....So it is pretended that such people want to fill a jar without a bottom to denote that such carnal dispositions are never able to fill their heart or satisfy their desire. (*Ovidius Moralizatus*: 115)

Ross writes in much the same way. All of Eve's children "are still drawing water in a sieve, which will never be filled; that is, still roiling and labouring for that which will never fill and content them: The Covetous man is still drawing riches, the Ambitious man honour, the Voluptuous man pleasures, the Learned man is still labouring for knowledge; and yet are they never full, but the more they draw the more they desire" (*Mystagogus Poeticus*: 44).

Not surprisingly, these husband-killing Belides were sometimes included in lists of bad wives (e.g., Brant, *Ship of Fools*: 64).

According to one tradition, one of the sisters, Hypermestra, did spare her husband, Lyncaeus; Ariosto (*Orlando Furioso*: 22.2), for example, refers to this.

Bibliography: DeWitt Starnes and E. W. Talbert, *Classical Myth and Legend in Renaissance Dictionaries* (1955): 221-222.

BELLEROPHON. Fulgentius—who was ultimately the source for most of the Medieval and Renaissance interpretations of Bellerophon and Chimaera—tells the story in this way:

> King Proteus had a wife named Anteia, who fell in love with Bellerophon. When she solicited him to adultery, he refused; she accused him before her husband. The latter ...sent him to kill the Chimaera; and Bellerophon slew it, seated on the horse Pegasus which had been born of the blood of the Gorgon....Homer in his narrative says this of Bellerophon: "devising upright thoughts, a most wise counsellor." He rejects lust, that is, Anteia, for *antion* in Greek means opposed....Then, too, Bellerophon, that is, good counsel, rides a horse which is none other than Pegasus, for *pegaseon*, that is, an everlasting fountain. The wisdom of good counsel is an everlasting fountain....Then he slew the Chimaera, with Chimaera for *cymeron*, that is, the surge of love....So too the Chimaera is depicted with three heads, because there are three stages of love—that is, the start, the continuation, and the end. For when love first comes, it makes a mortal attack like a lion...: "Lust is a ruler more forceful than the strength of a lion"....And the she-goat which is depicted in the center of the Chimaera is truly the embodiment of lust, because an animal of this species is most disposed to lust. (*Mythologies*; 3.1)

The "species" Fulgentius has in mind is probably the serpent. Dragons such as the Chimera were generally regarded as a species of serpent. And the lust of serpents was well known. Plutarch told a story that was often retold, as here by Sandys:

> And we read in Plutarch that sometimes Serpents have beene in love with women, manifesting all the signes of a wanton affection. As one with a maid of Aetolia, which nightly crept into her bed, gliding to and fro, and winding about every part of her body....This observed, the maid was forthwith removed by her Guardians. The serpent missing her for divers dayes together, at length found her out: who now not loving and gentle as accustomed, but horrid and ful of danger, leapt upon her, pinnioning her armes with his foldes, and lashing her thighs with the remainder of his length: yet with such an anger as seemed to be mixt with indulgency, as rather intending to chastize, then to hurt her. (*Ovid*: 424)

Valeriano retells the same story, in connection with his own assertion that the Chimera represents lust (*Hieroglyphica*: 147-148). Bernardus, too, identifies the Chimaera with lust: "*Chimaera* is a triform monster; the forepart is a lion, the midpart a goat, and the hindpart a serpent....[P]hilosophers interpret the Chimaera as passion offering the rage of a lion at the beginning (in sight, in encouragement), having the goatish and stinking practice of copulation in the middle, and the stings of serpents in the end (the pangs of penance and bad conscience)" (*On Virgil's Aeneid*: 6.287-288; see also 6.440-444; see also Lydgate, *Reson and Sensuallyte*: 3370-3382).

Sandys' account of Bellerophon and the Chimaera (*Ovid*: 446) follows Fulgentius closely; and Fraunce writes in much the same vein: "Chimera's upper part was like a Lyon, the middle like a Goate, the lowest like a Serpent, slaine by Bellerophon....Chimera, the type of inordinate luste...invadeth men fiercely like a

Lyon, then wantonly and lasciviously like a Goate, afterwards brings poysoned sorrow and repentance figured by snakes and serpents. Bellerophon sollicited to folly by Antia...constantly refused....He was called Bellerophon..., wise and prudent counsailer" (*Countesse of Pembrokes Yvychurch*: 28v-29r). Ripa makes the Chimera a figure for "the deformity of vice" (*Iconologie*: 1.167).

With this tradition in mind, we can understand Du Bartas's lament for humankind's spiritual blindness: "Mans eyes are sield-up with Cimmerian miste" (*Devine Weekes and Workes*: 531). And according to Ross, the story of Bellerophon's flight on Pegasus was intended to "encourage men to vertuous actions, and to sublime and heavenly cogitations" (*Mystagogus Poeticus*: 45).

From very early Christian times the Chimera was occasionally identified with the dragon/Satan of the book or Revelation, and so Bellerophon could be interpreted as a type of Christ. Methodius, bishop of Olympus, interpreted the story this way about the year 300 (Hanfmann 1980: 85-87).

According to Pindar (*Isthmian Odes*: 7.45-51), however, Bellerophon finally came to a bad end. His heroic successes so fed his pride that he mounted Pegasus again to fly up into the heavens. Zeus drove Pegasus wild with a gadfly, and Bellerophon fell to a miserable end. And so Bellerophon could also be understood as one who fell because pride led him to aspire too high. Conti interprets Bellerophon in this way, as an example of arrogance punished (*Mythologie*: 10, under *Bellerophon*). In aspiring to write of matters celestial, for example, Milton worries that he might be like Bellerophon:

> Descend from Heav'n Urania...
> Following [whom], above th' Olympian Hill I soar,
> Above the flight of Pegasean wing.
>   ...Up led by thee
> Into the Heav'n of Heav'ns I have presum'd,
> An Earthly Guest, and drawn Empyreal Air,
> Thy temp'ring; with like safety guided down
> Return me to my Native Element:
> Lest from this flying Steed unrein'd, (as once
> Bellerophon, though from a lower Clime)
> Dismounted, on th' Aleian Field I fall.
>   (*Paradise Lost*: 7.1-20)

Starnes and Talbert (1955: 240) note that Milton could have derived this understanding of Bellerophon from several of the Renaissance dictionaries. According to Theodulph's *Ecloga*, Bellerophon's flight on Pegasus was a type of the ascension of the Biblical Elias (2 Kings 2:6-13).

Bibliography: G. M. A. Hanfmann, "The Continuity of Classical Art: Culture, Myth, and Faith," in Kurt Weitzmann, *Age of Spirituality* (1980): 75-99; M. M. Lascelle, "The Rider on the Winged Horse," in *Elizabethan and Jacobean Studies Presented to F. P. Wilson* (1959): 173-198; David Leeming, "Chimera," in Malcolm South, *Mythical Creatures and Fabulous Beasts* (1987); DeWitt T.

Starnes and Ernest W. Talbert, *Classical Myth and Legend in Renaissance Dictionaries* (1955).

BELLONA was the Roman goddess of war. According to Fraunce, she was "Bellona, so called of Bellum, which is War, was a goddes, that entermedled with Martial affaires [as did Mars]. She is paynted like a furious woman, with a whippe in the one hand, and a firebrand in the other" (*Countesse of Pembrokes Yvychurch*: 39r). Tasso writes of "Bellona's dreadful rage" (*Jerusalem Delivered*: 7.63). She was sometimes said to be the wife or sister of Mars. Warlike as Minerva was, Christians often identified her with Bellona. A gloss on Bellona in the widely used Medieval schoolbook *Liber Catonianus* identifies Bellona as Minerva, for example (in Clogan 1968: 26). And Boccaccio wrote that "Minerva invented war, and therefore some call her Bellona" (*Genealogie Deorum*: 5.48; see also Spenser, *Shepheardes Calender*: E. K.'s gloss on Oct., 114; E. K.'s glosses appear in the original and all subsequent editions of Spenser's poem). But distinctions were sometimes made. Henkel and Schöne (1967: 1749) reprint a French emblem from the year 1539: We see Minerva has cast down Bellona, who holds the staff of a court jester; wise princes, we are to understand, recognize Bellona's counsels as folly. Here, for another example, is Lynche's commentary:

> Many have written also, that Bellona was goddesse of the warres, and the same as Minerva, but by their Statues and Images dedicated unto them, these differences doe appeare: By Minerva was understood and intended the wise councels and advised prudencie of Captaines and Officers, in managing their militarie affaires: and by Bellona were meant all bloudie strategems, massacres, surprises, executions, and fatall meetings of the enemie whatsoever..., she was held also to be the goddesse of wrath, furie, and anger...she was most commonly depictured with a flaming firebrand in her hand. (*Fountaine of Ancient Fiction*: Sii)

Milton seems to accept such a distinction. In *Paradise Lost* he likens the "noises loud and ruinous" that rise up out of hell to that noise made "when Bellona storms, / With all her battering Engines bent to rase / Some Capital City" (2.921-924).

   Bibliography: Paul Clogan, *The Medieval Achilleid* of Statius (1968); Arthur Henkel and Albrecht Schöne, *Emblemata: Handbuch zur Sinnbildkunst des XVI. und XVII. Jahrhunderts* (1967); Henry Lotspeich, *Classical Mythology in the Poetry of Edmund Spenser* (1932): 42.

BOREAS (Aquilo) was the North Wind, the sender of terrible storms, the harbinger of winter. As Surrey wrote, "In winters just returne...Boreas gan his raigne" ("In winters just returne"). It is in this sense that poets such as Spenser wrote of "fell Boreas" ("Ruins of Time": 16) or "blustring" Boreas (*Shepheardes Calender*: Feb., 226; see also Tasso, *Jerusalem Delivered*: 4.40; Shakespeare, *Troilus and Cressida*: 1.3.38). He was the son of Eos and Astraea, and the brother of Zephyr, the West Wind. He was said to have raped Orithyia, the daughter of

Erictheus. She bore him two sons, Zetus and Calais. The sons were known for their speed, and according to some accounts they had wings. Zetus and Calais went with the Argonauts in search of the Golden Fleece.

Bernardus sees Boreas as an allegorical figure for glory: "Boreas, the wind, is glory....Boreas is the father of Zetus and Calais since glory is the cause of poetry and of great works. For many place the fruit of virtue in glory. Indeed, poets greatly seek glory....Zetes and Calais help kill the Harpies—poets and Satirists and the examples of good work take away the capacity of avarice" (*On Virgil's Aeneid*: 6.289). In Bernardus's idiosyncratic version of the story, Zetes and Calais helped Hercules kill the Harpies. Probably the association of Boreas and glory grows out of the tradition that made Aeolus (the god of winds) an allegorical figure for fame (see **AEOLUS**); however, Berchorius associates Boreas with glory in a slightly different way: "Or say that Aquilo (or Boreas) signifies the tribulation which generates high men [i.e., Zetus and Calais]; for it creates winged holy, and contemplative men whose minds fly to the Golden Fleece—that is the glory of paradise—through desire" (*Ovidius Moralizatus*: 264).

For more wind allegory, see **AEOLUS, ZEPHYR**.

BRUTUS. The Trojan Brutus was unknown to the ancients; but since his invention in the twelfth century by Geoffrey of Monmouth (*History of the Kings of Britain*: 1.4-15), the English knew Brutus as the grandson of Aeneas and the eponymous founder of Britain—just as the Trojan Aeneas was the founder of Rome (this is, of course, the story of Virgil's *Aeneid*; see also Boccaccio, *Genealogie Deorum*: 6.57). Thus it was that Chaucer could refer to England as "Brutes Albyoun" (*Complaint*). By the sixteenth century Geoffrey's reliability was sometimes questioned, but Tudor poets and historiographers still relied on Geoffrey for their sense of early British history (Hamilton 1990: 329). Spenser, for example, recalls the felicitous reign of Brutus in his chronicle of British kings (*Faerie Queene*: 2.10.9-13). Indeed, Geoffrey's account of the antiquity of the British monarchy was an important ingredient of English thinking about monarchy right down to the time of the English Revolution in the seventeenth century (MacDougall 1982: 26). Milton refers to Brutus as one of England's kings in *Comus* (828).

For the allegorical implications of Britain's being founded by Trojans, see **TROY**.

Bibliography: A. C. Hamilton, *The Spenser Encyclopedia* (1990); Hugo MacDougall, *Racial Myth in English History* (1982).

BYBLIS, as Ovid told the story, "was smitten with a passion for her brother," Caunus (*Metamorphoses*: 9.455). When he ran from her in horror, she was changed into a fountain. Ovid tells us that "Byblis is a warning that girls should not love unlawfully" (454). She was sometimes included, then, in catalogues of *de casibus* lovers, as in Boccaccio's *Book of Theseus* (7.62; see, e.g., Taylor 1986).

She could also serve as an example of wanton passion and unnatural love. Boccaccio, for example, includes her in a list of those whom Love struck "with a wicked fire...Myrrha, Semiramis, Byblis, Canace, and Cleopatra" (*Fiammetta*: 20-21; see also *Ovide Moralisé*: 9.2077-2091). Tritonio includes her in his list of "The Libidinous" (*Mythologia*: 28), and Spenser compares her with the incestuous Myrrha (*Faerie Queene*: 3.2.41). Golding writes: "Cawne and Byblis are examples contrarie: / The Mayd of most outrageous lust, the man of chastitie" ("Epistle": 211-212). Sandys also interprets her as acting in a way "forbidden by the Law of Nature, as acknowledged by all Nations" (*Ovid*: 445).

Bibliography: Beverly Taylor, "Phyllis, Canacee, Biblis, and Dido: Keys to Understanding *The Minnegrotte* of Gottfried's Tristan," *Mediaevalia*, 8 (1982): 81-95.

C

CADMUS was the son of Agenor, King of Phoenicia. When Cadmus's sister Europa was abducted by Jupiter, Agenor sent Cadmus off to search her out. Eventually, Cadmus sought guidance from the Delphic oracle. This oracle advised him to search no longer for his sister, but rather to follow a certain cow and to found a city where the cow should lie down. Eventually, the cow did lie down; Cadmus then killed the dragon that guarded a nearby spring. Unfortunately, this dragon was the offspring of Mars, and so Cadmus earned the enmity of that god. This was then, the ominous beginning of the much-troubled city of Thebes (see **THEBES**).

Athena instructed Cadmus to sow the dragon's teeth. Where the teeth fell, soldiers grew up out of the ground, fully armed. The soldiers fought among themselves until just five lived. These soldiers were said to be the great ancestors of the Theban aristocracy. Cadmus married Harmonia, daughter of Mars and Venus. (Harmonia—or Harmony or Hermione—was often understood as a figure for the principle of harmony or consonance; see **MARS**; see Appendix A, "Music"). Finally, Cadmus and Harmonia were turned into serpents and entered Elysium in that form (e.g., Ovid, *Metamorphoses*: 3.1-137; Apollodorus, *Library*: 3.4.1-2).

The subsequent history of Thebes was unsavory, but Christians generally remembered Cadmus himself with favor. In the first place, the story of Cadmus was said to explain how the alphabet—and so, literacy and learning—came to Greece. "Cadmus son of Agenor brought letters from Phoenicia to Greece," wrote Isidore (*Etymologiarum*: 1.3.6), recalling Pliny (*Natural History*: 7.197). Ficino (*Philebus Commentary*: 29.18c), Sandys (*Ovid*: 149), and Ross (*Mystagogus Poeticus*: 51), among others, agreed. Pliny also gave Cadmus credit for bringing stone quarrying, mining, and gold smelting from Phoenicia (*Natural History*: 7.195, 197). Indeed, Cadmus was sometimes said to have brought the whole of civilized life to Greece; see, for example, Boccaccio (*Fates of Famous Men*: 7; *Genealogie Deorum*: 2.63). Lydgate is effusive on the subject:

> Thoruh his noble prudent purveiance
> He tauhte figures & lettris for to write,
> And made lawes off ful gret ordynance
> A-mong the Grekis, and sette governance
> Ther vicious liff bi virtu to restreyne.
> (*Falls of Princes*: 1.1955-1959)

According to the *Ovide Moralisé*, Cadmus's fight with the dragon was a figure for the philosopher's conquering the dragon of study in order to gain the fountain of philosophy (3.224-239). Cadmus was often mentioned as a type of Christ. Berchorius develops this type at considerable length: "Cadmus can signify Christ who by the command of his father came into the world to seek his sister—that is the human soul—whom Jupiter—that is the devil had seized from God the father" (*Ovidius Moralizatus*: 179). Berchorius goes on: the dragon "signifies the devil," the city which Cadmus founds is "the church," and so forth (180-183; see also Ross, *Mystagogus Poeticus*: 52). Sandys wrote that their marriage was "honoured by the presence of the Gods, & their bountiful endowments. So beloved of them is the harmony of exterior and interior beauty espoused to Virtue" (*Ovid*: 149).

But despite all this virtue, Cadmus and Harmonia were not beyond Dame Fortune's reach. Accounts vary as to why, but they did lose their kingdom. Thus Milton made Cadmus and Hermione a type of Adam and Eve (*Paradise Lost*: 9.505-510).

Cadmus could also be seen as a conventional *de casibus exemplum*: Ovid remarks, before beginning upon the catalogue of Cadmus's woes in old age: "But of a surety man's last day must ever be awaited, and none be counted happy till his death, till his last funeral rites are paid" (*Metamorphoses*: 3.135-137). For others who understood Cadmus as a *de casibus exemplum*, see the *Ovide Moralisé* (3.273-336), Boccaccio (*Fates of Famous Men*: 7-9), and Lydgate (*Falls of Princes*: 1.2052-2079).

Bibliography: Don C. Allen, *Mysteriously Meant* (1970): 164, 166, 181; Leonard Barkan, *The Gods Made Flesh: Metamorphoses and the Pursuit of Paganism* (1986): 42-46; Roberto Calasso, *The Marriage of Cadmus and Harmony* (1993); John P. McCall, *Chaucer among the Gods: The Poetics of Classical Myth* (1979): 89-91.

CADUCEUS was the rod of Mercury. Usually the rod is shown winged, with two serpents entwined. This staff is a part of a very old tradition; it seems to have come to the Greeks from the Middle East. Indeed, one finds something very like it in the Old Testament, where Moses set up a brazen serpent on a rod, that all who had been bitten by serpents might look upon it and be healed (Num 21:8-9; see also John 3:14). Virgil's account of Caduceus was widely known: "with this [Mercury] calls pale ghosts from Orcus and sends others down to gloomy Tartarus, gives or takes away sleep and unseals eyes in death; on this relying he drives the winds and skims the stormy clouds" (*Aeneid*: 4.242-246; see also Homer, *Odyssey*: 5.50).

Caduceus was often thought to bring peace and concord—and so in Botticelli's *Primavera* (fig. 13) we see Mercury wielding his Caduceus to expel the intrusive clouds from this scene of natural harmony (Lightbown 1989: 136). For Bernardus this had to do with the power of eloquence to persuade: "He is said to carry a wand with which he divides serpents, because he has the explanation by which he separates quarrellers and the purveyors of poisonous words" (*On Virgil's Aeneid*: on book 4). Ross understands the Caduceus in essentially the same way:

Mercury was painted with a rod in his hand wrapt about with two Serpents embracing each other: by which is signified, that eloquence must be joyned with wisdom, whereof the Serpent is the emblem: and where wisdom and eloquence are conjoyned there the State is well governed, which is signified by the rod or Scepter, the symbol of Government...for all anger and hostility falls to the ground when that rod doth mediate. (*Mystagogus Poeticus*: 263)

Caduceus could also be associated with peace without reference to eloquence, as we see in Fraunce: "the serpents, winding it about, are a signe of concord; and the rod itselfe was borne of those who intreated of peace, called thereof Caduceatores" (*Countesse of Pembrokes Yvychurch*: 38r). Spenser has this allegory in mind when he writes of Cambina:

> In her right hand a rod of peace shee bore,
> About the which two Serpents weren wound,
> Entrayled mutually in lovely lore,
> And by the tailes together firmely bound,
> And both were with one olive garland crownd,
> Like to the rod which Maias sonne doth wield,
> Wherewith the hellish fiends he doth confound.
>
> (*Faerie Queene*: 4.3.42; see also "Ruins of Time": 667)

According to Lotspeich (1932: 44), Spenser's immediate source for this is Conti (*Mythologie*: 5.5); see also Servius, where "Caduceus...is reason" (*In Virgilii Aeneidos*: 4.242).

Mercury could induce sleep with a touch of this rod; Pope gives this somniferous rod to the goddess Dulness,

> Who spread a healing mist before the mind,
> And, lest we err by Wit's wild, dancing light,
> Secure us kindly in our native night.
> Ah! still o'er Britain stretch that peaceful wand,
> Which lulls th' Helvetian and Batavian land.
>
> ("Dunciad": 1.152-156)

And from ancient times the Caduceus was associated with healing (e.g., Fraunce, 38r), as it is now with medical bills.

For the Caduceus and divine inspiration, see **MERCURY**.

Bibliography: Ronald Lightbown, *Botticelli: Life and Work* (1989); H.G. Lotspeich, *Classical Mythology in the Poetry of Edmund Spenser* (1932); Edgar Wind, *Pagan Mysteries of the Renaissance* (1968): 100, 197.

CAENIS was a beautiful maid who was raped by Neptune. Neptune told her then that he would give her whatever she might wish for. She asked to be changed into a brave man, so that she might never again be so taken advantage of. She was changed into a brave warrior, Caeneus. Caeneus was one of the bravest in the war of the Lapiths against the Centaurs, and sometimes he is mentioned as one of the Argonauts. The allegorical interpretation of the story was another version of the widely known allegory of male/female relations and male *virtus*/virtue (see **AMAZONS**). Here is Berchorius on Caenis/Caeneus: "Apply this to the many who are at first women—that is soft and feminine; but Neptune the god of the sea—that is the Father or the Holy Spirit—cohabits with them through grace and changes them into men—that is brave and stable persons" (*Ovidius Moralizatus*: 383). Sandys provides a secular, Euhemerist version of this allegory. Caenis was at first "a sloathfull and effeminate youth," who went on to become "a coragious and expert souldier" (*Ovid*: 563).

CALLISTO was best known during the Middle Ages and the Renaissance in Ovid's version of the story (*Metamorphoses*: 2.401-507; see also Hyginus, *Fabulae*: 177; Apollodorus, *Library*: 3.8.2): Callisto was an Arcadian nymph, a daughter of Lycaon. After swearing chaste fealty to Diana, Callisto was raped by Jupiter disguised as Diana. She managed to hide her shame until nine months into her pregnancy, at which time Diana urged her nymphs to bathe with her. And so Callisto's condition was discovered. Diana banished her from her company, and Juno revenged herself upon Callisto by turning her into a bear, eventually to be hunted by Callisto's own son, Arcas. Jupiter intervened, finally, and turned Callisto into the constellation Ursa Major and Arcas into Ursus Minor.

The story is one of the most pathetic in the *Metamorphoses*, a mood which Titian conveys in his two paintings of Callisto. But Callisto seems most often to have been understood by Medieval and Renaissance Christians in allegorical terms, as yet another example of the bestializing effect of lust (see Appendix B, "Bestialization"). Ross's interpretation would have been recognized as traditional throughout the Middle Ages and the Renaissance: "Calysto kept her maidenhood whilst she was employed in hunting, but giving her self to sleep and rest, lost it: exercise is the chief preserver of modesty, but idleness the mother of all wantonness and uncleanness....She is turned into a Bear for her adultery: by which we see, that they who give themselves to corporal uncleaness, degenerate into

Beasts" (*Mystagogus Poeticus*: 53; for the moral allegory of hunting, see **ADONIS**).

Since Jupiter assumed the form of Diana in order to approach Callisto without frightening her, Berchorius offers as one interpretation of the story that Jupiter is Christ who took on "human flesh and shape" in order to save mankind, whom Christ loved as Jupiter loved Callisto. But Berchorius also provides the more traditional interpretation:

She is changed from a woman into a bear because she loses her human shape—that is her rational way of thinking and manner of acting and takes on those of a bear, bestial and carnal. Then she acquires...a terrifying voice [i.e., a bear's growl]—that is, shameful and dishonest speech. When someone becomes a sinner, all good habits are changed in him. An example is Nabuchodnosor who was changed into a beast [Dan 4]. (*Ovidius Moralizatus*: 161-162)

For others who interpret Callisto as an *exemplum* of the bestializing effects of lust, see, for example, Burton (*Anatomy of Melancholy*: 3.2.3) and Sandys (*Ovid*: 112). In Chaucer's "Knight's Tale" (2056-2061) Callisto is one of the figures Emylye sees upon the wall of Diana's temple—one of the *de casibus* figures warning her of the fearful consequences of the loss of virginity.

Bibliography: Leonard Barkan, *The Gods Made Flesh: Metmorphosis and the Pursuit of Paganism* (1986): 201; Richard L. Hoffman, *Ovid and the Canterbury Tales* (1966): 82-85; Kathleen Wall, *The Callisto Myth from Ovid to Atwood: Rape and Initiation in Literature* (1988).

CALYPSO was a beautiful enchantress, one of the Pleiades, daughters of Atlas. In the *Odyssey* (1.13-87; 5.1-268; 7.244-269) it is on Calypso's isle that we first meet Ulysses. She had welcomed the shipwrecked hero to her isle; and she so loved him that she promised him eternal life if he would stay with her. She kept him for ten years, but Ulysses often wept, yearning for home. Finally, Athena prevailed upon Zeus to instruct Calypso to let Ulysses go.

At least as early as Plotinus, Calypso and her sister Circe were figures for sensual delights. This made particular sense since it was Athena (the goddess of wisdom) who was opposing Calypso. Plotinus:

"Let us flee to our own land," one might better urge. What is this flight and how shall we be born away? Just as Odysseus says he was delivered from a witch like Circe or Calypso, claiming—and I believe he hints at some further meaning—that it did not please him to stay, though he enjoyed visual delights and was in the presence of enormous beauty on the level of the senses. Our land is that place from which we came and our father is there. (*Enneads*: 1.6.8.16-21)

Lamberton (1989: 107) explains that for Plotinus, Ulysses' long journey home seems to be a figure for human striving after the realm of the spirit, "just as a man arrives in his well-governed land after a long journey" (*Enneads*: 5.9.1.20-21). Chaucer places Calypso alongside two other notorious love-sorceresses, Circe and Medea (*House of Fame*: 1271-1272). Pico wrote that "a man given over to his belly" is "blinded by his Calypso-like imagination...and delivered over to the senses" (*On the Dignity of Man*: 6). Gower makes Calypso and Circe co-rulers of the Isle of Sicily, both in love with Ulysses; they work together to transform Ulysses' men into beasts (*Confessio Amantis*: 6.1427-1453).

    Bibliography: Don C. Allen, *Mysteriously Meant* (1970): 91-96; Robert Lamberton, *Homer the Theologian* (1989); James J. Wilhelm, *The Cruelest Month. Spring, Nature, and Love in Classical and Medieval Lyrics* (1965).

CANACE was one of the daughters of Aeolus, king of Magnesia. Ovid tells the unpleasant story of her incestuous love for her brother, Macreus. When her father discovered their secret, he ordered that the defiled brother be exposed, to be eaten by "dogs and birds"; Canace he ordered to commit suicide (*Heroides*: 11). Canace thus came to be included in lists of *de casibus* lovers (see, e.g., Taylor 1986); Ausonius, for example, likens Canace to Phaedra, Dido, and Phyllis (*Epigrams*: 22); and in the *Fiammetta* Boccaccio provides a list of those whom Love molested "with a wicked fire...Myrrha, Semiramis, Byblis, Canace, and Cleopatra" (20-21). Chaucer's Man of Law mentions "thilke wikke ensample of Canacee" ("Man of Law's Tale": 78). Gower (*Confessio Amantis*: 3.143-360) is equally censorious.

    Bibliography: Beverly Taylor, "Phyllis, Canacee, Biblis, and Dido: Keys to Understanding *The Minnegrotte* of Gottfried's Tristan," *Mediaevalia*, 8 (1982): 81-95.

CASSANDRA was the daughter of Priam, king of Troy. As Apollodorus (*Library*: 3.12.5) and Servius (*In Virgilii Aeneidos*: 2.247) tell the story, Apollo loved Cassandra, and so he gave her the gift of prophecy. She did not reciprocate his love, however, and so he soured his gift: he cursed her, so that none should believe her prophecies. She is known in particular for her disregarded prophecies as to the doom of Troy. She was sometimes counted among the Sibyls: Bernardus (*On Virgil's Aeneid*: 6.9-13), for example, accords her this status; and Chaucer at one point refers to her as "Sibille" (*Troylus and Criseyde*: 5.1450). In the seventeenth century she was mentioned as a type of the Old Testament prophet Jeremiah (Allen 1970: 101). But Bacon made Cassandra an example of those who are so proud of their own wit as to "disdaine to submit themselves to the documents of Apollo, the God of Harmonie, whereby to learne and observe the method and measure of affaires, the grace and gravitie of discourse, the differences between the more judicious and more vulgar eares, and due times when to speake and when to be silent" (*Wisedome of the Ancients*: 1). Lemmi (1933: 191-192) suggests that Bacon's interpretation is in keeping with the roughness with which Cassandra delivers her awful prophecies to Ovid's Oenone (*Heroides*: 5.115-120) and Chaucer's Troylus (*Troylus and Criseyde*: 5.1513-1519).

   Bibliography: Don C. Allen, *Mysteriously Meant* (1970); Charles W. Lemmi, *The Classical Deities in Bacon* (1933).

CASTOR AND POLLUX (the Dioscuri, the Gemini, the Tyndarians). Castor and Pollux were sometimes said to be the twin sons of Leda and Tyndarus (e.g., Ovid, *Metamorphoses*: 8.301). More often they were said to be the twin sons born to Leda, after Jupiter had visited her in the guise of a swan; in this version they were born of a single egg, with their sister Helen (e.g., Apollodorus, *Library*: 1.8.2; Fulgentius, *Mythologies*: 2.13); sometimes Helen and Clytemnestra were said to have been born twins from a second egg. To name just three of Castor and Pollux's many exploits: They hunted the Calydonian Boar with Meleager (see **ADONIS** for the moral allegory of hunting); they sailed with the Argonauts; they fought with Jason and Peleus to defeat Iolcus. But Christians usually remembered them either because they were turned into stars (the Gemini, the Twins: the morning and the evening stars) or because of their affection for one another. Their story was said to explain certain astronomical facts. Here, for example, is Bernardus:

one reads that Castor and Pollux were brothers; Pollux was a god, and Castor was a mortal. Since indeed, Castor could not as a mortal live forever, it is said that Pollux shared his divinity with him and descended to the underworld so that Castor might ascend to the heavens. Some people interpret them as two stars, one of which has divinity because of its greater brilliance, and the other has mortality because of its lesser brilliance. And when Pollux descends to the lower hemisphere, Castor holds the higher, and thus Pollux descends to the underworld so that Castor may rise...for when one sets the other appears, and conversely. But, in a better way, we interpret these brothers to be the soul and the body, of which the soul is rational and immortal and thus a god, but the body is mortal. The soul endures the death of the body for a time, so that the body may then share the immortality of the spirit. For just as the soul dwells in this region of death by companionship with the body, so too the body dwells in the region of life by companionship with the soul. (*On Virgil's Aeneid*: 6.121; that birth meant a kind of death for the soul was one of the tenets of Neo-Platonism; for more on this, see **UNDERWORLD**.)

Another tradition had it that the twins, like their sister Helen, are figures for "disaster" (Fulgentius, *Mythologies*: 2.13) or "burning lustes" (Batman, *Golden Booke*: 22r).

   Renaissance Neo-Platonists, on the other hand, liked to contrast the two sets of twins. Since they loved one another so dearly, Castor and Pollux represented concord. The twin sisters represented discord: Helen was known to have caused the Trojan war; Clytemnestra was an adultress and murderer of her own husband (Wind 1968: 165-170). Just as Mars (discord) and Venus (concord) unite to produce Harmony (see **MARS**), so here discord and harmony are seen to issue from the same source.

In one story Castor and Pollux rape the two daughters of Leucippus; this story was sometimes understood—like the story of Ganymede ravished by Jupiter's eagle—as a figure for the soul's ascent to heaven (Seznec 1961: 105). Indeed, because of this ravishing, because of their own astral reincarnations, and because they were held to rule the two hemispheres of the heavens where the most privileged souls hoped to live after death, these twins were thought of as guides and protectors of apotheosized souls—the guides of the hopeful dead. As such, they frequently appeared in funerary art (Panofsky n.d.: 22, 36).

Bibliography: Erwin Panofsky, *Tomb Sculpture* (n.d.); Jean Seznec, *The Survival of the Pagan Gods* (1961); Edgar Wind, *Pagan Mysteries of the Renaissance* (1968); Chauncey Wood, *Chaucer and the Country of the Stars* (1970): 149-150.

THE CENTAURS were a vigorous race of creatures with the heads of men and the bodies of horses. Classical mythology provides more than one version of their origin. Bernardus's account agrees with that best known to the Middle Ages and the Renaissance: "we read in fables that Ixion desired to sleep with Juno and that she interposed a cloud which, receiving Ixion's seed, gave birth to the Centaurs, who were part men and part animals....[They are] called Centaurs, because they are partly rational and partly vicious, that is, because they are human in the forepart and bestial in the hind part" (*On Virgil's Aeneid*: 6.285-286).

Centaurs thus came to be used in various ways to suggest the double nature of human beings (e.g., Albricus, *De Deorum*: 22; Guido da Pisa, *Super Comediam Dantis*: 228; Conti, *Mythologie*: 7.5; Viana, *Ovid*: 9.17)—or the beasts human beings could become when reason slackened the reins (see Appendix B, "Bestialization"). Van Mander explains the assumptions at work in this tradition in the course of his explanation of the allegorical meanings of the horse: "The man who obeys reason is meant by the bridled horse....People who lead superficial lives are represented as half men and half horse....The licentious man is meant by the Centaurs, for (says one) not every man is a man, for he who gives himself to vice is a horse-man" (*Wtbeeldinghen der Figuren*: 114v). Centaurs could thus suggest human capitulation to any of the passions; but they were most commonly associated with lust, as in the *Chess of Love* commentary: the Centaur, we read, "was composed of two different forms, i.e., half human, insofar as he showed himself to be reasonable, and half horse, insofar as he showed himself to be lustful and deceived by carnal delight, like an animal" (522). Ross writes in the same vein: "Commonly as the Parents are, such be the Children; Ixion himself was given to leachery, and so were the Centaurs his Children; for which cause they were said to be half horses, intimating their insatiable lust, and proneness to Venery" (*Mystagogus Poeticus*: 227).

But the Centaurs were also known for their violence—especially drunken violence (see **LAPITHS** for the Centaurs' most famous drunken brawl). In the *Inferno* (12), for example, Dante puts Centaurs in charge of the tortures of the violent; Conti also associates the Centaurs with violence (*Mythologie*: 7.5).

Following Fulgentius (*Mythologies*: 2.14), Sandys links the Centaurs with the passion for glory: "Ixion is said to have begotten them on a Clowd, formed like, & mistaken for Juno....[They represent] the vaine pursute of imaginary glory, attempted by unlawful meanes; and the prodigious conceptions of Ambition: for from the navel downeward they carried the shapes of horses" (*Ovid*: 564). And Shakespeare's Lear thinks of his wicked daughters as Centaurs:

Down from the waist they are Centaurs,
Though women all above:
But to the girdle do the gods inherit,
Beneath is all the fiends'. (4.6.124-127)

Botticelli's *Pallas and the Centaur* (fig. 6) makes use of this traditional understanding of the Centaur. In this painting the Centaur seems to represent man's animal desires; the woman could be Minerva, pulling the head of the Centaur upwards, by way of making a Neo-Platonic point as to human aspirations for divine wisdom (Gombrich 1993: 69-72)—or the woman might be Camilla, a woman warior who devoted herself to Diana and so to chastity (Lightbown 1989: 146-152; for Camilla, see Virgil, *Aeneid*: 7, 9; Boccaccio, *Concerning Famous Women*: 37). In either case, the Centaur would stand in contrast to the ideal represented by the female figure. Ross's comment on the Centaurs is closely related: "Every regenerate man is in a sort a Centaur, to wit, a man in that part which is regenerate, and a beast in his unregenerate part....Where things are not ruled by Laws, Order and Civility, but carried headlong with violence & force, we may say that there is a Commonwealth of Centaurs" (*Mystagogus Poeticus*: 58; see also Wither, *Emblemes*: 103).

For closely related allegory having to do with bestiality, see **MINOTAUR**; for a virtuous Centaur, see **CHIRON**.

Bibliography: E. H. Gombrich, *Symbolic Images* (1993); Judith Kollman, "Centaur," in Malcolm South, *Mythical Creatures and Fabulous Beasts: A Source Book and Research Guide* (1987); Ronald Lightbown, *Botticelli: Life and Work* (1989); DeWitt Starnes and E. W. Talbert, *Classical Myth and Legend in Renaissance Dictionaries* (1955): 114-116.

CEPHALUS AND PROCRIS. There were many versions of the story of Cephalus and Procris. Ovid's was the one most familiar to Medieval and Renaissance Christians (*Metamorphoses*: 7.661-862; see also Hyginus, *Fabulae*: 189). Here is Sandys' paraphrase of Ovid, along with the traditional moral:

Cephalus...is said to have beene beloved and ravished by Aurora [the goddess of the dawn]; in that he usually spent the Morning in the woods, transported with the delight of hunting: To reject her; in fore-slowing his accustomed exercises, as not induring to be so long absent from his beloved wife: the foundation of his jealousies (here said to be infused by Aurora, or the practise of a rivall) an humor easily raised, and augmented by his owne example.

He decides, then, to test his wife, coming to her in disguise, as a lover:

he vainely attempts her with all the subtilties of a lover; til by multiplying of gifts, she seemes to him in the end to waver. When discovering himselfe and upbraiding her disloyalty; she overcome with shame and indignation to be so unworthily suspected and betrayed, abandoning her house, her husband, & for his sake the society of men; flyes unto the solitary woods, and devotes her selfe to the service of Diana.

Eventually, Cephalus manages to win her love again, and her forgiveness. But then Procris becomes jealous in her turn. She follows Cephalus when he goes out to hunt, thinking that he is going, really, to meet a lover. She hides in the bushes to watch, "and by rustling among the leaves is mistaken for a beast, and wounded to death by his javelin...the fable was deviced to deterr from ill-grounded jealousy, and to show how execrable they be who sow suspitions among the married; whose events are ever bitter, and not seldom tragical" (*Ovid*: 348-350). The same interpretation may be found, for example, in Bernardus (*On Virgil's Aeneid*: 6.445-447), Berchorius (*Ovidius Moralizatus*: 293), and Pettie, who tells the story as a warning to women that "sutch warying watching of your husbandes...is but a meane to make them fall to folly the rather" (*Petite Pallace*: 208). Shakespeare's bumpkins, then, are characteristically confused when they have Thisbe swear to her beloved Pyramus, "As Shafalus to Procrus, I to you" (*Midsummer Night's Dream*: 5.1.199).

   Bibliography: Leonard Barkan, *The Gods Made Flesh: Metamorphosis and the Pursuit of Paganism* (1986): 208-209.

CERBERUS, as Ross put it, was "Pluto's Dog, begot of Typhon and Echidna; he had three heads, and Snakes instead of hair, and lay in the entry of Hell" (*Mystagogus Poeticus*: 61). Because of his appetite for flesh he was often understood as a figure for the earth. Servius wrote, "Cerberus is the earth; for it is the devourer of all bodies" (*In Virgilii Aeneidos*: 6.395; see also Vatican Mythographer I: 57; Vatican Mythographer II: 11, 149). John of Garland followed Servius: "Cerberus is the earth which devours the flesh" (*Integumenta Ovidii*: 196); and Bernardus, for another example, wrote that Cerberus may be interpreted as, "the earth, whence his name is fitting. *Cerberus*, as if *caerberos*, that is, *carnem vorans*, 'devouring the flesh'" (*On Virgil's Aeneid*: 6.392; see also, e.g., Guido da Pisa, *Super Comediam Dantis*: 121, on Dante's meeting Cerberus in the *Inferno*: 6).

Cerberus could also be a figure for the earth in the moral sense; that is, he could be a figure for worldly things and for the associated sins: Ridewall wrote that "We understand Cerberus to mean earthly desires" (*Fulgentius metaforalis*: 103). Landino wrote that "if Cerberus be the earth, then who fails to understand that Virgil intended to signify the insatiability of the body by Cerberus's barking?" (*Disputationes Camuldenses*: 241; see also, e.g., Batman, *Golden Booke*: 12v; Fraunce, *Countesse of Pembrokes Yvychurch*: 27v).

Cerberus could also be a figure for the earth in nature allegory; in such contexts his three heads were usually understood as the three continents; see, for example, John of Garland (*Integumenta Ovidii*: 196), Bernardus (*On Virgil's Aeneid*: 6.384-391), the *Chess of Love* commentary (457), and Landino (*Disputationes Camuldenses*: 241; Allen 1970: 161).

Servius's etymology could also serve to make Cerberus a figure for death (e.g., Berchorius, *Ovidius Moralizatus*: 287) or the grave. Sandys: "His name doth signifie...a devourer of flesh; and allegorically is taken for the grave...the Grave is ever ravenous, but never satisfied" (*Ovid*: 343; see also Ross, *Mystagogus Poeticus*: 63).

Cerberus's proverbial ravenousness also made him a figure for avarice (e.g., Waleys, *Ovid*: 15), covetousness, or "the insatiableness of the body" in general (Landino, *Disputationes Camuldenses*, Stahel tr.: 237). Thus Dante puts Cerberus in charge of the gluttons in the Third Circle of the Inferno (6.1-21). Here is Sandys again: "Cerberus is the type of covetousness; tormented and mad with griefe, when inforced to bounty....He is faigned to have many heads, in that covetousnesse is the root of all the flagitious offences: to skluke in a darke Cave and in the passage to Hell; because no vice so obscures the understanding, nor leads a readier way to perdition" (*Ovid*: 343). Sometimes he was said to be a figure for covetousness because he was Pluto's dog, because some writers (e.g., Ross, *Mystagogus Poeticus*: 62) understood Pluto to be the god of riches (by conflating Pluto with Plutus; see **PLUTO**).

Hercules captured Cerberus as one of his twelve labors. Usually this was interpreted as one or another variation on the victory of Christ over the world or Satan—or spirit or virtue over the world/flesh (see **HERCULES: TWELFTH LABOR**). Heraclitus (*Allégories d'Homère*: 33.9) interpreted Hercules' defeat of Cerberus as his successful struggle with the three branches of philosophy: logic, natural philosophy, and moral philosophy!

Bibliography: Don C. Allen, *Mysteriously Meant* (1970); James Nohrnberg, *The Analogy of The Faerie Queene* (1976): 690-697; J. J. H. Savage, "The Medieval Tradition of Cerberus," *Traditio*, 7 (1949-1951): 405-410.

CERES (Demeter) was the daughter of Saturn and Ops (Rhea). She was a mother-earth goddess, a goddess of agriculture and of the rise of civilization associated with agriculture. She could thus serve as an allegorical figure for grain (e.g., Reynolds, *Mythomystes*: 170) and fertility, which is why she appears, for example, in the Temple of Venus in Chaucer's *Parliament of Fowls* (276). Plutus (the god of riches) was her son, since steady devotion to agriculture could produce wealth (see, e.g., Conti, *Mythologie*: 5.15).

Often Ceres allegorized the earth in accounts of the four elements (see Reid 1993: 468-469). We see her at work in this way on the title page of Sandys' *Ovid's Metamorphosis, Englished, Mythologized, and Represented in Figures* (fig. 16). Jupiter (the fiery ether) is in the upper left; Juno (air) is in the upper right; Neptune (water) is at the bottom right; and Ceres (earth) is in the bottom left with her signature cornucopia and a particularly motherly sort of cow (for a fuller explanation of this title page, see **APOLLO, MINERVA**). But because she could be identified with the earth, Ceres could also be interpreted as "the type of the earthly minded man" (Ross, *Mystagogus Poeticus*: 67).

Boccaccio writes of Ceres in Euhemeristic terms, as "a very ancient queen of Sicily, who had such great wisdom that after discovering how to till the soil she was the first among her people to tame oxen and accustom them to the yoke" (*Concerning Famous Women*: 5). Ceres could thus be understood as having ushered in the agricultural age, the age of cities. Boccaccio was not alone in thinking of this as a fall from the innocence of the Golden Age (see **THE FOUR AGES**). But Renaissance Christians were often more optimistic about civilization. Shakespeare has Ceres preside with Juno over the marriage masque in *The Tempest* (4.1)—Juno as the goddess of marriage, and Ceres as presiding over civilized nature, as opposed to Caliban and his pre-civilized rooting about for pig-nuts (Orgel 1975: 45-46).

The story of Ceres' loss of Proserpina to Pluto and the Underworld was usually interpreted as an explanation of the earth's alternating seasons of fertility and sterility (see **PROSERPINA**). And thus Ceres could serve as an allegorical figure for summer (for a list of paintings that work in this way, see Reid 1993: 468-469).

Because she was a goddess of the harvest, Ceres was associated with food in plenty. Thus it is that the narrator in Chaucer's *Parliament of Fowls* sees Ceres ("dining") and Bacchus ("drinking") in close company with Venus and Priapus, for according to an old proverb, "Venus freezes without Ceres and Bacchus" (McCall 1979: 61; Renger 1981).

Because she was a goddess of the earth and of fertility, Ceres was sometimes conflated with Cybele-Gaia-Rhea-Ops; see **CYBELE**.

Bibliography: Don C. Allen, *Mysteriously Meant* (1970): 164-165; John P. McCall, *Chaucer among the Gods: The Poetics of Classical Myth* (1979); Stephen Orgel, *The Illusion of Power: Political Theater in the English Renaissance* (1975); Jane Davidson Reid, *The Oxford Guide to Classical Mythology in the Arts, 1300-1990s* (1993); K. Renger, "'Sine Cere et Baccho friget Venus,'" in R. Preimesberger and J. Rasmussen, *Peter Paul Rubens Werk und Nachruhm* (1981); Rosemond Tuve, *Allegorical Imagery* (1966): 36, 228-229, 299-300.

CHARON was the misshapen being who ferried the souls of the dead across the fetid rivers of the Underworld. He charged for the passage, and so it was that the ancients were buried with a coin in their mouths. Fulgentius had it that Charon was a figure for "time, whence too he is called the son of Polydegmon, for Polydegmon in Greek is much knowledge" (*On the Content of Virgil*: 22). Fulgentius is commenting on Charon as he appears in Virgil's *Aeneid* (6.299), where Aeneas meets Charon in the course of his descent to the Underworld for knowledge; and so Fulgentius means, I think, that Charon is a figure for time insofar as time is necessary for learning, that older people are more likely to be wise than young people, that experience can be a teacher.   This is, at least, how Bernardus understands the allegory in *his* comment on Aeneas's descent: he reminds us that Aeneas's "journey is contemplation," and

Charon is said to be in Acheron, since a man of greater age sustains greater calamity....Charon speaks to Aeneas when an old man full of days and much time speaks to the rational person, and speaks first because old age is prudent and mindful of many things. Charon rebukes Aeneas—when a prudent old man sees someone's rational spirit traveling the path of contemplation, he fears lest he may be descending merely because of curiosity or for the love of temporal goods alone. (*On Virgil's Aeneid*: 6.384-391)

Dante descends into the *Inferno* for knowledge just as Aeneas did, and like Aeneas, Dante, too, meets Charon along the way. Dante describes Charon as "an old man, his hair white with age" (*Inferno*: 3.83); and so, following Fulgentius, Pietro Alighieri writes in his comment on this line, "Charon, that is, time" (*Commentarium*: 84, on *Inferno*: 3).

Bibliography: Ronnie Terpening, *Charon and the Crossing: Ancient, Modern, and Renaissance Transformations of a Myth* (1985).

CHIONE. There were several Chiones known to the ancients, but it was Chione, the daughter of Daedalion, who occasionally served the ends of Christian allegory. She was of surpassing beauty—so beautiful that both Apollo and Mercury lay with her, and so she bore twins, Philammon and Autolycus. "But," wrote Ovid, "what profits it...that she found favour with two gods...? Is not glory a bane as well? It has been a bane to many, surely to her! For she boldly set herself above Diana and criticized the goddess' beauty" (*Metamorphoses*: 11.315-322). Furious, Diana shot an arrow through Chione's tongue; and so she died with her proud tongue stilled. Chione could thus serve as a moral example, "signifying," as Fraunce put it, "that pride will have a fall" (*Countesse of Pembrokes Yvychurch*: 38r).

CHIRON, son of Saturn and Phillyra, was the most famous of the Centaurs. He was known for his mastery of astronomy, music, and medicine. Pliny wrote that "the science of herbs and drugs was discovered by Chiron" (*Natural History*: 7.197). He was remembered as the tutor of Aesculapius, the great physician-god of Greek mythology (e.g., Isidore, *Etymologiarum*: 3.71.36; Berchorius, *Ovidius Moralizatus*: 172), and for tutoring Achilles (e.g., Ovid, *Metamorphoses*: 6.126; Statius, *Achilleid*: 1.104-197; Dante, *Purgatorio*: 9.34-39; Gower, *Confessio Amantis*: 4.1963-2013). Thus it was that Chiron came to be a wisdom figure. Dante's Chiron is very wise (*Inferno*: 12.75-99), and as late as 1651 one Francis Bonomii entitled a book of moral emblems *Achilles' Chiron, or the Captain of Human Life*.

Chiron—horse in his lower parts, godlike in his reason—was also recognized as a figure for the human condition (e.g., the *Ovide Moralisé*: 2.3301-3376). Berchorius writes that Chiron figures forth "man who has a two-fold nature" (*Ovidius Moralizatus*: 172). Machiavelli (*Prince*: 18) remembers that Chiron was Achilles' tutor, and so makes Chiron a figure for the ideal prince, who must, like Chiron, combine the strength of the lion and the cleverness of the fox; Machiavelli is thus playing on the traditional allegory of the Centaur, that the Centaur is like human beings, half rational, half beast (see Ingman 1982). And here is Browne: "In briefe, we are all monsters, that is, a composition of man and beast, wherein we must endeavour to be as the Poets fancy that wise man Chiron, that is, to have the Region of Man above that of Beast, and sense to sit but at the feete of reason" (*Religio Medici*: 1.55).

For more on the allegory of Centaurs, see **CENTAUR**.

Bibliography: Heather Ingman, "Machiavelli and the Interpretation of the Chiron Myth in France," *JWCI*, 45 (1982): 217-225.

CIMMERIANS. Homer's Odysseus goes to the land of Cimmeria to seek the shade of Tiresias. Homer tells us that this is "the realm and region of the Men of Winter, / hidden in mist and cloud" (*Odyssey*: 11.15-16). These Cimmerians never see the sun. Ovid (*Metamorphoses*: 11.592) mentions Cimmeria as the land where Somnus, the god of sleep, lives his drowsy life. Erasmus wrote, "Deep obscurity or darkness of the mind they call Cimmerian gloom. Lactantius in...his *Divine Institutions* [5.3]: 'What a blind heart, a mind with all the darkness of what they call Cimmerian gloom!'" (*Adages*: 2.6.34). Erasmus also cites Jerome (*Against John of Jerusalem*: 44). Spenser writes that "A stonie coldness hath benumbd the sence" of those who refuse to understand poetry, "And dimd with darknesse their intelligence, / Darknesse more than Cymerians daylie night" ("Teares of the Muses": 253-255; see also Shakespeare, *Titus Andronicus*: 2.3.72).

CINYRAS was the first king of Cyprus; some traditions have it that his mother was Paphos, the daughter of Pygmalion and his erstwhile-ivory wife (e.g., Ovid, *Metamorphoses*: 10.299). In Ovid's story of the weaving contest between Minerva and Arachne, Minerva weaves into her tapestry stories that have to do with the punishment of presumption. Ovid writes that one of the four stories Minerva depicts is that of Cinyras's daughters. This corner of the tapestry "shows Cinyras bereft of his daughters; there, embracing the marble temple-steps, once their limbs, he lies on the stone, and seems to weep" (*Metamorphoses*: 6.98-100).

Berchorius guesses that the daughters had "said abusive things to Juno and despised her temple" and that it was thus Juno who "changed them into steps for the temple so they might remain there forever" (*Ovidius Moralizatus*: 251). Sandys understands the story to be a moral example of the dangers of presumption (*Ovid*: 289).

For Cinyras's equally unfortunate relations with another daughter, see **MYRRHA**. A few commentators, however, assumed that the Cinyras who fathered Myrrha is not the same as the Cinyras who fathered the presumptuous daughters (see, e.g., Sandys, *Ovid*: 289).

CIRCE was an island enchantress in book 10 of Homer's *Odyssey*; Ulysses' men drink from her cup and are changed into beasts. Already in classical times these transformations were interpreted allegorically, as the bestializing effects of the passions, and especially of lust. Horace understood the *Odyssey* in general, and the Circe episode in particular, as being about the importance of self-control. If Ulysses had drunk of Circe's cup, according to Horace, "he would have become the shapeless and witless vassal of a harlot mistress—would have lived as an unclean dog or a sow that loves the mire" (*Epistles*: 1.2.25-26). Heraclitus also interpreted her as a figure for pleasure or the sensual life; Ulysses overcomes her by his wisdom, and with the aid of Mercury, or "rational discourse" (*Allégories d'Homère*: 72-73). For Servius she was a "most radiant prostitute," a figure for libidinous desire (*In Virgilii Carmina Commentarii*: 7.19). According to Fulgentius, Ulysses was able to resist her because "wisdom scorns lust" (*Mythologies*: 2.9). These interpretations continue through the Middle Ages and the Renaissance with little variation (e.g., Vatican Mythographer II: 212). In the thirteenth-century pseudo-Ovidian "Elegy of the Flea," for example, the profane lover wishes to be metamorphosed "by Circe's drugs" into a flea so that he can wander at will over his lady's sweet person (in Brumble 1973: 148). And Lynche wrote that we are all tempted by "Circaean drugs, and lulled aspleepe by the villainous deceits of the sweet-seeming delights wherewith we are besotted" (*Fountaine of Ancient Fiction*: Qii; see also Wickram, *Ovid*: 145v; Bredero, *Lucelle*: 147-155). Harington recognized that Ariosto's Alcyna "alludes to Circes witchcraft" and that Alcyna's Isle, like Circe's, "signifieth pleasure and vanities of this world" (*On Orlando Furioso*: 47; for Alcyna as Circe, see Yarnall 1994: 127-130). Tasso's temptress is also like "false Circe" (*Jerusalem Delivered*: 4.86). And on the title page (fig. 16) of Sandys' *Ovid's Metamorphosis, Englished, Mythologized, and Represented in Figures* we see Circe and her bestializing transformations at the bottom of the picture, allegorically at the farthest remove from the apotheosis of the virtuous Hercules, there at the top. (For more on this title page, see **APOLLO**, **MINERVA**, and Appendix B, "Bestialization.") Milton makes Circe and Bacchus the parents of Comus, Milton's own allegorical figure for sensuality (*Comus*: 46-53; see Demaray 1966). Milton's Comus also plies a cup like Circe's, a "baneful cup...whose pleasing poison / The visage quite transforms of him that drinks" (524-526).

Even when the interpretation is Euhemeristic, as in the *Chess of Love* commentary, the moral allegory is the same:

Circe was...beautiful and supremely attractive, but she was so fortuned as to be supremely lustful...so she attracted and deceived young men by sweet looks, fair welcome, and fine speech, and maddened them so that sometimes they lost their minds from it. And that is why the fable pretends she made men become beasts. For too much pondering and setting one's heart on carnal delectations...is a bestial thing and inappropriate in reasonable men....That the companions of Ulysses were thus transformed into asses and pigs signifies to us that carnal delectation has regard to two senses, taste and touch. For the one lies in drinking and eating, and is signified by the pigs, who are gluttons. And the other lies in the deed of lust, which is signified by the asses. (605; see also 291; and Golding, "Epistle": 275-276)

Joining specific sins in this way with specific transformations was a popular pastime for allegorists; here, for example, is Boethius: "anyone whom you find transformed by vice cannot be counted a man....the man who is driven by avarice to seize what belongs to others is like a wolf; the restless, angry man...you will compare to a dog...; the lazy, stupid fellow is like an ass"—such, says Boethius, is the meaning of Circe's transformations of men (*Consolation of Philosophy*: 4.pr 3-mt 3; for Circe in Boethius, see O'Daly 1991: 207-219). Bernardus quotes from Boethius in order to make the same point about the bestializing effects of various sins (*On Virgil's Aeneid*: on book 3).

Essentially similar interpretations of Circe's transformations (sometimes with, sometimes without, reference to the meaning of individual animals) may be found in Boccaccio (*Concerning Famous Women*: 36; *Genealogie Deorum*: 4.14), Berchorius (*Ovidius Moralizatus*: 400-403), Erasmus (*Enchiridion*: 106), Fraunce (*Countesse of Pembrokes Yvychurch*: 47v), Whitney (*Emblemes*: 82), Conti (*Mythologie*: 6.6), Burton (*Anatomy of Melancholy*: 3.2.3), Milton ("Seventh Prolusion"), and Ross (*Mystagogus Poeticus*: 75). Tritonio includes Circe in his list of the "libidinous" (*Mythologia*: 28). Spenser has this tradition in mind when he describes the powers of Acrasia:

> These seeming beasts are men indeed,
> Whom this Enchauntresse hath transformed thus,
> Whylome her lovers, which her lusts did feed,
> Now turned into figures hideous,
> According to their mindes like monstruous.
> Sad end...of life intemperate.
>
> (*Faerie Queene*: 2.12.85)

Such interpretations were sufficiently well known that Circe could serve in Petrarchan love poetry as a point of comparison for the beloved and enchanting lady (e.g., Ronsard, *Des Amours* in *Les Oeuvres*, vol. 1: 161).

Because she was the daughter of Sol (the sun) and Perseis (daughter of Oceanus)—heat and moisture—Circe could also be associated with generation. Fraunce put it in this way: "She was called Circe, *à miscendo*, of mingling and tempring: for in the generation of bodies, these foure elements, as we call them, must needs bee tempered: which commixtion and composition is done by the influence and operation of the Sunne: and therefore Circe was borne of the Sunne and Perseis, the daughter of Oceanus" (*Countesse of Pembrokes Yvychurch*: 47v). And thus she could also be associated with the senses; for example, Fulgentius (*Mythologies*: 2.9) associates her with the sense of touch.

For the herb moly, which Mercury gave Ulysses to protect him from Circe's cup, see **ULYSSES**.

Bibliography: Leonard Barkan, *The Gods Made Flesh: Metamorphosis and the Pursuit of Paganism* (1986): 127; Leonora Leet Broadwin, "Milton and the Renaissance Circe," *MiltonS*, 6 (1974): 21-83; H. David Brumble, "John Donne's 'The Flea': The Implications of the Encyclopedic and Poetic Flea Traditions," *CQ*, 15 (1973): 147-54; John Demaray, "Milton's Comus: The Sequel to a Masque of Circe," *HLQ*, 29 (1966): 245-254; A. C. Hamilton, *The Spenser Encyclopedia* (1990); Gerard O'Daly, *The Poetry of Boethius* (1991); Rosemond Tuve, *Images and Themes in Five Poems by Milton* (1957); Judith Yarnall, *The Transformations of Circe: The History of an Enchantress* (1994).

CLEOPATRA, queen of Egypt, was famed for her beauty, her allure, and her ambition. She numbered both Julius Caesar and Mark Antony among her lovers. Since Antony lost his war with Octavian (later Caesar Augustus), the history of Rome subsequently tended to be written in such a way as to dispraise Antony. Small wonder, then, that his mistress should have been regarded as a wicked woman. Virgil regarded her as Antony's "shame" (*Aeneid*: 8.688). In the *Fiammetta* Boccaccio includes Cleopatra in a list of women whom Love molested "with a wicked fire...Myrrha, Semiramis, Byblis, Canace, and Cleopatra" (20-21). She was, Boccaccio wrote, "an object of gossip for the whole world." She was "almost the prostitute of Oriental kings." She led Antony to the excesses not only of lust, but of gluttony. It was for Cleopatra that Antony repudiated his proper Roman wife Octavia, Octavius's sister. And so, according to Boccaccio, were sown the "seeds of war between Octavian and Antony" (*Concerning Famous Women*: 86). De Mézières also held her responsible for this war, a war in which "so much human blood was shed that the sea was dyed crimson therewith" (*Letter to King Richard II*: 66r).

Chaucer includes Cleopatra in a list of *de casibus* lovers—a list that includes such notorious women as Biblis and Semiramis (*Parliament of Fowls*: 286-292). He is kinder to Cleopatra in the *Legend of Good Women*; this Cleopatra kills herself to be true to Antony, because he is never out of her "hertes remembraunce" (686). Whether we understand Shakespeare's Cleopatra to be a sympathetic figure or not, lusty she certainly was, envying as she did Antony's horse: "O happy horse, to bear the weight of Antony!" (*Antony and Cleopatra*: 1.5.21; see Appendix C, "Envying the Animals"). Shakespeare had probably consulted Cooper's *Thesaurus* (under *Cleopatra*; see Starnes 1955: 132), where he would have read that Cleopatra "exceeded in sumptuous gluttony" and that she brought Antony "into such dotage, that in following hir appetite, he aspyred unto the whole empire" and so entered into his disastrous war with Octavian.

Bibliography: DeWitt Starnes and E. W. Talbert, *Classical Myth and Legend in Renaissance Dictionaries* (1955); Beverly Taylor, "The Medieval Cleopatra: The Classical and Medieval Tradition of Chaucer's *Legend of Good Women*," *JMRS* (1977): 249-269.

CORINTH was known as a wealthy city as early as Homer (*Iliad*: 2.570; see also Strabo, *Geography*: 8.6.20). It was situated at the western end of the four-mile-wide isthmus linking the fertile Peloponnese to mainland Greece. A canal across the isthmus was considered as early as the sixth century B.C.; and when this project failed, Periander (c. 625-585 B.C.) built a paved, grooved road across the isthmus over which cargoes and even small ships could be carried. Substantial tolls could thus be collected on all goods moving across as well as up and down the isthmus. Corinth's wealth awakened the envy of less fortunate cities. The Athenian playwrights in particular made Corinth into a symbol of lechery. Aristophanes, for example, coined the word *Corinthize*, "to fornicate" (*Fragments*: 354); and sober Plato used the term "Corinthian girl" to mean a prostitute (*Republic*: 404d). The city was said to be devoted to Aphrodite—although modern historians have suggested that this was merely an ancient slander (Saffrey 1985), like Strabo's assertion that Corinth employed a thousand sacred prostitutes. But slander or no, the stories lived on. Shakespeare is referring to this tradition when he has Prince Hal say that because of all his rowdy doings, he is known as a "Corinthian" (*1 Henry IV*: 2.4.12). And here, for another example, is Burton: "It was that plenty of all things, which made Corinth so infamous of old....In that one temple of Venus a thousand whores did prostitute themselves, as Strabo writes...all nations resorted thither, as to a school of Venus" (*Anatomy of Melancholy*: 3.2.2.1).

Bibliography: *Anchor Bible Dictionary* (1992): under *Corinth*; H. D. Saffrey, "Aphrodite à Corinthe. Reflexions sur une idée recue," *RB*, 92 (1985): 359-74.

CORYBANTES were the ecstatic priests of Cybele and Dionysus. Cybele's priests were famous for their rites involving self-mutilation. Christians (e.g., Augustine, *City of God*: 7.25-26; Conti, *Mythologie*: 9.6; Sandys, *Ovid*: 478) saw clearly the connection between these self-mutilating eunuch priests and Attis, who emasculated himself out of frustrated love for Cybele (see **ATTIS**). Christians also knew the Corybantes for the fury of their rites. Augustine writes of these with horror (*City of God*: 7.25-26); and Conti wrote that "the name *Corybantes* comes from the Greek word *koryptein*, for they dance brandishing their arms and tossing their heads about like madmen" (*Mythologie*: 9.8). Spenser also makes a reference to "Cybeles franticke rites" (*Faerie Queene*: 1.6.15).

During the Renaissance, with the rise of state armies, the Corybantes—as armed priests—could serve to show that no occuption ought to consider itself exempt from military service. Here, for example, is Cartari: "These priestly Corybantes stand upright and armed to show that not only farmers, but also priests and rulers of cities and kingdoms must not remain seated and inactive, but that each of them should take up arms to to defend the country" (*Le Imagini*: 206).

CRASSUS.   Marcus Crassus (c. 112-53 B.C.) joined with Julius Caesar and Pompey to form Rome's first triumvirate. But ancient historians preferred to write about his avarice. He was well known as a real-estate speculator, for example. His practice was to take advantage of Rome's frequent fires and lack of a fire brigade. Crassus would buy burnt buildings for next to nothing, bring in his skilled team of slaves to rebuild and repair them, and then sell for a handsome profit. He was killed in the course of his campaign against the Parthians. The Parthians poured molten gold down his throat (Florus, *Epitome*: 3.11). Crassus thus came to serve as an *exemplum* of avarice. Orosius wrote that he was "a man of insatiable cupidity" (*History*: 6.13; see also Dante, *Purgatorio*: 20.116-117; Singleton 1973: 494; Gower, *Confessio Amantis*: 5.2068-2224; Chaucer, *Troylus and Criseyde*: 3.1387-1393; Brant, *Ship of Fools*: 3; Harington, *On Orlando Furioso*: 324; Burton, *Anatomy of Melancholy*: 2.3.3; and Coornhert, *Zedekunst*: 5.3.8).

Bibliography: John Boardman, *The Oxford History of the Classical World* (1986): 467; Charles S. Singleton, *Purgatorio, Commentary* (1973); DeWitt Starnes and E. W. Talbert, *Classical Myth and Legend in Renaissance Dictionaries* (1955): 216-217.

CRATES (c. 365-285 B.C.) was the son of Ascondas of Thebes. As a young man he went to Athens, where he was converted to the Cynic philosophy by Diogenes of Sinope. Accordingly, he determined to live a life of Cynic poverty, wandering from place to place preaching the good of poverty and independence. He was remembered, then, as an *exemplum*. Erasmus, for example, wrote the following warning as to the dangers of wealth: "If money falls to your lot without offering any impediment to a sound sense of values, use it....But if you are afraid you will lose peace of mind, then scorn this pernicious wealth; imitate that Crates of Thebes and hurl the offending burden into the sea rather than impede your way to Christ" (*Enchiridion*: 97; see also Brant, *Ship of Fools*: 3; Coornhert, *Zedekunst*: 5.3.8).

Crates was also famous for his control of the libidinous passion. Sandys, for example, quotes Crates as follows:

> Hard fare will famish love: if not, then will
> Time and long absence cure that fatall ill.

If neither of these remedies succeed,
Then take a halter; that will doe the deed.
(*Ovid*: 486)

CUPID (Anteros, Eros, Love). For Hesiod, Eros was the god of Love—but he was also the primal power of union without which the separate elements of the universe could never be joined. (See **VENUS** for more on the larger meanings of love.) For Hesiod, Eros was thus one of the three primal deities born of Chaos: Earth, Tartarus, and Eros (*Theogony*: 115-122; see also Plato, *Symposium*: 178). From very early times, then, Cupid was held to be the source of a wide range of phenomena—lust, love, and even the cohesion of physical elements. This wide conception of the powers of Cupid was still of interest to Bacon early in the seventeenth century, when he wrote a long essay entitled *On Principles and Origins, According to the Fables of Cupid and Coelum*:

The stories told by the ancients concerning Cupid, or Love...make mention of two Cupids, very widely differing from one another; one being said to be the oldest, the other the youngest of the gods. It is of the elder that I am now going to speak. They say then that this Love was the most ancient of all the gods, and therefore of all things else, except Chaos, which they hold to be coeval with him. He is without any parent of his own; but himself united with Chaos begat the gods and all things....[H]is principle and peculiar power is exercised in uniting bodies; the keys likewise of the air, earth, and sea were entrusted to him. (*On Principles and Origins*: 461)

Bacon would have known this idea's most famous expression, in Boethius (*Consolation of Philosophy*: 2.mt 8, quoted in **VENUS**); but he could have found the same in Ficino (*On Plato's Symposium*: 3.2), among others. Tradition thus assigned to Cupid a remarkably broad range of responsibilities; we should not be surprised, then, to find a correspondingly broad range of sometimes-conflicting traditions of iconography and allegory.

The Two Cupids Just as there was more than one Venus, so there was more than one Cupid. This goes back to classical times, when Anteros struggled with Eros in order to assure that love would be reciprocal (Merrill 1944; Panofsky 1962: 126). During the Renaissance some learned writers revived this interpretation of the two Cupids. Jonson, for example, wrote a masque called *A Challenge at Tilts*, wherein two Cupids strive for the title of *true* Cupid; then Hymen enters—Hymen was the god of marriage, and the masque was written for performance at a wedding—and judges that both must yield:

you are both true Cupids, and both the sonnes of Venus and Mars, but this the first-borne, & was called Eros. [Venus then bore another son,] Anteros: that with reciprocall affection, might pay the exchange of love...whereas if the one be deficient or wanting to the other, it fares worse with them both: This is the love, that Hymen requires, without which no marriage is happi....This is a strife, wherein you both winne, and begets a concord worthy all married minds emulation, when the lover transformes himselfe into the person of his belov'd, as you two doe now. (181-220; see also Cartari, *Imagini*, 1647 ed.: 259; Fraunce, *Countesse of Pembrokes Yvychurch*: 46r; Ferrand, *Treatise on Lovesickness*: 34)

But much more commonly the two Cupids, like the two Venuses, allegorized two kinds of love: spiritual and sensual. Thus Erasmus urges us to "Compare those two Venuses and Cupids of Plato: honorable love and sensual, that is, divine pleasure and lustful" (*Enchiridion*: 180-181). Erasmus is referring to the famous passage in Plato's *Symposium* that distinguishes between two kinds of Love, that is, two gods of love. According to Plato, there is first "the earthly Aphrodite's Love" who "does his work entirely at random." This god "governs the passions of the vulgar," for "whoever they may love, their desires are of the body rather than of the soul." And then there is "the heavenly Love" who "springs from a goddess...innocent of any hint of lewdness" (180d-181c; this passage is quoted at greater length under **VENUS**).

In *Cymbeline* Shakespeare can imply all that this tradition suggests as a comment upon Iachimo's visual rape of the chaste and faithful Imogen: Iachimo notices in Imogen's bedroom fireplace two andirons in the form of two Cupids (2.4.88; see Simonds 1992: 109-119). By the seventeenth century this allegory of the earthly and the divine Cupid had become so familiar that Quarles' emblems could routinely use the two Cupids as figures for Divine Love or Christ or the Spirit, on the one hand, and fleshly desire or the earthbound soul on the other. In one of these emblems (fig. 7), for example, we see Divine Love (always in Quarles identifiable by his halo) urging Human Love to give up his human pleasures, to resist its merely human cravings. In the emblem these human cravings are represented by the tobacco and the fleeting smoke; the Cupid of human desire is chained to the globe, unwilling to rise above earthly concerns and pleasures (Höltgen 1986: 33). We see much the same allegory in another of Quarles' emblems (fig. 17), where the earthly Cupid is drawn through the Labyrinth of the fallen world by the Cupid of spiritual love (see **LABYRINTH**). Alciati works in the same tradition (*Emblems*: 110).

At one extreme, in the seventeenth century, the bad Cupid could even be interpreted as an allegorical figure for the Devil, since both Cupid and the Devil tempt us to the sin of fornication (Arias 1992; for more on the two Cupids, see, e.g., Simonds 1992: 109-119).

The Blind Cupid Cupid never appeared as blind or blindfolded in ancient art; and the only poem in which he is described as blind is late and of doubtful authenticity. But suddenly, early in the twelfth century, Cupid began to be depicted as blind. In about 1215 Thomasin von Zerclaere wrote a didactic poem with a blind Cupid: "I am blind and I make blind" (*Der Wälsche Gast*, in Panofsky 1962: 105). Whoever originated it, this allegory became a commonplace. From this time until the seventeenth century, Cupid was often depicted as blind—or blindfolded, a detail that might begin with Boccaccio (*Genealogie Deorum*: 9.4; for the best account of the history and meaning of the blind Cupid, see Panofsky 1962: 95-128). Burton's commonsense explanation of Cupid's blindness may be taken as broadly typical:

Love is blind, as the saying is, Cupid's blind, and so are all his followers....Every lover admires his mistress, though she be very deformed of herself, ill-favoured, wrinkled, pimpled, pale, red, yellow, tanned, tallow-faced...a nose like a promontory, gubber-tushed, rotten teeth, black, uneven, brown teeth...; if he love her once, he admires her for all this, he takes no notice of any such errors or imperfections of body or mind. (*Anatomy of Melancholy*: 3.2.3; see also Bacon, *Wisedome of the Ancients*: 17)

Burton is following a well-worn path; see, for example, the *Chess of Love* commentary (362-363), and Brant (*Ship of Fools*: 13). An illustration of Cupid in Cartari's *Le Imagini* shows the blindfolded Cupid in his chariot, driving ranks of manacled lovers before him; Cupid's chariot is aflame with the fires of the passions (*Imagini*, 1647 ed.: 265).

With the rise of Neo-Platonism, Cupid's blindness could suggest the spiritual blindness that physical love can cause. The Cupid whom Chaucer's Palamon sees painted on the wall in the Temple of Venus is blind, for example ("Knight's Tale": 1965); Chaucer probably wants to suggest the essentially earthly nature of Palamon's love. Sidney, in the *Arcadia*, makes use of the notion of the blind Cupid in order to show in Neo-Platonic terms just how it is that Strephon and Claius are ennobled by love. They love the virtuous and beautiful maid Urania; Strephon and Claius feel no rivalry in their love for her, and so we are to understand that their love must be spiritual rather than physical:

hath not the onely love of her made us (being silly ignorant shepheards) raise up our thoughts above the ordinary levell of the worlde...? hath not the desire to seem worthie in her eyes made us when others were sleeping, to sit vewing the course of the heavens...? hath not shee throwne reason upon our desires, and, as it were given eyes unto Cupid? hath in any, but in her, love-fellowship maintained friendship betweene rivals, and beautie taught the beholders chastitie? (*Arcadia*: 1.1)

Cranach's *Cupid Unblindfolding Himself* (fig. 9) neatly illustrates what Sidney means by "giving eyes unto Cupid." Cranach's Cupid is lifting his (rather insubstantial) blindfold just as he rises up onto the toes of one foot, launching himself into flight. As he removes his blindfold, he ascends from the physical to the spiritual. His launching pad is a book, *Platonis Opera, The Works of Plato*. Cranach's painting thus encapsulates Medieval and Renaissance Platonic ideas—and especially the ideal of Platonic love (Panofsky 1962: 128). Van Mander wrote that Cupid's "blindness means...that some people, on account of the fire of love, lead improper lives, forgetting virtue and God" (*Wtlegginghe op den Metamorphosis*: 7v). The blind Cupid also appears in Spenser, in the Masque of Cupid staged in evil Busirane's castle of unlawful lust. Lest we doubt whether this be the Cupid of earthy or divine love, the masque's Cupid appears in a procession with (among others) Fury, Griefe, Dissemblance, Suspect, Daunger, Mischiefe, Mishap, Displeasure, Pleasaunce, and Cruelty:

> Next after her the winged God himselfe
> Came riding on a Lion ravenous,
> Taught to obay the menage of that Elfe,
> That man and beast with powre imperious
> Subdeweth to his kingdome tyrannous:
> His blindfold eyes he bad a while unbind,
> That his proud spoyle of that same dolorous
> Faire Dame he might behold in perfect kind;
> Which seene, he much rejoyced in his cruell mind.
> *(Faerie Queene*: 3.12.22)

Chapman associates the blind Cupid with darkness and "loves sensuall Emperie" ("Coronet for His Mistresse": 1).

But the blind Cupid was not invariably associated with earthly love. One Renaissance Neo-Platonist interpretation, for example, had it that Cupid was blind because love is beyond the intellect (Wind 1968: 51).

Cupid and Venus Cupid was often said to be the son of Venus (e.g., Cicero, *Nature of the Gods*: 3.59; Ovid, *Metamorphoses*: 1.463). But sometimes a distinction was made between Cupid the son of Venus and Cupid the primal deity. Bernardus provides one version of this distinction: "whenever you find Venus as the wife of Vulcan, the mother of Jocus and Cupid, interpret her as the pleasure of the flesh, which is joined with natural heat and causes pleasure and copulation" (*On Virgil's Aeneid*: on book 1; Horace, *Odes*: 1.2.34, invented Cupid's companion, Jocus; see de Tervarent 1958: 22.) It is as the son of Venus that we see Cupid in most of his important literary roles; de Meun, for example, specifies that the Cupid of the *Romance of the Rose* is Venus's son (10749). Bacon's allegorical interpretation of Venus and Cupid (written some three centuries after de Meun) could serve as a gloss on the *Romance*: "For Venus doth generally stirre up a desire of conjunction & procreation, and Cupid her sonne doth apply this desire to some individuall nature, so that the generall disposition comes from Venus, the more exact sympathy from Cupid" (*Wisedome of the Ancients*: 17). Venus, then, is love in general; Cupid inspires particular love ties. The basic distinction between general and particular love goes back at least to John the Scott (*Annotationes in Marcianum*: 8.8); and John is probably looking back to Augustine's distinction between "'lust'...the generic word for all desires," and "the many and various lusts, of which some have names of their own, while others have not" (*City of God*: 14.15).

But this idea of Venus as the "generall disposition" and Cupid as the "individuall" desire was important especially to the great Medieval poets of love: Alanus, de Meun, Lydgate (*Reson and Sensuallyte*), Chaucer, and Gower. It fits neatly with their firmly hierarchical sense of nature: as God is to Dame Nature,

Dame Nature is to Genius; as Dame Nature is to Genius, Venus is to Cupid (see **GENIUS, NATURE**). The *Chess of Love* commentary interprets their relation in the same way:

> If we wish then to consider well, we shall find that Venus...is no other thing than the concupiscible power, or a natural inclination that moves and incites us to desire and pursue lust and carnal delight. And this is why she is called the goddess of lust and of love. And her son Cupid, who is the god of love, is no other thing but concupiscence, or a secondary inclination that inclines and moves us to acquire and choose the person of the other sex without whom the desired accomplishment of delight could not be naturally achieved. And this election when it is proper, is perfected by love....And this is why he is called Cupido [L. *cupio*, "to desire"]. Because, then, concupiscence or this secondary inclination follows and depends on the first, for which it is ordained, Venus is called the mother of Cupid. (362)

Venus is thus the "general...desire" and "the cause of the second, particular desire that moves us to love one single woman before all others" (565).

The Cupid of earthly love could stand, allegorically, with Venus and Bacchus and various other gods in general opposition to Apollo and Diana: the forces of license and the passions in opposition to control, reason, and temperance. We may see this, for example, in a Neo-Platonic engraving after Baccio Bandinelli, *The Fray of Cupid and Apollo* (fig. 1; see **APOLLO** and **MINERVA** for more on this engraving). On the title page (fig. 8) of Jacob Cats' book of love emblems, Cupid is serving in much the same way. Cats' poem explains the allegory:

> See here the forest waste and all the sundry beasts....
> See here the people too, from all the distant lands....
> See here the black-skinned moor, the yellow Indian too...;
> All alike their appetites they serve....
> If our dull mind's not driven up to higher things...
> We follow down a darksome path where e'er the flesh us leads....
> Up, up, you human kind, climb up to reason wise....
> Live not as for the flesh, as do the beastial kind.
> *(Proteus*: 3)

All the people in their various degrees who flock to Cupid, sitting in his exotic arbor, are thus like the animals who similarly come to do Cupid homage. The human devotees, then, are at the same level as the rutting elk and the sniffing dogs just below Cupid. Justice, with her sword and balance scale, is there to suggest what will be the consequence of lives thus devoted to following Cupid; the Church, triumphing over Death, is there to suggest the spiritual alternative. And in Bronzino's *Allegory of Venus, Cupid, Folly, and Time* (fig. 23) we see that the delights of love promised by Cupid and Venus are but fleeting, impermanent, subject to the darker figures in the background, especially the ominously all-embracing figure of Saturn-as-Time. The figure along the margin, immediately behind Cupid, has been identified as syphilitic (Conway 1986).

Cupid stung by bees In Theocritus's nineteenth *Idyll* Cupid steals honey from a hive, and immediately learns that pain is a price we often pay for sweet delights. Alciati made an emblem of this (*Emblem*: 112; see also Heinsius, *Nederduytsche Poemata*: 42), and so this became a familiar allegorical device. The allegory here is close to that of Venus's rose, beautiful to behold but with hidden thorns painful to the touch (see **VENUS**).

Cupid's bow and arrows De Lorris's Lover tells us that he fell in love with his "Rose" in this way: "The God of Love, who had...followed me with drawn bow, stopped near a fig tree, and when he saw that I had singled out the bud that pleased me more than any of the others, he immediately took an arrow and...drew the bow—a wondrously strong one—up to his ear and shot at me in such a way that with great force he sent the point through the eye and into my heart" (*Romance of the Rose*: 1681-1691). Sandys interpretation of Cupid's bow and arrow—written some 400 years later—could serve as a gloss on de Lorris: "Bow and arrowes are given to Cupid," he wrote, "in that beauty wounds afarre off; and as an arrowe the body, so pierceth it in the heart through the eye" (*Ovid*: 73).

It was often said that Cupid had two kinds of arrows. Usually, the good arrows were gold, the bad lead. In de Lorris (*Romance of the Rose*: 907-984), for example, we find five gold and five lead arrows, and two bows as well. Both Lydgate (*Reson and Sensuallyte*: 5412-5522) and the *Chess of Love* commentary paraphrase de Lorris. Here is the *Chess of Love* commentary: "And the bows were of contrary nature, as were the arrows corresponding to them....One of the bows was beautiful...and the arrows that went with it were equally beautiful....The other bow was extremely ugly....And a great distinction between these two sets of arrows was that...the points of the first five were all of gold and the other five had lead points" (885). The commentary goes on to suggest that the five gold points correspond to the "five graces" that inspire love: "beauty, simplicity, generosity of soul, company, and sweet appearance." The five lead points, on the other hand, "are contrary to love and generative of ennuis, sorrow, and all pains, which are heavy and grevious....These five arrows, then, which are of contrary powers to the first five, signify five vices and inconveniences which often weary and disturb lovers...: pride, cruelty, shame, despair, and new thought" (895).

For Sandys the two kinds of arrows can also explain why it is that love is not always reciprocated: "Cupid drawes out of his quiver two arrowes of contrary effects: the one tipt with gold, the mettall of the Sunne, who heats our bloods and fills us with alactrity: the other with lead, belonging to Saturne, cold and melancholy: alacrity procures, and melancholy...extinguishes desires" (*Ovid*: 72). We find essentially the same explanation in, among others, Brant (*Ship of Fools*: 13).

Cupid's torch Cupid was often depicted as carrying a torch. This figured the heat of the passions, or as Fraunce put it, "his burning lampe" represented "the quickening light, and yet consuming heate of love" (*Countesse of Pembrokes Yvychurch*: 46r).

Cupid and Dame Fortune Because fleshly love is a species of earthly desire, because the object of fleshly love is, by definition, not spiritual, earthly lovers can never be certain of their love. They might enjoy their love one day and then be deprived of their chief delight the next. Earthly love was thus thought to be in the gift of Dame Fortune (see, e.g., Olsson 1992: 25-27). Dame Reason tries to explain this at some length to the Lover in de Meun's *Romance of the Rose* (5874-6978); finally, she urges the Lover to "despise the God of Love" and to "put no value on Fortune" (6873-6874). Lydgate explained the relation of Fortune and Cupid more succinctly:

> He is depeynte lich a blynd archer,
> To marke ariht failyng discrecioun,
> Holdyng no meseur, nouther ferr nor neer;
> But lik Fortunys disposicioun,
> Al upon happ, void off al resoun.
>
> (*Falls of Princes*: 1.6987-6991)

Cupid and Pan One myth had it that Cupid wrestled with Pan. Since Pan was a nature god, this myth was usually interpreted to mean that Cupid was the power that moved—or forced—nature to procreation; see, for example, the *Chess of Love* commentary (530-531) and Reynolds (*Mythomystes*: 173).

Cupid's vengeance Cupid was often thought of as vengeful: those who scorn love (and so, scorn Cupid), those who think themselves impervious to love (and so, impervious to Cupid's arrows), are likely to move Cupid to seek vengeance. Simply put, this convention is a joining together of the ancient idea that *no* one, not even the gods, can withstand Cupid's assault (e.g., Hesiod, *Theogony*: 120-122)—and the Christian idea that we are *all* susceptible to sin, and never more susceptible to sin than when we think ourselves safe. Erasmus expresses these ideas in terms of arming against sin: "as long as we serve in this body, we cannot get away from our weapons even by the width of a finger....We must never fail to post guard over the camp, never relax our vigilance, for our adversary never sleeps. On the contrary, when he is apparently quiet, when he pretends flight or truce, that is the time he is especially busy with his tricks" (*Enchiridion*: 46; for more on the moral allegory of arms and weapons, see **EPIC CONVENTIONS: The Arming of the Hero**).

And so, especially in the Petrarchan tradition, we find Cupid shooting his arrows for vengeance's sake or to punish the presumption of those who refused to recognize his power. Here, for example, is Petrarch: "I shall sing how...I lived in liberty while Love [i.e., Cupid] was scorned in my abode; then I shall pursue how that chagrined him too deeply, and what happened to me for that, by which I have become an example for many people" (*Rime sparse*: 23.4-9; see also 2.1-4; 3).

Many, many literary lovers fell in love in this way. Chaucer's Troilus scorns Love and lovers, for example:

> At which the God of Love gan loken rowe
> Right for despit, and shop for to ben wroken....
> Forthi ensample taketh of [Troylus],
> Ye wyse, proude, and worthi folkes alle,
> To scornen Love, which that so soone kan
> The fredom of youre hertes to hym thralle.
>
> *(Troylus and Criseyde*: 1.206-235)

And Shakespeare's proud Benedick and Beatrice are also lovers in this tradition (*Much Ado about Nothing*)—as are the men in *Love's Labours Lost* who foolishly imagine that they will be able to deny their amorous passions by shutting themselves up away from women, depriving themselves of sleep, and devoting themselves to study.

Cupid and Psyche: see **PSYCHE**.

Cupid and Rabbits: see **VENUS**.

Bibliography: Alison Adams, "Cupid and the Bees," *Emblematica* (1991) 5: 171-76; Judith Arias, "Don Juan, Cupid, the Devil," *Hispania*, 75 (1992): 1108-1115; Michael Bath, "Cupid and the Bees," in Peter M. Daly, *Andrea Alciato and the Emblem Tradition* (1989): 59-94; J. F. Conway, "Syphilis and Bronzino's London Allegory," *JWCI*, 49 (1986): 250-255; Guy de Tervarent, *Attributs et Symboles dans l'Art Profane, 1450-1600* (1958); Karl Josef Höltgen, *Aspects of the Emblem* (1986); Thomas Hyde, *The Poetic of Love: Cupid in Renaissance Literature* (1986); Henry Lotspeich, *Classical Mythology in the Poetry of Edmund Spenser* (1932): 48-50; Robert V. Merrill, "Eros and Anteros," *Speculum*, 19 (1944): 265-284; Kurt Olsson, *John Gower and the Structures of Conversion* (1992); Erwin Panofsky, *Studies in Iconology* (1962); Peggy Muñoz Simonds, "Eros and Anteros in Shakespeare's Sonnets 153 and 154: An Iconographical Study," *SSt*, 7 (1986): 261-286; Simonds, *Myth, Emblem, and Music in Shakespeare's Cymbeline* (1992); Edgar Wind, *Pagan Mysteries of the Renaissance* (1968).

CYBELE (Agdistis, Berecynthia, Cybebe, Dindymene, Earth, Gaia, Great Mother, Ops, Phrigia, Rhea, Terra, Vesta). Cybele's names are more complicated than her allegory. According to Hesiod, Gaia was the self-born, primal-elemental earth. She was the mother of Uranus (the sky), the mountains, and Pontus (the sea). By Uranus she went on to bear the Titans, the Cyclopes, Cronus, Rhea, and others. Rhea, by Cronus, bears Zeus, Hera, and other Olympian gods (*Theogony*: 125-164). Hereafter matters get rather complicated. The Greek Cronus came to be assimilated with the Roman god Saturn—but before this merger, Saturn had already long been married to an Italian fertility goddess named Ops. And so, as Saturn merged with Cronus, his wife's legends merged with Rhea's. Because Rhea-Ops was a mother- and earth-goddess, her legends were often conflated with those of Gaia. Isidore, for example, writes that "Terra is said to be Ops" (*Etymologiarum*: 14.1.1).

It is to this heady mixture that Cybele must be added. Among the ancient Greeks Cybele, too, was Earth, Mother Earth, or Great Mother—but not earth in the primordial sense of Gaia; rather Cybele was a fertility goddess. But mother and earth that she was, she, too, came to be conflated with Gaia-Rhea-Ops. When we add the names they received because of their association with certain places, Gaia-Cybele-Ops-Rhea-Berecynthia-Dindymene-Phrigia begins to sound more like a confederation than a goddess. Even Ceres (another mothering, fruitful earth goddess) and the motherly Roman goddess of the hearth, Vesta, were sometimes identified with Cybele (e.g., Lynche, *Fountaine of Ancient Fiction*: Miii; Fraunce, *Countesse of Pembrokes Yvychurch*: 8r)—and Macrobius suggests that Maia and Ops might be one (*Saturnalia*: 1.12.21-22). Cybele could be called Agdistis, too: there were two versions of the story of Attis, in one of which he was loved by Agdistis, in the other by Cybele (see **ATTIS**); and so Agdistis and Cybele came to be conflated.

Ross seems to wonder at this diversity as much as I do:

> Rhea was the daughter of Coelum [Sky, Uranus], her mother was Terra or Vesta; her husband was Saturn, she was the mother of all the gods.
> By Rhea is meant the earth...: she is called Ops, from wealth or help, because she affords all wealth....Cybele is from the Cymbals which she found out...so from the hills on which she is chiefly worshipped, she is called Idaea, Phrigia, Berecynthia, Dindymene, from her stability she is called Vesta. (*Mystagogus Poeticus*: 375)

Having begun by making Rhea the daughter of Terra—that is, Earth/Gaia, whom Ross identified with Vesta—Ross ends by identifying Rhea with Vesta.

Macrobius provides, less breathlessly, an overview of Cybele's responsibilities:

> Men believed that the goddess Ops was the wife of Saturn and that...the produce of the fields and orchards are thought to be the discovery of these two deities, who, when men have gathered in the fruits of the earth, are worshipped therefore as the givers of a more civilized life. Some too are of the opinion that Saturn and Ops represent heaven and earth, the name Saturn being derived from the word for growth from seed (*satus*), since such growth is the gift of heaven, and the name Ops being identified with earth, either because it is by her bounty (*ops*) that life is nourished or because the names come from the toil (*opus*) which is needed to bring forth the fruits of trees and fields. (*Saturnalia*: 1.10.19-20)

She could also figure forth charity or natural abundance, as we find in the *Chess of Love* commentary: "Cybele, Saturn's wife, is figured or painted beside him as an honorable old lady who is a great comfort to everyone, and especially to the poor, to whom she gives bread" (99; see also 110).

Despite the welter of names, the goddess's iconography is fairly consistent. We find, for example, that Isidore's description (*Etymologiarum*: 8.11.59-66) of Ops—whom Isidore conflates with Ceres—is closely paraphrased in Fraunce's account of Cybele:

She is covered with a Diadem bearing divers turrets; the circuit of her Crowne signifying the compas of the Earth, and her turrets the stately buildings of the same....Her garment is all wrought with flowers...noting that all such things proceede from the Earth. Her Chariot is drawne by Lions, on foure wheeles...the foure...seasons of the yeare....Her scepter is a signe of earthly pompe and dignitie....Isidorus maketh her hold a key in one hand; for that the earth is, as it were, closed and shut up in the winter, fostering then and cherishing in her lap the seede, till spring time come, and then she openeth her selfe. (*Countesse of Pembrokes Yvychurch*: 8v; see also Spenser, *Faerie Queene*: 4.11.28; Milton is referring to her "diadem bearing divers turrets" when he calls her "tow'red Cybele," in his "Arcades": 21)

The *Chess of Love* commentary interprets her more particularly in terms of nature allegory:

When we take Saturn as the first planet, we can very reasonably pretend that Cybele, or the earth, is his wife, because of the great influence the earth receives from this planet, by virtue of which she grows the fruits and vegetables on which man and animals live....We can say that she is the mother of [Jupiter, Juno, Neptune, and Pluto] and of all men generally, because the nourishment she gives to all creatures through the influence and power of the sky and planets, and principally of Saturn, for it is the highest and first of all of them, which engenders in the earth four kinds of human creatures according to the four kinds of complexions found in nature, which are corrupted into the four elements. And thus it is necessary that these four children, the elements, be included in the four complexions, and consequently, that the earth be their mother. (491-492)

Cybele was for Virgil (*Aeneid*: 6.784-787) and Ovid (*Fasti*: 4.179-372) a patron goddess of Rome—and so she came to be thought of, paradoxically, as a promoter of cities and civilization. She was, then, a goddess of both civilization *and* nature (Hawkins 1981).

See **JUNO, JUPITER, NEPTUNE**, and **PLUTO** for the specifics of the association of these gods with the four elements. For Cybele's ecstatic attendants and self-mutilating eunuch priests, see **CORYBANTES**.

Bibliography: Peter S. Hawkins, "From Mythography to Myth-Making: Spenser and the *Magna Mater* Cybele," *SCJ*, 12 (1981): 50-64; James Nohrnberg, *The Analogy of The Faerie Queene* (1976): 648-650; Maarten Vermaseren, *Cybele and Attis: The Myth and the Cult* (1977).

THE CYCLOPES were a race of uncouth, one-eyed giants in Homer's *Odyssey* (9; see also, e.g., Hesiod, *Theogony*: 139-146; Virgil, *Aeneid*: 3:616-681). Fulgentius wrote as follows of the Cyclopes:

The Cyclops is said to have one eye in its forehead because this wildness of youth takes neither a full nor a rational view of things, and the whole period of youth is roused to a pride like that of the Cyclops. So with the one eye in the head that sees and comprehends nothing but vanity. This is what the most wise Ulysses extinguishes: vainglory is blinded by the fire of the intellect....The blindness of adolescence follows youth's pride and indifference to reputation. (*On the Content of Virgil*: 15)

Bernardus says essentially the same (*On Virgil's Aeneid*: 3). Both Fulgentius and Bernardus base their interpretations on ingenious etymologies, but one suspects that they are really responding less to etymology than to the primitive wildness of the Cyclopes. Most writers did focus on this wildness (e.g. Erasmus, *Adages*: 1.10.69). Thus it is that Spenser's Hairy Carl, an allegorical figure for Lust, so much resembles the Cyclopes (Lotspeich 1932: 50). The cave-dwelling Hairy Carl has two eyes, but otherwise

> It was to weet a wilde and salvauge man,
> Yet was no man, but onely like in shape
> And eke in stature higher by a span,
> ...and his wide mouth did gape
> With huge great teeth, like to a tusked Bore
> For he liv'd all on ravin and on rape
> Of men and beasts; and fed on fleshly gore,
> The signe whereof yet stain'd his bloudy lips afore.
>   (*Faerie Queene*: 4.7.5)

Homer's Cyclopes Polyphemus is a man of "all outward power, / A wild man, ignorant of civility," a "caveman." The Hairy Carl is like him, too, when he rolls a stone over the mouth of his cave (*Faerie Queene*: 4.5.20). The Hairy Carl is a cannibal; Homer's Polyphemus was a cannibal: "Drunk, hiccuping, / he dribbled streams of liquor and bits of men" (*Odyssey*: 9.372-373).

Thus from Homer down to the seventeenth century, the Cyclopes were examples of humankind at its most brutish, a warning of what human beings would be without the guidance of reason, society, and law. Here, for example, is Sandys:

Now the Cyclops...were a salvage people given to spoyle and robbery; unsociable amongst themselves, & inhumane to strangers: And no marvaile; when lawlesse, and subject to no government, the bond of society; which gives to every man his owne, suppressing vice, and advancing vertue, the two maine columnes of a Common-wealth, without which it can have no supportance...: they therefore are to be numbered among beasts who renounce society, whereby they are destitute of lawes, the ordination of civility....But...this inhumane Monster, is surprised in his drunkennesse....In the person of Ulisses...wisdome is defigured...: in

Polyphemus, the folly of barbarous strength, infeebled with vices. (*Ovid*: 649-650; see also Ross, *Mystagogus Poeticus*: 87)

The story of the death of the Cyclopes was also interpreted allegorically, often as nature allegory. It seems that Aesculapius, the son of Apollo, was so successful at his doctoring that Jupiter was afraid that the natural order of things might be set askew, and so he struck him with a thunderbolt. Now, the Cyclopes were Jupiter's armorers—Brontes (Thunder), Steropes (Lightning), and Arges (Thunderbolt; or Pyrcmon, according to Virgil, *Aeneid*, 8.424-448). So when Jupiter killed Aesculapius with a thunderbolt, Apollo avenged his son by killing the Cyclopes. Fraunce's interpretation is typical: "Aesculapius was slayne by angry Joves thunder: Phoebus sory, and grieved for his sons death, slew in like sorte the Cyclopes, which made Joves thunder: that is the beames of the Sun, by degrees, doe consume that pestilent outrage of these contagious vapours and exhalations, causers of mortalitie" (*Countesse of Pembrokes Yvychurch*: 33r; see also Conti, *Mythologie*: 9.8).

For Polyphemus as a figure for New World peoples, see Quint (1993).

Bibliography: Melinda Lehrer, *Classical Myth and the "Polifemo" of Góngora* (1989); Henry G. Lotspeich, *Classical Mythology in the Poetry of Edmund Spenser* (1932); David Quint, "Voices of Resistance: The Epic Curse and Camões's Adamastor," in Stephen Greenblatt, *New World Encounters* (1993): 241-271; DeWitt Starnes and E. W. Talbert, *Classical Myth and Legend in Renaissance Dictionaries* (1955): 218, 149-150.

D

DAEDALUS was the fabulous inventor-artist of antiquity. He was born in Athens, but so jealous was he of the successes of his pupil (according to some accounts, his nephew) Talus (also known as Perdix or Calus) that he killed the boy (e.g., Apollodorus, *Library*: 3.15.8). Exiled from Athens, he found refuge with King Minos on the Isle of Crete. When Minos's wife Pasiphae fell in love with a bull, Daedalus made a wooden cow for her, wherein she could conceal herself to satisfy her unnatural passion. When Pasiphae conceived and bore the ferocious Minotaur, Daedalus constructed the Labyrinth, where Minos confined the Minotaur. It was also Daedalus who suggested to Ariadne the thread wherewith her lover Theseus might find his way out of the Labyrinth after killing the beast. For this treachery Minos imprisoned Daedalus and his son Icarus. But Daedalus made wings out of feathers and wax, and so he and his son were able to escape. Icarus, alas, forgot his father's warning and flew too close to the sun; the wax melted and he fell to his death (see especially Ovid, *Metamorphoses*: 8.155-259). Bruegel painted this last scene in his *Landscape with the Fall of Icarus* (fig. 15; see **ICARUS**).

Already in ancient times Daedalus's flight was associated with meditative flight. To fly high was to rise to the realm of Apollo, god of wisdom, learning, and music. This is implicit at the beginning of book 6 of Virgil's *Aeneid*: Aeneas "seeks the heights, where Apollo sits enthroned." Aeneas finds the cave where dwells the Sibyl, into whom Apollo "breathes a mighty mind and soul, revealing the future." Virgil makes this the place where Daedalus landed after his flight: "Daedalus, 'tis said, when fleeing from Minos' realm, dared on swift wings to trust himself to the sky; on his unwonted way he floated forth towards the cold North, and at last stood lightly poised above the Chalcidian hill. Here first restored to earth, he dedicated to thee, O Phoebus, the oarage of his wings and built a vast temple" (*Aeneid*: 6.9-19).

Christians generally regarded book 6—Aeneas's journey to the underworld for knowledge—as the most profound book of a profound poem. And here they found Daedalus, as it were, pointing the way for Aeneas. Bernardus comments: "Daedalus travelled the aerial paths with feathers and came to Apollo's temple—that is, by reason and intellect he contemplated the sublime and inwardly moved himself to philosophical study" (*On Virgil's Aeneid*: 6.14-34). Some 300 years later we find Landino commenting on Daedalus in much the same way. Daedalus built the temple of Apollo, writes Landino:

And what is it to build a temple for Apollo but to render oneself capable of acquiring wisdom? And indeed this is what we do when we bring our purified souls from all that is corporeal and fallible to a contemplation of the divine. And this is what Daedalus, a man instructed in all the finest arts, is able to do....[Daedalus] went neither by land nor by sea to the south (from our point of view, the lowest part of the world); but he went through the lofty air to the north. That is, there can be nothing lowly, nothing earthly, in the mind which is borne toward contemplation; it is rather directed to sublime and celestial things. (*Disputationes Camuldenses*: 206; Stahel tr.: 187)

Daedalus was thus sometimes listed with Phaethon driving the chariot of Apollo, Belerophon on Pegasus, and Endymion ravished by Diana—all of them figures for meditative flight (e.g., Ross, *Mystagogus Poeticus*: 45).

Since the Labyrinth could be interpreted as the World (see **LABYRINTH**), Daedalus's flight could be understood as escape from the bonds of sin, as in Berchorius: "Whoever mingles or binds himself in the labyrinth of the world or of sin through evil habits will seldom escape from there....If he wants to escape he must put on the wings of contemplation and fly up to celestial kingdoms through contemplation and pass over and transcend the sea of the changeful world by despising it" (*Ovidius Moralizatus*: 307). And Erasmus writes that Christian instruction will help us to extricate ourselves "from the labyrinthine errors of this world and, using these rules will like the thread of Daedalus" help us to find our way "back into the clear light of spiritual living" (*Enchiridion*: 83). In a similar vein Sandys explains that when Daedalus tells Ariadne how Theseus might make his way through the Labyrinth, Daedalus may be understood as "counsell and wisdom" (*Ovid*: 383).

The story of Icarus's fall was usually interpreted as demonstrating the dangers of straying too far from the Aristotelian mean between extremes (see **ICARUS**). In this context, Daedalus would, of course, be an *exemplum* of life lived near the virtuous mean (Koonce 1966: 162).

Daedalus could also serve simply as an *exemplum* of ingenuity: Isidore writes that Minerva herself aided him in his inventions (*Etymologiarum*: 19.8.1); Tritonio includes Daedalus in his list of the "ingenious" (*Mythologia*: 27). And Chaucer's mourning Man in Black says that not even Daedalus "with his playes slye" (*Book of the Duchess*: 570)—that is, his clever amusements—could sooth his grief. But perhaps Chaucer wants us to realize that the Man in Black might do better if he could rise up with Daedalus above his earthly attachments.

Christians thus usually interpreted Daedalus favorably, in one way or another—although negative interpretations do begin to appear in the Renaissance. Daedalus had, as Lemmi (1933: 109) notes, a rather unsavory reputation in ancient times, and with the revival of classical learning in the Renaissance, we find Daedalus being interpreted as a figure for envy or ingenuity-put-to-evil-ends (e.g., Tritonio's list of "The Envious"; Conti, *Mythologie*: 7.17; Bacon, *Wisedome of the Ancients*: 19).

For more on the episodes of Daedalus's story, see **ICARUS, MINOS, PASIPHAE**.

Bibliography: B. G. Koonce, *Chaucer and the Tradition of Fame* (1966); Charles W. Lemmi, *The Classical Deities in Bacon* (1933); Niall Rudd, "Daedalus and Icarus, from Rome to the End of the Middle Ages," and "Daedalus and Icarus, from the Renaissance to the Present Day," in Charles Martindale, *Ovid Renewed: Ovidian Influences on Literature and Art from the Middle Ages to the Twentieth Century* (1988).

DAMON AND PYTHIAS were examples of selfless friendship. Aquinas provides a typical version of the story:

When Dionysus, the tyrant of Syracuse, was about to slay one of the two friends, Damon and Pythias, the one who had been condemned asked for a few days' grace to enable him to go home and put his affairs in order; and the other of the friends offered himself as hostage against his return. But when the day of execution drew near, and the other did not return, everyone laughed at the stupidity of the hostage. But he declared himself sure of his friend's fidelity: and, in fact, at the appointed hour of execution, his friend returned. The tyrant greatly admired the fortitude of spirit shown by both, and in recognition of such steadfast friendship revoked the sentence, asking moreover, that he might be admitted as a third within the bonds of such friendship. But no matter how much they may desire it, tyrants can never win for themselves the joy of such friendship. Because they are concerned, not with the common good, but with their own satisfaction. (*On Princely Government*: 1.10)

DANAE was imprisoned in a tower by her father Acrarius, king of Argos, to keep her safe from any contact with men. Jupiter managed to get to her in the form of a shower of gold, and so Perseus was conceived. When her father discovered his daughter's condition, he put her and the child into a box and threw it into the sea (see, e.g., Hyginus, *Fabulae*: 63). Ovid regarded the story as one which reflects badly upon Jupiter; he has presumptuous Arachne weave this story into her tapestry, along with other stories disrespectful of the gods, such as the story of Jupiter assuming the form of a bull to rape Europa (*Metamorphoses*: 6.113). Christians, too, could interpret the story as an negative *exemplum*. For Rabanus the story shows us how women are likely "to be corrupted by gold" (*De Universo*: 429); and Berchorius interprets all of Arachne's stories as characteristic seduction stories: "Wanton men seem to act this way, for they beguile women in different ways" (*Ovidius Moralizatus*: 252; see also Fraunce, *Countesse of Pembrokes Yvychurch*: 14r; Batman, *Batman uppon Bartholomae*: 8.24; Ferrand, *Treatise on Lovesickness*: 6; Sandys, *Ovid*: 289; Ross, *Mystagogus Poeticus*: 90). This allegory is still to be found in Dutch paintings in the age of Rembrandt (Blankert et al. 1980: 92-93).

Elsewhere Berchorius interprets the story as a figure for the temptations of wealth in general: "Or say that Jupiter is the world which by means of gold—that is temporal wealth—corrupts Danae—that is the sinful soul—so that her father the devil shuts her up in the box of evil habit and sends her to wander through the sea of changeful life." But Berchorius also interprets Danae in a more favorable light. Like Boccaccio (*Eclogues*: 11.139-143) before him, Berchorius interprets the story as a type of the immaculate conception: "This girl can figure the glorious virgin who was guarded in the box of faith. There she was made pregnant by Jove—that is the Holy Spirit; and when a golden rain—that is the Son of God—descended into the bosom of her virginal womb she conceived Perseus—that is Christ, God and man. Psalm 71:6: 'He will come down like rain upon the fleece.' And so the father of this girl—that is the Jewish people—repudiated her with her son and rejected faith in her" (*Ovidius Moralizatus*: 218; see also Panofsky 1969: 145). Fraunce works a similar vein; the golden shower is God's grace: "Danae may represent mans soule, and Jupiters golden showre, the celestiall grace and influence derived into our mindes from above" (*Countesse of Pembrokes Yvychurch*: 14).

For the insistently typological Theodulph (*Ecloga*), Danae in the tower is a type of Daniel in the lion's den (Dan 6:1-28).

Bibliography: Leonard Barkan, *The Gods Made Flesh: Metamorphoses and the Pursuit of Paganism* (1986): 189-198; Albert Blankert et al., *Gods, Saints, and Heroes: Dutch Painting in the Age of Rembrandt* (1980); Erwin Panofsky, *Problems in Titian, Mostly Iconographic* (1969); Deborah Rubin, "Sandys, Ovid, and Female Chastity," in Jane Chance, *The Mythographic Art* (1990): 268-270; DeWitt Starnes and E. W. Talbert, *Classical Myth and Legend in Renaissance Dictionaries* (1955): 85-86.

DAPHNE (Dane) was changed into a laurel tree in order to escape the amorous advances of Apollo (e.g., Ovid, *Metamorphoses*: 1.452-567; Hyginus, *Fabulae*: 203). The *Chess of Love* commentary tells the story and glosses as follows:

there is more evil than good in love, as Ovid says....This can also clearly be shown by Phoebus, who loved [Daphne], daughter of Peneius, who had no taste for him....For Cupid, god of love, shot him in the heart with one of his arrows that had a gold point, which had a power generative of love. And on the contrary Love shot the maiden with a lead-pointed arrow, of which the power was to flee love and all carnal delight. And, therefore, Phoebus loved her...and pursued her very hard....Finally...she prayed the gods....And the gods...had pity on her and converted her into the form of a laurel....One could well explain this fable in more than one way....Firstly, it signified the strength and power of Love, which is so great and such that there is no one, no matter how wise...who cannot be completely surprised and conquered by love sometimes. And this is shown by Phoebus, whom the ancients called the god of wisdom, who was thus surprised....Secondly, it also signified to us...the strength of reason and virtue, which is so great and such that there is no lady or girl in the world, however beautiful and young she may be, or how strongly assailed, if she really wants to use reason, who cannot keep her chastity or virginity. (921-922; see also 571-573)

Daphne could thus serve as an example of determined chastity, as Golding and others agreed:

> As for example, in the tale of Daphnee turnd to Bay
> A myrror of virginitie appeere untoo us may,
> Which yeelding neyther untoo feare, nor force, nor flatterye,
> Doth purchace everlasting fame and immortalitye.
>
> ("Epistle": 67-70; see also Peele, *Arraignment of Paris*: 290; Sandys, *Ovid*: 73)

More often Daphne was a *de casibus* figure, one who died because of love. We see Daphne, for example, along the left-hand margin of Mantegna's *Triumph of Wisdom over the Vices* (fig. 19). Athena (Wisdom), Chastity, and Diana are chasing Venus and all the Vices she nurtures—Dalliance (*Otia*), Sloth, Hate, Suspicion, Avarice (Seznec 1961: 109). But Athena, alas, has come too late to save Daphne, already half transformed into the laurel. Chaucer also mentions Daphne as a *de casibus exemplum* ("Knight's Tale": 2061-2064; see also Bredero, "Apollo Speaks to the Netherlandish Youth": 170-182).

In the *Ovide Moralisé* Daphne was a type of the Virgin Mary: loved by God, her metamorphosis into a laurel was, allegorically, her winning of the crown of eternal glory (1.3215-3260). For Berchorius, Daphne was a figure for the good Christian: "She should flee occasions of sin by avoiding temptations and ask the goddess of the earth—that is Christ—to snatch her from the devil's hands by giving her another form" (*Ovidius Moralizatus*: 139). And here is Sandys: "Daphne is changed into a never-withering tree, to shew what immortall honour a virgin obtaines by preserving her chastity." And since Apollo is the sun, Sandys continues, it is appropriate that she became the laurel, "to fly his pursuit, in that [laurels] affect the shadow; and to repell the fire of lust, in not being scorched by the Sunne nor Lightning" (*Ovid*: 74).

And so the laurel is sacred to Apollo. And so, too, the laurel was associated with dreams. See, for example, Boccaccio (*Genealogie Deorum*: 7.29), who had read the following in Fulgentius: "the laurel...has been called the beloved of Apollo for the reason that those who have written on the interpretation of dreams...set forth in their books that if you place laurel on the head of sleepers, the dreams they see will come true" (*Mythologies*: 1.14).

Bibliography: Mary E. Bernard, *The Myth of Apollo and Daphne from Ovid to Quevedo* (1987); Jean Seznec, *The Survival of the Pagan Gods* (1961);

Wolfgang Stechow, *Apollo und Daphne* (1965); Rosemond Tuve, *Allegorical Imagery* (1966): 289.

DEMOGORGON is perhaps the only one of the gods as to whose nativity we can be certain. As Seznec (1961: 222) put it, "Demogorgon is a grammatical error become a god." It seems that Theodontius, an Italian philosopher who wrote some time between the ninth and the eleventh centuries, misunderstood a grammatical slip in the course of his reading. He mistook what should have been a reference to *Demiourgos*—the Demiurge, Plato's name in the *Timaeus* for the craftsman-god who ordered and made the material world—for *Demogorgon*. Boccaccio took this slender reference and turned Demogorgon into the father of all the gods, the first creator; Boccaccio's Demogorgon lives in the bowels of the earth (*Genealogie Deorum*: 1.Prohemium). Boccaccio's mistake has often been noted; indeed, Giraldi had already discovered the mistake in the sixteenth century ("Dedicatory Epistle" to *De deis gentium*; Nohrnberg 1976: 739).

But after all, Boccaccio's Demogorgon was, as mythology goes, not far from Plato's *Demiourgos*. For Boccaccio *Demo*gorgon was the *daemon*, the genius, the ordering spirit of the earth. In his own mythologizing summary of Plato on creation, Fraunce even recognizes *Demiurgon* as an alternate spelling for *Demogorgon*:

By Demogorgon, or peradventure, Demiurgon, is here understood that one & only creator of al, to whom Aeternitie is inseparably conjoined, sith himselfe is, was and will be eternall and everlasting. Chaos, in this eternall societie obteineth the third place, because she is that common, confused, and undistinct matter, which the ancient Philosophers made Co-eternall with the Creator: calling the one, the Father, the other the mother of al things formed; yet so, as they alwaies esteemed Demogorgon the chief and efficient, & Chaos only the subsequent and secondary cause in this procreation.

We begin to recognize traditional assumptions here as to the relationship of man to woman: The husband is the rational principle in marriage, the woman the irrational. The husband ought to control his wife, in the way that the reason controls the passions—and as Demogorgon-Demiurge exerts rational, ordering control over the chaos of earthly matter (for male/female allegory, see **AMAZONS**). Fraunce continues: "The reason why they joyned Chaos with the Creator as a companion from all eternitie, was this: They thought it proceeded from him by a certaine eternall generation: so proceeding, as eternall, because alwaies proceeding; yet so eternall, as proceeding, because not of her selfe proceeding, but from the procreator." Here Fraunce is making the age-old assumption that in generation the male is the active principle, the female the passive: the male's semen is the ordering principle; the female provides a vessel and matter. This conception of generation goes all the way back to Aristotle (e.g., *Generation of Animals*: 729a). Fraunce continues:

And as they made Chaos proceede from Demogorgon eternally without limitation of time, so they affirmed, that he afterwards framed all things of this unformed Chaos, not eternally, but in time. The tumult and uprore styrd up in the bowels of Chaos is her natural inclination and desire of bringing forth things variable and disagreeing. (*Countesse of Pembrokes Yvychurch*: 4v)

At any rate, Demogorgon came to be widely known during the Renaissance. Spenser's Demogorgon is like Fraunce's and Boccaccio's: He dwells "Downe in the bottome of the deepe Abysse," where he "The Hideous Chaos keepes" (*Faerie Queene*: 4.2.47; see also, e.g., Lynche, *Fountaine of Ancient Fiction*: Cii). Milton also refers to this tradition ("First Prolusion"; *Paradise Lost*: 2.965). It was thus that he was associated with that other great denison of the abyss, Satan. Marlowe's Faustus, for example, does his devilish conjuring by calling upon "Prince of the East, Beëlzebub, monarch of burning hell, and Demogorgon" (*Doctor Faustus*: 1.3.17-18). The clown, Robin, gets this a bit wrong when he tries to mimic Faustus's Latinate conjuring: "*o per se; deny orgon, gorgon*" (2.4.7).

Sometimes Demogorgon was said to personify, rather than control, Chaos. Van Mander, for example, wrote of the "Chaos that some called Demogorgon, father of all things and parent of all the gods" (*Wtlegginghe op den Metamorphosis*: 1r).

Bibliography: James Nohrnberg, *The Analogy of The Faerie Queene* (1976); Jean Seznec, *The Survival of the Pagan Gods* (1961).

DEUCALION AND PYRRHA. Deucalion was the Noah of Greco-Roman mythology. He was the son of Prometheus and the husband of Pyrrha. Jupiter spared them when he decided that the people of the Bronze Age were so wicked that they had to be wiped out by a great flood. Deucalion and Pyrrha rode out the flood in a big box. After nine days and nights, the waters abated. When they were again upon dry land, Deucalion and Pyrrha threw stones back over their shoulders, and these stones turned into human beings. Thus was the world repopulated. The story was best known to Medieval and Renaissance Christians in Ovid's version (*Metamorphoses*: 1.125-415; see also, e.g., Apollodorus, *Library*: 1.7.2). Ovid's characteristically Augustan contrast between hardness/cold/barrenness/death and softness/warmth/procreation/life (Fraenkel 1945) is at work here: Deucalion and Pyrrha are soft, yielding, *good* people—so good that they can make human beings of stones; they can make soft that which was hard, cold, and unyielding. Christians, however, tended to understand the story in the opposite way. For example, Isidore (*Etymologiarum*: 13.22.4), Berchorius (*Ovidius Moralizatus*: 135), and Conti (*Mythologie*: 8.19) all wrote that this race of human beings that grew up after the flood is as hard of heart as are the stones that bred them. Spenser also writes in this tradition:

For from the golden age, that first was named,
It's now at earst become a stonie one;

And men themselves, the which at first were framed
Of earthly mould, and form'd of flesh and bone,
Are now transformed into hardest stone:
Such as behind their backs (so backward bred)
Were throwne by Pyrrha and Deucalione.
                                    (*Faerie Queene*: 5.pr 2)

Deucalion was, of course, recognized as a type of Noah; see, for example, Theodulph (*Ecloga*), the *Ovide Moralisé* (1.2119-2158), Sabinus (*Fabularum Ovidii Interpretatio*: 31), Sandys (*Ovid*: 67), and Ross (*Mystagogus Poeticus*: 95). For Deucalion's release from the fires of love, see **LEUCADIAN ROCK**.

Bibliography: Leonard Barkan, *The Gods Made Flesh: Metamorphoses and the Pursuit of Paganism* (1986): 118, 134, 187, 284; Herman Fraenkel, *Ovid: Poet between Two Worlds* (1945); Charles Lemmi, *The Classical Deities in Bacon* (1933): 98-101.

DIANA (Artemis, Hecate, Lucina, Luna, Phoebe, Proserpina). During the Middle Ages and the Renaissance it was generally agreed that Diana (goddess of the moon) and Phoebus Apollo (god of the sun) were twins born to Jupiter's mistress Latona (Leto). Here is the *Chess of Love* commentary: "one could...pretend that the sun [Apollo] and the moon [Diana] were children of Jupiter and Latona, that is of fire and water, the sun because it has a masculine nature resembles fire more, and the moon, whose nature is more feminine, more resembles water" (597).

Diana was generally understood to be the goddess of virginity, or chastity. But as the goddess of the (changeable) moon, Diana had many aspects. The *Chess* commentator again:

The seventh planet is the moon, which was commonly enough called Diana by the ancients, and sometimes Proserpine, and Lucina, because of some different considerations....Diana...was figured by the ancients in the form of a lady who held a bow and an arrow in her hand....And this goddess had companies of nymphs and goddesses of the forest, mountains, fountains, and the ocean. And she also had a great company of horned satyrs, who were called the gods of the fields. This image can be explained easily enough. Therefore we should know that the moon has a special regard...over waters and all kinds of moistures and humors that can be turned into natural things. And therefore she is called the mother of humidity by the ancient philosophers. All this is sufficiently signified by the tide, which ebbs and flows twice in every natural day....[T]he image pretends that Diana was accompanied by nymphs and ladies of woods, mountains, fountains and the sea itself. That is, by the natural powers of these things, which are like goddesses of different kinds....And she was also accompanied by horned satyrs, i.e., by the powers of nature that govern the earth and sowings, which can be and were called gods of the fields by the ancients.

Shakespeare had such natural powers in mind at the end of *Midsummer Night's Dream*, when the fairies dash about blessing the marriage beds under the light of the new moon. The *Chess of Love* commentary continues:

Briefly, the moon was named differently because of her different influences in several places and on several things....she is called Luna in the sky....She is called Proserpine in respect of the earth, because she is the closest planet to the earth....She is also called Diana as far as her influence on woods and forests extends....Finally, because she has particular influence and great prerogatives in human generation, and rules and develops the child in the womb of its mother...she is called Lucina, goddess of childbirth. And also because she is of cold complexion, she is called goddess of chastity. (380-383)

Chaucer refers to these multiple aspects when he has Emelye invoke Diana thus:

O chaste goddesse of the wodes grene,
To whom bothe hevene and erthe and see is sene,
Queene of the regne of Pluto derk and lowe,
Goddesse of maydens.
("Knight's Tale," 2297-2300)

Among the many who reiterate such ideas are Lynch (*Fountaine of Ancient Fiction*: H) and Conti (*Mythologie*: 3.19). Fraunce adds to his account an explanation of that firebrand that Luna was often depicted as carrying. This brand denotes "either the pinching torments of child-birth...or the light which she afordeth for direction of men in the night season." Fraunce continues:

She is also called Hecate, signifieth an hundred: which simple & determinate number, is put for an infinite or great number: meaning that the moon hath many and infinite operations in and over these inferior bodies. She had three faces, called for that Trivia, Triformis, and Tergemina. For, in heaven she is called Luna, in the woods Diana, under the earth Hecate, or Proserpina. That of these three faces, which was on the right side, was the face...of a horse, figuring the swiftness of the Moone in ending her revolution. The left was of a dogge, noting that when she hideth her selfe from us she is then Proserpina with her hellish hounde: the middle was of a boare, signifying her jurisdiction in fields and forrests. (*Countesse of Pembrokes Yvychurch*: 42v-43r)

Hurst expressed this more succinctly in his introduction to his translation (1639) of Gombauld's *Endimion*. Diana is "Tria virginis...And that by reason of her three shapes, Coelestial, Terrestriall, and Infernall: when she shineth in Heaven, she is Cynthia, or Luna: when shee appeareth on Earth, Latonia virgo, or Diana; being resident in Hell, Hecate, or Prosperpina."

In summary, then, Diana had three aspects:

Luna In this aspect, Diana is the moon and the goddess of childbirth, a goddess of generation.

Diana In this aspect, she is the goddess of the hunt and of chastity. And Medieval and Renaissance readers would have recognized a connection between hunting and chastity. Love is most likely to strike those who are idle: in de Lorris's *Romance of the Rose* (685-690) and in Lydgate's *Reson and Sensuallyte* (4985), for example, Idleness is the porter at the gate of the Garden of Delight. In *Midsummer Night's Dream* the flower whose juice inspires love is called "love-in-idleness" (2.1.168). Hunting, on the other hand, could serve as a figure for the virtuous, manly life: "manly" in the sense of *(L.) virtus*, which meant both "manliness" and "virtue" (see **AMAZONS**). This is what Lydgate has in mind when he has Diana say that she is the goddess

> "Of chace also and of huntyng....
> This my crafte, in sothenesse,
> To eschewen ydelnesse,
> Which is to me most noyouse,
> Loth-som, and most odyouse."
>   (*Reson and Sensuallyte*: 2993-3002)

In *Gawain and the Green Knight* it is no coincidence that Gawain gets into love trouble when he stays home from the hunt (for more on the moral allegory of hunting, see **ADONIS, ATALANTA**).

Proserpina (or Hecate) In this aspect she is Pluto's wife; she is associated with the Underworld and the coming and going of spring (see **HECATE** and **PROSERPINA**).

To add to this welter, because she was born on the island of Delos, Diana sometimes takes the epithet "Delian," as when Spenser sings, "O Delian Goddesse" ("Virgils Gnat": 170). Sometimes Diana was called Cynthia, because she was born on Cynthus Hill; and thus it was that Cynthia came to be one of the allegorical names for the Virgin Queen, Elizabeth, as in Lyly's *Endymion*, Raleigh's *Cynthia* poems, and Spenser's "Colin Clouts Come Home Again" (164-167); Spenser also devised a character named Belphoebe—*(L.) bella*, "lovely" Phoebe—which, according to his "Letter to Raleigh," was to be an allegorical figure the virtue and the beauty of Elizabeth in her private, as opposed to her royal, person. Because she was the goddess of chastity, she was occasionally associated with the Virgin Mary (Berchorius, *Ovidius Moralizatus*: 75). More often she stood with such as Minerva and Apollo in opposition to those gods who represent earthly desires, as for example in Ficino (*On Plato's Symposium*: 6.1; quoted under *Bacchus*). We see these assumptions at work in a Neo-Platonic engraving after Baccio Bandinelli, *The Fray of Cupid and Apollo* (fig. 1), where Diana fights on Apollo's side, the side of rational restraint, in opposition to Cupid and the forces of license (for more on this engraving, see **APOLLO**). In another psychomachia, Andrea Mantegna's *Triumph of Wisdom over the Vices* (fig. 19), Diana accompanies Athena (Wisdom) as she routs Venus and the Vices that Venus mothers: Dalliance (*Otia*), Sloth, Avarice, Suspicion, Hate (Seznec 1961: 109).

Because of her several aspects, Diana was sometimes known as the Triple Goddess, or as Chaucer's Emelye puts it, the goddess of "thre formes" ("Knight's Tale": 2313). Thus is was that the *Ovide Moralisé* interpreted Diana as the Trinity (3.636-343).

For Diana's (the Moon's) love for the shepherd boy Endymion, see **ENDYMION**.

Bibliography: A. C. Hamilton, *The Spenser Encyclopedia* (1990): under *Belphoebe*; Richard Kay, *Dante's Christian Astrology* (1994): 17-37; Jean Seznec, *The Survival of the Pagan Gods* (1961); Kathleen Williams, "Venus and Diana: Some Uses of Myth in *The Faerie Queene*," in A. C. Hamilton, *Essential Articles for the Study of Edmund Spenser* (1972): 202-219.

DIDO (Elisa) and her beloved husband Sychaeus were the rulers of Tyre, until Dido's brother Pygmalion (not the sculptor Pygmalion; see **PYGMALION**) killed Sychaeus for his treasure. Dido and her followers then fled Tyre in ships. Eventually they landed on the north shores of Africa, where Dido founded Carthage. Two versions of subsequent events were known to the Middle Ages and the Renaissance. In the first version, which began with Justinus's *Epitoma historium Philippicarum*, Dido was a model of widowed chastity: She threw herself upon a funeral pyre rather than submit to a forced marriage with the North African king, Hiarbas. Tertullian cites this Dido as an example of pagan chastity. Playing on St. Paul's advice, Tertullian wrote that Dido "preferred 'to burn' rather than 'to marry'" (*Exhortation to Chastity*: 13; see also *To the Martyrs*: 4.5). Petrarch wrote that "by her own death she chose / to assure her virtue" (*Africa*: 3.530-531). In his profeminist *Concerning Famous Women*, Boccaccio writes that Dido is a "venerable and eternal example of constant widowhood" (40; see also Boccaccio, *Genealogie Deorum*: 6.53; Christine de Pizan, *City of Ladies*: 1.46; Cooper, *Dictionarium*: under *Dido*). Viana says that Virgil wrote disrespectfully of Dido out of "ignorance of her whole history"; Aeneas's love was "dishonest" (*Ovid*: 14.3). For Bredero, she was "pure Dido" (*Lucelle*: 1568; see also Sandys, *Ovid*: 647; for more on the chaste Dido, see Watkins 1995: 50-53, 78-80).

But she was more commonly remembered in Virgil's version: Aeneas and his storm-tossed Trojans are offered refuge in widow-Dido's Carthage. Forgetting now the husband she had mourned, Dido falls in love with Aeneas; then the gods send Mercury to remind Aeneas of his duty to found Rome, and so he sails away from Carthage. Dido throws herself upon a pyre in her grief. Since Aeneas's mission was divine, Dido represents a temptation to self-indulgence along the way. It was as this temptation that she was often remembered. Fulgentius, for example, comments upon Aeneas's descent to the underworld: "Then, too, Dido is seen, a shade now void of passion and its former lust. This lust, long dead of indifference, is tearfully recalled to mind as, now penitent, Aeneas reflects on wisdom" (*On the*

Content of Virgil: 22). Ausonius likened Dido to Phaedra, Canace, and Phyllis (*Epigrams*: 22), all women who suffered because they loved beyond the bounds of rational restraint. Donatus had disapproved of her in similar terms (*Interpretationes Virgilianae*: 4.172), as did Bernardus at greater length:

> Having buried his father, Aeneas goes hunting. Driven by storms into a cave, he dallies with Dido and there commits adultery. Receiving Mercury's counsel, he abandons this disgraceful way of life....By direct and allegorical narration Virgil describes the nature of young manhood. When Aeneas goes hunting...it signifies...vain endeavors which pertain to young manhood....Aeneas is driven to a cave by storms and rain, that is, he is led to impurity of the flesh and of desire by excitement of the flesh....This impurity of the flesh is called a cave, since it beclouds the clarity of mind....Mercury..."the activity of the mind"...warns and censures Aeneas because he finds him ignoring useful endeavor....Aeneas...leaves Dido and puts passion aside. Having been abandoned, Dido dies, and, burned to ashes, she passes away. For abandoned passion ceases and, consumed by the heat of manliness, goes to ashes. (*On Virgil's Aeneid*: 4)

Dante places Dido in the second circle of the Inferno, with the lustful (*Inferno*: 5.61-62; see also Dante, *Convivio*: 4.26.8; Pietro Alighieri, *Commentarium*: 117, in his commentary on *Inferno*: 5, discusses the controversy as to Dido's virtue). Boccaccio's early writings share Dante's low opinion of Dido. Several times he linked her with other examples of guilty lovers: For example, in the *Fiammetta* (19) he lists her with Paris, Helen, Clytemnestra, Aegisthus, Achilles, Scylla, Ariadne, Leander, the incestuous Myrrha—and the impassioned, desperate Fiammetta herself (it might here be worth mentioning that the extended title of Yong's 1587 English translation of this poem was *Amorous Fiammetta. Where in is sette downe a catalogue of all and singular passions of Love and jealosie, incident to an enamored yong Gentlewoman, with a notable caveat for all women to eschewe deceitfull and wicked Love*). In *Filocolo* Boccaccio lists Dido with Medea, Deianira, Phyllis, and Leander (4.83.3). It was only later that, led by Petrarch, Boccaccio came to regard Dido as an exemplar of chastity (Hollander 1977: 172-173).

In the *Ovide Moralisé*, where Aeneas is an allegorical figure for the "holy church," Dido figures forth the "perils" and the "diverse temptations" that the church has faced (14.527-30). And Harington, in his account of the "historical allegory" of book 7 of Ariosto's *Orlando Furioso*, writes that when the lascivious temptress Alcyna stays Rogero, this "alludeth to" Dido staying Aeneas (*On Orlando Furioso*: 55).

England's Elizabeth was sometimes referred to as Eliza/Elisa, and so as Dido. The best-known instance is Spenser's celebration of Elizabeth as Elisa in the April eclogue of *The Shepheardes Calender* (for other references, see McLane 1968: 47-60; for a history of attitudes toward Dido in classical and English literature, see Schmitz 1990: 17-45; Watkins 1995: 75-76).

For more on Dido, see **AENEAS**.

Bibliography: Robert Hollander, *Boccaccio's Two Venuses*, 1977); Paul E. McLane, *Spenser's Shepheardes Calender: A Study in Elizabethan Allegory* (1968); Götz Schmitz, *The Fall of Women in Early English Narrative Verse* (1990); Beverly Taylor, "Phyllis, Canacee, Biblis, and Dido: Keys to Understanding *The Minnegrotte* of Gottfried's Tristan,"*Mediaevalia*, 8 (1982): 81-95; J. Watkins, *The Specter of Dido: Spenser and Virgilian Epic* (1995).

DIOMEDES, son of Tydeus, was one of the greatest of the Greek heroes at Troy, and he figures largely in the *Iliad*. So glorious a warrior was Diomedes, according to Homer, that once, when the fury of battle was in him, he actually wounded the goddess Aphrodite, who was fighting on the Trojan side (*Iliad*: 5.120-417; see also, e.g., Apollodorus, *Epitome*: 4.2). He is one of the very few Greeks who come off well even in Virgil (Aeneas, the hero of the *Aeneid* and the founder of Rome, being, after all, a Trojan). According to Virgil, Diomedes sailed to Italy after the fall of Troy and founded the great city of Argyripa. Virgil has Diomedes, remembering the horrors of war, counsel movingly against war (*Aeneid*: 11.252-305).

In general, Medieval and Renaissance Christians also held Diomedes in high regard. Because Diomedes fought a god, Theodulph (*Ecloga*) recognizes him as a type of Jacob wrestling the angel (Gen 32:24-30). Berchorius wrote that because Diomedes fought and wounded Venus, he is a figure for "chaste men" (*Ovidius Moralizatus*: 408)—an allegory that goes back at least to Heraclitus, for whom Diomedes was "wisdom" in opposition to Venus, or "irrationality" (*Allégories d'Homère*: 30.4). In the *Chess of Love* commentary we find: "That Venus was wounded by Diomede means that the lust of the Trojans was reduced to nothing by the Greeks" (690). Lydgate also interprets Diomedes as an example of resistance to Venus/lust: in what follows, Diana (goddess of chastity) is urging a lover to resist Venus's blandishments:

> ageyn hir lust debate
> And haten hir of gretter hate
> Than ever dyde dyomede,
> Which with his swerde made her blede.
>
> *(Reson and Sensuallyte*: 4659-4662)

Christians also appreciated that Athena (goddess of wisdom) was Diomedes' patroness among the gods. Sidney mentions him as an *exemplum* of "wisdom and temperance" (*Defense of Poesy*: 15).

But Diomedes was also remembered as a deceiver: Diomedes helped Ulysses to decoy the youthful Achilles off to war and away from the safety of the isle of Skyros; and it was Diomedes and Ulysses again who devised the scheme of the Trojan Horse. Dante thus places Diomedes with Ulysses among the evil counsellors the *Inferno* (26.55-63). Chaucer (*Troylus and Criseyde*) and

Shakespeare (*Troilus and Cressida*) both described a cunning, deceitful Diomedes (see, e.g., Wood 1984: 139-142). And at least two Renaissance Flemish tapestries depict Diomedes the deceiver (Reid 1993: 347).

Sandys (*Ovid*: 657) understands Diomedes to have been punished for his presumption in wounding a god—and Sandys joins Bacon (*Wisedome of the Ancients*: 18) in interpreting Diomedes wounding Venus as a figure for misguided religious zeal!

For the other Diomedes, the barbarian Thracian king so justly slain by Hercules, see **HERCULES: NINTH LABOR**.

Bibliography: Jane Davidson Reid, *The Oxford Guide to Classical Mythology in the Arts, 1300-1990s* (1993); Jon Whitman, *Allegory: The Dynamics of a Medieval Technique* (1987): 47-55; Chauncey Wood, *The Elements of Chaucer's Troilus* (1984).

E

ECHO was best known to the Middle Ages and the Renaissance in Ovid's story of Echo and her disappointed love for Narcissus (see **NARCISSUS**). There was, however, another tradition, one in which Echo was beloved of Pan. In Longus's third-century version of this myth, Echo was a mortal wood-nymph, taught by the Muses to play on all the instruments and to sing. Concerned for her virtue, she fled from all males, gods or men, but she delighted to dance with the nymphs and sing in consort with the Muses:

Pan sees that, and takes occasion to be angry at the maid, and to envy her music because he could not come at her beauty. Therefore he sends a madness among the shepherds...and they tore her all to pieces and flung about them all over the earth her yet singing limbs. The Earth in observance of the Nymphs buried them all, preserving to them still their musical property, and they by an everlasting sentence and decree of the Muses breathe out a voice. And they imitate all things now as the maid did before, the Gods, men, organs [instruments], beasts. Pan himself they imitate too when he plays on the pipe; which when he hears he bounces out and begins to post over the mountains, not so much to catch and hold as to know what clandestine imitator that is that he has got. (in Hollander 1981: 7-8)

In Macrobius's version of the myth (*Saturnalia*: 1.22), Echo is married to Pan. Pan is the inventor of the seven-reed pipe, and so the creator of the sevenfold planetary music (see Appendix A, "Music"). Echo, echoing this music, is celestial harmony, an allegorical figure for the Music of the Spheres (Hollander 1981: 9-10). Echo and echoes thus become a way of talking about that poetry which arises out of natural yearnings, natural impulses, Pan being the god of nature. We see this most strikingly in Spenser's *Epithalamion* (18), with its repeated variations on "The woods shall to me answer and my Eccho ring"—variations that continue until the poet, his natural yearnings satisfied within the sanctified bounds of married love, begins to look forward to progeny—progeny that may inherit "heavenly tabernacles" (422). Now that his yearnings are spiritual, rather than natural, "The woods no more us answer, nor our eccho ring" (426; see Hamilton 1990, under *echo*).

Bibliography: A. C. Hamilton, *The Spenser Encyclopedia* (1990); John Hollander, *The Figure of Echo* (1981).

ENDYMION was a beautiful shepherd. In the version of the story best known to Christians, the Moon—or Diana (Cynthia, Phoebe), goddess of the moon—fell in love with him and came regularly to kiss him in his sleep (e.g., Apollonius, *Argonautica*: 4.57; Apollodorus, *Library*: 1.7.5). Already in classical times Endymion's ravishing was seen as an example of, or an allegorical figure for, apotheosis or spiritual ascent (Panofsky n.d.: 37). With the rise of Renaissance Neo-Platonism, Endymion was again frequently referred to in this connection. Fraunce's interpretation is typical: "Endymion...is a figure of the soule of man, kissed of Diana in the hill, that is ravished by celestiall contemplation" (*Countesse of Pembrokes Yvychurch*: 43v). Bacon agrees: The Moon coming to Endymion shows that "divine influences sometimes steal spontaneously into the understanding when at rest" (*De Augmentis*: 327). Chapman stoutly denies as ancient slander that Cynthia bore "fiftie children by Endimion"; no, rather Cynthia loved "Endimion for his studious intellect" ("Hymnus in Cynthiam": 491-494). It is in this tradition that Phoebe transports Endymion up to the heavens to learn good, Neo-Platonic "heavenly secrets" in Drayton's "Endimion and Phoebe." Gombauld's Endymion also "how farre are the Divine beauties different from these here below!" (*Endimion*: 19; see also Valeriano, *Hieroglyphica*: 627; Milton, "Seventh Prolusion").

For the version of the story that conflated Pan with Endymion, see **PAN**.

As Lemmi (1933: 180-181) notes, Endymion was also an example of those who profit from love or friendship; see, among others, Juvenal (*Satires*: 10.316-317), Bacon (*Wisedome of the Ancients*: 8), and Ross (*Mystagogus Poeticus*: 106).

Bibliography: Douglas Bush, *Mythology and the Renaissance Tradition in English Poetry* (1963): 156-160; E. S. Le Comte, *Endymion in England: The Literary History of a Greek Myth* (1944); Charles W. Lemmi, *The Classical Deities in Bacon* (1933); Erwin Panofsky, *Tomb Sculpture* (n.d.).

EPIC CONVENTIONS. Medieval and Renaissance readers thought of Epic poetry as the highest form of poetry. Homer's *Iliad* and *Odyssey*, Virgil's *Aeneid*, Statius's *Thebaid* and *Achilleid*, these and others were read as poetry of high moral seriousness. Elaborate commentaries were written, many of which treated the Greek and Roman epics allegorically, in such a way as to demonstrate their essential harmony with Christian doctrine. When Christian poets set out to write epics, they did so with a keen awareness of the classical models, an awareness that amounted in most cases to awed reverence.

There was considerable debate, especially during the Renaissance, as to just what an epic poem required. The details of this debate lie outside the purpose of this *Dictionary* (but see Donker and Muldrow 1982: 108-118). In practice, however, there was at least this general agreement: Poets announced to their readers that they were writing an epic by making use of what amounted to a kind of checklist of formulae—what have been called the "epic conventions." Very far from limiting the poets' inventiveness, the conventions provided them with devices for signaling a wonderful range of meanings, moods, distinctions, and intentions. Often the Christian poets turned the conventions to allegorical use. The following list suggests something of the richness of the variations inspired by the epic conventions.

High Seriousness Epics were written with gravity and in an elevated style; they dealt seriously with serious subjects. They told of princes and others of noble birth and high degree. But the notion of "high degree" was quite plastic enough, for example, to allow Milton's *Paradise Lost* to be about Adam and Eve: They were, before their fall, lords of all creation (Gen 1:28-31). And in their prelapsarian innocence, they were of the highest spiritual degree.

History Epics were supposed to be historical; the fiction was that there was no fiction. And it was to be the history of great peoples. *The Aeneid*, for example, was Virgil's history of the founding of New Troy, that was to become Rome. *The Iliad* told part of the history of the Trojan War. And so Spenser's *Faerie Queene* was a fictionalized history of King Arthur, Brutus and other English heroes—and typologically, the poem is frequently about the history of the Fall and Christ's redemption of humankind. Book 1 of *The Faerie Queene*, for example, is about the Red Cross Knight's abandonment of Una for the temptress Duessa; this is a type of the Fall of Adam and Eve. Spenser then tells of the Red Cross Knight's redeption; this is a type of human redemption. And the Red Cross Knight has his battle with the dragon; and this is a type of Christ's final conflict with Satan. Milton's *Paradise Lost* was the history of the war in heaven and the consequent fall of mankind in the Garden of Eden.

Invocations In Greek mythology the Muses were the goddesses who inspired poets. There were nine Muses, each responsible for a different kind of poetry (see **THE MUSES**). If a poet wanted to compose a love song, for example, he would pray to Erato, the Muse of love poetry. Even after poets stopped believing that their poems came to them from the Muses, the invocations continued: deaf though the Muses may have been to their prayers, the invocations still served usefully to alert readers as to the poet's intentions.

Calliope was the Muse to invoke when the poet wanted to "sing" an epic. Here, for example, is the invocation to Calliope at the beginning of the *Aeneid*: "Arms I sing and the man who first from the coasts of Troy, exiled by fate, came to Italy and Lavinian shores....Tell me, O Muse, the cause; wherein thwarted in will or wherefore angered, did the Queen of heaven drive a man, of goodness so wondrous, to traverse so many perils, to face so many toils" (1.1-11).

Because *Paradise Lost* was also supposed to be an epic, Milton began with an invocation—but Milton's was to be a Christian epic, and so he invokes not Calliope, but rather the "Muse" that inspired Moses to write God's law there on the top of Mt. Sinai. Milton, then, is playing with the convention, adapting it to his own purposes:

> Of man's first Disobedience, and the Fruit
> Of that Forbidden Tree, whose mortal taste
> Brought Death into the World, and all our woe,
> With loss of Eden, till one greater Man
> Restore us, and regain that blissful Seat,
> Sing Heav'nly Muse, that on the secret top
> Of Oreb, or of Sinai, didst inspire
> That Shepherd, who first taught the chosen Seed,
> In the Beginning how the Heav'ns and Earth
> Rose out of chaos.
>
> (*Paradise Lost*: 1.1-10)

Beings other than Calliope were often invoked along the way. If the poet is about to sing a love scene, for example, Erato might be invoked—or Venus. The poet might invoke Mars before describing a battle. As he begins book 4 of *Troylus and Criseyde* Chaucer invokes Mars *and* the Furies to aid him, "So that the losse of lyf and love yfere / Of Troylus be fully shewed here" (4.27-28). Clearly, Chaucer wants his audience to realize that the scenes he is about to describe are full indeed of suffering and strife.

In Medias Res

Epics begin *in medias res*—in the middle of things. Neither Homer's *Iliad* nor his *Odyssey* begins at the beginning. Homer begins *in medias res*. Then, well into the poem, he takes us back to tell us about the events that make up the beginning of the story. The *Odyssey*, for example, begins in the tenth year of Odysseus's wanderings; then, later in the poem, Odysseus tells about his years of wandering. The *Aeneid* begins with a storm at sea, a storm that nearly destroys Aeneas's ships. Only later do we hear about the sack of Troy and about Aeneas and his people fleeing from the city as it burned.

Thus it is that Spenser begins *The Faerie Queene* with the Red Cross Knight's battle with the dragon Error; only later do we find out how it was that he came to be on his quest. Milton begins his epic, too, *in medias res*.

Epic Gore Homer's descriptions of battle wounds are so detailed, so graphic, that some early scholars assumed that Homer must have been a field surgeon. Here are some typical passages of Homeric gore:

This man Meriones pursued and overtaking him struck in the right buttock, and the spearhead drove straight
on and passing under the bone went into the bladder.
He dropped, screaming, to his knees, and death was a mist about him.

(*Iliad*: 5.65-68)

But Tydeus' son in his hand caught
up a stone, a huge thing which no two men could carry
such as men now are, but by himself he lightly hefted it.
He threw, and caught Aineias in the hip, in the place where the hip-bone
turns inside the thigh, the place men call the cup-socket.
It smashed the cup-socket and broke the tendons both sides of it,
and the rugged stone tore the skin backwards.

(*Iliad*: 5.302-308)

Idomeneus stabbed Erymas in the mouth with the pitiless
bronze, so that the brazen spearhead smashed its way clean through
below the brain in an upward stroke, and the white bones splintered,
and the teeth were shaken out with the stroke and both eyes filled up
with blood, and gaping he blew a spray of blood through the nostrils
and through his mouth, and death in a dark mist closed in about him.

(*Iliad*: 16.345-350)

Epic gore thus became one of the conventions. Virgil seems to have been rather more squeamish than Homer—but still he did write in some epic gore (e.g., 10.780-83; 11.805-20). Spenser, too, included epic gore—often allegorical gore, as for example when the Red Cross Knight is struggling with the dragon Error:

Therewith she spewd out of her filthy maw
A floud of poyson horrible and blacke,
Full of great lumpes of flesh and gobbets raw,
Which stunk so vildly, that it forst him slacke
His grasping hold, and from her turne him backe:
Her vomit full of bookes and papers was,
With loathly frogs and toades, which eyes did lacke,
And creeping sought way in the weedy gras:
Her filthy parbreake all the place defiled has.

(*Faerie Queene*: 1.1.19)

The writers of mock epics, too, wrote in their epic gore, as Pope, for example, in "The Rape of the Lock":

The Peer now spreads the glittering forfex wide,
To enclose the Lock; now joins it, to divide.
Even then, before the fatal engine closed,
A wretched Sylph too fondly interposed;
Fate urged the shears, and cut the Sylph in twain
(But airy substance soon reunites again):

The meeting points the sacred hair dissever
From the fair head, forever and forever!
(3.147-54)

The Descent In book 11 of the *Odyssey* Odysseus sails to the end of the world, to reach the entrance to Hades. There he calls up the spirits of the dead, and there the shade of the Theban soothsayer Tiresias looks with his sightless eyes into Odysseus's future.

And so, in book 6 of the *Aeneid*, Virgil has Aeneas go to Hades. But Virgil is not content to allow Aeneas to remain above ground while he questions the shades. Virgil's Aeneas must go down into the bowels of the Underworld to hear what the shades can tell him. It is a harrowing journey. And so Aeneas's experience seems to say something about the human condition: We sometimes pay a terrible price for knowledge.

The commentators generally agree that Aeneas's descent had to do with knowledge and wisdom. Here, for example, is Fulgentius: "In book 6, Aeneas, reaching the temple of Apollo, goes down to the lower world. Apollo we call the god of learning, and he is also linked to the Muses. The shipwreck of unstable youth is now over and done with, and Palinurus lost overboard; Palinurus is...wandering sight." Fulgentius is remembering Aeneas's steersman, who is lost overboard in a storm at sea—after Aeneas had left Dido, whose allure Fulgentius interprets as "lust."   By leaving Dido, then, Aeneas conquers lust; the lost steersman is the leaving off of wandering ways. Aeneas is now ready for real learning. Fulgentius continues: "Having done with these matters, he reaches the temple of Apollo, that is, studious learning; and there he takes counsel on the course of his future life and seeks the way down to the lower world" (*On the Content of Virgil*: 18).

The commentators generally agreed that Virgil is at his most profound in book 6. (It is no coincidence that Petrarch's epic *Africa* follows Virgil in reserving book 6 for the descent to the underworld.) Bernardus (*On Virgil's Aeneid*), for example, devotes twice as much commentary to book 6 as he does to all the rest of the books of the *Aeneid* together.   Perhaps the most influential part of Bernardus's commentary on book 6 was his description of four kinds of epic descents:

The descent to the underworld is fourfold: the first is natural, the second is virtuous, the third is sinful, the fourth is artificial. The natural descent is the birth of man: for by it the soul naturally enters this fallen region and thus descends to the underworld and thus recedes from divinity and gradually declines into vice and assents to pleasures of the flesh; this is common to everybody. The second descent is through virtue, and it occurs when any wise person descends to mundane things through meditation, not so that he may put his desire in them, but so that, having recognized their frailty, he may thoroughly turn from the rejected things to the invisible things and acknowledge more clearly in thought the Creator of creatures. In this manner, Orpheus and Hercules, who are considered wise men, descended. The third is the descent of vice, which is common and by which one falls to temporal things...and does not turn away from them at all. We read that Eurydice descended in this way....The fourth descent is through artifice, when a sorcerer by necromantic operation seeks through execrable sacrifice a conference with demons. (*On Virgil's Aeneid*: 6.pref.; Nitzsche 1975: 45 suggests that Bernardus's source is Guillaume de Conches' glosses on Boethius's *Consolation*; Landino's account of the descents participates in this same tradition [*Disputationes Camuldenses*: 215-219]; see also Chance 1994: 449-450.)

For the first of Bernardus's four kinds of descent, the "natural" descent, the descent of the soul into the body, see **UNDERWORLD**.

The second kind, the virtuous descent, is best exemplified by Dante's descent into the Inferno: Dante descends in order that he might recognize the frailty of earthly things, so that he might, as Bernardus put it, "turn from the rejected things to the invisible things."

The third kind, the sinful descent, the fall to temporal things, is exemplified in the first book of Spenser's *Faerie Queene*, where the Red Cross Knight succumbs to the temptations of Duessa. But like Aeneas and Dante, he learns from his descent; specifically, he learns about the nature of sin and about his own moral vulnerability.

The fourth of Bernardus's kinds, the artificial descents, may also be found in book 1 of Spenser's *Faerie Queene*, when the sorcerer Archimago seeks out a black-magic charm with which to work his evil will upon the Red Cross Knight:

> Then choosing out few wordes most horrible,
> (Let none them read) thereof did verses frame,
> With which and other spelles like terrible,
> He bade awake blacke Plutoes griesly Dame,
> And cursed heaven, and spake reprochfull shame
> Of highest God, the Lord of life and light;
> A bold bad man, that dar'd to call by name
> Great Gorgon, Prince of darknesse and dead night,
> At which Cocytus quakes, and Styx is put to flight.
>   (1.1.37)

Milton worked several of these descents into *Paradise Lost*: there is Lucifer's literal descent to Hell; there is the fall of Adam and Eve (what Bernardus would call a "sinful" descent); Adam and Eve gain knowledge from their descent—and the poem looks forward to the descent of Christ into the flesh. Even Copernicus made use of this tradition: He described the astronomer's quest for knowledge as an epic descent (*Treatises*: 163-164).

Epic Simile The epic simile was one of the devices that contributed to the gravity of epic poetry. Epic similes are extended similes; a single simile may extend over five, ten, fifteen, even twenty or more lines. Here is a characteristic simile from Virgil:

the sailors, eager for flight, bring from the woods leafy boughs for oars and logs unhewn. One could see them moving away and streaming forth from all the city. Even as when ants, mindful of winter, plunder a huge heap of corn and store it in their home; over the plain moves a black column, and through the grass they carry the spoil on a narrow track; some strain with their shoulders and heave on the huge grains, some close up the ranks and rebuke delay; all the path is aglow with work. (*Aeneid*: 4.398-407)

Dante regarded his *Divine Comedy* as a kind of epic; one of the ways in which he signaled this intention was by the use of epic similes. Dante sees a group of souls on the Mount of Purgatory: "As sheep come forth from the fold by one and two and three, and the rest stand timid, bending eyes and muzzle to the ground; and what the first does the others also do, huddling themselves to it if it stops, simple and quiet, and know not why; so I saw then the head of that happy flock move to come on, and modest in countenance, in movement dignified" (*Purgatorio*: 3.79-87)

Catalogue of Participants In book 2 of the *Iliad* Homer simply calls a halt to the action and begins upon a list of the great men who fought at Troy. The list goes on for some four hundred lines. The original audiences for such epics would have been fascinated by the catalogues. We can imagine a noble family waiting eagerly for the mention of some great ancestor of their own who fought at Troy. But the catalogues numb the modern mind. Even in Roman times poets had fun with these catalogues. In his *Metamorphoses*, for example, Ovid told the story of Actaeon. Actaeon is out hunting when he happens upon Diana bathing in a forest pool. Angered, Diana turns Actaeon into a stag, and he is set upon by his own hounds. At this point Ovid waggishly stops the action to deliver himself of a ponderous catalogue of participants—the *dogs*:

And first come Melampus and keen-scented Ichnobates, baying loud on the trail—Ichnobates a Cretan dog, Melampus a Spartan; then others come rushing on swifter than the wind; Pamphagus, Dorceus, and Oribasus, Arcadians all; staunch Nebrophonus, fierce Theron and Laelaps; Pterelas, the swift of foot, and keen-scented Agre; Savage Hylaeus, but lately ripped up by a wild boar; the wolf-dog Nape and the trusty shepherd Poemenis. (*Metamorphoses*: 3.206-215)

He goes on to list thirty-six dogs!

But Virgil observes the convention with due seriousness in the *Aeneid* (7.641-817), and the convention was soberly observed as late as Milton, who provided a catalogue of the rebel angels—many of them recruited from the Old Testament, where they had served as gods of the Canaanites and Philistines (1.376-543). Milton thus makes allegorical use of the convention of the catalogue, to give us his sense of the Satanic nature of false gods.

Epic Epithet Homer often refers to the sea as "the wine-dark sea"; the god of war is sometimes "battle-insatiate Ares"; Diomedes is sometimes "Tydeus' son Diomedes"; Achilles is often "brilliant Achilles." And then there are "grey-eyed Athena," and "Zeus who gathers clouds before him," and "Odysseus, sacker of cities." Put very briefly, it seems that these epithets allowed an oral poet more easily to maintain his meter (for the effects of orality in epic poetry, see, e.g., Parry 1971; Toohey 1992: 11-16; see **HOMER, MUSES**). If two beats were necessary to make up a line about Achilles, for example, the poet would reach into his memory for the two-beat epithet for Achilles; if three beats were necessary in a line about Achilles, he would select the three-beat epithet for Achilles, and so forth (Lord 1981). Virgil was not an oral poet; he wrote epic epithets into the *Aeneid*, then, not because he "needed" them, but because they seemed to him to be a part of what it meant to write an epic: "Pious Aeneas," "ghastly Tisiphone," "Acestes, ripe of years," and "Gnosian Rhadamanthus." And so, we find epic epithets in the Christian epics as well: In Boccaccio's *Teseida*, for example, we read of "Nestor, son of Neleus," "subtle Mulciber," "battle-strong" Mars. In Spenser we find "false Duessa," "griesly Pluto." Milton gives us "Moloch, Scepter'd King," "The winged Hierarch," and "first Matron Eve."

The Arming of the Hero In the *Iliad* (18.368-616) Homer wants us to understand that Achilles is the most glorious of the heroes who fought at Troy. And so Achilles has armor that is far more wondrous than that of any of the other heroes. This armor was made by the god Hephaestus, and Homer describes it at some length. And so later epic poets include a long passage devoted to the arming of the hero with special armor. Virgil's Aeneas has armor made for him by the same god of the forge (*Aeneid*: 8.370-453). Spenser's Red Cross Knight, too, had special armor—allegorical armor; he was "Y cladd in mightie armes and silver shielde, / Wherein old dints of deepe wounds did remaine" (*Faerie Queene*: 1.1.1). In his "Letter to Raleigh" Spenser explains that this armor "is the armour of a Christian man specified by Saint Paul" (for more on Christian armor allegory, see Jeffrey 1992: 56-57). Here is the passage Spenser had in mind: "Put on the whole armour of God, that ye may be able to stand against the wiles of the devil....Stand therefore, having your loins girt about with truth, and having on the breastplate of righteousness....Above all, taking the shield of faith....And take the helmet of salvation, and the sword of the Spirit" (Eph 6:11-17).

The Gods in Control of Human Actions Homer and Virgil always made it clear that the gods were always in control, that Troy fell because of the wrath of Juno, that when the Trojans did well in the fighting it was because certain other gods took their part. Thus it is that we have the curious business of Saturn adjudicating between Venus and Mars at the end of Chaucer's "Knight's Tale" (2663-2699). For Chaucer the Christian conception of providence is implicit here. Other poets—especially Spenser and Milton—adapted this convention more explicitly to providence.

Bibliography: Jane Chance, *Medieval Mythography* (1994); Marjorie Donker and George Muldrow, *Dictionary of Literary-Rhetorical Conventions of the English Renaissance* (1982); Matthew Fike, *The Descent into Hell in The Faerie Queene*, Ph.D. dissertation, Univ. of Michigan (1988); David L. Jeffrey, *A Dictionary of Biblical Tradition in English Literature* (1992); Albert B. Lord, *The Singer of Tales*

(1981); Jane Chance Nitzsche, *The Genius Figure in Antiquity and the Middle Ages* (1975); Milman Parry, *The Making of Homeric Verse*, ed. Adam Parry (1971); William H. Porter, *Reading the Classics and Paradise Lost* (1993); Peter Toohey, *Reading Epic* (1992).

EPIMETHEUS was one of the Titans, the son of Iapetus, and the brother of Prometheus, Atlas, and Menoetius. After Prometheus had stolen the fire from Jupiter, Prometheus wanted to avoid the god's retaliation, and so he forbade Epimetheus to accept any gifts from Jupiter, since any gift might be a trick. But Jupiter offered Epimetheus Pandora and Epimetheus, unable to resist her beauty, took her for his wife. And so he was responsible for the woes that Pandora loosed upon mankind (see **PANDORA**). A second tradition also worked to Epimetheus's allegorical detriment: Plato had it that Epimetheus, "not a particularly clever person," was responsible for allotting faculties to the animals, while Prometheus alloted faculties to human beings (*Protagoras*: 320c-322a). For Proclus this meant that Prometheus "presided over the life of man, as Epimetheus over the life of the animals" (*Sur la République*: 2.53.10).

Most interpreters thus aligned Epimetheus in one way or another with worldly/fleshly things as opposed to things of the spirit/mind. Here is Ficino's Neo-Platonic version: "We can also refer to Epimetheus as the moon cherishing the body, that is, ensuring the safety of the species through Venus, and the individual through Jove. But we can refer to Prometheus as the sun cherishing the rational spirit especially: that is, ensuring through himself its power to perceive" (*Philebus Commentary*: 244). Bacon has something like this same contrast in mind. For Bacon it is Epimetheus who opens Pandora's fateful box. The gods gave Pandora

a goodly Box, full of all miseries and calamities....With this Box shee comes first to Prometheus, thinking to catch him, if peradventure, he should accept it at her hands, and so open it: which he neverthelesse, with good providence and foresight refused. Whereupon she goes to Epimetheus (who, though brother to Prometheus, yet was of a much differing disposition) and offers this Box unto him, who, without delay, tooke it, and rashly opened it...[and] all kinds of miseries came fluttering about his eares, being wise too late. (*Wisedome of the Ancients*: 26)

This is quite close to Erasmus's version of story (quoted below, under **PANDORA**), which is the earliest summary of the full Pandora story in Latin (Panofsky and Panofsky 1978: 17). Bacon provides the following moral interpretation:

this Fable doth delineate two conditions, or...examples of humane life, under the persons of Prometheus and Epimetheus: for they that are of Epimetheus his sect, are improvident, not foreseeing what may come to passe hereafter, esteeming that best which seems most sweete for the present, whence it happens that they are overtaken with many miseries, difficulties and calamities....But they that are Prometheus his schollers, are men endued with prudence, foreseeing things to come warily, shunning and avoyding many evils and misfortunes. (*Wisedome of the Ancients*: 26)

Ross also contrasts the two brothers. Prometheus may be understood as

Adams perfections...for he was quickened by Prometheus...that is Providence, and Minerva, that is wisdom; and this Providence or Prometheus was the son of Themis, that is, it was derived from his original justice; on him likewise was bestowed pardon, that is, all gifts or perfections: but as soon as he preferred the voice of the woman to the voyce of God, or Prometheus, he became Epimetheus; he lost his wisdom, providence, and other perfections. (*Mystagogus Poeticus*: 368-369)

Ross was not unusual in understanding Epimetheus as a pagan type of the fallen Adam.

    Bibliography: Erwin and Dora Panofsky, *Pandora's Box: Changing Aspects of a Mythical Symbol* (1978).

EUROPA was the beautiful maid abducted by Jupiter in the form of a bull (e.g., Moschus, *Idylls*: 2, "Europa"; Ovid, *Metamorphoses*: 2.835-877; *Fasti*: 5.605-616; Hyginus, *Fabulae*: 178). Dante likened himself to Europa when he was borne up in a dream to the heavens (*Paradiso*: 27.82-83; see Jacoff and Schnapp 1991). Dante, then, is thinking of spiritual ravishing. The *Ovide Moralisé* interprets the story in this same tradition: The story signifies Christ's redemption of the individual soul (2.5103-5138). Berchorius explains this allegory: "This girl signifies the soul, the spiritual daughter of God the king. Jupiter the supreme god signifies the Son of God who changed Himself into a beautiful bull—that is corporeal, mortal man by assuming human flesh and coming personally to the world—in order to have this virgin—that is the rational soul—he loved. This bull was beautiful, without stain or wrinkle" (*Ovidius Moralizatus*: 176-177).

    In van Heemskerck's *St. Luke Portraying the Virgin* (fig. 10), we see the bull and Europa carved into the base of St. Luke's bench. Van Heemskerck is assuming a Neo-Platonic interpretation of ascent: Jupiter carrying Europa up to the heavens was a figure for poetic/artistic inspiration. But there is also an iconographic double entendre here, since the ox was the animal traditionally associated with St. Luke (Panofsky 1972: 190).

    Another line of interpretation had it that the story was yet another example of bestialization (see Appendix B, "Bestialization"). Sandys is typical: "The gods themselves at once cannot love and be wise. Love like an inchanter deludes the eye of the minde with false apparitions: making that seeme noble, delightfull and profitable; which is full of dishonour, affliction and ruine....And behold our Jupiter becomes a beast to obtaine his bestiall desires" (*Ovid*: 123-124). This allegory goes all the way back to the classics—for example, Martial (*Epigrams*: 180)—and may still be found in Ross (*Mystagogus Poeticus*: 118) in the mid-seventeenth century.

Europa was the daughter of Agenor, King of Phoenicia. When she was abducted, Agenor ordered her brother, Cadmus, to find his sister and bring her home—or never return himself. Thus Europa was sometimes understood to be the object of a virtuous quest; see **CADMUS**.

Bibliography: Rachel Jacoff, "The Rape/Rapture of Europa: *Paradiso* 27," in Jacoff and Jeffrey Schnapp, *The Poetry of Allusion: Virgil and Ovid in Dante's Commedia* (1991); Erwin Panofsky, *Renaissance and Renascences in Western Art* (1972).

F

FAME in classical times was a winged female figure who allowed the reputation of the illustrious to live on. Horace wrote, for example, of a certain virtuous man: "him shall enduring fame bear on pinions that refuse to droop" (*Odes*: 2.2.7-8). But even in classical times there were already some who were skeptical of merely earthly fame. "What fame can you gain from the speech of men, or what glory that is worth the seeking?" asked Cicero in *The Republic*: "of how little value, indeed, is your fame among men...? Therefore, if you will only look on high and contemplate this eternal home and resting place, you will no longer attend to the gossip of the vulgar herd or put your trust in human rewards for your exploits. Virtue herself, by her own charms, should lead you on to true glory" (*Republic*: 6.19-23).

Such notions were easily assimilated by Christians, concerned as they characteristically were to distinguish what was outward and worldly from that which was inward and spiritual. (See **LUCRETIA** for Augustine's distinction between the Roman concern for honor as reputation and the Christian concern for honor as inward virtue.) Isidore, for example, wrote that Fame can be either good or bad, "For Fame sometimes pertains to successes, as in 'illustrious fame,' which is praise, and sometimes to evil deeds" (*Etymologiarum*: 5.27.26). As an example of bad fame, Isidore cites Virgil's Fame (or Rumor). Virgil had written that Fame is "of all evils the most swift. Speed lends her strength, and...soon she mounts up to heaven, and walks the ground with head hidden in the clouds." Virgil's evil Fame is a monstrous daughter of Earth, "who for the many feathers in her body has as many watchful eyes below—wondrous to tell—as many tongues, as many sounding mouths, as many pricked up ears" (*Aeneid*: 4.173-183; see also Ovid, *Metamorphoses*: 12.39-63). Virgil's many tongues and mouths become standard features of the iconography of Fame. In Cartari (*Imagini*, 1571 ed.: 397), for example, we see a picture of Bad Fame flying along with wings and trumpet in advance of the chariot of warlike Mars; she is covered with Virgil's little mouths and ears. And the stage direction at the beginning of Shakespeare's *2 Henry IV* reads "Enter Rumour painted full of tongues"; Rumour acts as Chorus in the play.

Boccaccio commented on the lines from Virgil, saying that Virgil should have used the word "infamy" rather than "fame": "For if fame is occasioned by virtue, then it should not be called evil" (*Genealogie Deorum*: 1.10). Boccaccio, like Isidore, wants to think in terms of "good fame" and "bad fame." Petrarch's *Triumphi* is a long poem that describes a hierarchical series of triumphs: the triumph of Cupid, Death's triumph over Cupid, Fame's triumph over Death, the Triumph of Time over Fame, the triumph of Eternity over Time—and finally, heavenly Fame, the eternal glory for which Christians strive, triumphs over all (Eisenbichler and Ianucci 1990).

During the Middle Ages Fame acquired a trumpet through which to broadcast her tidings. In Chaucer's *House of Fame*, for instance, Aeolus (god of the winds) serves as Fame's herald (see **AEOLUS**). Chaucer gives Aeolus two trumpets, one for good fame, one for bad; one is "Sklaundre...a blake trumpe of bras, / That fouler than the devel was"; the other, "Laude," is a "trumpe of golde" (1570-1688; see also Lydgate, *Falls of Princes*: 6.108-119). In Bruegel's *Triumph of Time* (fig. 24) we see Fame with her wings and trumpet riding on an elephant—elephants being known then as now for their mnemonic prowess (see **SATURN** for more on this engraving; for examples of elephantine feats of memory and learning, see, e.g., Bartholomaeus, *On the Properties of Things*: 18.42-44).

We see Good Fame and Bad Fame with their trumpets on the title page of Raleigh's *History of the World* (fig. 11). The woman on the left is Experience; she is full of years, and she casts her eyes down—toward the earth, the ground of experience. The woman on the right is Truth; she is young, or rather, timeless; she looks up toward the light. Good Fame and Bad Fame stand on either side of the globe, trumpeting forth their news. Bad Fame is covered with the tongues, mouths, and ears that Virgil gave her in the passage quoted above. This is clearer in some other representations of Bad Fame. The all-seeing eye of Providence looks out upon it all. The serene and hefty maid at the center is History, trampling death and oblivion underfoot. She is holding the world, a globe drawn in such a way as to suggest the whole sweep of history: the temptation of Adam and Eve, at the beginning of time, is in the upper right, there above the Caspian Sea. To the east of Europe, out in the Atlantic, is a battle at sea, an event from Raleigh's own time. History is holding up global history, as it were, before the eye of Providence. Raleigh, like Boethius, thinks of Providence as all-encompassing, complete, the whole history of the world, above Fame (for more on Boethius and Raleigh on the subject of Providence, see **FORTUNE**). In writing the history of the world, Raleigh is thus putting into written, chronological, narrative form that "history" that exists all at once and eternally in the mind of God, far above Fame.

Bibliography: Konrad Eisenbichler and A. A. Ianucci, *Petrarch's Triumphs*: Allegory and Spectacle (1990); B. G. Koonce, *Chaucer and the Tradition of Fame*

(1966); D. W. Robertson, Jr., "The Idea of Fame in Chrétien's *Cligés*," in Robertson, *Essays in Medieval Culture* (1980): 183-201.

THE FATES (Clothes, Moerae, Parcae) were three sisters. They were usually depicted as engaged in spinning, and hence were called *Clothes*, "spinners." Elaborating on a tradition that goes back to Hesiod (*Theogony*: 217-222), the *Chess of Love* commentary provides a typical account of the Fates:

These three dispose and order human life...Clotho, Lachesis, and Atropos. About these three the poets pretend that two, Clotho and Lachesis, continually spin. The first holds the distaff; the second draws and twists the thread, and elongates and extends it as far as she can. And the third is Atropos, who...is their extremely cruel enemy, ruining and destroying whatever of their work she can seize.

These goddesses, then, signify to us, properly enough, the estate and process of our human life. Clotho, first, who holds the distaff, signifies the beginning to us, i.e., the birth or the first generation of our bodies. Lachesis, who draws out the thread and pulls it, signifies the middle, i.e., the duration and continuation of our lives. And Atropos, who ruins and destroys all, signifies the end, i.e., death. (52; see also Fulgentius, *Mythologies*: 1.8; Isidore, *Etymologiarum*: 8.11.93)

The commentary places the Fates in Pluto's court in the Underworld. This, too, was a commonplace.

Hesiod had made the three sisters the daughters of the Night, but during the late Middle Ages and the Renaissance they were sometimes born of Demogorgon and primal Chaos. They were coeval, then, with the beginning of things, working out the pathways of necessity. Boccaccio (*Genealogie Deorum*: 1.5) and Spenser (*Faerie Queene*: 4.2.47-52), for example, associate them with Demogorgon and Chaos; Conti makes them daughters of Chaos (*Mythologie*: 3.6).

In classical times even Jupiter was commonly thought to be subject to the Fates' decrees. Homer suggests this (e.g., *Iliad*: 19.87; see also *Odyssey*: 22.413), as do Ovid (*Metamorphoses*: 5.532) and many others. But this was not invariable. Homer, for example, has Zeus consider changing Sarpedon's fate (*Iliad*: 16.432-438).

Christians, however, were likely to make careful distinctions between Fate and Providence (see, e.g., Wood 1970: 21-36). In doing so, they usually followed Boethius's formulation in *The Consolation of Philosophy*. Boethius's account of fate, free will, foreknowledge, and fortune was based on Christian-Platonic assumptions about the *real* world, which the mind and the spirit can perceive, and *this* world of mere seeming, this world of appearances, the world we perceive with our senses. Boethius calls the *real* world "the mind of God." Providence, then, is God's plan:

The generation of all things, and the whole course of mutable natures and of whatever is in any way subject to change, take their causes, order, and forms from the unchanging mind of God. This divine mind established the manifold rules by which all things are governed....When this government is regarded as belonging to the purity of the divine mind, it is called Providence; but when it is considered with reference to the things which it moves and governs, it has from very early times been called Fate.

Human beings, then, can see the workings of Fate even if they have no Christian awareness of Providence:

Therefore, whether Fate is carried out by divine spirits in the service of Providence, or by a soul, or by the whole action of nature, by the heavenly motion of the stars, by angelic virtue or diabolical cleverness...one thing is certain: Providence is the immovable and simple form of all things which come into being, while Fate is the moving connection and temporal order of all things which the divine simplicity has decided to bring into being. It follows, then, that everything which is subject to Fate is also subject to Providence, and that Fate itself is also subject to Providence. (*Consolation of Philosophy*: 4.pr 6)

In effect, Fate is all that non-Christians can see of Providence. This is what Bernardus had in mind when he wrote that "fate is the temporal outcome of things foreseen" (*On Virgil's Aeneid*: 6.45-47). Elsewhere Bernardus distinguishes between Urania's "Mirror of Providence," Dame Nature's "Table of Destiny," and Physis's "Book of Memory": "The Mirror of Providence was of vast circumference and boundless breadth, its surface extending forever, its shining glass such that whatever reflections it had once received no rubbing might erase, nor age make faint, nor destruction mar. There lived ideas and exemplars, not born in time and destined not to pass away in time. This Mirror of Providence is the eternal mind." Bernardus is describing Providence, which, as Boethius had written, is outside of time. The "ideas and exemplars" are the Platonic Forms; they are in the Mirror of Providence because they are a part of God's plan and, again, outside of time. The Table of Destiny, on the other hand, was "finite":

Here, in much the same manner as in the Mirror, appeared the shape of all creation, tinted with the hues of life. The difference between Mirror and Table was that the Mirror was particularly concerned with the unchanged state of heavenly natures, while the Table for the most part exhibited such products of the temporal order as were subject to change. Thence it is that Atropos, Clotho, and Lachesis, sisters obedient to Providence and fate, are assigned to keep a common careful watch, though in separate realms, over the workings of the universe. Atropos governs the sphere of the firmament, Clotho the planets' wandering, Lachesis the affairs of earth. Thus the Table of Destiny is nothing else but the sequence of those things which come to pass by the decrees of fate. (*Cosmographia*: 2.11)

For Bernardus, then, as for Boethius, Fate is the working out *in time* of the plan of Providence. And it is here that Bernardus locates the three sisters; he makes each sister responsible for the working out of Fate in a different sphere (Wetherbee's note on this line from his translation points out that the allegory here derives from Chalcidius, *Platonis Timaeus, Interpretate*: 144). All of this, Bernardus continues, can de deduced by looking at the effects of Fate and Providence in the world:

There remained the Book of Memory, written not in ordinary letters, but rather in signs and symbols, its contents brief and compressed into a few scant pages. In this brief compass the combined workings of Providence and fate could be deduced, and partially understood, but they could not be foreseen. For the Book of Memory is nothing else but the intellect applying itself to the study of creation. (*Cosmographia*: 2.11)

Ross's seventeenth-century comments on the Fates echo all this lore, in Ross's typical, wandering-eclectic fashion:

By these three sisters may be meant the threefold state of man in this world.

Of his birth...Of the continuance of his life...Of his death....Lachesis draws out the thred, Clotho wraps it about the spindle, Atropos cuts it off....By these three Sisters, called also Fates or Destinies, they signified the secret decrees of God, concerning mans birth, life, and death, therefore they made them the daughters of Jupiter and Themis, or Justice, because nothing befalls to us in this life, but by the decrees of God, grounded on his Justice; and because we should not pry too much into these decrees, they feigned these three Sisters to dwell in a dark cave, and to be the daughters of the night, and of Erebus [i.e., hell], because his judgments are a bottomless deep...and because his decrees are immutable, therefore they made the Fates the daughters of necessity. (*Mystagogus Poeticus*: 355)

The Fates were sometimes confused with the Furies; John the Scot, for example, wrote that "the Furies are called Clotho, Lachesis, and Atropos" (*Annotationes in Marcianum*: 364.14).

For more on Fate and Providence, see **FORTUNE**.

Bibliography: Henry G. Lotspeich, *Classical Mythology in the Poetry of Edmund Spenser* (1932): 58-59; DeWitt Starnes and E. W. Talbert, *Classical Myth and Legend in Renaissance Dictionaries* (1955): 340-386; Chauncey Wood, *Chaucer and the Country of the Stars* (1970).

FLORA was the goddess of the spring, flowers, and gardens—and so, of youth and the pleasures of youth. Thus it is that when a poet wants to let us know that he is feeling spring's promptings, that the green force is driving, Flora is likely to appear on the scene. Even dour Lydgate was not immune: After dreaming his dream of Nature and Genius, he wanders next morning out into a field full of flowers, "By vertu of the lusty quene, / Callyd Flora, the goddesse" (*Reson and Sensuallyte*: 920-921).

The best-known story having to do with Flora was first told by Ovid (*Fasti*: 5.183-212): A nymph of the fields named Chloris was raped by Zephyr; he then granted her eternal spring, made her goddess of the flowers, changed her name to Flora, and married her. Since Zephyr was the god of the west wind, the wind of spring, it seems clear that Ovid's myth has to do with the fructifying effects the warm winds of spring have upon the fields—we find Ross (*Mystagogus Poeticus*: 124-125) still interpreting the story in just this way in the seventeenth century. Botticelli's *Primavera* (fig. 13) depicts this transformation of Chloris into Flora:

Zephyr has Chloris in his grasp, even as she begins to merge with the flower-bedecked figure of Flora (Wind 1968: 115-116; Lightbown 1989: 137-140). The three figures on the right, then, show the cold earth metamorphosed by Zephyr—and these natural forces are related to the amorous promptings of Venus, who stands at the center of the painting.

Flora could thus serve with Nature, Genius, Venus, and other gods in nature and generation allegories (see, e.g., de Meun, *Romance of the Rose*: 8403 f.). In marriage paintings Renaissance brides were sometimes depicted in the guise of Flora (Panofsky 1969: 137-138). But given Christian attitudes toward sexuality, it is not surprising that Flora could be interpreted in less favorable terms. We find this as early as Lactantius (*Divine Institutes*: 1.20.6), who wrote that Flora was a wealthy prostitute who made Rome her heir and who was for this reason revered by the Romans. The slander was widely repeated (e.g., Boccaccio, *Genealogie Deorum*: 4.61; Pictorius, *Theologia Mythologica*: 28v; Fraunce, *Countesse of Pembrokes Yvychurch*: 27r; E. K.'s gloss on Spenser, *Shepheardes Calender*: March [E. K.'s glosses appear in the original and in all subsequent editions of Spenser's poem]; Giraldi, *De deis gentium*: 56; Ross, *Mystagogus Poeticus*: 124). Augustine wrote that the Roman Floralia, the festivities celebrating Flora, "are reckoned devout in proportion to their lewdness" (*City of God*: 2.27; see also Peacham, *Minerva Britanna*: 208; Ross, *Mystagogus Poeticus*: 125). Small wonder, then, that Alanus describes unnatural love as that love which will "blossom into vices, deflower the bloom of Flora" (*Complaint of Nature*: pr. 4.106). And when Spenser's Red Cross Knight has his lusty dream, it is Flora who gives the ivy garland to the False Una (*Faerie Queene*: 1.1.48). Elizabethan Protestants could mock nuns in such terms: Nuns claimed all to be brides of Christ, but to Protestant eyes they were more like unrepentent Magdalenes or devotees of the harlot Flora. This association was appealing also because of the Catholic inclination to associate the Virgin Mary with flowers (McGee 1987: 189-191).

Even the date of the Floralia, May 3, could convey allegorical meaning. Chaucer specified May 3 as the day on which Palamon escapes prison ("Knight's Tale": 1463) in order to suggest something about his cupidinous state of mind (McCall 1961). Chaucer must have had *something* in mind, since Pandarus suffered in his love on May 3 (*Troylus and Criseyde*: 2.50-63); and Chauntecleer disregards his dream and meets the fox on May 3 ("Nun's Priest's Tale": 3187-3197; for alternative allegorical interpretations of May 3, see Wood 1970: 87).

Sometimes poets simply refer to Flora metonymically, for spring, as when Milton refers to "Flora's earliest smells" (*Paradise Regained*: 2.365).

Bibliography: Ronald Lightbown, *Botticelli: Life and Work* (1989); Henry G. Lotspeich, *Classical Mythology in the Poetry of Edmund Spenser* (1932): 60; John P. McCall, "Chaucer's May 3," *MLN*, 76 (1961): 201-205; Arthur McGee, *The Elizabethan Hamlet* (1987); James Nohrnberg, *The Analogy of The Faerie Queene* (1976): 462-463; Erwin Panofsky, *Problems in Titian, Mostly Iconographic* (1969); Panofsky, *Renaissance and Renascences in Western Art* (1972): 192-200; Chauncey Wood, *Chaucer and the Country of the Stars* (1970).

FORTUNE was a goddess worshipped under many titles and in many aspects during Roman times. *Fortuna Publica* was the tutelary goddess of Rome; *Fortuna Caesaris* the protectress of Caesar; another goddess Fortune wore a crown in the shape of a city wall and was (in Roman times) the Protectress of such cities as Corinth. Usually she carried a cornucopia, to suggest the bounty she could provide when she chose; but she often had a ball or wheel as well, whose easy turning suggested her fickleness.   Sometimes she was depicted as blind.   Her popularity—and she was very popular among the Romans—suggests something about the Roman conception of the way the world works. But already in ancient times there were those who tried to limit Fortune's power.   One might show courage in the face of Fortune; Plato envisaged "a brave man who...confronts fortune with steadfast endurance and repels her strokes" (*Republic*: 399a-b). Others urged that her arbitrariness might be opposed with reason. Juvenal declared that "prudence" (*Satires*: 10.363) might counter her; Seneca counseled that one must believe that "the only good lies in that which is honourable. For anyone who deems other things to be good, puts himself in the power of Fortune, and goes under the control of another" (*Epistulae Morales*: 74.1).

It is impossible to know how long and with what degree of seriousness common Christians continued to invoke Fortune as the Romans had done. But a decisive change is reflected early in Christian books, pictures, and sermons—a change that in part grew out of the Roman Stoic response to Fortune. Augustine (*City of God*: 4.18-19), for example, pointed to certain logical contradictions in the Roman conception of Fortune. Christianity, with its God who knows all and ordains even the fall of the sparrow, leaves little room for Fortune. If we think we see her at work, this can only be an illusion.

Boethius provided the most influential explanation of this proposition. According to Boethius's Lady Philosophy, for those who can see beyond appearances, all is ordered, all is according to a plan:

Just as the craftsman conceives in his mind the form of the thing he intends to make, and then sets about making it by producing in successive temporal acts that which was simply present in his mind, so God by his Providence simply and unchangeably disposes all things that are to be done, even though the things themselves are worked out by Fate in many ways and in the process of time.

Therefore, whether Fate is carried out by divine spirits in the service of Providence, or by a soul, or by the whole activity of nature...one thing is certain: Providence is the immoveable and simple form of all things which come into being, while Fate is the moving connection and temporal order of all things which the divine simplicity has decided to bring into being. (*Consolation of Philosophy*: 4.pr 6)

Boethius transformed Fortune from a real goddess into a fictional-allegorical figure to personify not chance itself, but rather the human hope for prosperity and fear of adversity (Green 1962: xvii). Early in *The Consolation of Philosophy*, for example, Boethius is despairing. He cries out, "Oh God...We men are no small part of Your great work, yet we wallow here in the stormy sea of fortune" (1.mt 5). Lady

Philosophy assures him that he *imagines* Fortune to be in control because he is confused: "because you have forgotten how the world is governed, you suppose that these changes of your fortune came about without purpose. Such notions are enough to cause not only sickness but death" (*Consolation of Philosophy*: 1.pr 6). In his despair, Boethius sees only chaos, where in fact, Lady Philosophy assures him, there is order: "we can define chance as an unexpected event brought about by a concurrence of causes which had other purposes in view....Chance, too, which seems to rush along with slack reins, is bridled and governed by law" (*Consolation of Philosophy*: 5.pr 1-mt 1).

Only those who believe in chance could believe in Fortune or commit themselves to her. And so the stage was set for a thousand years: Fictional characters can manifest their inward spiritual state by announcing either that they were rejecting Fortune or embracing her. In general it can be said that after Boethius, when we find a character proclaiming himself to be suffering at the whim of Fortune—as Boethius does early in *The Consolation*—or when we find a character pledging his allegiance to Fortune, we are seeing a reflection of an inward spiritual state. For example, in one of his many moments of despair, the lover in de Lorris's portion of the *Romance of the Rose* speaks as follows: "But Love is so changeable that he robbed me of everything at once, when I thought that I had won. It is just as with Fortune, who puts discontent into the hearts of men but at other times caresses and flatters them. Her appearance changes in a short time: one hour she smiles, at another she is sad. She has a wheel that turns, and when she wishes she raises the lowest up to the summit, and with a turn plunges him who was on top of the wheel into the mud. And I am the one who is so turned" (3976-3991). The Lover realizes that Fortune and Cupid are fickle; but he does not turn away from them—and so his attitude toward Fortune characterizes him, in Boethian terms, as a worldling.

For Dante, Fortune is "an angelic intelligence" (Looney 1990: 87), something like Providence. This allegory is idiosyncratic—but even here the point is unexceptionably Boethian: Fortune "is much reviled even by those who ought to praise her, but do wrongfully blame her and defame her" (*Inferno*: 7.91-93)—those who blame her simply do not see that she works according to God's plan.

Chaucer's Pandarus provides a comic example of trust in Fortune. He encourages Troylus not to despair of his love precisely *because* Fortune is known to be fickle:

"Wostow not wel that Fortune ys comune
To every maner wight yn som degre?
And yet thou hast this comfort, lo, parde,
That as hire joyes moten overgone,
So mote hire sorwes passen everychone.

"For yf hire whiel stynte anythyng to torne,
Thanne cessed she Fortune anoon to be.
Now, sith hire whiel ny no wey may sojourne,

What wostow if hire mutabilite
Ryght as thiselven lyst wol don by the,
Or that she be not fer fro thyn helpynge?"
(Troylus and Criseyde: 1.843-853)

Fortune can still work in this way in the Renaissance. Edwards' cruel Dionysus is such a fool as to imagine that his power in this world is permanent: "My sword and power shall purchase my quietness," he says: "Fortune maketh all things subject to my power" (Damon and Pithias: 731, 735). And Tarquin is one of several characters in Shakespeare who choose to place themselves in Fortune's power. Pausing outside Lucretia's door, he begins to pray to the gods for a successful rape,

That his foul thoughts might compass his fair fair,
And they would stand auspicious to the hour,
Even there he starts: quoth he, "I must deflow'r;
The powers to whom I pray abhor this fact,
How can they then assist me in the act?
Then Love and Fortune be my gods, my guide!"
(Rape of Lucrece: 346-351)

What Boethius calls Fate, Raleigh calls Destiny—but Raleigh, too, agrees with Boethius: "Destinie or Necessitie is subsequent to Gods prouidence." And so, Raleigh writes, we must reject "that kind of Idolatrie, or God of fooles, called Fortune or Chance: a Goddesse, the most reverenced, and the most reviled of all other." Raleigh means that Fortune is most reverenced by fools—and most reviled by the philosophers. Fortune is "nothing else but a power imaginarie, to which the successe of humane actions and endeavors were for their varietie ascribed; for when a manifest cause could not bee given, then was it attributed to Fortune, as if there were no cause of those things, of which most men are ignorant" (History of the World: 1.1.15; for more on Raleigh's related views, see **FAME**).

Raleigh thus agrees with Boethius, de Lorris, Chaucer, and many others: Those who see Fortune at work are fools who are unaware of causes, fools who are unaware of providence and God's purpose.

Pandarus and Tarquin, as we have seen, both link Cupid and Fortune, but Fortune could, more generally, be associated with any yearning for, or reliance upon, earthly things. Fortune could also be connected to the Fates, as for example in Conti (Mythologie: 4.9); and because of her fickleness, Fortune could also be associated with the winds. There survives from the time of Elizabeth, for example, a preliminary sketch for a group of paintings that was to have been called Allegory of Fortuna; on the right and left margins of this sketch we find puffed-cheek figures blowing the winds through pursed lips (reproduced in Evett 1989: fig. 30).

Machiavelli seems at first to be at odds with this tradition; he seems to be proclaiming a pagan allegiance to Fortune: "I conclude then...that men are successful while they are in close harmony with Fortune." But he makes it clear that he means to make Fortune serve him, that he does *not* want to be a slave to Fortune: it is better to be impetuous than cautious, because "Fortune is a woman and it is necessary, in order to keep her under, to cuff and maul her...; therefore always, like a woman, she is the friend of young men, because they are less cautious, more spirited, and with more boldness master her" (*Prince*: 25).

For more on Providence, Fate, and Fortune, see **FATES**; for the close relationship between Fortune and love, see **CUPID**.

Bibliography: Orazio Bianco et al., *Il Tema della Fortuna nella Letteratura Francese e Italiana del Rinascimento* (1990); David Evett, "Some Elizabethan Allegorical Paintings: A Preliminary Inquiry," *JWCI*, 52 (1989): 140-166; Richard H. Green, "Introduction" to Boethius, *Consolation of Philosophy* (1962); A. C. Hamilton, *The Spenser Encyclopedia* (1990): under *Fortune*; Dennis Looney, *Inferno*, Canto VII," *LD*, 6 (1990): 82-92; James Nohrnberg, *The Analogy of The Faerie Queene* (1976): 307-311, 315-317; Howard R. Patch, *The Goddess Fortuna in Medieval Literature* (1927); Jon Whitman, *Allegory: The Dynamics of an Ancient and Medieval Technique* (1987): 111-121.

THE FOUR AGES (the Golden Age, the Silver Age, the Brass Age, and the Iron Age). Virgil's *Georgics*, Ovid's *Metamorphoses* (1.89-150), and Statius's *Silvae* provided the accounts best known to Christians of the Four Ages. The first age was a Golden Age of sinless simplicity, ruled over by Saturn. Then came the Silver Age, ruled by Jupiter, then the Brass Age, and finally the present, awful Iron Age. This conception of the large outline of human history was very widely known throughout the Middle Ages and the Renaissance. Boethius (*Consolation of Philosophy*: 2.mt 5), for example, paraphrases Virgil and Ovid on the Golden Age and the subsequent fall from acorn-eating innocence (for the Golden Age in Boethius, see O'Daly 1991: 179-188). Petrarch chastised the papal court at Avignon in these terms: "May fire from Heaven rain down on your tresses, wicked one, since doing ill pleases you so, who, after eating acorns and drinking from the river have become great and rich by making others poor" (*Rime sparse*: 136.1-4). There is much allegory in these few lines: The early church and the early popes lived thus in a prelapsarian age, an age of material simplicity and Christian innocence; the papal court of the present is fallen to Iron Age greed, self-seeking.

Boccaccio understood the course of human history in terms of the Four Ages. Boccaccio writes about these matters in his account of Ceres, whom he thinks of in Euhemeristic terms, as "a very ancient queen of Sicily, who had such great wisdom that after discovering how to till the soil she was the first among her people to tame oxen and accustom them to the plow." According to Boccaccio, then, it is this queen Ceres who ushered in the agricultural age, the age of cities:

I do not really know whether to praise or condemn [this] ingenuity. Who will condemn the fact that wild, wandering men were led out of the woods and into cities? Who will condemn the fact that men who were living like beasts were led to a better life?...But, to turn the argument around, who will praise the fact that the scattered multitudes living in the forests, accustomed to nuts, wild fruit, the milk of animals, the grass and rivers, having no worries, satisfied by the laws of nature, sober, modest and without deceit, enemies only of beasts and birds, were attracted to delicate and unknown foods? If we do not deceive ourselves, we shall see that because of these the door was opened to vices which had been in hiding for a long time....For this reason the fields, which had been common to all, began to have boundaries....From this came the words "mine" and "yours"....From this came poverty and slavery, as well as quarreling, hatred, bloody wars, and burning envy....And concupiscence, which up to that time had been dormant, began to rouse itself....I hardly know whether, or rather I do know that, those golden centuries, although primitive and uncivilized, were greatly to be preferred to our own age of iron and to all other centuries. (*Concerning Famous Women*: 5)

It is important to remember that Boccaccio is not writing an allegory. This is Boccaccio's best sense of the course of early human history. His conception of history *assumes* the Four Ages as its framework. (The details of Boccaccio's scheme derive from a passage in Vitruvius, *On Architecture*: 2.1, which Boccaccio quotes in the *Genealogie Deorum*: 12.70. All of this, according to Panofsky 1962: 40 derives ultimately from the Epicurean evolutionism whose classic expression is to be found in book 5 of Lucretius's *On The Nature of Things*.)

Clearly, Boccaccio was of two minds as to conditions during the Golden Age, an ambivalence that is often to be found in such discussions. See, for example, *The Wild Family* (fig. 12) by an anonymous fifteenth-century Netherlandish artist; this engraving aptly represents both the gentle simplicity of the Golden Age and its utter rudeness (for more on Renaissance ideas about wild men, see Simonds 1992: 136-169). Indeed, this ambivalence was so often felt that it was an easy mark for Shakespeare's Touchstone, who parodied such disquisitions in his comparison of the pastoral and the courtly life:

Truly, shepherd, in respect of itself, it is a good life; but in respect that it is a shepherd's life, it is naught. In respect that it is solitary, I like it very well; but in respect that it is private, it is a very vile life. Now, in respect it is in the fields, it pleaseth me well; but in respect it is not in the court, it is tedious. As it is a spare life (look you) it fits my humor well; but as there is no more plenty in it, it goes much against my stomach. (*As You Like It*: 3.2.13-21; for more on antipastoral sentiments in the Renaissance, see Lindenbaum 1986.)

Fraunce's conception of the Four Ages does not differ much from Boccaccio's, except that for Fraunce there were changes in nature as well as in human societies. With the passage of the Golden Age,

th'owld spring tyme Jupiter altred,
And chang'd it to a yeare, and new-made yeare he devuyded
In fowre parts, each part with a sev'rall season apoynted,
Warme Spring, hoate Sommer, cold wynter, changeable Autumme.
Then swelting doggstarre, then scalding breath of Apollo,
Then the northern Boreas caused better bowres to be builded.

Then ground gan to rebell, from a mother changd to a stepdame,
Naught but thorns and weeds of her owne accord she aforded.
(*Countesse of Pembrokes Yvychurch*: 2v-3r)

Fraunce is thinking of the fall from the Golden to the Silver Age as a type of Adam's fall. This was the common Christian understanding. For example, we find this interpretation in the *Ovide Moralisé* (1.827-936) and in Sandys' commentary on Ovid's account of the Four Ages:

The fiction of the foure Ages degenerating from better to worse, I should have thought, with others, to have beene derived from that Image in Daniel [2:36-44]; where the first Monarchie is presented by Gold, the second by Silver, the third by Brasse, and the fourth by Iron: had not Hesiod long before...by those names described them:

The Golden Age

The Golden Race of many languag'd men
The Gods first made, who heaven inhabit, when
The Scepter Saturne swaid: like Gods they
liv'd. [*Works and Days*: 109-111]

...Then was there neither Master nor Servant....Unforced Nature gave sufficient to all; who securely possess her undivided bounty....But this happy estate abounding with all felicities, assuredly represented that which man injoyed in his innocency: under the raigne of Saturne, more truly of Adam....

The Silver Age

[Jupiter] poyson first to spekled Serpents gave:
Taught Wolves to prey, and made the Ocean rave.
[Virgil, *Georgics*: 1.129-130]

And what was this but his connivency at wicked and licentious people, of whom he was glad to make use in the expulsion of his Father? Rebellion alwaies accompanied by liberty and out-rage: when nothing can better resemble those golden times then a free Common-wealth, ordred and maintained by well instituted lawes. But the silver Age is to be referred to the first Jupiter; which perhaps was Cain: A tiller of the Earth...a shedder of blood, a builder of Cities....In his time the people first fell from the worship of God, and through feare or flattery worshipped their King: envy, malice, and oppression...then entred the world....

The Brasen Age

The Brasen Age succeeded the Silver: for man grew not instantly superlative wicked, but degenerated by degrees, till imboldned by custome, through his insolencie and out-rage, he affrighted Astraea or Justice from the earth.

It was, Sandys continues, Astraea's departure that signaled the coming of the Iron Age:

The Iron Age

[The] Iron Age...is here so accurately described by our Poet; and withall those miseries which pursue it.

> Dejected Griefe, revengefull Cares, the rage
> Of Pale Diseases, melancholy Age,
> Base Beggery, ill-tempting Famine, Feare,
> Toyle, Death, and Furies, ever wander there.
> [Virgil, *Aeneid*: 6.274-277]
> (*Ovid*: 58-60)

Like Fraunce and most of the others who wrote about the Four Ages, Sandys is not much interested in the fine distinctions that separate the Silver from the Brass and the Brass from the Iron Age. Clearly, what is most important is the fall from the Golden to the Silver Age. As Reynolds put it, "What could they meane by their Golden-Age...But the state of Man before his Sin? and consequently, by their Iron age, but the worlds infelicity and miseries that succeeded [Adam's] fall?" (*Mythomystes*: 175-176). As late as 1732 Verburg could still confidently write that "no one still doubts today that Saturn was Adam" (*Gedaant-wisselingen van Ovidius*: 8).

Sometimes, however, the Four Ages were said to be figures for the four seasons (e.g., Berchorius, *Ovidius Moralizatus*: 129), or the four ages of individual human beings.

Often the Golden Age simply provided a way to talk about a time of glory: The rulers of sixteenth-century Florence, for example, liked to have their age described as a Golden Age (Puttfarken 1980). And in the seventeenth century Bredero recalls a time when there were great poets in Amsterdam; "Where is the Golden Age...gone?" he laments ("Broeders in Liefde Bloeyende": 9).

Arcadia was the place most often associated with the Golden Age; see **ARCADIA**.

Bibliography: Eugene R. Cunnar, "Fantasizing a Sexual Golden Age in Seventeenth-Century Poetry," in C. J. Summers and T. L. Pebworth, *Renaissance Discourses of Desire* (1993): 179-205; John Fleming, *The Roman de la Rose*: A Study in Allegory and Iconography (1969): 144-150; A. Bartlett Giamatti, *The Earthly Paradise and the Renaissance Epic* (1966); E. H. Gombrich, "Renaissance and the Golden Age," in *Norm and Form: Studies in the Art of the Renaissance* (1966); Harry Levin, *The Myth of the Golden Age in the Renaissance* (1969); Peter Lindenbaum, *Changing Landscapes: Anti-Pastoral Sentiment in the English Renaissance* (1986); Gerard O'Daly, *The Poetry of Boethius* (1991); Erwin Panofsky, *Studies in Iconology* (1962); Thomas Puttfarken, "Golden Age and Justice in Sixteenth-Century Florentine Political Thought and Imagery," *JWCI*, 43

(1980): 130-149; Peggy Muñoz Simonds, *Myth, Emblem, and Music in Shakespeare's Cymbeline* (1992); Roy Walker, *The Golden Feast: A Perennial Theme in Poetry* (1952).

THE FURIES (Dirae, Erinyes, Eumenides). For Hesiod (*Theogony*: 185) the Erinyes were daughters conceived upon Earth by the blood Cronus spilled when he castrated his father Uranus. The Furies were inhabitants of Erebus, the deepest precinct of Hades, and they were avengers of crimes, especially crimes against society and family. Aeschylus's *Eumenides* is named for these Furies, who tormented Orestes after he had killed his mother Clytemnestra. The incestuous parricide Oedipus also suffers their tortures, in Sophocles' *Oedipus at Colonus* (see also Virgil, *Aeneid*: 7.323-560). The Furies' names were fixed by the time of Apollodorus: Alecto, "the never resting," Tisiphone, the "avenger of murder," and Megaera, "the jealous one" (*Library*: 1.1.4).

In general, the Greeks recognized that the Furies were necessary to human societies. We see this clearly in the *Eumenides*, where even in Athens, with good Athenian law, the Furies are finally welcomed into the city. Fear of the Furies' torments was thought to act as a curb on human passions. This conception of the Furies—the torments, as it were, of the conscience—was largely forgotten during the Middle Ages; but we find it again in the Renaissance, when Landino, for example, wrote that "the Furies signify...that most violent distress of our minds—which disturbances present themselves as often as the sin which has been committed is remembered" (*Disputationes Camuldenses*: 250-251; Stahel tr.: 250). Thus it is that Shakespeare's Clarence, with blood on his conscience, dreams that he is seized by Furies (*Richard III*: 1.4.57; see also, e.g., Sandys, *Ovid*: 76).

In Roman times the Furies were not content merely to avenge crimes; they now began to incite crime as well. Ovid, for example, has the Furies brooding over the wedding of Tereus and Procne—a marriage that ended with rape, mutilation, child-murder, and cannibalism (*Metamorphoses*: 6.430-431). And in his account of the story of Myrrha's incestuous love for her father, Ovid writes that it could not have been Cupid who inspired such love; it was rather "One of the three sisters with a firebrand from the Styx and with swollen vipers" who blasted Myrrha (*Metamorphoses*: 10.313-314).

This notion that the Furies might tempt as well as punish was readily taken up by Christians. Alanus made the Furies the leaders of all the vices that come trooping out of Hell to attack the New Man:

Now that heavenly being and divine man had been perfected in entirety...harsh Alecto trembled at those reports....Therefore she laments that her abodes are inactive, and groans that groans are silent....Hence this aforesaid plague hastily calls together her kindred pestilences...: the ruler of darkness, the teachers of iniquity, inventors of crimes, masters of sin, injuries, thefts, plunderings....This whirlpool of sins, throng of vices...rushes into the Tartarean seats, where Erinys rules, Alecto commands, with Megaera prescribing the laws. (*Anticlaudian*: 8.3)

Christians were inclined to interpret the Furies as tempters not least because they easily associated the Furies' iconography (torches and snaky hair) and infernal habitation with the Devil. The Devil, after all, was also both tempter and punisher. In Tasso, for example, Alecto inspires war madness: "'Mongst them Alecto strewed wasteful fire, / Envenoming the hearts of most and least" (*Jerusalem Delivered*: 8.72). Sandys mentions this in the course of his commentary on Ovid's story of Myrrha: "Cupid (which is a desire of generation according to the order of Nature) denies to have kindled her unnatural flames: imputed to infernall Alecto, or the Divell, who begets in the impious soule, deserted by Virtue, such hellish affections" (*Ovid*: 485; see also E. K.'s comment on Spenser, *Shepheardes Calender*: Nov., 164). "What are the Furies," Sandys writes, "but the wicked desires and commotions of the minde?" (215). Sandys is working in a long-established tradition.

Waleys interpreted the three Furies with the three kinds of concupiscence: "By the Furies, it is said, the three kinds of concupiscence are understood...Avarice...Lechery...Ambition" (*Ovid*: 16). We find this same allegory in Trivet's commentary on Boethius's *Consolation*. The Furies were named as they were because of

three passions which produce many perturbations in the hearts of men, and at the same time make them transgress in such a way that they are not permitted to take any regard either for their fame or for any dangers that beset them. These are wrath, which desires vengeance, cupidity, which desires wealth, and libido, which desires pleasures. Hence they are called "avengers of crimes" because crimes are always accompanied by mental pain. And they may be ordered according to their etymologies, for *Alecto* means "incessant," and signifies cupidity; *Thesiphone* means "voice," and signifies libido; *Megaera* means "great contention," and signifies wrath. (as found in Robertson 1962: 474)

This tradition allows us to understand Chaucer's invocation of Tisiphone in the first stanza of *Troylus and Criseyde*: "Thesiphone, thow help me for t'endite / These woful vers, that wepen as I write." The invocation thus seems to suggest that the kind of love Chaucer will describe is that which Tisiphone/libido might inspire—the kind of love that leads to tragedy (Robertson 1962: 473-475; McCall 1955: 76; Wood 1984: 128; Heinrichs 1989). Fraunce (citing Lactantius) mentions this tradition, writing that the three Furies are "those three perturbations which tosse and turmoyle mens mindes, to weet, Wrath, Covetise, and Leachery" (*Countesse of Pembrokes Yvychurch*: 28v).

In a related tradition, the Furies were interpreted as the three stages of sin. Here, for example, is Bernardus (following Fulgentius, *Mythologies*: 1.7) on the Furies: "the Eumenides are the three daughters of Night and Acheron, namely Alecto, Tisiphone, and Megaera....The first is Alecto, who is interpreted as wicked thought; the second is Tisiphone, voice applied to wicked thought, and that is wicked speech; the third is Megaera, wicked deed" (*On Virgil's Aeneid*: 6.273-81). Henryson put it rather more succinctly:

Electo, migera, and thesaphany,
Ar nocht ellis, in bukis as we reid,
Bot wickit thocht, ill word, and thrawart deid.

("Orpheus and Eurydice": 476-478)

We find the same allegory in Neckam (*De Naturis Rerum*: 2.9) and John of Garland (*Integumenta Ovidii*: 199-200).

The Furies were sometimes conflated with the Harpies (e.g., Lynche, *Fountaine of Ancient Fiction*: Pii; Ross, *Mystagogus Poeticus*: 48) and, less frequently, with the Fates (e.g., John the Scot, *Annotationes in Marcianum*: 364.14). See **FATES, HARPIES**.

Bibliography: Katherine Heinrichs, "The Denizens of Hades in the Love Poems of the Middle Ages," *Neophil*, 73 (1989): 593-604; Robert Hollander, *Allegory in Dante's Commedia* (1969): 239-244; John P. McCall, *Classical Myth in Chaucer's Troilus and Criseyde* (1955); D. W. Robertson, Jr., *Preface to Chaucer* (1962); Chauncey Wood, *The Elements of Chaucer's Troilus* (1984).

G

GANYMEDE was the son of Tros, the founder of Troy. So beautiful was this boy that Jupiter took him up to the heavens to serve as his cup bearer. In some versions Jupiter assumes the form of an eagle to fetch Ganymede; in others he sends an eagle (e.g., Virgil, *Aeneid*: 5.252-257). Occasionally Ganymede is remembered as "wanton Ganymede" (Shakespeare, *Two Noble Kinsmen*: 4.2.15), or even as an emblem of sodomy (Peacham, *Minerva Britanna*: 48). But he was more often thought of in loftier ways. For the Neo-Platonist Philo, Ganymede was an allegorical figure for the divine logos (Dillon 1985). And some Roman sarcophagi bore the image of Ganymede and the eagle to depict the ascent of the soul after death (Panofsky 1962: 214; Panofsky n.d.: 37). The most common Medieval and Renaissance understanding of Ganymede seems clearly related to these favorable interpretations. There is Dante's first dream on the Mount of Purgatory, for example:

At the hour near morning when the swallow begins her sad lays, perhaps in memory of her former woes, and when our mind, more a pilgrim from the flesh and less captive to thoughts, is in its visions almost divine, I seemed to see, in a dream, an eagle poised in the sky, with feathers of gold, its wings outspread, and prepared to swoop. And I seemed to be in the place where Ganymede abandoned his own company, when he was caught up to the supreme consistory; and I thought within myself, "Perhaps it is wont to strike only here, and perhaps disdains to carry anyone upward in its claws from any other place." Then it seemed to me that, having wheeled a while, it descended terrible as a thunderbolt and snatched me upwards as far as the fire: there it seemed that it and I burned; and the imagined fire so scorched me that perforce my sleep was broken. (*Purgatorio*: 9.13-33)

Dante begins with a reference to Philomela, who was ravished by Tereus and then transformed into a swallow. And then the eagle takes Dante up—ravishes him as Ganymede was ravished by Jupiter. The eagle takes Dante up in this dream vision to see the cleansing fire at the top of the Mount of Purgatory. For Dante, then, the ravishing of Ganymede is an allegorical figure for divine contemplation, for spiritual ascent. Landino's commentary on the *Divine Comedy* confirms this:

> Ganymede, then, signifies the human mind, loved by Jupiter, which is the Supreme Being. Ganymede's companions [left behind when he was taken up] represent the soul's other faculties, which are the vegetal and sensorial souls. Jupiter...raises the mind of man to heaven with the eagle...and abandoning his companions, the vegetal and sensorial souls, is, as Plato says, removed from the body, and forgetting bodily things, it concentrates on the contemplation of heavenly secrets. (*La Commedia*: 172)

Chaucer's *House of Fame* begins with a respectful parody of Dante/Ganymede's spiritual flight. Fraunce's interpretation of Ganymede seems to be quite close to Dante's, Chaucer's and Landino's: "Others, by the ravishing of Ganymede by Jupiter, understand the lifting up of mans minde from these earthly toyes, to heavenly conceipts" (*Countesse of Pembrokes Yvychurch*: 33r). See also, for example, the *Chess of Love* commentary (117), Dolce (*Transformationi*: 223), Viana (*Ovid*: 10.11), Conti (*Mythologie*: 9.13), Alciati (*Emblems*: 4), Sandys (*Ovid*: 481), Reynolds (*Mythologie*: 152), and finally Ross, who writes that "The quick-sighted Eagle, is Divine contemplation or meditation, by which Ganimedes, the soul, is caught up to Heaven" (*Mystagogus Poeticus*: 131).

For a standard account of spiritual ravishing, see Bonaventure's *Mind's Road to God*: "on mental and mystical ravishment in which repose is given to the soul which rises toward God in ecstatical love" (7).

Ganymede also occasionally served as a figure for man's nearness to God in general, not just in time of meditation. Henkel and Schöne (1967: 1726), for example, reprint a German emblem from 1531 which shows Ganymede riding the eagle; the accompanying verse explains that "Whosoever with all his might, heart, and judgment holds fast to God, the same may certain be that he'll never be far from God."

Bibliography: John Dillon, "Ganymede as the Logos: Traces of a Forgotten Allegorization in Philo?" *ClasQ*, 31 (1985): 183-185; Arthur Henkel and Albrecht Schöne, *Emblemata: Handbuch zur Sinnbildkunst des XVI. und XVII. Jahrhunderts* (1967); John Hollander, *Allegory in Dante's Commedia* (1969): 146-147; Gerda Kempter, *Ganymed: Studien zur Typologie, Ikonographie und Ikonologie* (1980); Erwin Panofsky, *Tomb Sculpture* (n.d.); Panofsky, *Studies in Iconology* (1962); James Saslow, *Ganymede in the Renaissance* (1986).

GENIUS (Daemon) was a very ancient god indeed. He had his beginnings in ancient animistic beliefs and in the worship of household spirits. Among the Greeks and Romans each human being, each creature, even every *thing* was said to have its individual Genius (or daemon, for the Greeks; see, e.g., Plato, *Statesman*: 271d). Every human being was born with an individual Genius. Each family had its individual Genius; each place had its Genius (the *genius loci*);

marriage beds, schools, marketplaces, each had its individual Genius. Livy (*Ab urbe condita libri*: 21:62) records that the frightened citizens of Rome offered up no fewer than five sacrificial victims to Rome's Genius in the hope that the god might protect the city from warlike Hannibal in 217 B.C. It was in this sense, then, that Martianus referred to Minerva as the "guiding genius" of all the universe (*Marriage of Philology and Mercury*: 6.567). As Ripa put it, "it is not only human beings alone that have Genii, but insensible things as well" (*Iconologie*: 1.68).

All of these individual Genii came to be a way of accounting for the wide diversity of human inclinations. Here is Horace's explanation: "Of two brothers one prefers...idling and playing and the anointing of himself; the other, wealthy and untiring, from dawn to shady eve subdues his woodland farm with flames and iron plough. Why so, the Genius alone knows—that companion who rules our star of birth, the god of human nature, though mortal for each single life, and changing in countenance, white or black" (*Epistles*: 2.2.183-189). This Genius, allegorized, was still current in the Renaissance. Erasmus explains all of this, and provides a sketch of the classical antecedents, in the course of his disquisition on the term "evil Genius":

this is the name we give to those whom we blame for our misfortunes, for the most part, and it remains in common speech to the present day. There are people who have such an unlucky effect on others that they can really appear to be their evil destiny, and born to destroy them. The proverb, however, seems to have arisen from the view of the ancients that each person had two attendant spirits whom they called *daemones*—and not people only, but also places and buildings are said to have spirits—and one of these plots our destruction while the other tries to come to our aid. Empedocles thought this, according to Plutarch's quotation in his essay "On Tranquility of Mind" [15]....And indeed our own theologians (following the ancients, I imagine) attribute to each person from the very beginning of his life two *genii* which they call angels; one is our friend, and...the other is evil. (*Adages*: 1.1.72; see also, e.g., Rabanus, *De Universo*: 435; Albricus, *Allegoriae Poeticae*: 17r-v; Fraunce, *Countesse of Pembrokes Yvychurch*: 29r; Ross, *Mystagogus Poeticus*: 133)

Genius was associated with engendering from very early times. Indeed, the god's Latin name shares the Indo-European root *gen* with *engender*, *generation*, and (after a consonant shift) *kin*, *kind*, (Ger.) *kinder*, and many other words (Shipley 1984: 129-133). For some classical authorities, such as Horace, this was because we are each born—engendered—with an individual Genius (see, e.g., Macrobius, *Saturnalia*: 1.19.17; Servius, *In Virgilii Aeneidos*: 6.743). But Genius was also very early thought of as the god of generation—in addition to being each individual's tutelary spirit. Augustine, arguing against Roman religion in *The City of God*, saw a contradiction in this: "What is Genius? [Varro wrote,] 'He is the god who is set over, and has the power of begetting, all things'"—however, Augustine continues, Varro also wrote "that Genius is the rational soul of every one, and therefore exists separately in each individual" (7.13).

But by the time of Augustine, Genius's long and active career as a god was drawing to a close. There followed a period of relative inactivity, disturbed only by the passing reference of the theologian or scholiast. Then in the twelfth century Genius began his climb to the heights of his fictive and allegorical career in the late Middle Ages and the Renaissance. Genius owed his resurrection to Bernardus, who gave Genius an important role in his *Cosmographia*. Remembering the classical traditions that each individual thing had its Genius and that Genius was a god of engendering, Bernardus made Genius the translator of the Platonic Forms into individual shapes—that is, into individuals. Bernardus wrote that Genius was "devoted to the art and office of delineating and giving shape to the forms of things. For the whole appearance of things in the subordinate universe conforms to the heavens, whence it assumes its characteristics, and it is shaped to whatever image the motion of the heavens imparts" (*Cosmographia*: 2.3). For Bernardus, then, Genius provided each individual creature with its inclinations (or "instincts," as we would say), because Genius translated the universal Forms into individuals. Each individual's Genius, then, provided all his desires, as we find in another passage from Bernardus:

For no one is without natural concupiscence. Whence one reads in poems that there is a certain genius, a god of human nature, which is born and dies with a man, as Horace says: "a god of mortal human nature in each head" [*Epistles*: 2.2.188-189]. We understand that to be the natural appetite which dominates human nature, and it is called Eurydice, that is, the appetite for the good, for it is given in order to seek the good. (*On Virgil's Aeneid*: 6.119-120; for Eurydice as natural concupiscence, see **ORPHEUS**)

Since most later poets and naturalists understood Nature to be the repository of the Platonic Forms, Genius became Nature's regent. Nature preserved the Forms immutable; Genius was responsible for translating these Forms into individuals—individual goats, gnats, horses, and human beings. To those who followed Bernardus, this meant that Genius was not just concerned with engendering; he was the provider of the whole range of inclinations that belong to human beings because they are human beings. Essentially, this is the way Genius works in Alanus's *Complaint of Nature*, Gower's *Confessio Amantis* (for Genius in Gower, see Olsson 1992), and in Spenser's *Faerie Queene* (2.12.47-49).

In these writers, then, we must remember that Genius is limited. Because he is responsible for *natural* inclinations, he cannot be expected to understand matters theological. In this tradition Nature is limited in the same way. Alanus's Dame Nature explains this: "I know in order that I might believe; [Theology] believes in order that she may know. I assent by perceiving and knowing, she perceives by assenting. I barely see the things that are visible, she comprehends in their reflection things incomprehensible...I, almost like a beast, walk the earth, she serves in secret heaven" (pr. 3; for more on levels of understanding, see **NATURE**).

But if Nature and Genius cannot rise to an understanding of what Theology knows, they can rise above Venus, even oppose her (Economou 1970: 204). For the Venus of earthly love urges unbridled passion; she urges love *no matter what*. Genius and Nature, on the other hand, since they provide the whole range of humankind's inclinations, also provide the promptings of reason, since rationality is a part of the Form of humankind. Of course, the Fall has confused those divinely instituted inclinations, as Alanus's Dame Nature complains in *The Complaint of Nature*.

Batman provided a brief summary of the relevant Neo-Platonic notions before going on to write his explanation of Genius:

> The Platonikes report, that all the bodyes belowe, are Ideadit or conceited by the uppermost Idees or conceits: and they define an Idea to be one, simple, pure, unchangeable, indivisible, incorporall, & everlasting forme above bodies, soules, and mindes, and the same to be the nature of all Ideas. And first they place the Idees, in the very goodnes it selfe, that is in God, by the manner of the cause, to be differing onely among themselves, by certaine relative reasons: leest whatsoever is in the world, shuld be alone with out any varietie, and yet to agree among themselves in essence, that God may not be a manifold substance. Secondly, they place them in the very intelligible part, that is in the soule of the world, properly by formes, & moreover differing one from another in perfect formes: so that all the idee or conceipts in God, are one forme, but in the soule of the world many: they are placed in the mindes folowing or joined to the body [i.e., the body of the world] or severed from the body, severed now more & more by a certaine participation, & by degrees: they place in nature, as it were certaine seeds of formes below infused from the Idee. Finally, they place them in matter, as shadowes.

Now, the correspondence between the Forms in the world soul and the individuations of those Forms in the world's body continue after the seeds are sown, "so that every kinde, hath a celestiall figure agreeing unto him: from whence also, proceedeth unto him, a mervailous power." The power of these correspondences, Batman continues, is limited only by

> the qualitie of the matter...For after this sort things even of one kinde, are founde more or lesse mightie, according to the impurity or misorder of the matter. For all the influences of the heavens may be hindred by the unabilytie of the matter....Wherefore the sight of heavenly things, is the cause of all the noble vertue, that is in the kindes belowe. (*Batman uppon Bartholomae*: 170; for the most part, this book is Batman's translation of Bartholomaeus Anglicus's *De Proprietatibus Rerum*; but the sections having to do with Genius were Batman's own additions.)

Batman cites the German occultist Cornelius Agrippa (1486?-1535) as his source.

Genius lingers on in our talk of how our children have a *genius* for this or that; and we still talk about *the spirit of a place*. The Christian custom of naming children after saints is probably a survival of the ancient belief in an individual helping spirit, or genius.

Daemon did not always mean "Genius." Sometimes, for example, it was simply a term for "demigod," as in Vives (*Of the Citie of God*: 10.21).

Bibliography: H. David Brumble, *The Allegorical Figure Genius*, Ph.D. Dis., Univ. Of Neb. (1970); G. D. Economou, "The Character Genius in de Lille, de Meun, and Gower," *ChauR*, 4 (1970): 203-210; Economou, *The Goddess Natura in Medieval Literature* (1972): 90-123; J. Chance Nitzsche, *The Genius Figure in Antiquity and the Middle Ages* (1975); K. Olsson, *John Gower and the Structures of Conversion* (1992); H. J. Rose, "On the Original Significance of the Genius," *ClasQ*, 17 (1923): 57-60; J. Shipley, *The Origins of English Words* (1984); W. Wetherbee, "Introduction" to his tr. of Bernardus Silvestris, *Cosmographia* (1973); D. T. Starnes, "The Figure Genius in the Renaissance," *SRen* 2 (1964): 234-244.

THE GIANTS. According to Hesiod (*Theogony*: 178-186) Gaia (the Earth) conceived when the blood of her husband Uranus (the Sky) fell to the ground after he was castrated by Saturn. The Giants were the awful fruit of this unnatural union. For Ovid these Giants were "serpent-footed" monsters, each with a hundred hands (*Metamorphoses*: 1.182-186; *Fasti*: 5.37). According to a late-classical tradition, the Giants rebelled against Jupiter and the other gods (see, e.g., Apollodorus, *Library*: 1.6.1-2; Ovid, *Metamorphoses*: 1.151-162).   In this war, the Gigantomachia, the gods enlisted the aid of Hercules, because an oracle had warned them that they could not kill the Giants without the aid of a mortal.

Christians usually associated the Giants, in one way or another, with pride. Thus they could be a type of the Tower of Babel or of presumptuous Lucifer and his rebel angels (see, e.g., *Ovide Moralisé*, 1.1185-1202). In Dante we find the image of one of the Giants, Briareus, graven into a paving stone on the Terrace of Pride, alongside other *exempla* of pride such as Arachne, Niobe, and the rebel angel Satan (*Purgatorio*: 12.25-46; see also *Inferno*: 31.98; for Dante's allegorical giants, see Dronke 1986: 50-55). Cervantes' Don Quixote was also aware of this tradition: "It is for us to slay pride," he says, "by slaying giants" (*Don Quixote*: 2.8; see also Fulgentius, *On the Content of Virgil*: 22; Pietro Alighieri, *Commentarium*: 416-417, on *Inferno*: 31; and van Mander, *Wtlegginghe op den Metamorphosis*: 4r-v).

Christians sometimes interpreted the Gigantomachia as a figure for the conflict between the body and the mind. Here, for example, is Bernardus: "They are called *gigantes*, 'giants,' as if *gegantes*, 'engendered from the earth'; their bodies are created naturally from the earth and nourished by its food....We say that the gods are knowledge and virtue. The Giants therefore declare war on the gods when bodies oppress knowledge and virtue. The Giants are defeated when bodies are mortified" (*On Virgil's Aeneid*: 6.322-324).

Fraunce writes that the Giants were "furious and unruly by reason of the superaboundant store of unbridled humors" and that they figure forth "nothing else but an obstinat and selfe-wild conceite and desire grounded in the minde, and not removeable. These allegorically are seditious and rebellious subjects in a common wealth or schismaticall and haereticall seducers in the Church" (*Countesse of Pembrokes Yvychurch*: 9r; see also Sabinus, *Fabularum Ovidii Interpretatio*: 14-15). Reynolds interprets the Giants in much the same way (*Mythomystes*: 169).

In all of this we should recognize that the outward form of the Giants mirrors their inward spiritual state. Sandys explains this at some length: the Giants were said to be "of a vast proportion," or rather they were "so called of their monstrous

Mindes" (*Ovid*: 61). Most of the giants treading their fearsome, heavy way through Medieval and Renaissance literature reflect these same allegorical notions. Spenser's Orgoglio comes immediately to mind; he may be understood allegorically in much the same way as the Giants—and like them (and the Titans), "The greatest Earth his uncouth mother was" (*Faerie Queene*: 1.7.9). Such giants were also related to the "giants in the earth" of Genesis, the giants whose lust for "the daughters of men" (Gen 6:4) brought on the flood. As Jerome put it, "the impiety of the giants brought on the shipwreck of the entire world" (*Letters*: 50; see Nohrnberg 1976: 264-267 and Dronke 1986: 32-55).

The Giants were often confused or conflated with the Titans: both Titans and Giants were giants, after all; and both rebelled against Jupiter. This conflation may be found all the way from Horace (*Odes*: 3.4.53) and Hyginus (*Fabulae*: 150) to Peele (*Arraignment of Paris*: 254-255) and Ross (*Mystagogus Poeticus*: 404-405).

For more on the allegory of giants, see **TITANS, TYPHOEUS, URANUS**.

Bibliography: Peter Dronke, *Dante and Medieval Latin Traditions* (1986); Henry Lotspeich, *Classical Mythology in the Poetry of Edmund Spenser* (1932): 63-64; James Nohrnberg, *The Analogy of The Faerie Queene* (1976); Janis Pallister, "Giants," in Malcolm South, *Mythical Creatures and Fabulous Beasts: A Source Book and Research Guide* (1987).

GLAUCUS of Anthedon was a humble fisherman who ate of a certain grassy herb and so became immortal. As Ovid tells the story, Glaucus no sooner ate of the herb than he "yearned with desire for another element" (*Metamorphoses*: 13.945-946), and so he leapt into the sea, where he was transformed into a fish-tailed sea god. Later he fell in love with Scylla, but his amorous hopes were ruined by the jealous enchantress Circe.

Since the roiling, changeable sea was so commonly associated with the passions, Glaucus was sometimes interpreted—as were other sea gods (see **NEPTUNE, PROTEUS**)—as a figure for the passions or the effects of the passions. Fulgentius, for example, wrote that we can interpret Glaucus's love for the temptress Scylla as lust, "for Glaucus is the Greek for one-eyed, whereby we call blindness glaucoma. For anyone who loves debauchery is blind" (*Mythologies*: 2.9; see **SCYLLA AND CHARYBDIS**). To leave the land for watery chaos is to descend to lust and debauchery. Renaissance Neo-Platonists transformed this descent to lust into another version of the soul's descent into the body (see **UNDERWORLD**). Tasso wrote that "Glaucus, who leapt into the sea, is the rational soul, which descends into the body, where it mixes with the sensitive and vegetable souls which are necessary to the body" (*Dialoghi*: 3.275-276). Fraunce provides a rather free paraphrase of Tasso and then adds a bit of moral allegory:

The tale is...expounded by Tasso...where by the deified Glaucus, he understandeth the intellectual part and facultie of man: by the sea wherein he fisheth, the body of all bodily matters, being...subject to continuall alteration like the sea: by his fishing, the discoursing and sylogisticall reasoning of Intellectus...: by the herbe which he did bite, the heavenly delite of contemplation, whereby he was made a God: by the casting of himselfe into the sea, his comming and descending from the quiet rest of contemplation, to the variable sea of action and operation....Glaucus, by tasting the herbe, leapeth into the sea, together with his fishes: that is, yeelding to the inchaunting force of pleasure, he so drowneth himselfe in the Aphrodisian sea of sensuality, that he becomes altogether beastlike. (*Countesse of Pembrokes Yvychurch*: 21v-22r; see Appendix B, "Bestialization")

One part of Fraunce's interpretation of Glaucus makes Glaucus a figure for the deification of man by "the heavenly delite of contemplation." This, too, seems to have been traditional. We find Dante in the *Paradiso* comparing his own yearning for spiritual change to this change of Glaucus. Dante fixes his eyes on Beatrice: "Gazing upon her I became within me such as Glaucus became on tasting of the grass that made him sea-fellow of the other gods. The passing beyond humanity may not be set forth in words: therefore let the example suffice any for whom grace reserves that experience" (1.67-71; see Hollander 1969: 216-220; Brownlee 1993: 116).

Boccaccio interprets Glaucus as a type of the Christian convert, specifically as a type of Peter, another fisherman (*Eclogues*: 11; Boccaccio explains the allegory in his comment on this eclogue, quoted in Smarr's tr.: 236). Sandys provides a secular version of the same allegory: Glaucus is an example of how even the humble can achieve immortality if they excel "in commendable arts" (*Ovid*: 616).

There were several other Glaucuses: Glaucus son of Minos and Pasiphae was drowned in a honey pot; Glaucus son of Antenor helped Paris abduct Helen. Glaucus son of Hippolochus was one of the Greek heroes at Troy; he traded his gold armor for Diomedes' bronze—an exchange which, according to Cooper (*Dictionarium*: under *Glaucus*), was proverbial for a bad trade.

Bibliography: Kevin Brownlee, "Dante and the Classical Poets," in Rachel Jacoff, *The Cambridge Companion to Dante* (1993); Douglas Bush, *Mythology and the Renaissance Tradition in English Poetry* (1963): 83-86; Robert Hollander, *Allegory in Dante's Commedia* (1969).

THE GOLDEN CHAIN (Great Chain of Being). At the beginning of book 8 of the *Iliad*, Zeus boasts of the greatness of his power. He taunts the other gods to let down from the sky a golden chain—a "cord of gold" in Lattimore's translation—and try, all of them, to pull Zeus down. He could, he warns them, pull them all up whenever he chose: "I could drag you up, earth and all and sea and all with you" (8.18-27)—Zeus at one end, and all the gods and the world at the other end of a golden chain.

Plato turns Homer's innocent figure of speech into allegory: the Golden Chain is "the sun, and signifies that so long as the heavens and the sun continue to move round, all things in heaven and earth are kept going, whereas if they were to be bound down and brought to a stand [as Jupiter threatens to do in Homer], all things would be destroyed" (*Theaetetus*: 153c). Heraclitus also glosses Homer's golden chain as a figure for Jupiter's connection to the whole of creation (*Allégories d'Homère*: 36.2). Plotinus (*Enneads*: 1.1.8) develops this into an allegorical veil for one of the central ideas of Neo-Platonism, the idea of the World-Soul and of the indissoluble connection between this World-Soul and God.

The idea and the Neo-Platonic allegory of the Golden Chain seems to have descended to the Middle Ages through Macrobius. The world has a "Soul," he wrote, and we can call this World-Soul "Mind":

Accordingly, since Mind emanates from the Supreme God and Soul from Mind, and Mind, indeed, forms and suffuses all below with life, and since this is the one splendor lighting up everything and visible in all, like a countenance reflected in many mirrors arranged in a row [Virgil, *Aeneid*: 6.726-32], and since all follow on in continuous succession, degenerating step by step in their downward course, the close observer will find that from the Supreme God even to the bottommost dregs of the universe there is one tie, binding at every link and never broken. This is the golden chain of Homer which, he tells us, God ordered to hang down from the sky to the earth. (*On the Dream of Scipio*: 1.14.14-15; see also Ficino, *Opera Omnia*: 1049; Pico, *Heptaplus*: 5.proem; Conti, *Mythologie*: 2.5; Milton, *Paradise Lost*: 2.105; "Second Prolusion")

Bodin (*Colloquium*: 32) assumes the same allegory and adds the suggestion that the Golden Chain is a type of Jacob's Ladder (Gen 28:12-13).

A similar allegory hung upon another Golden Chain, this one also derived from the *Iliad* (15.18-22), where Jupiter binds Juno with a Golden Chain. Fraunce provides a clear statement of the allegory:

Homer maketh Jupiter binde Juno with a golden chayne, hanging two great masses of Iron at her heeles, and that she thus tied could be loosed by none, but by himself: Juno is the ayre, the two weights of Iron, be the earth and water, betweene which two & the Superior bodies she hangeth chayned: & this golden chayne is the coherent concatenation and depending of things united so in order, as none but only the almighty Jupiter can dissolve the same. (*Countesse of Pembrokes Yvychurch*: 15r)

This idea goes back as far as Heraclitus (*Allégories d'Homère*: 40) and Proclus (*Sur la République*: 1.193.10); see also Chaucer ("Knight's Tale": 2987-2993), Giraldi (*De deis gentium*: 158), Valeriano (*Hieroglyphica*: 631), and Milton ("Second Prolusion"; *Paradise Lost*: 3.1005).

Another interpretation, much less widely known, had it that the Golden Chain was a figure for ambition (Conti, *Mythologie*: 2.5; Spenser, *Faerie Queene*: 2.7.46).

Bibliography: George D. Economou, *The Goddess Natura in Medieval Literature* (1972): 16-17, 114, 149; A. O. Lovejoy, *The Great Chain of Being* (1936); Emil Wolff, *Die goldene Kette. Die Aurea catena Homeri in der englischen Literatur* (1947).

THE GORGONS were three horrible sisters, Sthenno, Euryale, and Medusa. Isidore's comment is brief, but it carries the same moral freight as most of what comes later: The Gorgons are "serpent-haired harlots who turn those who look upon them to stone" (*Etymologiarum*: 11.3.29). Bernardus's interpretation is typical of the more elaborated Medieval and Renaissance interpretation of the Gorgons:

the Gorgons...were the three daughters of Phorcys, the god of the sea....These three are said to have had only one common eye, which they shared among themselves. We read that Perseus killed [Medusa] with the help of Pallas and Mercury....Phorcys is the god of the sea, the spirit which rules in the flesh (as we interpret the sea)....He begets three daughters: the first is bad desire (called Sthenno)—weakness, because the first weakness is to wish evil; the second is concealing the good (Euryale), which is wicked speech because it conceals the good by detraction; the third is wicked practice (...Medusa)—terror, because we fear her more than the others. *Gorgon* is the name common to them..., since they attend the flesh....Perseus is interpreted as virtue. With the help of his sister Pallas and his brother Mercury (wisdom and eloquence), he kills the third wicked sister (wicked act). (*On Virgil's Aeneid*: 6.289)

The *Chess of Love* commentary also had a good deal to say about Medusa and her sister Gorgons:

The poets also say that Medusa had the head of a serpent, and some say and pretend that because Neptune was so taken and deceived by his love for Medusa from the time he saw her in the temple of Pallas [at a time when she was a beautiful young woman], because of the beauty of her pleasant hair, he was moved out of all measure to ravish her by force, and so the goddess changed Medusa's hair into serpents. And this may be what is meant by the serpent's head....Moreover, the poets said that Medusa transformed those who looked at her into stones, i.e., that those who stopped to consider her beauty and countenance so dawdled in wonder and were so troubled that there was no more sense, or movement, or understanding left in them than in a stone....

This terrible monster portrayed on the shield of Pallas signifies to us that the wise and doughty man should use all his strength to conquer all sins and flee vices as things more terrible and abominable than any monster whatsoever, and especially carnal delectation, which transforms the mad men who dally too intently with it into stones. (402-404)

Landino's comment is essentially similar: the Gorgons are "the allurements of passion," by which "the foolish are said to be turned into stone," while "on the other hand, the prudent easily make an end of such pleasures with Pallas's shield and Mercury's sword" (*Disputationes Camuldenses*: 235-236). Tritonio includes Medusa in his list of the "libidinous" (*Mythologia*: 28). For Reynolds, she is an example of the punishment of "Contempt of the gods" (*Mythomystes*: 169). Peele assures us that the Gorgons are "wealth and beauty," which "turn men to stones" (*Arraignment of Paris*: 280; see also Batman, *Golden Booke*: 21r; and Ross, *Mystagogus Poeticus*: 140).

Fraunce repeats the two stories about how Medusa came by her snaky hair, and then gets down to his own version of the moral allegory:

Some, by the three Gorgons, note the three faculties of the soule in man: Medusa, of the three sisters, was only mortall, figuring the sensible and living power, common to beasts, beheaded by Perseus, that is, kept under by the good Genius or celestial grace. The second was Stheno, the reasonable facultie of the soule, the third Euryale, the light infused and intellectuall part. They turne the beholders into stones: for we must kill Medusa, all perturbations, and be in that respect, as dead as stones, else we cannot enjoy this intellectuall light....Others understand the earth and earthly affections by Gorgon, dashed and daunted by Perseus borne of Jove, that is, assisted by his heavenly helpe and influence. (*Countesse of Pembrokes Yvychurch*: 29r)

There was another Gorgon, too, one of Homer's monsters. He is mentioned by Lucan (*Civil War*: 6.744). During the Renaissance this monster was sometimes conflated with Demogorgon.

For more Gorgon allegory, see **PERSEUS**; for the winged horse born of the blood of the Gorgons, see **PEGASUS**.

Bibliography: Judith Suther, "The Gorgon Medusa," in Malcolm South, *Mythical Creatures and Fabulous Beasts: A Source Book and Research Guide* (1987).

THE GRACES (Charites). After Hesiod there were generally said to be three Graces, the three sisters "Aglaea, and Euphrosyne, and lovely Thaleia" (*Theogony*: 907). Seneca was the most important classical source. He tells us,

Why the Graces are three in number and why they are sisters, why they have their hands interlocked...and why they are clad in loose and transparent garb. Some would have it appear that there is one for bestowing a benefit, another for receiving it, and a third for returning it....Why do the sisters hand in hand dance in a ring which returns upon itself? For the reason that a benefit passing in its course from hand to hand returns nevertheless to the giver...and it is fitting that there should be nothing to bind or restrict them, and so the maidens wear flowing robes, and these, too, are transparent because benefits desire to be seen. (*De Beneficiis*: 1.3)

For Seneca there is thus a triple rhythm of generosity: giving, accepting, and returning.

Those who represented the Graces as nudes—as Cossa does in his *Venus and Her Children* (fig. 26)—were following Servius, who wrote that the Graces "are nude because Graces must be free of deceit," and that "one is depicted from the back, and two face us for this reason, that for every kindness issuing from us, two return" (*In Virgilii Aeneidos*: 1.720). Fulgentius (*Mythologies*: 2.1) repeats both parts of Servius's allegory. One of E. K.'s glosses on Spenser's *Shepherd's Calender* combines Seneca and Servius:

The Graces be three sisters, the daughters of Jupiter....Whom the Poets feyned to be the Goddesses of al bountie and comelines, which therefore...they make three, to wete, that men first ought to be gracious and bountiful to other freely, then to receive benefits at other mens hands curteously, and thirdly to requite them thankfully: which are three sundry Actions in liberalitye. And Boccace saith, that they be painted naked...the one having her backe toward us...as proceeding from us: the other two toward us, noting double thanke to be due to us for the benefit we have done. (*Shepheardes Calender*, E. K. on April, 109 [E. K.'s glosses appear in the original and in all subsequent editions of Spenser's poem]; see also Batman, *Golden Booke*: 18r)

And there were other meanings for the Graces. In his commentary on Dante's *Inferno* (2.49-126), for example, Landino interprets Mary, Lucy, and Beatrice as types for the Three Graces, and the Three Graces as allegorical figures for the three aspects of divine grace, as Augustine defined them. But we are not to disregard the poets, says Landino, for the poets have also written about three aspects of grace, or the Three Graces:

Hesiod in his *Theogony* writes that there are three Graces....They are Jove's daughters, which means all graces come only from God....Their names are Aglaia, Euphrosyne, Thalia. In Greek *aglaos* signifies brilliance, and surely it is God's grace alone that illuminates our dark spirit; *Euphrosine* means happiness, and grace is the sole source of our happiness; *Thalia* means verdant and flourishing, and truly heavenly grace makes verdant our souls, and makes them flourish....Two of the Graces turn toward the first; and indeed, souls must look to the brilliance of God's grace for joy and health. (*La Commedia*: 20v)

In another tradition the Three Graces had to do not with Senecan-Stoic liberality, but with love. And thus they were sometimes daughters not of Jupiter (as in Hesiod), but of Venus. The *Chess of Love* commentary suggests this, for example, and so the Three Graces can be "the three guilts or three vices"—or more commonly three "degrees" of love:

The first degree lies in looking at and seeing the beloved. For by looking is love begun and the eye primarily chooses the beloved. The second degree is in getting better acquainted with the beloved by sweet talks and beautiful words and prayers. And the third degree is in touching the beloved and in using her all according to one's will, as one should desire in good love, perfect and loyal....
    That the two young damsels were looking at the first, and she did not look at them, but turned her back to them, signifies to us that these first two degrees of love tend toward the third...and it is commonly the end of all their intent and they are simply ordained for it. (351-352)

This would seem to be an elaboration upon Bernardus (*On Martianus Capella*: 3.869-870). Conti also associates the Graces with love, and more specifically, with procreation and with fruitfulness in general (*Mythologie*: 4.15).
    They could also exemplify love's perversion: Homer (*Odyssey*: 8.364) says that the Graces comforted Venus after Vulcan publicly revealed her unfaithfulness

(see **MARS**). Jonson understood this comfort to be sexual; the Graces were thus "Tribade," or Lesbian—and thus the episode was an instance of Venus's easy virtue ("The Forrest": 10).

But the Graces are nowhere more important than they are to the Neo-Platonists, for whom Seneca's description of the dance of the Graces takes on new meaning. The dance embodied the Neo-Platonic law of procession, rapture, and return. For example, Christian Neo-Platonists delighted to find indications of the trinity—or of relatable triune configurations—in the Platonic opus and in nature (see, e.g., Pico, *Conclusiones*: 23-26). Thus it was that Ficino glossed the Graces as the divine trinity, Jupiter-Apollo-Venus (*Opera Omnia*: 536; see Allen 1984). Ficino says even of the eye, ear, and mind, "these are those three Graces" of whom Orpheus sang, for they allow us to appreciate beauty: the mind perceives the beauty of the soul, the eye senses physical beauty, and the ear "that pure, powerful, and perpetual pleasure which we experience in musical melody" (*On Plato's Symposium*: 5.2).

Wind (1968: 113-127) argues that the dance of the Graces in Botticelli's *Primavera* (fig. 13) represents just such a triad, where Chastity (the central Grace) is turned toward Voluptuousness (on the left) by Beauty. Cupid, Love, provides the impetus—and Mercury is there as the "leader of the Graces" (for other interpretations of Botticelli's Graces, see Seznec 1961: 207-209; Lightbown 1989: 127-136).

Pico and Ficino sometimes made the Graces allegorical figures for various astrological groupings: Neptune, Jupiter, and Pluto; or Mercury, Sol, and Venus, for example (Gombrich 1993: 56-58).

Bibliography: Michael J. B. Allen, "Marsilio Ficino on Plato, the Neoplatonists and the Christian Doctrine of the Trinity," *RQ*, 37 (1984): 555-584; E. H. Gombrich, *Symbolic Images* (1993); A. C. Hamilton, *The Spenser Encyclopedia* (1990): under *Graces*; Ronald Lightbown, *Botticelli: Life and Work* (1989); Erwin Panofsky, *Renaissance and Renascences in Western Art* (1972): 193-197; Jean Seznec, *The Survival of the Pagan Gods* (1961); DeWitt Starnes and E. W. Talbert, *Classical Myth and Legend in Renaissance Dictionaries* (1955): 88-93; 258-259; Edgar Wind, *Pagan Mysteries of the Renaissance* (1968).

H

HAEMUS AND RHODOPE were brother and sister, and incestuous lovers. So audacious was their love that they dared call one another Juno and Jupiter, and so they were punished by being transformed into mountains. Haemus and Rhodope could thus serve as examples of presumption. Ovid's Athena, for example, weaves their story into her tapestry in order to instruct proud Arachne as to the consequences of presumption (*Metamorphoses*: 6.87). Berchorius commented that "They should be changed into mountains because they can be called inflated and swollen" in their pride (*Ovidius Moralizatus*: 250). And here is Sandys' gloss on the story: "Pallas, to shew her rival Arachne what she was to expect for her presumption...delineates Haemus and Rhodope, both begotten of one father; and in love with each other: insomuch that Haemus called his sister Juno, and Rhodope her brother Jupiter: for which praesumption, they were fained to be by the angry Gods converted into these Thracian mountaines" (*Ovid*: 287).

THE HARPIES. Hesiod (*Theogony*: 265-269) tells us that there were two Harpies, Aello and Ocypetes, daughters of Thaumus and Electra (Electra the daughter of Oceanus and Tethys, not Electra, daughter of Agamemnon and Clytemnestra). Their names—"Storm-swift" and "Swift-flier"—associated them with the gods of the winds, especially Boreas (e.g., Fraunce, *Countesse of Pembrokes Yvychurch*: 28v; Ross, *Mystagogus Poeticus*: 48); and because their mother Electra was the daughter of Oceanus, the Harpies were also often attendant upon Neptune (e.g., the *Chess of Love* commentary, 446-447; Viana, *Ovid*: 7.2). Later tradition usually made the Harpies three. Bernardus's description would have been widely acceptable: "the three Harpies are maidens who are covered with feathers of birds, have sharp claws, and feel hunger in their bellies; the first is Aello, the second Ochiroe, the third Celaeno." Bernardus goes on to tell the story of the Harpies plaguing the avaricious Phineus (for the Harpies as devils in punishing Phineus, and for Jason as a type of Christ in setting Phineus free from these afflictions, see **PHINEUS**); Bernardus concludes that the Harpies are figures for greed: "*Arpia* in Greek is...'greed'" (*On Virgil's Aeneid*: 6.289; see also Viana, *Ovid*: 7.2; Peacham, *Minerva Britanna*: 115). Dante perches Harpies in the trees of the suicides in the *Inferno* (13.10-15). Sandys calls the Harpies "the dogges of Jupiter: the ministers of his wrath upon the covetous, who are ever their owne tormentors" (*Ovid*: 331; see also the *Chess of Love* commentary, 447; Fraunce, *Countesse of Pembrokes Yvychurch*: 28v). Shakespeare seems to have this kind of allegory in mind at the end of the fourth act of *The Tempest*, when Prospero calls up spirits to punish Stephano, Trinculo, and Caliban. The stage direction reads: "A noise of hunters heard. Enter divers spirits, in shape of dogs and hounds, hunting them about; Prospero and Ariel setting them on." (This scene recreates the Harpies' stripping of the Trojans' tables in Virgil's *Aeneid*: 3.225-228; see also Milton, *Paradise Regained*: 2.401-405).

Because they were sometimes interpreted in this way, as ministers of divine punishment, they were sometimes conflated with the Furies. Thus it is that Lynche describes first the Furies and then the Harpies: "Poets have also in some sort annexed unto these furies, as partaking something of their natures, those monsters which are called Harpiae, for that the Ancients beleeved, that these also were employed by the gods in punishing the sinnes of mortall men" (*Fountaine of Ancient Fiction*: Piii; see also, e.g., Ross, *Mystagogus Poeticus*: 48).

The Harpies also appeared fairly frequently in Italian Renaissance paintings: Filippino Lippi's *Virgin with Saints* (1498) and *St. Sebastian* (1503), for example. In such paintings the Harpies seem to represent the paganism that Christianity superseded (Wittkower 1963: 291).

During the Middle Ages, harpies were sometimes assumed to exist as a real species of bird. De Mézières, for example, claimed knowledge of a Harpy: "in the desert of India...near the sea, there exists a great bird called the harpy, cruel beyond belief, which has the face of a man and is a bird of prey. This cruel bird kills at the sight of the first man it meets." For de Mézières, "speaking figuratively," the bird is a warning against the cruelty of war (*Letter to King Richard II*: sub. 5).

Bibliography: Don C. Allen, *Mysteriously Meant* (1970): 150, 154, 220; Anthony DiMatteo, "'The Figure of this Harpy': Shakespeare and the Moralized Ovid," *NQ*, 38 (1991): 70-72; Beryl Rowland, "Harpies," in Malcolm South, *Mythical Creatures and Fabulous Beasts: A Source Book and Research Guide* (1987); Rudolf and Margot Wittkower, *Born under Saturn: The Character and Conduct of Artists* (1963).

HARPOCRATES. There was among the Egyptians a child god, Horus, who was represented with his finger in his mouth, to suggest his childish nature. The Greeks and Romans misunderstood this; they saw a finger *at* the mouth, and so was born the Greco-Roman god of silence, Harpocrates. As the ancients came to interest themselves in divine mysteries, Harpocrates achieved larger importance: He enjoined silence when mysteries were about to be expounded. We still find him exercising this function in Martianus (*Marriage of Philology and Mercury*: 90, 728). This tradition was alive even in the sixteenth and seventeenth century: Pictorius (*Apotheoseos*: 113), Ross (*Mystagogus Poeticus*: 146), and Sandys each mention it. Here is Sandys: "He who is here mentioned with his finger on his mouth [Ovid, *Metamorphoses*: 9.692] was called Harpocrates, the God of Silence: intimating how sacred mysteries were not to be divulged" (*Ovid*: 448). Pictorius, Ross, and Sandys also go on to retail the following slander from Augustine: "And since in every temple where Iris and Serapis were worshipped there was also an image which, with finger pressed on the lips, seemed to warn men to keep silence, Varro thinks that this signifies that it should be kept secret that they had been human" (*City of God*: 18.5).

Bibliography: Jean Seznec, *The Survival of the Pagan Gods* (1961): 294-296; Edgar Wind, *Pagan Mysteries of the Renaissance* (1968): 12.

HEBE (Dia, Ganymeda). Hebe was the daughter of Jupiter and Juno, sister of Mars (Hesiod, *Theogony*: 923). She was also a cupbearer for the gods—until, as one late tradition had it, she tripped and fell while making her rounds. In falling she exposed her private parts to general view, and the gods were so offended by this that Ganymede was brought up to take her place.

The Romans in particular associated her with *Iuventus*, or youthful vigor. She was thus thought of as a goddess of youthful beauty—and so seventeenth- and eighteenth-century painters often depicted their young female subjects as Hebe (Reid 1993: 490-491). And she was associated with the spring. Here, for example, is Ross: "Hebe was wont to be painted in the form of a child, clothed with a rich garment of divers colours, & wearing garlands of flowers in her head: By this they represented the nature of the Spring, which is the infancy & beauty of the year, clothed with party-coloured fields and meadows, & graced with delightful and fragrant flowers" (*Mystagogus Poeticus*: 150). Since she was thus a personification of spring, her fall could be understood as a figure for the coming of autumn. Reynolds, for example, writes that one of the "obviouser kinde of truths in Nature" was

Hebe's stumbling and falling with the Nectar-bowle in her hand, and thereby discovering her hidden parts to the gods, as she served them at their boord, meaning the nakednesse of the trees and plants in Autumne, when all their leaves are falne from them by the downefall or departure of the Spring, which their Hebe (or goddesse of youth, as the Aunciensts called her, because the Spring renewes and makes young all things) meanes. (*Mythomystes*: 170-171)

And since she was associated with spring, she was also associated with fertility. Thus it was that Hebe was one of the gods Spenser invoked in his prayer for children at the end of the "Epithalamion" (405).

As early as Homer (*Odyssey*: 11.609) Hebe was said to have been Hercules' wife (see **HERCULES: Apotheosis and Marriage to Hebe**), Hercules being wedded to her after his apotheosis. This was the sign, as it were, and the source of his immortality. Sandys: "This Hebe was held for the Goddesse of youth, her name importing as much; and to have beene married unto Hercules in Heaven,...signifying how strength and youth are to concurre in those, who are quallified for noble achievements" (*Ovid*: 443).

Hebe was occasionally interpreted in moral-allegorical terms, as, for example, here in Ross:

Hebe fell in her younger years, and when she was at a feast; youth and feasting are dangerous temptations, and occasions for falling: young peoples feet are slippery; youth is more apt to fall then old age....If Jupiter did not spare his own daughter which he had of Juno, but thrust her out of her office, and drove her from his presense when she fell; then let not the children of God think, that they are more privilidged from punishment when they fall. (*Mystagogus Poeticus*: 150-151)

In late classical times, Juno was said to have conceived Hebe without benefit of a father (e.g., Ovid, *Metamorphoses*: 9.416). I cannot resist mentioning that this was sometimes said to have been managed, as Ross put it, "only by eating of Lettice....Juno conceived not, till she had eat of the Lettice; by this perhaps, did they intimate, that Lettice accidently is the cause of fecundity; for...Lettice, or the seede thereof is good against the Gonorrhea, and also for nocturnal pollution in sleep, which are hinderances to procreation" (*Mystagogus Poeticus*: 151; see also Stephanus, *Dictionarium*: under *Hebe*).

Bibliography: Jane Davidson Reid, *The Oxford Guide to Classical Mythology in the Arts, 1300-1990s* (1993).

HECATE was a goddess with wide-ranging powers in ancient times. She could grant victory in war, athletics, and eloquent debate; she was sometimes regarded as the instrument or conduit of other gods' powers; she conferred the power of increase on flocks of cattle and sheep (see Hesiod, *Theogony*: 411-452; Spenser, *Faerie Queene*: 7.3.6). She was a protectress of youth, and thus associated in particular with Artemis and Apollo. She came also to be associated—sometimes conflated—with Proserpina. As Servius wrote, "Hecate possesses the powers of three deities, Luna, Diana, and Proserpina" (*In Virgilii Aeneidos*: 6.118). Thus she was often represented as a goddess in three persons or with three heads. But she came more and more to be linked with magic, sorcery, and witchcraft; and so she figured in the stories of Medea and Circe.

Virgil made Hecate a guide in the underworld: "Hecate...taught me the gods' penalties," says Tisiphone in Hades, "and guided me through all" (*Aeneid*: 6.564-565). Bernardus, along with most other Medieval and Renaissance readers of Virgil, interpreted Aeneas' journey through the underworld as a descent for wisdom (for the allegory of descents, see **EPIC CONVENTIONS: The descent**), and so he comments on Hecate as follows:

Hecate is the goddess having a hundred powers; people say she is the moon which has infinite effects [i.e., because the moon changes]. Here we interpret her to be divine wisdom, which is called Hecate, that is, a hundred powers since she contains in herself ideas of infinite things. Hecate controls understanding in the lower world, since wisdom subsumes understanding in temporal matters because wisdom knows them perfectly, and wisdom by knowing the divine transcends understanding. By the testimony of Boethius, understanding grasps all those inferior powers of the soul [*Consolation of Philosophy*: 5.pr 4]. There are four powers of the soul, and the superior knows all the inferior, but the reverse does not hold. (*On Virgil's Aeneid*: 6.118)

But the association with underworld-sorcery was more common among Christian allegorists. Spenser's evil sorcerer Archimago, for example, creates his phantasm-temptress with the aid of Hecate (*Faerie Queene*: 1.1.43-44). And Shakespeare has Macbeth's three witches subject to Hecate (3.5; see also 2.1.54).

HECTOR was the eldest son of Priam. He was renowned as the bravest, the most honorable of the Trojans. According to Homer, Hector and his fellow Trojan Polydamas were born on the same night; Hector became the greatest in battle, Polydamas the wisest in counsel (*Iliad*: 12.210-229; 18. 249-283). Between them, then, they possessed the qualities necessary in a great leader (Curtius 1963: 171; Nohrnberg 1976: 62-63). During the late Middle Ages and the Renaissance Hector was frequently depicted in tapestries, on castle walls, in stone carvings, and in carved fireplaces as one of the Nine Worthies, the most honorable men of the ages (McKendrick 1991: 78-79). Pageants of the Nine Worthies were frequently mounted as popular entertainments at Christmas and other festive seasons. Shakespeare parodies these in *Love's Labour's Lost* (5.1-2); Furness's *Variorum* edition of the play includes an example of a Nine Worthies pageant. Furness also briefly describes other Nine Worthies pageants, from the fifteenth to the seventeenth centuries (282-284; for more on the Nine Worthies, see Hölgen 1959, Kellogg 1990). The list of the Worthies usually included three Jews (Joshua, David, and Judas Maccabeus), three Christians (King Arthur, Charlemagne, and Godfrey of Bouillon), and three pagans (Hector, Alexander the Great, and Julius Caesar). The list did vary—Shakespeare, for example, put Pompey and Hercules on the list—but Hector was always included.

Hector was thus an example of the honorable man—Christine de Pizan writes of Hector as the ideal knight, for example (*L'Epitre*: 1, 88, 90-93). But Hector's honor was sometimes thought of as limited, as honor in the eyes of the world merely (see **FAME, LUCRETIA**); Shakespeare seems to make Hector an example in this way of the limitations of honor in *Troilus and Cressida* (Lynch 1987); this is perhaps clearest in 2.2, where Hector first explains why Helen ought to be sent back to the Greeks—and then concludes in this way:

> yet ne'er the less,
> My spritely brethren, I propend to you
> In resolution to keep Helen still,
> For 'tis a cause that hath no mean dependance
> Upon our joint and several dignities.
>   (2.2.189-193)

Hector decides to ignore morality in favor of honor; the result, of course, was the destruction of Troy.

Hector's wife Andromache, daughter of the Theban king Eëtion, was known as a paragon of loyalty and wifely virtue, as for example, in the *Ovide Moralisé* (13.3060-3088).

Bibliography: Ernst R. Curtius, *European Literature and the Latin Middle Ages* (1963); H. H. Furness, ed., *A New Variorum Edition of...Love's Labour's Lost* (1932); K. J. Hölgen, "Die 'Nine Worthies,'" *Anglia*, 77 (1959): 279-309; Judith Kellogg, "Christine de Pizan as Chivalric Mythographer," in Jane Chance, *The Mythographic Art* (1990): 100-124; Stephen J. Lynch, "Hector and the Theme of Honor in *Troilus and Cressida*," *UCrow*, 7 (1987): 68-79; Scot McKendrick, "*The Great History of Troy*: a Reassessment of the Development of a Secular Theme in Late Medieval Art," *JWCI*, 54 (1991): 43-82; James Nohrnberg, *The Analogy of The Faerie Queene* (1976).

HECUBA was queen of Troy at the time of the Trojan War. She was the mother of Troy's princes, Troy's greatest heroes, and so she watched her sons and her daughter die, and she watched her city burn. She was known, then, for the greatness of her grief. As Ovid told her harrowing story (*Metamorphoses*: 13.404-571), Hecuba sees her daughter Polyxena torn from her side to be sacrified on the funeral pyre of Achilles; and she sees the spear-torn body of her son Polydorus washed up on the beach. This transforms her, from a dignified and loving mother into a maddened beast: Barking like a dog, she tears out the eyes of Polymestor, the Thracian king who had killed her son, and throws herself into the sea. For Ovid she is thus an example of how our passions can transform us into something less than human. Dante mentions her as an example of transforming madness (*Inferno*: 30.16-21; see also, e.g., Guido da Pisa, *Super Comediam Dantis*: 617). Boccaccio wrote that Hecuba is "a true example of misery...a great illustration of how prosperity perishes" (*Concerning Famous Women*: 68; for a history of Hecuba in classical and early English poetry, see Schmitz 1990).

For another example of the bestializing effects of mourning, see **MELEAGER**; see also Appendix B, "Bestialization."

Bibliography: Götz Schmitz, *The Fall of Women in Early English Narrative Verse* (1990).

HELEN was the famously beautiful daughter of Leda and Jupiter. She was the wife of the Greek king Menelaus, but she was stolen away by the Trojan prince Paris, and so became the occasion for the Trojan war. Homer's treatment of Helen is ambivalent: Paris is called "Evil" and "woman crazy" for taking her (*Iliad*: 3.39); but King Priam accepts Helen, blaming the gods rather than her (3.161-170). Helen herself despises Paris for his weakness as a warrior—but still she goes off to be with Paris while other warriors carry on the battle (3.421-448). But Medieval and Renaissance Christians tended simply to regard Helen as culpable. She was thus "the adulteress [who] shatters both worlds with grief," nothing less than a "seedbed of scandal and strife" (Fulgentius, *Mythologies*: 2.13). Petrarch called her "bane of earth and source of woes / past count" (*Africa*: 6.79-80; for a brief history of her unsavory reputation, see Schmitz 1990: 60-66). She could thus serve as a warning as to the terrible consequences that could ensue from unbridled passions. Here is Boccaccio:

Helen was known to the entire world as much for her lustfulness as for the long war which resulted from it....All Greece was aroused by Helen's wantonness....Paris having been slain...Helen entered into wedlock again and married [Paris's brother] Deiphobus, as if...she had not sinned sufficiently the first time.

Finally, as an attempt was being made to achieve with treachery what it did not seem possible to do with arms, Helen, who had been in charge of the seige, strove as best she could against the Trojans in order to help in their destruction and to return into the good graces of her first husband. (*Concerning Famous Women*: 35)

Conti (*Mythologie*: 6.23) writes that in choosing Helen, Paris is choosing lust. Ross minces no words; her beauty was only outward,

for she had a deform'd soul, playing the strumpet, not only in her younger years with Theseus...but also being married to Menelaus, forsook him, and became a whore to Paris; and not content with him, committed incest with Gorythus, the son of Paris and Oenone; afterward betrayed the city of Troy to the Grecians, and treacherously caused her husband Deiphobus to be murdered in his bed by Menelaus....Thus we see, that outward beauty of the body, without the inward graces of the mind, is but a gold ring in a Swines snout. (*Mystagogus Poeticus*: 161)

This tradition provides the moral coordinates for understanding, for example, Spenser's *Hellen*ore and *Pari*dell (*Faerie Queene*: 3.9); and it explains the venom of Shakespeare's Diomedes as he addresses Paris:

You like a lecher out of whorish loins
Are pleas'd to breed out your inheritors.
    ...Hear me, Paris:
For every false drop in her bawdy veins
A Grecian's life hath sunk; for every scruple
Of her contaminated carrion weight,
A Troyan hath been slain.
                (*Troilus and Cressida*: 4.1.64-73)

For the judgment of Paris, whereby he won Helen as Venus's gift, see **PARIS**; for more on the consequences of his dalliance with Helen, see **TROY**.

Bibliography: Robert Lamberton, *Homer the Theologian* (1989): 199-200; James Nohrnberg, *The Analogy of The Faerie Queene* (1976): 114-119, 257-260, 572-574; Götz Schmitz, *The Fall of Women in Early English Narrative Verse* (1990); Mihoko Suzuki, *Metamorphoses of Helen* (1989).

HERCULES (Alcaeus, Alcides, Amphitryonid, Heracles, the Oetean, the Tirynthian). The stories of Hercules' exploits are among the oldest and most numerous in Greco-Roman mythology. He was the son of Jupiter by Alcmene, and so he often suffered from jealous Juno's enmity. Indeed, most of his heroic feats were trials imposed upon him by Juno; thus his name, *Heracles*, "renowned through Hera" (this etymology was well known; see, e.g., Sandys, *Ovid*: 424). He was usually pictured wearing the skin of the Nemean Lion and carrying a club. At the end of his difficult life, Hercules threw himself onto a funeral pyre at the top of Mt. Oeta, and Jupiter took him up into the heavens, married him to Hebe (the goddess of eternal youth), and made him one of the gods. What follows is an account of those Hercules stories which received the most attention during the Middle Ages and the Renaissance (see, e.g., LeFèvre, "Le prouesses et vaillances du preux Hercules," the last 6 chapters of book 1 and book 2 of *Le recueil des hystoires de Troyes*).

The Serpents in the Cradle
Sandys tells the story and provides a typical explanation:

Juno is said to have sent two serpents to destroy him in his cradle; who strangled them both before he was so old as to know them....By which they would have us to know, that those who are markt for great actions, and are covetous of a virtuous prayse; should betimes...exercise their fortitude in subduing of pleasures; which infeeble the mind, and destroy it with serpentine embracements. Nor is pleasure and lust unaptly expressed by serpents; not onely for their naturall subtilty and inveterate hatred to man; but also for their inbred lasciviousnes. (*Ovid*: 424)

(When Sandys speaks of the serpent's "naturall subtilty and inveterate hatred to man," he is of course remembering the serpent in Eden, Gen. 3.) Fraunce had earlier explained the allegory more succinctly: "In his infancie he strangled two snakes; the meaning is, that he began even then to represse wantonnes" (*Countesse of Pembrokes Yvychurch*: 46v). And for Ross, Hercules slew the serpents of "malice and envy" (*Mystagogus Poeticus*: 168).

Hercules at the Crossroads
Early in his life, Hercules once found himself at a crossroads, where he had to choose either the road of pleasure or the perilous road of self-sacrifice and virtue. A painted woman, Vice, urges him to take the easy way; another woman, Virtue,

frankly explains the difficulties and the glory that lie along the way she advises. Hercules chooses the way of Virtue. The first author of the story—and so the author of the first personification allegory in the West—seems to have been the fifth-century B.C. Sophist Prodicus (Whitman 1987: 22). The story was not entirely unknown to the Middle Ages; Peter of Blois refers to the story in a mid-twelfth century poem about the conflict between reason and love (Dronke 1984: 298-299). But during the Renaissance, Hercules at the crossroads became one of the best-known Hercules stories. It was very often represented in paintings during the Renaissance (see Panofsky 1930; Reid 1993: 527-529 lists thirty such depictions from 1500 to 1650). Whitney provides a typical version of the story and a typical interpretation:

> When Hercules, was dowtfull of his waie,
> Inclosed rounde, with vertue, and with vice:
> With reasons firste, did vertue him assaie,
> The other, did with pleasures him entice...
> Till at the lengthe, Alcides thus begonne
>
> Oh pleasure, thoughe thie waie bee smoothe, and faire...
> Yet can I heare, of none that have bene there,
> That after life, with fame have been renoum'de:
> For honor hates, with pleasure to remaine,
> Then houlde thy peace, thow wastes thie winde in vaine.
>
> But heare, I yeelde oh vertue to thie will,
> And vowe my selfe, all labour to indure,
> For to ascend the steepe, and craggie hill,
> The toppe whereof, whoe so attaines, is sure
> For his rewarde, to have a crowne of fame.
>   (*Emblemes*: 40)

Whitney writes that fame was Hercules' motive, but Hercules was not seen as self-seeking in this. As Brant wrote, it was virtue that motivated Hercules: He avoided the woman who promised "lust and vice," while the woman pointing to the difficult way warned Hercules:

> She said: "No joy I promise you,
> No rest, and labors not a few,
> On virtue you will virtue heap
> And recompense eternal keep.
>   (*Ship of Fools*: 107)

In *The Pilgrim's Progress* (74) Bunyan has the pilgrim Christian face such a choice. And in *The Merchant of Venice* Bassanio's choice of the lead casket is just such a choice as Hercules had made before him. "I stand for sacrifice," says Portia to Bassanio as he surveys the caskets: "Go, Hercules" (3.2.57-60). Wither makes Hercules an emblem for this motto: "When Vice and Vertue youth shall wooe, / Tis hard to say, which way 'twill goe": the emblem shows Hercules rejecting a masked temptress in favor of a robed and bearded man who offers the book of wisdom (*Emblemes*: 22). We find Hercules as an allegorical figure for philosophical wisdom as early as Heraclitus (*Allégories d'Homère*: 34.7).

We are to understand, then, that all of Hercules' difficult trials followed upon this choice.

The Twelve Labors

Juno managed things in such a way that Hercules was bound to perform certain labors imposed upon him by Eurystheus, king of Mycenae. The number was set at twelve as early as the fifth century B.C., with only occasional variations. The twelve labors were sometimes interpreted in terms of the twelve zodiacal signs (Norhnberg 1976: 396-402). Erasmus provides a more common, explicitly Christian interpretation of Hercules' labors: "if the labors of Hercules show you that you achieve heaven by honest effort and tireless industry—are you not learning by means of fable the precepts offered by philosophers and divines as authorities on how to live?" (*Enchiridion*: 106).

Here follows the most commonly agreed-upon list of the Twelve Labors.

FIRST LABOR
The Slaying of the Nemean Lion

The Nemean Lion had an impenetrable hide, and it lived in a cave with two entrances. The lion was thus thought to be invulnerable. Hercules blocked up one of the entrances and then went into the cave and strangled the lion. He then clothed himself in the lion's skin. For Fraunce, the lion represents "wrath, pride, and crueltie" (*Countesse of Pembrokes Yvychurch*: 46v); and Ross writes that Hercules' struggle with the Nemean Lion is an allegory of the Christian's struggle against "the Lion of anger" (*Mystagogus Poeticus*: 168). We find much the same in Salutati (*De Laboribus Herculis*: 3.8.9-10), Berchorius (*Ovidius Moralizatus*: 330), and Ripa (*Iconologie*: 1.168).

SECOND LABOR
The Hydra

The Hydra was a nine-headed swamp monster—and one of the heads was immortal. Every time Hercules cut off one of the Hydra's heads, two new ones would grow up in its place. Eventually Hercules seared each bloody stump in turn with a torch, and then he dealt with the immortal head by weighing it to the ground with a great boulder. The Hydra was a useful creature for Christian allegorists. Its many heads seemed to suggest something quintessential about sin. See **HYDRA**.

THIRD LABOR
The Erymanthian Boar

Hercules was to bring back this giant boar alive. He tired the creature out by chasing it out into a snowfield, and then running it to exhaustion. Salutati interpreted Hercules here as "perfect heroic virtue opposing bestiality" (*De Laboribus Herculis*: 3.18.6; see Appendix B, "Bestialization"). For Ross this boar was "the Boar of Wantonness" (*Mystagogus Poeticus*: 168).

FOURTH LABOR
The Ceryneian Hind

With its golden horns and its brazen hooves, this animal, too, was to be brought back alive. Hercules finally managed this by wounding the hind in the neck after a long chase. Fraunce writes that by overcoming "the mighty Hart, he freed mens hearts from feare" (*Countesse of Pembrokes Yvychurch*: 46v).

FIFTH LABOR
The Birds of Lake Stymphalus

These birds were sometimes said to have been man-eaters, with brass claws and beaks and with feathers that could be shot as projectiles. The birds were protected, too, by the dense thicket in which they lived. Hercules managed to drive them out of this thicket with a brass rattle, and then he killed them with his arrows. Salutati (*De Laboribus Herculis*: 3.13.3) followed Boccaccio (*Genealogie Deorum*: 13.1) in conflating these nasty birds with the Harpies. Salutati goes on to explain that the birds are figures for those "delectations which excite the affections without rational moderation." Hercules, the virtuous man, kills the birds with his arrows, the "acumen of reason" (3.13.9).

SIXTH LABOR
The Girdle of Hippolyta

Hercules was sent to capture the girdle of Hippolyta (also known as Antiope), the queen of the Amazons. This he managed only after killing the queen in the course of a fierce battle with the whole army of the Amazons. Salutati (*De Laboribus Herculis*: 3.35) provides an extended version of the traditional interpretation: the Amazons in general and Antiope in particular, represent the libidinous passions; in overcoming them, Hercules represents the virtuous man's rational control of these passions. (For what it might mean to conquer Amazons, see **AMAZONS**.)

SEVENTH LABOR
The Augean Stables

Augeas, king of Elis, possessed a huge herd of cattle. Hercules was required to clean the stable of all its dung in a day. This he accomplished by the simple expedient of turning the course of the river Alpheus through the stable. As Erasmus wrote, the Augean stables became a "proverbial allegory, used of a person or thing that is filthy beyond measure" (*Adages*: 2.4.21).

EIGHTH LABOR
The Cretan Bull
Accounts vary as to the origin of this bull; but all agree that it was terrible in its ravages upon the island of Crete. Hercules was to bring the bull to Mycenae, alive. He subdued the bull so completely that he was able to ride across the sea on its back. He then hoisted the bull to his shoulders and carried it to Mycenae, where he released it. The bull then continued its depredations in its new neighborhood until, finally, Theseus killed it.

NINTH LABOR
The Mares of Diomedes
Diomedes, the king of Thrace and a son of Mars, owned four mares that fed on human flesh. Diomedes delighted to feed to these horses the strangers who landed in his country. Hercules was to bring these horses back to Eurystheus. Hercules managed to do so only after killing Diomedes and a number of other Thracians. Apollodorus (*Library*: 2.5.8) and Boccaccio (*Genealogie Deorum*: 13.1), among others, tell the story.

Because he had killed so cruel a tyrant as Diomedes—and other cruel tyrants such as Busiris (a guest-killing king of Egypt) and Hippocoon (a Spartan usurper)—Hercules came to be thought of as a defender of justice, a champion against tyrants (e.g., Guido da Pisa, *Super Comediam Dantis*: 649). Spenser, for example, wrote that Artegall was like Bacchus and Hercules in this way:

> Such first was Bacchus, that with furious might
> All th'East before untam'd did overronne,
> And wrong repressed, and establisht right,
> Which lawlesse men had formerly fordonne.
> There Justice first her princely rule begonne.
> Next Hercules his like ensample shewed,
> Who all the West with equall conquest wonne,
> And monstrous tyrants with his club subdewed;
> The club of Justice dread, with kingly powre endued.
> (*Faerie Queene*: 5.1.2)

Spenser seems to be following Horace (*Odes*: 3.3) in seeing Bacchus and Hercules as putters-down of tyrants (Lotspeich 1932: 69). See also Berchorius (*Ovidius Moralizatus*: 333) and Sandys: "Hercules better deserved a Deity then all the rest of the Heroes: who conquered nothing for himself; who ranged all over the world, not to oppress it, but to free it from oppressors and by killing of Tyrants and Monsters preserved it in tranquility" (*Ovid*: 439).

TENTH LABOR
The Oxen of Geryon
Geryon was a winged giant with three bodies. He owned a huge herd of red oxen. Hercules' task was to bring this herd back to Mycenae. This meant a long

quest, for Geryon dwelt on an island in the far west. After many adventures Hercules reached this island and killed Geryon, the oxherd Eurytion, and his giant dog Orthrus. Hercules then had to herd the oxen all the way back to Mycenae, and this again involved him in many adventures. Hercules raised the pillars of Hercules (Gibraltar and, across the straits, the Rock of Ceuta) on this journey. Upon his return, Eurystheus sacrificed the red oxen to Juno. According to Bernardus, the monster has three bodies because "allegorically, Geryon signifies the man of vice who is urged on by three types of vice: latent, manifest, and habitual" (*On Virgil's Aeneid*: 6.289).

ELEVENTH LABOR
The Golden Apples of the Hesperides
Eurystheus directed Hercules to bring to him the golden apples of the Hesperides. These were apples Gaia had given to Juno as a wedding present when Juno married Jupiter. The apples grew on trees planted in the garden of the gods near Mount Atlas. To guard the apples, Juno placed in the garden a hundred-headed dragon and the Hesperides, nymphs and daughters of the Night (Hesiod, *Theogony*: 214). Hercules managed to bring these apples to Eurystheus only after many adventures—but after all this, Eurystheus knew not what to do with them. Hercules then presented the apples to Athena. For allegorical interpretations, see **THE HESPERIDES**.

TWELFTH LABOR
Descent to Hades for Cerberus
Hercules' task was to bring the great dog Cerberus up out of Hades. Along the way Hercules freed Theseus. (Theseus and his friend Pirithous had foolishly gone down to Hades to take Proserpina away to be a wife for Pirithous; Pluto made them prisoners for their pains.) Hercules won permission from Pluto to take Cerberus to the regions above, but only on condition that Hercules take Cerberus without using any weapons. And so Hercules restrained the dog with the strength of his arms alone. When Hercules returned to Mycenae with Cerberus, Eurystheus was so frightened that he hid himself in a great jar. Hercules then returned Cerberus to Hades.

This story was interpreted in several ways. Albricus wrote that Hercules controlling Cerberus shows that "reason and a virtuous spirit conquer cupidity and earthly sins" (*De Deorum*: 22). Bernardus comments at greater length, but in the same tradition:

Hercules descended to the underworld, but since he was a demigod, the return lay open to him, and he dragged the chained gatekeeper Cerberus with him. Hercules signifies the virtuous person....He descended to the underworld when by contemplation he came to temporal things, but since he was a demigod, rational and immortal in spirit, irrational and mortal in body, he returned from these things when he rose again to heavenly matters. (*On Virgil's Aeneid*: 6.392)

For Bernardus, Hercules—half man and half god—is thus an allegorical figure for the human condition: even virtuous human beings descend occasionally, as Hercules did, to things irrational and earthly. But just as Hercules finally relinquished Cerberus and "rose again to heavenly things," so it can be with us lesser human beings (more at **CERBERUS**).

A better-known allegorical interpretation had it that Hercules' descent into Hades was a type of Christ's Harrowing of Hell (e.g., Ross, *Mystagogus Poeticus*: 172, quoted below under **Hercules in General**). (Between his crucifixion and resurrection, Christ went down to hell, or limbo, in order to rescue forth the virtuous souls who had died before the crucifixion, according to a tradition that grew out of Ephesians 4:9 and I Peter 3:18; the complete story goes back to the fifth-century apocryphal Gospel of Nicodemus.) Here is Berchorius: "Or say that Cerberus signifies death which has three heads because it devours skin, flesh, and blood. It is said to be the gate-keeper of hell because through it a sinner is drawn to hell and kept there. Hercules—that is Christ—conquered this dog by rising" (*Ovidius Moralizatus*: 287-288; see also 118, 120; see also Boccaccio, *Eclogues*: 10.147-148).

Hercules Wrestles with Antaeus: see ANTAEUS.

Hercules and Cacus
Cacus, with his three heads and his breath of fire, was a son of Vulcan. While Hercules was driving back to Eurystheus the cattle he had stolen from Geryon (his tenth labor), Cacus stole eight of the beasts and hid them in his cave. He cleverly pulled them by their tails all the way, to make it seem that the tracks led away from the cave. Hercules managed to discover the cattle, kill Cacus, and lead the cattle out of the cave. The story was often interpreted as being a type of the struggle of good and evil (e.g., Fulgentius, *Mythologies*: 2.3; Albricus, *Allegoriae Poeticae*: 49v, *De Deorum*: 22; Salutati, *De Laboribus Herculis*: 3.30.5) or, more specifically, Christ's struggle with the devil for human souls. Berchorius's comment is rather more ingenious than most:

Cacus...stole the cattle of Hercules and Evander but led them into his cave backwards so he would not be detected and made a great amount of smoke so they could not be seen. Thus he fooled many men and concealed the stolen cattle. Hercules finally drew him out and killed him. The devil seems to be such a robber. After he has stolen cattle—that is the faithful of the church—from Hercules—that is Christ—he is accustomed to make them move backwards; for those who have been stolen and subjugated to the devil's rule do not know how to proceed along the way of morals but are accustomed to proceed backwards through oblique and perverse intention....Cacus—that is the devil—conceals them in the cave of snares and beclouds them with the smoke of pride and hypocrisy. So it is necessary that Hercules...bring them out. (*Ovidius Moralizatus*: 336; see also, e.g., Boccaccio, *Eclogues*: 11.206-208)

Salutati worked with the implications of Cacus's Vulcanic cave, where "darkness mixed with fire"; this is a figure for the "turbulent passions" (*De Laboribus Herculis*: 3.30.17).

The story could also be understood more specifically as a type of Christ's Harrowing of Hell (see *Twelfth Labor: Descent to Hades for Cerberus*).

Hercules Fighting the Pygmies: see PYGMIES.

Hercules in Love with Iole: see IOLE.

Hercules Frees Prometheus

Hercules' quest for the golden apples of the Hesperides was interrupted by several other adventures. Along the way, for example, he slew Antaeus and freed Prometheus. Bacon provides an interpretation of the freeing of Prometheus:

It is true greatness to have in one the frailty of a man, and the security of a God....This would have done better in poesy, where transcendences are more allowed. And the poets indeed have been busy with it; for it is in effect the thing which is figured in that strange fiction of the ancient poets, which seemeth not to be without mystery; nay, and to have some approach to the state of a Christian; that Hercules, when he went to unbind Prometheus (by whom human nature is represented) sailed the length of the great ocean in an earthen pot or pitcher; lively describing Christian resolution, that saileth in the frail bark of the flesh through the waves of the world. (*On Adversity*: 386)

Hercules in Love with Omphale

Omphale was a widowed queen of Lydia. According to one classical tradition, Hercules was forced to sell himself into servitude for three years in order to purify himself after coming into conflict with Apollo. It was Omphale who purchased him, and he spent three years ridding her kingdom of robbers and other pests. But in the version best known to Christians, Hercules—the "distaff Hercules"—subjected himself to Omphale for love. For Christians, Hercules' fawning love for Omphale was his best known lapse from virtue. The power of love was such that even Hercules could be subdued by love. Hercules thus could serve as an *exemplum* of the unreasonable lover. Fulgentius's commentary was typical of what was written about Hercules and Omphale all the way to the seventeenth century:

the virtue of Hercules fought hard in the battle against lust. For the allure of woman is greater than the world, because the greatness of the world cannot overcome him whom lust tightly held: it attacked through the evil of a woman his virtue which could not be secured by nature. For Hercules fell in love with Omphale, who persuaded him both to soften the delicate shrunken parts of fibers and to whirl the spindle round finely with his thumb....[H]e is conquered by lust....This shows that lust can conquer even virtue that is still unconquered. (*Mythologies*: 2.2; see also, e.g., Salutati, *De Laboribus Herculis*: 3.26)

The story was often represented in pictures, more than once, for example, by Cranach. Peacham's verses could serve as a description of, and gloss upon, Cranach's painting of *Hercules and Omphale* (1537):

Alcides heere, hath throwne his Clubbe away,
And weares a Mantle, for his Lions skinne,
Thus better liking for to passe the day,
With Omphale, and with her maides to spinne,
 To card, to reele, and do such daily taske,
 What ere it pleased, Omphale to aske.

That all his conquests wonne him not such Fame,
For which as God, the world did him adore,
As loves affection, did disgrace and shame
His virtues partes. How many are there more,
 Who having Honor, and a worthy name,
 By actions base, and lewdnes loose the same.
      (*Minerva Britanna*: 95)

And here is Sidney's comment on the story: "So in Hercules, painted with his great beard, and furious countenance, in a womans attyre, spinning, at Omphales commaundement, it breeds both delight and laughter: for the representing of so straunge a power in Love, procures delight, and the scornefulnesse of the action, stirreth laughter" (*Defense of Poesy*: 40). For essentially the same interpretation, see Tasso (*Jerusalem Delivered*: 16.3), Sidney (*Arcadia*: 1.12.2), Fraunce (*Countesse of Pembrokes Yvychurch*: 47r), Spenser (*Faerie Queene*: 5.8.2), and Nichols (1823, vol. 1: 462). Shakespeare is probably alluding to this tradition when he has Cleopatra fondly recall a time when she had "put her tires and mantle" on Antony, while she "wore his sword Philippan" (*Antony and Cleopatra*: 2.5.22-23; for another woman who dresses like a man, see **SEMIRAMIS**).

Hercules' Love for the Youth Hylas: see HYLAS.

Hercules and Deianira
 While Hercules was in Hades seeking Cerberus, he met the shade of a prince named Meleager. Meleager implored Hercules to marry and protect his sister Deianira when he returned to the upper world. This Hercules promised; but when he sought Deianira out, he found that the river god Achelous also wished to marry her. Hercules then fought Achelous for her hand. River gods, like sea gods (see **PROTEUS**), often had the power to change their shape; and so when Hercules pressed him, Achelous changed himself first into a serpent and then into a bull. Finally, Hercules defeated the bull/Achelous by pressing him to the ground and breaking off one of his horns. The Naiades took up the horn and made it flow with fruits and flowers; this was the origin of the Horn of Plenty.

The fight with Achelous was allegorized in several different ways, but usually the victory over Achelous was in some way a victory over vice or sin (see Lemmi 1933: 159-161). Here, for example, is Berchorius:

So the daughter of the King of Calydonia—that is the human soul, the daughter of the Father—had been linked to the horned Achelous—that is the devil—through sin and joined to him in marriage through sinful pleasures. The Son of God is called Hercules whose fortitude is like a rhinocerous'. Hercules conquered and subdued the one who at one time was a snake through deceit and at another a bull through wantonness. He broke his horn of power and thus freed the human soul from him and joined her to himself through grace. Psalm 74:11: "I will break the horns of sinners." (*Ovidius Moralizatus*: 323-324)

And Ross interprets Achelous as a warning: "They who turn themselves into wanton Bulls, and spend their horn, that is, their strength on women or wine, are at last choaked with melancholly, and hydropical humors" (*Mystagogus Poeticus*: 6). Sandys is a good deal more restrained than Berchorius or Ross, but he does associate Achelous in the form of the serpent with the serpents Hercules killed in his cradle—and these serpents figured forth "pleasure and lust" (*Ovid*: 424). Sandys goes on to interpret the story in terms of nature allegory, where Hercules controlling the river god is a figure for controlling the river, turning it to human purposes: "he restrained the river with bancks, extenuating his force by digging of sundry trenches, & draining those grounds which his overflowes had surrounded; whereby they became extraordinary fruitfull; which here is deciphered by the horne of Plenty" (*Ovid*: 425).

After defeating Achelous, Hercules departed with Deianira. Soon they came upon a river, where the centaur Nessus served as ferryman. In Ovid's version, Nessus urges Hercules to swim across and leave Deianira to cross in the boat. When Hercules is safely on the opposite shore, Nessus sets about to ravish Deianira. Hercules then shoots the centaur with an arrow poisoned with the blood of the Hydra. Ovid writes that Nessus, dying, muttered, "I shall not die unavenged," and so he gave his blood-soaked tunic to Deianira as a gift, assuring her that it was potent to revive waning love (*Metamorphoses*: 9.131-133). Later, when Hercules had taken Iole as his mistress, Deianira bethought herself of the shirt and gave it to Hercules, as she hoped, to win him back. The shirt burned his flesh terribly, and so Hercules threw himself onto a funeral pyre atop Mount Oeta.

In general, Christians did not look upon Deianira with favor. Theodulph (*Ecloga*) understands Hercules and Deianira as types of Samson and Delilah (Judges 16:4-18). The *Chess of Love* commentary interprets the story as a warning to women who practice magic. More commonly, Deianira was an *exemplum* of jealousy (e.g., Golding, "Epistle": 205) and Hercules here as a *de casibus* lover. Here, for example, is de Meun: "Hercules had many struggles: he conquered twelve horrible monsters, and when he had overcome the twelfth he could never finish with the thirteenth, his sweetheart Deïaneira, who, with her poisonous shirt, lacerated his flesh, all enflamed with the poison. His heart had already been made mad with love for Iole. Thus Hercules, who had so many virtues, was subdued by a woman" (*Romance of the Rose*: 9191-9202).

Apotheosis and Marriage to Hebe

Christians generally saw Hercules as being Christlike in his ascension and apotheosis—especially since Christ, too, was taken up into heaven from a mountaintop (Luke 24:51; Acts 1:9). This was, then, yet another way in which Hercules and Christ were associated—in this case as early as the second century (e.g., Justin Martyr, *Apologies*: 1.22). After Hercules' apotheosis, Jupiter married him to Hebe. Fraunce's comment was typical: "Hebe, they say, married Hercules; the fame of valyant and heroical personages, is ever florishing" (*Countesse of Pembrokes Yvychurch*: 33r). Boccaccio, too, had written of her in connection with "perpetual freshness," which is ever "associated with the deeds of famous men" (*Genealogie Deorum*: 9.2).

See also **HEBE**.

Hercules in General

In general Hercules was usually interpreted as an *exemplum* of the virtuous man: Juvenal contrasted "the sorrows and labours of Hercules" with all of "Sardanapalus' downy cushions and women and junketings" (*Satires*: 10; the reference is to Assurbanipal, the famously effeminate and luxury-loving king of Assyria, 668-631 B.C.); Boethius lists Hercules' Twelve Labors as examples of the virtuous struggle with fortune: "Indeed, virtue gets its name from that virile strength which is not overcome by adversity" (*Consolation of Philosophy*: 4.pr 7-mt 7; for the allegory of male virtue, see **AMAZONS**). Hercules' "Strength denotes virtue," wrote Bernardus, and his "beauty denotes glory" (*On Virgil's Aeneid*: 6.392). Guido da Pisa (*Super Comediam Dantis*: 646) explained the inimical relations between Juno and Hercules by interpreting Juno as the active life, in contrast with Hercules, the life devoted to contemplation and virtue. Mantegna, on the other hand, in the fresco ceiling for the *Camera degli Sposi*, juxtaposed images of Hercules with those of Orpheus and Arion, in order to suggest the proper balance of the active life figured by Hercules and the contemplative life figured by Orpheus and Arion (Welles 1990: 115). And in a Neo-Platonic engraving after Baccio Bandinelli, *The Fray of Cupid and Apollo* (fig. 1), we see Apollo, Diana, and Hercules (reclining with his signature club) opposing Bacchus and Venus: reason and temperance in opposition to license and the passions (see **APOLLO**). Hercules functions in much the same way on the title page (fig. 16) of Sandys' *Ovid's Metamorphosis, Englished, Mythologized, and Represented in Figures*. We see Venus and Cupid (in the middle, along the left margin) standing opposite Athena. To follow Athena, to restrain the desires figured forth by Venus and Cupid, is to soar aloft with Hercules. And so we see Hercules (again with his club) at the top of the picture, soaring off to heavenly glory. To follow Venus without restraint is to succumb to Circe, whom we see at the bottom of the picture, making beasts of Ulysses' men (for more on this title page, see **MINERVA, APOLLO**).

Shakespeare has this allegory in mind when he has Hercules forsake Antony on the eve of battle: Antony's *virtus* has succumbed to the charms of Cleopatra (*Antony and Cleopatra*: 4.3.16).

Hercules was often said to have been a pagan type of Christ (e.g., Guido da Pisa, *Super Comediam Dantis*: 652). Ross, for example, develops this type at some length:

Our blessed Saviour is the true Hercules, who was the true & only son of God..., who was persecuted out of malice [as Hercules was persecuted by Juno], and exposed to all dangers, which he overcame: he subdued the roaring Lion, that red Dragon, that tyrant and devourer of mankinde, the devil; he subdued the Hydra of sin, the Antaeus of earthly affections: he by his Word supported the world; Satan is that Cacus, that Sea-monster, from whom by Christ we are delivered; it is he only that went down to hell, and delivered us from thence, he alone travelled through the torid zone of his fathers wrath; he purged the Augean stable of Jewish superstition, and heathenish profanation...; who at last was burned, but not consumed by the fire of his Fathers wrath: who...was received up into glory, & exalted above the heavens. (*Mystagogus Poeticus*: 171-172)

Other Traditions

There was also a tradition of Hercules as a figure for eloquence or as an example of the eloquent man. Bernardus, for example, interprets the story of Hercules and Cerberus in this way: "Cerberus figures eloquence....Hercules drags out the chained Cerberus when he comprehends eloquence in precepts and other rules" (*On Virgil's Aeneid*: 6.392). And here is Fraunce: "Sometimes Hercules is paynted olde and balde, with his club, bow, and shafts, & smal chaynes or wyres drawen from his toung, to othermens eares: signifiying, that his sweete toung wrought more, then his strong body: and that aged eloquence is most piercing and avayleable, as Homer maketh manifest under the person of olde Duke Nestor" (*Countesse of Pembrokes Yvychurch*: 47r). Alciati (*Emblems*: 181), Valeriano (*Hieroglyphica*: 339), and many others give Hercules these chains of eloquence (see also Becker 1991: 58-60).

We have seen (see *Eleventh Labor*) that Fraunce associated the Zodiac with Hercules and his quest for the golden apples of the Hesperides. But Hercules had long been associated for other reasons with the Zodiac—and with the sun. "Hercules," wrote Macrobius, "does not differ in essence from the sun, for he is that power of the sun which gives to the human race a valor after the likeness of that of the gods" (*Saturnalia*: 1.20.6). Twelve hundred years later, Sandys is writing in the same tradition:

Hercules is also taken for the Sun; as his twelve labours by Porphery for the twelve signes in the Zodiack. Hercules, saith Macrobius, is the power of the Sun, which actuates virtue in the minde of man to the similitude of the Gods, nor was Baeotia the country of Alcmena, nor he at the first called Hercules; but long after was honoured with that name; meriting by his admirable fortitude to be stiled the God of virtue. For what signifies Hercules but the Glory of the Aire? and what is the Glory of the aire, but the Suns illumination, which expelleth the Spirit of Darknesse? (*Ovid*: 440; see also, e.g., Vos, *De Theologia Gentili*: 383-384)

With all of this, it is not surprising that the great ones of the Renaissance should have exulted in comparisons of themselves with Hercules. This was especially the case with monarchs, who rejoiced to think of themselves as opposing tyranny and as leading their subjects by their eloquence; see, for example, Ronsard's "Au Roy Charles IX," which compares the King Charles to Hercules at embarrassing length; Ronsard's "Pour le Roy Habillé" works in the same way. For many other sixteenth-century examples of this allegory, see Jung (1966: 159-185).

In the time when Christianity still felt Roman paganism to be its great rival, there were numerous treatises written to demonstrate the evils and the limitations of Roman religion, morality, and statecraft. The best-known work of this kind is of course Augustine's *City of God*. In this tradition, Hercules was interpreted as the example of *pagan* virtue, as distinct from Christian virtue. Hercules was thus an example of the debilitating limits of Roman conceptions of morality (see, e.g., Nees 1991: 47-109).

Bibliography: J. Becker, "Amphion and Hercules in Amsterdam: Vondel's Bijschrift op Diedrick Sweelinck," *SL*, 33 (1991): 49-68; Maria M. Donato, "Hercules and David in the Early Decoration of the Palazzo Vecchio," *JWCI*, 54 (1991): 83-98; Peter Dronke, *The Medieval Poet and His World* (1984); Karl Galinsky, *The Herakles Theme...from Homer to the Twentieth Century* (1972); Marc-René Jung, *Hercule dans la Littérature Française du XVIe Siècle* (1966); Charles Lemmi, *The Classical Deities in Bacon* (1933); Henry G. Lotspeich, *Classical Mythology in the Poetry of Edmund Spenser* (1932); Lawrence Nees, *A Tainted Mantle: Hercules and the Classical Tradition in the Carolingian Court* (1991); John Nichols, *The Progresses and Public Processions of Queen Elizabeth*, 3 vols. (1823); James Nohrnberg, *The Analogy of The Faerie Queene* (1976); Erwin Panofsky, *Hercules am Scheidewege* (1930); Jane Davidson Reid, *The Oxford Guide to Classical Mythology in the Arts, 1300-1990s* (1993); E. M. Waith, *The Herculean Hero in Marlowe, Chapman, Shakespeare, and Dryden* (1962); Elizabeth B. Welles, "Orpheus and Arion as Symbols of Music in Mantegna's *Camera degli Sposi*," *SI*, 13 (1990): 113-144; Jon Whitman, *Allegory* (1987).

HERMAPHRODITUS AND SALMACIS (Androgenes and Salmacis). In Hermaphroditus was combined both his parents' names—Hermes and Aphrodite—and their beauty. In Ovid's version of the story, the boy bathed in "a pool of water crystal clear." The nymph of this pool, Salmacis, looked upon Hermaphroditus "and longed to possess what she saw." She offered to kiss the boy, but he rejected her, diving into the inviting waters. Salmacis followed him into the pool and clung to him, refusing to let him go. She prayed to the gods that they might never be parted. The gods grant her prayer, and their bodies "were merged in one, with one face and form for both." Thus, says Ovid, "the fountain of Salmacis is of ill-repute...it enervates with its enfeebling waters and renders soft and weak all men who bathe therein" (*Metamorphoses*: 4.285-388).

The *Chess of Love* commentary explains the story in two ways. I quote at length, partly because it seems to me that this commentary gives some insight into how the story of Venus and Adonis might have been understood. First, the commentary interprets the story as an allegorical explanation of the nature of the sexual impulse:

That Hermaphroditus came to bathe in this powerful and much cared for fountain of nature signifies to us that the masculine power descends there and comes upon it in the hour of generation, and there begins to demonstrate its mastery and strength, on the one hand. And Salmacis, on the other hand, jumps back into the fountain to keep Hermaphroditus company, i.e., for the feminine power returns to the place of generation, for it certainly wishes to have the lordship and to attract the male power to its inner being, but the male power does not want to agree, but always sticks to its proper nature of overcoming and conquering the feminine power. And thus there is a sort of struggle between these two powers, for the feminine power always by its nature means to engender a female, and the masculine power, on the contrary, a male. And it is also the well-ordered intention of nature that either a male or a female should result from this fountain. (646)

The commentary's second interpretation is moral:

One could also well say to the profit of morals that Hermaphroditus signifies the young men who have their eye and heart on the vanities of the world and idleness, and who wish to dive wholly into the fountain of delectation. And this is enough signified to us by what this fable pretends as to his being the son of Mercury and Venus. For according to the astronomers, when Mercury and Venus are joined together in the sky they incline their human hearts to these things. And Salmacis signifies the young girls who love the pleasures of the world in the same degree and want to run everywhere to feasts and games. By which it often happens that a damsel will see a youth [as it were] bathing in the fountain who will seem pleasant and agreeable to her, whom she will love so furiously that by her own motion and without any modesty she will jump into the fountain with him and offer him everything, heart, body and love. And the boy will at first be embarrassed and strongly want to refuse this offer.

Finally, she also sometimes joins herself to him and draws him and embraces him so that they become as one, so that they cannot separate or disjoin themselves, but wish to remain united. And thus the boy becomes effeminate and more than half turned into a woman. (648; see also *Ovide Moralisé*: 4.2224-2389)

This moral explanation was the most common. Boccaccio (*Genealogie Deorum*: 3.21), for example, and Ross (*Mystagogus Poeticus*: 172) both mention the effeminizing effects of drinking at the pool of Salmacis. Peele writes how "Salmacis resembling ydleness, / Turns men to women all through wantoness" (*Arraignment of Paris*: 280-281). This notion of the emasculating effect of love was widely recognized (see, e.g., the grotesque emasculating himself in the bottom right-hand corner of Bruegel's *Lechery* engraving, fig. 20; see **ATTIS**; see also Stone 1977: 497). For Golding,

Hermaphrodite and Salmacis declare that idlenesse
Is cheefest nurce and cherisher of all voluptuousnesse,
And that voluptuous liyfe breedes sin.
                              ("Epistle": 113-115)

Sandys' interpretation is like the *Chess* commentary's in that it combines moral allegory with an explanation of the sexual impulses:

The fine nymph Salmacis delighting only to adorne her person, to couch in shades, and bathe in her owne fountaine, burnes in desire with the son of Hermes and Aphrodite partaking the names and the beauties of either....Sensual love is the deformed issue of sloth and delicacy: and seldome survives his inglorious parents....Salmacis clinges about the surprized youth like a serpent, till both become one body. The reason why lovers so strictly imbrace; is to incorporate with the beloved, which sith they cannot, can never be satisfied. (*Ovid*: 206-207)

The notion that lovers try to unite themselves into one was of particular interest to Neo-Platonists, since Plato had written in the *Symposium* (189d-191e) that human beings were originally bisexual: so, when lovers long to unite themselves with the beloved, they are in fact yearning for primal human unity (see Ficino, *On Plato's Symposium*: 5.1; Nohrnberg 1976: 604-605).

One Medieval tradition had it that Hermaphroditus represented the dangerous feminization (i.e., the perversion) of Mercury's role as god of eloquence—Hermaphroditus, then, could serve as a figure for eloquence put to lascivious ends (Chance 1994: 275).

For Dolce, Hermaphroditus was an allegorical figure for "the miraculous union of the soul with God...by contemplation" (*Transformationi*: 102)!

Bibliography: Jane Chance, *Medieval Mythography* (1994); A. C. Hamilton, *The Spenser Encyclopedia* (1990): under *Hermaphrodite*; James Nohrnberg, *The Analogy of The Faerie Queene* (1976); Lawrence Stone, *The Family, Sex and Marriage in England 1500-1800* (1977); Raymond B. Waddington, "The Poetics of Eroticism: Shakespeare's 'Master Mistress'," in C. J. Summers and T. L. Pebworth, *Renaissance Discourses of Desire* (1993): 13-28.

HERO AND LEANDER. Hero was a maiden of Sestus, very much in love with Leander of Abydos. Alas, the waters of the Hellespont stretched between the two lovers. Leander would swim the Hellespont to embrace his love, but finally he drowned in a storm. Hero, despairing, drowned herself. The story could serve, then, as a morally neutral example of the power of love (e.g., Spenser, "Hymne of Love": 231). But in the most widely known version of the story, Ovid has Hero say to Leander, "I cannot be patient for love! We burn with equal fires" (*Heroides*: 19.4-5)—and so it is not surprising that Hero and Leander were usually understood as examples of the dangers of immoderate love. Boccaccio (*Fiammetta*: 19), for example, linked Hero and Leander with Dido, Paris, Helen, Clytemnestra,

Aegisthus, Achilles, Scylla, and Ariadne, all as examples of guilty love. The *Chess of Love* commentary likened Hero and Leander to Pyramus and Thisbe: "Briefly, such mad loves commonly end in bitter sorrow and in some surpassing misfortune." Hero and Leander thus serve as "an example...of the danger that lies in such loves" (686).

Bibliography: Douglas Bush, *Mythology and the Renaissance Tradition in English Poetry* (1963): 121-136; Götz Schmitz, *The Fall of Women in Early English Narrative Verse* (1990): 90-98.

THE HESPERIDES were daughters of the Night, according to Hesiod (*Theogony*: 214); others make them daughters of Zeus or Atlas. They lived in the garden of the gods, which was planted in the far west of the world, on the border of Oceanus. The Hesperides were there to guard a tree of golden apples given to Hera as a wedding gift. They were aided in this work by a dragon (e.g., Ovid, *Metamorphoses*: 4. 631-648; Apollodorus, *Library*: 2.5.11)—and in some accounts by Typhon and Echidna. One of the twelve labors King Eurystheus assigned to Hercules was the theft of three of these golden apples. When Hercules did finally manage to steal them, he brought the apples to Eurystheus, who could think of nothing to do with them. Hercules then decided to give the apples to Athena.

These apples frequently appeared in temptation stories: Hippomenes used the golden apples to tempt Atalanta (see **ATALANTA**); and one of the golden apples is the prize Paris is to award in the story of the choice of Paris (see **PARIS**). Thus it is that Ross urges us to "take heed that the golden apples of worldly pleasure and profit, which Hippomenes, the Devil, flings in our way, may not hinder our course" (*Mystagogus Poeticus*: 36). Because the golden apples acquired these unsavory connotations, Hercules' giving the apples to Athena (the goddess of wisdom) could be interpreted as another *exemplum* of contempt for worldly pleasures, as in Ripa: "in the Roman Capitol stands a bronze statue of Hercules vested in the skin of a lion. He holds a club in his right hand and in the left three golden apples, gotten from the Garden of the Hesperides. By this is signified three kinds of heroic virtues....The first is the moderation of anger; the second is temperance; and the third is the contempt for voluptuousness and the pleasures of the world" (*Iconologie*: 1.168).

In a second line of interpretation the golden apples could be a type of knowledge or learning (Nohrnberg 1976: 335). Here is Fulgentius:

Hercules took golden apples from the garden of the Hesperides: there are said to be four Hesperides, namely, Aegle, Hespera, Medusa, and Arethusa, whom in Latin we call study, intellect, memory, and eloquence, for the first task is to study; the second, to understand; the third, to remember what you have understood; and the final one to adorn with eloquence what you have remembered. It is, therefore, in this fashion that manliness seizes the golden jewel of learning. (*On the Content of Virgil*: 20; see **AMAZONS** for the allegory of manly virtue)

Guido da Pisa's comment is in this same tradition: "Hercules, it may be said, figures forth the wise man, who overcomes the dragon, which is sensuality, and wins the golden apples, which is to acquire the delights of wisdom" (*Super Comediam Dantis*: 648).

The story could also be understood in relation to astrology. Berchorius makes this connection (*Ovidius Moralizatus*: 331), as do Conti (*Mythologie*: 7.7) and Fraunce:

Hesperides, the daughters of Hesperus, are the starres: their garden is in the weast, wherein grow golden apples: for such is the nature of the starres, to glister like gold, and seeme round in shew like apples. They grow in the weast, because the stars never appeare, but when the sun setteth, and that is in the weast....The never-sleeping Dragon, that watcheth these apples & keepeth the garden, is the cyrcle, called Signifier [i.e., the Zodiac; Pliny had called the Zodiac "signifier" in *Natural History*: 2.3.9]. Hercules brought these into Grece, that is, he brought Astrologie into his countrey. (*Countesse of Pembrokes Yvychurch*: 46v-47r)

The Garden of the Hesperides was thought of as perpetually fruitful, as existing in a perpetual spring. Thus it was that during the Renaissance, the Hesperides were associated with the earthly paradise, as in Herrick's *Hesperides*. And because the Hesperides were usually regarded as islands, the Fortunate Isles, they became an Elisabethan and Stuart commonplace for England itself, as we see again in Herrick's *Hesperides*. Jonson's masque *The Fortunate Isles and Their Union* plays elaborately with this idea of England as the Hesperides in order to praise James, the first king of all Britain (Coiro 1985).

This perpetual fruitfulness also associated the Garden of the Hesperides with Venus. This is, for example, probably the garden we see in Botticelli's *Primavera* (fig. 13). Botticelli depicts the Apples as citrus in keeping with a rationalization of the myth that goes all the way back to the third century B.C., that the Golden Apples were, in fact, citrus fruit, exotics in the Greco-Roman world (Lightbown 1989: 126).

Bibliography: Ann Coiro, "Herrick's *Hesperides*: The Name and the Frame," *ELH*, 52 (1985): 311-336; Ronald Lightbown, *Botticelli: Life and Work* (1989); James Nohrnberg, *The Analogy of The Faerie Queene* (1976).

HIPPOLYTUS was the son of Theseus and the Amazon Hippolyta (Antiope in some versions). He was devoted to the hunt. When he refused the amorous advances of his stepmother Phaedra, she accused him of rape. Theseus called upon Neptune to punish the supposed rape, and the god sent forth a sea-monster, which frightened Hippolytus's chariot horses. Hippolytus was thrown from the chariot and dragged to death. According to Virgil (*Aeneid*: 7.761-782) and Ovid (*Metamorphoses*: 15.497-546), Aesculapius then restored him to life.

Because he devoted himself to the hunt, and spurned love, Hippolytus came to be an *exemplum* of male chastity (see **ADONIS** for the moral allegory of hunting). Hippolytus was one of the examples Ferrand evinced to demonstrate that hunting can be a cure for love melancholy (*Treatise on Lovesickness*: 37).

Because he was falsely accused by a seductress, he could be a type of Joseph, who had fled the adulterous advances of Potiphar's wife (Gen 39). We see this in art as early as the sixth century (Hanfmann 1980: 84); Alanus refers to the type as well (*Anticlaudian*: 7.2), as does Sandys (*Ovid*: 710).

Since he was resurrected, Hippolytus was irresistible as a type of Christian spiritual renewal (e.g., Dante, *Paradiso*: 17.46-48; see Brownlee 1993: 117)—or as a type of Christ. Boccaccio recalls "how Hippolytus' / gashed limbs after three days rose up alive" (*Eclogues*: 11.210-211). And here is Ross:

Christ is the true Hippolytus, who lived a single, chast, & holy life, giving himself to spiritual hunting of souls; he was falsly accused by the Jewish Synagogue, his malicious step-mother; and was condemned to death by his heavenly Father: not for his own offences, for he was innocency it self....But because he became our surety, his blessed body was torn worse than that of Hippolytus; he went down to hell and died, but was restored back to life, and arose the third day. (*Mystagogus Poeticus*: 178-179; for Christ's Harrowing of Hell, see **HERCULES: TWELFTH LABOR**)

Already in classical times Phaedra was an *exemplum* of those who love dangerously, beyond the restraint of reason (e.g., Ovid, *Heroides*: 4). Ausonius, for example, places Phaedra in a list of *de casibus* lovers, along with Dido, Canace, and Phyllis (*Epigrams*: 22). Lydgate includes her in a list of unnatural lovers: Narcissus (self-love), Myrrha (incestuous love), Pygmalion (love of an image), Tereus (rape), Pasiphae (bestial love), and others (*Reson and Sensuallyte*: 4300-4344). See also the *Chess of Love* commentary (670) and Dolce (*Transformationi*: 320).

For the story of Hippolytus being brought back to life by Aesculapius, see **AESCULAPIUS**.

Bibliography: Kevin Brownlee, "Dante and the Classical Poets," in Rachel Jacoff, *The Cambridge Companion to Dante* (1993); Henry Lotspeich, *Classical Mythology in the Poetry of Edmund Spenser* (1932): 69-70; James Nohrnberg, *The Analogy of The Faerie Queene* (1976): 175, 270, 279.

HOMER. We seem, alas, to know less and less about Homer as the centuries roll by. Modern scholars are uncertain as to whether Homer was literate (e.g., Lloyd-Jones 1992), uncertain as to how much of the *Iliad* and the *Odyssey* Homer composed—uncertain, even, as to whether there *was* a Homer, a single author of the two great epics (e.g., Jensen 1980). Medieval and Renaissance Christians, on the other hand, knew their Homer more clearly. He was certainly the author of the *Iliad* and the *Odyssey*; he was blind; he wrote history; and he was divinely inspired. His poems were deeply profound and profoundly allegorical. Images of Homer survive from the late fourth century that suggest that Christian Neo-Platonists of this period could think of Homer as being like Christ in his spirituality (Hanfmann

1980: 78). Even during the Middle Ages—when his poems were unavailable, when he was known only by his reputation—Homer was still revered. Dante referred to him as the "sovereign poet" (*Inferno*: 4.88).

To demonstrate the continuity of such traditions, Lamberton (1989: 8-10) discusses the title page of Chapman's translation (c. 1614) of the *Odyssey* (fig. 14), where we see Homer assimilated with Tiresias. The central figure wears the poet's laurels; he is Homer. But he is surrounded by the shades of the poets—the profile of Dante on the left is the most recognizable. This is a reference to one of the stories of Tiresias. Homer's Circe promises that Odysseus will meet Tiresias in the underworld:

> You shall hear prophecy from the rapt shade
> of blind Teiresias of Thebes, forever
> charged with reason even among the dead;
> to him alone, of all the flitting ghosts,
> Persephone has given a mind undarkened.
> (Odyssey: 10.495-499)

The script around the head of Homer in the engraving—"*Solus sapit hic homo*," "This man alone is wise"—and the script over the shades—"*Reliqui vero Umbra moventur*," "The others truly are moving shades"—are adapted from this passage. (Plato recognized that Tiresias was the only shade in the Underworld capable of reason: *Meno*: 100a; *Republic*: 3.386d.) The shades hovering about Homer/Tiresias are crowned with laurel, and so we must associate them with the company of poets that Dante meets in the fourth canto of the *Inferno*. Dante tells us that Homer leads this group, an idea that goes back at least to Pythagoras. The engraving, then, merges the Homer of the *Inferno* with the Tiresias of the *Odyssey* underworld. And so we are to understand that Homer, in his blindness, was able to see with no merely earthly eyes, that he was inspired by a transcendent vision—like Homer's own creation Demodocus, the blind bard of the eighth book of the *Odyssey* (on the superiority of blindness to earthly seeing, see Wind 1968: 53-80). In the engraving Homer's blind eyes are raised to heaven; he is seeing with the eye of the spirit. Minerva, goddess of wisdom, sits in the foreground on the left, gesturing toward Homer, thus showing Ulysses (a hero famous for his wisdom and restraint) the way to wisdom. Cooper (*Dictionarium*: under *Homer*) explains Homer's blindness in these same allegorical terms.

This interpretation of Homer's blindness, that it is related to the eye of the spirit and divine inspiration, is at least as old as Proclus (*Sur la République*: 1.193-194), and it was still current in the seventeenth century (e.g., Reynolds, *Mythomystes*: 151-152). The idea that Homer was a self-consciously mystical-allegorical poet goes back to Heraclitus (e.g., *Allégories d'Homère*: 1-3). It must be with this tradition in mind that Petrarch mentions his own "wretched blindness" in the course of the invocation that begins his epic, *Africa* (1.23): Petrarch wants to associate himself with Homer the inspired poet.

Plato (*Phaedrus*: 243a-b) wrote that Homer and Stesichorus were both guilty of disparaging love, since both had written of Helen's dalliance. According to Plato, both were punished with blindness. Ficino (*Letters*, vol. 1: 37; vol. 3: 10) recalls this tradition in the course of his own Neo-Platonic praise of love.

For more on blindness, Homer, Tiresias, and spiritual sight, see **TIRESIAS**. See also Don C. Allen (1970: 102-105) for an account of the seventeenth-century English scholarship that associated Homer with the prophets of the Old Testament. For more on Homer's singing, see **MUSES**.

Bibliography: Don C. Allen, *Mysteriously Meant* (1970); G.M.A. Hanfmann, "The Continuity of Classical Art: Culture, Myth, and Faith," in Kurt Weitzmann, *Age of Spirituality* (1980): 75-99; Minna Skafte Jensen, *Homeric Question and the Oral-Formulaic Theory* (1980); Robert Lamberton, *Homer the Theologian* (1989); Hugh Lloyd-Jones, "Keeping up with Homer," *NYRB*, 39, no. 5 (1992): 52-57; Edgar Wind, *Pagan Mysteries of the Renaissance* (1968).

HYACINTHUS was a beautiful boy beloved by Apollo. There are various accounts of his death, the most common being that he was killed by the errant flight of a discus thrown by Apollo (e.g., Ovid *Metamorphoses*: 10.163-219). Apollo then immortalized the boy by turning him into the flower Hyacinth. Hyacinthus could thus be interpreted, like Ganymede, as an example of the virtuous union of God and a human being. In the *Ovide Moralisé* this took the following form: "By Hyacinthus, without doubt, are intended all the apostles and the martyrs, all of whom God loves" (10.3444-3447). And here is Sandys: "The Poets, shaddowing under their fables Philosophicall and Theologicall instructions, by the love of Gods unto boyes express the graciousnesse of simplicity and innocency: and like little children, or not at all, must we ascend the celestiall habitations" (*Ovid*: 482).

But Hyacinthus, like Daphne, could also be interpreted as a *de casibus* lover (e.g., Brant, *Ship of Fools*: 13; Fraunce, *Countesse of Pembrokes Yvychurch*: 45r). This would account for Milton's placing the flower Hyacinth in the bower of Adam and Eve only *after* the fall (*Paradise Lost*: 9.1041).

Bibliography: James Nohrnberg, *The Analogy of The Faerie Queene* (1976): 513-514.

THE HYDRA (Idra) was usually represented in classical times as a serpent with many heads—anywhere from five to a hundred. Its very breath could kill; but it was dangerous especially because, should a hero manage to cut off a head, the Hydra could quickly grow a replacement. It was Hercules who finally managed to kill the Hydra, as one of his twelve labors.

Bernardus understood Hercules as a figure for wisdom, and so Hercules' struggle with the Hydra was the struggle with "ignorance" and its "many ambiguities" (*On Virgil's Aeneid*: 6.287-288; repeated by Salutati, *De Laboribus Herculis*: 3.5). Viana seems to be working in this same tradition: the Hydra is "sophistical arguments"; but Viana also interprets the Hydra as "sensuality" (*Ovid*: 9.19). And this was the way most Medieval and Renaissance Christians understood the struggle with the Hydra, as a figure for the struggle with sin or the passions. Some writers associated the Hydra with some particular sin. Fraunce, for example, made the Hydra a figure for Envy: "Hercules...overcame Hydra, the almost invincible, & still breeding beast, Envy. Hydra lurked in moores & fennes; Envy creepeth on the ground, in base and abject brests" (*Countesse of Pembrokes Yvychurch*: 46v). And Ross wrote of "the Hydra of Drunkenness" (*Mystagogus Poeticus*: 168). Other writers interpreted the struggle with the many-headed beast as representing the struggle with the passions in general. Erasmus, for example:

when we are enticed by wickedness, we should pray repeatedly for God's help....[T]o devout men temptations are sometimes not hazardous, but even fruitful in the maintenance of virtue. And, finally, we are taught that when all the rest of the passions have been subjugated, only the infirmity of empty glory lies in ambush, even in the midst of virtues; and this is like that Hydra of Hercules, a monster tenacious of life and spawning by means of its own wounds; one which, even at the very end, when all other labors have been finished, can scarcely be suppressed. But persistent labor overcomes all difficulties. (*Enchiridion*: 7)

Bibliography: James Nohrnberg, *The Analogy of The Faerie Queene* (1976): 140-141, 690-691.

HYLAS, a handsome youth, was a favorite of Hercules. They were voyaging with the Argonauts when Hylas, ashore to fetch water from a spring, was swept away by nymphs, who desired him for his beauty. When the Argonauts sailed on, Hercules stayed behind to search for Hylas (see, e.g., Theocritus, *Idylls*: 13; Apollodorus, *Library*: 1.9.19; Cooper, *Thesaurus*: under *Hylas*). Hylas and Hercules could thus serve as examples of true friendship (e.g., Ronsard, "L'Hylas"; Spenser, *Faerie Queene*: 4.10.27)—or of sodomy and immoderate affection (e.g., Ross, *Mystagogus Poeticus*: 181, 183).

Because he was ravished by dieties, Hylas—like Europa, Ganymede, the Leucippides (see **CASTOR AND POLLUX**), and Endymion—could be seen as a figure for spiritual ascent. For this reason Hylas sometimes appeared in classical funerary art (Panofsky n.d.: 37).

Bibliography: Erwin Panofsky, *Tomb Sculpture* (n.d.).

HYMEN (Hymenaeus, Imeneus). Hymen was the god of marriage. He was said to preside at marriages, and songs were sung to him on these occasions. He was god of lawful marriages only. John of Salisbury, for example, distinguished between Hymen and Cupid: "it is Hymen that loves light; it is Cupid with his swift shafts that kindles the furtive flame and lurks in nooks and corners" (*Policraticus*: 8.11). Hymen's absence could suggest something untoward or unpropitious in a marriage. In the best-known example of this, Ovid (*Metamorphoses*: 6.429) mentions that Hymen was not present at the marriage of Tereus and Procne—a marriage that ends with rape, murder, and cannibalism. Sandys mentions this tradition (*Ovid*: 298), as does Ross (*Mystagogus Poeticus*: 187). Thus it was that Christian poets came to invoke Hymen if they wanted to suggest that a certain marriage was right, lawful, and propitious.   Spenser does this in his "Epithalamium" (140), for example; and Shakespeare's Prospero urges Ferdinand and Miranda to enter chastely into marriage, "As Hymen's lamps shall light you" (*Tempest*: 4.1.23). Sometimes in Medieval literature the poet intends some irony in the invocation of Hymen. This is certainly the case when Chaucer's Merchant assures us that "Ymeneus that god of weddyng.../ Saugh nevere his lyf so myrie a wedded man" as the libidinous and soon-to-be-cuckolded Januari ("Merchant's Tale": 1730-1731). Chaucer must intend irony, too, when he has Troylus thank Hymen for the felicity of his extramarital union with Criseyde (*Troylus and Criseyde*: 3.1258).

Hymen was occasionally said to be the son of a Muse (see, e.g., Martianus, quoted below); more often he was said to be the son of Venus and Bacchus (e.g., Vatican Mythographer III: 11.2; Boccaccio, *Genealogie Deorum*: 5.26). The *Chess of Love* commentary explains that Hymen was one of Venus's three sons by Bacchus: Jocus, "the god of games and worldly solace"; Cupid, the god of love; and Hymen, "the god of weddings." Hymen thus signifies reasonable, lawful love "for the profit of generation" (561; Boccaccio, *Genealogie Deorum*: 5.26; see also **JOCUS**).

Hymen could also stand as a figure for union in a larger sense. Thus it is that Martianus begins his *Marriage of Philology and Mercury* with a paean to Hymen: "Sacred principle of unity....You bind the warring seeds of the world with secret bonds and encourage the union of opposites by your sacred embrace. You cause the elements to interact reciprocally, you make the world fertile; through you, Mind is breathed into bodies by a union of concord which rules over Nature, as you bring harmony between the sexes and foster loyalty by love" (1).   Martianus is allegorizing the Platonic idea that the universe is made up of "seeds," or elements, which any act of creation brings together in harmony. (In his note to this passage, Stahl cites Plato, e.g., *Timaeus*: 32c, *Gorgias*: 508a; and Macrobius, *On the Dream of Scipio*: 2.2.16-19, as Martianus's sources. For more on the allegory of Martianus's Hymen, see Dronke 1974: 100-105; for more on cosmic harmony, see Appendix A, "Music.") As the god of marriage, Hymen could serve as a figure for this bringing together of elements. The ideas here are very close to Boethius, in the famous passage in *The Consolation*, where we read that Love holds "the conflicting seeds of things...in everlasting law," that Love maintains the "harmonious order of things" (2.mt 8). Jonson's masque *Hymenaei* makes use of much the same Neo-Platonic allegory: The marriage of the king is related to the harmonious union of the universe (Starnes and Talbert 1955: 154).

Bibliography: Peter Dronke, *Fabula: Explorations into the Uses of Myth in Medieval Platonism* (1974); George Economou, *The Goddess Natura in Medieval Literature* (1972): 84-90; Jane Chance Nitzsche, *The Genius Figure in Antiquity and the Middle Ages* (1975): 99-106; DeWitt Starnes and E. W. Talbert, *Classical Myth and Legend in Renaissance Dictionaries* (1955).

I

ICARUS and his father Daedalus were imprisoned by king Minos. Daedalus made wings out of wax and feathers for himself and his son, so that they could escape by flight. Daedalus warned Icarus not to fly too close to the sun, lest the sun melt the wax. But Icarus disregarded his father's warning, and he fell to his death in the sea. The earliest and most common interpretation was that Icarus was an example of pride; we find this allegory in the writers of antiquity (e.g., Lucian, *Essays in Portraiture*: 21; it must be said that the emperor Nero seems to have been oblivious to this allegory; fond as Nero was of "snuff theater," he had this scene staged in the arena; the actor hit the ground close enough to spatter Nero with his blood; see Plass 1995: 74). And we find the same allegory in the Christian era (e.g., the *Ovide Moralisé*: 8.1579-1708).

Bruegel's *Landscape with the Fall of Icarus* (fig. 15) could certainly have been understood according to this same interpretation. The painting seems to suggest an analogy between Icarus (whom we see just as he enters the water) and the great sea-going ship; for the ship, seemingly so mighty and yet so frail in the face of storms and rock, was also a traditional figure for pride (see Isaiah 2:12-16). For example, Camões (*Lusiads*: 6.78) writes that the Portuguese explorers, sailing so far and conquering so much, are like the rebellious Giants in their presumption; and Camões's comparison of sea-going men and rebellious Giants goes back at least to Statius (*Silvae*: 3.2.61-66; see Quint 1993: 263, 271). Whitney (*Emblemes*: 11) also associates sea-going ships with pride.

Bruegel's painting also suggests an analogy between Icarus and the shepherd, who gazes up at the sky with his mouth agape while his sheep wander the dangerous cliffs. The Good Shepherd left the ninety and nine to look for the one sheep that was lost (Matt 18:12); in the case of Bruegel's shepherd, it is the ninety-nine that have strayed. The shepherd stands in contrast to the plowman, who is carefully making his furrows even, his eyes firmly fixed on the work at hand. The shepherd, not content with his place in the divinely instituted order of things, is like Icarus. Golding's comment on Ovid's story seems almost to have been written with Bruegel in mind:

We also lerne by Icarus how good it is too bee
In meane estate and not too clymb too hygh, but to agree
Too wholsome counsell: for the hyre of disobedience is
Repentance when it is too late for thinking things amisse.
                                        ("Epistle": 177-180)

Whitney's comment on the fall of Icarus also seems apposite to Bruegel:

Heare, Icarus with mountinge up alofte,
Came headlonge downe, and fell into the Sea....
Let suche beware, which paste theire reache do mounte,
Whoe seeke the thinges, to mortall men deny'de,
And searche the Heavens, and all the starres accoumpte...
With blusshinge nowe, theire weakenesse rightlie weye,
Least as they clime, they fall to theire decaye.
                                        (*Emblemes*: 28)

Such allegory was sufficiently well known that the humanist who advised the builders of the Amsterdam Town Hall suggested that Icarus's fall be depicted in the decoration of the Bankruptcy Court as a warning against high-flying ambition (Gombrich 1993: 8).

In Alciati (*Emblems*: 104), Icarus is a warning against that species of pride that induces us to seek after the secrets of heaven. The opening Chorus of Marlowe's *Doctor Faustus* tells us that Faustus, with all his learning, was "swoll'n with cunning of a self-conceit," until "His waxen wings did mount above his reach, / And melting, heavens conspired his overthrow" (20-22).

A second, closely related interpretation of Icarus took hold as Christians began to give voice to Aristotelian and Horatian notions of the middle way. At least as early as Berchorius we find the story of Icarus interpreted in such terms:

If he descends too low...through desire for earthly goods, his wings of power and temporal nobility will be made heavy and destroyed and his spiritual wings—that is virtues and inclination—will be weighed down by the storms and waves of the sea—that is the delights of the world. If he raises himself through presumption or pride more than is just...or seeks a higher position beyond the sufficiency of his person the interior wings—virtues—are burned and the exterior wings—that is nobility and worldly power—are loosed and destroyed little by little. The presumptuous are also accustomed to fall in their habits through misfortunes and to be drowned finally in the sea of delights....In short, it is true in all matters that the middle avails more than the extreme. (*Ovidius Moralizatus*: 310)

Nearly 300 years later, Sandys put it more succinctly: "This fable applaudes the golden Meane, and flight of virtue betweene the extreames. Icarus falls in aspiring" (384). Henkel and Schöne (1967: 1617) reprint an emblem from 1531 that makes the same point, that virtue lies in the Middle Way. Van Veen's emblem of Icarus bears the legend, "Virtue consists in the mean" (*Horatii Emblemata*: 18). For two of many other versions of this interpretation, see Bacon (*Wisedome of the Ancients*: 27) and Conti: "Therefore he urged Icarus, as they were about to fly off...that the middle way is best....Neither did the poets preserve the memory of these matters except to show us that there is no safety in excess" (*Mythologie*: 7.16).

Bibliography: E. H. Gombrich, *Symbolic Images* (1993); Arthur Henkel and Albrecht Schöne, *Emblemata: Handbuch zur Sinnbildkunst des XVI. und XVII. Jahrhunderts* (1967); Charles Lemmi, *The Classical Deities in Bacon* (1933): 109-117; Paul Plass, *The Game of Death in Ancient Rome* (1995); David Quint, "Voices of Resistance: The Epic Curse and Camões's Adamastor," in Stephen Greenblatt, *New World Encounters* (1993): 241-271; Niall Rudd, "Daedalus and Icarus, from Rome to the End of the Middle Ages," and "Daedalus and Icarus, from the Renaissance to the Present Day," in Charles Martindale, *Ovid Renewed: Ovidian Influences on Literature and Art from the Middle Ages to the Twentieth Century* (1988); John H. Turner, *The Myth of Icarus in Spanish Renaissance Poetry* (1976).

IO, a Naiad, was Jupiter's mistress for a time. Jupiter transformed her into a lovely heifer in order to hide her from Juno's wrath. But jealous Juno set hundred-eyed Argus to guard her. Jupiter determined to set Io free, and so sent Mercury to slay Argus. This should have been impossible, since watchful Argus never closed all his eyes at once. Mercury, however, charmed him to sleep with his Caduceus and with his playing upon the pipes, and then cut off Argus's head. Juno took up the head and transformed those hundred eyes into the eyes on the tail of her bird, the peacock.

Berchorius's comment on this story was typical: "Or say that Jupiter is the devil who does not wish that Io—that is the soul with which he fornicates by sin—be known or drawn back by Juno—that is by the Church—and so changes her into a heifer—that is makes her a sinner and carnal and alien from all spirituality" (*Ovidius Moralizatus*: 142). The *Chess of Love* commentary had it that "she who had earlier been noble, fresh, and a virgin was transformed into a vile woman and enslaved like a true beast" (377; see also Bredero, *Lucelle*: 156-158). Sandys' comment is in the same tradition:

That Jupiter, the mind of man falling from Heaven, and joyning with Io, the body in a clowd is turned into a beast: and forgetfull of his owne originall; and captivated by his vices: when of more maturity in age and judgement, Mercury is sent to kill Argus, in that Reason bridles and subdues the exorbitancies of the affections. Then Juno lets loose the Furies, the stings of the Conscience....This horror begets repentance, repentance reformation, by which he is restored to his former beauty, and becomes like the Gods through his sanctity and integrity. (*Ovid*: 76)

Already in classical times Io began to be identified with Isis (Apollodorus, *Library*: 2.1.3-4; see **ISIS**).

Bibliography: Leonard Barkan, *The Gods Made Flesh: Metamorphoses and the Pursuit of Paganism* (1986): 16-17, 194-196.

IOLE was the daughter of Eurystheus, the king of Mycenae, the king who imposed upon Hercules the tasks known as the Twelve Labors of Hercules. According to one tradition, it was this Iole with whom Hercules fell in love, rather than Omphale (Skretkowicz 1980). The consequences for Hercules were often described in much the same way as they were in the case of his love for Omphale. De Meun, for example, writes that Hercules was as "mad" in his love for Iole as Samson was for Delilah (*Romance of the Rose*: 9183-9202). Indeed, Iole and Omphale were sometimes conflated (Nohrnberg 1976: 359): Cooper, for example, wrote that Iole was "the daughter of Eurytus King of Aetolia, whome Hercules loved so much, that he served hir in a womans appareil, and spanne on a distaffe" (*Dictionarium*: under *Iole*). Spenser (*Faerie Queene*: 5.5.24) also writes of Iole as though she were Omphale, as does Tasso (*Jerusalem Delivered*: 16.3). But Omphale or Iole, the lesson was the same; here is Boccaccio on Iole:

To Hercules' eternal shame...by vanquishing Alcides, she triumphed over all those monsters which he had conquered....This pestilential passion usually creeps upon delicate girls, and very often it seizes lustful and idle young men, because Cupid scorns seriousness and is a great worshipper of wantonness. Therefore, the fact that it entered Hercules' hard breast is a far greater marvel than the deeds he himself had performed. This must instill great fear in men...when it is clear what a strong and powerful enemy threatens them. We must therefore be vigilant. (*Concerning Famous Women*: 21)

Bibliography: James Nohrnberg, *The Analogy of The Faerie Queene* (1976); Victor Skretkowicz, "Hercules in Sidney and Spenser," *NQ*, 225 (1980): 306-310.

IRIS was the goddess of the rainbow and Juno's special messenger. As Fraunce put it, "As Mercury is Jupiters messenger, so is Iris Junoes" (*Countesse of Pembrokes Yvychurch*: 16r; see also Shakespeare, *Tempest*: 4.1.60-100). In Ovid, for example, when Juno wanted to reveal to Alcyone that her beloved Ceyx had died, she said, "'Iris, most faithful messenger of mine, go quickly to the drowsy house of Sleep, and bid him send to Alcyone a vision in dead Ceyx's form to tell her the truth about his fate.' She spoke; and Iris put on her cloak of a thousand hues and, trailing across the sky in a rainbow curve, she sought the cloud-concealed palace of the king of Sleep" (*Metamorphoses*: 11.585-591).

Fulgentius explains that Juno (goddess of riches), is associated with Iris and the rainbow because the rainbow, like "fortune, though at first glance brightly colored, soon after fades away" (*Mythologies*: 2.1; see also Vatican Mythographer II: 6). But Christians could also interpret Iris and her rainbow as a type of the

Biblical rainbow (Gen 9:12-13) and so a figure for God's providence and covenant. Probably Shakespeare has this in mind when he makes Iris the active agent of the marriage masque in the *Tempest* (4.1; see Orgel 1975: 46).

Others connected Iris with the air, since in nature allegory Juno represented the air (see **JUNO**). Bernardus thus suggests that Iris is in charge of "aerial storms" (*On Virgil's Aeneid*: on book 1). And Berchorius explains that Juno is associated with Iris, "because the rainbow and the nymphs—that is the clouds—are engendered in the air" (*Ovidius Moralizatus*: 82).

Ovid (*Metamorphoses*: 14.85) and Virgil (*Aeneid*: 5.604-644) both write that it was Iris whom Juno sent to persuade the Trojan women to burn Aeneas's ships, so that they might stay in happy Sicily, rather than pursue their difficult destiny. While the women are being urged to burn the ships, the men are some distance off, engaged in manly athletic contests. Bernardus's comment on the episode assumes our familiarity with the tradition that allegorically associated *vir*ile pursuits (*L.*, *vir*, "man") with *vir*tue (see **AMAZONS**). He comments as follows:

the Trojan women at the urging of Iris...burned the ships, because while the spirit is exercised in virtue, the frailties of the flesh (which are the Trojan women) will dare in the heat of passion to violate the society and friendship of Aeneas, thus frustrating honest desires which wish to bring them to Italy, that is, to growth.

They do this at Iris's persuasion. Iris, who is multicolored and placed opposite to the sun, figures the senses, which are...contrary to reason. (*On Virgil's Aeneid*: on book 5)

Bibliography: Stephen Orgel, *The Illusion of Power: Political Theater in the English Renaissance* (1975).

ISIS AND OSIRIS. Isis was an important Egyptian deity, wife and sister of Osiris and mother of Horus. In Hellenic times her cult spread to become important to the Greeks as well. She was variously identified with a number of the Greek goddesses. Diodorus, for example, equates Isis with Demeter, and Osiris with Dionysus:

Osiris when translated is Dionysus, and Isis is more similar to Demeter than to any other goddess....Osiris was the first, they record, to make mankind give up cannibalism; for after Isis had discovered the fruit of both wheat and barley...and Osiris had also devised the cultivation of these fruits, all men were glad to change their food....And...he was the first to drink wine and taught mankind at large the culture of the vine and the use of wine. (*Bibliotheca Historia*: 1.13-154)

Already in classical times, Isis was identified with Io (Apollodorus, *Library*: 2.1.3; Hyginus, *Fabulae*: 145); and this was the identification most commonly remembered by Christians. Early in the Christian era, for example, Lactantius is aware of the association: "And so that she might escape the wrath of Juno, as she was then...she is said to have swum across the sea and to have come into Egypt, and there, when her former appearance was recovered, she became the goddess who is now called Isis" (*Divine Institutes*: 1.11). Some 1,300 years later van Mander's (*Wtlegginghe op den Metamorphosis*: 8r) and Sandys' (*Ovid*: 74-75) accounts are much the same.

There were several stories as to just how Io came to Egypt. Ross's version may be taken as typical, at least in its ingenuity. He recounts how Jupiter had fallen in love with Io and turned her into a cow in order to hide her from jealous Juno, and how Juno set hundred-eyed Argus to guard cow-Io. Jupiter then sent Mercury to kill Argus, "and Juno in revenge, sent a Gad-bee to sting her, which made Io run mad up and down the World, till she came to Egypt; where she recovered her owne shape again, and was there called Isis, and married to Osyris" (*Mystagogus Poeticus*: 206).

But much of what was written about Isis during the Middle Ages and the Renaissance had nothing overtly to do with Io. Plutarch had written a whole treatise on Isis and Osiris, and he invested her with a wide range of meaning. For Plutarch she was the daughter of Reason or Wisdom: "Many writers have held her to be the daughter of Hermes, and many others the daughter of Prometheus, because of the belief that Prometheus is the discoverer of wisdom and forethought, and Hermes the inventor of grammar and music" (*Isis and Osiris*: 352.a-b). This allowed Plutarch to associate her with order (see Appendix A, "Music"): "if we revere and honour what is orderly and good and beneficial as the work of Isis and as the image and reflection and reason of Osiris, we shall not be wrong" (376f-377a; for more on Isis and law and order in ancient times, see Kee 1983: 116-119). But in Plutarch's Platonic scheme, this was the good and beneficence of a right-ordered creation. Plutarch again:

Isis is, in fact, the female principle of Nature, and is receptive of every form of generation, in accord with which she is called by Plato [*Timaeus* 49a, 51a] the gentle nurse and the all-receptive, and by most people has been called by countless names, since, by force of Reason, she turns herself to this thing and that and is receptive of all manner of shapes and forms....For creation is the image of being in matter, and the thing created is a picture of reality.

According to an Egyptian myth known to the Greeks and Romans, Osiris was killed by his evil brother Typhon. Typhon placed his remains in a box and sent it floating down the Nile. Plutarch continues his account of Isis by allegorizing upon this myth:

It is not, therefore, out of keeping that they have a legend that the soul of Osiris is everlasting and imperishable, but that his body Typhon oftentimes dismembers and causes to disappear, and that Isis wanders hither and yon in her search for it, and fits it together again; for that which really is and is perceptible and good is superior to destruction and change. The images from it with which the sensible and corporeal is impressed, and the relations, forms, and likenesses which this takes upon itself, like impressions of seals in wax, are not permanently lasting, but disorder and disturbance overtakes them, being driven hither from the upper reaches, and fighting against Horus, whom Isis brings forth, beholden as the image of the perceptible world. (*Isis and Osiris*: 372e-373a)

Macrobius wrote rather more simply, "Isis is the earth, or the world of nature, that lies beneath the sun; and so the whole body of the goddess is thickly covered with a series of breasts, because everything that exists draws its sustenance and nourishment from the earth or world of nature" (*Saturnalia*: 1.20.18).

Isis was thus thought of as a goddess of agriculture, or even as Nature—especially in relation to fertile Egypt. Cartari makes her the "Genius of Egypt" and the goddess of Nature (*Imagini*, 1571 ed.: 118). Ross agrees: "By Isis may be meant the Genius or nature of the soil of Egypt, as her picture sheweth, which moveth a timbrel with her right hand, shewing thereby the coming of Nilus" (*Mystagogus Poeticus*: 207).

Spenser's conception of Osiris and Isis was largely influenced by Plutarch (*Isis and Osiris*) and Diodorus (*Bibliotheca Historia*: 1.11-15; see Lotspeich 1932: 73). For Spenser, Osiris was a type of the just king, while Isis had to do with Equity or Justice—an association that goes all the way back to Aristotle (Stump 1982). Here is Spenser:

> Osyris, whilest he lived here,
> The justest man alive, and truest did appeare.

> His wife was Isis, whom they likewise made
> A Goddesse of great powre and soverainty,
> And in her person cunningly did shade
> That part of justice, which is Equity.
> (*Faerie Queene*: 5.7.2-3)

Bibliography: A. C. Hamilton, *The Spenser Encyclopedia* (1990): under *Isis*; A. Kent Hieatt, *Chaucer, Spenser, Milton: Mythopoeic Continuities and Transformations* (1975): 135-145; Howard C. Kee, *Miracle in the Early Christian World* (1983); Henry G. Lotspeich, *Classical Mythology in the Poetry of Edmund Spenser* (1932); Peggy Muñoz Simonds, *Myth, Emblem, and Music in Shakespeare's Cymbeline* (1992): 98-101; Donald V. Stump, "Isis versus Mercilla: The Allegorical Shrines in Spenser's Legend of Justice," *SSt*, 3 (1982): 87-98.

IXION, king of the Lapiths, was the son of Mars or Phlegyas and the father of the Centaurs. Ross's version of the Ixion stories would have been widely recognized as typical:

He was the son of Plegias, who having murthered his father-in-law, went up and down the earth as a vagabond: at last Jupiter did pity him, and expiating his crime, received him into heaven; where he began to fall in love with Juno, desiring the use of her body, but Jupiter understanding this, presented to him a cloud, having the shape of Juno; of this cloud the Centaurs were procreated; therefore Ixion was sent down again to the earth, where bragging that he had lain with Juno, he was by Jupiters thunder cast down to hell, where, being tyed to a wheel, he is continually whirled about. (*Mystagogus Poeticus*: 225)

He came thus to be an *exemplum* of ambition and pride, both for his monstrous ingratitude to Jupiter and for presuming to desire Juno. As Fulgentius had written a thousand years earlier, the story of Ixion shows "that all who aspire to dominion by arms and violence are one moment held aloft and the next cast down, like a wheel which at no time has a fixed high point" (*Mythologies*: 2.14). Fraunce wrote that Ixion is "plagued in hell, for his ambitious and aspyring arogancie" (*Countesse of Pembrokes Yvychurch*: 29r). The wheel was like Fortune's wheel, bringing down what it had raised up. The *Chess of Love* commentator makes something like the same allegorical point: "He is eternally fastened to a wheel that never stops turning and will never be at rest. This is the punishment the ambitious bear, for they never cease from turning from one advantage to another...and always seek different turns by which to climb...to greater dignities than before" (485).

His fathering of the Centaurs—half human, half animal—also suggested the unnaturalness of his desires (see **CENTAURS**, Appendix B, "Bestialization"). Landino, for example: "Centaurs are rightly thought to be the offspring of Ixion, who...put justice aside as worthless and...broke...the bond of humanity....Although in the beginning his thoughts may display something of humanity, they descend at last into a kind of savagery and wildness" (*Disputationes Camuldenses*: 235).

When Virgil's Aeneas descends to the Underworld, he sees Ixion among the sufferers (*Aeneid*: 6:601). In Ovid's account of the Underworld, we see four men suffering their hellish torments: Ixion, Tantalus, Sisyphus, and Tityus (*Metamorphoses*: 4.456-463). These four thus became the conventional Four Blasphemers in subsequent poetic journeys to the Underworld (e.g., de Meun, *Romance of the Rose*: 19279; Conti, *Mythologie*: 6.17-20; Spenser, *Faerie Queene*: 1.5.35; see Panofsky 1962: 217; see **SISYPHUS, TANTALUS, TITYUS**).

Infrequently, Ixion was explained as a figure in nature allegory. Here is Bernardus:

we read in fables that Ixion desired to sleep with Juno and that she interposed a cloud which, receiving Ixion's seed, gave birth to the Centaurs, who were part men and part animals. We therefore interpret Ixion as the sun....Juno...is called the earth....Ixion wishes to lie with Juno when the sun sends both its heat and dryness below. Juno interposes clouds when the earth produces mist against the approaching heat. After the heat of the sun mixes with this moisture, temporal goods are produced and are therefore called Centaurs, because they are partly rational and partly vicious, that is, because they are human in the forepart and bestial in the hindpart. (*On Virgil's Aeneid*: 6.285-286)

Bibliography: Charles Lemmi, *The Classical Deities in Bacon* (1933): 101-103; Erwin Panofsky, *Studies in Iconology* (1962).

J

JANUS was the god with two faces. According to a Roman legend, Janus saved Rome when it was near overrun by the Sabines. According to Macrobius, "the Sabines were just about to burst in through the open gate when (so the story goes) a great stream of water came gushing in a torrent through it from the temple of Janus, and large numbers of the enemy perished, either scalded by the boiling heat of the water or overwhelmed by its force and depth. It was therefore resolved to keep the doors of the temple of Janus open in time of war, as though to indicate that the god had gone forth to help the city" (*Saturnalia*: 1.9.15; see also Lucan, *Civil War*: 1.62). Thus it is, for example, that Fulgentius writes of "warlike Janus" (*Ages of the World and Man*: 14); and thus it is that, when Tasso's fierce Argantes decides to go to war "with fell rage and hate," he "seem'd of Janus' church t'undo the gate" (*Jerusalem Delivered*: 2.90). Janus was also "the first to strike coins" (Macrobius, *Saturnalia*: 1.7.21).

But most often Janus was remembered as the Roman god of doorways, with one of his faces looking inward, the other outward. Ovid wrote that because he has in charge all comings and goings, all openings and closings, "The guardianship of this vast universe" is in Janus's hands; Janus even "regulates the comings and goings of Jupiter himself" (*Fasti*: 1.117-126). According to Macrobius, "At Rome all doorways are under the charge of Janus....He is represented as carrying a key and a rod, as the keeper of all doors and a guide on every road" (*Saturnalia*: 1.9.7). His two faces could even represent the human progression from savagery to civilization (Allen 1970: 258).

Janus's guardianship of doorways explains, of course, why Janus is invoked when Chaucer's Pandarus enters Criseyde's palace (*Troylus and Criseyde*: 2.77)—but two-faced as he was, Janus was also associated with deception and lechery; and so there is probably something unintentionally self-revealing in Pandarus's invocation of Janus (Robertson 1962: 256). That Janus was a deceiver-god was well known. Greene interpreted Janus in this way, for example; he had Achilles refer to Janus as the god of deceit ("Euphues His Censure": 163; see also, e.g., Ross, *Mystagogus Poeticus*: 198-199). And Shakespeare's most vile deceiver, Iago, swears his false oath "by Janus" (*Othello*: 1.2.33).

For Bernardus, Janus was "the eternal wisdom of God" (*On Martianus Capella*: 5.842). In a closely related allegory, Neckam writes that Janus could be Prudence, which looks both before and after (in Robertson, 1962: 256). And this is still the interpretation we find in Alciati (*Emblems*: 18) and in Wither, where Janus signifies God, "To whom, all hidden things are truely knowne"—God, who "Beholds, at one aspect, all things that are, / That ever shall be, and that ever were." Wither continues:

> But, in a Morall sense, we may apply
> This double-face, that man to signifie,
> Who (whatsoere he undertakes to doe)
> Lookes, both before him, and behinde him, too.
> (*Emblemes*: 138)

And for the Neo-Platonist Pico, Janus symbolized the "celestial souls" that animate the universe. "In ancient poetry," he wrote, "these souls were signified by the double-headed Janus, because being supplied like him with eyes in front and behind, they can at the same time see the spiritual things and provide for the material" (in Wind 1968: 201).

According to a late Euhemerist interpretation, Janus was really Noah. Here, for example, is Reynolds: "What can be plainer then that by their Janus they ment Noah..., whome they give two faces to, for having seene both the old and new world; and which his name (in Hebrew, Iain, or wine) likewise confirmes,—Noah being....the first inventor of the use of wines?" (*Mythomystes*: 175; see also van Mander, *Wtlegginghe op den Metamorphosis*: 101r). As late as 1732 Verburg could confidently assert that "today no one still doubts that Saturn was Adam, and Janus, Noah" (*Gedaant-wisselingen van Ovidius*: 8).

Bibliography: Don C. Allen, *Mysteriously Meant* (1970); Charles Lemmi, *The Classical Deities in Bacon* (1933): 61-74; D. W. Robertson, Jr., *Preface to Chaucer* (1962); Edgar Wind, *Pagan Mysteries of the Renaissance* (1968).

JASON, son of Aeson, was numbered among the most glorious of the mythic heroes. Like Achilles, Jason was given over to the centaur Chiron for his education. By the time he reached manhood, his wicked uncle Pelias had deprived him of his right to rule Iolcos; it was this same Pelias who imposed upon Jason the quest for the Golden Fleece—a quest from which Pelias was confident Jason would never return. Sandys tells the story of the origin of the Golden Fleece:

Phrixus with his sister Helle, to avoid the cruelty of their father Athamas, provoked by the treachery of their Stepmother Ino, were mounted, as was fained, by the compassionate Gods on a Ram with a golden fleece, and carryed swiftly through the aire: when fearful Helle fel from his back into that straight of the sea, which is of her called the Hellespont. But Phrixus arriving at Colchos, in gratitude sacrificed the Ram to Jupiter (converted into that Caelestial Signe) and hung up his fleece in the Grove of Mars. (*Ovid*: 331)

Jason soon had a ship, the Argo; and he called together a band of heroes, the Argonauts. This was usually reckoned a sizeable contingent; Hyginus's catalogue of the Argonauts covers most of three pages (*Fabulae*: 14). Aeetes, king of Colchos, was the keeper of the Golden Fleece. He told Jason that he could have the fleece—providing he could plough the field of Mars with a brace of fire-breathing oxen, sow the field with teeth taken from a certain dragon, and then defeat the armor-clad warriors who would spring from those seeds. And then, of course, Jason would have to deal with the dragon that guarded the fleece. But Aeetes' daughter Medea, a sorceress, fell in love with Jason and so helped him to cope with his perils and capture the Fleece. She fled her father's kingdom with Jason and bore him sons. But Jason came to love Creusa, daughter of Creon. Medea's revenge was terrible: Armed with her magic, she killed Creusa, and then she killed the sons she had borne Jason. This story of Medea's revenge is told vividly by Euripides in his *Medea* and by Seneca in his. Apollonius (*Argonautica*) tells the whole story of the Argonauts; Ovid's version of the story features a particularly ferocious Medea (*Metamorphoses*: 7.391-403).

Christians interpreted Jason sometimes positively, sometimes negatively. For Dante, Jason's arduous voyage for the Golden Fleece is a type of Dante's own voyage to God, to paradise (Hollander 1969: 220-225). Berchorius wrote that the minds of "contemplative men...fly to the golden fleece—that is the glory of Paradise—through desire" (*Ovidius Moralizatus*: 264). Berchorius also interprets Jason as a type of Christ in the Harrowing of Hell:

the argonaut Jason—that is Christ...came to the island of hell [where] he overcame fire-breathing bulls—that is demons—and conquered the vigilant dragon—that is Lucifer—and carried back from there the golden fleece—that is the spoil of holy souls. The golden fleece which was guarded by a dragon signifies the group of holy souls which was held captive in hell by the devil. (*Ovidius Moralizatus*: 268; for Christ's Harrowing of Hell, see **HERCULES: TWELFTH LABOR**)

Berchorius also interprets Jason as a type of Christ in saving Phineus from the afflictions of the Harpies (see **PHINEUS**). Another widespread tradition made Jason, like Hercules, an example of manly virtue. Philip the Good, Duke of Burgundy, had this tradition in mind when he founded the knightly Order of the Golden Fleece in 1430—an order, by the way, which was particularly associated with the idea of (as distinct from the practice of) the crusades. Golding, too, understood Jason in this way:

The good successe of Jason in the land of Colchos
    ...doo give too understand
That nothing is so hard but peyne and travell doo it win,
For fortune ever favoreth such as boldly doo begin.
                            ("Epistle": 142-146)

Peacham makes Jason an emblem for courage in the face of necessary dangers (*Minerva Britanna*: 54; see also Fraunce, *Countesse of Pembrokes Yvychurch*: 47r); for Dolce, Jason was a man "eager to acquire true glory and honor" (*Transformationi*: 157).

On the other hand, as the seducer of Medea, Jason was understood as an *exemplum* of the dangers of irrational love. Dante places Jason among the Seducers and Pandars in the Inferno (18.85). In the *Chess of Love* commentary we find that the story shows "how powerful and effective the force of love is, which conquers both nature and reason" (615). It was for such reasons that Tritonio includes Jason in his list of "The Perfidious" (*Mythologia*: 29).

Medea was usually a figure for "lascivious love" (Dolce, *Transformationi*: 168) or sorcery. Tritonio places her in his list of "The Libidinous" (*Mythologia*: 280). And she is often to be found in lists of bad wives (e.g., Lydgate, *Reson and Sensuallyte*: 4329-4332; Brant, *Ship of Fools*: 64). Berchorius makes her an *exemplum* of "corrupt love" (*Ovidius Moralizatus*: 277). Even in his profeminist *Concerning Famous Women*, Boccaccio interprets the story of Medea as demonstrating that our eyes often "place the shameful ahead of the sacred, the false ahead of the true....These ignorant eyes are captivated, attracted, seized, and held by beauty even if dishonorable, by lascivious motions, by youthful wantonness, and by corroding vices. And since the eyes are the gates of the spirit, through them lust sends messages to the mind, through them love sighs and lights blind fires" (16; see also Boccaccio, *Genealogie Deorum*: 4.12).

The *Chess of Love* commentator (617-622) interprets the story of Jason's quest for the Golden Fleece as an allegory of the quest for love, after the fashion of the lover's quest for the rose in de Meun's *Romance of the Rose*—but the commentator goes on to equate the love of Jason and Medea with the disastrous love of Paris and Helen (623). Then the commentator continues: "That Medea was such a great enchantress...can be related against some bad women who...know how to enchant and attract men, so that these women make in those whom they bemuse the darkness of ignorance, the winds of pride, the lightnings and thunders of burning concupiscence, the rains and sleets of grief and sorrow" (624). Ross put it more simply: "In Medea we may see the nature of lust, jealousie, and cruelty" (*Mystagogus Poeticus*: 267).

Fraunce, on the other hand, writes that "when Jason gives himselfe over to filthines, then doth Medea, good counsel, flie away in her chariot drawne by winged Dragons, noting wisdom and policie" (*Countesse of Pembrokes Yvychurch*: 47r).

Christine de Pizan, champion as she was of education for women, praises Medea for her learning (*City of Ladies*: 2.56.1).

In Renaissance alchemical circles, the Golden Fleece could serve as a symbol of alchemy or hermetic art (e.g., van Mander, *Wtlegginghe op den Metamorphosis*: 62r; see also Faivre 1993).

Jason was also known as one of the heroes who hunted the Calydonian boar (see **MELEAGER**).

Bibliography: Antoine Faivre, *The Golden Fleece and Alchemy* (1993); John Hollander, *Allegory in Dante's Commedia* (1969); Henry Lotspeich, *Classical Mythology in the Poetry of Edmund Spenser* (1932): 38-39; John P. McCall, *Chaucer among the Gods: The Poetics of Classical Myth* (1979): 112-116.

JOCUS (Iacchus, Jacchus, Jest, Mirth).   Originally Jocus was a minor deity associated with the Eleusian mysteries; he seems to have originated, in fact, from the word cried out by initiates during the rituals, *Iacchus!* *Iacchus* was close enough to *Bacchus* (Dionysus's title), that Iacchus was sometimes one of the names of Dionysus. But things took a turn with Horace. In a brief passage Horace (*Odes*: 1.2.34) wrote that Venus had two sons, Jocus, "Mirth," and Cupid, "Desire" (see also Prudentius, *Psychomachia*: 1.432-439). It was then left to Alanus to invent an extended account of the origins of the two brothers. Dame Nature is speaking:

While in her wild fornication she was continuing the illicit actions of concubinage with the adulterer [Antigenius; see **GENIUS**], she conceived offspring from him, and became the parent of a bastard for a son...Mirth [*Jocus*]....To Dione [i.e., Venus], then, were given two sons, divided by their differences in kind, unlike by law of their birth, dissimilar in the marks of their qualities, ill-agreeing in the variance of their occupation. For Hymen, who is related to me by the bond of brotherhood from the same mother, and whom a stock of excellent worth produced, begot to himself from Venus a son Cupid. (*Complaint of Nature*: pr. 5.235-250)

Hymen is the god of marriage, and so for Alanus, Cupid is a figure for natural desire, the sort of desire that is sanctified by marriage, the sort of desire that is naturally procreative: Alanus's Dame Nature recognizes Cupid as natural. But Antigenius is an allegorical figure for unnatural inclinations, just as his bastard child, Jocus is a figure for unnatural sexual desire—the kind of desire that is merely selfish, merely interested in pleasure (Nitzsche 1975: 100-102). It is in this sense that Jocus is "barren."

The *Chess of Love* commentary also associates Jocus with unreasonable love, but with a rearranged family tree:

Venus had three sons by the god Bacchus, of which one was Jacchus, the god of games and worldly solace. And this is the one called Deduit in *The Romance of the Rose*. The second is called Cupid, the god of love, and the third is named Hymen, the god of weddings. Certainly some say that Jacchus signifies the delectation of embracing and kissing; and that

Cupid, further, signifies the delectation of fully accomplishing the delight desired unreasonably; and that Hymen signifies the delight desired precisely as reason teaches and for the end nature intends in it, i.e., for the profit of generation. (562)

For the commentator, then, Jocus is "This general and first inclination...which thus moves and impels us all, male and female, to carnal delight for the said purpose Nature intends in it" (856; see also 566, 926).

Little was said of Jocus during the Renaissance.

Bibliography: George Economou, *The Goddess Natura in Medieval Literature* (1972): 87-93; Jane Chance Nitzsche, *The Genius Figure in Antiquity and the Middle Ages* (1975); Erwin Panofsky, *Studies in Iconology* (1962): 98.

JUNO (Hera, Lucina, Saturnia). As the wife and sister of Jupiter, Juno was the queen of the gods. An account of the allegorical understanding of Juno might best begin with the story of the Choice of Paris. Paris had to choose which of three goddesses, Athena, Venus, and Juno, ought to win the prize of a golden apple (for the origin of this apple, see **ATE**). Athena offered Paris wisdom; Venus offered Helen; and Juno offered worldly dominion. Paris gave the prize to Venus. Fulgentius's interpretation was widely influential: "Philosophers have distinguished a threefold life for mankind, by which they mean first the meditative; second, the practical; and third, the sensual—or as we call them in Latin, the contemplative, the active, the voluptuary." Venus, of course, was the voluptuary, Athena the meditative, and Juno the active life. Fulgentius went on to describe the active life:

The second kind of life led is the active one, so eager for advantages..., insatiable for possessions,...it has no stability because it does not go about things honorably....They put Juno in charge of the active life....She is said to rule over dominions, because this kind of life is much concerned with riches; she is depicted with a scepter, because riches and dominions are close kin. They say that Juno has her head veiled, because all riches are always hidden; they chose her as the goddess of birth, because riches are always productive and sometimes abortive. They also place the peacock in her patronage, because the whole acquisitive life of power is always looking to adorn its appearance. (*Mythologies*: 2.1)

Much of this allegory is worked out at length in Peele's *Arraignment of Paris*.

Juno was often associated, then, with all manner of things of the world. Augustine, for example, could interpret Aeneas's long struggle with Juno allegorically, as the struggle with evil, since the poets had represented Juno "as hostile to virtue, and jealous of men of mark aspiring to the heavens" (*City of God*: 10.21). Landino is still working in this tradition in his interpretation of book 4 of the *Aeneid*: Aeneas is tempted to stay in Carthage "to spend the long winter in debauchery" with Dido—but Landino reminds us that Carthage was Juno's city, and so there is also Juno's temptation, the temptation to rule: "it is a rare mortal who overcomes Juno, ...the desire to rule others" (*Disputationes Camuldenses*: 186; see also Ficino, *Philebus Commentary*: appendix 3).

The ancient Greeks knew that Hera often chafed within the bounds of her marriage to Zeus (see, e.g., Pantel 1992: 40-42). And with all of Jupiter's amours, there were many stories of Juno's jealousy (e.g., Ovid, *Metamorphoses*: 1.601-667; 2.466-530). Juno was proverbial for her "infinit spight and jealousie" (Lynche, *Fountaine of Ancient Fiction*: Pii; see also Ross, *Mystagogus Poeticus*: 366).

The peacock was Juno's bird. According to the *Ovide Moralisé* (1.4099-4150), the Argus eyes on her peacock's tail figure the vanities of the world (see also Boccaccio, *Genealogie Deorum*: 9.1). Sandys talks about Juno in relation to her peacock:

Juno is drawne into Heaven by her yoaked Peacocks: in whose traine, as formerly fained, she had fixed the eyes of Argus,...deciphering proud and ambitious men who attempt high things; riches, which morally is Juno, being their tutelar Goddesse; having need of many eyes to sentinel their wealth....The varietie of her colours shew the many vicissitudes of Fortune, which infest their mindes with cares and feares, who seeme to others so absolutely happy. (*Ovid*: 113; see also Fraunce, *Countesse of Pembrokes Yvychurch*: 15r-15v)

Lydgate, too, wrote of Juno as the "chefe goddesse of rychesse" (*Reson and Sensuallyte*: 1286; among many others, see, e.g., Boccaccio, *Genealogie Deorum*: 9.1, Conti, *Mythologie*: 2.5; for Rembrandt's *Juno* as the goddess of wealth, see Held 1969: 98-103).

But things of the world were not always regarded as necessarily evil; and most writers recognized that the active life, fraught though it may be with dangers, need not necessarily lead to evil. Societies must needs have governors; money could accomplish good works. And so Juno could represent the benificent side of dominion and money—or at least she was sometimes morally neutral. During a pageant staged for Elizabeth at Kenilworth, for example, it was Juno who bestowed jewels and raiment upon the queen (in Nichols 1823, vol. 1: 469). But another allegorizing entertainment, this one at Norwich in 1578, made the more familiar point. Juno appeared before Elizabeth and declaimed as follows:

Is Juno rich? no, sure she is not so:
She wantes that wealth, that is not wanting heere:
Thy good gets thee friends, my welth wins many a foe;
My riches rustes, thyne shine passing cleere.
Thou art beloved of subjectes farre and nye,
Which is such wealth as money cannot bye.
                    (as found in Nichols 1823, vol. 2: 160)

In nature allegory, Juno was a figure for the air. Saturn could thus be understood as the creator or source of the four elements, since he was the father of Jupiter (fire—the fire of the upper air, often distinguished from earthly fires), Juno (air), Neptune (water), and Pluto (earth). See, for example, Cicero (*Nature of the Gods*: 2.66), Heraclitus (*Allégories d'Homère*: 41.6-12), Vatican Mythographer II (7), Pietro Alighieri (*Commentarium*: 243, on *Inferno*: 14; Petrarch (*Rime sparse*:

41.12-13), "Le Commentaire de Copenhague de l'*Ovide Moralisé*" (390), the *Chess of Love* commentary (54, 414), and Sandys (*Ovid*: 113). This was a commonplace, although sometimes gods changed elements, as, for example, on the title page (fig. 16) of Sandys' *Ovid's Metamorphosis, Englished, Mythologized, and Represented in Figures*. Jupiter (the fiery ether) is in the upper left corner with a fiery salamander; Juno (air) is in the upper right; Neptune (water) is at the bottom right; and Ceres (earth) is at the bottom left (for more on this title page, see **APOLLO, MINERVA**).

In one of her aspects, Juno was Lucina, goddess of childbirth. (Cicero, *Nature of the Gods*: 2.69, distinguishes between Lucifera, one of the aspects of Diana, and Lucina, one of the aspects of Juno. He saw that both were etymologically related to *L. lucere*, "to shine"; and both were responsible for childbirth. But during the Middle Ages and the Renaissance, this distinction was not always observed. Both Juno and Diana could be called Lucina; see **DIANA**.) Augustine, for example, mentions the belief that Juno was in charge of births (*City of God*: 7.2-3); Fraunce provides this explanation: "Juno...is the Lady of marriage, and governesse of child-birth, called therefore Lucina...sith she, as a coelestial midwife, helpeth to bring forward the children *in lucem*, into light" (*Countesse of Pembrokes Yvychurch*: 15r).

Juno's role as the goddess of marriage was well known: Virgil mentions this (*Aeneid*: 4.166); it is as the goddess of married women that Juno aids Alcyone in Chaucer's *Book of the Duchess* (108-152); Juno presides over the marriage masque in Shakespeare's *Tempest* (4.1); see also Boccaccio (*Genealogie Deorum*: 9.1), Conti (*Mythologie*: 2.5), Spenser ("Epithalamion": 390-397), and many others.

Juno is sometimes called Saturnia, because she was Saturn's daughter.

Bibliography: Margaret J. Ehrhart, *The Judgment of the Trojan Prince Paris in Medieval Literature* (1987); Ehrhart, "Christine de Pizan and the Judgment of Paris," in Jane Chance, *The Mythographic Art* (1990): 125-156; Julius Held, *Rembrandt's Aristotle* and Other Rembrandt Studies (1969); John Nichols, *The Progresses and Public Processions of Queen Elizabeth*, 3 vols. (1823); Pauline Schmitt Pantel, *From Ancient Goddesses to Christian Saints* (1992).

JUPITER (Jove, Zeus). Jupiter was the son of Saturn and Cybele and the brother and husband of Juno. He was the greatest of the gods, the chief god of the Pantheon; consequently Christians often made him an allegorical figure for God (e.g., Berchorius, *Ovidius Moralizatus*: 132; the *Chess of Love* commentary, 822-823) or for Christ (e.g., Dante, *Purgatorio*: 6.118; Mutianus, *Briefwechsel*: 28). Indeed, in the seventeenth century, "Jove" became a standard euphemism for God, since the name of the Christian God was forbidden by law from being uttered on the English stage (Simonds 1992: 294).

In nature allegory, Jupiter could figure forth a kind of air that was higher, purer than the air we breathe—a refined ether combining fire and light. This distinction between two kinds of air was already recognized in classical times. Cicero, for example, explains that Juno is the sister and wife of Jupiter because "There is an affinity between the air and aether and they are closely linked together" (*Nature of the Gods*: 2.66; see also Heraclitus, *Allégories d'Homère*: 41.6-12; van Mander, *Wtlegginghe op den Metamorphosis*: 4v-5r). For Waleys, Jupiter was thus the "superior fire" (*Ovid*: 4). For Isidore this meant that Jupiter could allegorize two elements and his wife Juno the other two: Jupiter stands for "fire and air, while Juno is interpreted as water and earth" (*Etymologiarum*: 8.11.69; see also Hugh of St. Victor, *Didascalicon*: 1.10). But most Christians would have identified the four elements with the four children of Saturn. Fulgentius works this out at the beginning of his *Mythologies* (1.3-5; see Vatican Mythographer II: 2, 207). The *Chess of Love* commentary makes the same distinctions: "Saturn...sired four children, three sons and a daughter, by whom some wish to understand the four elements or the gods who had lordship over the four elements. Jupiter...fire, or the sovereign air....Juno...was understood as the lower air....Neptune...is the sea....And the fourth is Pluto who is the earth or the god of the earth" (54; see also 414).

We see all this illustrated on the title page (fig. 16) of Sandys' *Ovid's Metamorphosis, Englished, Mythologized, and Represented in Figures*: Jupiter (the fiery ether) is in the upper left corner with a fiery salamander; Juno (air) is in the upper right; Neptune (water) is at the bottom right; and Ceres (earth) is at the bottom left (for more on this title page, see **APOLLO, MINERVA**). Sandys later elaborates this nature allegory (*Ovid*: 113); and the same subject is treated by Fraunce (*Countesse of Pembrokes Yvychurch*: 13v) and many others (with Pluto, Cerberus, or Cybele sometimes substituting for Ceres as earth). Given his connection with the fiery ether (and given his place at the head of the gods), it is not surprising that Jupiter was sometimes seen as a personification of the sun itself (e.g., Dante, *Purgatorio*: 29.120).

Because of his etherial eminence and his association with the Christian God, Jupiter could stand with Apollo, Minerva, and Diana in general opposition to Venus, Bacchus, and various other gods: the forces of control and temperance in opposition to license and the passions. This is the meaning of a Neo-Platonic engraving after Baccio Bandinelli, *The Fray of Cupid and Apollo* (fig. 1; see **APOLLO** for more on this engraving).

Some of this is reflected in the astrological thinking about Jupiter. Gower explains the influence of Jupiter at some length:

> ...Jupiter the delicat,
> ...causeth pes and no debat.
> For he is cleped that Planete
> Which of his kinde softe and swete
> Attempreth al that to him longeth;
> And whom this planete underfongeth
> To stonde upon his regiment,
> He schal be meke and pacient
> And fortunat to Marchandie
> And lusti to delicacie....

> This Jupiter is cause also
> Of the science of lyhte werkes....
> Bot in Egipte of his offices
> He regneth most in special...
> For ther no stormy weder falleth,
> Which myhte grieve man or beste,
> And eke the lond is so honeste
> That it is plentevous and plein...
> And upon such felicite
> Stant Jupiter in his degre.
>
> (*Confessio Amantis*: 7.907-934)

We can see many of these ideas represented in the drawing of Jupiter by the Master of the Amsterdam Cabinet, where Jupiter "rides a pacing horse. His emblem, a lamb, is repeated on both his banner and on his horse's 'sack.' From his position in the heavens between Sagittarius and Pisces, he governs archers, hunters, falconers, judges, lawyers and scholars. His nature is warm and his children are handsome, well-dressed, good-humored and ingenious" (Filedt Kok 1985: 222). Gower and the Master could, on the whole, have agreed with Burton's estimate of Jupiter's influence: "If Jupiter domineers, they are more ambitious, still meditating of kingdoms, magistracies, offices, honours, or that they are princes, potentates, and how they would carry themselves, etc." (*Anatomy of Melancholy*: 1.3.1.3; see also Neckam, *De Naturis Rerum*: 1.7).

Ficino, in the course of a discussion of astrological influence, wrote that it was Jupiter who gave to mankind the art of ruling (*On Plato's Symposium*: 5.13)—a notion that was sufficiently well known that, among the Neo-Platonists, Jupiter could signify the active life, as opposed to the contemplative life, signified by Saturn (see, e.g., Pico, *Conclusiones*: 49.9; *On a Poem of Platonic Love*: 8; quoted below, under **SATURN**).

Jupiter's planetary influence was clearly related to Jupiter's "hot and moist" influence upon the bodily humors. Here, for example, is the *Chess of Love* commentary: "Finally, Jupiter is contrary to Saturn in all his nature. While Saturn is cold and dry and the signifier of sadness, anguish, old age, and death, as was said, Jupiter is on the contrary, hot and moist without moderation and is the signifier of amplitude, delectation, youth, and life" (107; see also Bartholomaeus, *On the Properties of Things*: 8.12). The notion that "Jupiter is contrary to Saturn" goes back to Jupiter's rebellion against his father Saturn (see **THE FOUR AGES, SATURN**).

Jupiter was also known for his sexual appetites. Isidore (*Etymologiarum*: 8.11.34-35) writes of Jupiter's "lewdness" in connection with his rape of Europa (see **EUROPA**) and of Danae (see **DANAE**). Jupiter transformed himself into a bull to carry off Europa and into a shower of gold to make his way to the lap of fair Danae (see **DANAE, EUROPA**). Petrarch likens himself to Jupiter in the *Rime sparse* (23), since he, too, finds himself transformed by his sexual appetites (Sturm-Maddox 1983). Often this allegory was put more strongly: Jupiter could serve as an example of bestializing effects of passion (e.g., Golding, "Preface": 95-96). Burton is typical: "The major part of lovers are carried headlong like so many brute beasts," he writes, "as Jupiter into a bull" (*Anatomy of Melancholy*: 3.2.3; see also 3.3.1.2). Jupiter's transformation into a swan in order to rape Leda could work allegorically in the same way: "Although love of lust is shamefull in all men," wrote Fulgentius, "it is never worse than when it is involved with honor," as in the case of Jupiter's degrading lust for Leda (*Mythologies*: 2.13; see also Vatican Mythographer III: 3.6; see **LEDA** for favorable interpretations of this myth). Such "lovetricks," wrote Fraunce, transformed Jupiter "into sundry shapes of brute beasts: for this immoderate lust and wantonnes, is not onely beastlike it self, but maketh them also beasts which give themselves over thereunto" (*Countesse of Pembrokes Yvychurch*: 13v). This seems to explain why Spenser has the stories of Jupiter's transformations graven upon the walls of Busirane's castle of unlawful lust:

> Therein was writ, how often thundring Jove
> Had felt the point of his [Cupid's] hart-percing dart,
> And leaving heavens kingdome, here did rove
> In straunge disguize, to slake his scalding smart;
> Now like a Ram, faire Helle to pervart,
> Now like a Bull, Europa to withdraw.
> *(Faerie Queene*: 3.11.30)

Jupiter's animal was the eagle, as Chaucer found when Jupiter's eagle took him up to heaven in *The House of Fame* (605-609). Fraunce's explanation for the eagle's association with Jupiter is typical: "The Aegle is his bird, as being, by report, never tutcht with thunder, but looketh directly on the burning beames of the sunne, and is King of birds, as Jupiter is Monarch among the Gods" (*Countesse of Pembrokes Yvychurch*: 13v; see also Conti, *Mythologie*: 1.2).

Jupiter was particularly important to the Neo-Platonist cosmologists, where he was interpreted as a figure for the world soul; and since the world soul was infused throughout the universe, Jupiter could have a wide range of related meanings. We find this, for example, in Bernardus's comment on Jupiter as he appears in the sixth book of the *Aeneid*:

Jupiter is to be taken...in diverse ways. As the superior fire, whence it is said, "from Jove, the origin of the Muses." As the spirit of the world, whence it is said, "Everything is filled with Jove." As the planet, whence, after Saturn, Jupiter is said to be first in the order of the planets. As the Creator, whence he is called "omnipotent Jupiter." As the human soul in this poetic fiction [i.e., in the *Aeneid*]. And according to this interpretation we say first the world, since it is ruled by Jove, and then man, who is moved by the soul. Thus man is called Microcosmus, the lesser world. In this world, heaven is the divine nature of the spirit from which the Aloides [the two giant sons of Neptune who rebelled against the gods] wish to cast out Jove. (*On Virgil's Aeneid*: 6.580-584)

Ficino, too, writes about Jupiter as the world soul. In Ficino's system Saturn's father, the Sky, is "the first principle of the sky and of all things"; Saturn, or Cronos, is "a divine intelligence begotten immediately by God. This intelligence Porphyry calls 'the reason or word of God the father'" (Allen's tr. provides this note: "The source of the Neoplatonic Kronos/Nous identification is Plotinus' *Enneads* 5.1.4; it derives in turn from Plato's *Cratylus* 396bc"). As Ficino continues, Saturn, in turn, is the father of Jupiter:

Out of this divine intelligence [i.e., Saturn] a certain living spirit is granted to the universal mechanism of the world; a spirit, indeed, which is borne above the waters, that is, above the flowing matter of the world. In the *Timaeus* [30b] Plato calls the spirit "the world's soul";...in the *Phaedrus* "Jove, the lord of who sets the winged chariot into motion in the sky" [*Phaedrus*: 246e]. In this dialogue the world's soul will be called by Plato "the intelligence," "the all-governing wisdom," "the queen of earth and sky," "Jove" (in whom dwells royal intellect and royal soul). (*Philebus Commentary*: 136)

Lynche put all this rather more succinctly: "The Neoplatonickes understand by Jupiter the soule of the world" (*Fountaine of Ancient Fiction*: Iiii).

For Jupiter's rebellion against Saturn and the end of the Golden Age, see **THE FOUR AGES** and **SATURN**; for Jupiter as the Platonic Form of fire and Vulcan as material fire, see **VULCAN**; for Jupiter and Io, see **IO**.

Bibliography: Leonard Barkan, *The Gods Made Flesh: Metamorphoses and the Pursuit of Paganism* (1986): 189-206; J. P. Filedt Kok, *Livelier Than Life: The Master of the Amsterdam Cabinet..., ca. 1470-1500* (1985); Richard Kay, *Dante's Christian Astrology* (1994): 187-217; Robert Lamberton, *Homer the Theologian* (1989): 219-221, 246-247; Henry Lotspeich, *Classical Mythology in the Poetry of Edmund Spenser* (1932): 75-76; Peggy Muñoz Simonds, *Myth, Emblem, and Music in Shakespeare's Cymbeline* (1992); Sara Sturm-Maddox, "Petrarch's Laurel and Jove," in Aldo S. Bernardo and Anthony L. Pellegrini, *Dante, Petrarch, Boccaccio: Studies in the Italian Trecento in Honor of Charles S. Singleton* (1983): 255-271.

L

THE LABYRINTH was built by Daedalus at King Minos's behest, as a place to conceal the terrible Minotaur. Here is Virgil's description: "in high Crete 'tis said the Labyrinth held a path woven with blind walls, and a bewildering work of craft with a thousand ways, where the tokens of the course were confused by the indiscoverable and irretraceable maze" (*Aeneid*: 5.588-591).

Allegorically, the Labyrinth was in one way or another likened to the uncertainties of life in this world. Boccaccio, for example, wrote of the "wretched valley" which lovers are wont to think of as "the Court of Love." But it is "a 'labyrinth'...because men become as trapped in it as they did in that of old, without ever knowing the way out" (*Corbaccio*: 14). As Guido da Pisa phrased it: "Allegorically...the labyrinth signifies the world, full of all fallacies and error" (*Super Comediam Dantis*: 222). That is, the Labyrinth could signify the World, in the theological sense. As Berchorius wrote, "it often happens that when someone thinks to escape from the labyrinth of the world...he puts himself in there more strongly....Whoever mingles or binds himself in the labyrinth of the world or of sin through evil habits will seldom escape from there" (*Ovidius Moralizatus*: 307).

Sandys, like many other mythographers, described basically the same allegory in nontheological terms: "By a Labyrinth the Ancient deciphred the perplexed condition of man, combred and intangled with so many mischiefes: through which impossible to passe without the conduct of wisdome, and exercise of unfailing fortitude" (*Ovid*: 382; see also Conti, *Mythologie*: 7.9; Dinet, *Hieroglyphiques*: 385). Thus it is that Tasso's Rinaldo, ensnared by a temptress, is pent up in a castle "With doors and entries false a thousand fold; / A labyrinth they made that fortress brave" (*Jerusalem Delivered*: 16.1). And Spenser can thus call his wood of Error a "labyrinth" (*Faerie Queene*: 1.1.11); it is in this wood that the Red Cross Knight loses his way (see Blissett 1989).

This seems to have been one of the reasons for building labyrinths into the pavements—or depicting them on the walls—of Medieval churches and cathedrals. This practice was particularly widespread in twelfth-century France and Italy, but the oldest known example is in the basilica of Reparatus at Orleansville, in Algeria, from about the fourth century. Some of the other churches with labyrinths are the Cathedral of Cremona (eighth or ninth century), the church of San Michele Maggiore at Pavia (tenth century), Chartres Cathedral (twelfth century), and Amiens and Rheims Cathedrals (thirteenth century). The labyrinth in Chartres is the largest extant, measuring forty feet in diameter. A tenth-century labyrinth in the church of San Savino at Piacenza was accompanied by a legend in Latin hexameters to the effect that "the labyrinth represented the world we live in, broad at the entrance, but narrow at the exit, so that he who is ensnared by the joys of this world, and weighed down by his vices, can regain the doctrine of life only with difficulty" (in Matthews 1922). In this spirit Erasmus wrote that Christianity allows us to escape "from the labyrinthine errors of this world" (*Enchiridion*: 83). One of Quarles' emblems (fig. 17) shows us a labyrinth working in the same allegorical way: The Cupid of divine love is at the top of a tall tower, leading our pilgrim through the labyrinth-world by a taut line; others are lost in the labyrinth; one is led by a dog (for more on the Labyrinth in the emblem tradition, see Pinkus 1993).

Some of the labyrinths in the churches might have been used for purposes of penance: The penitent would seek the Jerusalem at the center of the labyrinth instead of going on an actual pilgrimage (Matthews 1922; Santarcangeli 1974: 272-301; Kern 1982: 206-218).

Sometimes, however, "pilgrims" would find a Minotaur at the center of their Labyrinth; this might suggest the antithesis of the Heavenly City; the center of the Labyrinth would be a type of hell, at the spiritual-geographic center of the world. Pilgrims could thus show their contempt for the world by stepping on the Minotaur (Demaray 1991: 26). Berchorius was aware of such traditions; he interpreted the story of Theseus and the Labyrinth as a type of Christ's Harrowing of Hell (for the Harrowing of Hell, see **HERCULES: TWELFTH LABOR**):

The lot of the human condition was such that the Athenians conquered by Minos—that is Lucifer in the person of Adam—were sent one after another to those minotaurs and were devoured by them body and soul....Wisdom 2:1: "No man has been known to have returned from hell." But Theseus—that is Christ—the son of the king held it to be necessary to descend to those minotaurs because of the mortality he had accepted. He...went out free from there through his resurrection, and returned as victor. He led with him Ariadne the daughter of Minos—that is human nature the daughter of Adam which lay in limbo. (*Ovidius Moralizatus*: 304)

For more Labyrinth allegory, see **MINOS, MINOTAUR, THESEUS**.

Bibliography: William Blissett, "Caves, Labyrinths, and *The Faerie Queene*," in G. M. Logan et al., *Unfolded Tales: Essays on Renaissance Romance* (1989): 281-311; John G. Demaray, *Cosmos and Epic Representation* (1991); Penelope

Doob, *The Idea of the Labyrinth from Classical Antiquity through the Middle Ages* (1990); Hermann Kern, *Labytrinthe* (1982); W. H. Matthews, *Mazes and Labyrinths: Their History and Development* (1922); David Ormerod, "*A Midsummer Night's Dream*: The Monster in the Labyrinth," *ShakS*, 11 (1978): 39-52; Karen Pinkus, "Philology and Emblems," *SI*, 15 (1993): 177-196; Paolo Santarcangeli, *Le livre des labrinthes: Histoire d'un mythe et d'un symbole* (1974).

LAODAMIA (Ladomya) was the wife of Protesilaus, the first Greek killed at Troy. Homer mentions Laodamia, with her "cheeks torn for grief" (*Iliad*: 2.700). Ovid suggests that Laodamia killed herself to join her husband in death (*Heroides*: 13). Thus it was that Jerome included her, along with Penelope, Lucretia, Alceste, and Portia, in a short list of virtuous wives: "Laodamia's praises are also sung by the poets, because, when Protesilaus was slain at Troy, she refused to survive him" (*Against Jovinianus*: 1.45). And so, she became an *exemplum* of wifely virtue. Chaucer, for example, has Dorigin mention her in a list of faithful wives ("Franklin's Tale": 1445).

THE LAPITHS were a Thessalian people. There were Lapiths numbered among the Argonauts (see **JASON**) and the hunters of the Calydonian Boar (See **MELEAGER**). But they were best known for their battle with the Centaurs (e.g., Ovid, *Metamorphoses*: 12.210-535). The Lapiths were celebrating the marriage of their king, Pirithous, to the lovely Hippodamia; the Centaurs, present as wedding guests, became drunk and increasingly obnoxious, until one of the Centaurs, Eurytus, tried to make off with the bride. Eventually—after what can best be described as an epic barroom brawl—the Lapiths and Pirithous's great friend Theseus managed to drive the Centaurs off.

In general, this battle was seen as a struggle wherein the rational element, figured by the Lapiths and Theseus, gains control over the passionate or bestial element, figured by the Centaurs (see Appendix B, "Bestialization"). Thus it is that Spenser's description of the house of Ate (goddess of discord) includes "the relicks of the drunken fray, / ...which sent away / So many Centaures drunken soules to hell" (*Faerie Queene*: 4.1.23). The story could also serve, more simply, to allow us "too understand / The beastly rage of drunknesse" (Golding, "Epistle": 247-248).

LEDA was one of the beautiful mortals for whom Jupiter lusted. He assumed the form of a swan to have his way with her (e.g., Ovid, *Metamorphoses*: 6.109). This much of the story was often interpreted as an example of bestial desire (see **JUPITER**; see also Appendix B, "Bestialization"). But this story was sometimes interpreted in terms of spiritual ravishing (for other spiritual ravishings, see **DANAE, ENDYMION, EUROPA, GANYMEDE**).

Leda was usually said to have born four children from two eggs: Helen (see **HELEN**) and Clytemnestra (see **AGAMEMNON, AEGISTHUS**) from the one, and Castor and Pollux from the other (see **CASTOR AND POLLUX**).

Bibliography: Judson B. Allen, "The Allegorized Mythography of Johannes Calderia," in *ICNLS*, 4 (1981): 390-398.

LEUCADIAN ROCK (Leucata Petra). Ovid tells the story of Sappho of Lesbos, the poet of love: she loved young Phaon; but he did not requite her love, and so she sought some remedy for her pain. A Naiad appeared before her and said,

"Since thou art burning with unrequited flame, Ambracia is the land thou needs must seek. There Phoebus from on high looks down on the whole wide stretch of sea—of Actium, the people call it, and Leucadian. From here Deucalion, inflamed with love for Pyrrha, cast himself down, and struck the waters with body all unharmed. Without delay, his passion was turned from him...and Deucalion was freed from the fires of love. This is the law of yonder place. Go straightway seek the high Leucadian cliff, nor from it fear to leap!" (*Heroides*: 15.163-172)

This tradition was revived during the Renaissance; Burton assures us that the leaping cure was well known:

Our old poets and phantastical writers have many fabulous remedies for such as are lovesick....But the most famous is Leucata Petra, that renowned rock in Greece, of which Strabo writes [*Geography*: 10]...from which rock if any lover flung himself down headlong, he was instantly cured. Venus after the death of Adonis...came to the temple of Apollo to know what she should do to be eased of her pain; Apollo sent her to Leucata Petra, where she precipitated herself, and was forthwith freed. (*Anatomy of Melancholy*: 3.2.5.4; see also Sandys, *Ovid*: 611)

Burton numbers Jupiter and Deucalion among those who were cured by leaping from the rock (see Ovid, *Epistulae*: 21.163-172, for the story of Deucalion's leap). Spenser's Malbecco makes such a leap, but so spent is this old man by his lechery that he manages no more than a sad parody of the Leucadian cure:

> Still fled he forward, looking backward still,
> Ne stayd his flight, nor feareful agony,
> Till that he came unto a rockie hill,
> Over the sea, suspended dreadfully....
> From thence he threw himselfe dispiteously,
> All desperate of his fore-damned spright,
> That seem'd no helpe for him was left in living sight.
>
> But through long anguish, and self-murdring thought
> He was so wasted and forepined quight,

That all his substance was consum'd to nought...
That on the rockes he fell so flit and light,
That he thereby receiv'd no hurt at all.
(Faerie Queene: 3.10.56-57)

But this falling from a high rock came to be a cure for more than just lover's despair. Sappho's leap suggested something more nearly universal to the poets. Ariosto—one of Spenser's sources for the story of the rock—makes this explicit in his account of Ariodantes, who was driven by love's pain: He did "leape downe headlong from the rock."

But as we see men oft with rash intent
Are desperate and do resolve to die,
And straight do change that fancie and repent,
When unto death they do approch more nie:
So Ariodant to drowne himselfe that ment,
Now plung'd in sea repented by and by,
And being of his limbes able and strong,
Unto the shore he swam againe ere long.

And much dispraising in his inward thought,
This fond conceit that late his minde possest.
(Orlando Furioso: 6.5-6)

Harington's commentary on these lines recognizes the allusion to the Leucadian Rock (On Orlando Furioso: 39). We see this tradition in Shakespeare's King Lear, where Edgar allows his blind and despairing father to think that he is going to leap off a high cliff: "Why I do trifle thus with his despair," Edgar explains, "Is done to cure it" (4.6.33-34).

For some, however, Sappho's leap from the Leucadian Rock was simply an example of the dangers of love madness (e.g., Ferrand, Treatise on Lovesickness: 2).

The rock seems to have been named after the Nereid Leucothea: Ino sought to raise with her own children the child Bacchus—her sister Semele's child by Jupiter (see **SEMELE**). Jealous Juno made Ino mad, and in her madness, Ino killed her own child Melicertes and then leaped from a rock into the sea now known as the Ionian Sea. She was transformed into the Nereid Leucothea and was thenceforth known for rescuing sailors (e.g., Homer, Odyssey: 5.333-353, 458-462).

LUCRETIA was the wife of Tarquinius Collatinus. She was famed for her chastity; but she was raped by Sextus, son of Tarquinius Superbus, King of Rome. Lucretia told her husband of the outrage and then committed suicide. Legend had it that this led to a popular uprising, led by Junius Brutus, and so to the fall of the Tarquin kings. This, in turn, meant the establishment of the Roman Republic.

There were two main lines of interpretation of the story (for a history of attitudes toward Lucretia up to the Renaissance, see Schmitz 1990: 76-104). For some Lucretia was an example of married chastity. Jerome (*Dialogue against Jovinianus*: 1.45) and Tertullian (*To the Martyrs*: 4.4; *Exhortation to Chastity*: 13) understood her in this way; and here is Boccaccio:

As her relatives consoled her while she cried wretchedly, she took out a knife that she had under her dress and said: "Although I absolve myself of the sin, I do not free myself from the punishment, and in the future no woman will live dishonorably because of Lucretia's example." Having said these words, she drove the knife into her innocent breast....She cleansed her shame harshly, and for this reason she should be exalted with worthy praise for her chastity, which can never be sufficiently lauded. Because of her action, not only was her reputation restored, which a lewd young man had tried to destroy with the stain of sin, but Rome was made free. (*Concerning Famous Women*: 46)

Gower also praised her (*Confessio Amantis*: 8.2639); and for Chaucer she was one who "loved clennesse and eke trouthe" (*Legend of Good Women*: 1860; see also Brant, *Ship of Fools*: 64; Cooper, *Dictionarium*: under *Lucretia*; Harington, *Apologie of Poetrie*: 8).

Augustine began a second tradition, where Lucretia was an example of the Roman—as distinct from the Christian—sense of honor. In a society known for its sexual laxness, Augustine writes, Lucretia was a noble Roman famed for her faithfulness to her husband. And after the rape:

What shall we call her? An adulteress, or chaste? There is no question which she was. Not more happily than truly did a declaimer say of this sad occurrence: "Here was a marvel: there were two, and only one committed adultery." Most forcibly and truly spoken. For this declaimer, seeing in the union of the two bodies the foul lust of the one, and the chaste will of the other, and giving heed not to the contact of the bodily members, but to the wide diversity of their souls, says: "There were two, but the adultery was committed only by one."

Since Lucretia was raped, she was innocent. In Tarquin there was "foul lust"; but Lucretia was of "chaste will." There was certainly "contact of the bodily members"; but since Lucretia's will did not consent, she retained her unspotted chastity. For Augustine, then, the morality of an act has to do with the choice of the will. But for the Romans, honor had to do with reputation—and so, Augustine continues, Lucretia committed suicide: "this matron, with the Roman love of glory in her veins, was seized with a proud dread that, if she continued to live, it would be supposed she willingly did not resent the wrong that had been done her. She could not exhibit to men her conscience, but she judged that her self-inflicted punishment would testify to her state of mind" (*City of God*: 1.19).

For Augustine Lucretia was thus a moral exemplar only until she committed suicide. Then she became a martyr to that misguided Roman "love of glory," what Augustine elsewhere calls Rome's characteristic "vice, namely, the love of praise" (*City of God*: 5.13). Vives, a Renaissance commentator on Augustine, continues the argument: "The Romaine Nation were alwaies most greedy of glory....And Ovid saith of Lucrece, in his *Fasti*: 'Conquer'd with feare to loose her fame, she fell' [2.810]....for our [Christian] glory is this (saith Saint Paul 2 Cor. 1.12) the testimony of our consciences. And this the Stoikes and all the heathenish wise men have ever taught" (*Of the Citie of God*: 1.18)

Don C. Allen (1968: 58-76) and Battenhouse (1969: 10-41) argue that Shakespeare's view of Lucretia in "The Rape of Lucrece" is in essential agreement with Augustine—but Allen also points out that "For the sixteenth century the tragedy of Lucrece was a kind of casuistic problem, a matter of legal gamesmanship for canon lawyers," some of whom argued that she was innocent, others that she must have been guilty of some degree of lust.

The story was sometimes cited as an example of the potentially disastrous effects of individual lack of control might have upon a whole society: Tarquin's lust brought on the fall of the Roman kings. Petrarch, for example, cites the story of Lucretia along with the story of Helen and Troy to make this point (*Remedies for Fortune*: 1.72).

Bibliography: Don C. Allen, *Image and Meaning* (1968); Roy Battenhouse, *Shakespearean Tragedy: Its Art and Its Christian Premises* (1969); Ian Donaldson, *The Rapes of Lucretia: A Myth and Its Transformations* (1982); Götz Schmitz, *The Fall of Women in Early English Narrative Verse* (1990).

LYCAON, for the Middle Ages and the Renaissance, was that king of Arcadia who received Jupiter as his guest only to feed him human flesh. In most accounts he did this in order to see whether Jupiter really was a god. Enraged, Jupiter overthrew the table, struck Lycaon with a bolt of lightning, and turned him into a wolf. In Ovid (*Metamorphoses*: 1.177-243), it is in response to Lycaon's wickedness that Jupiter determines to destroy mankind by flood. Lycaon is thus one of Brant's examples of blasphemy (*Ship of Fools*: 87). For Regius, Lycaon's "terrible barking teaches us to be ready with our prayers" (*Ovid*: 4). Sandys' comment may be taken as broadly typical:

This fable of Lycaon was devised to deterre from impiety, treachery, & inhospitality; as also to excite to the contrary virtues: since the Gods, though disguized, are alwaies present; punishing, and rewarding, according to our actions. In this, as in the rest, [Ovid] proportions the transformation to the quality of the transformed....The Sinnes of men drew on (in which our poet concurres with Moses) the general Deluge. (*Ovid*: 65-67)

Much the same interpretation may be found, for example, in Conti (*Mythologie*: 9.9). And Burton makes Lycaon's metamorphosis one of his examples of what happens to human beings when they behave like "brute beasts" (*Anatomy of Melancholy*: 3.2.3; see also, e.g., Golding, "Preface": 94-96).

Bibliography: Leonard Barkan, *The Gods Made Flesh: Metamorphoses and the Pursuit of Paganism* (1986): 24-27.

Fig. 1. *The Fray of Cupid and Apollo, with All the Gods Present,* engraving after Baccio Bandinelli (1545), Paris, Louvre (*Cabinet des Estampes*).

Fig. 2. Title page for Alexander Ross, *Mystagogus Poeticus, or The Muses Interpreter* (London, 1648). Courtesy of the Beinecke Rare Book and Manuscript Library, Yale University.

Fig. 3. *Aristotle and Phyllis*, Master of the Amsterdam Cabinet (c. 1488), drypoint, Coburg, Veste Coburg. Courtesy of the Kunstsammlungen der Veste Coburg.

Fig 4. *Aristotle and Phyllis*, Aquamanile (c. 1400), bronze, New York, The Metropolitan Museum of Art. Courtesy of the Metropolitan Museum of Art, Robert Lehman Collection, 1975 (1975.1.1416), all rights reserved.

Fig. 5. *The Fair at Hoboken*, Peter Bruegel the Elder (c. 1559), engraving, Brussels, Bibliothèque royale Albert Ier (Cabinet des Estampes Bruxelles). Courtesy of the Bibliothèque royale Albert Ier (Royal Library of Albert I, Department of Prints).

Fig. 6. *Pallas and the Centaur* (c. 1482), Sandro Botticelli, Florence, Galleria degli Uffizi. Courtesy of the Galleria degli Uffizi.

IV.

Quam graue ſeruitium eſt, quod leuis eſca parit.

Fig. 7. Book 2, Emblem 4, in Frances Quarles, *Emblemes* (Cambridge, 1643). Courtesy of the Beinecke Rare Book and Manuscript Library, Yale University.

Fig. 8. Title page for Jacob Cats, *Proteus, ofte Minne-beelden Verandert in Sinne-beelden* (Rotterdam, 1627), Chicago, Newberry Library. Photo courtesy of The Newberry Library.

Fig. 9. *Cupid Unblindfolding Himself* (c. 1525–1530), Lucas
Cranach the Elder, Philadelphia, Philadelphia Museum of Art.
Courtesy of the Philadelphia Museum of Art: John G. Johnson
Collection.

Fig. 10. *St. Luke Portraying the Virgin* (1532), Maerten van Heemskerck, Haarlem, Frans Hals Museum. Courtesy of the Frans Hals Museum, Haarlem–Holland.

Fig. 11. Title page for Sir Walter Raleigh, *The History of the World* (London, 1614). Courtesy of the Beinecke Rare Book and Manuscript Library, Yale University.

Fig. 12. *Wild Family* (1480), anonymous Netherlandish artist, engraving, Paris, Louvre (*Cabinet des Estampes*), E. de Rothschild collection (inventory number 288 LR).

Fig. 13. *Primavera* (c. 1484), Sandro Botticelli, Florence, Galleria degli Uffizi. Courtesy of the Galleria degli Uffizi.

Fig. 14. Title page for Chapman's translation of the *Odyssey* (London, 1614?).
Courtesy of the Beinecke Rare Book and Manuscript Library, Yale University.

Fig. 15. *Landscape with the Fall of Icarus* (probably c. 1558), Peter Bruegel the Elder, painting, Brussels, Musées Royaux des Beaux-Arts. Courtesy of the Musées Royaux des Beaux-Arts.

Fig. 16. Title page for George Sandys, *Ovid's Metamorphosis Englished, Mythologiz'd, and Represented in Figures* (Oxford, 1632). Courtesy of the Beinecke Rare Book and Manuscript Library, Yale University.

Fig. 17. Book IV, Emblem 2, in Frances Quarles, *Emblemes* (Cambridge, 1643). Courtesy of the Beinecke Rare Book and Manuscript Library, Yale University.

Fig. 18. *Mars and Venus* (1578), Veronese, New York, The Metropolitan Museum of Art. Courtesy of The Metropolitan Museum of Art, John Kennedy Fund, 1910 (10.189), all rights reserved.

Fig. 19. *Triumph of Wisdom over the Vices* (c. 1499–1502), Andrea Mantegna, painting, Paris, Louvre. Photo © R.M.N. Photo courtesy of the Museés Nationaux–Paris.

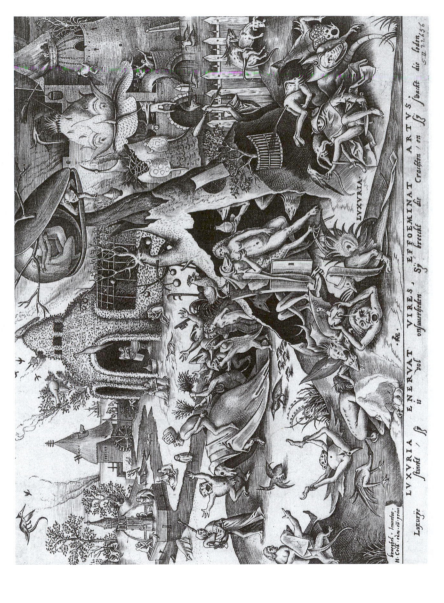

Fig. 20. *Lechery* (1557), Peter Bruegel the Elder, engraving, Brussels, Bibliothèque royale Albert Ier (Cabinet des Estampes Bruxelles). Courtesy of the Bibliothèque royale Albert Ier (Royal Library of Albert I, Department of Prints).

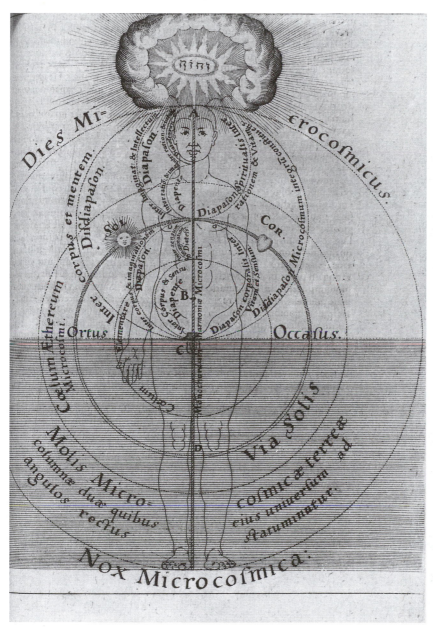

Fig. 21. *The Relationship of Man to the Macrocosm*, illustration in Robert Fludd, *Tomus Secundus De Supernaturali . . . Microcosmi historia* (n.p., 1619). Courtesy of the Beinecke Rare Book and Manuscript Library, Yale University.

Fig. 22. *Man of War seen between Two Galleys, with the Fall of Phaethon* (probably 1565), Peter Bruegel the Elder, engraving, Brussels, Bibliothèque royale Albert Ier (Cabinet des Estampes Bruxelles). Courtesy of the Bibliothèque royale Albert Ier (Royal Library of Albert Ier, Department of Prints).

Fig. 23. *Allegory of Venus, Cupid, Folly, and Time* (probably c. 1540–1545). Bronzino, London, National Gallery. Reproduced by courtesy of the Trustees, The National Gallery, London.

Fig. 24. *The Triumph of Time* (1574), Peter Bruegel the Elder, engraving, Brussels, Bibliothèque royale Albert Ier (Cabinet des Estampes Bruxelles). Courtesy Bibliothèque royale Albert Ier (Royal Library of Albert I, Department of Prints).

Fig. 25. *Drunken Silenus* (1626), Jusepe de Ribera, Naples, Museo e Gallerie Nazionali di Capodimonte. Courtesy of the Museo Nazionali di Capodimonte.

Fig. 26. *Venus and Her Children* (1470), Francesco del Cossa, Ferrara, Palazzo Schifanoia. Courtesy of the Musei Civici Arte Antica.

Fig. 27. *Sacred and Profane Love* (c. 1515), Titian, Rome, Galleria Borghese. Courtesy of the Galleria Borghese.

M

MARS (Ares, Gradivus). Mars was the son of Juno, by her touching of a spring flower, according to one tradition, or by Jupiter, according to another. Both Romans and Greeks recognized that Mars was a bloodthirsty god, but the Romans were rather more inclined to revere him than were the Greeks. A warlike people, the Romans recognized him as the father of Romulus and Remus, founders of Rome.

Mars served Christian poets and artists as an allegorical figure for wrath, violence, and violent inclinations. "Mars is named for death [*L., mors*]," wrote Isidore (8.11.51). Mars' influence is well described in the *Chess of Love* commentary on Mars:

> Mars, who is the third god and the third planet after Saturn, is pictured in the similitude of a savage madman who has a red and terrible face, and a cruel one to look at. He is placed in a chariot and always has a helmet on his head. He carries in his hand a big whip or a big club, and also, a wolf was painted before him.
>
> If we wish to consider this picture well, we will find that it clearly presents the nature and properties of Mars to us. For this planet is hot, dry, and of a choleric complexion by nature. Thus it disposes human hearts and inclines them as much as it can to wars, battles, and all discords....And this is why Mars is figured...in the similitude of a furious and raging man full of great ill will and desiring to revenge himself for all injury. (126-127)

The astrological drawing of Mars by the Master of the Amsterdam Cabinet could almost be an illustration of this passage (in Filedt Kok 1985: 222). Burton's account of Mars' influence is in this same tradition: "If Mars [predominate], they are all for wars, brave combats, monomachies, testy, choleric, harebrain, rash, furious, and violent in their actions. They will feign themselves victors, commanders, are passionate and satirical in their speeches, great braggers, ruddy of colour" (*Anatomy of Melancholy*: 1.3.1.3).

But the passion Mars inspired was not always condemned. Romans thought of Mars as having two faces: Mars turned a savage face to Rome's enemies in times of war; Mars looked with his tranquil face upon Rome when he presided over civic peace (see Plass 1995: 34-35). It was thus sometimes assumed that the passion itself was neutral; the passion Mars inspired could only be judged in relation to the cause in which it was engaged. This classical notion of the two aspects of Mars continued into the Middle Ages and the Renaissance. When Boccaccio's Theseus goes to war with Thebes, for example, the knights on both sides invoke Mars: "The horses quivered and the confident knights all shouted, 'Oh, Mars, now your harsh blows will appear. Now your art will be revealed'" (*Book of Theseus*: 2.54). When Boccaccio writes that Theseus "burned all over with wrath" (2.60), we are to understand that it is Mars who inspires this passion. But Boccaccio makes it clear that Theseus and his Athenian knights are fighting a good and selfless battle against proud, wicked Creon; and thus we are given to understand that Mars' influence upon Theseus is not malign. Chaucer's "Knight's Tale" describes the same episode; when Chaucer's Theseus takes up the grieving widows' cause, he does so under the banner of Mars:

> The rede statue of Mars, with spere and targe,
> So sheyneth in his white baner large,
> That alle the feeldes glyteren up and doun.
> ("Knight's Tale": 975-977)

Chaucer's Arcite later invokes Mars; this, however, is not the Mars of the just war. The icons in this temple are an outward manifestation of Arcite's inward spiritual state:

> Ther saugh I first the dirke ymaginyng
> Of Felonye, and al the compassyng;
> The crueel Ire, reed as any gleede;
> The pykepurs, and eek the pale Drede;
> The smylere with the knyfe under the cloke...;
> The tresoun of the mordrynge in the bedde;
> The open werre, with woundes al bibledde....
>   The statue of Mars upon a carte stood
> Armed, and looked grym as he were wood....
> A wolf ther stood biforn hym at his feet
> With eyen rede, and of a man he eet.
> ("Knight's Tale": 1995-2048)

Erasmus provides a clear explanation of this kind of thinking. He argues against the Stoics who wanted human beings to extirpate "all perturbations" of the passions; no, says Erasmus:

the passions are not to be extirpated but controlled, for...some of [the passions] are useful because they have been implanted by nature as a kind of incentive and spur to virtue, as anger contributes to courage, envy to industry, and so on....The first thing you must do, therefore, is to understand all these agitations of the mind; then you must realize that there are none so turbulent that they cannot be curbed by rational control or channeled in the direction of virtue. (*Enchiridion*: 68)

During the Renaissance we see the good Mars, for example, in the entertainments at Killingworth Castle for Elizabeth in 1575. A masque was presented in which the gods gathered to give their gifts to the queen. Mars gave "Captainz of good conduct, men skylfull in feats of armz, pollitik in stratagemz, good coroage in good quarelz, valiant and wizehardy: abandoning pikquarrells and ruffianz" (in Nichols 1823, vol. 1: 469).

One of the best-known myths about Mars was that of his love for Venus. Vulcan, the god of the forge, the unlikely, misshapen husband of Venus, caught the lovers in bed with a finely wrought net, in most versions a net of gold. The net held Venus and Mars in lewd embrace for the gods to laugh at. As Ovid tells the story, Venus and Mars are guilty lovers. The Sun was the first to see "the shame of Mars and Venus." The Sun then "revealed her sin" to Vulcan. When Vulcan's trap is sprung, "There lay the two, disgracefully...and for a long time this story was the talk of heaven" (*Metamorphoses*: 4.171-189; see also *Art of Love*: 2.561-600).

The story could, of course, serve as a moral example: the consequences of adultery (e.g., *Ovide Moralisé*: 4.1577-1629). But in this context we should remember the classical and Christian allegorical sense of manhood: the word "virtue," and the Latin *virtus* from which it derives, have *vir*, "man," as their root. To be *vir*tuous, then, was to behave like a man (see **AMAZONS, HERCULES: Hercules in General**). As Boethius put it, "virtue gets its name from that virile strength [*virtus*] which is not overcome by adversity" (*Consolation of Philosophy*: 4.pr 7). Thus, it was that Arnolphe of Orléans interpreted Venus overcoming Mars as "virtue [*virtus*] overcome by libidinousness" (*On Ovid*: 210), or "the reason by the flesh," as Agostini put it (*Ovid*: 35). For Christine de Pizan the story is a warning against lechery and covetousness (*L'Epitre*: 231). The *Chess of Love* commentary is in the same tradition—and this account of the story is typical as well in its treatment (following Ovid, *Art of Love*: 2.561-600) of Vulcan as an *exemplum* of the foolish, jealous old husband:

Briefly, this fable signifies to us on first glance the mad love of the world that is common enough. For we often see two people love each other so madly and for so long that even though they are accused and seen by the sun, i.e., reason, and made fun of by the gods, i.e., the wise and everybody, they cannot part from each other, but wish thus to live and remain as they are....For Vulcan, i.e., the fire of their concupiscence and their bad habit, binds couples together with a net that holds them like very hard steel and binds them as strongly as brass, so that they cannot separate or disjoin themselves. And this thing is most especially and frequently seen in...young, beautiful, amorous girls given in marriage to Vulcan, i.e., to a rude husband, ill-mannered, base, old, and jealous....And so they betray them with Mars, whom they choose and love above all, i.e., with noble lovers who are valiant, daring, and devoted to arms. (502-503)

Fraunce's comment is closely related:

Venus, that is to say, Wantonnes, joyned with Mars, which noteth hoate and furious rage, giving themselves over to excessive and inordinate pleasure; are by Phoebus, figuring the light of reason, accused to Vulcan, who representeth naturall heate; which is weakned by this inordinate lust....Vulcan sheweth them both to be mockt of the Gods: the naturall heate complayneth, as it were, and sheweth to all the other faculties (called gods by reason of their heavenly frame and function) his decay and impotencie: whence foloweth of necessitie the impayring of all the other faculties. (*Countesse of Pembrokes Yvychurch*: 39r)

Brant made much the same moral point rather more succinctly: Had it not been for the folly of passion, "Mars in chains would never lie" (*Ship of Fools*: 13; see also Greene, "Perymedes": 89; Sandys, *Ovid*: 203). As Nohrnberg (1976: 511-512) has shown, Mars' dalliance with Venus was the model for several similar scenes in Renaissance poetry: in book 16 of Tasso's *Jerusalem Delivered*, for example, Rinaldo plays Mars to Armida's Venus; and Spenser's Verdant loses his *virtus* to Acrasia in the Bower of Bliss:

> His warlike arms, the idle instruments
> Of sleeping praise, were hong upon a tree,
> And his brave shield, full of old moniments,
> Was lowly ra'st, that none the signes might see;
> Ne for them, ne for honour cared hee,
> Ne ought, that did to his advauncement tend,
> But in lewd loves, and wastfull luxuree,
> His dayes, his goods, his bodie he did spend:
> O horrible enchantment, that him so did blend.

Guyon and the Palmer rush upon Acrasia and Verdant and throw a "subtile net" over them—a net like Vulcan's—and "So held them under fast" (*Faerie Queene*: 2.12.80-81). Shakespeare's treatment of Antony and Cleopatra (in *Antony and Cleopatra*) also seems intended to recall the unmanning of Mars and the lovers' eventual public embarrassment (Bate 1993: 201-205).

In order to get about the business of dallying with Venus, Mars had, of course, to lay aside his arms. This scene—ripe with allegorical significance—was often represented in pictures of Mars and Venus (see, e.g., Veronese's *Mars and Venus*, fig. 18). The putting aside of armor could recall St. Paul's description of the spiritual armor of the Christian: "Put on the whole armour of God, that ye may be able to stand against the wiles of the devil....Stand therefore, having your loins girt about with truth, and having the breastplate of righteousness...the shield of faith...and the sword of the Spirit" (Eph 6:11-17; see Jeffrey 1992: 56-57).

More often, however, the story was understood to suggest the moderating influence Venus has on Mars. In this tradition, the love of Venus and Mars produces the child Harmonia (e.g., Hesiod, *Theogony*: 934-937; Ovid, *Metamorphoses*: 3.132; Plutarch, *Isis and Osiris*: 48; Apollodorus, *Library*: 3.4.2). For Heraclitus (*Allégories d'Homère*: 69.7-11) the myth figured the creative harmony that arises out of the concord of love and discord (for related allegory, see **CASTOR AND POLLUX**).

The Renaissance Neo-Platonists in particular were fascinated by the implications of this myth. Pico, for example, was convinced that beauty was a concord arising out of discords, an "amicable enmity." But if there is to be creation and concord, love must overcome discord and strife—otherwise nothing would hold together (see **VENUS**). Without love in this large sense, Pico wrote, there can be "no composition":

In these compositions the Union necessarily predominates over the contrariety; otherwise the Fabrick would be dissolved. Thus in the fictions of Poets, Venus loves Mars: this Beauty cannot subsist without contrariety; she curbs and moderates him....And in Astrology, Venus is plac'd next to Mars...to abate his malignancy. If Mars were alwayes subject to Venus...nothing would ever be dissolved. (*Platonick Discourse upon Love*: 26)

Panofsky writes of a related vogue in sixteenth-century Italy for paintings of "elegant couples masquerading as Mars and Venus" (1962: 162-163). And according to Wind (1968: 89), Veronese's *Mars and Venus* (fig. 18) is a working out of just these ideas: softened by Venus, warlike Mars has laid his sword and helmet by; Cupid binds Mars to Venus—a softened reminder of Vulcan's binding net and of the more ominous chain that binds Mars to Venus in some moral-allegorical pictures (e.g., Cossa's *Venus and Her Children*, fig. 26).

Sandys' interpretation is clearly influenced by the Neo-Platonists—but he also takes astrology and moral allegory into account (for more on the astrological meaning of this story, see Wood 1970: 112-120, and Schreiber 1975: 525-528). According to Sandys, the adultery of Venus and Mars

carries this astrological sence: that those who are borne in the Conjunction of Mars and Venus are prone to inordinate affections. Mars sometimes descendeth beneath the Sun, and Venus for a part of the yeare ascendeth above him, as it were to meete with each other: whose conjunction may then be said to be discovered by the Sunne, when he ceaseth to obscure them by the proximity of his greater splendor. Vulcan bindes them in a net: that is, with too much fervor subdues their operations. For the star of Mars is hot; and that of Venus moderate moist; whereof generation consists....Proceede we a little with the influencies of these Plannets: Mars is malignant, but approaching Venus subdues his malignity: Mars exciteth greatnesse of spirit and wrath in those whose nativity he predominates; Venus impeacheth not that virtue of magnanimity, but the vice of anger: Venus ruling infuseth the effects of love; and Mars conjoyning, makes the force of that love more ardent: wherefore those that are borne under that conjunction are most fervently amorous....Mars likewise signifies strife, and Venus friendship; which as the ancients held, were the parents of all things. But morally adulteries are taxed by this fable; which how potent soever the offenders, though with never so much art contrived, and secrecy concealed, are at length discovered by the eye of the Sun, and exposed to shame and dishonour. (*Ovid*: 202-203; much the same astrological meaning is adduced by the *Ovide Moralisé*: 4.1488-1537)

Chaucer's Wife of Bath explains her own concupiscence in just such terms of astrological influence: she is "al Venerian / In feelyne, and myn herte is Marcien" ("Wife of Bath's Tale": 609-610).

Bibliography: Jonathan Bate, *Shakespeare and Ovid* (1993); J. P. Filedt Kok, *Livelier Than Life: The Master of the Amsterdam Cabinet, ca. 1470-1500* (1985); David L. Jeffrey, *A Dictionary of Biblical Tradition in English Literature* (1992); Richard Kay, *Dante's Christian Astrology* (1994): 137-186; John Nichols, *The Progresses and Public Processions of Queen Elizabeth*, 3 vols. (1823); James Nohrnberg, *The Analogy of The Faerie Queene* (1976); Erwin Panofsky, *Studies in Iconology* (1962); Paul Plass, *The Game of Death in Ancient Rome* (1995); Earl G. Schreiber, "Venus in the Medieval Mythographic Tradition," *JEGP*, 74 (1975): 519-535; Melvin Storm, "The Mythological Tradition in Chaucer's *Complaint of Mars*," *PQ*, 57 (1978): 323-335; Edgar Wind, *Pagan Mysteries of the Renaissance* (1968); Chauncey Wood, *Chaucer and the Country of the Stars* (1970).

MARSYAS was a satyr. It was Minerva who first made the shepherd's pipe, but she threw the pipes away when the gods laughed at her as she played, because she looked ridiculous with her cheeks puffed out. Marsyas found the pipes where they lay, and he came to play so well upon them that he presumed to think his music better than Apollo's (see Appendix A, "Music"). Apollo, playing upon the lyre, challenged Marsyas to a contest with the Muses as judges. (In some versions of the story, the song contest was judged by King Midas.) Apollo won—and so he flayed Marsyas alive. The ancients sometimes expressed sympathy for Marsyas—Lucian, for example, has Hera say that Marsyas would have bested Apollo in the contest, "if the Muses had chosen to judge fairly" (*Dialogues of the Gods*: 18). But Christians best knew Marsyas as an *exemplum* of punished pride—like Niobe, Arachne, the Pierides, Prometheus, Phaethon, and Icarus. Berchorius, for example, says that the story "appertains in the case of many who oppose themselves to prelates and rulers" (*Ovidius Moralizatus*: 260; see also Golding, "Epistle": 121-125). In this same tradition, Sandys wrote that Marsyas is a figure for "ambition and vaine-glory, which delight in loud shouts and applauses: but virtue and wisdom have a sweeter touch, though they make not so much noise in popular opinion" (*Ovid*: 296-297; see also Reynolds, *Mythomystes*: 169).

Apollo's contest with Marsyas was also understood as allegorizing the antagonism between two kinds of music and two kinds of instruments, the wind instruments and the stringed instruments (see Appendix A, "Music"). "It means in the rationalized form of the Greek myths the realm of inhibition, of reason, of measure—in the literal Pythagorean sense of measuring strings and intervals, and in the metaphorical sense of *mesure*—as opposed to the realm of blind passion: in short, the antagonism between Apollo and Dionysus" (Winternitz 1979: 152). Plato, for example, discusses just what sort of music ought to be allowed in his Republic. The Ionian and the Lydian modes must not be allowed, for these are "convivial modes...modes that are called lax." Only the Dorian and the Phrygian modes are to be permitted, for these musical modes "fittingly imitate the utterances and the accents of a brave man who is engaged in warfare or in any enforced business....Leave us these two modes...that will best imitate the utterances of men failing or succeeding, the temperate, the brave." Plato goes on to characterize this distinction between easeful music and the music that inspires bravery and temperance: "We are not innovating, my friend, in preferring Apollo and the instruments of Apollo to Marsyas and his instruments" (*Republic*: 398e-399e).

Fulgentius revealed "the hidden sense" of the story:

The story is shown to be associated with musicians..., for musicians have established two stages for their art, adding a third as it were of necessity...that is, singing, plucking the lyre, or playing the flute....But the flute could strictly fulfill only the lowliest role in the art of music....So it was according to the art of music that Minerva discovered the double flute, which anyone skilled in music despises for the poverty of its sounds. They are said to have laughed at her puffed out cheeks because...anyone at all skilled laughs at her harshly blowing; and so Minerva, that is, wisdom, reproaching herself, throws it away, and Marsyas picks it up. For Marsyas in Greek is *morosis*, that is, a solitary fool, for wanting to place the flute in musical effect above the lyre; whence he is depicted with a hog's tail. (*Mythologies*: 3.9)

Vatican Mythographer III (10.7) also contrasts the foolishness of Marsyas and the wisdom of Minerva, who discarded the flute. Thus, when Dante invokes Apollo at the beginning of the *Paradiso*, he asks that he might sing as did Apollo when the god defeated Marsyas (1.19-21). Sandys' comment is in the same tradition: Marsyas is

called a Satyre, for his rude and lascivious composures: who finding the flute, which Minerva had cast away...was the first of mortalls that played thereon: and so cunningly, that he presumed to challenge Apollo with his Harpe....It is said that Minerva threw the flute away, not only for deforming her face, but that such musique conferreth nothing to the knowledge of the Mind; presented by that Goddesse, the patronesse of wit and learning. The fiction of the Satyres punishment was invented not only to deterre from such self-exaltation: but to dehort the Athenians from the practise of an art so illiberall, whereunto the Thebans were generally addicted. To which purpose thus spake Alcibiades: "Let the Thebans play on the flute, who know not how to speake: but for us Athenians, we have Pallas and Apollo for the Patrons of our country; of whom, in times past, the one threw away the pipe, and the other uncased the piper." (*Ovid*: 295-296)

In less complicated fashion, Marsyas could also serve simply as a point of comparison for someone who played music badly, as in Udall, where it is said of the braggart Ralph Roister Doister's extempore songs, "Foolishe Marsias nere made the like, I suppose!" (2.1.30).

Bibliography: Emmanuel Winternitz, *Musical Instruments and Their Symbolism in Western Art* (1979); Anne Weis, *The Hanging Marsyas and Its Copies* (1992); Peggy Muñoz Simonds, *Myth, Emblem, and Music in Shakespeare's Cymbeline* (1992): 52-59, 296, 355-356.

MELEAGER, son of Oeneus of king of Calydon and Althaea, was one of the most renowned of the Greek heroes. He sailed with the Argonauts, for example—but he was best known to Christians (as he had been to antiquity) for leading the hunt for the Calydonian boar (for the moral allegory of hunting, see **ADONIS**). As Ovid tells the story (*Metamorphoses*: 8.270-546), Oeneus once neglected to offer up his sacrifice to Diana. In her wrath Diana sent a monstrous boar to ravage the kingdom. Meleager organized a star-studded band of heroes to hunt the boar: Theseus and Pirithous, the Lapiths, Castor and Pollux, Achilles' father Peleus, the youthful Nestor, and Atalanta, among others. After a fierce struggle, Atalanta managed to wound the boar with an arrow; and finally it was Meleager who delivered the fatal spear thrust. Meleager thus deserved the trophy of the boar's skin, but he gave it to Atalanta, in honor of her arrow shot. His mother's brothers then accused him of being blinded by lovesickness, and so they took the skin for themselves. Meleager killed them in his rage. His mother raged at this murder of her brothers. Now, when Althaea had born Meleager, the Fates had determined that his span of life should be no longer than that of a log then upon the fire. Althaea had quickly taken that log out of the fire at the time, to preserve her son's life; now, lusting for vengeance, she thrust the log into the fire, and so her son soon died.

Since Maleager hunted the boar to save the Calydonians and since his reward was death, Berchorius interprets him as a type of Christ: "At last his mother—the synagogue—burned him to death by means of the tree of the cross" (*Ovidius Moralizatus*: 314). But in an alternative interpretation, Berchorius asks us to "Note how endless evils came to be because of the love of women" (313). Sandys moralizes upon Diana's punishment of Calydon: "there is no evil befalls unto man, but either proceeds from his omission of divine duties, or actual impiety" (*Ovid*: 386). Dolce makes Meleager a figure for "piety" (*Transformationi*: 190).

Meleager's sisters so mourned his death that they were turned into birds. Here is Ross: "By this...they would signifie, that too much sorrow makes men degenerate from their own nature, and for the present to be void of reason" (*Mystagogus Poeticus*: 278). Since it springs from the passions, mourning, like love, can bestialize (for another example of the bestializing effects of mourning, see **HECUBA**; see also Appendix B, "Bestialization").

MENEPHRON (Monophron) is mentioned by Ovid as one who committed "incest after the wild beasts' fashion" (*Metamorphoses*: 7.386-387). Thus Menephron was occasionally mentioned as an *exemplum* of lust or unnatural love. The *Chess of Love* commentary provides both story and allegory:

Monophron...loved his mother with mad love, and however it was, wanted to lie with her. And therefore the fable pretends that Jupiter changed him into a bull. And it was thus pretended because of his outrageous and base lust. And in truth such love is mad and unreasonable and seems in some way to be against nature, and especially in our human species, which should rule all its desires and concupiscence by reason. (667)

Lydgate's Diana, for another example, recites a list of the "many meschefs that felle in the gardyn of Deduit" (*Reson and Sensuallyte*: 4227). She includes (among others) the stories of Narcissus, Pygmalion, Pasiphae, Myrrha, Phaedra, Tereus, Medea, and Menephron:

> Menafron,
> In poetis as ye may lere,
> Lovede his owne moder dere
> Ageyn naturys ordynaunce,
> To fulfillen hys pleasaunce.
>
> (*Reson and Sensuallyte*: 4290-4294)

Small wonder that Tritonio includes Menephron in his list of "The Libidinous" (*Mythologia*: 28).

MERCURY (Hermes, Cylennius, Psychopompus). Mercury was the son of Jupiter and Maia (one of the Pleiades). He may usually be recognized by his broad-brimmed hat or helmet, his winged sandals, his purse, and his rod, Caduceus. In classical times, because he managed to steal his brother Apollo's cattle on the afternoon of his own birth, Mercury came to be the god of thieves and trickery. But he was more widely revered for other things. He was known especially as the messenger god—and so he was the god of eloquence. For his youth and vigor, he was the god of gymnastics, boxing, and some other sports. He loved human dealings, barter, trade, shipping—and so he was the god of merchants. He was the god of sleep and dreams; he could put to sleep with a touch of his rod. It was he who invented both the lyre and the pipes: Plutarch wrote that Mercury was "the inventor of grammar and music" (*Isis and Osiris*: 352a-b). Mercury was the god of the arts.

Because he was the god of eloquence and of deception, he came also to be associated with casuistry—the essential nature of the legal profession being impervious to the march of time. During the Middle Ages it was not forgotten that eloquence sometimes finds itself in the service of deception. Indeed, Isidore wrote, "it is said that Mercury first invented deception" (*Etymologiarum*: 8.9.33), and most of what Fulgentius says about Mercury has to do with Mercury's patronage of thieves and merchants (*Mythologies*: 1.18; see also Bartholomaeus, *On the Properties of Things*: 8.15; Bodin, *Colloquium*: 190; Golding, "Preface": 65-66). Shakespeare's rogue Autolycus was "litter'd under Mercury," and so is a thief and gambler (*Winter's Tale*: 4.3.23-31).

But Mercury's association with persuasive eloquence (e.g., Heraclitus, *Allégories d'Homère*: 59.1-2) and the arts was also remembered to his credit: Lydgate, for example, associates him with "Prudent Marchaundes," "eloquence," the "craft of calculacion," "wysdam and science" (*Reson and Sensuallyte*: 1691-1702; see also Batman, *Batman uppon Bartholomae*: 8.27). This was particularly so because of the influence of Martianus Capella's *Marriage of Philology and Mercury*. This book was one of the most widely read books in the Middle Ages; it was still in demand in 1599, when Hugo Grotius published a new edition—and late in the seventeenth century none other than Leibniz planned to edit Martianus anew (Curtius 1963: 38). The book was a compendium of knowledge of the seven liberal arts, clothed in elaborate allegory. The controlling allegory was that Mercury, or eloquence, was marrying Philologia, or learning; the quadrivium was marrying the trivium. In his commentary on *The Marriage of Philology and Mercury*, Bernardus wrote that the marriage signified the conjunction of discourse/Mercury and reason/Philology (*On Martianus Capella*: 2.40). Any learned Roman would have understood the appropriateness of a marriage of learning and eloquence. Cicero's *De oratore* defined the ambitions of a Roman gentleman right down to the time of the collapse of the Empire. Cicero argued that the orator was more exalted even than the philosopher, because the orator his mastery of the entire range of human knowledge with consumate rhetorical skills. Even after the Empire fell, when "it was pointless for schools to maintain the pretense of preparing young rhetoricians for a career in politics. Nevertheless, during the Middle Ages rhetorical studies and classical literary models continued to engage the attention of students because they constituted the only academic curriculum familiar to the Roman world" (Stahl et al. 1971: 24-25).

Some of these assumptions are still at work in a drawing of Mercury by the Master of the Amsterdam Cabinet (for the image and description, see Filedt Kok 1985: 224). The Master draws Mercury at the top of the page, riding a richly caparisoned horse across the sky. Beneath the rider the Master depicts the children of Mercury: clockmaker, organ maker, painter, goldsmith, sculptor, and teacher. (Even here, however, there may be some suggestion of Mercurial deception: The master sculptor's smiling wife is handing a beguiling cup of wine to a young journeyman sculptor.) But Mercury was soon to experience a decline in his labors as god of the arts. After Ficino, Neo-Platonists came to see melancholy—and so Saturn—as essential to the artistic temperament (as we see in Dürer's engraving of *Melancholia*). But if Ficino took away from Mercury his connection to the arts, he gave Mercury another important role. Mercury was associated with that "celestial inspiration" which leads to divine contemplation:

So it's said that when Ulisses had been given a certain flower by Mercury, that is, light from God through an angel, he escaped the poisoned cups of Circe; that is, he escaped the allurements of corporeal love which transforms the human soul out of a man into a beast, that is, out of the reason into the sense. So at some point through this flower Ulisses is said to have escaped both the poisons of pleasure and the worries of ambition, and attained the secret mysteries of things divine. (*Philebus Commentary*: 448; see also Sandys, *Ovid*: 121)

Botticelli's *Primavera* (fig. 13) could have been understood to represent Mercury at work in something like this way. Here we see Mercury with his staff Caduceus as he "drives the winds and skims the stormy clouds" (Virgil, *Aeneid*: 4.245-246). This cloud skimming was understood allegorically at least as early as Boccaccio, who wrote that Mercury had the power to skim away mental as well as sky-born clouds (*Genealogie Deorum*: 12.52; 3.20). And so Botticelli's Mercury skims away clouds, pointing upward, beyond the world of the senses, moving the cloudy veils to allow us glimpses of good, Neo-Platonic, Hermetic knowledge (Wind 1968: 122-126; but also see, e.g., Lightbown 1989: 134-137). Burton provides a homely version of this tradition: "Mercurialists are solitary, much in contemplation, subtle, poets, philosophers, and musing most part about such matters" (*Anatomy of Melancholy*: 1.3.1.3).

Part of what made such ideas attractive to the Neo-Platonists was Mercury's role as Psychopompus, "accompanier of souls," an idea that goes back to Homer's *Odyssey* (5.46; 24.1-100)—and an idea that was brought to grotesque allegorical life in the Roman arenas when the corpses of the slain gladiators were dragged out through the Gate of Death by attendants costumed as Charon and Mercury (Plass 1995: 43). Sandys comments on this tradition: "For Mercury taught that no man came into the World, or went out of it, without divine appointment: and therefore was Mercury said to passe betweene Jupiter and Pluto, fetching Ghosts from the under-shadowes, & carrying them thither. So in that dreames were held to be inspired from above...[they called] that divine inspiration Mercury (the messenger betweene God and man)" (*Ovid*: 121; see also van Mander, *Wtlegginghe op den Metamorphosis*: 9r; for more on Mercury as a guide, see Bowen 1985).

With all of this, it is not surprising that Mercury could allegorize wise counsel, or the wisdom necessary to control the passions (e.g., Seznec 1961: 102). According to Bernardus, for example, when Circe tempted Ulysses with her bestializing charms, the hero "thwarted her by the counsel of Mercury" (*On Virgil's Aeneid*: on book 3). In the *Aeneid* it is again Mercury who warns Aeneas to leave the lovely Dido and continue upon his divinely appointed mission to found Rome. And again Bernardus comments:

Mercury is eloquence when he seeks marriage with Philology. For eloquence without wisdom is little help, and indeed it is often harmful....And thus he is also called Hermes, that is, *interpres*, "explanation." For *Hermenia* is *interpretatio*, "interpretation."

Mercury warns and censures Aeneas because he finds him ignoring useful endeavor....Mercury chides Aeneas, who leaves Dido and puts passion aside. (*On Virgil's Aeneid*: on book 4)

By virtue of his association with eloquence, learning, and wise counsel, Mercury was counted with those gods—Apollo, Saturn, and Diana—who stood for rational control and temperance, as opposed to Venus, Bacchus, and Vulcan, promoters of license and the passions. We see this, for example, in a Neo-Platonic engraving after Baccio Bandinelli, *The Fray of Cupid and Apollo* (fig. 1; see **APOLLO** for more on this engraving).

Ross's long commentary on Mercury provides a good summary of much of what was generally understood:

He is called [the Messenger], for speech, whereof he is said to be god, runs between man and man...and Merchants by this trade with each other: therefore he is called the God of Merchants....[H]e taught the Egyptians all Arts and Sciences; he taught men to leave their rudeness, and become civil and religious: therefore they make him still to be waiting upon the gods, especially upon Jupiter....They made him winged both in his head and feet, to shew...the nimbleness of their wits, tongues, and fingers, who are born under that star.

Mercury was said to be able to calm storms, Ross continues, because

so doth Mercury, or eloquence, pacifie a stormy and tempestuous State....I find that Mercury is painted in some pictures not only with winged head and feet, but also with a Purse in his hand: to shew that he is the god of gain, which is not got but by diligence, expedition, and wit....By Mercury may be understood the desire for knowledge....Our blessed Saviour is the true Mercury, the Son of God, the Word of the Father, the Messenger of the Angel of the Covenant...the God of Order and Harmony, the Prince of Peace, who by his Cross, as the true Caduceus, hath reconciled all things in heaven and earth. (*Mystagogus Poeticus*: 262-266).

One of the reasons Christians thought of Mercury as a type of Christ was that he gave the healing, soul-preserving herb moly to Ulysses, to preserve him from the charms of Circe; see **ULYSSES**.

Mercury was sometimes called the Cylennian, after Mt. Cylennius, where he was born.

For Mercury and Herse, see **HERSE**; for Mercury slaying Argus, see **IO**; for Mercury's serpent-twined staff, see **CADUCEUS**.

Bibliography: C. Balavoine et al., *Mercure a la Renaissance* (1988); Barbara Bowen, "Mercury at the Crossroads in Renaissance Emblems," *JWCI*, 48 (1985): 222-229; Ernst Robert Curtius, *European Literature and the Latin Middle Ages* (1963); A. C. Hamilton, *The Spenser Encyclopedia* (1990): under *Mercury*; Richard Kay, *Dante's Christian Astrology* (1994): 38-65; Ronald Lightbown, *Botticelli: Life and Work* (1989); Paul Plass, *The Game of Death in Ancient Rome* (1995); Jean Seznec, *The Survival of the Pagan Gods* (1961); Janet Levarie Smarr, "Mercury in the Garden: Mythographical Methods in the *Merchant's Tale* and *Decameron* 7.9," in Jane Chance, *The Mythographic Art* (1990): 199-214; William Harris Stahl et al., *Martianus Capella and the Seven Liberal Arts*, vol. 1 (1971); Edgar Wind, *Pagan Mysteries of the Renaissance* (1968).

MIDAS was a mythical king of Phrygia. Two Midas stories were important to the Middle Ages and the Renaissance. The first was the familiar story of Midas's touch: Bacchus tells Midas that anything he wishes for will be granted him. Midas asks that everything he touches might turn to gold—but, alas, he cannot turn the gift off. When he sits at table, his food turns to gold; when he takes up his cup to drink, the wine turns to gold. Finally, Midas implores Bacchus to take back the gift, and Midas is freed by washing himself in the river Pactolus (e.g., Ovid,

Metamorphoses: 11.100-145). For Ovid and later writers, Midas was an obvious example of avarice. Dante (*Purgatorio*: 20.106-108) mentions him in this way, for example. And Sandys wrote that "Midas is the image of a covetous man; who while he seekes to augment his riches, denies to himselfe the use of his owne, and starves in abundance" (*Ovid*: 522-523). Thus it is that when Shakespeare's Bassanio rejects the golden casket, he says, "Hard food for Midas, I will none of thee" (*Merchant of Venice*: 3.2.102); he will choose the leaden casket—and self-sacrifice—instead.

The second Midas story was employed more often by Christian allegorists. The story seemed to them to say something about spiritual as opposed to merely physical perception. According to Ovid, Midas no sooner escaped from his first difficulty than he fell into another. Hating wealth now, Midas "haunted the woods and fields, worshipping Pan, who has his dwelling in the mountain caves. But stupid his wits still remained, and his foolish mind was destined again as once before to harm its master....There, while Pan was singing his songs...and playing airy interludes upon his reeds...he dared speak slightingly of Apollo's music in comparison with his own." A song contest ensued, and Midas decided that Pan's squeaking music was the better. Ovid continues: "The Delian god did not suffer ears so dull to keep a human form, but lengthened them out and filled them with shaggy, grey hair....Human in all else, in this one feature was he punished, and wore the ears of a slow-moving ass" (*Metamorphoses*: 11.146-193).

In some versions of the story, it is the contest between Marsyas and Apollo that Midas misjudges. In both versions, Midas tries to hide his ears, but cannot keep them long a secret.

The allegorical interpretation of the story built first upon traditional normative assumptions about different modes of music (see Appendix A, "Music"). The *Chess of Love* commentary, for example, discusses Midas in the course of its treatment of the different modes of music (283). But more generally, Midas had to do with a want of higher, or spiritual, discernment, as for example in Fulgentius: "King Midas judged between these two contestants, for Midas...is said to have asses' ears, because being totally lacking in discernment he is in no way different from an ass" (*Mythologies*: 3.9). Thus it is that the Wife of Bath's deafness ("General Prologue": 446) should be understood allegorically, as being like Midas's ass's ears: both are spiritually deaf (see Allen and Gallacher 1970, Robertson 1984).

In this same tradition, Sidney likens Midas to those whose who are deaf to the spiritual import of poetry: "But if...you bee borne so neare the dull-making Cataract of Nilus, that you cannot heare the Planet-like Musicke of Poetrie; if you have so earth-creeping a mind that it cannot lift itselfe up to looke to the skie of Poetrie, [then you deserve] the Asses eares of Midas" (*Defense of Poesy*: 46). And Sandys wrote that in the story of the judgment of Midas,

Pan presents illiterate rusticity; Apollo a mind imbued with the divine endowments of art and nature. Midas an ignorant Prince, unable to distinguish betweene that which is vile and excellent; and therefore preferrs the one before the other; for which he is justly branded by the learned with the ensignes of folly....For there is a twofold harmony or musick; the one of divine providence, and the other of humane reason. To humane judgement (which is as it were to mortall eares) the administration of the World, of the creature, and more secret decrees of the highest sound harsh and disconsonant; which ignorance, though it be deservedly markt with the eares of an asse, yet is it not apparant, or noted for deformity by the vulgar. (*Ovid*: 524)

Bacon, too, made use of this same distinction, between godlike and merely human understanding. Bacon wrote that the story of the music contest between Apollo and Pan

conteines a wholesome instruction, which may serve to restraine mens reasons and judgements with the reines of sobriety from boasting and glorying in their gifts. For there seemes to be a two-fold Harmonie, or Musicke: the one of divine providence, and the other of humane reason. Now to the eares of mortals, that is to humane judgement, the administration of the world and the creatures therein, and the more secret judgements of God, sound very hard and harsh; which folly albeit it bee well set out with Asses eares, yet notwithstanding these eares are secret, and doe not openly appeare, neither is it perceived or noted as a deformity by the vulgar. (*Wisedome of the Ancients*: 6)

Bibliography: Judson B. Allen and Patrick Gallacher, "Allisoun through the Looking Glass: Or Every Man His Own Midas." *ChauR*, 4 (1970): 99-105; D. W. Robertson, Jr., "The Wife of Bath and Midas," *SAC*, 6 (1984): 1-20.

MINERVA (Athena, Bellona, the Tritonian). According to the best-known story, the goddess Minerva sprang fully armed from the head of Jupiter. Among the ancients she had many roles: Armed as she was, she was regarded as a kind of female Mars, though she was more discriminating than Mars, promoting only just wars. (She could also be distinguished in this way from Bellona, the Roman goddess of war with whom she was sometimes conflated.) She was the patroness of spinning and weaving (see **ARACHNE**); she made the fields fruitful; she was even thought of as the goddess who sends the dew. Macrobius (*Saturnalia*: 3.4.8) identified her with the highest of the three kinds of air, or ether: Juno was the lowest air, Jupiter the middle air, and Minerva the highest (see also Martianus, *Marriage of Philology and Mercury*: 567)—although it was Jupiter who was most commonly associated with the highest ether.

Minerva was, however, best known for another, related loftiness: She was the goddess of wisdom, cleverness, wit, and learning. Already in classical times she was identified with universal reason (Buffière 1956: 281, 288); she was the Greek equivalent of the Hebrew Sophia concept (e.g., Proverbs 1, 8:22-31). And these associations continued with the Christians. The best early example is perhaps Martianus, who wrote of Minerva as the "bearer of all knowledge," as the "intelligence and perspicacity of Fate, guiding genius of the universe...ardent flame and founder of learning...; with anxious foresight you form the wise man's judgement; you are the pinnacle of reason, the holy Mind [the *nous*] of Gods and men" (*Marriage of Philology and Mercury*: 567).

Fulgentius explains Minerva in the course of his discussion of the choice of Paris (see **PARIS**), which he interprets as an allegory of the choice that human beings must make among the three kinds of life, the intellectual (Minerva), the active (Juno), and the voluptuous (Venus): "The first or intellectual life we name in honor of contemplative wisdom; thus they say that she was born from the head of Jove, because the intellect is situated in the brain; and she was armed, because she is full of resource. They associate her with the Gorgon, worn on her breast as a symbol of fear, just as the wise man bears awe in his breast to guard against his enemies" (*Mythologies*: 2.1).

This interpretation was often paraphrased (e.g., *Courte of Sapyence*: 1758-1764; Fraunce, *Countesse of Pembrokes Yvychurch*: 40r). Berchorius also paraphrased Fulgentius, adding what were common variations:

I say that Minerva signifies wisdom and the life of a wise man which is born from the brain of Jove—that is from the divine mind itself....She is armed because wisdom or the wise man should in all respects be armed with virtues. He should also have the shield of fortitude and patience, the lance of rectitude and justice, the helmet of sobriety and temperance, the olive of piety and mercy, the owl of humility....She also ought to have an owl, a bird which hides itself from the day—that is flight from the presence of men and concealment of her virtues. She is also said to have an olive which is the sign of peace and which pours out oil—that is peace, concord, love and also pity and compassion. (*Ovidius Moralizatus*: 79, 81; see also the *Chess of Love* commentary: 386-388, 405, 536; Peacham, *Minerva Britanna*: 188)

Berchorius is describing Minerva's armor in such a way as to recall St. Paul's well-known allegory of Christian armor: "Put on the whole armour of God, that ye may be able to stand against the wiles of the devil....Stand therefore, having your loins girt about with truth, and having on the breastplate of righteousness...the shield of faith...and...the sword of the spirit" (Eph 6:11-17; see Jeffrey 1992: 56-57). Lydgate describes Minerva in this same tradition:

> First on her hede, be governaunce,
> A bryght helme of a-temperaunce....
> In her ryght honde she had a spere,
> Which named was, in sothfastnesse,
> The egal launce of ryghtwysnesse....
> A myghty shelde of pacience
> Ther-with to make resistence
> Ageyn al vices.
>
> (*Reson and Sensuallyte*: 1187-1203)

Minerva was often understood in this way, as a figure for the restraint of the passions.

The story of Minerva's birth—Jupiter swallowed his pregnant wife Metis, and so Minerva was born from his head (e.g., Apollodorus, *Library*: 1.3.6)—was interpreted allegorically as early as Heraclitus (*Allégories d'Homère*: 19.8-9). Fulgentius, as we have seen, says that this birth associates Minerva with "contemplative wisdom." Conti writes in the same tradition: "Jupiter espoused Metis, which is to say counsel....Jupiter swallowed this pregnant woman and gave birth from his head, because the head is the principle seat of reason and human discourse. Pallas is born from this reason and human discourse" (*Mythologie*: 1.2; see Bacon, *Wisedome of the Ancients*: 30, for a slightly idiosyncratic version of this allegory; for Bacon on Metis, see Lemmi 1933: 164-167).

Another version of the story left Metis out, saying simply that Minerva was born from the head of Jupiter. But the allegorical interpretation was usually the same. Guido da Pisa, for example, wrote that she was born from the head of Jupiter because she is "the contemplative life, which is the means by which we come to know God" (*Super Comediam Dantis*: 112; see also Vatican Mythographer I: 124; Albricus, *Allegoriae Poeticae*: 36r). In the seventeenth century Ferrand is still referring to the brain as "the citadel of Athena" (*Treatise on Lovesickness*: 3).

In Andrea Mantegna's *Triumph of Wisdom over the Vices* (fig. 19) we see Minerva dressed in her battle gear, accompanied by Diana and Chastity, putting to rout "Venus, mother of all the Vices, who are shown swarming in a stagnant pool—Dalliance (Otia), Sloth, Hate, Suspicion, Avarice" (Seznec 1961: 109). Along the left-hand margin of the picture, we see Daphne, who has already been turned into a laurel tree; Daphne thus provides a warning as to the dangers of the passions Venus inspires. We see a more complicated working out of the same assumptions on the title page (fig. 16) of Sandys' *Ovid's Metamorphosis, Englished, Mythologized, and Represented in Figures*. Jupiter (the fiery ether) is in the upper left with the salamander, which was thought to thrive in fire; Juno (air) is in the upper right; Neptune (water) is at the bottom right; and Ceres (earth) is at the bottom left with a particularly motherly sort of cow. Sandys explains the allegory in the first lines of the poem that follows the title page:

Fire, Aire, Earth, Water, all the Opposites
That strove in Chaos, powrefull Love unites;
And from their Discord drew this Harmonie,
Which smiles in Nature: who, with ravisht eye,
Affects his owne made Beauties. But, our Will,
Desire, and Powres Irascible, the skill
Of Pallas orders; who the Mind attires
With all Heroick Vertues: This aspires
To Fame and Glorie; by her noble Guide
Eternized, and well nigh Deifi'd.
But who forsake that faire Intelligence,
To follow Passion, and Voluptuous Sense;
That shun the path and Toyles of Hercules;
Such, charm'd by Circe's luxurie, and ease,

Themselves deforme: 'twixt whom, so great an ods;
That these are held for Beasts, and those for Gods.

Venus, then, as the power of love, can harmonize the elements; but she also inspires desires. To restrain these desires is to follow Minerva, who appears in suitably martial garb opposite Venus. Minerva's restraint allows us to follow in the path of Hercules, whom we see "Deifi'd" (and bearing his signature club) soaring above the scene. At the bottom of the picture we see the alternative: Circe and bestialization (see Appendix B, "Bestialization").

Minerva could thus be the individual's guide—reason controlling the passions—as we see in the following lines by Peacham:

Lo Pallus heere, with heedefull eie doth leade;
Ulisses in his travaile farre and neere:
That he aright, might in his journey treade,
And shunne the traine of Error, every where:
 N'ought had Ulisses, ever brought to passe,
 But this great Goddesse, his directresse was.

  ...it doth wisely show,
With all our actions, Wisedome should remaine.
(Minerva Britanna: 69)

Thus it is that she appeared in psychomachias, as for example in an engraving after Baccio Bandinelli, *The Fray of Cupid and Apollo* (fig. 1). Here Venus, Cupid, and Vulcan (their armorer) do battle with Jupiter, Minerva, Mercury, and Saturn (for more on this engraving, see **APOLLO**). Ficino opposes Priapus and Bacchus with Diana and Minerva in just this same way (*On Plato's Symposium*: 6.1; quoted under **BACCHUS**).

For Medieval Neo-Platonists, Minerva's association with wisdom could make her a figure for Noys—Bernardus's "true Minerva" (*Cosmographia*: 1.1)—a combination of Divine Providence, the Biblical Wisdom, Providence, and the locus of the Platonic Forms (see Silverstein 1948-49: 110-112, and the Introduction to Wetherbee's tr. of Bernardus's *Cosmographia*: 39-40). Alanus, following Bernardus, also associates Noys and Minerva (*Anticlaudian*: 2.7). Her name Tritonia suggested to others "threefold apprehension," or three ways of knowing: "of God, called intellectible; of souls, called intelligible; of bodies, called natural. And the name of wisdom by right belongs to these three alone" (Hugh of St. Victor, *Didascalicon*: 2.18; Taylor's note to this passage points to the ninth-century Remigius of Auxerre as Hugh's source for this interpretation; see also Bernardus, *On Martianus Capella*: 6.133-143 for a related interpretation).

For Renaissance Neo-Platonists Minerva played a variety of other allegorical roles, all of them similarly associated with things of the spirit/knowledge/ mind/Forms: for example, Reynolds makes her "Ideall beauty" (*Mythomystes*: 151); for Ficino she is one scale in a Neo-Platonic ladder of knowing (e.g., *In Phaedrum*: 118).

For the shield of Minerva, see **PERSEUS**. For Minerva/Athena's association with the city of Athens, see **ATHENS**. For the goddess of war with whom Minerva was sometimes conflated, see **BELLONA**.

Bibliography: Félix Buffière, *Les Mythes d'Homère: la Pensée Grecque* (1956); Margaret J. Ehrhart, *The Judgment of the Trojan Prince Paris in Medieval Literature* (1987); Ehrhart, "Christine de Pizan and the Judgment of Paris," in Jane Chance, *The Mythographic Art* (1990): 125-156; David L. Jeffrey, *A Dictionary of Biblical Tradition in English Literature* (1992); Charles Lemmi, *The Classical Deities in Bacon* (1933); Jean Seznec, *The Survival of the Pagan Gods* (1961); Theodore Silverstein, "The Fabulous Cosmogony of Bernardus Silvestris," *MP*, 46 (1948-1949): 156-162; Rudolf Wittkower, "Transformations of Minerva in Renaissance Imagery," *JWCI*, 2 (1938-1939).

MINOS. According to the version best known to the Middle Ages and the Renaissance, Minos was the son of Jupiter and Europa and the king of Crete. But already in Homer there are two distinct traditions for Minos. He is, on the one hand, "King Minos whom great Zeus received / every ninth year in private council" (*Odyssey*: 19.184-185). This Minos was thought to receive laws for Crete direct from Zeus. And this Minos was thought to have been the framer of the older Cretan constitution. Thus it was that for Homer Minos is judge in Hades (*Odyssey*: 11.568-571. And in a later legend, which seems to have originated with Plato (*Gorgias*: 523-527; see also *Apology*: 41a), Minos served with his brothers Rhadamanthus and Aeacus as judges of the dead in the underworld. Virgil mentions Minos as such a judge (*Aeneid*: 6.432-434), as does Servius (*In Virgilii Aeneidos*: 6.566). This tradition survived into the Middle Ages and the Renaissance, as we see, for example in de Meun (*Romance of the Rose*: 19839-19864) and Lynche, who paraphrased Plato as follows:

[Jupiter said,] my pleasure is, that my three sonnes, two of them borne in Asia, being Minos and Rhadamantus, and another in Europe, which is Eacus, standing in a certain greene meade, out of which do part and are divided two severall waies, the one into Hell, and the other into Elisium (for so we may call them) shall bee appointed there as Judges of the soules of mortals, Rhadamante judging those of Asia, and Eacus those of Europe. And that, if it fortune that any doubt or undecided scruple, shall arise between them, that then the same bee referred presently unto Minos....This (sayeth Plato) was the order and decree of Jupiter....First upon the examination of their sins, Rhadamantus and Eacus sate together in two yron chaires, holding in either of their hands a white rod. And Minos (divided from them both) was seated all alone, holding in his hand a golden scepter, who seemed to meditate and ponder with a musing & sad countenance upon the punishments, torments, or pleasures, to be denounced & due to the offenders. (*Fountaine of Ancient Fiction*: Pi-Pii)

Less commonly, the judges were thought each to judge a different range of sins: According to John of Garland, Minos judged sins of the "mind"; Rhadamanthus those of the "voice" (i.e., sins of speaking: slander, etc.); Aeacus judged sinful "acts" (*Integumenta Ovidii*: 201-202).

In another tradition, Homer could call Minos "the grim king" (*Odyssey*: 11.320); and on the Attic stage he was presented as a cruel tyrant—hardly surprising, since Minos was thought to have conquered Athens and demanded as tribute seven boys and seven virgins every nine years to be thrown into the Labyrinth, there to be eaten by the Minotaur (see **MINOTAUR**).

Dante seems to combine Virgil's judge with the Cretan tyrant when he makes Minos, "horrible and snarling," the judge of souls in the second circle of Hell (*Inferno*: 5.4); Pietro Alighieri, commenting on this passage, interprets judge Minos as "remorse of conscience" (*Commentarium*: 111); see also Chaucer's "Juge infernal, Mynos, of Crete Kynge" (*Legend of Good Women*: 1886). The "creull judge" Spenser mentions in "Virgils Gnat" (27) is probably Minos (Lotspeich 1932: 82; for more on Minos and the law in Spenser, see Nohrnberg 1976: 410-412). Later interpreters combined the two allegorical traditions to make Minos an *exemplum* of the Fall and redemption, as for example, in Ross:

> By Minos the son of Jupiter, may be meant Adam, the son of God; Minos was a just King, and was Lord both of the Island Creta, and of the sea: so Adam was created with justice, and had dominion given him both over Sea and Land, over the beasts and fishes; Minos married with Pasiphae, the daughter of the Sun; and Adam was betrothed, that is endowed with knowledge and understanding, which is the light of the mind; ...but this Pasiphae or knowledge of man fell in love with the Bull, that is, with Satan and his cunning suggestions, and by this means the Minotaur, or monster of sin, was procreated, being the deformed issue of Satan, and mans corrupted nature, and so his soule and knowledge became a captive, and was inclosed in the Labyrinth, or involved with innumerable difficulties, and inextricable till Christ came, a greater conqueror than Theseus, who killed the Minotaur of sin, which had devoured mankind, and delivered us who were in worse condition than the Athenians, from the domineering power of that all-devouring monster. (*Mystagogus Poeticus*: 293)

Sandys had offered something like the same interpretation (*Ovid*: 383). Tritonio included Minos in his list of "The Cruel" (*Mythologia*: 18)—along with such figures as Tereus, Medea, and Lycaon—but he also listed Minos with "The Prudent," because Minos was able to resist the advances of Scylla (31).

Bibliography: Henry Lotspeich, *Classical Mythology in the Poetry of Edmund Spenser* (1932); James Nohrnberg, *The Analogy of The Faerie Queene* (1976).

MINOTAUR. King Minos's wife Pasiphae fell in love with a bull. The terrible fruit of this unnatural passion was the Minotaur, a monster with the head of a bull and the body of a man. King Minos promptly built the great Labyrinth to hold the Minotaur.

The monster Minotaur was generally interpreted as the allegorically appropriate result of what Virgil called a "monstrous love" (*Aeneid*: 6.26). The

Minotaur became a standard figure for human bestiality (e.g., Orosius, *History*: 1.13; Guido da Pisa, *Super Comediam Dantis*: 220; Dinet, *Hieroglyphiques*: 385; see Appendix B, "Bestialization"). Sandys provides a succinct statement of the typical allegorical interpretation: "for so brutish and violent are the affections when they revolt from the obedience of Virtue; producing Minotaures and monsters, by defaming Nature through wicked habit, and so become prodigious" (*Ovid*: 383).

The Minotaur was misshapen, then, for precisely the same reason that we find grotesques in Bruegel's *Lechery* engraving (fig. 20). To succumb to lechery—to allow the reason to be controlled by the passions—is to sink to the level of the beasts. For Bruegel's grotesques as for the Minotaur, the outward form mirrors the inward spiritual shape. Since rebels against a king were analogous to the flesh rebelling against the spirit, rebels against the king could be associated with Minotaurs (e.g., Shakespeare, *1 Henry VI*: 5.3.189).

Theseus came to Crete and killed the Minotaur. Berchorius's interpretation may be taken as widely typical: "he has conquered this beast, ...he has triumphed over the flesh or the devil" (*Ovidius Moralizatus*: 305-306). The Minotaur embroidered on Theseus's pennant in Chaucer's "Knight's Tale" (978-980) seems to work in the same way; it recalls Theseus's triumph over the product of Pasiphae's lust—and so Theseus stands as a normative figure in a tale that describes the tragic consequences of uncontrolled passions (Green 1960: 132; see also Ross, quoted under **MINOS**).

For the meaning of the Minotaur in the Labyrinth, see **LABYRINTH**.

Bibliography: Michael J. Curley, "Minotaur," in Malcolm South, *Mythical Creatures and Fabulous Beasts: A Source Book and Research Guide* (1987); Richard H. Green, "Classical Fable and English Poetry," in Dorothy Bethurum, *Critical Approaches to Medieval Literature* (1960): 110-133; M. E. Lamb, "*A Midsummer Night's Dream*: The Myth of Theseus and the Minotaur," *TSLL*, 21 (1979): 478-491; David Ormerod, "*A Midsummer Night's Dream*: The Monster in the Labyrinth," *ShakS*, 11 (1978): 39-52.

MORPHEUS. For Ovid, dreams were the sons of Somnus, god of sleep: When we dream, we see the sons of Somnus acting in their various guises. Morpheus was usually said to be the son who enacts the human roles. Phobetor "takes the form of beast or bird or the long serpent"; Phantasos "puts on deceptive shapes of earth, rocks, water, trees, all lifeless things," and so forth (*Metamorphoses*: 11.633-643). This division of responsibilities was widely remembered (see, e.g., Berchorius, *Ovidius Moralizatus*: 373-374; Boccaccio, *Genealogie Deorum*: 1.31; and Gower, *Confessio Amantis*: 4.3039-3051; van Mander, *Wtlegginghe op den Metamorphosis*: 87r-v). To some, Ovid's division suggested a hierarchy of dreams. Sandys, for example, wrote that Ovid divides dreams "into three kinds; the one imitating the Rationall, the other the Animall, & the third the inanimate." Sandys went on to explain that Morpheus was in charge of rational dreams, "Phobetor or Feare" produced nightmares of "beasts & Monsters," and Phantasos produced dreams "of the imagination" (*Ovid*: 532-533). But Christians usually neglected Phobetor and Phantasos, leaving all the work of dream production to sleepy Morpheus. Marlowe, for example, has Abigail pray to "gentle sleep" (i.e., Somnus) that he might direct Morpheus to give her a "golden dream" (*Jew of Malta*: 2.1.35-37).

Following Macrobius (*On the Dream of Scipio*), Christians often sought to distinguish between good and bad dreams, between dreams that offered real warnings or wisdom and those dreams which were merely phantasms—or worse, tempting visions. In this tradition, poets could make Morpheus the author of a dream in order to suggest that it was *not* heaven-sent. Chaucer makes just this distinction in the proem to book I of the *House of Fame*, for example (Koonce 1966: 46-57). But the best known instance must be in Spenser (*Faerie Queene*: 1.1.39-50), where the evil Archimago gets from Morpheus the dream of "unwonted lust" (49) with which he deludes the Red Cross Knight.

Often Morpheus was conflated with Somnus. For example, Chaucer calls "Morpheus...the god of slepe" (*Book of the Duchess*: 136-137; for Chaucer's use of Morpheus in *The House of Fame*, see McCall 1979: 55-58); and Spenser does the same (*Faerie Queene*: 1.1.39-44; 2.7.25).

Bibliography: B. G. Koonce, *Chaucer and the Tradition of Fame* (1966); Henry Lotspeich, *Classical Mythology in the Poetry of Edmund Spenser* (1932): 82-83; John P. McCall, *Chaucer among the Gods: The Poetics of Classical Myth* (1979); James Nohrnberg, *The Analogy of The Faerie Queene* (1976): 122, 126.

THE MUSES (The Aonians, Aionides, Pierians, Pierides). The Muses were the sisters who provided poetic inspiration. It was no easy matter for an illiterate bard to sing very long narrative poems in complicated meters. It seemed quite reasonable to assume that such feats could be accomplished only with divine aid. Thus it was that Homer—who was either an illiterate bard himself or a near heir—invokes the Muse: "Sing, goddess, the anger of Peleus' son Achilleus" (*Iliad*: 1.1; to appreciate the wonder of illiterate bards bringing forth "songs" like the *Iliad* and the *Odyssey*, to appreciate what might be called the mechanics of the Muses, see Parry 1971 and Lord 1981; see also Jensen 1980 and Lloyd-Jones 1992).

Homer here invokes one Muse; in the *Iliad* (2.484-493) he invokes many Muses; in the *Odyssey* (24.64) he mentions nine Muses. Hesiod also made them nine: "the Olympian Muses, daughters of Zeus the aegis-holder....For nine nights did wise Zeus lie with [Mnemosyne, or Memory], entering her holy bed." There were rival traditions among the ancients as to the parentage of the Muses. Some made them daughters of Uranus and Gaia, or of Harmonia. But the notion that Memory should be the mother of the Muses seems to open a window upon the past—memory would have been crucially important to oral poets. Hesiod continues: "And when a year had passed...she bare nine daughters, all of one mind, whose hearts are set upon song and their spirit free from care, a little way from the topmost peak of snowy Olympus. There are their bright dancing places." Hesiod goes on to name the Muses: "Cleio and Euterpe, Thaleia, Melpomene and Terpsichore, and Erato and Polyhymnia and Urania and Calliope, who is the chiefest of them all" (*Theogony*: 52-79).

There were rival versions; but in general, tradition followed Hesiod, both as to the number of the Muses and as to their names (see, e.g., Apollodorus, *Library*: 1.3.1; for the Muses in early Christian art, see Hanfmann 1980: 76-78). There was, however, less agreement as to just how the responsibilities were divided among the Muses. As the following table indicates, there are two main lines of interpretation: one that goes back to the classics (e.g., Ausonius), identifying individual Muses with particular poetic modes, and a second, beginning with Fulgentius (*Mythologies*: 1.15), which identifies each Muse with a particular stage of learning. Although Fulgentius's was the dominant interpretation of the Muses during the Middle Ages, there were occasional Medieval references to the classical division of the Muses' labors: Fulgentius himself, for example, refers at one point to Thalia as "the Muse of comedy" (*Mythologies*: pro); and Chaucer seems to invoke Clio because she is the Muse of history (*Troylus and Criseyde*: 2.8-14).

I include Bernardus (*On Virgil's Aeneid*: 6.9) in the table as typical of the Medieval commentators who followed or adapted Fulgentius's allegory (but see also, e.g., Boccaccio, *Genealogie Deorum*: 11.2; the *Chess of Love* commentary: 150-151; Giovanni del Virgilio, "Espositore delle *Metamorfosi*": 66-68); indeed, Bernardus's commentary on the Muses is sometimes difficult to understand without a knowledge of Fulgentius. In some quarters Fulgentius's interpretation lingered on well after the waning of the Middle Ages: as the table shows, Ross (*Mystagogus Poeticus*: 301) was still reflecting Fulgentius in the mid-seventeenth century:

1. Clio:

Ausonius (*Appendix to Ausonius*: 3): "Clio, singing of famous deeds, restores times past to life." Clio was often thought of as the Muse of history.

Fulgentius: "First is Clio, standing for the first conception of learning, for *cleos* is the Greek for fame." History was thought of as Fame's recording instrument (see **FAME**).

Bernardus: "thought leading to learning."

Ripa (*Iconologie*: 2.72-76): "this Muse is called Clio...which signifies praise, or possibly...glory...because the invention of history is attributed to this Muse." In the illustration that accompanies this passage in Ripa, Clio appears with a volume of history and a trumpet, to trumpet forth fame. (The figures of Good Fame and Bad Fame on the title page of Raleigh's *History of the World*, fig. 11, have trumpets for the same reason.)

Ross: "*Clio* from [the Greek for] glory, for great is the glory of learning."

2. Euterpe:

Ausonius: "Euterpe's breath fills the sweet-voiced flutes." She inspired pastoral poetry.

Fulgentius: "Second is Euterpe, whom in Greek we call well pleasing," for the second step of learning is "to delight in what you seek."

Bernardus: "proper desire" to learn.

Ripa: "Euterpe, from the Greek word signifying agreeable or pleasant...from the marvelous contentment provided by the *belles Lettres*." She is pictured wearing a garland of flowers, playing upon the flute, with other musical instruments at her feet. She is associated with instrumental music and dialectic.

Ross: "*Euterpe*, from [the Greek for] delightful, for there is no delight comparable to that of learned men."

3. Melpomene:

Ausonius: "Melpomene cries aloud with the echoing voice of gloomy tragedy."

Fulgentius: "Third is Melpomene...that is, applying persistent thought."

Bernardus: "perseverance in thinking."

Ripa: She is the Muse of tragedy. In the illustration her aspect is "grave, in accord with the subject of tragedy." She bears the crown, dagger, and scepters as "emblems of the bad and good fortune of man."

Ross: "*Melpomene* [from the Greek for] making melody, for the life of a Scholar is still chearful and melodius."

4. Thalia:

Ausonius: "Thalia rejoices in the loose speech of comedy."

Fulgentius: "Fourth is Thalia, that is, growth" in learning.

Bernardus: "the giver of ability."

Ripa: She is the Muse of comedy; she holds in her hands the comic masks.

Ross: "*Thalia*, from [the Greek meaning] to grow green, for Learning will still flourish, and never wither."

5. Polyhymnia:

Ausonius: "Polymnia expresses all things with her hands and speaks by gesture." This generally came to mean that she was the Muse of rhetoric.

Fulgentius: "Fifth is Polyhymnia..., as we say, making much memory."

Bernardus: "memory for retention."

Ripa: Polyhymnia "is depicted with pearls on her head, a white robe, the right hand raised in the gesture of the orator, and in the left is a scroll"; all of this is suggestive of the "precepts of rhetoric, which employ invention, disposition, memory, and delivery."

Ross: "*Polymnia*, from [the Greek, meaning] no mens minds are so full of melody and spiritual comforts as the minds of learned men."

6. Erato:

Ausonius: "Erato bearing the plectrum harmonizes foot, song, and voice in the dance."

Fulgentius: "Sixth is Erato, that is, *euronchomoeon*, which in Latin we call finding the same"; that is, "to discover in yourself something resembling what you remember."

Bernardus: "the discovery of likenesses."

Poliziano: invokes Erato as he begins to write of love: "You have sole rule over love poetry" (*Stanze*: 1.69).

Ripa: "She is crowned with myrtle and roses, having in the right hand a lyre [see, e.g., the amorous lyre in fig. 26], and in the left a bow. Before her is a little Cupid with torch and bow....She is crowned with the Myrtle and Roses, because she treats of amorous subjects. The plant and flower are symbols, the one and the other being sacred to Venus and Cupid."

Ross: "*Erato*, from [the Greek for] love, for the more a man knows learning; the more he loves it."

7. Terpsichore:

Ausonius: "Terpsichore with her lyre stirs, swells, and governs the emotions."

Fulgentius: "Seventh is Terpsichore, that is pleasant filling"; i.e., one feels pleasantly satisfied after learning, as after a good meal.

Bernardus: "delight in studying."

Ripa: "She is crowned with a garland and bears a harp...in the semblance of a dancer." She was often thought of as the Muse of the dance.

Ross: "*Terpsichore*, from [the Greek meaning] to delight in singing or dancing, for the songs, dancing, and mirth of learned men are within themselves."

8. Urania:

Ausonius: "Urania examines the motions of the heaven and stars." The Muse of astronomy, then.

Martianus: she gives the gift of "a gleaming mirror...a mirror in which Psyche could recognize herself and learn her origins" (*Marriage of Philology and Mercury*: 7; As the Muse of Astronomy, Urania was associated with the stars; Psyche, or the individual soul—see **PSYCHE**—was thought to have its beginning among the stars).

Fulgentius: "Eighth is Urania, that is, heavenly, for after judging, you select what to say and what to reject."

Bernardus: "the heavenly Muse, which is understanding."

Ripa: "She is dressed in the color of the sky. She is crowned with stars, and holds a globe in her two hands." She is the Muse of astronomy.

Du Bartas: Du Bartas's poem "Urania" (*Devine Weekes and Workes*: 528-542) is a kind of dialogue, wherein Urania urges that Du Bartas accept *her* inspiration for his poetic endeavors. She says,

I graunt, my learned Sisters warble fine,
And ravish millions with their Madrigalls:
Yet all, no lesse inferiour unto mine,
Then Pies to Syrens, Geese to Nightengalls. (16)

The idea is that Urania inspires divine poetry, the kind of poetry David sang:

> The chain of Verse was at the first invented
> To handle onely sacred Misteries
> With more respect: and nothing else was chanted
> For long time after in such Poesies.
> So did my David on the trembling strings
> Of his devine harpe, onely sound his God:
> So milde-soul'd Moses, to Jehovah sings
> Jacobs deliverance from th'Egiptians Rod. (48-49)

Urania could thus serve Christians as the Muse-equivalent of the Holy Ghost. Thus it is, for example, that Dante (*Purgatorio*: 19.37-42) and Milton (*Paradise Lost*: 7.1-15; see Steadman 1984: 115-140; Haan 1993) invoke her as their source of inspiration for divine subjects.

Ross: "*Urania*, from [the Greek for] the heaven for learning came from thence, and the minds of learned men are there, and not upon earthly things."

9. Calliope:

Virgil (*Aeneid*: 9.525): invokes Calliope as the Muse of epic poetry.

Ausonius: "Calliope commits heroic songs to writing."

Fulgentius: "Ninth is Calliope, that is, she of the excellent voice"; that is, "to make known in attractive form what you select."

Bernardus: "the best voice."

Ripa: She is "young and crowned like her companions. On her left arm she bears several garlands of laurel, and she bears on her right hand three books. These are the *Odyssey*, the *Iliad*, and the *Aeneid*. She wears a crown of gold on her head, because she is the worthiest and the foremost of the Muses."

Ross: "*Calliope*, from [the Greek for] a good voice, there is no outward voice so charming and melodious as the inward voice of knowledge in the mind."

Accounts of the Muses' attributes also varied widely, although Ripa's *Iconologia* (first edition, 1593) went a long way toward standardizing these.

The Muses were also associated with the music of the spheres (see Boyancé 1946; see also Appendix A, "Music"). This goes back to Plato and to the following passage from Macrobius (Macrobius is conflating Muses and Sirens):

> In a discussion in the *Republic* [10.617b] about the whirling motion of the heavenly spheres, Plato says that a Siren sits upon each of the spheres, thus indicating that by the motions of the spheres divinities were provided with song....Moreover, cosmogonists have chosen to consider the nine Muses as the tuneful song of the eight spheres and the one predominant harmony that comes from all of them. In the *Theogony*, Hesiod calls the eighth Muse Urania because the eighth sphere, the star-bearer, situated above the seven errant spheres, is correctly referred to as the sky; and to show that the ninth was the greatest, resulting from the harmony of all sounds together, he added: "Calliope...is preeminent among all." (*On the Dream of Scipio*: 2.3.1-2)

Martianus worked out a scheme that associated each Muse with a particular sphere:

The upper spheres and the seven planetary spheres produced a symphony of the harmonious notes of each....indeed...[each Muse] took her position where she recognized the pitch that was familiar to her. For Urania was attuned to the outermost sphere of the starry universe, which was swept along with a high pitch. Polymnia took over the sphere of Saturn; Euterpe controlled that of Jove; and Erato, that of Mars...; while Melpomene held the middle region, where the sun enhanced the world with the light of flame. Terpsichore joined the golden Venus; Calliope embraced the Cyllenian's [i.e., Mercury's] sphere; Clio set up as her lodging the innermost circle—that is, the moon's....Thalia was left sitting on earth's flowery bosom. (*Marriage of Philology and Mercury*: 27; Zecher 1993 discusses this association of particular Muses with particular spheres as it was worked out in sixteenth-century French poetry.)

Landino (*Disputationes Camuldenses*: 223), Conti (*Mythologie*: 10. under *Muses*), and many others also associated the Muses with the music of the spheres. Sandys wrote much in the same vein as Martianus, while changing the correspondences a bit:

The Muses are also taken for the Inteligences, of the Coelestiall Spheares; which...doe make a diversity of sounds; and consequently (according to Pythagoras) an incredible harmony. Yet this saith Macrobius is not to be heard, in that so vast a sound cannot enter at the narrow labyrinth of the eare....Calliope is the melody which results from the rest of the spheares: Urania, of the Spheare of the fixed Starres, so named of her dignity: Polymnia of Saturn, for the memory of antiquity, which he exhibits in his cold and dry quality: Terpsichore of Jupiter, propitious to mortalls: Clio of Mars, for the thrist of glory: Melpomene of the Sunne, in that of all the World the moderator: Erato of Venus, in regard of love: Euterpe of Mercury, for the honest delights among serious affaires: Thalia of the Moone for the vigour which she infuseth by her humidity. (*Ovid*: 248; Fraunce; *Countesse of Pembrokes Yvychurch*: 33v, has same listing)

Lynche is one of many others (e.g., Ficino, *On Plato's Symposium*: 5.13) who follow Macrobius in this. Lynche is also typical in associating Apollo with the Muses:

The auncients when they intended to set down how the liberall arts, and all other sciences, depended one upon the other, and were as it were knit and coheared together, depictured the Muses, holding one another by the hand and heedfully dauncing (as it were in a round) lead and guided by Apollo: which meaneth that superiour light and understanding, which illuminateth and enknowledgeth the intellectuall parts of man. The heavens (according to the opinion of the Platonickes) have every one their severall Muse, called by them oftentimes Syrens, as most harmoniously and sweetly singing, alluded unto the celestial orbes, which in number are likewise nine, and have their motions as they receive their severall powers from the son. (*Fountaine of Ancient Fiction*: Eiii)

The association with Apollo is already found in the Homeric Hymn "To the Muses and Apollo." And the idea that Apollo—god of the sun, source of divine illumination—was the leader of the Muses was important to Christian commentators. For example, the anonymous fourteenth-century "Commentaire de Copenhague de l'*Ovide Moralisé*" (400) makes Apollo a figure for God inspiring Christian religious music—as David had been inspired to sing and play upon the lyre. The title page of Ross's *Mystagogus Poeticus* (fig. 2) shows the Muses surrounding Apollo—all of them ready to inspire Ross in his work as an allegorizing mythographer (for Apollo, music, and the Muses among the Renaissance Neo-Platonists, see Cheney 1993).

The Muses could serve as figures for "the Nine Notable Sciences...[or] the nine liberal arts" (*Chess of Love* commentary: 155). They could also figure forth good or bad poetry. In the first prose section of Boethius's *Consolation of Philosophy*, Lady Philosophy drives away "the Muses of poetry" who inspired Boethius to bewail his plight in the self-pitying, spiritually myopic first poem. "They kill the fruitful harvest of reason," scolds Lady Philosophy, "with the sterile thorns of the passions." Lady Philosophy calls these Muses "Sirens," and she drives them out: "Leave him to be cured and made strong," she says, "by my Muses." Good and bad poetry: good and bad Muses.

But Boethius's reference to Muses of bad poetry was unusual. Much more commonly the Muses are figures for good poetry. "God the Father," wrote Ross, "hath given wings to the Muses, that they might soar on high in heavenly raptures" (*Mystagogus Poeticus*: 301). As representing good poetry, the Muses could be contrasted with the Sirens (see **SIRENS**) or with the Pierides, who foolishly engaged in a song contest with the Muses (see **PIERIDES**)—but, confusingly, the Muses themselves were occasionally referred to as Pierians or even Pierides, after "the mount Pierus, where they were borne" (Fraunce, *Countesse of Pembrokes Yvychurch*: 33v; see also, e.g., Petrarch, *Africa*: 9.156).

Bibliography: Pierre Boyancé, "Les Muses et l'harmonie des sphères," in *Mélanges dédiés à la mémoire de Félix Grat* (1946); Girolami Cheney, "The Chamber of Apollo of the Casa Vasari," *SI*, 15 (1993): 135-176; Ernst Curtius, *European Literature and the Latin Middle Ages* (1963): 228-246; Estelle Haan, "From Helicon to Heaven: Milton's Urania and Vida," *RS*, 7 (1993): 86-107; A. C. Hamilton, *The Spenser Encyclopedia* (1990): under *Muses*; G. M. A. Hanfmann, "The Continuity of Classical Art: Culture, Myth, and Faith," in Kurt Weitzmann, *Age of Spirituality* (1980): 75-100.

Minna Skafte Jensen, *Homeric Question and the Oral-Formulaic Theory* (1980); Hugh Lloyd-Jones, "Keeping up with Homer," *NYRB*, 39, no. 5 (1992): 52-57; Albert B. Lord, *Singer of Tales* (1981); Henry Lotspeich, *Classical Mythology in the Poetry of Edmund Spenser* (1932): 83-85; Milman Parry, *The Making of Homeric Verse*, ed. Adam Parry (1971); John Steadman, *Milton's Biblical and Classical Imagery* (1984); Carla Zecher, "Pagan Spirituality and Christian Passion: The Music of the Spheres in Sixteenth-Century French Cosmological Poetry," *FrF*, 18 (1993): 297-317.

MYRRHA (Smyrna). In Ovid's version of the story, Myrrha conceives a "vile passion" for her father Cinyras, King of Cyprus. So debased is she that she envies the animals their freedom: "Other animals mate as they will," she laments, "nor is it thought base for a heifer to endure her sire, nor for his own offspring to be a horse's mate; the goat goes in among the flocks which he has fathered....Happy they who have such privilege!" (*Metamorphoses*: 325-328; see Appendix C, "Envying the Animals"). Torn by guilt and despairing of winning her father's consent, she decides upon suicide. She is prevented by her old nurse, who then devises a scheme that brings Myrrha to her father's bed under cover of dark, and when he is fuddled with wine. Sadly, she conceives, and is eventually transformed into a tree, the myrrh tree. Her child, Adonis, is born through the bark of the tree.

She thus became an *exemplum* of unnatural, bestial desire, or of the power of lust. Alanus, for example, includes her in his rather extensive catalogue of unnatural lovers: "Myrrha, roused by the stings of myrrh-breathing Venus, fallen from the affection of a daughter to a lust for her father, filled and renewed with her father the office of her mother" (*Complaint of Nature*: pr. 4.115-119). Boccaccio includes her in a list of those whom Love struck "with a wicked fire...Myrrha, Semiramis, Byblis, Canace, and Cleopatra" (*Fiammetta*: 20-21; see also *Eclogues*: 15.104-105). And Tritonio includes her in his list of the "libidinous" (*Mythologia*: 28).

Sandys' commentary is typical: "Cupid (which is a desire of generation according to the order of Nature) denies to have kindled her unnatural flames: imputed to infernall Alecto, or the Divell, who begets in the impious soule, deserted by Virtue, such hellish affections." Sandys goes on to comment on Myrrha's nurse: "Bodin observes that Witches for the most part are old women (not one among an hundred a man) as more easily seduced by the Divell in regard of their melancholy and envy. Though Myrrha at the first was ashamed to confesse so detested a guilt; yet could the experienced old woman discover it to be love." And so on—enough to allow us to recognize this nurse as a type of the worldly Old Woman who encourages and aids the desires of her young female charge. Just such a nurse helped Semele (see **SEMELE**). And there is the old woman who acts as a go-between for the Lover in the *Romance of the Rose* (de Meun retells the story of Myrrha and mentions that it was "a strange trick for the old woman to allow the king to lie with his daughter," *Romance of the Rose*: 21196). There is the Nurse in *Romeo and Juliet*. Spenser's Britomart also has a nurse (see especially *Faerie Queene*: 3.2.30-36), one who seems to be directly descended from Ovid's Myrrha's nurse (Nohrnberg 1976: 447). And then there is the nurse in an anonymous English poet's titillating, moralizing retelling of the Myrrha story, *The Scourge of Venus* (1614). When the nurse in this poem recognizes that Myrrha is lovesick, she encourages the girl to tell all:

> I have bene wanton once as well as you,
> Now yet by age, am altogether dull,
> I have been love-sicke, as you may be now,

Of toyes and love-trickes i was wondrous full,
How strange so ere thy case do therefore stand,
I can and will redresse it out of hand. (p. 245)

But let us return to Sandys: "Cyneras, full of wine, is tempted and deceaved by the Nurse. Wine is a spur unto Venus, and prodigall cups besot the understanding." For Sandys, Myrrha's transformation is an allegory of repentance; she is "changed into a tree...by the compassionate Gods, who accept of her repentance: and although insensitive, sheds bitter teares (meant by the odorous Gum which distilleth from thence) for her former transgressions" (*Ovid*: 485-489). This, too, was already familiar allegory. The *Chess of Love* commentator, for example, had written:

And the history says that...the gods, who had pity on her, transformed her into the form of a tree that bears myrrh, which tree, because of the great sorrow and bitterness of this young lady still distills and weeps a very acid and very bitter drop which is called myrrh....This narration...means that this damsel repented of the evil she had done and wept her misdeed all the days of her life. Or it means that she was ruined by it and died poor in great sorrow and bitterness. (665-666)

Thus, when Chaucer tells us that the tears of Troylus and Criseyde are as bitter as those shed by "The woful Myrra thorugh the bark and rynde" (*Troylus and Criseyde*: 4.1139), the simile probably ought not to be taken as morally neutral.

Boccaccio's account of the story (*Genealogie Deorum*: 2.52) cites Fulgentius, whose allegory has largely to do with nature:

The myrrh is a kind of tree from which the sap oozes out; she is said to have fallen in love with her father. These same trees are found in India, glowing with the heat of the sun; and since they always said that a father is the sun of all things, by whose aid the growth of plant life develops, so she in this fashion is said to have fallen in love with her father....It is told of her that she gave birth to Adonis because *adon* is the Greek for sweet savor. So they say that Venus fell in love with him because this kind of liquid is so very fiery; so, too, Petronius Arbiter says that he drank a draught of myrrh to arouse his sexual desires. (*Mythologies*: 3.8)

It is in this sense, then, that Alanus refers to "myrrh-breathing Venus" in the passage quoted above.

Bibliography: James Nohrnberg, *The Analogy of The Faerie Queene* (1976).

N

THE NAIADS were the Nymphs of the watery places: each stream, each spring, each pool had its Naiad. Spenser once calls the Muses Naiads, "which the glorie be / Of the Pierian streams" ("Virgils Gnat": 25-26).

NARCISSUS was the beautiful boy who fell in love with his own reflection in a pool, and so rejected poor doting Echo. Ovid's version of the Narcissus and Echo story in the *Metamorphoses* (3.339-510) was the one best known to the Middle Ages and the Renaissance. It is also one of the most affecting and insightful of Ovid's many stories. Ovid's Echo has all the yearnings of pubescence—along with the painful inarticulateness, self-doubt, and feelings of rejection that are the special burdens of budding youth. Echo has been cursed by the goddess Juno; she can speak only by echoing what she hears:

Now when she saw Narcissus wandering through the fields, she was inflamed with love and followed him by stealth; and the more she followed, the more she burned by a nearer flame...Oh, how often does she long to approach him with alluring words and make soft prayers to him! But her nature forbids this, nor does it permit her to begin....By chance the boy, separated form his faithful companions, had cried: "Is anyone here?" and "Here!" cried Echo back. Amazed, he looks around in all directions and with loud voice cries "Come!"; and "Come!" she calls him calling...."Here let us meet," he cries. Echo, never to answer sound more gladly, cries: "Let us meet"; and to help her own words she comes forth from the woods....But he flees at her approach....But still, though spurned, her love remains and grows on grief....She hides in woods and is seen no more upon the mountain-sides; but all may hear her, for voice, and voice alone, still lives in her. (*Metamorphoses*: 3.370-401)

Ovid's Narcissus suffers punishment for mocking Echo—and all the other girls who had loved him in vain. The goddess Nemesis arranged that he should fall in love with his own reflection in a clear pool. And so Narcissus "loves an unsubstantial hope and thinks that substance which is only shadow" (3.417). Finally, he pines away by the side of the pool, dies, and is transformed into a flower, the narcissus.

For the Augustan Ovid, Narcissus is wrong for his lack of feeling, for his coldness. But most of those who read the story during the Middle Ages and the Renaissance understood the moral differently. For Christians, self-love—and so, the story of Narcissus—had essentially to do with love of the world. To love the self *is* to love the world—or "the false mirror of this world," as the *Ovide Moralisé* (3.1909) put it; self-love thus stood in opposition to *caritas*, "charity" in the Christian sense. Boccaccio, for example, wrote that the water of the pool is "insubstantial worldly pleasures" (*Genealogie Deorum*: 7.59). For Caxton the story shows "How soone is come to naught the vayn Beaute of the peple. He is a grete foole that for this Beaute that soone passeth leseth the love pardurable" (*Ovid*: comment on book 3). For Conti, Narcissus is an *exemplum* of the consequences of lasciviousness and of glorying in the body (*Mythologie*: 9.16). And here is Ross:

he is much like men of this world, who dote not upon the substance of true Happiness, but on the shadows thereof, upon worldly riches, honours, pleasures, beauty, which are but empty vanities, which when they embrace, they find they embrace but the shadow....Narcissus was turned into a flower of his own name, which, as Pliny sheweth, is dangerous for the stomach, and causeth vomiting, and loosness; an enemy also to the head and nerves, causing...stupidity, which might be the reason perhaps; why the greeks write that whilst Prosperpina was gathering of Narcissus she was ravished by Pluto....Eccho fell in love with Narcissus, Eccho may signifie bragging, or vain words, which with pride or self-love is always enamoured. (*Mystagogus Poeticus*: 307-308).

Lydgate had also associated Narcissus with "Presumtuous pride" (*Falls of Princes*: 1.5668).

The pool into which Narcissus gazed was usually remembered as a fountain during the Middle Ages and the Renaissance, as we see in the early manuscript illuminations of *The Romance of the Rose* (see, e.g., Fleming 1969: figs. 5, 24, 25; see also fig. 59 in Dahlberg's tr. of the *Romance*). The *Chess of Love* commentary spoke of "the fountain of Narcissus, which some call the fountain of love, and which is very often called the perilous fountain" (938). De Lorris's Lover explains why this fountain might be thought of as "perilous":

Whoever admires himself in this mirror can have no protection, no physician, since anything he sees with his eyes puts him on the road of love. This mirror has put many a valiant man to death, for the wisest, most intelligent and carefully instructed are all surprised and captured here. Out of this mirror a new madness comes upon men: Here hearts are changed; intelligence and moderation have no business here, where there is only the simple will to love....For it is here that Cupid, son of Venus, sowed the seed of love..., here stretched his nets and placed his snares to trap young men and women; for Love wants no other birds. Because of the seed that was sown this fountain has been rightly called the Fountain of Love. (*Romance of the Rose*: 1571-1597)

After saying all this, the Lover does look into the fountain of Narcissus—and so falls in love with the Rose. Thus de Lorris makes clear the connections between the fountain of Narcissus, self-love, and sexual love (see also de Lorris's contemporary, Thibaut, "A Enviz Sent Mal Qui Ne l'a Apris": 36). The Lover's own gloss on the Narcissus story—that it is an *exemplum* warning ladies not to neglect their duties to their sweethearts (*Romance of the Rose*: 1507-1510)—is probably best understood as one of the Lover's characteristic, obtuse non sequiturs (Fleming 1969: 96). Looking into the fountain of Narcissus is one of the stages of love in Lydgate's *Reson and Sensuallyte* as well (5751-5752).

Among the Renaissance Neo-Platonists, too, Narcissus was associated with carnal love. And the reflection in the pool allowed a characteristic Neo-Platonic point as to what is *real*: Ficino, for example, wrote "that tragic fate of Narcissus" had to do with the general pitiable condition of mankind:

Narcissus, who is obviously young, that is, the soul of rash and inexperienced man. *Does not look at his own face*, that is, does not notice its own substance and character at all. *But admires the reflection of it in the water and tries to embrace that*; that is, the soul admires in the body, which is unstable and in flux, like water, a beauty which is the shadow of the soul itself. *He abandons his own beauty, but he never reaches the reflection*. That is, the soul, in pursuing the body, neglects itself, but finds no gratification in its use of the body. For it does not really desire the body itself; rather, seduced, like Narcissus, by corporeal beauty, which is an image of its own beauty, it desires its own beauty. And since it never notices the fact that, while desiring one thing, it is pursuing another, it never satisfies its desire. For this reason, *melted into tears, he is destroyed*; that is, when the soul is located outside itself in this way, and has sunken into the body, it is racked by terrible passions and, stained by the filths of the body, it dies. (*On Plato's Symposium*: 6.17; Ficino is following Plotinus, *Enneads*: 1.6.8)

The fountain of Narcissus was related to the whole line of fountains from which worldlings hope to quench their thirst—fountains that stand in contrast with the fountain that is Christ. This tradition goes back to the Biblical story of Christ and the Samaritan woman at the well: "Jesus answered and said unto her, Whosoever drinketh of this water shall thirst again: But whosoever drinketh of the water that I shall give him shall never thirst; but the water that I shall give him shall be in him a well of water springing up into everlasting life. The woman said unto him, Sir, give me this water, that I thirst not, neither come hither to draw" (John 4:13-15). Already in the Old Testament there is a distinction between two kinds of water: "For my people have committed two evils; they have forsaken me the fountain of living waters, and hewed them out cisterns, broken cisterns that can hold no waters" (Jer 2:13; for more on the allegory of fountains and cisterns, see Jeffrey 1992: 457-459).

Tasso describes such a perilous fountain, a fountain of "danger and of deadly pain," where

two naked virgins bathe and dive,
That sometimes toying, sometimes wrestling stood....
And 'ticing baits laid forth of lust and love:

These naked wantons, tender, fair and white,
Moved so far the warriors' stubborn hearts,
That on their shapes they gazed with delight;
The nymphs applied their sweet alluring arts,
And one of the above the waters quite
Lift up her head, her breasts, and higher parts,
And all that might weak eyes subdue and take.

Fortunately, Tasso's warriors escape these temptations:

Straight armed reason to his charge upstarts,
And quencheth lust and killeth fond desire.
                                    (*Jerusalem Delivered*: 15.57-66)

Spenser's Bower of Bliss is furnished with a fountain modeled on Tasso's (*Faerie Queene*: 2.12.71)—and we find a visual analogue in Bruegel's *Lechery* engraving (fig. 20).

Since the fountain reflected the beauty of Narcissus, the story of Narcissus was also related to mirror allegory. Spenser, for example, writes about "Venus looking glass" (*Faerie Queene*: 2.1.8), upon looking into which Britomart becomes more foolish than Narcissus (2.2.44).

Female Petrarchan poets sometimes used Echo as a poignant analogue for themselves; see, for example, Gaspara Stampa (*Rime*: 124, 152).

For the Echo beloved of Pan, see **ECHO**.

Bibliography: Calvin R. Edwards, "The Narcissus Myth in Spenser's Poetry," *SP*, 74 (1967): 63-88; John V. Fleming, *The Roman de la Rose*: A Study in Allegory and Iconography (1969); Frederick Goldin, *The Mirror of Narcissus in the Courtly Love Lyric* (1967); A. C. Hamilton, *The Spenser Encyclopedia* (1990): under *Narcissus*; David Jeffrey, *A Dictionary of Biblical Tradition in English Literature* (1992); Charles Lemmi, *The Classical Deities in Bacon* (1933): 183-185; Louise Vinge, *The Narcissus Theme in Western Literature up to the Early Nineteenth Century* (1967).

NATURE (*Physis*). Medieval and Renaissance ideas about Dame Nature look back to Plato's creation myth in the *Timaeus*. Here Plato divides Nature (*physis*, translated by the Latin *natura*) into three levels:

we must acknowledge that one kind of being is the form which is always the same, uncreated and indestructible, never receiving anything into itself from without, nor itself going out to any other, but invisible and imperceptible by any sense, and of which the contemplation is granted to intelligence only. And there is another nature of the same name with it, and like to it, perceived by sense, created, always in motion, becoming in place and again vanishing out of place, which is apprehended by opinion jointly with sense. And there is a third nature, which is space and is eternal, and admits not of destruction and provides a home for all created things. (*Timaeus*: 51e-52c)

There is, then, a level at which the Platonic Forms have their true being; at another level the Forms are made use of in the business of generation; and then there is a third level, "a home for all created things." Elsewhere in the *Timaeus* Nature is spoken of as a kind of grand repository of all the Forms. This "universal nature...receives all bodies," and yet, Plato continues, "she never departs at all from her own nature and never, in any way or at any time, assumes a form like that of any of the things which enter into her; she is the natural recipient of all impressions....But the forms which enter into and go out of her are the likenesses of eternal realities modeled after their patterns in a wonderful and mysterious manner." Nature then impresses these forms upon matter, which is itself utterly devoid of any form of its own:

For if the matter were like any of the supervening forms, then whenever any opposite or entirely different nature was stamped upon its surface, it would take the impression badly, because it would intrude its own shape. Wherefore...those who wish to impress figures on soft substances do not allow any previous impression to remain, but begin by making the surface as even and smooth as possible. (*Timaeus*: 50b-51b)

Nature is thus at once the eternal, immutable keeper of the Forms and god's agent in stamping those Forms upon matter: She is both the keeper of the Form of horse-hood *and* the power that stamps the corresponding shape onto matter to make earthly horses, snorting and galloping in the flesh.

This conception of nature descended to the Middle Ages through Chalcidius's fourth-century translation (with commentary) of the first half of the *Timaeus* (see, e.g., Curtius 1963: 108)—and so the *Timaeus* spawned numerous other hierarchical divisions of nature: John the Scot, for example, wrote a whole volume on *The Division of Nature*; Guillaume de Conches divided nature into three levels, the "eternal," the "perpetual," and the "temporal" (*On Boethius*). Hugh of St. Victor, following Guillaume, divided nature into the same three levels:

But since we have already spoken so many times of "nature," it seems that the meaning of this word ought not to be passed over in complete silence....Men of former times, we find, have said a great deal concerning "nature"....So far as I am able to conclude from their remarks, they were accustomed to use this word in three special senses, giving each its own definition.

In the first place, they wished by this word to signify that archetypal Exemplar of all things which exists in the divine Mind, according to the idea of which all things have been formed; and they said that nature was the primordial cause of each thing, whence each takes not only its being but its "being such a thing" as well. To the word in this sense they assigned the following definition: "nature is that which gives to each thing its being."

In the second place they said that "nature" meant each thing's peculiar being, and to "nature" in this sense they assigned this next definition: "The peculiar difference giving form to each thing is called its nature"....

The third definition is this: "Nature is an artificer fire coming forth from a certain power to beget sensible objects." (*Didascalicon*: 1.10; see also 1.6-9)

Loosely speaking, the Christians' Dame Nature was a personification of such ideas. She thus had very wide responsibilities indeed. She was more than the Mother Nature whom our own Thoreaus hasten to meet in the woods on the weekend: as keeper-of-the-Forms, she was responsible for immutably preserving the Form of goat-hood, the Form of horse-hood—and the Form of humanity. This meant that she was also in charge of preserving immutable the human moral-hierarchical order: Natural Law (for a clear summary of characteristic Christian thinking on Natural Law, see Aquinas, *Summa Theologiae*: 2.1, qu. 94).

We see this kind of thinking already in Statius: when Theseus decides to fight Thebes, he urges his men into battle in the name of Nature: "'Soldiers, who will defend with me the laws of nations and the covenant of heaven...! For us, 'tis clear, stands the favour of all gods and men, Nature our guide...: for [our enemies] the troops of Furies, that Thebes has marshalled....Onward in warlike spirit, and trust, I pray you, in a cause so noble!'" (*Thebaid*: 12.642-648). Crime or sin is thus no mere breach of a merely human covenant: crime, sin—indeed, any disturbance of the divinely instituted, hierarchical order of Nature—is un*natural*.

And so we come to Alanus's widely influential *Complaint of Nature*. (Alanus's conception of Nature was heavily influenced by Bernardus's *Cosmographia*). Here Nature is a personification of the second of Guillaume's and Hugo's three levels: She was herself created, and so she is not the "Eternal"; but she is without end, and so she is "Perpetual." She is keeper of the Forms. Alanus shows us the these Forms upon her robe:

A garment, woven from silky wool and covered with many colors, was as the virgin's robe of state. Its appearance perpetually changed with many a different color and manifold hue....On it, as a picture fancied to the sight, was being held a parliament of the living creation. There the eagle....There the hawk, chief of the realm of the air, demanded tribute from its subjects with violent tyranny....The ostrich, disregarding a worldly life for a lonely, dwelt like a hermit in solitudes of desert places....The duck and the goose wintered, according to the same law of living, in their native land of streams....These living things, although as it were in allegory moving there, seemed to exist actually.

We see the Forms of hawk-hood, ostrich-hood, duck-hood, goose-hood, each behaving perfectly in accord with the immutable law of Nature for its species. As Alanus continues, we find that the Form of humanity is also to be found on her robe. There is on her robe an image of man; in this image "man laid aside the idleness of sensuality, and by the direct guidance of reason penetrated the secrets of the heavens." Avoidance of sensuality, reasonable life: this is the Form of humanity, just as flying south for the winter is the Form of the species for ducks.

But just here, alas, Alanus sees the effects of the Fall: "Here the tunic had undergone a rending of its parts, and showed abuses and injuries. But elsewhere its parts were united in unbroken elegance, and suffered no discord nor division" (*Complaint of Nature*: pr. 1.204-349; see also Milton, *Paradise Lost*, 9.780-783). This is, precisely, Nature's complaint.

Alanus's Dame Nature was also in charge of nature at the third level, "the temporal," the earthly, the level at which things take on the shapes we can recognize with the senses, the level at which things come into being and then pass away. This is the level at which the Forms are individuated. In Alanus's scheme, this work is delegated to Genius (see **GENIUS**). Nature is God's viceregent; Genius is Nature's.

Nature functions essentially according to this description from Alanus through de Meun's *Romance of the Rose*, Chaucer (e.g., *Parliament of Fowls*), Gower's *Confessio Amantis*, and all the way to Spenser's "Mutabilitie Cantos." Van Mander's engraving *Nature Teaching* (reproduced in Leesberg 1993/1994: fig. 27) works along these same lines: Dame Nature (identifiable by her multiple breasts) is instructing Man by directing his attention to the stone tablets of the Law of Moses. The point would seem to be that *these* laws are natural law, as distinct from the law of the spirit which is promulgated in the New Testament.

For more nuanced discussions of Dame Nature and her antecedents, see Curtius (1963: 106-127), Wetherbee's Introduction to his edition of Bernardus's *Cosmographia*, Dronke (1980 and 1974: esp. 122-125), Economou (1972), Stock (1972: 63-87), and Knowlton (1920, 1921). For the classical tradition of personifying Nature, see Economou (1972: 40-48); Economou draws particular attention to the following: a third- or fourth-century Orphic hymn to *Physis*, Apuleius (*Metamorphoses*: 11.5), Statius (especially *Thebaid*: 12.642-648), and Claudian (e.g., *Rape of Proserpine*: 1.248-251, 3.18-32).

For Isis as a personification of Nature, see **ISIS AND OSIRIS**.

Bibliography: Ernst Curtius, *European Literature and the Latin Middle Ages* (1963); Peter Dronke, *Fabula: Explorations into the Uses of Myth in Medieval Platonism* (1974); Dronke, "Bernard Silvestris, Natura, and Personification," *JWCI*, 43 (1980): 16-31; George D. Economou, *The Goddess Natura in Medieval Literature* (1972); A. C. Hamilton, *The Spenser Encyclopedia* (1990): under *Nature*; E. C. Knowlton, "The Goddess Nature in Early Periods," *JEGP*, 19 (1920): 224-253; Knowlton, "Nature in Middle English," *JEGP*, 20 (1921): 186-207; Marjolein Leesberg, "Karel van Mander as a Painter," *Simiolus*, 22 (1993/1994): 5-57; L. D. Roberts, *Approaches to Nature in the Middle Ages* (1982); Brian Stock, *Myth and Science in the Twelfth Century* (1972).

NEMESIS. Hesiod wrote that "deadly Night bare Nemesis to afflict mortal men" (*Theogony*: 223). She was sometimes understood as divine punishment in general, but more often as the punishment due to those who try to rise above their station in the divinely established order of things. Macrobius wrote that "we worship"

Nemesis "to keep us from pride" (*Saturnalia*: 1.22.1). As Sandys summarized her powers, Nemesis was "severe and inexorable to the proud and arrogant, who are too much elated with the indowments of nature, or felicities of fortune" (*Ovid*: 157). In ancient times Nemesis was represented with wings, for the swiftness of her revenge; with a bridle and measuring rod, to enforce control and measure in all things; and with the sword of vengeance. The emblem of Nemesis in Alciati includes the bridle and this motto: "We should injure no one by word or deed" (*Emblems*: 27). And here is Ross:

Nemesis is painted with a bridle and a ruler, by which is represented Gods justice in curbing and holding in of wicked men....Hence some have thought Nemesis and Justice to be the same; which they paint like a Virgin of a truculent aspect, quick-sighted, sad, holding a ballance in one hand, and a whip or rod...in the other to shew that Justice must not be partial...[and that she is] terrible to the wicked. (*Mystagogus Poeticus*: 309)

Nemesis was sometimes identified with the sun (e.g., Macrobius, *Saturnalia*: 1.22.1; Ross, *Mystagogus Poeticus*: 310).

    Bibliography: Charles Lemmi, *The Classical Deities in Bacon* (1933): 176-177.

NEPTUNE (Poseidon) was a son of Saturn and thus a brother of Jupiter. Christians made occasional references to some of Neptune's legends, but he was important mainly because he was the god of the sea, and thus a figure for one of the four elements. Cicero had explained this allegory: Jupiter is the ether, the heavens, sometimes spoken of as the purest kind of fire; Juno is the air; Dis (Pluto) is the earth; and "the whole realm of the sea was given to Neptune, the brother of Jupiter" (*Nature of the Gods*: 2.66). This was a commonplace; we find the same allegory in Fulgentius (*Mythologies*: 1.2-4), Bernardus (*On Virgil's Aeneid*: on book 1), the *Chess of Love* commentary (54, 414, 431), Sandys (*Ovid*: 113), and Ross (*Mystagogus Poeticus*: 311)—albeit with some variations as to which god represented what. For example, on the title page (fig. 16) of Sandys' *Ovid's Metamorphosis, Englished, Mythologized, and Represented in Figures* we see Jupiter (the fiery ether) at the upper left; Juno (air) is in the upper right; Neptune (water) is at the bottom right with his signature trident; Ceres at the bottom left represents the earth (for more on this title page, see **APOLLO, MINERVA**).

    Neptune was interpreted in other ways as well. The Neo-Platonic Proclus, for example, wrote that Neptune could be interpreted as "the Angelic Intellect, who contains in himself the Forms of all things engendered" (*Sur la République*: 1.112.26-30). Proclus has in mind the changeableness of the sea—remember the many forms the sea-god Proteus can assume—and the sea as primal chaos. This roiling chaos was frequently associated with the equally chaotic human passions. So, the seas and their gods were likened to the famous changeability of the passions (see **GLAUCUS, PROTEUS**). "The ocean," as Salutati put it, "is sensuality" (*De Laboribus Herculis*: 3.7). Here is the *Chess of Love* commentary:

the sea very properly signifies the pleasures and delights of the world and especially the delights of lust, for several reasons, and especially for two similitudes. First, as the sea is all full of diverse dangers, so the delights of this world are mingled with so many great dangers that no one could sufficiently number them....Secondly, as the sea is bitter and displeasing to the taste, so are the delights mentioned above when they are fully known. (344)

The *Chess* commentator elsewhere concludes that Neptune is a figure for "intelligence," because he controlled the sea, just as the higher reason controls the passions (see e.g., Seznec 1961: 94). Landino is working in this tradition when he interprets Neptune as "higher reason" in the course of his gloss on the passage early in Virgil's *Aeneid* (1.124-141), where Neptune chastises Aeolus, the god of the wind that tosses Aeneas's ships (the winds were also associated with the mutability of the passions; see **AEOLUS**):

Neptune became disturbed by the enormity of the tempest....The poets always thought of Neptune as the supreme god of the sea. I say the "supreme god" because there are also other gods in the waters, as, indeed, the appetite has many powers presiding over it—it is moved by the judgment of the senses or of the inferior reason, but the supreme command is reserved to the superior reason. (*Disputationes Camuldenses*: 164-165; Stahel tr.: 120; see also, e.g., Ridewall, *Fulgentius metaforalis*: 93)

But often Neptune was thought of not as controlling the sea/passions, but rather as a figure for the sea/passions. Eustathius (*Commentarii ad Homeri Odysseam*) interprets him in this way, for example: Neptune is the passions that Odysseus (Christ) must overcome on his difficult voyage. Berchorius wrote in the same tradition: "Through Neptune I perceive the who is called the god of this world's sea because he rules there" (*Ovidius Moralizatus*: 89). Berchorius has in mind the Biblical association of the sea with primal chaos and sin: "Save me, O God; for the waters are come into my soul....I am come into deep waters, where the floods overflow me" (Psalms 69:1-2; see also Psalms 18:16; 32:6; 46:3). The Four Great Beasts in Daniel's vision rise up out of the sea (7:3), as does one of the evil seven-headed beasts in John's Revelation (13:1-9; see Jeffrey 1992: 818-819).

Neptune's trident was interpreted in ingenious ways. Servius's account was well known: The trident was three forked because "the sea is said to be a third part of the world, or because there are three kinds of water, seas, streams, and rivers" (*In Virgilii Aeneidos*: 1.137; see also Sabinus, *Fabularum Ovidii Interpretatio*: 33). Vatican Mythographer II (9) and Vatican Mythographer III (5.1) sagely note that Neptune's trident stood for water's three properties: Water is "liquid, fecund, and drinkable."

For Poseidon's contest with Athena for the city of Athens, see **ATHENS**.

Bibliography: David L. Jeffrey, *A Dictionary of Biblical Tradition in English Literature* (1992); Jean Seznec, *The Survival of the Pagan Gods* (1961); Brenda Thaon, "Spenser's Neptune, Nereus and Proteus: Renaissance Mythography Made Verse," *ICNLS*, 4 (1981): 630-637.

NIOBE was the daughter of Tantalus and Dione; she married Amphion, king of Thebes. She bore him children, six boys and six girls, according to Homer (*Iliad*: 24.603-606), ten and ten, or five and five, according to others. Christians usually remembered Ovid's numbers, seven and seven. Whatever the number, Niobe was puffed up with pride; and she made the mistake of boastfully comparing her children with Latona's mere two. Latona then calls upon her children, Apollo and Diana, to avenge the slight—and they kill all Niobe's children. In Ovid's version of the story (*Metamorphoses*: 6.146-312)—the version most widely known by Christians—Niobe was a figure for presumption; and she was proud of more than her children. It is not surprising, then, that Dante should have made Niobe one of the *exempla* of pride graven into the walkway on the terrace of pride in the *Purgatorio* (12.40). Berchorius's comment on Ovid emphasizes that this story "can be allegorized against those who are too proud" (*Ovidius Moralizatus*: 256; see also Alciati, *Emblems*: 67; Golding, "Epistle": 123). And Sandys' paraphrase of and comment on Ovid may be taken as typical of many Christian allegorizations of the story:

Niobe in times past had knowne Arachne, yet could not be admonished by her example, but exceeded her in insolency: proud of her high parentage, and of her husband Amphion; both descending from Jupiter....Niobe glories besides in her beauty, her riches, her dependancy, but especially in her children; exalting herself above the reach of fortune, or degree of a mortall, affects divine honours: enraged at those which were given to an other....She now supresseth the sacrifices of Latona: who complaining to Apollo and Diana; Niobe, by the slaughter of her children...is left a childlesse, despised, and desolate widdow; congealing with sorrow into a statue of marble....

Niobe is said to be the daughter of Tantalus, and Taygeta, one of the Pleiades, or rather Euryanassa, that is of Avarice and Riches, which engender pride in the hearts of Mortalls: from whence proceeds the contempt both of God and man, and an insolent forgetfulnesse of humane instability. (*Ovid*: 292-293)

Ross provides a slightly altered genealogical allegory, to make the same point: "Tantalus was covetous, & Amphion rich; when wealth and covetousness meet together, they bring forth Niobe, that is pride, insolence, and contempt of God himself" (*Mystagogus Poeticus*: 317).

We should also remember that Niobe was the Queen of Thebes—and that Thebes was well known for its sinful ways (see **THEBES**; Hoffman 1966: 153).

Because of the greatness of her loss, she was also known for her weeping (e.g., Shakespeare, *Hamlet*: 1.2.149; *Troilus and Cressida*: 5.10.19).

Bibliography: Richard L. Hoffman, *Ovid and The Canterbury Tales* (1966).

O

OCYRRHOE was Chiron's daughter. As Ovid tells the story (*Metamorphoses*: 2.635-675), Ocyrrhoe received the gift of prophecy at birth, but she offended the gods when, against the gods' command, she told the child Aesculapius what the gods had in store for him. They turned her into a mare to punish her. Berchorius first makes the story into a lesson about envy: "This fable can be allegorized against the envious who cannot hear any good prediction about someone without being angry." And then he suggests that it might also have to do with young people who "are sometimes changed into horses because they finally degenerate from their former goodness and become lascivious and wanton...and are despoiled of their human shape—that is of their rational condition and habits" (*Ovidius Moralizatus*: 171-172).

More commonly, the story was, rather more simply, a warning to those who yearn after the mysteries (e.g., *Ovide Moralisé*: 2.3204-3222). Here is Golding: "The fable of Ocyroee by all such folk is told / As are in searching things too come too curious and too bold" ("Epistle": 94-95; see also, e.g., Sandys, *Ovid*: 119).

OEDIPUS was the King of Thebes; unawares, he killed his father and married his mother. Ross gives us the story in a version that would have been widely recognized as typical:

He was the Son of Laius, King of Thebes, and Jocasta; his father understanding by the Oracle, that he should be killed by his own Son, delivered him to his shepherd to be murthered, who pitying the child, bored two holes through his feet, and so hung him by the feet on a tree; but...the King of Corinths [i.e., Polybius's] shepherd, passing that way, took down the Child, and bestowed him on his Queen being childless, who bred him as her own Son, but when the Child grew up, he went to Phocis, and there lighting on his Father Laius, unawares in a tumult killed him; and going to Thebes, he lighted on Sphinx, whose riddles he untied: afterwards he married Jocasta, not thinking she was his Mother, but when he understood that he had killed his Father, and married his Mother, being highly displeased with himself, he put out his own eyes. (*Mystagogus Poeticus*: 331-332)

He had two sons by Jocasta, Eteocles and Polynices—the "fatal progeny" (Spenser, *Faerie Queene*: 5.11.25) whose fratricidal strife led to the fall of Thebes. Fulgentius commented at length on the story of Oedipus: His birth is a figure for "licentiousness"; in the killing of his father Oedipus is a figure for the soul of sinning man extinguishing "the sacred light" with which souls enter into the world (*Super Thebaiden*, quoted at length under **THEBES**). More than a thousand years later, Ross's interpretation is largely in agreement with Fulgentius: "Oedipus...may thank his Father for his wounded feet, but he may thank himself for his blinded eyes: our Father Adam by his sin hath made us unable to walk in the ways of God, and we, by our voluntary blindness, have made our selves unable to see the Sun of Righteousness, so that our actual blindness is the sequel of our Original lameness" (*Mystagogus Poeticus*: 332).

When Chaucer's Pandarus first seeks out Criseyde to tell her of Troylus's love, he interrupts her reading of the "romaunce" of Thebes. Criseyde tells Pandarus that "we han herd how that Kyng Layus deyde / Thorugh Edyppus his sone, and al that dede" (*Troylus and Criseyde*: 2.101-102). Probably Chaucer expected his readers to be aware of traditional allegorical interpretations of the story, and so we should probably recognize that there is something morally obtuse in Pandarus's easy dismissal of the story, his failure to recognize parallels with the situation of Troy.

During the Middle Ages, Oedipus became (like Judas) a figure for despair, because he put out his own eyes in response to his sin (Edmunds 1976; Patterson 1991: 412-413).

With Oedipus's skill at solving riddles in mind, Ficino makes Oedipus a kind of Neo-Platonic seer, a man who knew secret things: "I have not given what is holy to dogs or pigs," Ficino wrote. "On the other hand...I have revealed to men like Oedipus as many secret things as I myself have seen; however, to all the ignorant I have given them completely veiled" (*Letters*, vol. 3: 10; see also vol. 4: 27).

For Oedipus's daughters, Ismene and Antigone, see **ANTIGONE**; for Oedipus's sons, Eteocles and Polynices, and for their city, see **THEBES**.

Bibliography: Lowell Edmunds, "Oedipus in the Middle Ages," *AnA*, 22 (1976): 140-155; Edmunds, *Oedipus: The Ancient Legend and Its Later Analogues* (1985); Lee Patterson, *Chaucer and the Subject of History* (1991).

ORION was a giant and a mighty hunter. Like most of the other classical (and Biblical) giants, he was proud in proportion to his size. Apollodorus (*Library*: 1.4.5) has him challenging Diana to a contest of quoits, for example. Others had it that Orion attempted to rape Opis, one of Diana's votaries, or Diana herself (e.g., Hyginus, *Fabulae*: 195). Diana sent a giant scorpion to kill Orion—and that scorpion still chases Orion through the skies, where both were transformed into constellations. Already in classical times Orion was thus understood as an example of presumption. Horace draws the moral thus: "Brute force bereft of wisdom falls to ruin by its own weight. Power with counsel tempered, even the gods make greater. But might that in its soul is bent on all impiety, they hate" (*Odes*: 3.4.65-68). Conti also moralizes on Orion's impious "arrogance" (*Mythologie*: 8.14).

One of the Orion stories seems almost to have been devised with Christian allegorizers in mind: Orion ravished fair Merope; her father got Orion drunk and then put out his eyes; Orion snatched up Vulcan's apprentice (or Vulcan himself in another version), put him on his shoulders to serve as his eyes, and bade the boy guide him to the east, where the rays of the rising sun healed his eyes (e.g., Apollodorus, *Library*: 1.4.3-4). Here is Ross:

Orion, for ravishing of Merops...lost his eyes...and for his pride and bragging his skill was killed by Diana; thus we see, that lust and pride seldom go unpunished. Orion recovered his sight by Vulcan's help, in counselling, and conducting him through the Sea to the East, towards the Sun: we shall never recover our spiritual eye-sight, which we lost by our spiritual fornications, but by the fiery zeal of the Spirit conducting us through the sea of Repentance to Christ the Sun of Righteousness. (*Mystagogus Poeticus*: 335)

I blush to call attention to another tradition, at least as old as Hyginus (*Fabulae*: 195), that Orion was engendered in the Earth (Gaia) by the urine of Jupiter, Neptune, and Mercury. Probably Hyginus assumed an etymological connection between *L. urina* and Orion—and a reference as well to the wet, foul weather that comes with the rising of the constellation Orion. Certainly this is the way Isidore (*Etymologiarum*: 3,71.10), for example, and Ross (*Mystagogus Poeticus*: 334-335) understood this etymology. See Bartholomaeus (*On the Properties of Things*: 8.24) for an account of the storms and other meteorological effects of the constellation Orion. These effects were well known: Petrarch, for example, mentions that "armed Orion shatters the unfortunate mariners' tillers and shrouds" (*Rime sparse*: 41.10-11); and Boccaccio referred to winter as that time when "Orion / still rules the sky at night" (*Eclogues*: 8.30-31; see also Milton, *Paradise Lost*, 1.305). Conti elaborated upon this tradition, interpreting the story of Orion as a veiled symbolic account of the interaction of water (Neptune), air (Jupiter), and sun (Apollo)—the drama of the natural circulation of water by evaporation and rainfall:

through the combined power of these three Gods arises the stuff of wind, rain and thunder that is called Orion. Since the subtler part of the water which is rarefied rests on the surface it is said that Orion had learned from his father how to walk on the water. When this rarefied matter spreads and diffuses into the air this is described as Orion having come to Chios which place derives its name from "diffusion (for *chéein* means to diffuse). And that he further attempted to violate Aerope (sic) and was expelled from that region and deprived of his lights—this is because this matter must pass through the air and ascend to the highest spheres and when the matter is diffused throughout that sphere it somehow feels the power of fire languishing....

They say that he was killed by Diana's arrows for having dared to touch her—because as soon as the vapours have ascended to the highest stratum of the air so that they appear to us touching the moon [i.e., Diana] or the sun, the power of the moon gathers them up and converts them into rains and storms, thus overthrowing them with her arrows and sending them downwards; for the power of the moon works like the ferment that brings about these processes. Finally they say that Orion was killed and transformed into a celestial constellation—because under this sign storms, gales and thunders are frequent. (*Mythologie*: 8.14, tr. in Gombrich 1993: 121)

Such allegory explains the presence of Orion in the statuary of Renaissance fountains (see e.g., Gombrich 1993: fig. 4).

Bibliography: E. H. Gombrich, *Symbolic Images* (1993).

ORPHEUS, son of the Muse Calliope, played upon the lyre and cithera so cunningly that he could charm men and beasts to his will. This was full of meaning: The divinely instituted ordering force in the universe was commonly thought of as Harmony; and so Orpheus and the other singers, Amphion and Arion, could figure forth this harmonizing, ordering force. Just as Orpheus, Arion, and Amphion could charm people, animals, and even inanimate nature, so did God's Harmony maintain order in the universe (see Appendix A, "Music"). Martianus, for example, explains Orpheus in this connection (*Marriage of Philology and Mercury*: 907-908, quoted under **ARION**).

But Orpheus was also a type of the poet, musician, and singer. One ancient tradition made Orpheus the ancestor of Homer and Hesiod. At least as early as Plato, Orpheus was not just a type of the poet, but specifically the type of the mystical-allegorical poet (see, e.g., Reynolds, *Mythomystes*: 152-153; see Hollander 1977: 83-86; Lamberton 1989: 28-29; for more on Orpheus as the type of the poet, see Segal 1989). Theodulph (*Ecloga*) makes Orpheus specifically a type of David playing upon the lyre. And so, down through the Middle Ages and the Renaissance, Orpheus was usually associated in one way or another with the struggle of the spirit against the yearnings of the flesh or of nature. Boethius's Lady Philosophy sings of this:

Happy is he who can look into the shining spring of good; happy is he who can break the heavy chains of the earth.

Long ago the Thracian poet, Orpheus, mourned for his dead wife. With his sorrowful music he made the woodland dance and the rivers stand still. He made the fearful deer lie down bravely with the fierce lions....

But as the sorrow within his breast burned more fiercely, that music which calmed all nature could not console its maker....[H]e went to the regions of hell. There he sang sweet songs to the music of his harp....

Hell is moved to pity when, with his melodious prayer he begs the favor of those shades....At last, the judge of souls, moved by pity, declares, "We are conquered. We return to this man his wife, his companion, purchased by his song. But our gift is bound by the condition that he must not look back until he has left hell." But who can give lovers a law? Love is a stronger law unto itself. As they approached the edge of night, Orpheus looked back at Eurydice, lost her, and died.

This fable applies to all of you who seek to raise your minds to sovereign day. For whoever is conquered and turns his eyes to the pit of hell, looking into the inferno, loses all the excellence he has gained. (*Consolation of Philosophy*: 3.mt 12; for Orpheus in Boethius, see O'Daly 1991: 188-207)

Lady Philosophy is urging Boethius to keep his mind fixed on things of the spirit, to turn away from merely material concerns. Certainly this is how Chaucer understood the passage. Chaucer provides the following glosses in his translation of Boethius: "sovereyn day" is the "clernesse of soveryn god"; to turn the eyes "into the putte of helle" is "to sette his thowhtes in erthly thinges"; to look back at the inferno is to regard "the lowe thinges of the erthe" (*Boece*: 3.mt 12; see also, e.g., Salutati, *De Laboribus Herculis*: 4.7). Indeed, during the Middle Ages Eurydice (or Heurodis) was sometimes said to have been carried off to hell in the first place by the "Noonday Demon" of the Vulgate translation of Psalms 90:5 (KJV 91:5; see Dronke 1966). And here is Bernardus:

We interpret Orpheus to be wisdom and eloquence....He is said to be the son of Apollo and Calliope, that is, of wisdom and eloquence....Orpheus has a harp, that is, rhetorical speech in which diverse colors as if diverse strings resound. With his soothing remedy he urges sluggards to honest work, calls the unstable to constancy, calms the truculent; and therefore it is said that he draws out rocks, stops rivers, and calms beasts. Eurydice is his wife, that is, he is naturally joined to natural appetite. For no one is without natural concupiscence....We understand that to be the natural appetite which dominates human nature, and it is called Eurydice, that is, the appetite for the good, for it is given in order to seek the good. She wanders about the meadow, that is, she errs through the earthly things which in a way flourish and immediately dry up....Eurydice treads on a serpent in the fields (in this earthly life she encounters temporal good). The serpent is called temporal good because it crawls through lower things, and, although it appears beautiful, it is deadly. The serpent's bite poisons her: the delight of temporal good infects sense. Having received the cause of death (delight in temporal good), she is drawn to the underworld (she is led away to temporal things and abandons heavenly matters). Moved by desire for his wife, Orpheus goes to the underworld: he descends by thought to temporal matters so that, once he has seen their fragile nature, he may withdraw his appetite from them....After he has sung for a while (after he has there exercised wisdom and eloquence), he regains his wife (he removes appetite from earthly matters) with the stipulation that he will lose her if he looks back (if he thinks again about the temporal). (*On Virgil's Aeneid*: 6.119-120)

Henryson's "Orpheus and Eurydice" is also in this tradition; here Henryson points the moral:

The perfyte wit, and eik the fervent luve
We suld haif allway to the hevin abuve;
Bot seildin thair our appetyte is fundin,

It is so fast within the body bundin;
Thairfoir dounwart we cast our myndis E,
Blindit with lust, and may nocht upwartis fle.
(449-454)

John of Garland (*Integumenta Ovidii*: 67), the *Chess of Love* commentary (1215-1216), Salutati (*De Laboribus Herculis*: 4.28-30), Fraunce (*Countesse of Pembrokes Yvychurch*: 47v), Valeriano (*Hieroglyphica*: 632), Ross (*Mystagogus Poeticus*: 338), and many others provide essentially the same moral allegory. Dante plays hauntingly on this tradition. When Dante's beloved and trusted Virgil vanishes at the end of the *Purgatorio*, Dante is much moved: "But Virgil had left us bereft of himself, Virgil sweetest father, Virgil to whom I gave myself for my salvation" (30:49-51). His language seems intended to recall Orpheus's mournful call after Eurydice in Virgil's *Georgics* (4.525-527); and so we are to understand that Dante's loss of Virgil—who represents something like human reason or natural philosophy—is like Orpheus's loss of Eurydice, or earthly attachments (see Jacoff 1991; Ball 1991: 32). Tritonio, less subtle, includes the Orpheus who turned toward Eurydice in his list of the "libidinous" (*Mythologia*: 28). Chaucer's Criseyde would seem thus to be saying more than she knows when she likens Troylus and herself to "Orpheus with Erudice" (*Troylus and Criseyde*: 4.791; for the application of this Eurydice allegory to domestic life, see San Juan 1992).

But Bernardus associated Orpheus with eloquence as well as wisdom. And indeed, the Orpheus myth was widely regarded as indicating what are, really, the role and powers of music and poets. Reynolds interprets the story of Orpheus and Eurydice, for example, in such a way as to suggest the powers of allegorizing poets. The Moderns, Reynolds argues, are neglecting the spiritual/allegorical understanding:

And I am fully of opinion...that the Ignorance of this Art, and the worlds mayme in the want or not understanding of it, is insinuated in the Poets generally-sung fable of Orpheus, whom they faigne to have recovered his Euridice from Hell with his Musick, that is Truth and Equity from darkenesse of Barbarisme and Ignorance with his profound and excellent Doctrines; but, that in the thicke caliginous way to the upper-earth, she was lost againe, and remaines lost to us that read and understand him not, for want meerely of the knowledge of that Art of Numbers that should unlocke and explane his Mysticall meanings to us. (*Mythomystes*: 159)

But Orpheus was most often thought of in relation to Pythagorean conceptions of music. Here, for example, is Macrobius:

Every soul in this world is allured by musical sounds so that not only those who are more refined in their habits, but all the barbarous peoples as well, have adopted songs by which they are inflamed with courage or wooed to pleasure; for the soul carries with it into the body a memory of the music which it knew in the sky [that is, the music of the spheres], and is so captivated by its charm that there is no breast so cruel or savage as not to be gripped by the spell of such an appeal. This, I believe, was the origin of the stories of Orpheus and

Amphion, one of whom was said to have enticed the dumb beasts by his song, the other the rocks. They were perchance the first to attract in their song men lacking any refinement and stolid as rocks, and to instill in them a feeling of joy. Thus every disposition of the soul is controlled by a song. For instance, the signal for marching into battle and for leaving off battle is in one case a tune that arouses the martial spirit and in the other one that quiets it. (*On the Dream of Scipio*: 2.3.7-9; see also Bernardus, *On Martianus Capella*: 5.120-130)

Orpheus was widely associated with music's ability to transform human states of mind. (See, for example, the *Chess of Love* commentary: 1214-1215) And thus Orpheus also came to stand for the civilizing triumph of art over nature. Aquinas writes of Orpheus in this way, for example (*In Aristotelis de Anima*: 1.lect. 12, *ad* 1.5.410b 28; see Pépin 1970: 109-110). And in Mantegna's elaborate fresco ceiling for the *Camera degli Sposi* we find images of Orpheus and Arion alongside images of Hercules: "Thus juxtaposed, Hercules can be seen to represent the highest achievements of active life, while Orpheus and Arion, *vates* and inventors of music and poetry, represent the most exalted forms of artistic and contemplative life. Translated into the ideal of a good ruler, this symbolic coupling indicates that the exercises of war and good government should be balanced by the cultivation of the finer arts of poetry and music" (Welles 1990: 115). When Spenser's Piers speaks of poetry's utility in curbing "The lust of lawlesse youth," he mentions Orpheus by way of example (*Shepheardes Calender*: "October," 19-29). Another example: a description of the house and gardens at Gorhambury, where Elizabeth was entertained in 1577 in the course of one of her progresses:

Over a gate leading into the Orchard, which had a garden on one side and a wilderness on the other, under a statue of Orpheus stood these verses:

> Of yore how frightful did this place appear,
> Here howl'd wild beasts, and satyrs frolick'd here,
> When luckily for me this Orpheus came,
> Whose heav'nly art has smooth'd my rugged frame,
> For withered stocks, gave these fair spreading-trees,
> And rais'd a shade that deities might please.
> Labours like his my Orpheus here employ,
> Oh may we both each other long enjoy!
> (in Nichols 1823, vol. 2: 59)

Sandys, looking back to Horace, extends this same idea:

Orpheus...with the musick of his harp and voice, attracts even beasts and senceless trees to heare and admire him. The morall of which fable may parallell with that...of Amphion: where of Horace in his art of Poetry [391-401]:

> Orpheus, the gods interpreter, from blood
> Rude men at first deter'd, and savage food:
> Hence said to have Tigers and fell Lyons tam'd.

Amphion so, who Theban bulwarks fram'd
T'have led the stones with musick of his lute,
And mild requests. Of old in high repute
Publique from privat, sacred from profane,
To seperate; and wandering lust restraine
With matrimoniall tyes; faire Citties raise,
Lawes stamp in Brasse. This gave the honourd bayes
To sacred Poets, and to verse their prayse.
                                    (*Ovid*: 476)

In fact, in one story Orpheus calmed an outbreak of civil strife among the
Argonauts (Apollonius Rhodius, *Argonautica*: 1.492 f.), a story remembered by
Conti (*Mythologie*: 7.14) and Spenser (*Faerie Queene*: 4.2.1), among others. Ross,
too, associates Orpheus with the governing and civilizing of "rude and ignorant
people" (*Mystagogus Poeticus*: 338).

From very early times Orpheus could stand as a figure for Christ. Christ and
Orpheus were alike in being Psychopompi, leaders of souls out of death and hell.
Thus it was that Orpheus often figured in Christian funerary art as early as the
second century A.D. (See Friedman 1970: 43; Friedman's fig. 1 reproduces a
second-century Orpheus-Christ fresco. Friedman provides a comprehensive
treatment of Orpheus in the Middle Ages. Ohly 1978: 133 cites an example of
Christ-Orpheus typology from twelfth-century Germany.) As late as 1634
Calderón's *The Divine Orpheus* pits Aristeo (Satan) against Orpheus (Christ) in a
struggle for the soul of Eurydice (mankind). Orpheus the poet-prophet was also a
type of the prophet Moses (e.g., Pico, *Opera Omnia*, vol. 2: 1374).

According to Ovid (*Metamorphoses*: 10.87-92), Orpheus shunned all women
after the loss of Eurydice—and turned to boys instead. He was thus associated with
homosexuality, and more particularly with pederasty (Bate 1993: 51-55).

For the Bacchae's murder of Orpheus, see **BACCHAE**.

Bibliography: Robert Ball, "Theological Semantics: Virgil's *Pietas* and
Dante's *Pietà*," in Rachel Jacoff and Jeffrey Schnapp, *The Poetry of Allusion:
Virgil and Ovid in Dante's Commedia* (1991): 19-36; Jonathan Bate, *Shakespeare
and Ovid* (1993); Kristy Cochrane, "Orpheus Applied: Some Instances of His
Importance in the Humanist View of Language," *RES*, 19 (1968): 1-13; A. Leigh
DeNeef, "The Poetics of Orpheus: The Text and a Study of *Orpheus His Journey
to Hell (1595)*," *SP*, 89 (1992): 20-70; Peter Dronke, "Eurydice, Heurodis, and the
Noon-day Demon," *Speculum*, 41 (1966): 22-29; John B. Friedman, *Orpheus in the
Middle Ages* (1970); Robert Hollander, *Boccaccio's Two Venuses*, (1977); Rachel
Jacoff, "Intertextualities in Arcadia: *Purgatorio* 30.49-51," in Jacoff and Schnapp
(1991): 131-144; Robert Lamberton, *Homer the Theologian* (1989); John Nichols,
The Progresses and Public Processions of Queen Elizabeth, 3 vols. (1823); Gerard
O'Daly, *The Poetry of Boethius* (1991); Friedrich Ohly, "Typologische Figuren aus
Natur und Mythus," in Walter Haug, *Formen und Functionen der Allegorie* (1978);
Jean Pépin, *Dante et la Tradition de l'Allégorie* (1970); Rose Marie San Juan,
"Mythology, Women and Renaissance Private Life: The Myth of Eurydice in

Italian Furniture Painting," *AH*, 15 (1992): 127-145; Charles Segal, *Orpheus: The Myth of the Poet* (1989); Peggy Muñoz Simonds, *Myth, Emblem, and Music in Shakespeare's Cymbeline* (1992): 334-363; John Warden, *Orpheus: The Metamorphosis of a Myth* (1982); Elizabeth B. Welles, "Orpheus and Arion as Symbols of Music in Mantegna's *Camera degli Sposi*," *SI*, 14 (1990): 113-144.

P

PAN (Inuus, Sylvanus) was the god of the shepherds (Theocritus, *Idylls*: 1.15-18; Virgil, *Eclogues*: 2.31-36). He was also known as Sylvanus, because he was god of the woods (*L. silva*, woods). But Macrobius was typical in insisting that Pan was much more than this:

The attributes with which Pan (or Inuus, as he is called) is represented enable those who are the better endowed with understanding to perceive that he himself is the sun...not that he is the lord of the forest but the ruler of all material substance....The horns, then, and the long, hanging beard...are symbols of the nature of the light by which the sun illumines the expanse of sky above and brings brightness to the parts that lie below. (*Saturnalia*: 1.22.2-4; see also Albricus, *De Deorum*: 9)

Ross's more detailed account is typical of interpretations of Pan from the time of Macrobius down to the seventeenth century:

He was the god of shepherds, and finder out of the Pipe or Cornet; red faced, horned like an Oxe, footed like a goat, rough and hairy on his thighs and legs.

By Pan may be meant the Universe, as the word *pan* [all] sheweth: therefore they feigned him to be begot of the seed of all Penelopes woers, because the world is composed of the seeds of all things...: his red face shewed the colour of the heavens, his long beard signified the masculine vertue of the fire and air, in the production of things; he wore the spotted skin of a red Dear, to represent the starry heaven....by his shepherds crook in one hand may be meant that providence by which the world is guided....By Pan some understand the Sun, for his horns signifie the Sun-beams....he was chiefly worshipped by the Arcadians...because that Country most abounded in shepherds, who called him the Lord of the Woods, or of the Universe, rather....Pan was much given to lust and venery, therefore they feign that he was begot of Mercury in the form of a Goat....perhaps they might signifie that the Sun whom they meant by Pan...stirs up venery, and desire of procreation in all sensitive creatures, namely in the Spring, when he cometh towards us, and his heat is moderate....Pan and Bacchus were constant companions....[W]ine excites lust, and seldom do Wine and Venery part company. (*Mystagogus Poeticus*: 351-353)

Ribera's *Drunken Silenus* (fig. 25) depicts a particularly nasty Pan, one clearly suggestive of the animal appetites (for more on this painting, see **SILENUS AND THE SILENI**. Pan's "crooked, rough, and deformed lymmes," wrote Fraunce, "are the foure Elements, and the bodies thereof made, which, compared with those above, are altogeather rude and homely" (*Countesse of Pembrokes Yvychurch*: 10v).

Isidore and many others provided the same etymology for Pan as does Ross—Milton speaks of "Universal Pan" (*Paradise Lost*, 4.266)—and basically the same iconology. Sandys' account is very like Ross's, although Sandys goes into a bit more detail as to Pan's relation to procreative urges: "he followes the Nymphs with insatiate lust, for that the world doth continually procreate, wherein moisture is chiefly requisite, as a matter most fit and proper for generation: Man being the greater worlds most exact epitome" (*Ovid*: 658). Sandys is assuming familiarity with the idea that human beings are microcosms of the universe, the macrocosm, as we see in Robert Fludd's picture of *The Relationship of Man to the Macrocosm* (fig. 21). Sandys concludes his account of Pan with this translation of Alciati:

> Men worship nature by the name of Pan
> A man halfe-goat, withall, a God halfe-man.
> Above a man, where sacred reason raignes;
> Borne in the heart and toured in the braines.
> Belowe a Goat, since nature propogates
> By coiture, in all whom life instates.
> Rough Goates, as other animals, expresse
> Ranke luxury, and brutish lusts excesse.
> Some say that wisedome governes in the heart;
> Some in the braine; none in the nether part.
> (*Ovid*: 658-659, quoting Alciati, *Emblems*: 97)

Bacon's myth-allegory is often idiosyncratic, but his account of Pan is in many ways traditional. Pan is a figure for Nature, and so Pan's human-and-animal body may be understood as an allegory of Nature in general and of human nature in particular:

Nature is also excellently set forth with a biformed body, with respect to the differences betweene superiour and inferiour creatures....This description of his body pertaines also to the participation of Species, for no naturall beeing seemes to be simple, but as it were participating and compounded of two....As for example; man hath somthing of a beast: a beast something of a plant: a plant something of a inanimate bodie, so that all naturall things are in very deed biformed. (*Wisedome of the Ancients*: 6; see also Valeriano, *Hieroglyphica*: 93, 475)

In one Pan story, the god entices Diana (the Moon) into the woods with a dewy fleece. Virgil tells the story in the *Georgics*: "'Twas with the gift of such snowy wool, if we may trust the tale, that Pan, Arcadia's god, charmed and beguiled thee, O Moon, calling thee to the depths of the woods; nor didst thou scorn his call" (3.391-393). Virgil is actually confusing Pan with Endymion (as was already recognized by Servius, *In Bucolica et Georgica*, in his comment on Virgil's lines). But the allegorical interpretation could be quite different. The story of Diana coming to Endymion was usually thought to be a figure for divine contemplation; Pan luring Diana was usually interpreted as nature allegory. Here is Fraunce: "Pan enticed the Moone into the woods, by giving her a faire fleece of white wooll: that is to say, nature doth induce and perswade the soule, by the gift of sensible bewty, to come downe into this world of generation, and propagation signified by the wood" (*Countesse of Pembrokes Yvychurch*: 43v).

Since he was the god of shepherds, Pan was—at least as early as Boccaccio (*Eclogues*: 10.149-150)—sometimes a figure for Christ, the good shepherd. Here is Rabelais's Pantagruel giving his opinion as to the true identity of Pan: "'I would interpret it to be about that Great Savior of the faithful, Who was ignominiously slain in Judaea by the iniquity of the pontiffs, doctors, priests, and monks of the Mosaic Law. And the interpretation does not seem preposterous to me, for He may rightly in the Grecian tongue be called Pan, seeing that he, is our All....He is the good Pan, the great Pastor'" (*Gargantua and Pantagruel*: 4.28; see also, e.g., Spenser, *Shepheardes Calender*: May, 54, and E. K.'s note on July, 49; E. K.'s glosses appear in the original and in all subsequent editions of Spenser's poem).

For Pan's song contest with Apollo, see **MIDAS**; for Pan and his son, Silenus, see **SILENUS AND THE SILENI**.

Bibliography: Charles Lemmi, *The Classical Deities in Bacon* (1933): 61-74; James Nohrnberg, *The Analogy of The Faerie Queene* (1976): 196, 219-221, 764-766.

PANDORA was the very image of feminine beauty. According to the earliest traditions, Pandora was made of water and earth by Prometheus, the maker of mankind. Most Christians, however, knew the version of the story that goes back to Hesiod (*Works and Days*: 57-101; *Theogony*: 570-590): Pandora was fashioned by Hephaestus, at Zeus's command. She was to be the instrument of Zeus's vengeance upon Prometheus and the human beings Prometheus had created and presumptuously provided with divine fire. Fearful of just such vengeance, Prometheus warned his brother Epimetheus against accepting such a gift from the gods. But when Epimetheus saw Pandora, born down to him by Hermes, he could not resist her beauty—Hesiod calls her "the beautiful evil" (*Theogony*: 585). All too soon Pandora opened the jar which Zeus had given her and so released all the miseries of human existence. In ancient times, then, she was the essential temptress (e.g., Pantel 1992: 362, 376).

Since Hesiod was not available in Latin until 1471, the Middle Ages knew nothing of Pandora and her fatal jar; indeed, Panofsky (1978: 3) asserts that Pandora never appears at all in Medieval art. The following passage from Erasmus was the first Latin summary of the entire Pandora story:

Jupiter, angry at Prometheus because of the stolen fire he had abstracted from heaven and handed over to the mortals, and wishing to take his revenge by a similar fraud, commanded Vulcan to form out of clay, as skillfully as he could, the image of a maiden. This done, he asked all the gods and goddesses each to bestow a gift upon this image; hence, it appears, the maiden was named Pandora. This maiden, then, showered with all the gifts of beauty, grooming, intelligence, and eloquence, was sent to Prometheus with a box, it too, most beautiful in shape but concealing within every kind of calamity. Prometheus refused this present and admonished his brother not to accept any present delivered in his absence. Pandora returns, captivating Epimetheus and presenting the box to him. As soon as he [or she] had opened it, so that the evils flew out, and as soon as he had realized that Jupiter's gifts were "no-gifts," he surely became a wise man too late. (*Adages*: 2.233; in Panofsky, 1978: 16)

Pandora was thus a pagan type of Eve. Reynolds is typical: "What other can Hesiod's Pandora, the first and beautifullest of all women, by whome all evils were dispersed and spred upon the earth, meane then Moses his Eve?" (*Mythomystes*: 175; see also van Mander, *Wtlegginghe op den Metamorphosis*: 3r). And here is Bacon:

it is a common, but apt, interpretation, by Pandora to be meant pleasure & voluptuousnes, which (when the civill life is pampered with too much Arte, and culture, and superfluitie) is ingendred, as it were, by the efficacy of fire, and therefore the worke of voluptuousnes is attributed unto Vulcan, who also himselfe doth represent fire. From this doe infinite miseries, together with too late repentance, proceed and overflowe the minds, and bodies, and fortunes of men. (*Wisedome of the Ancients*: 26)

Much less commonly, Pandora was interpreted in terms of nature allegory. According to van Mander, "Vulcan made Pandora, that is the heat and the moderation of moisture, these making the year fruitful" (*Wtlegginghe op den Metamorphosis*: 3r).

Bibliography: Erwin and Dora Panofsky, *Pandora's Box* (1978); Pauline Schmitt Pantel, *From Ancient Goddesses to Christian Saints* (1992).

PARIS (Alexander) was the Trojan prince who abducted Helen, and so brought on the Trojan war (e.g., Homer, *Iliad*: 3 and passim). Paris was the second son of King Priam and Hecuba. Hecuba dreamed that she was giving birth to a firebrand that would destroy Troy, and so the seer Aesacus foretold that Paris would bring on the destruction of Troy. Instead of killing the child, as she was told to do, Hecuba exposed him on Mt. Ida. There he was found and raised by shepherds, who named him Alexander (e.g., Apollodorus, *Library*: 3.12.5).

While Paris was thus a shepherd, Jupiter decided that it was he who should decide which of the three goddesses, Juno, Athena, or Venus, should win a golden apple, inscribed "For the fairest" (for the origin of this apple, see **ATE**). Juno offered him worldly power; Athena offered wisdom and victory in battle; Venus offered the love of the most beautiful woman in the world, Helen. Paris chose Venus (e.g., Apollodorus, *Epitome*: 3.1-5). Even in classical times, Paris was thus a proverbial figure for lust (see, e.g., Cicero, *Nature of the Gods*: 3.91). Proclus suggested that in choosing Venus Paris chose "the erotic" life, rather than Hera, "the regal" life, or Minerva, "the philosophic" (*Sur la République*: 6.108-109.5). Fulgentius elaborates upon this tradition:

Philosophers have distinguished a threefold life for mankind, by which they mean first the meditative; second, the practical; and third, the sensual—or as we call them in Latin, the contemplative, the active, the voluptuary....The poets explain...that Jove could not judge among these, perhaps because they did not perceive that the judgment of this world has preordained limits, for they believed man was made with free will; wherefore, if Jove had judged as God, in condemning two lives he would have committed the world to only one kind.   But they pass the decision over to man, to whom a free choice is owed. But...Paris...did a dull and stupid thing and, as is the way of wild beasts and cattle, turned his snail's eyes towards lust rather than...virtue or riches. (*Mythologies*: 2.1; see also Vatican Mythographer II: 206)

Boccaccio (*Genealogie Deorum*: 6.22) cites this passage from Fulgentius as a source for his interpretation. The *Chess of Love* commentary also interprets Paris as choosing "the delicate or voluptuous life" rather than the active or the contemplative life (538; see also Vatican Mythographer III: 11.21-22; Guido da Pisa, *Super Comediam Dantis*: 111-112; Christine de Pizan, *L'Epitre*: 43; Lydgate, *Reson and Sensuallyte*: 5884-5900; Ficino, *Philebus Commentary*: 446-454; and Landino, *Disputationes Camuldenses*: 121, 127; for the Neo-Stoic allegorical interpretation of Juno as the Active Life, see Chance 1994: 426). A thousand years after Fulgentius, Whitney's verses follow the same tradition:

With kingdomes large, did Juno make her sute,
And Pallas nexte, with wisedome him assaide,
But Venus faire, did winne the goulden fruite.
No princelie giftes, nor wisedome he did wey,
For Bewtie, did comaunde him to obey.

The worldlie man, whose sighte is alwaies dimme,
Whose fancie fonde eache pleasure doth entice,
The shaddowes, are like substance unto him,
And toyes more deare, them thinges of greatest price:
But yet the wise this judgement rashe deride,
And sentence give on prudent Pallas side.
(Emblemes: 83)

Paris was often spoken of as "effeminate" (for more on the emasculating effects of lust, see **HERMAPHRODITUS**).   Paris and Helen are Clement's examples of the dictum: "artificial beauty turns women into harlots, and makes men effeminate and adulterous" (*Christ the Educator*: 3.2.13; see also Viana, *Ovid*: 12.9). Peele's *Arraignment of Paris* makes the same allegorical point—while also suggesting that, had he remained a *shepherd*, Paris was little likely to be tempted by offers of glory and great learning. For Spenser, Paris was the shepherd

> That left his flocke to fetch a lasse,
> Whose love he bought to deare...
> And with lewde lust was overlayd.
> (*Shepheardes Calender*: July, 147-151)

Berchorius's comment on the story is a variant on this tradition: "Or say that these three goddesses are the three powers of the soul. Pallas is reason which has wisdom. Juno is memory which has the riches of knowledge. Venus is the will which is the mistress of pleasures. Paris signifies sinners and foolish men who obey the will and despise the other powers of the soul. They refuse to follow memory and reason and offer the apple of their heart to their concupiscence" (*Ovidius Moralizatus*: 380).

Because he had already sworn his love to the shepherdess Oenone when Venus offered him Helen, Paris was also remembered as an example of the faithless lover (e.g., Chaucer, *House of Fame*: 399; de Meun, *Romance of the Rose*: 13215-13228; Spenser, *Faerie Queene*: 3.9.36). Ovid tells the story in the *Heroides* (5); Heywood's *Oenone and Paris* follows Ovid fairly closely, contrasting the country nymph Oenone from the worldly, coquettish Helen (see, e.g., Schmitz 1990: 66-68).

Ovid has Paris carve Oenone's name in the bark of a poplar (*Heroides*: 5.27; De Meun, *Romance of the Rose*: 13224), the tree of mourning (see, **PHAETHON**).

Many commentators considered the Judgment of Paris to be especially significant because of its tremendous effects: since Helen was the bribe that Venus offered Paris, his choice—which is to say, his lust—meant war and annihilation for Troy. This is an interpretation of the story that probably goes all the way back to the Pythagoreans (Lamberton 1989: 35). Horace, for example, wrote that the story has to do with "the passions of foolish kings and peoples" (*Epistles*: 1.2.8; see also Athenaeus, *Deipnosophistae*: 12.510c). Alanus wrote that, "Broken by love, Paris, cooked in Venus' fire, makes war in the service of Venus, while he divests the role of fighter" (*Anticlaudian*: 1.5). Sandys had it that it is "No marvaile then, though the successe were tragicall, when Pleasure was preferred before Glory and Virtue" (*Ovid*: 557).

There are some interesting variations among the Neo-Platonists.   In Montemayor's *Diana*, for example, there is a debate about the meaning of the Judgment of Paris; and one character argues that the choice of Venus was "not to be understood of corporall beautie, but of the intellectual beautie of the mind" (81).

For more on Paris and Helen, see **HELEN**; for the consequences of their dalliance, see **TROY**.

Bibliography: Jane Chance, *Medieval Mythography* (1994); Margaret J. Ehrhart, *The Judgment of the Trojan Prince Paris in Medieval Literature* (1987); Ehrhart, "Christine de Pizan and the Judgment of Paris," in Jane Chance, *The Mythographic Art* (1990): 125-156; Robert Lamberton, *Homer the Theologian* (1989); James Nohrnberg, *The Analogy of The Faerie Queene* (1976): 720-723; Götz Schmitz, *The Fall of Women in Early English Narrative Verse* (1990).

PASIPHAE was the wife of Minos, King of Crete. She fell in love with a bull. The inventor Daedalus made for her a wooden cow wherein to conceal herself, and so the Minotaur was conceived—the fruit of this bestial passion. (According to one of the Roman historians, the emperor Nero had this scene enacted in the arena: the audience saw a real Pasiphae inside a wooden cow, mounted by a bull; see Plass 1995: 74.) Thus Pasiphae was generally a figure for unnatural, lustful love. Thus Ovid likened her to incestous Myrrha—and has Pasiphae feel jealous envy of heifers (*Art of Love*: 1.289-325; see Appendix C, "Envying the Animals"). Alanus, for example, wrote that Pasiphae, like Helen, was an unnatural lover. This woman, "driven by the madness of inordinate lust, in the form of a cow corruptly celebrated her bestial nuptials with a brute animal, and, concluding with a viler error, ended by the miscreated enormity of the bullock" (*Complaint of Nature*: pr. 4.111-114). Dante speaks of this as "the infamy of Crete" (*Inferno*: 12.12). In the *Purgatorio* (26.40-41) he links Pasiphae's lust for a bull with the unnatural love of the Sodomites. Boccaccio understood the story as an example of "how the vice of bestiality is occasioned in us" (*Genealogie Deorum*: 4.10; see also *Esposizioni sopra Dante*: 12.2.7; see Appendix B, "Bestialization"). Spenser follows Boccaccio and Alanus in this:

> Yet playd Pasiphae a more monstrous part,
> That lov'd a bull, and learnd a beast to bee;
> Such shamefull lusts who loaths not, which depart
> From course of nature and of modestie?
> (*Faerie Queene*: 3.2.41)

Tritonio includes Pasiphae in his list of the "libidinous" (*Mythologia*: 28). Sandys comments on her unnatural lust:

Pasiphae the daughter of Sol and Persis, is the Soule of man; inriched with the greater reason and knowledg, by how much the body is more sublimated by the virtue and efficacy of the Sun; Persis being that humidity whereof it is ingendred. This Soule espoused to Minos (Justice and Integrety) where carried a way with sensual delights, is said to forsake her lawful husband, and to committ with a Bull: for so brutish and violent are the affections when they revolt from the obedience of Virtue; producing Minotaures and monsters, by defaming Nature through a wicked habit, and so become prodigious. Nor possible to get out of that intricate Labyrinth of Vice, without the counsell and wisdom of Dedalus, imparted by Ariadne, or sincere affection. (*Ovid*: 383)

Bibliography: Don C. Allen, *Mysteriously Meant* (1970): 194, 199, 227; Paul Plass, *The Game of Death in Ancient Rome* (1995); Jean Seznec, *The Survival of the Pagan Gods* (1961): 172, 224.

PEGASUS, the winged horse, was born from drops of blood spilled when Perseus slew the Gorgon. A blow from the hoof of Pegasus on Mount Helicon made flow a fountain called the Hippocrene; both mountain and fountain were sacred to the Nine Muses. Thus Pegasus was associated with the Muses, as in the following passage from Fulgentius. When he set out to kill the Chimaera, Bellerophon was

seated on the horse Pegasus which had been born of the blood of the Gorgon....Then, too, Bellerophon, that is, good counsel, rides a horse which is none other than Pegasus, for *pegaseon*, that is, an everlasting fountain. The wisdom of good counsel is an everlasting fountain. So, too, is Pegasus winged, because he looks down on the whole nature of the world with a swift perception of its designs. Then, too, he is said to have opened up the fountain of the Muses with his heel, for wisdom supplies the Muses with a fountain. (*Mythologies*: 3.1)

Pegasus was thus associated with flights of poetic inspiration (Lascelle 1959) and with fame (e.g., Vatican Mythographer I: 130; Vatican Mythographer III: 14.3; Guido da Pisa, *Super Comediam Dantis*: 184; Lascelle 1959). Remembering the Hippocrene, Petrarch speaks of writing poetry as "making a river flow from Helicon" (*Rime sparse*: 7.8). Spenser provides a traditional explanation of the connection between Pegasus, fame, and the poets:

> But fame with golden wings aloft doth flie,
> Above the reach of ruinous decay,
> And with brave plumes doth beate the azure skie,
> Admir'd of base-born men from farre away:
> Then who so will with vertuous deeds assay
> To mount to heaven, on Pegasus must ride,
> And with sweet Poets verse be glorifide.
> ("Ruins of Time": 421-427)

Spenser eulogizes Sidney with reference to the same tradition ("Ruins of Time": 645-658). Sandys' comment on Ovid's Pegasus might serve as well for a gloss on Spenser: "the fountaine Hippocrene, late raised by the hoofe of Pegasus, and therefore so called....may be thus interpreted: How Pegasus, or Fame, as soone as borne in the mouthes of mortalls, beginneth to fly: and raise the Muses fountain in Parnassus, by ministring an argument to the Poet to sing the illustrious actions of men" (*Ovid*: 247).

Spenser and Sandys agree that Pegasus-Fame provides the *matter* for poets—but especially Spenser seems to suggest that Pegasus might figure poetic inspiration itself. This seems related, for example, to Conti's suggestion that Bellerophon's flight on Pegasus is the life devoted to reason (*Mythologie*: 9.4). Evidently by the seventeenth century Pegasus came to suggest a different kind of inspiration: Wither laments that foolish moderns know nothing of Pegasus "Untill, a Taverne-signe, they saw it made"; Wither then goes on to say that the true meaning of "this old Emblem" is "winged contemplation" (*Emblemes*: 105).

Berchorius, citing Fulgentius, agrees that Pegasus can signify fame; but he provides a second interpretation as well. Here Perseus is Christ, who at last "ascended on Pegasus—that is his body glorified through the Resurrection—when at his Ascension he flew to Paradise" (*Ovidius Moralizatus*: 222-223). In a related tradition, Pegasus could represent the Holy Ghost (see Wind 1968: 252-253).

For Bellerophon riding Pegasus, see **BELLEROPHON**.

Bibliography: M. M. Lascelle, "The Rider on the Winged Horse," in *Elizabethan and Jacobean Studies Presented to F.P. Wilson* (1959): 173-198; Edgar Wind, *Pagan Mysteries of the Renaissance* (1968).

PELEUS AND THETIS. Thetis was a sea goddess, the most famous of the Nereids, and the mother of Achilles. An oracle prophesied that she would bear a son who would be greater than his father; and so Jupiter, who had desired her, was suddenly anxious to marry her to a mortal, Peleus. All of the gods were invited to their marriage—save only the goddess Discord (e.g., Ovid, *Metamorphoses*: 11.215-265). Fulgentius told the story in this way:

They say that Thetis signifies water, whence the nymph took her name. Jove as God married her to Peleus, and *pelos* in Greek is *lutum*, mud, in Latin. Thus they wish to produce a man commingled with water, whereby they say that Jove wished to lie with Thetis but was prevented by the thought that she would produce one greater than himself who would drive him from his rule; for if fire, that is Jove, mingles with water, it is put out by the power of the water. So in the union of water and the earth, that is, of Thetis and Peleus, discord alone is not invited, for the reason that there must be concord between the two elements for a man to be produced: their coming together shows that Peleus stands for earth, that is, the flesh, and Thetis for water, that is, fluid, and Jove who married the two for fire, that is, the spirit...the conceiving of man from the blending of the elements....Jove is said to have summoned all the gods to the wedding because the heathen believed that in a human being separate gods gained possession of separate parts—for instance, Jove, the head; Minerva, the eyes; Juno, the arms; Neptune, the breast; Mars, the waist; Venus, the kidneys and sex organs; Mercury, the feet. (*Mythologies*: 3.7)

The nature allegory here was long lived. The *Chess of Love* commentary (557-558) followed Fulgentius closely; and Fraunce wrote that the marriage "noteth the generation of things, for *pelos* is slyme, and Thetis water, whereof all things are made, yet by an efficient; and therefore all the gods were at the wedding, except

Discord, the only cause of dissolution" (*Countesse of Pembrokes Yvychurch*: 5v). Sandys provides a virtual paraphrase of Fulgentius; but since Sandys prizes clarity rather more highly than does his mythographic predecessor, it might be well to quote at least a few lines from Sandys: "there is no discord betweene Peleus and Thetis, for of the concord of these two elements man is begotten: of Peleus the flesh, and of Thetis the humors, both quickned by the soule, or the fire of Jupiter" (*Ovid*: 526). Thus it was that Renaissance Dutch painters could employ the marriage of Peleus and Thetis in wedding paintings (Blankert et al. 1980: 58).

For Discord's rolling the golden apple at this wedding, see **ATE**. For the story of Thetis dipping Achilles in the Styx, see **ACHILLES**.

Bibliography: Albert Blankert et al., *Gods, Saints, and Heroes: Dutch Painting in the Age of Rembrandt* (1980); P. Grootkerk, *The Wedding of Peleus and Thetis in Art and Literature of the Middle Ages and Renaissance*, PhD. dissertation, Case Western Reserve Univ. (1975); James Nohrnberg, *The Analogy of The Faerie Queene* (1976): 746-747.

PENELOPE was the clever, faithful wife of Ulysses. Despite the eagerness of many suitors, she waited for her husband through the ten years of the Trojan War and then through the ten years it took him to find his way back to Ithaca. Her faithfulness was proverbial in classical times as well as in the Middle Ages and the Renaissance. Ovid, for example, contrasts the adultress Helen with faithful Penelope (*Heroides*: 1); Jerome mentions her as such an example (*Against John of Jerusalem*: 1.45); and here is Vatican Mythographer II: "Ulysses innocently passes by [Circe's isle]; this is wisdom contemplating libidinousness. And he has to wife Penelope, who is said to be chaste, for always wisdom is married to chastity" (212). According to Dante's fourteenth-century commentators, since Ulysses was often associated with wisdom, Penelope—always busy with her weaving—was a figure for the active life (as opposed to the contemplative life). Boccaccio calls her "a woman of untarnished honor and inviolate chastity, and a holy and eternal example for women" (*Concerning Famous Women*: 38). Gower's sense of her virtue was typical:

> Penolope that on was hote,
> Whom many a knyht hath loved hote...
> Bot sche, which hath no worldes joie
> Bot only of hire housebonde,
> Whil that hir lord was out of londe,
> So wel hath kept hir wommanhiede,
> That al the world thereof tok hiede.
> (*Confessio Amantis*: 8.2621-2630)

Surrey was one of many poets in the Renaissance who saw Penelope in this same way. Surrey praises his beloved: "And thereto hath a trothe as just / As had

Penelope the fayre" ("Geve place, ye lovers"; see also Shakespeare, *Coriolanus*: 1.3.82).

There was, however, another version of the story, in which the god Pan was born of Penelope—conceived of the seed of all (*L. pan*, "all") her suitors! Ross refers to this interpretation: "By Pan may be meant the Universe, as the word *pan* sheweth: therefore they feigned him to be begot of the seed of all Penelopes woers, because the world is composed of the seeds of all things" (*Mystagogus Poeticus*: 351). But this was not widely accepted. Bacon, for example, mentions it only to dismiss it, reminding us of her reputation for "matronly chastity" (*Wisedome of the Ancients*: 6).

PENTHEUS was the king of Thebes and the son of Agave, one of the Bacchae. As Euripides (*Bacchanals*) and Ovid (*Metamorphoses*: 11.1-43) tell the story, when Bacchus returned in triumph from his eastern conquests, Pentheus refused to allow Bacchus's followers—the Bacchae—to worship him. Pentheus then found that his soldiers were powerless to prevent the Bacchae from their ecstasies. Pentheus then went himself to spy on the bacchanals. But the Bacchae found him out and, led by Agave, they killed him in their frenzy.

The story of Pentheus could thus suggest the power and the danger of sexual passion. Boccaccio was probably referring to this tradition when he included a character named Pentheo in the *Teseida* (Hollander 1977: 181). Berchorius (*Ovidius Moralizatus*: 197) regarded Pentheus as a martyr—and as an example of the difficulties that lie in the way of the good person who tries to reproach or reform sinners. For John of Garland, Pentheus was the "studious man" distracted—torn apart, as it were—by the senses (*Integumenta Ovidii*: 169-180). During the Renaissance the story came to be a warning to rulers, as in Conti: "Pentheus, the son of Echion and Agave daughter of Cadmus, the king of Thebes, was determined to exterminate the mysterious secrets and sacrifices and orgies and Bacchanals, which were execrable profanations....But it is hazardous for princes and kings to abolish on the instant dissoluteness and intemperance which have been long practiced" (*Mythologie*: 5.14). Sandys made something like the same point with less sympathy: "Pentheus affords a miserable example....Wise Princes should rather indeavor to pacifie, then violently oppose a popular fury: which like a torrent beares all before it" (*Ovid*: 169). Sandys goes on to write that Pentheus could even be interpreted as "the image of an implacable Tyrant."

Bibliography: Robert Hollander, *Boccaccio's Two Venuses* (1977).

PERSEUS had the formidable task of slaying Medusa, one of the three monstrous sisters known as the Gorgons. Perseus was aided in this endeavor by Mercury and Minerva. With their help, he acquired winged sandals and the helmet of Pluto, which made the wearer invisible. Once Perseus found Medusa, Minerva held up a shield of highly polished bronze (or crystal, in some versions) to reflect away the gaze of Medusa, which could turn men to stone. Perseus was thus able to cut off the head of Medusa (e.g., Ovid, *Metamorphoses*: 4.605-803; Apollodorus, *Library*: 2.4.1-5; Hyginus, *Fabulae*: 63, 64).

For Fulgentius, "Perseus with the help of Minerva...is manliness aided by wisdom" (*Mythologies*: 1.21; see also Vatican Mythographer II: 113). Perseus's "manliness" here is *L. virtus*, which combined the notions of *vir*, "man," and *virtue* (see **AMAZONS, HERCULES: Hercules in General**). Berchorius was one of many who developed this idea. Perseus was sent to kill the Gorgons:

Against the danger of being turned into stone he took the crystal shield of Pallas and wings along with the sickle-like sword of Mercury and went to the dwelling of the monsters beyond Mount Atlas. Around this dwelling he found men and animals turned to stone. When one of the sisters handed their common eye to another, Perseus put out his hand and stole the eye. Afterwards...he looked at their location and appearance in his mirror-like shield. He directed himself with it so he could look at them and kill them....These serpent-like monsters can signify evil, beautiful women who are serpent-like—that is of an evil nature....Those who see them are turned into stones; for men are made stones—that is insensible—by the sight of women....But Perseus...[had] the shield of Pallas who is the goddess of wisdom—that is wisdom and discretion [and] the wings of Mercury who is a god who can fly—that is celestial contemplation....Above all, he should not look at these women with pleasure but flee their sight by avoiding the occasion of sin and look at their form...only in the shield of Pallas—that is in the scripture, which is the shield of wisdom. (*Ovidius Moralizatus*: 219-220)

The reflective or crystal shield of Minerva was sometimes associated with contemplation (e.g., Pictorius, *Apotheoseos*: 45).

Boccaccio provides a full fourfold allegory for the story of Perseus:

Jove's son Perseus, according to the poetic fictions, killed the Gorgon and flew up victorious into the air. This may be understood superficially in its literal, historical sense. If in its moral sense, it shows the wise man's triumph over vice and attainment of virtue. In addition, allegorically it designates the contempt of the pious mind for worldly delights and its elevation to the celestial. Anagogically, the fable figures forth Christ's ascension to his Father and his victory over the Prince of the world. (*Genealogie Deorum*: 1.3; for Perseus as type of Christ, see also, e.g., Ross, *Mystagogus Poeticus*: 359)

Harington provides a similar fourfold interpretation. He explains first the historical/literal level, then the moral allegory, where Perseus, "a wise man, sonne of Jupiter endewed with vertue from above, slayeth sinne and vice, a thing base and earthly; signified by Gorgon, and so mounteth up to the skie of vertue." Then Harington explains what the story means "in the kind of Allegorie":

the mind of man being gotten by God, and so the childe of God killing and vanquishing the earthlinesse of this Gorgonicall nature, ascendeth up to the understanding of heavenly things, of high things, of eternal things; in which contemplation consisteth the perfection of man....It hath also another Theological Allegorie; that the angelicall nature, daughter of the most high God the creator of all things; killing & overcomming all bodily substance, signified by Gorgon, ascended into heaven. (*Apologie of Poetrie*: 4-5)

Sandys also comments on Ovid's story of Perseus and Medusa. He writes that Perseus was sent by "the compassionate Pallas" to slay Medusa, because "she transformed who soever she lookt on, into marble." Perseus,

spying Medusa a sleepe in the mirror of his shield, he cut off her head before her sisters could awake; from whose blood up-sprung Crysaor, and the winged horse Pegasus. This fable declares that no great action should be taken in hand without the advice of Pallas, which is wisdome. That the equity of the cause is chiefly to be considered: for what more...noble then to suppresse a tyranny; under which the people lie prostrate; deprived of life and vigour, as under the aspect of Medusa?....Pegasus, a flying horse, ascends from the blood of Medusa: expressing that fame, which flies through the mouthes of men, and celebrates victorious virtue. Perseus is also taken for the reasonable soule...Medusa, lust and the inchantments of bodily beauty, which stupifies our senses, make us altogether unusefull, and convert us as it were into marble. (*Ovid*: 221)

Sandys was not alone in associating Perseus with the suppression of tyranny. The Duke of Anjou, for example, "was to be a true Perseus" by delivering Brabant from tyranny and "reigning by law and reason" (in Nichols 1823, vol. 2: 375).

During the Middle Ages, Perseus, as the courageous rescuer of Andromeda, could serve as an example of knighthood (see Tuve 1966: 35-36). For more on Perseus and Andromeda, see **ANDROMEDA**.

Bibliography: Charles Lemmi, *The Classical Deities in Bacon* (1933): 156-159; John Nichols, *The Progresses and Public Processions of Queen Elizabeth*, 3 vols. (1823); Rosemond Tuve, *Allegorical Imagery* (1966).

PHAETHON persuaded his father, Apollo, to allow him to drive the chariot of the sun. But he could not control the horses, and so the chariot came too near the earth and burned it. In Ovid's version, Jupiter then

thundered, and, balancing in his right hand a bolt, flung it from beside the ear at the charioteer and hurled him from the car....Phaethon, fire ravaging his ruddy hair, is hurled headlong and falls with a long trail through the air....The Naiads in that western land consign his body, still smoking with the flames of that forked bolt, to the tomb and carve this epitaph upon his stone:

HERE PHAETHON LIES: IN PHOEBUS' CAR HE FARED, AND THOUGH HE GREATLY FAILED, MORE GREATLY DARED. (*Metamorphoses*: 2.309-328)

There is a warning implicit in Ovid's version of the story, but the epitaph makes it clear that Ovid admired Phaethon's daring. Some later commentators also gave Phaethon's flight a favorable interpretation; Ross, for example, wrote that the story was meant to "encourage men to vertuous actions, and to sublime and heavenly cogitations" (*Mystagogus Poeticus*: 45).

Most Medieval and Renaissance allegorists, however, concentrated on the warning. Fulgentius saw Phaethon as one who fell for "aspiring" (*Mythologies*: 1.16); Dante compared proud churchmen to Phaethon (*Letters*: 11.4, 5-8; see Pépin 1970: 112-113); Lydgate wrote of Phaethon's "presumpsion" (*Reson and Sensuallyte*: 4206; see also Caxton, *Ovid*: comment on book 2). And Golding wrote that in this story Ovid meant to express

> The nature of ambition blynd, and youthfull wilfulnesse.
> The end whereof is miserie, and bringeth at the last
> Repentance when it is to late that all redress is past.
>   ("Epistle": 72-74)

Berchorius saw the story as showing that "virtue is in the mean" (*Ovidius Moralizatus*: 154). *Ovide Moralisé* (2.689-730) and Berchorius (*Ovidius Moralizatus*: 160) treat Phaethon as a type of proud aspiring Lucifer and his revolt in heaven. Elsewhere, the *Ovide Moralisé* interprets Phaethon as the Antichrist (2.914-1012). In this same tradition, Milton's description of Satan's descent from the outer shell of the universe to the Orb of the Sun (*Paradise Lost*: 3.526-590) recalls Ovid's description of the flight of Phaethon (Harding 1946: 89).

Bruegel's engraving of Phaethon (fig. 22) associates Phaethon with sea-going ships, which were allegorical figures for pride (see **ICARUS**). The swan with the odd, human face is Cycnus. According to Ovid, Cycnus was Phaethon's cousin and friend, and he mourned Phaethon's death bitterly:

He, abandoning his kingdom...went weeping and lamenting along the green banks of the Eridanus....And as he went his voice became thin and shrill; white plumage hid his hair and his neck stretched out from his breast. A web-like membrane joined his reddened fingers, wings clothed his sides, and a blunt beak his mouth. So Cycnus became a strange new bird—the swan. But he did not trust himself to the upper air and Jove, since he remembered the fiery bolt which the god had unjustly hurled. His favorite haunts were the still pools and spreading lakes; and...he chose the water for his home, as the opposite of flame. (*Metamorphoses*: 2.370-380; Petrarch, in the *Rime sparse*: 23.58-63, likens himself to Cycnus, since like the swan-Cycnus his mourning takes the form of song)

Allegorically, Cycnus provides a moral contrast for Phaethon. See, for example, the *Ovide Moralisé* (2.1136-1131) and Berchorius, where Lucifer and Phaethon are struck with "the bolt of eternal fire." It is this fire which Cycnus fears: "In order to avoid it we should shed tears through remorse and be changed into a bird—that is into a spiritual man—through confession and change in our actions. We should be covered with white feathers because of a chaste external life" (*Ovidius Moralizatus*: 160). Sandys is content merely to point out that Cycnus was not "mounting aloft, as detesting Jupiter" (*Ovid*: 111); that is, Cycnus did not mount aloft because he detested worldly power (Jupiter).

During the Renaissance the story of Phaethon was often given a political interpretation, as in this passage from Fraunce about inappropriate youthful ambition:

The ethicall moralization...may be this: Phaethon, a youth, and therefore unable to governe, will needes be a magistrate: but alas, it is too great a burden for his weake shoulders....The government and administration of a common wealth or kingdome, is a heavenly charge....It is also as heavy as heavenly. The beginning and climing up, is hard and difficult: the top thereof is subject to a thousand perills and dangers, which make even the most experienced, much to feare: and the descent or comming downe is headlong....But ambition can heare no reason, and Phaethon will needs sit in his fathers chariot....This chariot is the glorious type of earthly honor and dignitie.....When all is come to al, Phaetons ambitious conceit, gaines naught but this, to comfort his destruction, that when by his aspiring, he hath procured his owne overthrow, men may say after his death, This fellow caried a brave minde, and shott at mighty matters....The like folly and fall was that of Icarus. (*Countesse of Pembrokes Yvychurch*: 35v-37r)

Sandys' comment is in the same tradition: "This fable to the life presents a rash and ambitious Prince, inflamed with desire of glory and dominion" (*Ovid*: 106; see also Golding, "Epistle": 75). Shakespeare makes use of this allegory on several occasions, as for example in *3 Henry VI*, when the proud and aspiring Duke of York is taken prisoner: "Now Phaeton hath tumbled from his car" (1.4.33; see also *Richard II*: 3.3.178).

Phaethon was so sadly mourned by his sisters, the Heliades, that they were transformed into poplars, their tears into amber (*Metamorphoses*: 2.340-366), because, as Sandys put it, "Great sorrowes stupifie" (*Ovid*: 110). The poplar was thus associated with mourning. In De Meun's version of the story of Venus and Adonis, for example, we are to see allegorical foreshadowing when Venus courts Adonis under a poplar tree (see also, e.g., Fraunce, *Countesse of Pembrokes Yvychurch*: 45r).

Bibliography: Joseph A. Dane, "Chaucer's Eagle's Ovid's Phaeton: A Study in Literary Reception," *JMRS*, 11 (1981): 71-82; Davis Harding, *Milton and the Renaissance Ovid* (1946); B. G. Koonce, *Chaucer and the Tradition of Fame* (1966): 164-166; Henry G. Lotspeich, *Classical Mythology in the Poetry of Edmund Spenser* (1932): 99-100; Jean Pépin, *Dante et la Tradition de l'Allégorie* (1970); Rosemond Tuve, *Allegorical Imagery* (1966): 317-318.

PHILEMON AND BAUCIS. According to Ovid (*Metamorphoses*: 8.611-724), Philemon and Baucis were an exemplary old married couple. When Jupiter and Mercury wandered through their country in human form, they were received hospitably only by this pair. And so Philemon and Baucis were spared when the gods destroyed all their neighbors with a great flood. Their humble dwelling was changed into a magnificent temple, and, when they prayed that even death might not separate them, they were changed together into trees. Berchorius (*Ovidius*

Moralizatus: 315-316) interprets them as examples of hospitality and their story as a type of Lot's entertaining angels unawares (Gen 19). Tritonio includes them in his list of "The Hospitable."

Bibliography: Manfred Beller, *Philemon und Baucis in der europäischen Literatur* (1967).

PHILOMELA, PROCNE, AND TEREUS.   As Ovid told the story (*Metamorphoses*: 6.412-674), Procne married Tereus, the king of Thrace, and bore him a son, Itys. Tereus then raped her sister Philomela, cut out her tongue to prevent her telling what had occurred, and hid her away in a tower. Philomela contrived to tell her story by weaving it into a tapestry. When Procne came to know of her husband's perfidy, she decided upon a terrible revenge: she and her sister cut Itys into pieces, cooked the bits, and served them to Tereus. When Tereus discovered what had been done, he leapt up to revenge himself upon the two women—and Philomela was changed into a nightingale, Procne a swallow. Tereus himself was changed into a hoopoe.

This last is a clear instance of an outward manifestation of the inward, spiritual state (see Appendix B, "Bestialization"), for the hoopoe was a particularly nasty bird, as we find in Hugh of Fouilloy's *Aviarium*: "The Greeks call [this bird] hoopoe because it alights on human feces, and feeds on stinking dung. The bird is exceedingly filthy, is helmeted with a broad crest, is always lingering in tombs, and on human feces." Whence Hrabanus says, "This bird symbolizes wicked sinners, men who continually delight in the filth of sins" (57; Hugh is quoting first Isidore, *Etymologiarum*: 12.7.66, and then Rabanus Maurus, *De Universo*: 252). For Ovid, then, Tereus was a very bad man, one who had "confused all natural relations" (*Metamorphoses*: 6.537). The *Chess of Love* commentary interprets accordingly:

And briefly, this was pretended because they fled, one here and another there, because of their confusion and shame over the misadventure, in the way birds fly...from one region to another. Because Procne fled into a tower into which she thrust herself, it was pretended that she was changed into a swallow, because swallows willingly live in towers.

And Philomela fled to a wood where she hid, and so it was pretended that she changed into a nightingale because these birds willingly inhabit woods....The fable says that Tereus was changed into a hoopoe because it has a topknot of plumage on its head, a high crest like a helmet....The hoopoe also willingly makes its nest in excrement and ordure and willingly remains in such feces.

And one can also say that Tereus was gross and base for indulging thus in the vice of lust, which is a stinking, excremental, and abominable thing. (674-675)

As Pettie interprets the tale, all three were changed to birds, "meaninge they were not worthy humaine shape or the use of reason" (*Petite Palace*: 55). Burton makes Tereus's transformation one of his examples of the bestializing effects of lust (*Anatomy of Melancholy*: 3.2.3). And here is Ross: "There are two violent affections which make men shake off all humanity; the one is impotent lust, the other inordinate desire of revenge. We see what lust did in Tereus, and how desire of revenge prevailed in Progne" (*Mystagogus Poeticus*: 399).

When the poets write of warbling nightingales and swallows, then, their songs are often meant to remind us of the sad effects of uncontrolled passions. Thus it is that Chaucer's Pandar hears but does not heed a swallow's song:

> The swalwe Proigne with a sorowful lay,
> Whan morwe com gan make hire waymentyne,
> Whi she forshapen was; and ever lay
> Pandare abedde, half yn a slomberynge.
>
> (*Troylus and Criseyde*: 2.64-66)

But this allegory was more commonly applied to nightingales. Statius, for example, wrote that the nightingale's song is a "plaint" uttered "in mutilated speech" to decry "the treachery of the wedding bower and Tereus' cruel deed" (*Thebaid*: 12.478-480). At the end of the day that Pandar disregarded the swallow's song, Criseyde lay in bed thinking of Troylus. Obtuse in her blissful anticipations, she heard a nightingale:

> A nyghtyngale upon a cedre grene
> Under the chambre wal there as she lay
> Ful loude sang ayen the mone shene,
> Peraunter, yn his bryddes wyse, a lay
> Of love, that made hire herte fressh and gay.
> That herkened she so longe yn good entente,
> Til at the laste the dede slep hire hente.
>
> (*Troylus and Criseyde*: 2.918-924; see McCall 1979: 38)

Clanvowe's *Booke of Cupide* is a debate between a cuckoo and a nightingale as to the merits and dangers of love. Clanvowe probably wants us to remember the story of Philomela as the nightingale sings sweetly of love's pleasures. Ariosto, for another example, places a nightingale on Alcyna's isle of lechery (*Orlando Furioso*: 6.21). And Peacham wrote that this bird sings "In sweetest tunes, her bitter Fate" (*Minerva Britanna*: 209). In the anonymous, early seventeenth-century English mock epic *The Scourge of Venus*, Myrrha fantasizes about bedding her father; it is night, and every creature is asleep, "Save Philomell, that sings of Tereus rape / And Myrha plotting some incestious scape" (p. 242). Milton refers to the "poor hapless Nightingale" (*Comus*, 566). All three birds, Sandys wrote, "are said to have certaine articulate notes, whereby they expresse their infortunities: which I omit to rehearse, since they no way accord with our language" (*Ovid*: 302; for Philomela in literature, from Ovid to Caxton, see Schmitz 1990: 48-60).

But Philomela and Procne could also represent poetry and oratory, respectively, as we find in Sandys:

The Nightingall & Swallow are alluded to Poetry & Oratory: called sisters because there is in both a similitude of Harmony: the one affecting solitary places; sequestred from the converse of men, but frequented by Gods & Muses; differing in argument, as in affection, from the other: who delights in cities, exercising her eloquence before tribunals, in Senates, and assemblies. Yet as the Nightingall excells the Swallow in sweetnesse, skill, and variety; so doth Poesy Oratory. (*Ovid*: 302-303; see also, e.g., Ross, *Mystagogus Poeticus*: 399)

The ravishing of Philomela and the ravishing of Ganymede were both figures for the rapture of spiritual ascent, for divine contemplation (see **GANYMEDE**). Dante, for example, mentions the swallow singing "her sad lays, perhaps in memory of her former woes," just before he is, like Ganymede, ravished up to heaven by an eagle (*Purgatorio*: 9.13-14).

In some versions of the story, Procne becomes the nightingale, Philomela the swallow.

Bibliography: J. E. Gellink-Schellekens, *The Role of the Nightingale in Middle English Poems and Bird Debates* (1984); John P. McCall, *Chaucer among the Gods: The Poetics of Classical Myth* (1979); Götz Schmitz, *The Fall of Women in Early English Narrative Verse* (1990).

PHINEUS. Christians were most likely to know the story of Phineus in something like the way Sandys tells it: "Phineus...having pulled out the eyes of Crambus and Orythus, his sons by Cleopatra daughter to Boreas and Orythia, at the instigation of their stepmother Idaea...was struck blind himselfe by the divine vengeance for his unnaturall cruelty: the Harpies being sent to devoure his foode and contaminate his table." Phineus was rescued from the Harpies by Jason's Argonauts. Sandys goes on to provide the conventional allegorical interpretation:

Phineus therefore is said to have lost his sight, and to suffer perpetual famine, in that so blinded with avarice that he could not see into himselfe, nor afford those necessaries to life, which is contented with a little: the Harpyes called else where his daughters, that is, his covetous desires, not suffering him to eate of the meat, which was set before him, himselfe polluting it with his sordid disposition.

The Harpies, Sandys continues, are thus "the dogges of Jupiter: the ministers of his wrath upon the covetous, who are ever their owne tormentors" (*Ovid*: 330-331). This allegory was already well known during the Middle Ages; Bernardus, for example, had written that "Phineus signifies the greedy person" (*On Virgil's Aeneid*: 6.289).

Sandys really is not far from Berchorius's typological interpretation:

Phineus can signify Adam who at the insistence of Eve—our step-mother—killed all his sons—us—and subjected us to death, punishment, and sin when at the insistence of his wife he sinned. Thus he is blind because he is deprived of the light of grace and ejected from the light of paradise and sent into the fog of the world....The harpies, cruel and filthy birds—that is demons—are sent to punish and test. They take from him the foods of virtue and stain the table of his heart with the filth of evil thoughts.   But the argonaut Jason—that is Christ—came to the hospitality of the blind king—that is Adam—in the ship of a virgin's womb....Thus he put to flight those dogs—that is devils. (*Ovidius Moralizatus*: 267-268)

Bibliography: DeWitt Starnes and E. W. Talbert, *Classical Myth and Legend in Renaissance Dictionaries* (1955): 218, 398-400.

THE PHOENIX was a bird that was regenerated from its own ashes. The Phoenix was described fairly consistently from the first account by Herodotus (*History*: 2.72-73) to Ovid (*Metamorphoses*: 15.391-407) and Pliny (*Natural History*: 10.2), down to the seventeenth century. Batman's translation of Bartholomaeus Anglicus is typical:

Phenix is a bird, and there is but one of that kinde in all the wide worlde....The Philosopher speaketh of this bird and saith, that Phenix is a bird without Make, & liveth iii hundred, or v hundred yeares: when the which yeares be passed, she feeleth her owne default and feeblenesse, and maketh a nest of right sweet smelling stickes, that be full drye, and in Summer when the western winde bloweth, the stickes and the neast be set on fire with burning heate of the Sun, and burneth strongly, then this bird Phenix commeth wilfully into the burning neast, and is there burnt to ashes, among these burning stickes, and within three dayes a little worme is gendered of the ashes, and waxeth little and little, and taketh feathers, and is shapen and turned into a bird. (*Batman uppon Bartholomae*: 12.14)

Batman goes on to cite Ambrose (*On the Decease of His Brother Satyrus*: 2.59) as authority that the Phoenix is a figure for resurrection. He might have cited other Fathers as well; indeed, Ambrose himself was paraphrasing this passage from Tertullian: "The Lord has declared that we are worth more than many sparrows: if we are not also worth more than many phoenixes, this is no grand thing. Can men die permanently, while Arabian birds are sure of a resurrection?" (*De resurrectione*: 13.4). Thus from the early days of Christianity the Phoenix was a figure for the resurrection—perhaps even in the New Testament (Jeffrey 1992: 611). And this allegory continued current down through the Middle Ages (see Schiller 1971, vol. 2: figs. 489, 571). And it was still current in the seventeenth century, when Sandys wrote that with the story of the Phoenix illustrates "the immortality of the soule, and resurrection of the body" (*Ovid*: 707; see, e.g., Simonds 1992: 233-236).

But the Phoenix could also be interpreted as a reminder of nature's ability to perpetuate species, as we see in this passage from de Meun:

There is always a single phoenix that lives, up until its end, for five hundred years. [And when] Death devours the phoenix, the phoenix still remains alive....It is the phoenix in its ideal form that Nature reshapes into individuals; and this common form would be entirely lost if the next phoenix were not left alive. All things under the circle of the moon have this very same mode of being, so that if one of them can remain, its species so lives in it that Death can never catch up with it. (*Romance of the Rose*: 15977-16004)

A sixteenth- and seventeenth-century emblem tradition associated the Phoenix with learning and fame, since great learning was rare as the Phoenix and lived on as did the Phoenix (Becker 1991: 54-55).

In Chester's *Loves Martyr* the Phoenix becomes an allegorical figure for perfect female love, as the Phoenix and the Turtle (perfect male love) die together in the fire, each sacrificing the self entirely. The Phoenix thus became a figure for selfless, Platonic love. Several poets wrote poems that were published in an appendix to *Loves Martyr*, poems that make similar allegorical use of the Phoenix (e.g., Jonson, *The Forrest*: 10, 11; "The Phoenix Analysde"; "Ode"; Shakespeare, "The Phoenix and the Turtle").

Bibliography: *Anchor Bible Dictionary* (1992): under *Phoenix*; J. Becker, "Amphion and Hercules in Amsterdam: Vondel's Bijschrift op Diedrick Sweelinck," *SL*, 33 (1991): 49-68; R. van den Broek, *The Myth of the Phoenix: According to Classical and Early Christian Traditions* (1972); David L. Jeffrey, *A Dictionary of Biblical Tradition in English Literature* (1992); Douglas A. McMillan, "Phoenix," in Malcolm South, *Mythical Creatures and Fabulous Beasts: A Source Book and Research Guide* (1987); Gertrud Schiller, *Iconography of Christian Art* (1971); Peggy Muñoz Simonds, *Myth, Emblem, and Music in Shakespeare's Cymbeline* (1992).

PHRIXUS was the man who fixed the Golden Fleece to an oak tree in the wood of Mars. Sandys tells the story of Phrixus as he knew it from Ovid (*Fasti*: 3.851-876; see also Boccaccio, *Genealogie Deorum*: 13.68; Conti, *Mythologie*: 6.9):

Phrixus with his sister Helle, to avoid the cruelty of their father Athamas, provoked by the treachery of their Stepmother Ino, were mounted, as was fained, by the compassionate Gods on a Ram with a golden fleece, and carryed swiftly through the aire: when fearful Helle fel from his back into that straight of the sea, which is of her called the Hellespont. But Phrixus arriving at Colchos, in gratitude sacrificed the Ram to Jupiter (converted into that Caelestial Signe) and hung up his fleece in the Grove of Mars. (*Ovid*: 331)

Phrixus was interpreted as a figure for meditative flight; here, for example, is Ross: "The Poets by the fictions of Bellerophon riding in the air, upon a winged horse, of Phryxeus riding on a Ram over the Sea, of Daedalus flying in the ayr, of Phaeton riding in the Chariot of Phoebus, of Endymion with whom the Moon was in love. By these fictions, I say they did encourage men to vertuous actions, and to sublime and heavenly cogitations" (*Mystagogus Poeticus*: 45).

PHYLLIS AND DEMOPHON were best known in Ovid's version (*Heroides*: 2): Phyllis, daughter of King Lycurgus of Thrace, welcomed Demophon when he was shipwrecked on their shores. She fell in love with Demophon; they married; and he sailed back to his native Athens, vowing soon to return. When he did not keep his promise, Phyllis decided to kill herself. Demophon thus became an example of infidelity; and Phyllis became a *de casibus* love figure (e.g., Taylor 1982). Chaucer, for example, puts her in a list that includes Dido, Medea, and Ariadne, among others (*House of Fame*: 388-407; see also Ausonius, *Epigrams*: 22, and Lydgate, *Reson and Sensuallyte*: 4333-4334). According to another version of the story, Phyllis was changed into an almond tree. The *Chess of Love* commentary reads as follows: "Phyllis was changed into an almond tree....For the almond tree bears two kinds of almonds, some sweet, and some bitter, and this signifies to us that love contains in itself joy and pain....By this history, taken literally, it clearly appears to the purpose of Diana that it is not safe to immerse oneself too deeply in love" (680).

For the Phyllis whom Aristotle doted upon, see **ARISTOTLE**.

Bibliography: Beverly Taylor, "Phyllis, Canacee, Biblis, and Dido: Keys to Understanding *The Minnegrotte* of Gottfried's Tristan," *Mediaevalia*, 8 (1982): 81-95.

THE PIERIDES (Pieria) were the nine daughters of king Pierus. As Ovid (*Metamorphoses*: 5.294-678) tells the story, Pierus presumptuously gave his daughters the names of the nine Muses, and they grew up to be so vain of their skill in song that they challenged the Muses to a contest. The Pierides sang of battle of the Titans and the gods—a song ascribing "undeserved honour to the giants, and belittling the deeds of the mighty gods" (*Metamorphoses*: 5.319-320), a song that mirrored the Pierides' own presumption. For the Muses, Calliope sang of Ceres and Proserpina, a song that had to do with planting and regeneration. Soundly defeated, the Pierides were changed into magpies.

Like Arachne, then, the Pierides were figures for presumption. Thus it is that, as he begins the *Purgatorio*, Dante hopes that Calliope will accompany his song "with that strain whose stroke the wretched Pies felt so that they despaired of pardon" (1.9-12). Singleton's note, in his translation of the poem, points out that it is fitting that this first canto, which has to do with Dante's humility, should begin with the Pierides. The *Ovide Moralisé* (5.1763-1832) and Berchorius (*Ovidius Moralizatus*: 232-233) also understood the Pierides as figures for presumption (see also Lynche, *Fountaine of Ancient Fiction*: Eiii). Sandys provides a clear statement of this interpretation:

The Pye is the hierogliphick of unseasonable loquacity: deciphering those illiterate Poetasters (by the Satyre called the Pye-poets) who boast of their own composures, and detract from the glory of the learned. Justly therefore are the Pierides changed into those silvan scoulds, for their arrogancy and impudence: but above all for extolling the flagitious Gyants, and vilifying the Gods, since Poesy in regard of her originall, inspired into the mind from above, should chiefly, if not onely, be exercised in celebrating their praises; as here exemplified by the Muses. (*Ovid*: 263)

The contest between the Pierides and the Muses was also used to draw a distinction between good and bad poetry (see, e.g., Wood 1970: 201-202). As we see in the Sandys passage, above, the Pierides were also wrong for singing songs that extolled "the flagitious Gyants"—the Giants themselves were figures for presumption (see **GIANTS**)—while "vilifying the Gods." Ross mines the same allegorical vein:

Seeing the Muses are Jupiters daughters, and came from heaven, and are perpetual Virgins; by which is intimated their divine original, purity, and modesty, 'tis an injury to the sacred study of Poetry to call scurrilous and wanton versifiers by the name of Poets, whereas Poetry is a divine gift, the end whereof is to praise and honour God the Father of it; who therefore hath given wings to the Muses, that they might soar on high in heavenly raptures: and that they might flee away from the company of such chattering Mag-pies. (*Mystagogus Poeticus*: 301)

The Muses were occasionally called Pierides (Harty 1981); see **MUSES**.

Bibliography: K. Harty, "Chaucer's Man of Law and the 'Muses that Men Clepe Pierides,'" *SSF*, 18 (1981): 75-77; Chauncey Wood, *Chaucer and the Country of the Stars* (1970).

PLUTO (Dis, Erebus, Hades, Plutus). The Greek god Hades was son of Saturn and Rhea. He was the god of the Underworld and the dead (Homer, *Iliad*: 5.394-400, 15.187-193, 20.61-67; Hesiod, *Theogony*: 455, 765-778, 850). But in Roman mythology, Pluto had his beginnings as an earth god, a fertility god; and this association lingered on in various ways after Pluto had come to be identified with Hades. Bernardus, for example, wrote that "The god of Erebus is called Pluto, that is, the earth, because the heaviness of the earth dominates the fallen world" (*On Virgil's Aeneid*: on book 1; Pluto was called Erebus only rarely; for Christians, Erebus was usually synonymous with the Underworld). We find much the same in the *Chess of Love* commentary: "Saturn...sired four children, three sons and a daughter, by whom some wish to understand the four elements or the gods who had lordship over the four elements. Jupiter...fire, or the soverign air....Juno...was understood as the lower air....Neptune...is the sea....And the fourth is Pluto who is the earth or the god of the earth" (54; see also 414).

For Christians, this association of Pluto with earth and the fallen world (see also Waleys, *Ovid*: 16) would have made all the more attractive the conflation of Pluto and Plutus, the god of wealth. Plutus and Pluto were sometimes conflated even in ancient times; but the idea that the underworld might be associated with riches and the earth would have been particularly appealing for Christians, of course. Here, for example, is Fulgentius: "They also say that Pluto was the ruler of a quarter of the earth (for *plutos* in Greek they call riches), believing that riches were assigned only to the earth" (*Mythologies*: 1.5). Thus it was that Dante had Pluto guarding the Fourth Circle, the circle of the avaricious (*Inferno*: 7.1-15). Pietro Alighieri commented on this passage as follows:

And as [Dante] in other circles had fashioned a Demon who represented the diabolical passion itself, so now he shows himself meeting just such a demon in Pluto, who the poets say was the son of Saturn and Cybele, and who stands for the element earth. He is said to be *Dis* or *Dite*, because riches are said to be born in the earth and from the earth. Consequently avarice comes from the earth or because of the earth. (*Commentarium*: 138, on *Inferno*, 7)

The same identification of Pluto and Plutus may be found in Boccaccio (*Genealogie Deorum*: 8.6), Conti (*Mythologie*: 2.9), Giraldi (*De deis gentium*: 273), Batman (*Golden Booke*: 12v), Shakespeare (*Troilus and Cressida*: 3.3.197), Reynolds (*Mythomystes*: 170), and in the following passage from Ross: "Plutus or Pluto....'Tis not without cause that the same who is god of hell, is also god of riches; for the riches, gold, and silver, which we so much sweat and labour for, are near hell in the bowells of the earth...; besides, covetous rich men have a hell within them....and I am sure that no god is now held in so much veneration as wealth" (*Mystagogus Poeticus*: 364-365). Chaucer seems to have such ideas as this in mind when he has Pluto come to the aid of the avaricious Januari ("Merchant's Tale": 2225-2263; see Olson 1961).

Among the Renaissance Neo-Platonists, Pluto could function as an emblem of occult knowledge, because Pluto's subterranean world is secret and hidden, just as is occult knowledge (Wind 1968: 280-281). And, of course, Christians could identify Pluto with the devil, lord of hell (see, e.g., the *Chess of Love* commentary: 479).

For the story of Pluto and Proserpina, see **PROSERPINA**.

Bibliography: Paul A. Olson, "Chaucer's Merchant and January's 'Hevene in Erthe Heere,'" *ELH*: 28 (1961): 203-214; Richard L. Hoffman, *Ovid and the Canterbury Tales* (1966): 154-157; Edgar Wind, *Pagan Mysteries of the Renaissance* (1968).

PLUTUS, in Hesiod's *Theogony* (969-974), is the child of Demeter and Iasion. He was the god of wealth, whom Jupiter blinded because in making his gifts, Plutus was as likely to favor the wicked as the virtuous (see, e.g., Theocritus, *Idylls*: 10.19-22). For example, in the course of the entertainments for Elizabeth at Killingworth Castle in 1575, the gods convened to give their gifts to the queen: "Blind Plutus, bags of moony, Custumerz, Exchaungers, Bankers, store of riches in plate and coyn" (in Nichols 1823, vol. 1: 469). But during the Middle Ages and the Renaissance, Plutus was usually identified with, or seen as one aspect of, Pluto (See **PLUTO**).

Bibliography: John Nichols, *The Progresses and Public Processions of Queen Elizabeth*, 3 vols. (1823).

PODALIRIUS was a physician, like his more famous father Aesculapius. Podalirius attended the Greeks during the siege of Troy. According to one tradition, Podalirius healed Philoctetes of a wound that had supperated for ten years—and this allowed Philoctetes to bring to Troy the bow and arrows of Hercules, to which he had fallen heir upon the death of the hero (e.g., Apollodorus, *Epitome*: 5.8). Podalirius, again like his father, could thus be associated with Christ the physician. Spenser, for example, compares Podalirius's healing of Philoctetes to the holy Hermit's healing of the (spiritual) wounds inflicted by the Blatant Beast (*Faerie Queene*: 6.1).

PRIAPUS. In classical times statues of Priapus were often found in gardens, where the size, prominence, and altitude of the little god's erection made it clear enough that he was a god of fertility. He was regarded as a comic grotesque at least as early as Ovid (*Fasti*: 1.415-440), who tells the story of Priapus's attempt upon a sleeping nymph, Lotis: at the crucial moment Lotis was awakened by a braying ass, and all the gods laughed at Priapus's discomfiture. Ross tells the story of Priapus's origin in such a way as would have been familiar in ancient times: "He was the son of Bacchus and Venus, begot by him, when he returned from the Indies, for then Venus fell in love with him, and crowned him with roses: but when she was brought to bed of Priapus, he was so deformed a child, because of Juno's inchantments, that Venus slighted him; he was the god of gardens" (*Mystagogus Poeticus*: 366). Much of Ross's commentary may be taken as typical of what was written about Priapus during the Middle Ages and the Renaissance:

Priapus is begot of Bacchus and Venus, because wine and lust are the main causes of procreation. Venus fell in love with Bacchus, after his return from the Indies; to wit, when he was idle; for while he was employed in his expedition against the enemy, he had no thoughts of Venus: this was David's case when he fell in love with Bathsheba [2 Sam 11]....Priapus was a misshapen, deformed child, thus God doth often punish the inordinate lust of the Parents with the deformity of their Children....Priapus was called the god of Gardens, because he was the Son of Bacchus, that is of the Sun, and of Venus, that is of moysture, to shew that all trees, herbs, fruits, and plants are ingendred and maintained by the Suns heat, and their radical moysture....Other things may be here written of Priapus, but for modesties sake I forbear them. (*Mystagogus Poeticus*: 366-367)

Priapus was thus an apt figure for lust, and so Boccaccio is probably telling us something about the nature of Palaemon's love when "Priapus held the highest place" in the temple of Venus in which Palaemon prays that he might win Emilia (*Book of Theseus*: 7.60). Batman wrote that Priapus "betokeneth lust, otherwyse called the God of Lecherye....The poets faine Priapus to be the sonne of Venus, which is Lust following carnal desyre" (*Golden Booke*: 19v).

Priapus could also serve as a figure for sensuality in general (see, e.g., Ficino, *On Plato's Symposium*: 6.1; quoted under **BACCHUS**; see also Ficino, *Three Books on Life*: 1.7.1-12). This allegory would seem to account for Priapus's domination of Januari's garden in Chaucer's "Merchant's Tale" (2034-2037) and for his presence in the temple of Venus in "Parliament of Fowls" (253-258).

Rabanus (*De Universo*: 428) identifies Priapus with the Moabite fertility god Baal; Rabanus is remembering the vivid Old Testament descriptions of Baal's lascivious festivals (Hos 2:9-13).

Bibliography: Emerson J. Brown, "Priapus and the *Parlement of Foulys*," *SP*, 72 (1975): 258-273; Richard L. Hoffman, *Ovid and the Canterbury Tales* (1966): 154-157; Joseph A. Salemi, "*Priapus* by Pietro Bembo: An Annotated Translation," *Allegorica*, 5 (1980): 81-103.

PROMETHEUS was one of the Titans, the son of Iapetus, brother of Epimetheus, Atlas, and Menoetius. Fulgentius's version of the Prometheus story was widely known:

They say that Prometheus made man of clay, but made him without soul or feeling. Minerva, in her admiration pledged this office, that if there were anything desired by way of heavenly gifts, he might ask it to assist his task....She brought away the workman, bearing him up to the sky...and when he saw all the heavenly substance of life stirred up in flaming vapors, he secretly attached a stick of fennel to the wheels of Phoebus's chariot and stole some fire; implanting this in the puny breast of man he gave his body life. Thus they describe how he was bound and endlessly exposed his liver to a vulture....I take Prometheus to be...divine foresight. By such divine foresight, and Minerva as heavenly wisdom, man was made and the divine fire they wanted they explain to us as the soul divinely inspired. (*Mythologies*: 2.6; see also, e.g., van Mander, *Wtlegginghe op den Metamorphosis*: 3r; for classical sources, see, e.g., Hesiod, *Theogony*: 507-616; Apollodorus, *Library*: 1.7.1-2; Hyginus, *Fabulae*: 54, 142, 144)

The idea that Prometheus might be identified with "divine foresight"—or providence for Medieval and Renaissance Christians—goes back at least to Plutarch (*Isis and Osiris*) and Plotinus (see Lamberton 1989: 103) and survives as late as Ross (*Mystagogus Poeticus*: 368; see also Ficino, *Philebus Commentary*: 240; Sabinus, *Fabularum Ovidii Interpretatio*: 7). But for Fulgentius the story of Prometheus is most importantly an allegorical account of the creation of human beings—mortal beings, but with something of the divine in them. Servius, on the other hand, understood Prometheus Euhemeristically, as a great king, one who civilized men (*In Bucolica et Georgica*: 6.42). Augustine understood Prometheus as did Servius: "He is reported to have formed men out of clay, because he was esteemed the best teacher of wisdom" (*City of God*: 18.8). Van Mander (*Wtlegginghe op den Metamorphosis*: 6r) also interprets Prometheus as a wisdom figure. Boccaccio might be said to combine the two views:

Prometheus may be interpreted as having a two-fold nature, just as created man has. First, then, he is the true and all-powerful God, who made man out of clay....Second, he is the Prometheus-the-man, who...inherited regal power from his father Japhet; but being young and in love with learning, he abdicated in favor of his brother Epimetheus and removed himself to Assyria where he associated with the most renowned Chaldeans of the day. Thence he withdrew to the top of Mount Caucasus, where he studied the course of the stars and many other things. Coming down from the mountain, he began teaching astrology and the customs of civilized life to his fellow men, who were then entirely barbarous. He labored so successfully that he left them in a civilized state. (*Genealogie Deorum*: 4.44)

This was already conventional well before Boccaccio (see, e.g., Vatican Mythographer I: 1). Lemmi (1933: 128-129) notes that Bacon's allegorical account of Prometheus (*Wisedome of the Ancients*: 26) combines Boccaccio and the following passage from Conti:

Prometheus...is mind, which foresees things long before they happen. Epimetheus is the knowledge we acquire after the fact, and his daughter is repentance....In truth men were at first primitive; they knew nothing of ploughing or any other art—But gradually experience and necessity taught them to do better—In truth daily discomfort made them prudent—Hence it is said that Prometheus or prudence discovered fire; and by means of this, later, all the arts. For indeed, there is no art which does not depend upon fire....The ancients tell us that Jove, enraged at the invention of Fire, sent all sorts of evil to men; for there is no calamity that does not arise from voluptuousness, which is served by many arts. Indeed, together with the arts there arose kings, and war and robbery, and anxiety and all the distresses of life....

It is said that Prometheus offered to God flesh in one oxhide, bones in another; for with the coming of voluptuousness and luxuries, not only are right and law sacrificed to convenience, but even the gods come to be held in contempt. Few indeed are those who care more for the worship of God than for fat and profits....

It is said that the eagle of Jove incessantly tears at Prometheus's liver, because the minds of men are always distracted with various cogitations....Prometheus's liver is said to have grown at night in proportion as it was devoured by day because nature determines alternate times of quiet and of anxiety and cogitation. (*Mythologie*: 4.6; tr., Lemmi)

Conti and Bacon were not the first to suggest that Prometheus brought sin and grief into the world. Horace had interpreted him in this way:

Iapetus' daring son by impious craft brought fire to the tribes of men. After fire was stolen from its home in heaven, wasting disease and a new throng of fevers fell upon the earth, and the doom of death, that before had been slow and distant, quickened its pace....No ascent is too steep for mortals. Heaven itself we seek in our folly, and through our sin we let not Jove lay down his bolts of wrath. (*Odes*: 1.3.27-40)

And Statius lamented the "dread Promethean skill" (*Thebaid*: 11.468) which allowed humans to aspire to things beyond the life of simple piety. Christians could thus understand Prometheus as a type of Adam. Milton, for example, wrote that we cannot hear the music of the spheres because of the presumption of Prometheus's robbery, "which brought so many evils upon men, and at the same time deprived us of that felicity which we shall never be permitted to enjoy as long as we wallow in sin and are brutalized by our animal desires" ("Second Prolusion"; see Appendix A, "Music").

But Christians also remembered Prometheus for his refusal of Pandora's gift. Erasmus's interpretation was widely known: "And if you regard with suspicion the benign look of fortune, do as Prometheus did. Decline the treacherous box and hurry on, free and unimpeded, toward that one and only Good" (*Enchiridion*: 97). Sometimes Prometheus is contrasted with his brother Epimetheus in this way. For example, one of Ross's interpretations of Prometheus him makes him a type of the prelapsarian Adam and Epimetheus a type of the fallen Adam (*Mystagogus Poeticus*: 368-369; see also **EPIMETHEUS**).

Less commonly, the two brothers were contrasted in terms of mental awakening, as for example in such mythographers as Boccaccio, who distinguished between Vulcan, personifying the "elemental," or physical, fire that mankind uses for practical purposes, and the torch of Prometheus lit at the wheels of Phoebus's chariot. This torch carries the "celestial fire," which stands for the "clarity of knowledge infused into the heart of the ignorant" (*Genealogie Deorum*: 12.70). But to gain this Promethean clarity of knowledge is to be tortured as Prometheus was tortured: One must give up happiness and peace of mind. And so on the left of Piero's painting we see the ignorantly happy, earth-bound Epimetheus bathed in light, reaching up to the beautiful Pandora. On the right we see Prometheus, his face in melancholy shadow, gazing skyward (Panofsky 1962: 50). In some contexts, then, Prometheus can be a figure for contemplation. A related tradition was that of the astrologer-Prometheus, as we see in this passage from Ross: "By Mercury may be understood the desire for knowledge, which bound Prometheus the Astronomer to Caucasus, that the Eagle might feed upon his heart; by this they did signifie the care and solicitude which the Astronomer took in remaining upon that hill in the night time to observe the motions of the stars" (*Mystagogus Poeticus*: 265).

For other episodes of Prometheus's story, see **EPIMETHEUS, PANDORA**.

Bibliography: Robert Lamberton, *Homer the Theologian* (1989); Charles W. Lemmi, *The Classical Deities in Bacon* (1933); Linda Lewis, *The Promethean Politics of Milton, Blake, and Shelley* (1992); Erwin Panofsky, *Studies in Iconology* (1962); Olga Raggio, "The Myth of Prometheus, Its Survival and Metamorphoses up to the Eighteenth Century," *JWCI*, 21 (1958): 44-62; Raymond Trousson, *Le thème de Prométhée dans la littérature européenne* (1976).

PROSERPINA (Persephone) was the daughter of Jupiter and Ceres and the wife of Pluto, according to the genealogy best known to the Middle Ages and the Renaissance. Far the most important story regarding Proserpina was that of her abduction by Pluto. In Ovid's version Venus instructed Cupid to prevent Proserpina from maintaining her vow of chastity, and so he shot an arrow at Pluto. Pluto then saw Proserpina playing and gathering flowers near a shaded forest pool, where "spring is everlasting" (*Metamorphoses*: 5.391). On the instant he loved her, and so carried her off, down to the Underworld. Sandys paraphrases and comments on Ovid's story:

Ceres...is taken for corne: her Proserpina for the fertility of the seed...: begotten by Jove, that is, by the aetheriall virtue and clemency: when corupting, and dying (for even that which groweth dies before it bee quickned.) Shee was said to be ravished by the earth or Pluto: and then when gathering of flowres, in regard of the fertility, and temperate ayre, of Silicia, producing flowres in all seasons. Ceres is said to have wandred all the world over in search of her daughter: because of the obliquity of the Zodiack, which causeth Summer at severall times in severall countries; without whose fervor the Corne cannot ripen; and to have sought her with two torches kindled at Aetna, in regard of the superior and inferior heat; the one nourishing that part, which is above the Earth; the other what is under....Ceres, full of indignation for her Proserpine, strikes the Earth with barrennes.

Ceres is then told that her daughter has been ravished down to hell:

This known, she ascends into heaven, and complaines unto Jupiter, who signeth Proserpina's returne; provided, that since her descent she had tasted of nothing: meaning, as some suppose, if she had not lost her virginity...because a rape so consummated is no way repairable but by marriage....But Proserpina having eaten seven graines of a Pomegrannet (a fatall liquorishnesse, which retaines her in Hell; as the Apple thrust Evah out of Paradice...) [Ceres'] hopes were made frustrate. (*Ovid*: 254-257)

Sandys' association of Eve with Proserpina was a familiar bit of mythological typology. Dante, for example, had seen a fair lady in the earthly paradise near the top of the Mount of Purgatory. She "went singing and culling flower from flower, with which all her path was painted." He likened the lady to Proserpina "at the time her mother lost her, and she the spring" (*Purgatorio*: 28.34-51). Such associations arose from Ovid: "Ceres was resolved to have her daughter back. Not so the fates; for the girl had already broken her fast, and while, simple child that she was, she wandered in the trim gardens, she had plucked a purple pomegranate hanging from a bending bough" (*Metamorphoses*: 5.533-536). That a hitherto innocent virgin should pluck a desirable fruit while wandering in a garden where "spring is everlasting," was irresistible to Christian allegorists. Thus it was that Proserpina was understood to have been herself culpable—even though Pluto took her off against her will. And thus it was that Proserpina could be for Berchorius a figure for fallen human nature (*Ovidius Moralizatus*: 286), or as he elsewhere describes her, Proserpina is "evil"; she is Pluto's queen, and she "rules on a sulphur throne—that is in the filthy heart of a sinner" (*Ovidius Moralizatus*: 100). The *Chess of Love* commentator wrote in a similar vein: "Persephone, i.e., avarice, a very vile, vituperable thing, worthy of being married to Pluto, is seated beside him in hell as lady and queen" (463-464). Spenser was working in this tradition when he has Mammon tempt Guyon to avarice in the Garden of Proserpina—a garden that was probably suggested to Spenser by Claudian's description (*Rape of Proserpine*: 2.285 f.) of the garden that Pluto hoped would delight Proserpina. In this garden grew enticing golden apples—and other things less inviting:

> There mournfull Cypresse grew in greatest store,
> And trees of bitter Gall, and Heben sad,

Dead sleeping Poppy, and black Hellebore...,
Mortal Samnitis, and Cicuta bad,
With which th'unjust Atheniens made to dy
Wise Socrates.

(Faerie Queene: 2.7.52)

Spenser also distinguishes between Proserpina and Persephone, making the latter one of the Furies (e.g., "Virgils Gnat": 422; E. K.'s comment on *Shepheardes Calender*: Nov., 164; E. K.'s glosses appear in the original and in all subsequent editions of Spenser's poem; see Lotspeich 1932: 103).

Sandys provides a clear statement of the commonest understanding—going all the way back to the classics—of the nature allegory associated with Proserpina:

Jupiter, compassionating Ceres, decreeth that her daughter should live six months with her husband, and as long with her mother. For the seede, which is Proserpina, while the Sun is on the south for the Aequinoctiall, lies hid in the earth, which is Pluto: but when he travells through the Northerne signes, it shouteth up and growes to maturity; and then Proserpina is said to be above with Ceres. As also because the Moone (which is taken for Proserpina) hath halfe of the yeare her dominion in our hemisphere: being the Lady of the night. (*Ovid*: 260)

For three of the many others who understood the story of Proserpina as an allegory for the alternation of winter and summer, see Alanus (*Complaint of Nature*: pr. 2), Dolce (*Transformationi*: 135), and Reynolds (*Mythomystes*: 170). And so Proserpina could serve as an allegorical figure for spring (for a list of paintings that work in this way, see Reid 1993: 468-469). But Proserpina's alternation between upper and lower worlds could also be understood as a figure for the waxing and waning of the moon. Bernardus, for example, understood the story in this way:

the goddess of Erebus is Proserpina, whom Pluto carried off, and he takes her back to the upper world for half the month, and he does not permit her to leave him for the other half....Pluto (the earth) seizes her (the moon), since the earth by giving heaviness to the moon keeps it away from the ethereal region....For half the month Proserpina is sent to the upper world, and for the other half she is united with her husband, because the moon for half the month is seen in the upper hemisphere, and for half it is in the lower region of the earth. (*On Virgil's Aeneid*: 6.138)

This is an unusual interpretation, but the association of Proserpina with the moon was general (e.g., the *Chess of Love* commentary: 463).

As a figure for the moon, Proserpina was usually thought of as one aspect of Diana (see **DIANA**); Proserpina was also sometimes conflated with Hecate (see **HECATE**).

Bibliography: Richard L. Hoffman, *Ovid and the Canterbury Tales* (1966): 154-157; Charles Lemmi, *The Classical Deities in Bacon* (1933): 74-91; Henry G. Lotspeich, *Classical Mythology in the Poetry of Edmund Spenser* (1932); James Nohrnberg, *The Analogy of The Faerie Queene* (1976): 335, 356-357, 576-577;

Jane Davidson Reid, *The Oxford Guide to Classical Mythology in the Arts, 1300-1990s* (1993).

PROTEUS was regarded in classical times as a very ancient sea god, and as Neptune's shepherd of the sea.   Like other sea gods, he had the gift of prophecy—and the ability to take whatever shape he pleased.   This ability he exercised especially in attempts to escape those who came to ask him questions. Only by catching hold of Proteus and clinging tight could questioners force him to foretell the future for them (e.g., Homer, *Odyssey*: 4.353-564; Hyginus, *Fabulae*: 119).

Heraclitus (*Allégories d'Homère*: 64-65) and Proclus associated the many-formed Proteus with "the Forms of all things engendered" (*Sur la République*: 1.112.26-30).   This interpretation was widely credited during the Renaissance: Giraldi defines Proteus in this way, for example (*De deis gentium*: 228), as does Ross: "Proteus was thought to be the first god, as his name sheweth: therefore Orpheus calls him the first born, by which they meant the first matter, which is capable of all forms; from this arose the fiction of Proteus his many shapes: and because Thales held water to be the first matter or principle of all things, therefore Proteus was made god of the Sea" (*Mystagogus Poeticus*: 374).   This idea, that Proteus was a personification of matter in its relation to the Platonic forms, Ross could have found in Conti (*Mythologie*: 8.8) and Bacon (*Wisedome of the Ancients*: 13), among others.   Indeed, after citing numerous examples all the way up to Goethe and Joyce, Nohrnberg concludes that "we are dealing here with a kind of orthodoxy" (1976: 584).   Nohrnberg argues that Spenser's realm of Proteus is related to this tradition; it is a sub-marine Garden of Adonis (1976: 581).

Other mythographers, however, were more likely to concentrate on Proteus's powers of truth-telling and prophecy.   Thus Augustine could understand Proteus as a figure for truth:

Proteus...plays in poetry the role of truth which no one can hold if, deceived by false representations, he slackens or lets loose the bonds of understanding.   It is these representations which, because of our association with corporeal things, do their best to fool and deceive us through the senses...even when we have already grasped truth and hold it, so to speak, within our hands. (*Against the Academics*: 3.6; see also Theodulph, *Carmina*: 332).

Ross also interpreted Proteus Euhemeristically—a tradition that went back to Herodotus (*History*: 2.112, 118): Proteus was perhaps a "King of Egypt, a wise politick man, and a great Prophet" (*Mystagogus Poeticus*: 371; see also Sandys, *Ovid*: 525).   Typically, Ross suggests other possibilities as well.   He repeats, for example, an idea that began with Augustine (*City of God*: 10.10), that Proteus might have been a prophet inspired by the devil, a prophet "by a Diabolical act" (*Mystagogus Poeticus*: 371).   Berchorius also associates Proteus with "hypocrites, false friends, and flatterers" (*Ovidius Moralizatus*: 152).   Spenser seems to have both traditions—diabolical Proteus and false Proteus—in mind when he writes of evil Archimago's genius for disguise:

> For by his mightie science he could take
> As many formes and shapes in seeming wise,
> As ever Proteus to himselfe could make.
> *(Faerie Queene*: 1.2.10)

But Proteus was most often associated with falseness and deception in matters of love. Indeed, according to Nohrnberg Proteus was a "type of the seducer" (1976: 593), as we see in the following advice to the seducer from Ovid's *Art of Love*:

various are the hearts of women; use a thousand means to waylay as many hearts....Hearts have as many fashions as the face has features; the wise man will suit himself to countless fashions, and like Proteus will now...be a lion, now a tree, now a shaggy boar. These fish are caught with spears, those with hooks; these ones are dragged with taut ropes in bulging nets....And so comes it that she who has feared to commit herself to an honourable lover degrades herself to the embraces of a mean one. (1.755-770)

Thus de Meun, writing about the course of love, likens False Seeming to Proteus, both being known for "fraud and guile" (*Romance of the Rose*: 11181-11183). This tradition accounts as well for Shakespeare's Proteus, a faithless would-be seducer in *Two Gentlemen of Verona*.

Sea gods in general were associated with the passions. Bernardus, for example, writes that Triton (the son of Neptune) "is vexation of the flesh. He is called the god of the sea since he dominates the body. He is said to blow a trumpet, since bodily vexation vents itself vocally in wailing, that us, weeping" (*On Virgil's Aeneid*: book 1; see also **NEPTUNE, GLAUCUS**). And so Proteus, too, could be understood as a personification of the passions, or cupidity. Here is Clement of Alexandria:

The soul consists of three parts. The intelligence, which is also called the reason, is the inner man....The part in which anger resides is akin to the beasts and lives close to madness. The third part, desire, takes many forms and is more changeable than Proteus the sea god, assuming a different form for every different occasion, seeking satisfaction in adultery, promiscuity, and seduction.

Clement explains this by quoting and commenting upon Homer's account of Proteus:

"At first, he [Proteus] turned into a bearded lion," retaining only his adornment, the hair of his chin which proved his manhood. "Then into a serpent and a leopard and a huge boar." Vanity degenerated into immorality. Finally, his human nature is evident no longer, not even in the appearance of a lordly beast, but he "turned into flowing water, and into a tree high and leafy" [Homer, *Odyssey*: 4.359]. The passions are poured out, pleasures sprout forth, and beauty withers and falls to the ground—more quickly than the leaf—when the violent storms of lust blow upon it. (*Christ the Educator*: 3.1.1)

Nohrnberg (1976: 594-595) argues that this tradition explains the behavior of Spenser's Proteus, who first rescues Florimell from the lecherous fisherman and then lusts for her himself, there in the "Fishers wandring bote, / That went at will, withouten carde or sayle" (*Faerie Queene*: 3.8.31). Nohrnberg cites Boccaccio (*Genealogie Deorum*: 7.9) and Erasmus, among others. Here is Erasmus, who proceeds by quoting and glossing Virgil's *Georgics* (4.406-442):

when the mind seethes with furious upheavals you must, with every resource at your command, stick with and bind fast that Proteus of yours with tough chains, even as

> into marvelous shapes he changes himself
> Into fire and ravening beast and flowing river.

And what, pray, is so Protean as the emotions and desires of fools....Is this not a neatly appropriate bit which the most accomplished of all poets has written?

> Then varying shapes will mock you, and the likenesses of beasts;
> For suddenly he will become a bristly swine, a malevolent tiger,
> A scaly dragon, a tawny-throated lioness.
> Or he will make the crackling sound of flames.

But remember what follows:

> Nevertheless, my son, the more shapes he assumes
> The more tightly you must draw his bonds.
> (*Enchiridion*: 77)

Bibliography: A. Bartlett Giamatti, *Exile and Change in Renaissance Literature* (1984): 115-150; A. C. Hamilton, *The Spenser Encyclopedia* (1990): under *Proteus*; Charles Lemmi, *The Classical Deities in Bacon* (1933): 91-98; James Nohrnberg, *The Analogy of The Faerie Queene* (1976): 580-599; Brenda Thaon, "Spenser's Neptune, Nereus and Proteus: Renaissance Mythography Made Verse," *ICNLS*, 4 (1981): 630-637.

PSYCHE was the heroine of a story first told by Apuleius (*Metamorphoses*: 5-6). She was the daughter of a king and queen, and so beautiful that while many men worshipped her for her beauty's sake, none dared declare his love. After Psyche undergoes some trials, none less than Cupid himself falls in love with her. He visits her only in the dark of night. And he withholds from her his identity, warning her that should she ever see him, she would lose him utterly. Enraptured, she agrees to this—but finally, overcome by curiosity, she one night holds up a lamp to see her lover while he sleeps. Alas, a drop of the hot oil falls on Cupid, who awakes to banish her from his sight, to be evermore a fugitive. Venus forces trials upon Psyche, to punish her presumption in rivalling Venus's own beauty. But at length, Psyche's marriage to Cupid was restored by Jupiter's command.

Even this brief summary is sufficient to suggest how fertile this story must have been for allegorizers. In the fifth century Martianus wrote that Psyche was the daughter of Sol (the sun, Apollo) and "Entelechia" (*Marriage of Philology and Mercury*: 7). By this abstruse bit of Aristotelian philosophicoreligious allegory, Martianus meant to suggest that the human soul (Psyche) is the product of the divine potentiality (the divine fire, Sol, the sun) and the Aristotelian *Entelechia*, "actuality." Put another way, the human soul is thus a making actual of the divine potentiality, an incarnation of the divine fire (see Stahl's note in his tr. of the passage; see also Dronke 1974: 100-118). For Fulgentius Psyche's parents are "God and Matter...the world":

Psyche in Greek is called the spirit....Venus envies her as lust; to her she sends greed (*cupiditatem*) to do away with her; ...greed...links itself to her, as it were in marriage. It persuades her not to look upon its countenance, that is, not to learn the pleasure of greed (thus Adam, although possessing sight, does not see himself as naked until he eats of the tree of covetousness)....She produces a lamp from beneath the bed, that is, reveals the flame of desire concealed in her breast....She is said to have burned it by the bubbling over of the lamp because all greed grows hot to the extent that it is desired and marks the flesh with the stain of sin. (*Mythologies*: 3.6)

For Fulgentius, then, the story is a type of the Fall, with Venus and Cupid combining to play the serpent to Psyche's Adam.

After Fulgentius, the story seems to have been largely unavailable until it was recirculated in Italy in the fourteenth century (Schlam 1990). Boccaccio's account of the story mentions the various trials Venus imposes upon Psyche. The best known of these trials required Psyche to go down into the Underworld to bring back a bit of Proserpina's beauty. She does manage to get from Proserpina a box containing such a fragment—but on her way back she succumbs to the temptation to look inside the box. She faints as the vapors are released and is saved only by the intervention of Cupid, who reseals the box. Here is Boccaccio's interpretation of the allegory, beginning with a reference to Martianus's allegory:

Psyche is interpreted as the soul. Thus she is said to be the daughter of Apollo—that is, the Sun...for God is the true light of the world...who created the human soul with reason....There were two older sisters born, of whom one is the vegetative soul, the other the sensible soul....and joined to her is pure Love, which maintains the divine rational-element in the soul. Finally...she achieves the consummation of divine joy and contemplation, and is united with her lover forever, and shedding all mortal things, she is born into eternal glory. From this love Pleasure is born, that is, eternal joy and gladness. (*Genealogie Deorum*: 5.22)

For Boccaccio, Psyche is thus a kind of female Hercules: After many trials, she is taken up into heaven, where she is joined in spiritual/divine love with the god of love. And Pleasure—no merely earthly pleasure—is the fruit of this marriage. Spenser, in turn, paraphrases these ideas in the *Faerie Queene* (3.6.50-51; and see Allen 1968: 26-31 on Spenser's use of Psyche in *Muiopotmos*).

Bibliography: Don C. Allen, *Image and Meaning* (1968); Peter Dronke, *Fabula: Explorations into the Uses of Myth in Medieval Platonism* (1974); James A. McPeek, "The Psyche Myth and *A Midsummer Night's Dream*," *SQ*, 33 (1982): 433-448; Carl C. Schlam, "Apuleius in the Middle Ages," in A.S. Bernardo and S. Levin, *The Classics in the Middle Ages* (1990): 363-369; Peggy Muñoz Simonds, *Myth, Emblem, and Music In Shakespeare's Cymbeline* (1992): 78-92; Luisa Vertova, "Cupid and Psyche in Renaissance Painting before Raphael," *JWCI*, 42 (1979): 104-121.

PYGMALION was a king of Cyprus who carved a statue of a beautiful woman and then fell in love with it. Medieval and Renaissance Christians usually knew the story as Ovid told it:

> with wondrous art he successfully carves a figure out of snowy ivory, giving it a beauty more perfect than that of any woman ever born. And with his own work he falls in love. The face is that of a real maiden....Often he lifts his hands to the work to try whether it be flesh or ivory....He kisses it and thinks his kisses are returned. He speaks to it, grasps it and seems to feel his fingers sink into the limbs when he touches them....Now he addresses fond words of love, now brings it gifts pleasing to girls....He drapes its limbs also with robes, puts gemmed rings upon its fingers and a long necklace around its neck....All these are beautiful; but no less beautiful is the statue unadorned. He lays it on a bed spread with the coverlets of Tyrian hue, calls it the consort of his couch, and rests its reclining head upon soft, downy pillows, as if it could enjoy them.

Pygmalion prays in Venus's temple that he might have a wife like his "ivory maid." Venus then brings the statue to life—much to Pygmalion's delight:

> The ivory grew soft to his touch and, its hardness vanishing, gave and yielded beneath his fingers....The lover stands amazed....Yes, it was real flesh!....The maiden felt the kisses, blushed and, lifting her timid eyes up to the light, saw the sky and her lover at the same time. The goddess graced with her presence the marriage she had made; and ere the ninth moon had brought her crescent to the full, a daughter was born to them, Paphos. (*Metamorphoses*: 10.247-297; see also Apollodorus, *Library*: 3.14.3)

Ovid has fun with love-smitten Pygmalion's amorous attentions to his statue. One thinks of twentieth-century bachelors and their inflatable dolls—indeed, in the story's prurient Greek original, Pygmalion copulates with the statue (Segal 1989: 85). But as Ovid continues, it becomes clear that Pygmalion is one of his normative characters. Ovid has Pygmalion's story follow that of the Propoetides, the world's first prostitutes: "and as their shame vanished and the blood of their faces hardened, they were turned with but small change into hard stones" (*Metamorphoses*: 10.238-242). The prostitutes, then, were hard of heart and barren of womb. They become stones, while Pygmalion's warm and loving nature makes even the hardness of ivory come to life and good Augustan fruitfulness (see Fraenkel 1945; but see also Segal 1989: 85-90).

Medieval Christians tended to understand Ovid's story differently. For Boccaccio the story is an allegory wherein we see a "bashful virgin" led to "concupiscence" (*Genealogie Deorum*: 2.49). Near the end of de Meun's *Romance of the Rose*, for another example, the Lover approaches an image of his Beloved. The Lover compares the beauty of this image with the image carved by Pygmalion, and so tells the story—in a version that adds considerable detail to the comic business of Pygmalion's lovemaking: Pygmalion said,

"When I want to ease myself, to embrace and kiss, I find my love as rigid as a post and so very cold...."

Then Pygmalion knelt, his face wet with tears, and offered his gage as amends to her. But she cared nothing for the gage....Thus Pygmalion strove, but in his strife, was neither peace nor truce. He could not remain in any one condition. He either loved or hated, laughed or cried; he was either...tormented or calm. He would dress the image in many ways....Then he would undress her and try the effect on her of a dress of silk, sendal, or *melequin*, or of a *moiré* in indigo.

He tries jewelry of every description, and more: "He gave careful attention to dressing her feet. On each foot he put a shoe and a stocking cut off prettily at two fingers' length from the pavement....He brought her fresh flowers." The Lover sings to her, and he plays for her on no less than twenty different instruments, everything from organs to bagpipes. He even dances for her (*Romance of the Rose*: 20895-21214).

Robertson has argued that de Meun's Pygmalion is an *exemplum* of the idolatrous lover, the lover whose reason was completely overcome by his lechery: He cannot see his beloved for what she is, and she becomes more important to him than even things of the spirit. "An 'idol' is thus not always a tangible image of wood or stone," Robertson writes, "it may be an image in the mind. And such mental images are typically those formed on the basis of feminine beauty, the *phantasmata* of Cupid. Thus the inner idols of Wisdom 14 and Isaias 44 may be taken as figures for inner idols constructed in the mind by the desire of the idolater" (1962: 99; see also Tuve 1966: 262-263; Fleming 1969: 85-86; Olsson 1992: 136-137; and Dahlberg's note in his translation: 423; but see also, e.g., Camille 1991: 325-337). Some of the Medieval illuminators of the *Romance of the Rose*, for example, seem to have understood the story in this way (see, e.g., Camille, 1991: 319; Fleming, 1969: fig. 22). The connection between Pygmalion and idolatry was still current in the sixteenth century, when one of the unnamed authors in Tottel's *Miscellany* called Pygmalion's statue "his idol" ("The Tale of Pygmalion"), and when Marston satirized foolish, unrequited lovers:

And fondly doting, oft he kist her lip.
Oft would he dally with her Ivory breasts.

No wanton love-trick would he over-slip,
But still observ'd all amorous beheasts.
     Whereby he thought he might procure the love
     Of his dull Image, which no plaints coulde move.

Looke how some peevish Papists crouch, and kneele
To some dum Idoll with their offering,
As if a senceless carved stone could feele
The ardor of his bootles chattering,
     So fond he was, and earnest in his sute
     To his remorsles Image, dum and mute.
                    ("The Metamorphosis of Pigmalion's Image":13-14)

But whether or no de Meun's Pygmalion is specifically an idolatrous lover, he is certainly an *exemplum* of the maddened, unrequited lover. Petrarch understands the story this way, and so he envies Pygmalion because, once his statue became flesh, once it yielded, Pygmalion "received a thousand times what I yearn to have just once!" (*Rime sparse*: 78.12-14). The *Chess of Love* commentary makes this interpretation explicit:

One could also very well say more generally that a man who has chosen a lady or a girl from among the others, whom he loves with true, perfect love, willingly has her beauty and form figured and portrayed in his imagination so that they cannot properly leave his memory. And according to this, one can properly say that he loves his image.

And because ladies and girls are found strange at first sight, and are not easily conquered by gifts or by prayers, but are commonly found unyielding, it is not marvelous if they are haughty, proud, and full of denial and refusal from the beginning, or perhaps they are ashamed and this is right. Especially young girls are afraid of being dishonored, flee the danger, are very much on guard, and hold themselves closely so that they are colder than ivory or marble.

And thus one can suitably enough say that a man finds a mute image in which he cannot find any pleasure or comfort, any more than if she were of ivory or some other insensate matter.

Finally, it can well happen by the cunning of the lover and his fine words, by his loyalty and perseverance continued secretly and wisely, and because the goddess Venus shows her mastery and strength there, that he will find his beloved compliant, familiar, and all ready to do his will. (662-663)

Most poets and scholars would have agreed with the *Chess* commentary in regarding Pygmalion as a negative *exemplum*. For Berchorius the story becomes an allegory for succumbing to lust:

at last it happens that Venus the goddess of wantonness—that is concupiscence of the flesh—interposes herself and changes this dead image into a living woman. She causes that chaste woman to feel the goads of the flesh and changes her from a good person into a foolish one. (*Ovidius Moralizatus*: 356)

Lydgate (*Reson and Sensuallyte*: 4277-4344) includes Pygmalion in a catalogue of such unnatural lovers as Narcissus (self-love), Pasiphae (bestial love), Myrrha (incestuous love), Phaedra (incest), Tereus (rape), and Menaphron (incest). Tritonio includes Pygmalion in his list of the "libidinous" (*Mythologia*: 28).

There was another, less well known Pygmalion: Dido's evil brother. He killed her husband, Sychaeus, the king of Tyre, and assumed the throne. Dido then fled with some of her people to the north coast of Africa, where she founded Carthage. Dante remembers him as "Pygmalion, whom insatiate lust of gold made traitor, thief, and parricide" (*Purgatorio*: 20.103-105).

Bibliography: Michael Camille, *The Gothic Image: Ideology and Image-Making in Medieval Art* (1991); John V. Fleming, *The Roman de la Rose*: A Study in Allegory and Iconography (1969); Herman Fraenkel, *Ovid: Poet between Two Worlds* (1945); T. D. Hill, "Narcissus, Pygmalion, and the Castration of Saturn: Two Mythographic Themes in the *Roman de la Rose*," *SP*, 71 (1974): 404-426; Kurt Olsson, *John Gower and the Structures of Conversion* (1992); D. W. Robertson, Jr., *Preface to Chaucer* (1962); Charles Segal, *Orpheus: The Myth of the Poet* (1989); Rosemund Tuve, *Allegorical Imagery* (1966).

PYGMIES were said in ancient times to have waged war upon the cranes (or storks). Homer, for example, mentions these wars in the *Iliad* (3.6). There were varying accounts as to the source of this enmity: Sometimes it was said to have been because Oenoe (or Pygmae or Gerana), a Pygmy queen, neglected to worship Juno as she ought; sometimes the Pygmies as a people were thought to have been neglectful in this way. In either case, even in ancient times the Pygmies served as examples of presumption. In Ovid, for example, the story of the Pygmies is one of the stories Minerva weaves into her tapestry in her weaving contest with proud Arachne, "that her rival might know by pictured warnings what reward she may expect for her mad daring....A second corner shows the wretched fate of the Pygmaean queen, whom Juno conquered in a strife, then changed into a crane, and bade her war on those whom once she ruled" (*Metamorphoses*: 6.83-92).

In Berchorius's gloss on this passage, the queen is a figure for the "women who glory in their own beauty" (*Ovidius Moralizatus*: 250). Sandys' interpretation of the queen's vanity is closer to Ovid's intention: "Shee, the male line failing, became the Queene of that nation: adored by her subjects, as if more then mortall, for the excellency of her feature. Wherewith she pleased her selfe so much, that shee began to neglect the service of the Gods, but especially Juno's: who...transformed her into a Crane; and made her war with her owne nation, as a punishment for her arrogancy: and to be a punishment unto those who had given her undue honours" (*Ovid*: 287). Milton probably wants us to remember the Pygmies' presumption when he writes that Satan's throng was "numberless, like that Pigmean Race" (*Paradise Lost*, 1.780).

Another tradition had it that the Pygmies—not having learned their lesson, alas, as to the dangers of vanity and presumption—once went to war against

Hercules. In Cranach's paintings of this mighty conflict, the Pygmies are made to look particularly ridiculous in their vainglory. Cranach seems to have looked to Alciati for his inspiration (van Hasselt-von Ronnen 1970). Whitney (also following Alciati) summarizes the event:

> But foolishe dwarffes? theire force was all to smalle,
> For when he wak'de, like gnattes he crush'd them all.

> This warneth us, that nothinge paste our strengthe
> Wee should attempte: nor anie worke pretende,
> Above our power: lest that with shame at lengthe
> Wee weaklinges proove, and fainte before the ende.
> The pore, that strive with mightie, this doth blame;
> And sottes, that seeke the learned to defame.
>
> (*Emblemes*: 16; see also Shakespeare, *King John*: 5.2.135)

Dinet, on the other hand, understood the Pygmies to be completely given over to "voluptuousness, delights, and concupicences," and so interpreted the story as "virtue" (Hercules) defeating "voluptuousness" (*Hieroglyphiques*: 486-487).

See Dudley and Novak (1972: 263) for a thirteenth-century debate on the existence of Pygmies (decision: affirmative) and the question of their humanity (decision: negative).

Bibliography: C. J. van Hasselt-von Ronnen, "Hercules en de Pygmeën bij Alciati, Dossi, en Cranach," *Simiolus*, 4 (1970): 13-18; Edward Dudley and Maximillian Novak, *The Wild Man Within: An Image in Western Thought from the Renaissance to Romanticism* (1972).

PYRAMUS AND THISBE loved one another—"he, the most beautiful youth, and she the loveliest maid of all the East" (Ovid, *Metamorphoses*: 4.55-56). They lived in Babylon in neighboring houses, but their parents did not consent to their marriage. And the lovers were separated by a wall; they could manage only to whisper back and forth through a hidden chink—that same chink immortalized in Shakespeare's play of Pyramus and Thisbe (*Midsummer Night's Dream*: 5.1.108-354). Eventually, they ran off to meet in the woods, at Ninus's tomb, under a spreading mulberry tree. Thisbe comes first to the appointed place, but she is frightened off by a lioness. The lioness tears "with bloody jaws" (*Metamorphoses*: 4.104) the cloak which Thisbe had let fall in her flight. This bloody cloak Pyramus sees when he reaches the spot. Convinced that his love has been devoured, he kills himself. Then Thisbe returns, only to find her lover's bleeding corpse. She kills herself in turn.

Usually the story was seen as an example of the dangers of immoderate love. Indeed, Alanus seems to have been altogether carried away by his imaginings of just how immoderate the love of Pyramus and Thisbe might have been.

Immoderate lovers are unnatural lovers—and so Alanus makes Pyramus a sodomite! "Not only does Pyramus seek the kisses of Thisbe through a chink, but no small opening of Venus pleases him" (*Complaint of Nature*: mt. 1.56-57). The *Chess of Love* commentary more moderately condemns the lovers' immoderation:

And however one sees it, the end of love is most commonly sad and painful. And the history of Pyramus and Thisbe...shows this to us well....The history, then, recounts that these two loved each other with a supremely strong and immoderate love....

This history enough confirms that in the life of love joy and grief, good and evil are always intermingled, that, however the beginning may be, the end of love is easily painful. (653-655)

According to this same commentator, the mulberry—whose fruit became black, according to Ovid, when the blood of Pyramus soaked into the ground at its roots—itself comes to figure forth the same moral: "The trees also that bear fruit of different kinds that is sometimes white and sweet, and other times black and bitter, signify the joy and sorrow, and the good and evil generally found in the life of love, in which life these two contraries are always intermingled by its own nature" (653; see also Lydgate, *Reson and Sensuallyte*: 3954-4001).

Tritonio is content simply to include Pyramus in his list of the "libidinous" (*Mythologia*: 28); Golding says that Pyramus and Thisbe exemplify "The headie force of frentick love whose end is woe and payne" ("Epistle": 109-110; see also Sabinus, *Fabularum Ovidii interpretatio*: 138-139).

Bibliography: Emerson Brown, Jr., "*Hortus Inconclusus*: The Significance of Priapus and Pyramus and Thisbe in the *Merchant's Tale*," ChauR, 4 (1970): 31-40; Niall Rudd, "Pyramus and Thisbe in Shakespeare and Ovid," in D. West and T. Woodman, *Creative Imitation and Latin Literature* (1979); Franz Schmitt-von Muhlenfals, *Pyramus und Thisbe: Rezeptionstypen eines Ovidischen Stoffes in Literatur, Kunst, und Muzik* (1972).

PYTHON was a great serpent/dragon. According to Ovid (*Metamorphoses*: 1.434-440), Python was engendered of the fertile slime that was left after Deucalion's flood. The assumption was that certain creatures could be spontaneously generated in, for example, the mud of the Nile. Putrefaction was usually seen as an important aspect of such spontaneous generation. (Aristotle provides the classic explanation of spontaneous generation: *Generation of Animals*: 762a) But once generated, Python took up residence in the near neighborhood of Apollo's oracle at Delphi, and so eventually Apollo shot the dragon with his arrows. Since Apollo was the god of the sun and since he was associated with light and wisdom, his killing of Python is usually seen as some version of the victory of good over evil or wisdom over error. Here, for example, is Berchorius: "The serpent signifies the flesh which with the poison of its pleasures presses down and fills the entire world" (*Ovidius Moralizatus*: 136-137). Others associated Python with error, or "false credulity," as Vatican Mythographer III put it (8.1). Spenser must have had Python in mind as a model for his dragonness Error; her vomit teemed with loathly books, papers, frogs, and toads, as though from the Nile's "fertile slime" (*Faerie Queene*: 1.1.13-26; see Nohrnberg 1976: 138). Sandys also associates Python with error (and with the putrefaction usually associated with spontaneous generation): "The word [*python*] signifies putrefaction: and because the Sunne consumes the putrefaction of the Earth, his beams darting from his orbe like arrowes; with his arrows he is said to have killed Python. So serpentine Error by the light of truth is confounded" (*Ovid*: 71).

Remembering the story of the tempter serpent in the Garden of Eden (Gen 3), Christians, of course, associated dragons and serpents with the Devil. And so Python could be seen as a type of the Devil. When Milton's Satan is transformed into a crawling serpent, for example, he is "Now Dragon grown," larger than "Huge Python" (*Paradise Lost*, 10.529-31).

One story had it that Juno entrusted the upbringing of her monstrous son Typhon to Python (see Fontenrose 1959: 70-93 for an account of the ancient connection between Python and Typhon).

Bibliography: Joseph Fontenrose, *Python* (1959); James Nohrnberg, *The Analogy of The Faerie Queene* (1976).

R

THE RIVERS OF THE UNDERWORLD (Acheron, Cocytus, Lethe, Phlegethon, and Styx). The Underworld was, if not a pleasantly, at least a well-watered place. The Cocytus, Lethe, Phlegethon, and Styx all emptied their noisome floods into great, marshy Acheron. On their way to the Underworld, the shades of the dead crossed over these rivers in Charon's boat. Book 6 of Virgil's *Aeneid* provided the description of the Rivers of the Underworld best known to Christians (see also Plato, *Phaedo*: 112e-114a). In his commentary on the *Aeneid*, Landino interprets Aeneas's journey to the Underworld as being undertaken for wisdom (see **EPIC CONVENTIONS: The descent**), and so Aeneas's passage across the rivers is a figure for the contemplation of sin in all its foulness:

From our concupiscence, as from a spring, flows the water which makes up the Stygian swamp. (Indeed, it is from concupiscence that there first comes the thought, and then the action, by which we sin.) Following is Acheron, the swifter river, for by it is expressed the impulse to foul deeds, and this is only aroused after the thought....And it is because the "will" makes its transit into vice under the direction of this kind of "deliberation" on sin that there are customarily placed in the river a "little boat" and its "sailor" [i.e., Charon and his boat]. After this transit (that is, after the sin has been committed) there follows sorrow, which is what the Styx signifies. After that, greater mourning, which is Cocytus. (*Disputationes Camuldenses*: 236-237; Stahel tr.: 230-231; see also Fraunce, *Countesse of Pembrokes Yvychurch*: 27v-28r)

Usually such ideas are at work in allegorical interpretations of the crossing, and of the rivers themselves: *usually* the rivers have something to do with sin or the awareness of sin, or with matter, as opposed to spirit (Panofsky 1962: 204). But the details of the allegory vary considerably from writer to writer—as do the physical descriptions of the rivers.

Acheron

Acheron was sometimes described as a river, sometimes as a marsh. Fulgentius wrote that "This river is, as it were, the seething emotions of youthful acts; it is muddy because youths do not have clear-sighted or mature judgment" (*On the Content of Virgil*: 22). But most commentators associated Acheron with sorrow, in accordance with an etymology that goes back to classical times. Bernardus, for example, interprets Acheron as sorrow (*On Virgil's Aeneid*: 6.proem), and so, to cross Acheron is to go "into the quiet life of the cleansed" (6.313-320). In a related interpretation, the commentary on *The Chess of Love* glosses Acheron as "despair" (475). Berchorius's interpretation has also to do with despair: "Acheron is interpreted 'without salvation' because in that place there is neither salvation nor...hope" (*Ovidius Moralizatus*: 103). Conti provides an extended explanation of the connection between Acheron and sorrow (*Mythologie*: 3.1). Sometimes this sorrow for sin was associated with "conscience" (e.g., Fraunce, *Countesse of Pembrokes Yvychurch*: 28r).

Cocytus

Bernardus wrote that Cocytus "means lamentation," because whoever goes to hell will lament, "either repenting his delights or suffering punishment" (*On Virgil's Aeneid*: 6.132-135). Berchorius: Cocytus "is interpreted 'sorrow' because in that place is sorrow about others' good and the sorrowful incitement of envy" (*Ovidius Moralizatus*: 103; see also Milton, *Paradise Lost*: 2.579).

Lethe

Christian commentators agreed with the mythographers of antiquity that Lethe had to do with forgetfulness. But they suggested new kinds of forgetfulness. Alanus wrote that since the Fall, human beings have been "drunk with the Lethean cup of sensuality" (*Complaint of Nature*: pr. 4.277). Bernardus seems to have had the same allegory in mind: Lethe signifies "the oblivion of the mind forgetful of the majesty of its own divinity" (*On Virgil's Aeneid*: 6.proem). And Berchorius: "There is Lethe which is interpreted 'forgetfulness' because in that place is forgetfulness of God and of all that pertains to salvation" (*Ovidius Moralizatus*: 102).

But Lethe could also signify other kinds of forgetting. At the end of his ascent of the Mount of Purgatory, for example, Dante passes through the river Lethe; it is the water of baptism, and so he loses even the memory of his sins (*Purgatorio*: 33.94-102). It is in this same sense that Donne prays in one of his Holy Sonnets for a "heavenly Lethean flood" to drown his "sinnes blacke memorie" ("If Poysonous Mineralls"). Another tradition had it that lovers could recover their sanity by drinking of Lethean waters. Here is the *Chess of Love* commentary:

those who pay attention to good deeds and forget the bad are happy. And therefore Ovid says in his *Remedy of Love* [551-554] that it was the custom a long time ago to have a temple at Rome, or near it, to which young lovers and maidens went to pray and make their offering to Letheus, the god who caused mad love to be forgotten, to implore that forgetfulness when they were too maddened by love and wanted to get out of it. (465)

Burton mentions this same tradition (*Anatomy of Melancholy*: 3.2.5.4).

Phlegethon

For some writers the Phlegethon was a river of water (e.g., Ovid, *Metamorphoses*: 5.544); but as its etymology suggests (*Gk. phlegein*, "to burn"), it was often described as a river of fire (e.g., Virgil, *Aeneid*: 6.550-551; Statius, *Thebaid*: 4.523; Servius, *In Virgilii Aeneidos*: 6.265; Spenser, *Faerie Queene*: 1.5.33). Thus Phlegethon was often associated in particular with the fiery passions. Bernardus writes that Phlegethon is "the fires of the angry" (*On Virgil's Aeneid*: 6.proem). Dante saw the fires of the Phlegethon in that circle of the Inferno where suffer the violent against God, nature, and art (14.133-134). Landino too associates Phlegethon with wrath (*Disputationes Camuldenses*: 248). Boccaccio associates this river with sin's "excitement to fury" (*Genealogie Deorum*: 3.16). Thus it is that Spenser's furious Pyrochles complains that he is consumed: The ghost of the damned "In flaming Phelegeton does not so felly rost" (*Faerie Queene*: 2.6.50; Nohrnberg 1976: 303). Milton refers to "fierce Phlegeton" (*Paradise Lost*, 2.580). Sandys' comment is in the same tradition:

Consonant to the truth was that opinion of the Poets, how virtue and vice in another world had their rewards and punishments....From whence sprung their fictions of the infernall rivers, and abysse of Tartarus. Acheron...corresponding with the ayre and Meridian, purging by sorrow and anxiety: Phlegeton with fire and the Orient, punishing wrath and concupiscence, by a more violent fervor: Styx and Cocytus with the Earth and Occident afflicting hatred by teares and lamentations. (*Ovid*: 211)

Occasionally we find the Phlegethon associated with some other fiery passion. The *Chess of Love* commentary says that "this river signifies ambition to us" (469); and Berchorius suggests that Phlegethon is appropriate for the punishment of "ardent desire" (*Ovidius Moralizatus*: 106).

Styx

Bernardus interprets the Styx as "hatred" (*On Virgil's Aeneid*: 6.proem). The *Chess of Love* commentary had it that the Styx "signifies sorrow and displeasure," which arise from sin (482). For Berchorius the Styx is "punishment and eternal sadness," because Styx is "a swamp of hell and is interpreted 'sadness'" (*Ovidius Moralizatus*: 93).

There was a separate tradition having to do with swearing by Styx. Hesiod wrote that if any god should swear by the waters of the Styx and be forsworn, "For nine years he is cut off from the eternal gods" (*Theogony*: 798). Statius refers to this tradition (*Thebaid*: 8.21-45); de Meun has Cupid (*Romance of the Rose*: 10838) and Jupiter (13133) both swear by Styx; Spenser has Diana swear by Styx

(*Faerie Queene*: 3.6.24); and Peele has Minerva, Juno, and Venus all swear by Styx (*Arraignment of Paris*: 1195-1225).

   Bibliography: James Nohrnberg, *The Analogy of The Faerie Queene* (1976); Erwin Panofsky, *Studies in Iconology* (1962).

S

SATURN (Cronus). According to the genealogy best known to the Middle Ages and the Renaissance, Saturn's father was Uranus (Sky), his mother, Gaia (Earth). Saturn married his sister Rhea and begot Hestia, Jupiter, Ceres, Juno, Pluto, and Neptune (see, e.g., Hesiod: *Theogony*: 453-456). Saturn's mother prophesied that one of his children would depose him, and so he devoured all his children, except Jupiter, whom Rhea contrived to save. Eventually, Jupiter was able to force his father to disgorge his children; with their aid, Jupiter overthrew Saturn. Saturn then went in exile to Italy, where he introduced the art of agriculture and where he ruled over the Golden Age, the first of the Four Ages, "that first age, which with no one to compel, without a law, of its own will, kept faith and did the right...; men knew no shores except their own....Then spring was everlasting" (Ovid, *Metamorphoses*: 1.89-107). Old as he was, he was often depicted as lame, leaning on a crutch.

All of this proved fertile ground for the allegorizers. The *Chess of Love* commentary provides a good overview of much of the typical Saturn allegory:

We must know that Saturn is sometimes taken for...the first planet; sometimes he is taken for time, and also sometimes for the power of prudence; and according to different fables he is differently explained.

Briefly one can easily understand and explain the above-mentioned things literally by saying that Saturn is the highest of all the planets and the first below the firmament, and that some of the ancients therefore called him the first god and the father of the other gods....[T]he scythe is properly given to him. This is...because the scythe...cuts down and cancels the trees and grass to which it can attain, and everything else, too, that it encounters, suddenly and without distinction.

In the same way death destroys and annihilates whatever it can attain. (99-103)

The identification of Saturn with time, and time's devastations, probably goes back to a pre-Hellenic age, when Cronus, father of the gods, came to be associated with *chronus*, "time" (Shipley 1984: 264; see Panofsky 1962: 62-93 for Cronus, Saturn, and the figure of Time). Cicero, for example, wrote as follows:

Men have believed it to be Saturn who rules the cyclic courses of the times and seasons. In Greek the nature of this god is expressed in his name. He is called Kronos, which is the same as Chronos, and means a lapse of time, just as our Roman name "Saturn" means "sated with years". In mythology he is said to have devoured his own children, just as age eats up the passing years and is fed but never satiated as the years go by. (*Nature of the Gods*: 2.64; see also, among many others, Rabanus, *De Universo*: 428)

Heraclitus wrote that it was appropriate that Saturn/Cronus should be both Time and the father of all things—that is, the father of the four elements: Jupiter, Juno, Neptune, and Pluto, "for it is absolutely impossible that things should come into being without the [existence of] time" (*Allégories d'Homère*: 41.6-9).

   The iconography of Cronus—who castrated his father Uranus with a pruning hook—was readily adapted to the Roman scythe-bearing god Saturn, a god of the harvest (see **URANUS** for the associated nature allegory). But there came to be some confusion as to just who castrated whom. Early Greek tradition had it that it was Cronus who castrated his father, Uranus; and this tradition did survive into the Christian era (e.g., Macrobius, *Saturnalia*: 1.8.6-8; Isidore, *Etymologiarum*: 8.11.77; Fraunce [quoted below]; van Mander, *Wtbeeldinghen der Figuren*: 112r). But at least as early as Plotinus (*Enneads*: 3.5.2), we also find Saturn/Cronos being castrated by *his* son Jupiter (Wind 1968: 135). Indeed, this was the most common understanding from Plotinus to the mid-seventeenth century (see, e.g., Guillaume de Conches, *On Macrobius*: 6, 7c; Bartholomaeus, *On the Properties of Things*: 8.12; the *Chess of Love* commentary: 107; Ross, *Mystagogus Poeticus*: 75).

   Fulgentius wrote that Saturn carries a scythe for good reason: "either because every season turns back on itself like the curved blades of scythes or on account of the crops" (*Mythologies*: 1.2). Van Mander explained Saturn's relation to time and the heavens in this way: "By Saturn is understood the time which was established by the heavens [i.e., the sun, stars, etc.], because before the heavens were, there was no time, as Plato has explained in his *Timaeus*" (*Wtlegginghe op den Metamorphosis*: 3v). And here is Ross:

Saturn is nothing else but Time, which is the son of Coelum and Thetis, because Time is measured by the motion of the Heavens and likewise by the motion, or ebbing and flowing of the Sea....Saturn was painted like an old man bare-headed, in a ragged garment, holding a hook and a key in his hand, devouring of his Children; by which they did understand the antiquity & long continuation of Time....The ragged Garment shews that Time wears and consumes all things: which was also meant by his devouring of his children, and by the hook or sickle which he hath in his hand. (*Mystagogus Poeticus*: 378-379; see also Macrobius, *Saturnalia*: 1.8.10; Isidore, *Etymologiarum*: 8.11.31; Bernard of Utrecht, *Kommentar über Theoduli "Ecloga"*: 19; Boccaccio, *Fates of Famous Men*: 6; Pictorius, *Apotheoseos*: 79; Fraunce, *Countesse of Pembrokes Yvychurch*: 45r)

Bronzino's *Allegory of Venus, Cupid, Folly, and Time* (fig. 23) assumes just this sense of Saturn-as-Time. All the delights of love, as figured forth by Venus and Cupid in the foreground, are called into question by the darker figures that surround them, especially old Saturn as all-destroying Time. Love—earthly love, merely physical love—is ephemeral. Bruegel makes this point in his allegorical engraving of *Lechery* (fig. 20) by placing two lovers in a bubble, there in the aphrodisiac clam shell at the top of the blasted tree. In Bruegel's *Triumph of Time* (fig. 24) we see Time tricked out as Saturn at the center of the engraving: He has the tattered clothing associated with Saturn, and we see him devouring a child. All of the artifacts of human endeavor are being trampled by Time's chariot—and we see that all is devastation where Time has passed. There can be naive enjoyment of earthly pleasures only where Time has not yet passed: See the lovers hand in hand and the dancing around the Maypole on the right hand side of the engraving, where Time's chariot is headed. What remains, blowing her signature trump, is Fame—or History, as van Mander might put it, since "the writing of history was begun in the time of Saturn" (*Wtbeeldinghen der Figuren*: 112r; for more on the engraving, see **FAME**).

After discussing Saturn's meaning in relation to time, the *Chess of Love* commentary goes on to relate Saturn's planetary influence to the humors:

> Then we must consider that Saturn is naturally cold and dry in power and so has a special influence on the earth, which is also cold and dry by nature. ....He also has regard to melancholy which is, among human beings, also cold and dry. And because of this he signifies all sorts of maladies engendered by melancholy and by such cold, gross, and viscous humours.
>
> And generally he signifies death, especially sudden and strange death....He also signifies the season of autumn, which is naturally deathlike and sickly. And he signifies old age by semblance. And finally all things excessively cold agree with him. (100-101; see also John of Salisbury, *Policraticus*: 2.19)

A drawing of *Saturn* by the Master of the Amsterdam Cabinet (for the image and despcription, see Filedt Kok 1985: 221-222) illustrates these ideas. The Master depicts Saturn as a thin old man, riding a horse across the sky. The malign influence of the planet Saturn was thought to explain the inequalities and misfortunes that are suffered in this world (e.g., Batman, *Batman uppon Bartholomae*: 8.23). The poem that accompanies the drawing describes Saturn's children as "pale, hard, cold, sad and old" (in Filedt Kok 1985: 221). In the drawing we see some of these unfortunates: a cripple, prisoners, men executed on gallows and wheel, and a knacker busily disemboweling a worn-out horse. The knacker's pants have sagged a bit, and the smell wafting forth has attracted a pig, Saturn's animal. Even this association of Saturn with evil smells was traditional. In Batman, for example, we find that Saturn "loveth stinking beasts and uncleane" (*Batman uppon Bartholomae*: 8.23). Since Saturn's element is the earth, the Master includes a farmer among his children.

Chaucer is one of many others, then, who associated Saturn with misfortune and tragedy. In "The Knight's Tale" (2684-2685), for example, it is Saturn who calls up the fury to make Arcite's horse throw and mortally wound him; in *The Legend of Good Women* (2596-2599) Ypermestra dies in prison under Saturn's influence. Gower, too, wrote of Saturn's malevolent influence:

> Saturnus, whos complexion
> Is cold, and his condicion
> Causeth malice and crualte
> To him the whos nativite
> Is set under his governance.
> For alle hise werkes ben grevance
> And enemy to mannes hele.
>
> (*Confessio Amantis*: 7.937-943)

The identification of Saturn with melancholy was wide spread; indeed, we still speak of "Saturnine" personalities. Bartholomaeus (*On the Properties of Things*: 8.12) writes about this, and Batman's translation of Bartholomaeus helped in the spread of such ideas (*Batman uppon Bartholome*: 8.23; see also Shakespeare, *Much Ado about Nothing*: 1.3.11; *Two Noble Kinsmen*: 5.4.62). Burton cites Ptolemy as one of his authorities for the following account: "if Saturn be predominant in his nativity, and cause melancholy in his temperature, then he shall be very austere, sullen, churlish, black of colour, profound in his cogitations, full of cares, miseries, and discontents, sad and fearful, always silent, solitary" (*Anatomy of Melancholy*: 1.3.1.3). Aristotle had contended that Melancholy was the temperament essentially associated with artistic genius (*Problemata*: 7.953a). The Middle Ages never entirely forgot Aristotle's notion, but in this period melancholy was generally regarded as a merely physical disorder. Then, late in the fifteenth century, Ficino's *De vita triplica* returned to Aristotle, arguing that the melancholy of those born under Saturn was nothing less than a divine gift, essential to human greatness: "Not only those who take refuge in Jupiter, but also those who wholeheartedly and sincerely concentrate on that divine contemplation which is signified by Saturn, will escape the latter's pernicious influences and only enjoy his benefits....To the spirits that dwell in the spheres of the sublime Saturn himself is a benevolent father" (in Panofsky 1955a: 167; see also Ficino, *Philebus Commentary*: 242).

Pico made Saturn and Jupiter figures for the contemplative and the active lives: "Saturn signifies the intellectual nature, which alone is capable of understanding and contemplation. Jupiter signifies the active life which consists of ruling, administering, and moving" (*On a Poem of Platonic Love*: 8; see also *Conclusiones*: 49.9). And so during the Renaissance, Saturn replaced Mercury as the patron-god of the arts. "The most illustrious members of the Florentine circle—among them, besides Ficino, Pico della Mirandola and Lorenzo the Magnificent—referred to themselves, only half playfully, as 'Saturnians,' and they discovered to their immense satisfaction that Plato, too, had been born under the sign of Saturn" (Panofsky 1955a: 167; see also Wittkower 1963: 102-104). Spenser's Phantastes, for example, was a personification of the imagination, and so Spenser made him a Saturnian melancholic. Phantastes was

> A man of yeares yet fresh, as mote appere,
> Of swarth complexion, and of crabbed hew,
> That him full of melancholy did shew;
> Bent hollowbeetle browes, sharp staring eyes,
> That mad or foolish seemd: one by his vew
> Mote deeme him borne with ill disposed skyes,
> When oblique Saturne sate in the house of agonyes.
> *(Faerie Queene*: 2.9.52)

Saturn was often associated with prudence (McCall 1979: 172-173), as we have seen in the passage quoted above from the *Chess of Love* commentary. He was also a wisdom figure. Neckam, for example, explains the connection in this way: The planet Saturn's orbit around the sun—three years—was longer than that of the other planets; this suggested age, and so wisdom (*De Naturis Rerum*: 1.7). When Dante and Beatrice rise from the sphere of Jupiter to the sphere of Saturn, they leave behind all material concerns and enter into the realm of contemplation (*Paradiso*: 21). Ficino also associates Saturn with contemplation (e.g., *In Phaedrum*: 100)—and with such Neo-Platonic conceptions as "the Angelic Mind" (*On Plato's Symposium*: 5.12), with "universal reason" (*In Phaedrum*: 102), and even with "the reason or word of God the father" (*Philebus Commentary*: 134). Ficino regarded Saturn as the special guide of those seeking good, Neo-Platonic wisdom: "For Saturn himself is (to speak Platonically) in place of Jupiter to the spirits inhabiting the sublime sphere, just as Jupiter is the helping father to people leading ordinary lives" (*Three Books on Life*: 3.22.37-38). Saturn was thus sometimes included with Apollo and Diana, all of them known for their restraint of the passions, sometimes in opposition to Venus and Bacchus and various other gods. They stood for the forces of control and temperance in opposition to license and the passions. This is the meaning of a Neo-Platonic engraving after Baccio Bandinelli, *The Fray of Cupid and Apollo* (fig. 1; see **APOLLO**).

Saturn devouring his children was sometimes understood as a figure for the devastations of time, as we have seen in Ross, above, and in the Bruegel engraving of *The Triumph of Time* (fig. 24). But there were also more complex interpretations, which linked the devouring of the child with Jupiter's castration of Saturn. Fraunce, for example, wrote that Saturn, "that is, Tyme, with his sithe...cut off his fathers manlike parts: of which, cast into the sea, Venus was borne. So Saturne destroyeth, Venus bringeth foorth; and both are necessary for the continuall propagation of these inferior bodies, sith the corruption of one, is the generation of another" (*Countesse of Pembrokes Yvychurch*: 45r).

This nature allegory was an outgrowth of Saturn's labors of old as a god of agriculture. Some of the children of Saturn in the Master of the Amsterdam

Cabinet's drawing of Saturn described above, for example, are engaged in farming. The *Chess of Love* commentary explains the matter in this way:

For he moves, maintains, and governs the earth according to the astronomers. He even disposes and prepares the sowings of the earth for good fructifying. And some say that this is because he comforts the sown seeds by coldness, which concentrates their natural heat in them. And by this they are preserved from putrefaction and unnatural corruption until the sun later returns to put them in order and perfect them by his warmth. (100)

For Saturn as the father of the four elements, see **URANUS**; for Saturn's rule during the Golden Age, see **THE FOUR AGES**.

Bibliography: Raymond Klibansky, Erwin Panofsky, and Fritz Saxl, *Saturn and Melancholy* (1964); J. P. Filedt Kok, *Livelier Than Life: The Master of the Amsterdam Cabinet, ca. 1470-1500* (1985); Richard Kay, *Dante's Christian Astrology* (1994): 218-242; John P. McCall, *Chaucer among the Gods: The Poetics of Classical Myth* (1979); Erwin Panofsky, *The Life and Art of Albrecht Dürer* (1955a); Rudolf and Margot Wittkower, *Born under Saturn: The Character and Conduct of Artists* (1963).

THE SATYRS were usually depicted as human from the waist up and like either a goat or a horse from the waist down. They were spirits of the wild, uncivilized life in the woods. With their impressive penises perpetually erect, they spent their days carousing and making music in the company of Bacchus and lying in wait for woodland nymphs. As Fulgentius wrote of them, "the Satyrs are depicted with goats' horns, because they can never satisfy their lust" (*Mythologies*: 3.1; van Mander, *Wtbeeldinghen der Figuren*: 115r)—goats being known for their insatiable sexual appetites (for more on goats and lechery, see **PAN**). Berchorius says that the lustful are "bestial as satyrs. Such a one was Mohammed who seemed to assert that he is a satyr because in his Alkoran he asserted that in that task he had power. A satyr is an animal of human form which is untiringly licentious" (*Ovidius Moralizatus*: 252). Ribera's *Drunken Silenus* (fig. 25; see **SILENUS AND THE SILENI**) is a nice indication of the unfortunate company Satyrs were thought to keep.

During the Renaissance, the Satyrs could also stand for the physical, as distinct from the spiritual, aspect of human beings. This would seem to explain Spenser's Satyrane, for example, whose father was a Satyr, his mother human. Satyrane, then, is part human, part animal—like all of humankind. He was raised by his father: "He noursled up in life and manners wilde, / Emongst wild beasts and woods, from lawes of men exilde." But when Una—who represents the Church—sojourns among the Satyrs, they would as soon worship her ass as herself, for they are creatures solely of Nature, and so by definition cannot understand things of the spirit. Satyrane, on the other hand, since he possesses human reason, *is* able to learn Una's "discipline of faith and veritie" (*Faerie Queene*: 1.6.23-31;

see Nohrnberg 1976: 218-224). In something like the same way, Veronese's painting of *Mars and Venus* (fig. 18) includes a Satyr in the ruined arch. According to Neo-Platonist assumptions, Veronese's Satyr would suggest not that the scene below is "licentious," but rather that, quite simply, the animal passions are at work in Mars and Venus; they are feeling the natural promptings to love (see, e.g., Wind 1968: 272-275).

By extension, as Golding wrote, the Satyrs could represent "The playne and simple country folke that every where abyde" ("Preface": 76; see also Sandys, *Ovid*: 199).

Burton lumps Satyrs together with the other woodland sprites: "Terrestrial devils are those lares, genii, fauns, satyrs, wood-nymphs....Some think it was they alone that kept the heathen people in awe of old, and had so many idols and temples erected to them....Some put our faeries into this rank" (*Anatomy of Melancholy*: 1.2.1.2).

Fauns were usually thought of as being close in meaning to the Satyrs (see, e.g., Lotspeich 1932: 59).

Renaissance writers associated Satyrs with satire, because they (wrongly) assumed that *satire* was etymologically connected to *Satyr* (see Donker and Muldrow 1982: 181-186).

Bibliography: Thomas H. Carpenter and Christopher A. Faraone, *Masks of Dionysus* (1993): 45-49, 207-220; Marjorie Donker and George Muldrow, *Dictionary of Literary-Rhetorical Conventions of the English Renaissance* (1982); Paul Grootkerk, "Satyr," in Malcolm South, *Mythical Creatures and Fabulous Beasts: A Source Book and Research Guide* (1987); A. C. Hamilton, *The Spenser Encyclopedia* (1990): under *Faunus, Styrane, Satyrs*; Henry Lotspeich, *Classical Mythology in the Poetry of Edmund Spenser* (1932); James Nohrnberg, *The Analogy of The Faerie Queene* (1976); Edgar Wind, *Pagan Mysteries of the Renaissance* (1968).

SCYLLA AND CHARYBDIS were monsters lying in wait for sailors, one on either side of the Strait of Messina. Homer (*Odyssey*: 11.107-108) and Ovid (*Metamorphoses*: 7.62-65) describe the peril: Sailors who try to avoid the one fall prey to the other. Fulgentius allegorized Scylla as follows:

They say that Scylla was a most beautiful maiden loved by Glaucus....Circe...thought much of him and, growing jealous of Scylla, put magic herbs in the pool in which she was accustomed to bathe. When she immersed herself in it her loins were filled with wolves and wild sea dogs. For Scylla in Greek is said to be...violence. And what is violence but lust? Glaucus loves this lust, for Glaucus is the Greek for one-eyed, whereby we call blindness glaucoma. For anyone who loves debauchery is blind....And Scylla is explained as the symbol of a harlot...; she is truly filled with wolves and dogs, because she cannot satisfy her private parts with inroads of any other kind....Ulysses also sailed harmlessly past her, for wisdom scorns lust. (*Mythologies*: 2.9)

In general, later commentators followed Fulgentius. Vatican Mythographer III wrote that "Ulysses' safe passage past Scylla shows that lust cannot conquer wisdom" (11.8). De Meun associated "treacherous Charybdis, repellant but attractive," with the perils of love (*Romance of the Rose*: 4293-4304); Landino wrote that the two women represent "great desires" (*Disputationes Camuldenses*: 151); Erasmus associated Charybdis with "greed" (*On Disclaiming the World*: 137); Golding associated Scylla with lust ("Epistle": 169); and here is Sandys:

Scylla represents a Virgin; who as long as chast in thought, and in body unspotted, appeares of an excellent beauty....But once polluted with the sorceries of Circe; that is, having rendred her maiden honour to bee deflowred by bewitching pleasure, she is transformed into a horrid monster. And not so only, but endeavours to shipwracke others...upon those ruining rocks, and make them share in the same calamities. That the upper part of her body, is feigned to retaine a humane figure, and the lower to be bestiall; intimates how man, a divine creature, endued with wisdome and intelligence, in whose superior parts...that immortal spirit resideth...can never so degenerate into a beast, as when he giveth himselfe over to the lowe delights of those baser parts of the body, Dogs and Wolves, the blind & salvage fury of concupiscence....The dangerous sailing betweene Scylla and Charybdis, commends the safetie of the middle course, and deterres from other extremitie. (*Ovid*: 645-646)

It is no wonder, then, that Milton's allegorical figure Sin—born from the head of Satan as an upside-down version of Minerva (Wisdom) born from the head of Jupiter—is described in such a way as to recall Scylla: Sin is a "Snaky Sorceress" who once shone "heav'nly fair" until, made pregnant by her father Satan, her "nether shape thus grew / Transformed" (*Paradise Lost*: 2.724-785; Harding 1946: 96).

Sandys' suggestion that sailing between Scylla and Charybdis "commends the safetie of the middle course" had long been a commonplace. We find this allegory, for example, in de Mézières' advice to King Richard II during the Hundred Years' War:

Most worthy and devout King, it lies in the power of the free-will of both you and your brother of France to choose....[In] a certain region of the sea there are two rocks, two whirlpools, two great hazards, and it is prudent that ships which chance to find themselves in the midst of these perils should steer between the two rocks, for if they depart ever so slightly from a middle course, they will be lost. These two dangers are called...the one Scylla and the other Charybdis. (*Letter to King Richard II*: 60-61; see also, e.g., van Mander, *Wtlegginghe op den Metamorphosis*: 96v)

Such interpretations gave expression to the ideal of the Aristotelian (and Horatian) mean. See, for example, Conti (*Mythologie*: 8.12) and Bacon, for whom Ulysses' passage between Scylla and Charybdis is like the story of Icarus, an example of the "the Middle-way" (*Wisedome of the Ancients*: 27).

For Ulysses' temptation by Scylla and Charybdis, see **ULYSSES**; for Glaucus's love of Scylla, see **GLAUCUS**.

Bibliography: Davis Harding, *Milton and the Renaissance Ovid* (1946); James Nohrnberg, *The Analogy of The Faerie Queene* (1976): 291.

SEMELE was the daughter of Cadmus, king of Thebes, and Harmonia. According to Ovid's account, Semele was one of Jupiter's mortal lovers. But jealous Juno appeared to her disguised as Semele's nurse Beroe and advised her to win from her lover the promise of a boon; she should ask to see Jupiter in all his divine splendor. (For the tradition of bad advice from worldly, old nurses, see **MYRRHA**.) Semele naively followed this advice—only to be consumed by flames when Jupiter appeared in flashes of lightning. She was some months pregnant at this time with Jupiter's son, Bacchus. According to Ovid, "The babe still not wholly fashioned is snatched from the mother's womb and (if report may be believed) sewed up in his father's thigh, there to await its full time of birth" (*Metamorphoses*: 3.310-312).

This story was sometimes understood as an allegorical account of the production of wine. Here is Reynolds:

Or what can Jupiters blasting of his beloved Semele, after his having defloured her, and the wrapping of his sonne he got on her (Bacchus or wine) in his thigh after his production, meane other than the necessity of the Ayres heate to his birth in the generation, and (after a violent pressure and dilaceracion of his mother the Grape) the like close imprisoning of him also, in a fit vessell, till he gaine his full maturity and come to be fit aliment? (*Mythomystes*: 170)

Sandys understood Semele "Theologically," as a figure for presumptuous curiosity, an example of "how those who search too curiously and boldly into the divine Majesty, shall be oppressed with the glory and brightnesse of the same" (*Ovid*: 153). Semele was also interpreted as an *exemplum* of lust, for which see **BACCHAE**.

For Dante, Semele's transformative experience of divine Jupiter is a type of his own transformative experience of the incarnate Christ (*Paradiso*: 21.4-12; 23.28-33; see Brownlee 1993: 117).

Bibliography: Kevin Brownlee, "Dante and the Classical Poets," in Rachel Jacoff, *The Cambridge Companion to Dante* (1993): 100-119.

SEMIRAMIS. The Semiramis of legend was a warrior queen of Assyria and the founder/builder of Babylon (e.g., Ovid, *Metamorphoses*: 4.58). (The figure behind this legend was probably Sammuramat, wife of the Assyrian king Shamshi-Adad V; she ruled as regent from 810 B.C. to 805 B.C.) But despite these accomplishments, she had an unsavory reputation (Parr 1970; Samuel 1944). Diodorus accuses her of cunningly usurping her husband Ninus's throne (*Bibliotheca Historia*: 2.20); Orosius—a combative Christian historian from the fifth century, who was widely read throughout the Middle Ages—added other sins as well. According to Orosius, Babylon was at this time the world's *only* warlike nation. Soon after she assumed her husband's bloody throne, Semiramis "added Ethiopia to her empire by war and drenched it with blood....Such action at that time, namely, to persecute and slaughter peoples living in peace, was even more cruel and serious than it is today, because at that time there were neither the incentives for war abroad, nor such great temptation to exercise cupidity at home." Unnatural woman that she was, she also began dressing like a man (see **AMAZONS**; for other women who dress like men, see **HERCULES: Hercules in Love with Omphale**). Orosius continues:

This woman, burning with lust and thirsting for blood, in the midst of unceasing adulteries and homicides, after she had slaughtered all whom summoned by royal command she had delighted by holding in her adulterous embrace, finally, after shamelessly conceiving a son and impiously abandoning him, and after later having incestuous relations with him, covered up her private disgrace by a public crime. For she decreed that between parents and children no reverence for nature in the conjugal act was to be observed and that each should be free to do as he pleased. (*History*: 1.4)

Orosius, who knew the Old Testament of course, could readily understand such enormities—for if Semiramis built Babylon, it was she who was responsible for the monstrous presumption of the Tower of Babel: "And they said, Go to, let us build us a city and a tower, whose top may reach unto heaven" (Gen 11:4). Here is Fulgentius's paraphrase of Orosius:

at that time there sprang up through infamous design the walls of Babylon, which Semiramis is said to have erected in swollen ferment of vainglory....she was the executioner of her own lovers and the mistress of those doomed to death; then came the height of her lust: as she flamed with desire for her own son...and she became his bride....Just as the vastness of the tower was raised up to the skies, so the period of man's youth is inflated by ambition....Semiramis was inflamed with the ardor of consuming lust, and so is youth fired to immoderate excesses by the flame of desire. (*Ages of the World and Man*: 3)

Dante derived his sense of Semiramis's sins from this tradition: "She was so given to lechery that she made lust licit in her law, to take away the blame she had incurred. She is Semiramis" (*Inferno*: 5.55-58). When Chaucer's Man of Law calls the Sultan's wicked mother "Virago, thou Semyrame the secounde" ("Man of Law's Tale": 359), he is condemning her unseemly mannishness as well as her more general wickedness. There was even a tradition that had her lusting for the sexual attentions of a certain horse; Rabelais has this tradition in mind when he links Semiramis with bull-loving Pasiphae at the bestial end of the scale of lust (*Gargantua and Pantagruel*: 3.34). Shakespeare's remarkably cruel and unnatural Tamora, Queen of the Goths, is compared to Semiramis (*Titus Andronicus*: 2.3.118-119).

But not all authorities were so harsh. Boccaccio, for example, is willing to admire her for her military prowess, although he, too, laments that she was "constantly burning with carnal desire" (*Concerning Famous Women*: 2; see also

Fiammetta: 20-21). Christine de Pizan recognizes Semiramis for her remarkable feats: "greater courage and more marvelous and memorable deeds have never been recorded about any man" (*City of Ladies*: 1.15.1). Christine remembers her incest, but assures us that Semiramis was no less honorable for this, since there were as yet no laws against incest! Some other, later commentators also treat her favorably: Sandys, for example, mentions her glorious conquests, but makes no reference to depravity of any kind (*Ovid*: 201).

Another, narrower tradition made Semiramis a type of the Virgin Mary! This was because Semiramis was supposed for a time to have been shut up in a tower, and so she was a type of Mary in the temple. See the Netherlandish woodblock *Speculum Humanae Salvationis* (15; see also Wilson and Wilson 1984: 151).

Bibliography: Johnstone Parr, "Chaucer's Semiramis," *ChauR*, 5 (1970): 57-61; Irene Samuel, "The Legend of Semiramis through the Middle Ages," *MH*, 2 (1944): 32-44; Adrian Wilson and Joyce Wilson, *A Medieval Mirror: Speculum Humanae Salvationis* 1324-1500 (1984).

SENECA. From the Middle Ages to the Renaissance, Seneca was often regarded as a Christian. It seems that a correspondence between Seneca and St. Paul was regarded as genuine during the Middle Ages—and it circulated in more than 300 manuscripts. Jerome, for example, provided this testimonial:

> Lucius Annaeus Seneca of Cordova...was most continent of life. I would not place him in the catalogue of saints if I were not encouraged by letters read by many between Paul and Seneca and Seneca and Paul. Although he was Nero's teacher and most powerful in his time, he says in them he would like to be regarded by his fellow citizens as Paul was by the Christians. He was put to death by Nero two years before Peter and Paul won martyrs' crowns. (*Liber de viris illustribus*: 662; in Allen 1970: 47)

Augustine, Abelard, Peter of Cluny, and Petrarch are among those who regarded Seneca as a Christian. Erasmus attacked the authenticity of the letters in his 1529 edition of Seneca, but the belief in Seneca's Christianity lingered on in some quarters until the mid-seventeenth century (Allen 1970: 47-51).

Bibliography: Don C. Allen, *Mysteriously Meant* (1970).

SIBYLS were priestesses, almost always of Apollo, who pronounced oracles. The most famous of the Greek Sibyls was she of Erythrae, in Lydia. She was said to have lived for the lifetime of nine men. Sometimes this Sibyl was said to be the same as the most famous of the Italian Sibyls, the Sibyl of Cumae. The Sibyl of Cumae lived in, and pronounced her oracles from, a cave. Apollo, seeking to seduce her, had offered her whatever she wished; she wished for long life—but forgot to ask for eternal youth. And so she lived out her long years, ever more shrunken. Her oracle's voice, however, remained powerful (see Ovid, *Metamorphoses*: 14.101-153). This was the Sibyl whom Virgil's Aeneas consulted at the beginning of book 6 of the *Aeneid*: "good Aeneas seeks the heights, where Apollo sits enthroned, and a vast cavern hard by, hidden haunt of the dread Sibyl, into whom the Delian seer breathes a mighty mind and soul, revealing the future" (6.9-11). It is this Sibyl who guides Aeneas on his descent to the Underworld. According to Bernardus, "The Sibyl is indeed...'divine counsel,' which we take to be understanding, which is called counsel: by it man consults with himself. It is called divine because understanding is nothing else than the comprehension of divine matters" (*On Virgil's Aeneid*: 6.9-13; see also Landino, *Disputationes Camuldenses*: 205).

Often the Sibyls were thought of as pagan equivalents of the Old Testament prophets. Augustine writes confidently that "This sibyl of Erythrae certainly wrote some things concerning Christ which are quite manifest," and he goes on to quote at length from "a Greek manuscript" of the sibyl's prophecy (*City of God*: 18:23; see also Rabanus, *De Universo*: 420-421; see Dronke 1990 and 1974: 62-65 for the literary/philosophical reasoning that underlay the idea that the pagans could utter truths beyond their own knowing). Voragine's *Golden Legend* (Dec. 25) assures us that—on the very day that the star appeared to the three Magi—the Tibertine Sibyl prophesied to the Emperor Augustus of the birth of Jesus. *The Mirour of Mans Salvacioun* puts Voragine into verse: "And Crist shewed nought his birth unto the Jewes onely, / Bot to the payens also, of his aboundant mercy." And so, when the mighty Emperor Augustus sought the Sibyl to ask if any one would ever be greater than he,

> A sercle of gold at Rome aboute the sonnebeme sawe she
> Thilk day that Crist was borne in the land of Judee;
> Als in that cercle sho se the fairest mayden sitting,
> A faire sonover alle other in hire swete armys halsing.
> To the emperoure Octavian thilk Sibille shewed that thing,
> And saide over his estate that day was borne a king.
> (1085-1098)

Thus it was that Roger van der Weyden's *Bladelin Altarpiece* (c. 1460) juxtaposes the two annunciations—the annunciation to the Sibyl in the West and that to the Magi in the East—in panels on either side of a nativity scene (see, e.g., Blum 1969: 19). And thus it was that in the fifteenth century ten Sibyls were depicted in the pavements of the Siena cathedral.

We also see Sibyls, this time in matched portraits with the prophets, on the exterior panels of Jan and Hubert van Eyck's *Ghent Altarpiece*, which was complete in 1472. On the left are Zachariah and the Erythrean Sibyl, on the right Micah and the Cumean Sibyl. On the scrolls we read their prophecies of the glory of the Virgin Mary and the Incarnation of Christ (Panofsky 1966: 207-208; for more on the Sibyls as pagan prophets of Christ, see de Lubac 1964: 247-249). The Sibyls entered into the Medieval cycle plays for the same reason. In *The Procession of the Prophets*, for example, one of *The Wakefield Mystery Plays*, a Sibyl prophesies of the coming of Christ along with Moses, David, and Daniel.

The windows (c. 1500) of the Cathedral of Auch are in this tradition. The whole history of the world is in these windows, as it is in the cycle plays; and here, too, we find the prophets and the Sibyls, foretelling the coming of Christ (Male 1958: 136-138). Michelangelo also used Sibyls in this way, juxtaposing Sibyls with the prophets on the Sistine Chapel ceiling. Sandys also associates the Sibyl with "the will of the Allmighty revealed by his prophets" (*Ovid*: 648).

Some, however, did regard the Sibyls as suspect; Ross, for example, wrote that they were "diabolical and divinatory by evil spirits, which they carried about with them in divers shapes" (*Mystagogus Poeticus*: 306).

Bibliography: Shirley N. Blum, *Early Netherlandish Triptychs* (1969); Henri de Lubac, *Exégèse Médiévale: Les Quarte Sense de L'Ecriture* (1964); Peter Dronke, *Fabula: Explorations into the Uses of Myth in Medieval Platonism* (1974); Dronke, *Hermes and the Sibyls* (1990); Emile Male, *Religious Art from the Twelfth to the Eighteenth Century* (1958); Erwin Panofsky, *Early Netherlandish Painting* (1966).

SILENUS AND THE SILENI. Silenus was the father of Satyrs; he was often said to be the son of Pan. He was also the adoptive father of Bacchus. Silenus had a human form, although he was sometimes depicted with pointed ears. Ovid describes Silenus as that "old man who, drunk with wine, supports his staggering limbs on his staff, and clings weakly to his misshapen ass," following in Bacchus's train (*Metamorphoses*: 4.26-27). Sandys provides a typical explanation Silenus and his namesake Sileni:

The Silenii were no other then old Satyres: but one here mentioned more famous then the rest...and tutor unto Bacchus. Lucian [*Dionysus*: 2] describes him to be old and bald, riding for the most part on an Asse: low of stature, unwildly fat, with an over growne belly: his eares long and erected....He is fained an attendent on Bacchus, big bellied, reeling, and old: because immoderate drinke puffs up the body, making the head light, and the feete inconstant, producing also untimely age, by extinguishing the naturall with adventitious heat...and to ride on an asse: because habituall drunkennesse besots the sences, and dulls the understanding. (*Ovid*: 200)

Ribera's *Drunken Silenus* (fig. 25) participates in this tradition. Here Silenus's sagging belly and puddling flesh suggest his unbridled appetites. The braying ass invites comparison with bestial Silenus. The wreath of grape leaves—and the abundance of wine—suggest his association with Bacchus and, again, his appetites. A particularly goatish old Pan supports his son's head. In the foreground, on the right, we see Pan's shepherd's crook and a tortoise. The tortoise is there both to identify Pan, to whom the tortoise was sacred, and to suggest sloth (Felton and Jordan 1982: 109).

Bacon interpreted the Sileni and the Satyrs as "youth and old age" (*Wisedome of the Ancients*: 6). But there was another, more flattering, tradition of Silenus as sage. This tradition goes back Virgil's *Eclogue* 6, where shepherd lads come upon old Silenus in a cave in a bibulous sleep. They bind him with his garlands. "Smiling at the trick," Silenus promises to sing for them if they free him—and so he sings to rival even Orpheus, singing of the creation of the world and other weighty matter, even "All the songs that old Phoebus rehearsed." Ariosto makes use of this allegory: when Orlando awakens, cured of his love-madness, despising now the temptress Alcyna, he is likened to Silenus waking and being freed from his bonds:

> Thus being to his former wits restord,
> He was likewise delivered cleane from love....
> Now onely he applies his wits to prove,
> That fame and former glory to recover,
> Which he had lost, the while he was a lover.
>
> (*Orlando Furioso*: 39.59; see Harington on these verses:
> *On Orlando Furioso*: 332)

Another tradition had its beginnings in Plato's *Symposium* (215-217), where Alcibiades likens Socrates to certain statuettes of Silenus in use at the time, statuettes that could be opened up to reveal images of the gods. In the Renaissance, then, very occasionally, Silenus could suggest that beauty (or wisdom) could lie within an ugly exterior. Erasmus, for example, suggests that "the Holy Scriptures, like the Silenus of Alcibiades, conceal their real divinity beneath a surface that is crude and almost laughable" (*Enchiridion*: 105).

Bibliography: Thomas H. Carpenter and Christopher A Faraone, *Masks of Dionysus* (1993): 217-218, 233; Craig Felton and William B. Jordan, *Jusepe de Ribera lo Spagnoletto, 1591-1652* (1982).

SIRENS were female monsters who tempted sailors to destruction by the sweetness of their songs. There were two main lines of allegorical interpretation of the Sirens, one concentrating on them as temptresses, the other on the nature of their song. The temptress allegory is based, ultimately, on Homer's account of the Sirens: Odysseus plugs his men's ears with wax, has himself tied to the mast, then sails past the Sirens, able to hear their ravishing songs but safe from succumbing to them (*Odyssey*: 12.40-58, 159-200; see also Apollonius, *Argonautica*: 4.891 f.; and Virgil, *Aeneid*: 5.864-865). Horace, for example, writes of the Sirens as temptresses (*Epistles*: 1.2.23). According to Fulgentius there were three of these Sirens:

The Sirens are named as deceivers in Greek, for the allure of love is interpreted in three ways, by song or by sight or by habit: some creatures are loved for [the pleasure of their song], some for beauty of appearance, and some for pleasant habits....Ulysses...[i.e.,] wisdom...both hears and sees, that is, recognizes and sizes up and still passes by the Sirens, that is, the allures of pleasure. (*Mythologies*: 2.8)

This was the most common interpretation of the temptress Sirens. Dante's dream of the Siren in the *Purgatorio* is in this tradition:

"I am," she sang, "I am the sweet Siren who leads mariners astray in mid-sea, so full am I of pleasantness to hear...." Her mouth was not yet shut when a lady, holy and alert, appeared close beside me to put her to confusion. "O Virgil, Virgil, who is this?" she said sternly....He seized [the Siren] and laid her bare in front, rending her garments and showing me her belly: this waked me with the stench that issued therefrom. (19.19-33)

Virgil's stripping of the Siren recalls the stripping of the Whore of Babylon: "But the time will come when the ten horns and the beast will turn against the prostitute, and strip off all her clothes and leave her naked" (Rev 17:16). For Boccaccio, too, the Sirens were temptresses; he makes them part woman, part fish (the classical Sirens had been part woman, part bird): in their upper parts, they are beautiful virgins, while below they are fishlike, showing the true nature of "libidinous concupiscence" (*Genealogie Deorum*: 7.20; see also Vatican Mythographer III: 11.9; Lydgate, *Reson and Sensuallyte*: 6753 f.). Two centuries later Daniel's poem "Ulysses and the Siren" is working in this same tradition. The poem is a dialogue: The Siren tempts Ulysses with promises of ease and pleasure; Ulysses responds that toil leads to honor.

The temptress Sirens came to be synonymous with mermaids, as Chaucer explains:

But it was wonder lyk to be
Song of meermaydens of the see,
That for her synging is so clere,
Though we meermaydens clepe hem here
In Englisshe, as in our usaunce,
Men clepe hem sereyns in Fraunce.
                    (*Romaunt of the Rose*: 679-84)

Sirens were also mermaids for Batman (*Batman uppon Bartholomae*: 18.97), Spenser (*Faerie Queene*: 2.12.30), among others, and Shakespeare:

O, train me not, sweet mermaid, with thy note,
To drown me in thy sister's flood of tears,
Sing, siren, for thyself, and I will dote.
                    (*Comedy of Errors*: 3.2.45-47)

Similarly, Shakespeare's Venus finds herself tempted by Adonis's "mermaid voice" (*Venus and Adonis*: 429). Alciati's interpretation of the temptress Sirens blends woman, bird, and fish: "Birds without wings, and girls without legs, and fish without a mouth, they nevertheless sing with their lips....because lust carries with itself many monsters....The muses tear off their feathers, and Ulysses mocks them. That is to say, scholars have nothing to do with a harlot" (*Emblems*: 116).

This association of Sirens with lust was a commonplace. Petrarch cries out that he ought to avert his eyes from his beloved and so close his ears to the Sirens' song (*Rime sparse*: 207.82). We find the same allegory in Medieval English sermons (Owst 1966: 186). Erasmus, for another example, wrote that the prickings of lust are "extremely deadly Sirens whom scarcely anybody has escaped except those who kept their distance" (*Enchiridion*: 183-184; *On Disclaiming the World*: 137; see also Tasso, *Jerusalem Delivered*: 15.57). Bacon's chapter on Sirens is entitled "Sirens, or Voluptuousness" (*Wisedome of the Ancients*: 31). Sandys' explanation of the Sirens' grotesque form is in accord with such allegorical interpretations: "This double forme expresseth the angelicall and brutish nature in man" (*Ovid*: 259; for the same moral allegory in seventeenth-century Spain, see Smith 1984). Less censoriously, Ronsard ("Chant des Serenes") makes the allurements of the Sirens' song the allurement of love.

But the temptress Sirens could suggest earthly desires other than lust, as they do for example in Ficino (*Letters*, vol. 4: 27), where they are associated with the seductions of flattery. For Fraunce, they are the lust for fame: Some of Ulysses' men, he writes, "drawen away with ambition and vayn-glorie, would have yeelded to the deceiptfull sweetness of the Syrenes, had not their Capten stopped their eares with waxe" (*Countesse of Pembrokes Yvychurch*: 48r). And Golding makes listening to the Sirens' song a figure for reading Ovid literally, reading merely for the enjoyment of the sometimes bawdy stories. This passage comes at the end of his "Preface" to his translation of the *Metamorphoses*—a preface wherein he points to traditional allegorical interpretations of individual stories—many of which suggest the dangers of fleshly desires:

> Now too thintent that none have cause heereafter too complaine
> Of mee as setter out of things that are but lyght and vaine:
> If any stomacke be so weake as that it cannot brooke,
> I give him counsell too absteine untill he bee more strong,
> And for too use Ulysses feat ageinst the Meremayds song.
> Or if he needes will heere and see and wilfully agree
> (through cause misconstrued) untoo vice allured for too bee:
> Then let him also marke the peine that dooth therof ensue,
> And hold himself content with that too his fault is due.
>   (213-222)

The second tradition of Siren allegory is based on Plato's Sirens: in the vision of Er the vault of the heavens is composed of eight spheres, "and up above on each of the rims of the circles a Siren stood, borne around in its revolution and uttering one sound, one note, and from all the eight there was a concord of a single harmony" (*Republic*: 617b). Among the early Pythagoreanizing Neo-Platonists, this passage gave rise to a conception of benevolent Sirens (Lamberton 1989: 37). Proclus, for example, comments upon these Sirens as follows:

He called them "Sirens" to indicate that the harmony they impart to the rings is always bound to the material world, but he called them "celestial Sirens" in order to distinguish them from the Sirens within, which he himself elsewhere agrees that Odysseus sailed past, as in Homer's story [Plato, *Phaedrus*: 259a]....There are likewise Sirens in Hades, which [Plato] clearly mentions in the *Cratylus* [403d], saying they will not leave Hades because they are bewitched by the wisdom of Pluto.

Thus there are three classes of Sirens by Plato's own account: the celestial ones belonging to Zeus; the ones that function in this world, belonging to Poseidon; and the chthonic ones belonging to Pluto. All three produce a physical harmony, tied to matter, for the Muses are specifically granted the noetic harmony. This is why they are said to conquer the Sirens and crown themselves with their feathers, for they draw the Sirens up into contact with them and fasten the Sirens' own unruly powers to their wisdom. (*Sur la République*: 2.238.21-239.14, in Lamberton 1989: 231-232)

Macrobius (*On the Dream of Scipio*: 2.3.1) understands Plato's harmony of the Sirens to be the music of the spheres (see Appendix A, "Music"); Vatican Mythographer III (11.9), citing Plato and Macrobius, also associates the Sirens with the music of the spheres; Ficino (*Letters*, vol. 2: 15) and Lynche follow this tradition, as well: "The heavens (according to the opinion of the Platonickes) have every one their several Muse, called by them oftentimes Syrens, as most harmoniously and sweetly singing, alludeth unto the celestial orbes, which in number are likewise nine" (*Fountaine of Ancient Fiction*: Eiii).

See **MUSES** for more on the equation of Sirens and Muses. As figures for (or inspirers of) bad poetry, the Sirens could be contrasted with the Muses (see **MUSES**). The Sirens could also serve as allegorical figures for persuasive rhetoric and flattery (e.g., Conti, *Mythologie*: 7.13; see Nohrnberg 1976: 687-688).

Bibliography: Ruth Berman, "Sirens," in Malcolm South, *Mythical Creatures and Fabulous Beasts: A Source Book and Research Guide* (1987); John Hollander, *Allegory in Dante's Commedia* (1969): 136-144; Hollander, "*Purgatorio* XIX: Dante's Siren/Harpy," in Aldo S. Bernardo and Anthony L. Pellegrini, *Dante, Petrarch, Boccaccio: Studies in the Italian Trecento in Honor of Charles S. Singleton* (1983); Robert Lamberton, *Homer the Theologian* (1989); James Nohrnberg, *The Analogy of The Faerie Queene* (1976); G. R. Owst, *Literature and Pulpit in Medieval England* (1966); Paul Julian Smith, "Quevodo and the Sirens: Classical Allusion and Renaissance Topic in a Moral Sonnet," *JHP*, 9 (1984): 31-41.

SISYPHUS was best known for his punishment in Hades. Homer describes this in book 11 of the *Odyssey*, when Odysseus makes his descent into Hades:

Then Sisyphos in torment I beheld
being roustabout to a tremendous boulder.
Leaning with both arms braced and legs driving,
he heaved it toward a height, and almost over,
but then a Power spun him round and sent

the cruel boulder bounding again to the plain.
Whereon the man bent down again to toil,
dripping sweat, and the dust rose overhead.
(11.598-605)

Homer does not say why Sisyphus must endure this punishment, and later legends provide conflicting accounts. Apollodorus, for example, wrote that Sisyphus was punished "for the sake of Aegina, daughter of Asopus; for when Zeus had secretly carried her off, Sisyphus is said to have betrayed the secret to Asopus, who was looking for her" (*Library*: 1.9.3; see also Pausanius, *Description of Greece*: 2.5.1). Ovid suggests that Sisyphus was punished for his "tricks and fraud" (*Metamorphoses*: 13.32); Hyginus makes him guilty of "impiety" (*Fabulae*: 60). Christian commentators also disagreed as to Sisyphus's sins, but they were alike in seeing him as an example of the sinner justly punished. De Meun's Dame Nature, for example, complains that fallen mankind "alone works against my laws...; there is nothing that can satisfy him." And Sisyphus is one of her examples of the consequences of breaking Nature's laws. Will mankind, Dame Nature wonders, "role the millstone along the surface of the rock, then go find it to roll it again, never to cease, as you did, O wretched Sisyphus?" (*Romance of the Rose*: 19191-19322). And here is Ross: "The work of Sisyphus is like the work of worldly men, they toyl night and day for pleasures, honours, profit, but the work is never at an end; and when they think to end, they are but beginning" (*Mystagogus Poeticus*: 387). For Christians there was, then, something in the repetition of Sisyphus's endless labors that seemed to teach the lesson Jesus tried to teach the Samaritan woman at the well: "Jesus answered and said unto her, Whosoever drinketh of this water shall thirst again: But whosoever drinketh of the water that I shall give him shall never thirst; but the water that I shall give him shall be in him a well of water springing up into everlasting life" (John 4: 13-14).

The *Chess of Love* commentary makes Sisyphus an example of the punishment of those who "vary in their affections and are inconstant of purpose" (486). For Erasmus, "the rock of Sisyphus convinces you that ambition is troubled and harassed" (*Enchiridion*: 106).

Accounts and depictions of Sisyphus often group him with three others who suffer famously in the Underworld: Ixion, Tantalus, and Tityus (see **IXION**, **TANTALUS**, **TITYUS**). These were known as the Four Blasphemers or the Four Condemned.

T

TANTALUS, was king of Phrygia and the father of Niobe and Pelops. He offended the gods, and so was thrown down into Hades for eternal punishment. Some say that he told the secrets of the gods (e.g., Apollodorus, *Epitome*: 2.1); others, that he cut his son Pelops into pieces and served him to the gods to see if they were indeed omniscient (e.g., Ovid, *Metamorphoses*: 6.402-411); and there were other versions as well. Sources also vary as to the nature of his punishment. Apollodorus combines the two most commonly mentioned punishments, that he was held up to his neck in water he could not drink, with fruits he could not eat just out of reach and that he had a great stone perpetually hanging just above his head, ready to fall.

The allegorical interpretations of Tantalus, on the other hand, were virtually unanimous. He was regarded as an *exemplum* of greed or avarice by Horace (*Satires*: 1.1.68-79), Macrobius (*On the Dream of Scipio*: 1.10.13), Lydgate (*Reson and Sensuallyte*: 6479-6483), Erasmus (*Adages*: 2.6.12; *Enchiridion*: 106), Alciati (*Emblems*: 85), and Harington (*Apologie of Poetrie*: 7). For Spenser, too, he was "greedie Tantalus" whose punishment should an "Ensample be of mind intemperate" (*Faerie Queene*: 2.7.60; see Nohrnberg 1976: 333-334). And Whitney wrote:

> The covetous man, this fable reprehendes,
> For chaunge his name, and Tantalus hee is,
> Hee dothe abounde, yet sterves and nothing spendes,
> But keepes his goulde, as if it weare not his:
> With slender fare, he doth his hunger feede,
> And dare not touche his store, when hee doth neede.
> *(Emblemes*: 74)

As an allegorical figure for cupidity, Tantalus also served in a number of Medieval poems as an analogue for the sufferings of infatuated lovers (Heinrichs 1989).

Tantalus was often placed with three others suffering punishments in the Underworld; these were sometimes known as the Four Blasphemers or the Four Condemned (see **IXION, TANTALUS, TITYUS**).

Bibliography: Katherine Heinrichs, "The Denizens of Hades in the Love Poems of the Middle Ages," *Neophil*, 73 (1989): 593-604; James Nohrnberg, *The Analogy of The Faerie Queene* (1976).

THEBES was the chief Mycenaean city in central Greece. It was said to have been a pleasant place, with good water and abundant trees. But the city had a most unfortunate history. This was the city Oedipus ruled after he had killed his father and married his mother (see **OEDIPUS**). Subsequent events at Thebes were at least as unsavory. After Oedipus blinded himself and was banished from the city, it was decided that his sons, Eteocles and Polynices, would rule in alternating years. Eteocles ruled first, with Polynices going out into exile. When the year ended, Eteocles refused to cede the kingdom to his brother, and so Polynices gathered together seven kings of Greece, who swore vengeance upon Eteocles. (These are Aeschylus's *Seven against Thebes*.) When battle was joined, there was terrible carnage: all of the kings were killed except Adrastus. Finally, the brothers met in single combat and destroyed each other. Creon rose up as the new ruler. He refused to allow the kings to be buried. The wives of the kings besought Theseus, king of Athens, for aid (see **THESEUS, ATHENS**). Theseus finally defeated Creon.

Statius's *Thebaid* was the most important version of the story of Thebes for the Middle Ages and the Renaissance (but see also, e.g., *Le Roman de Thèbes* and Lydgate's *Siege of Thebes*). And Fulgentius's *On the Thebaid* was the most important allegorical commentary (but see also, e.g., Lactantius Placidus's commentary on the *Thebaid*; see Anderson 1988; Clogan 1985, 1988). Here follows an abridgment of Fulgentius's commentary:

Now the kernel can be extracted from the husk. Thebes is the soul of man. Laius is sacred light. Thus Laius ruled in Thebes, that is, sacred light in the soul of man. Furthermore, he had a wife named Jocasta, that is, pure joy. Jocasta is well named, for as her husband rules so she like a wife is subject to him. Oedipus being born is licentiousness. Just as joy, pure and at first undefiled sinks to the defilement of licentiousness, so Jocasta gave birth to Oedipus. When he grows up, that is, the soul of man asserting its strength, he kills his father, that is, puts out the sacred light which in its munificence had provided the very occasion for his birth. For his wife he takes his own mother in marriage. From this incestuous union are produced what have neither manliness nor yet the appearance of manliness, namely the two daughters [manliness was a figure for *virtue*—L., *vir*, man; see **AMAZON**]. Other creatures are produced having the appearance of manliness, but not manliness itself, namely the two sons, one of them called Eteocles and the other Polynices. Eteocles is destruction of morals, that is, greed, whereby morals are destroyed, for it is the origin and root of all evils. Polynices conquering many in this world is lust, to which many yield. As these sons grow up, that is greed and lust in the soul of man, their father blinds himself in his grief, that is the licentious mind tortures itself, horror-stricken at its sin.

First Boccaccio in the *Teseida* and then Chaucer in "The Knight's Tale" recreate these fratricidal brothers in Palamon and Arcite; and both poets follow the commentary tradition in making the brothers examples of the disastrous effects of misordered love (see, e.g., Anderson 1988: 82, 211-212).

To return to Fulgentius's commentary: Polynices seeks the help of Greek kings, the Seven against Thebes—that is, the worldly learning for which the Greeks were famous. The seven Greek kings are thus, "the seven liberal arts...worldly knowledge." They are led by Adrastus. "This king of Greece is philosophy, to which all worldly wisdom is subject." But in the context of Fulgentius's commentary, this is not flattering, since Polynices simply wants all the learning of the Greeks to aid him in the form of cunning:

Finally, the brothers, that is greed and lust, meet in single combat and destroy each other; but as these vices are destroyed, so in the mind there uprises pride [i.e.,] Creon. [The] wives of the kings, that is human feelings, which had formerly been subject to the kings, beseech Theseus, that is, God. Theseus fights with Creon, as God teaches that pride is conquered by humility. By such a struggle with vice was Thebes, that is, the soul of man, left shattered; but it is freed when the grace of God comes to its aid.

Fulgentius's commentary was widely known. But Thebes was also known more simply for the peculiar, nasty, animalistic intensity of its crimes and bloodshed (Patterson 1991: 75-78). Thus Dante calls wicked Pisa a "new Thebes" (*Inferno*: 33.89). And in the *Teseida* Boccaccio's Arcites, himself a Theban prince, laments Thebes' bloody history: "'Our ancestors, who were born of the teeth sown by Cadmus, son of Agenor, harbored such mutual hatred that they killed one another without regard for brotherly love.'" Arcites is recalling the story of Cadmus. In the course of founding the city of Thebes, Cadmus killed Mars' dragon and then, on Athena's instruction, sowed the teeth of the dragon. Immediately, armed men sprouted up; they fought among themselves, until only five remained. And these five Cadmus admitted into his newly founded Thebes (see **CADMUS**). Arcites continues his lament: "'Athamas killed his children, so enraged was Tisiphone against him!'" Athamas had married Ino, one of the daughters of Cadmus, and had become King of Thebes. Tisiphone, one of the three Furies, so possessed him that he killed one of his own children in his madness. Arcites continues: "'Latona killed the children of Amphion as they stood around Niobe their grieving mother. Spiteful, unfriendly Juno made Semele burn wretchedly. Everyone knows what the madness of Agave and her companions was like'" (*Book of Theseus*: 5.57-58). (In a frenzy of Bacchic ecstacy, Agave killed her son Pentheus, another unfortunate Theban; see **BACCHAE, PENTHEUS**.)

Arcites' history of Theban woe goes on to include Oedipus, Creon, Eteocles, and Polynices. Chaucer's "Knight's Tale" is based on Boccaccio's *Teseida*, and so it, too, is set against the backdrop of Thebes. Chaucer encourages us to see the Theban princes Palamon and Arcite as analogous to the fratricidal Polynices and Eteocles (for the meaning of Thebes to Chaucer, see, e.g., McCall 1979: 90-91). Spenser had this sense of Thebes in mind when he placed a monument to "fatall Thebes" in the house of Ate, goddess of discord—"Hard by the gates of hell" (*Faerie Queene*: 4.1.20,22).

Sandys contrasts the passionate, inarticulate Thebans with the Athenians, who were devoted to Apollo and Athena, and thus to measure, wisdom, and control (*Ovid*: 295-296).

For the story of the building of the walls of Thebes, see **AMPHION**, for the earlier history of the city, see **CADMUS**.

Hunting was said to have been particularly important to Thebes. John of Salisbury, for example, wrote that "The Thebans...were the first to decree that the knowledge of hunting should be imparted to all. They in particular formulated the rules of this profession, or shall we call it vice?" (*Policraticus*: 1.4).

Bibliography: David Anderson, "Theban History in Chaucer's *Troilus*," *SAC*, 4 (1982): 109-133; Anderson, "Mythography or Historiography? The Interpretation of Theban Myths in Late Mediaeval Literature," *Florilegium*, 8 (1986): 113-139; Anderson, *Before the Knight's Tale: Imitation of Classical Epic in Boccaccio's Teseida (1988);* Paul M. Clogan, "Lactantius Placidus' Commentary on the *Thebaid*," *ICNLS*, 6 (1985): 25-32; Clogan, "The Renaissance Commentators on Statius," *ICNLS*, 7 (1988): 273-280; John P. McCall, *Chaucer among the Gods: The Poetics of Classical Myth* (1979); Lee Patterson, *Chaucer and the Subject of History* (1991).

THESEUS was one of the greatest of the mythic heroes. He was born a prince of Troezen. As a young man he journeyed to Athens, disposing of such nasty tyrants and enemies of travelers as Procrustes along the way (Ovid, *Metamorphoses*: 7.430-452). Plutarch understands Theseus as an example of a man who *chose* to do great and difficult things: "Theseus, out of his own free-will, without any compulsion, when he might have reigned in security at Troezen in the enjoyment of no inglorious empire, of his own motion affected great actions" (*Lives*: "Comparison of Romulus with Theseus"). After his arrival in Athens Theseus continued upon this heroic course: He volunteered to be one of the young Athenians who had to be sent every nine years as tribute to cruel Minos, king of Crete. Theseus was then thrown with the other youths into the Labyrinth, to be eaten by the Minotaur. But Theseus had won the love of Minos's daughter, Ariadne; and she gave him a ball of thread which he was to let out as he sought the Minotaur and to follow back to the light after killing the monster. Theseus promised to marry Ariadne, but he forsook her on the Island of Naxos. In some legends he leaves her at the behest of the gods; in others, this is mere faithlessness. And there were other stories, too, of passionate escapades; he was said to have abducted Helen, for example.

But he came to rule Athens and all of the country around. He was thus remembered as the founder of the Attic State and as the man who brought unity and thus strength to his people. Plutarch again:

forming in his mind a great and wonderful design, he gathered together all the inhabitants of Attica into one town, and made them one people of one city, whereas before they lived dispersed, and were not easy to assemble upon any affair for the common interest. Nay, differences and even wars often occurred between them, which he by his persuasions appeased....Yet he did not suffer his state, by the promiscuous multitude that flowed in, to be turned into confusion and be left without any order or degree, but was the first that divided the Commonwealth into three distinct ranks, the noblemen, the husbandmen, and artificers. (*Lives*: 15-16)

During the Middle Ages and the Renaissance, then, Theseus could stand as either a positive or a negative *exemplum*. Thus Boccaccio makes him come to the end of his life as a *de casibus* figure, grieving for his son Hippolytus, and driven into exile by "the ungrateful Athenians": "What good did his royal lineage do him? What good the glory acquired by his valor? What good his strength? And what did his kingdom avail against hard-hearted Fortune?" (*Fates of Famous Men*: 23). Chaucer writes of Theseus's "grete untrouthe of love" (*Legend of Good Women*: 1890); Tritonio includes him in his list of "The Perfidious" (*Mythologia*: 29); and Spenser writes that Theseus is "condemned to endlesse slouth by law" (*Faerie Queene*: 1.5.35). Theseus's rape of Helen, late in his life, could be cited as an example of the power of love/lust (e.g., Ferrand, *Treatise on Lovesickness*: 19).

Modern critics sometimes interpret Shakespeare's *Midsummer Night's Dream* with reference to this "Theseus who, as any half-way educated person in the Renaissance could tell you, was a notorious rapist" (Bate 1993: 136). Other moderns have interpreted the play with reference to the good Theseus (e.g., Olson 1957). Probably Shakespeare wants us to remember both—but probably we are to think of the Theseus who is incapable of controlling his passions as being the *young* Theseus. In his youth, the play suggests, even Theseus had difficulty controlling his passions. But now Theseus is capable of rational control. Now he is marrying; now Theseus is ruling Athens. Probably Shakespeare wanted to suggest that the play's four youthful, passionate lovers can change in the way that Theseus changed. At the end of the play, they leave the woods for Athens and marriage.

Christians did more often remember the good Theseus. Fulgentius, for example, ends his commentary *On the Thebaid* with Theseus's conquest of Thebes: Theseus is God conquering the human pride, so that the grace of God can bring salvation. (This commentary is quoted at length, above, under **THEBES**.) For Bernardus, too, Theseus is a type of God: "Theseus is called divine and good, for *theos* is *deus*, 'god,' and *eu* is *bonus*, 'good.' We interpret Theseus as the rational and virtuous man. He descends to the underworld according to the descent of virtue" (*On Virgil's Aeneid*: 6.122-123; see **EPIC CONVENTIONS: The descent**).

The "descent" Bernardus has in mind is Theseus's descent to Hell to aid his friend Pirithous in his attempt to abduct (or rescue, in some versions) Proserpina, wife of Pluto. Even this, then, could be allegorized to the good; indeed, Theseus was remembered with Pirithous as an example of perfect friendship (e.g., Virgil, *Aeneid*: 6.393; Ovid, *Metamorphoses*: 8.303, 405-406; Spenser, *Faerie Queene*: 4.10.27; see also Nichols 1823, vol. 3: 281; Hoffman 1966: 52-56).

Like Hercules, Theseus was sometimes interpreted as a type of Christ (e.g., Berchorius, *Ovidius Moralizatus*: 290; Conti, *Mythologie*: 7.10; Ross, *Mystagogus Poeticus*: 401), or for God, as we have seen. But most often he was the ideal ruler (e.g., Golding, "Epistle": 155-156), vigorous in war, strong in his dealings with his nobles, compassionate with the poor. Theseus was sometimes called the founder of knighthood, in a development of Plutarch's idea that it was Theseus who first divided a society into the three estates (e.g., Higden, *Polychronicon*: 2.381-95; Lydgate, *Falls of Princes*: 1.4398-4400). And he was the ruler of *Athens*, the city devoted to Athena, the city of the philosophers—Socrates, Plato, Aristotle. Here is Boccaccio: "The city of Athens was once the light of Greece, for it was the celebrated nurse of philosophers, poets, and orators. It also had very famous kings; and Theseus...was fated perhaps to be the greatest of them all" (*Fates of Famous Men*: 19; see also Lydgate, *Falls of Princes*: 1.4243-77; see also Olson 1986: 62-63).

Ruler of the city of Athena, selfless knight—for John of Garland (*Integumenta Ovidii*: 364) Theseus represented the ideal but rarely achieved balance of the active and contemplative lives. Conti calls Theseus "the wisest man of his age" (*Mythologie*: 7.10). This is the Philosopher-king of Boccaccio's *Teseida*, Chaucer's "Knight's Tale," and Shakespeare's *Midsummer Night's Dream*—the king whose victories over the Amazons and Thebes allegorized the victory of the reason/spirit over the flesh, an example of human valor and prudence.

Sometimes Theseus was called Hercules, "To signefie," Lydgate explained, "This name in conquest all other doth excell" (*Falls of Princes*: 1.4374-4375).

For more on the episodes of Theseus's story, see **AMAZONS, ARIADNE, ATHENS, HIPPOLYTUS, LABYRINTH, MINOS, MINOTAUR, THEBES**.

Bibliography: Jonathan Bate, *Shakespeare and Ovid* (1993); Richard L. Hoffman, *Ovid and The Canterbury Tales* (1966); John Nichols, *The Progresses and Public Processions of Queen Elizabeth*, 3 vols. (1823); Paul A. Olson, "*A Midsummer Night's Dream* and the Meaning of Court Marriage," *ELH*, 24 (1957): 95-119; Olson, *The Canterbury Tales and the Good Society* (1986); David Ormerod, "*A Midsummer Night's Dream*: The Monster in the Labyrinth," *ShakS*, 11 (1978): 39-52; Melvin Storm, "From Knossos to Knight's Tale: The Changing Face of Chaucer's Theseus," in Jane Chance, *The Mythographic Art* (1990): 215-231.

TIRESIAS was the blind soothsayer of Thebes. Stories varied as to how he came by his blindness. According to one version he was watching his mother Athena bathing in a pool, when she splashed water into his eyes and thus blinded him; she then gave him the gift of prophecy in order to compensate him for the loss of his sight (Callimachus, *Hymns*: "The Bath of Pallas").   Ovid's version (*Metamorphoses*: 3.316-338) was, however, much more widely known: Jupiter and Juno were arguing as to whether the man or the woman had the greater pleasure in lovemaking.   They decided to allow Tiresias to decide the issue, since he was the only person who had experienced sex both as a man and as a woman.   It seems that Tiresias had once seen two serpents coupling and hit them with his staff.   The serpents punished him by changing him into a woman.   After seven feminine years, he happened again upon coupling serpents; he hit them again with his staff, and again his sex was reversed.   So when the question was posed to him, he was ready with the answer: Women had more pleasure in sex than men.   Juno, not the most even-tempered of the gods, was furious that the judgment should have gone against her, and so she struck Tiresias blind.   Jupiter then gave him the gift of prophecy, in compensation for the loss of his merely physical eyes.

Already in antiquity the story of Tiresias suggested something about different ways of seeing.   And this distinction was basic to most of the allegorical uses of Tiresias by Christians.   Berchorius provides a homely instance of the tradition: "For the loss of worldly consolation is the occasion of spiritual wisdom and of meditation on the future.   Matthew 11:5: 'The blind see'....Or say that where the exterior powers are lacking the interior ones become more acute and where the eyes of the body are shut the mind is raised high to think" (*Ovidius Moralizatus*: 193).   Reynolds, Neo-Platonist that he is, provides a rather loftier statement (paraphrasing Pico) of the same idea:

The object of this Celestiall or Intellectuall Love...is the excellency of the Beauty of Supernall and Intellectual thinges: To the contemplation whereof, rationall and wise Spirits are forcibly raised and lifted aloft...in an Extaticke manner, and...cry out..."Ope thine eyes, ope them wide, raise and lift them aloft." ...many, with the fervent love of the beauty and excellence of intellectual things, have been so raized above all earthly considerations as they have lost use of their corporall eyes.   Homer...with seeing the ghost of Achilles, which inspired him with that Poeticke fury, that who with understanding reades shall find to containe in it all intellectuall contemplation, was thereby deprived (or faigned to bee deprived) of his corporall eye-sight, as one that seeing all things above, could not attend to the heeding of triviall and meaner things below.   And such rapture of the spirit is exprest...in the fable of Tyresias...who for having seene Pallas naked (which signifies no other then that Ideall beauty, whence proceeds all sincere wisdome, and not cloathed or covered with corporall matter) became sodainly blind, and was by the same Pallas made a Prophet; so as that which blinded his corporall eyes opened to him the eyes of his understanding, by which he saw not only all things past, but also all that were to come. (*Mythomystes*: 150-151; on the superiority of blindness to merely earthly seeing, see Wind 1968: 53-80)

Tiresias could thus serve as a type of the ecstatic poet in general and for blind Homer in particular (see **HOMER**).

But Tiresias was sometimes interpreted in ways that had nothing to do with his powers as a seer.   The commonest of these interpretations seems to have had its beginnings with Fulgentius, who interpreted the story of Tiresias's judgment in terms of nature allegory. The ancients, he says,

took Teiresias as an allegory of time....Thus in springtime, which is masculine because at that season there is a closing and immovability of plants, when he saw before him the creatures coupling and struck at them with his staff—that is in the heat of temper, he is turned into the feminine gender, that is, into the heat of summer. They took summer to be in the form of a woman because at that season all things blossom forth with their leaves. And because there are two seasons for mating, spring and autumn, having stopped their conceiving he returned again to his former appearance. For autumn so strips all things in its masculine guise. (*Mythologies*: 2.5)

For paraphrases of this passage, see, for example, Bernardus (*On Martianus Capella*: 3.554), Berchorius (*Ovidius Moralizatus*: 192), and Sandys (*Ovid*: 155).

The story of Tiresias was also understood morally. Berchorius (*Ovidius Moralizatus*: 191), for example, interprets Tiresias's metamorphosis from man to woman as an instance of the loss of *virtus*: Latin (*vir*, "man") for "manliness" and for "virtue" (for male/female allegory, see **AMAZONS**). Golding understands Tiresias's judgment of the dispute between Jupiter and Juno as a warning to "inferior folk in any wise to shun / To judge betweene their betters least in peril they doo run" ("Epistle": 103-104).

For Tiresias in the Underworld, see **HOMER**.

Bibliography: Robert Lamberton, *Homer the Theologian* (1989): 8-10; Edgar Wind, *Pagan Mysteries of the Renaissance* (1968).

THE TITANS were the children—six brothers and six sisters—of Uranus (the Sky) and Gaia (the Earth). The names of the better-known Titans were Hyperion, Iapetus, Oceanus, Saturn, Mnemosyne, Tethys, and Themis. Their offspring could also be called Titans; Hyperion's son Sol (the Sun), for example, was often called a Titan. Uranus shut the Titans up in the depths of Earth, and so Gaia urged her children to rebel against their father. Saturn took the lead, cutting off his father's privates with a sickle (see **SATURN**). Hesiod (*Theogony*: 154-185) provides the classic account of their complicated wars; but with some exceptions (e.g., Conti, *Mythologie*: 6.21) Christians tended to look past such details. In the main they remembered the Titans for their rebellious pride, and so their allegorical uses are usually identical with those of the Giants. Indeed, Giants and Titans were often conflated. Both Titans and Giants were outsized rebels, after all. See, for example, Horace (*Odes*: 3.4.53), Hyginus (*Fabulae*: 150), Peele (*Arraignment of Paris*: 254-255), and Ross (*Mystagogus Poeticus*: 404-405).

For more on giants, Giants, presumption, and rebellion, see **GIANTS**.

Bibliography: A. C. Hamilton, *The Spenser Encyclopedia* (1990): under *Titans*.

TITHONUS was usually said to have been the brother of Priam. Bacon's version of the story is typical:

Tithonus was the paromour of Aurora, who (desirous ever to enjoy his company) petitioned Jupiter that he might never dye, but (through womanish oversight) forgetting to insert this clause in her petition, that he might not withall grow old and feeble, it followed that he was onely freed from the condition of mortality, but for old age, that came upon him in a marvelous and miserable fashion, agreeable to the state of those who cannot die, yet every day grow weaker and weaker with age. Insomuch that Jupiter (in commiseration of this his misery) did at length metamorphose him into a Grasshopper.

Bacon goes on to suggest that Tithonus ought to be interpreted as a figure for "pleasure, which in the beginning, & as it were in the morning [Aurora being the goddess of the dawn] seemes to be so pleasant and delightfull that men desire that they might enjoy & monopolize it for ever unto themselves, unmindful of that Satiety and loathing, which (like old age) will come upon them before they bee aware" (*Wisedome of the Ancients*: 15). Tithonus could thus be understood as having experienced an ironic fulfillment of earthly desire. Horace had made him an example of the vanity of human wishes (*Odes*: 2.16.30; see also Conti, *Mythologie*: 6.5, and Ross, *Mystagogus Poeticus*: 402). Spenser's misshapen, lustful Malbecco is a type of Tithonus, having been "granted a kind of parody of immortality" (Nohrnberg 1976: 640). Spenser might also be alluding to this allegorical tradition when he refers to Tithonus on the morning of the third and final day of the Red Cross Knight's battle with the dragon:

> The joyous day gan early to appeare,
> And faire Aurora from the deawy bed
> Of aged Tithone gan her selfe to reare....
> Then freshly up arose the doughtie knight,
> All healed of his hurts and woundes wide.
> (*Faerie Queene*: 1.11.51-52)

Since the Knight's three-day battle with the dragon is a type of Christ's three-day battle with Satan and death—the three days between the crucifixion and the resurrection—Tithonus stands as an ironic inversion of the eternal life Christ's resurrection made possible.

See also **AURORA**.

Bibliography: James Nohrnberg, *The Analogy of the Faerie Queene* (1976).

TITYUS was one of the four great sinners—the Four Blasphemers—who suffer eternal punishment in Hades: Tityus, Tantalus, Ixion, and Sisyphus (see **IXION, SISYPHUS, TANTALUS**). He was the son of Jupiter and Elare. According to Apollodorus, Jupiter got Elare with child; then "after he had debauched her," mindful of Juno's jealousy, Jupiter hid Elare under the earth. There she bore the giant Tityus. Eventually, this monster attempted to rape Latona, the first wife of Jupiter and the mother of Diana and Apollo: "But she called her children to her aid, and they shot him down with their arrows. And he is punished even after death; for vultures eat his heart in Hades" (*Library*: 1.4.1). More commonly, it is Tityus's liver that the vultures eat: The liver was thought to be the seat of the passions. From ancient times, then, this torture was seen as a figure for the gnawing pains occasioned by the passions—especially that of love (see, e.g., Lucretius, *On the Nature of Things*: 3.982 f.). As Ferrand put it in his *Treatise on Lovesickness*, "the liver is the hearth of this fire and the seat of love," as is "reconfirmed by the poets who devised [the myth] of the vulture assiduously gnawing at the liver of Tityus in punishment for his attempted rape of the goddess Leto" (8).

Tityus was also essentially of the earth. Born deep under ground, Tityus was sometimes referred to as "the earth-born" or, as in Homer (*Odyssey*: 11.577) and Virgil (*Aeneid*: 6.595), a son of the earth. This association with the earth, his lechery, and his gnawed liver combined to make him a natural *de casibus exemplum* of lust. Here is Berchorius's comment on Tityus, for example: "the wanton man gives his liver—that is his desire—to vultures, that is to carnal acts which devour and consume him and take from him his life, reputation, and wealth. Once devoured, he is made whole again because the wanton man is continually renewed in his evil dispositions and the goad of the flesh...renews itself through him" (*Ovidius Moralizatus*: 113). The *Chess of Love* commentary is in the same tradition:

the vultures always gnaw his gizzard and devour it completely, and when it is all eaten it grows back by the third day, and then on the return of the vultures it is assailed more fiercely than before, and devoured again....This is the pain by which the lustful are ravaged, their vitals, i.e., hearts, desires, and affections, are always given to the vultures to eat. That is, to carnal desires, which completely devour not only their bodies but also their substance and even their reputations. And worse yet, when all is consumed, their mad affection and desire for these delights gushes up again and is renewed, and so eternally devours them. (488-489)

Thus when Chaucer's Pandarus compares Troylus's sufferings with those of Tityus, he is probably telling us more than he knows about the nature of Troylus's love (*Troylus and Criseyde*: 1.786).

It is allegorically appropriate that Diana (chastity) and Apollo (wisdom) slay Tityus, because, as Sandys put it, Tityus "is said to be the son of the Earth of his earthly affections; and in opposition to the heavenly seed." And he was so huge "in regard of the large extension of lust" (*Ovid*: 211).

Bibliography: Katherine Heinrichs, "The Denizens of Hades in the Love Poems of the Middle Ages," *Neophil*, 73 (1989): 593-604.

TROY (Ilium) was the great city in the northeast of what is now Turkey. It was the city of King Priam and Queen Hecuba. Troy was best known for its disastrous war with the Greeks. When the Trojan prince Paris went on his delegation to the

Greeks, he fell in love with Helen, the wife of the Greek king Menelaus. Paris abducted his love, the Greeks decided that they must win her back and get revenge, and so began the famous ten-year siege of Troy. This war was certainly the most important event in classical mythology: The *Iliad* describes events of the war; the *Odyssey* is about Odysseus's return from the war; the *Aeneid* is about the founding of Rome by Trojan refugees; and Ovid, too, wrote at length about this war (*Metamorphoses*: 11-15). The war was almost as important in the Christian imagination as it had been for the Greek and Roman. The story of Troy was taken as history.

In general Christians ascribed the fall of Troy not to destiny, but to pride and criminal lust. And it was not Paris alone, but the whole city which acted in such a way as to bring about its destruction. Bernardus provides a good sense of these assumptions:

Troy was destroyed...by a horse. The horse, enclosing many Greeks, was taken into the city, and, when the Trojans were asleep, the horse released the hidden Greeks into the city....The horse also signifies lechery....The horse has this meaning because in this animal lechery flourishes especially....The horse holds an infinite number of Greeks, since lechery contains various vices such as incest, adultery, fornication, and harlotry....The Trojans sleep when they do not exercise knowledge and virtue....When the exercise of virtue is halted, wantonness, prodigality and avarice come forth from lechery....The Greeks are smuggled into the city and set it in flames when vice overcomes the body with the heat of its burning after the flesh consents to vice. (*On Virgil's Aeneid*: 6.515-516)

The idea of Troy's pride goes back at least to Virgil, who speaks of "proud Illium" (*Aeneid*: 3.2); Dante also wrote of "the all-daring pride of the Trojans" (*Inferno*: 30.14). Horace wrote that the story of Troy "embraces the passions of foolish kings and peoples" (*Epistles*: 1.2.8). Petrarch was among many who developed such ideas along allegorical lines: "Now all this tumult, this ruin, this destruction in which the voluptuous city, victim of its own passions, struggles between the fires kindled by libidinousness and the sword of anger occurs fitly at night to denote the darkness of human error and the blackness in which our life, buried in sleep and drenched in wine, is ignorantly and drunkenly immersed" (in Don C. Allen 1968: 73). And here is the *Chess of Love* commentary: "That Aeneas was a son of Venus secretly shows us that the Trojans were lustful. That Venus was wounded by Diomede, means that the lust of the Trojans was reduced to nothing by the Greeks" (690). Raoul de Presles, in his commentary on *The City of God*, wrote that Troy fell because it neglected Pallas (wisdom) in favor of fleshly lusts (I, sig. A, viii *recto*). Golding put the matter strongly:

The seege of Troy, the death of men, the razing of the citie,
And slaughter of king Priams stock without remorse or pitie,
...do declare
How heynous wilfull perjurie and filthie whoredome are
In syght of God.
                              ("Epistle": 242-246)

But in order really to understand what Troy meant during the Middle Ages and the Renaissance, one must realize that it was generally accepted that Rome was not the only kingdom founded by Trojans. Merovingian scholars assured their countrymen, for example, that the Franks were descended from the Trojan Francus (Seznec 1961: 19). The Pearl Poet wrote that Trojan Ticius founded Tuscany and that Trojan Langobard founded Lombardy (*Sir Gawain and the Green Knight*: 1.11-12). And Britain, of course, was founded by another Trojan, Brutus, grandson of Aeneas (see **BRUTUS**). Geoffrey of Monmouth tells this story as early as the twelfth century. And it was Geoffrey who derived the old name for London, Trinovantum, from *Troia Nova*, "New Troy" (*History of the Kings of Britain*: 1.17; see Tatlock 1950: 111). Geoffrey was also the first of many to point to British customs that were supposed to have come to Britain with the Trojans (3.1). A fifteenth-century handbook of London customs asserts as a thing well known that London was founded before Rome and that the city "possesses the liberties, rights, and customs of the ancient city of Troy and enjoys its institutions" (in Riley 1861: 54). In 1591 Queen Elizabeth was entertained by a song that called her the "beauteous Quene of second Troy" (in Nichols 1823, vol. 3: 108). Indeed, this myth held sway in England for some 500 years, at least from the time of Geoffrey in the twelfth century until the time of the Revolution in the seventeenth century (MacDougall 1982: 26; see also Patterson 1991: 90-94).

For Europeans in general, and for the English in particular, to read of Troy and its fall was thus to read a warning as to the danger to the state, to the common weal, of private passions (McCall 1962: 264; Robertson 1968: 2-3). This would explain the extended reference to Troy at the beginning of act 3 of Sackville and Norton's *Gorboduc*: Just as Troy fell because Paris did not control his passions, so Gorboduc's Britain will fall because of the passions of Porrex and Ferrex. And this must be one of Shakespeare's reasons for having his Lucrece contemplate the "skilful painting" of Troy (*Rape of Lucrece*, 1366-1568): Just as Troy fell because of the lust of Paris and Helen, so King Tarquin's Roman kingdom will fall because Prince Tarquin raped Lucrece.

But Troy could also be understood—especially by the Renaissance Neo-Platonists—as a figure for the individual's response to love and lust. Landino provides a nice instance of this interpretation. After first explaining Plato's distinction between the two Venuses, "one heavenly, the other earthly," Landino writes that it is the Venus of heavenly love who leads Aeneas out of "burning Troy, that is, away from the heat of fleshly pleasures" and then, coming finally to Italy "after many errors, is coming to true wisdom." Paris, on the other hand, is selfishly dedicated to such pleasures and so, being "one with Troy, he perishes" (*Disputationes Camuldenses*: 125-127). Calcagni's gloss is closely related: Troy is this world, out of which Aeneas ascends by a Neo-Platonic ladder (*Lectiones Antiquae*: 2.555-559).

For more on the causes and meaning of the war, see **HELEN, PARIS**.

Bibliography: Don C. Allen, *Image and Meaning* (1968); Hugh A. MacDougall, *Racial Myth in English History* (1982); John P. McCall, "The Trojan

Scene in Chaucer's Troilus," *ELH*, 29 (1962): 263-275; Scot McKendrick, "*The Great History of Troy*: a Reassessment of the Development of a Secular Theme in Late Medieval Art," *JWCI*, 54 (1991): 43-82; John Nichols, *The Progresses and Public Processions of Queen Elizabeth*, 3 vols. (1823); Lee Patterson, *Chaucer and the Subject of History* (1991); H. T. Riley, *Liber Albus: The White Book of the City of London* (1861); D. W. Robertson, Jr., *Chaucer's London* (1968); Jean Seznec, *The Survival of the Pagan Gods* (1961); J. S. P. Tatlock, *The Legendary History of Britain* (1950).

TYPHEUS (Typhon) was a gigantic monster who rebelled against Jupiter. Hesiod is the ultimate source for most of the Typheus lore. In the *Theogony* Typheus is the son of Gaia (the earth) and Tartarus (the lowest region of the world, as far below Hades as the earth is below the heavens; see also Ovid, *Metamorphoses*: 5.321-360). Most later descriptions of Typheus are variations—at first or second hand—on this passage from Hesiod: "From his shoulders grew an hundred heads of a snake, a fearful dragon, with dark, flickering tongues, and from under the brows of his eyes in his marvelous heads flashed fire, and fires burned from his heads as he glared. And there were voices in all his dreadful heads which uttered every kind of sound unspeakable" (*Theogony*: 820-827). Apollodorus provides what must be the most fearsome description of Typheus: He was immense, taller than "all the mountains....One of his hands reached out to the west and the other to the east." He was human in his shape only down to his thighs. "From the thighs downward he had huge coils of vipers," and he was winged, and "fire flashed from his eyes" (*Library*: 1.6.3).

Typheus was said to have fathered a remarkable number of monsters: among others, the dog Cerberus, the Hydra, the Nemean Lion, the dragon of the Hesperides, and the Chimera. But he was best known for his ferocious rebellion against the gods. Only Jupiter and Athena dared stand against him. Eventually, Jupiter overcame Typheus by hurling thunderbolts at him, then burying him under a mountain. And this was the origin of volcanoes and the dangerous winds (Hesiod, *Theogony*: 855-870; Servius, *In Virgilii Aeneidos*: 3.578; Boccaccio, *Genealogie Deorum*: 4.22; Conti, *Mythologie*: 6.22; Ross, *Mystagogus Poeticus*: 404).

This Typheus was often conflated with Typhon, of whom we first read in *The Homeric Hymns* (311 f.). Hera, it seems, was enraged that Zeus should have conceived and born Athena on his own, without her. In her envious fury she asked the aid of the Tartaran regions, that *she* might conceive and give birth without her husband. She did conceive and bore the monster Typhon. Hera gave the child to the dragoness Python to be reared. (Hyginus, *Fabulae*: 152, makes Typhon the son of Tartarus and Tartara, a darksome goddess Hyginus seems to have invented.) Since eventually this Typhon, like Typheus, rebelled against Zeus, later traditions usually made the monsters one.

Christian allegory usually understood ugliness as an outward manifestation of an inward spiritual state; and Renaissance writers—Typheus/Typhon was not much mentioned during the Middle Ages—tended to be authoritarian. It is hardly surprising, then, that Christians should have interpreted the rebel Typheus unfavorably. For Conti he was "the fury of ambition" (*Mythologie*: 6.22). Bacon associates him with that particular species of ambition, rebellion:

This Fable seemes to point at the variable fortune of Princes, and the rebellious insurrection of Traytors in a State. For Princes may well be said to be maried to their dominions, as Jupiter was to Juno: but it happens now & then, that being deboshed by the long custome of empyring & bending towards tyrany, they endevor to draw all to themselves, and (contemning the counsell of their Nobles and Senatours) hatch lawes in theire owne braine, that is, dispose of things by their owne fancie and absolute power. The people (repyning at this) study how to create and set up a cheefe of their owne choise....[T]here followes a kind of murmuring or discontent in the State, shadowed by the infancie of Typhon, which being nurst by the naturall pravitie and clownish malignity of the vulgar sort (unto Princes as infestious as Serpents) is againe repaired by renewed strength, and at last breakes out into open Rebellion, which...is represented by the monstrous deformity of Typhon: his hundred heads signifie their devided powers. (*Wisedome of the Ancients*: 2)

Not surprisingly, he was also interpreted as a type of the rebel angel Satan (e.g., Lavinius, *Metamorphoses*: 11v, col. a). Thus it is that Milton likens Satan to Typhon (*Paradise Lost*: 1.196-200). And here is Ross:

he was about to shut Jupiter out of his Kingdom: but he was shot with his thunder, and thrust under the Isle Inarime, or, as some write, under the hill Aetna in Sicily....The Devil is the very Typhon, who by his pride opposed God, and was thrust down to hell: the greatness of Typhons body argues the greatness of Satans power; his snaky hands and serpentine feet do shew, that his actions and ways are cunning and deadly....The Pope is another Typhon: the Son of earth; for he hath turned Christs heavenly Kingdom into an earthly Monarchy; he makes war against heaven, by opposing Gods Ordinances....But it was Juno, the goddess of wealth, that produced this monster out of the earth, and it was wealth that raised the Pope to that pride and greatness, by which he hath troubled the world ever since. (*Mystagogus Poeticus*: 404-405)

In Neo-Platonic terms, baneful Typhon could be a figure for the destructive, disorderly tendencies inherent on the World-Body. Plutarch explains Typhon in this allegorical way in his essay *Isis and Osiris*: Typhon's destructiveness is held in check by Isis, the principle of generation (Hankins 1971: 77-78).

Despite his titanic proportions, Typheus was not, properly speaking, one of the Titans. The Titans were the sons of Gaia and Uranus. Neither, properly speaking, was gigantic Typheus one of the Giants, who were the sons of Gaia, born of the blood of castrated Uranus. But since all of these figures—Titans, Typhon, Typheus, and Giants—were outsized rebels, they were often conflated. See **GIANTS, TITANS.**

Bibliography: John E. Hankins, *Source and Meaning in Spenser's Allegory* (1971); Charles Lemmi, *The Classical Deities in Bacon* (1933): 162-164.

U

ULYSSES (Odysseus) was the most cunning of the heroes who fought at Troy. Homer (in the *Iliad*) quite evidently prized the valor of Achilles above the cunning of Ulysses. For Virgil, Ulysses was the archenemy of the Trojans, a man driven by "malice" (*Aeneid*: 2.90). Devoted to Virgil as he was, Dante followed Virgil in condemning Ulysses (*Inferno*: 26.56). Ovid, on the other hand, treated Ulysses favorably in *The Metamorphoses* (13); and Horace in his *Epistles* makes Ulysses "an instructive pattern" of the "power of worth and wisdom." Ulysses is

that tamer of Troy, who looked with discerning eyes upon the cities and manners of many men, and while for self and comrades he strove for a return across the broad seas, many hardships he endured, but could never be o'erwhelmed in the waves of adversity. You know the Sirens' songs and Circe's cups; if, along with his comrades, he had drunk of these in folly and greed, he would have become the shapeless and witless vassal of a harlot mistress—would have lived as an unclean dog or a sow that loves the mire. (*Epistles*: 1.2.17-26)

Statius (*Achilleid*) also wrote favorably of Ulysses. And already among the Greek Neo-Platonists, Porphyry and Numenius, Ulysses's odyssey was understood allegorically as a journey of the spirit. Porphyry understood "Odysseus as the symbol of man escaping the physical universe (the sea) to return...to the place where there is not even any memory of the physical universe" (Lamberton 1989: 130). On the whole, it was this favorable view of Ulysses that prevailed during the Middle Ages and the Renaissance.

Homer's first allegorical interpreter, Heraclitus (*Allégories d'Homère*: 70, 73.10, 75), interpreted Ulysses as wisdom struggling against the vices. This developed into an enduring tradition. Fulgentius, for example, wrote that "Ulysses in Greek is for *olonxenos*, that is, stranger to all; and because wisdom is a stranger to all things of this world, so Ulysses is called crafty"; and Ulysses was able to sail harmlessly past the temptations of Scylla, "for wisdom scorns lust; he had a wife called Penelope the chaste, because all chastity is linked to wisdom" (*Mythologies*: 2.8-9). Boethius cites Ulysses' struggle with Polyphemus as an example of a virtuous struggle against fortune: "Indeed, virtue gets its name from that virile strength [*L. vir*, 'man'] which is not overcome by adversity" (*Consolation of Philosophy*: 4.pr 7-mt 7; for the allegory of *vir* and *virtus*, see **AMAZONS**; for Ulysses in Boethius, see O'Daly 1991: 224-227). For some of the many others who wrote along these same lines, see Boccaccio (*Genealogie Deorum*: 4.14; 11.40), the *Chess of Love* commentary (657), Conti (*Mythologie*: 9.1), Golding ("Epistle": 248-249), and Viana (*Ovid*: 13.12). And then there is Hall's curious pamphlet, *Wisdoms Conquest. or, An explanation and Grammaticall Translation of the thirteenth Book of Ovids Metamorphoses, containing that curious and Rhetoricall contest between Ajax and Ulysses...where is set forth to the life the power of Valour, and the prevalence of Eloquence.* Hall assures us that "The scope and drift of this Fable and fiction is, to shew the folly of those, who preferre Strength before Policy...and Weapons before Wisdome" (3).

Brant also wrote of Ulysses:

> Ulysses was uncanny shrewd
> That he took neither drink nor food
> Until the sorceress he deceived
> And all his comrades he relieved....
> Thus many a hardship he'd elude
> By wisdom sage, by counsel shrewd.
> (*Ship of Fools*: 108)

Cooper, citing Plutarch, wrote that Homer's two poems "comprehendeth both the partes of man. For in *Ilias* he describeth strength and valiantnesse of bodie, in *Odyssea* he doth set forth a perfite patterne of the minde" (*Dictionarium*: *sub* "Homer"). For Richard Edwards, Ulysses was, quite simply, "a perfect wise man" (*Damon and Pithias*, 443). Spenser wrote that "Homere...in the persons of Agamemnon and Ulysses hath ensampled a good governor and a virtuous man, the one in his *Ilias*, the other in his *Odysseis*" ("Letter to Raleigh"). And for Sidney, Ulysses was an example of "wisdom and temperance" (*Defense of Poesy*: 15).

According to Homer (*Odyssey*: 10.310-327) and Ovid (*Metamorphoses*: 14.291), Mercury delivered to Ulysses an herb, moly, which protected him from Circe's drugs. For Heraclitus moly was "wisdom," just what was needed to "protect Ulysses and assure the victory over the drugs of Circe" (*Allégories d'Homère*: 73.10). The early Christians tended to conflate Wisdom and Logos, and so they were much interested in this soul-healing herb, which they interpreted as a figure for the Logos, the Word, the power of Christ/Mercury to heal the spirit (Rahner 1971: 179-224). Milton names this herb "haemony" and cites it as a specific against the wiles of the Circe-like Comus (*Comus*: 630-649; see Harding

1946: 63-64; Steadman 1984: 141-159). In Alciati, on the other hand, moly figured eloquence (*Emblems*: 182).

For other episodes of the Ulysses story, see **AEOLUS, AJAX, CALYPSO, CIRCE, CYCLOPES, PENELOPE, SCYLLA AND CHARYBDIS, SIRENS**; for Ulysses and the healing, soul-preserving herb moly, see **MERCURY**.

Bibliography: Don C. Allen, *Mysteriously Meant* (1970): 90-102; Davis P. Harding, *Milton and the Renaissance Ovid* (1946); John Hollander, *Allegory in Dante's Commedia* (1969): 114-123, 140-143; Robert Lamberton, *Homer the Theologian* (1989); Gerard O'Daly, *The Poetry of Boethius* (1991); Hugo Rahner, *Greek Myths and Christian Mystery* (1971); John Steadman, *Milton's Biblical and Classical Imagery* (1984).

UNDERWORLD (Hades). The accounts of the Underworld best known to Christians were those of Homer (*Odyssey*: 11), Virgil (*Aeneid*: 6), and Ovid (*Metamorphoses*: 4.432-511; 10.1-63). But whatever description they read, it was easy for Christians to see the Underworld as a pagan version of their own hell, a correspondence most famously elaborated in Dante's *Inferno*. But the Underworld was also interpreted, by Neo-Platonists, as a figure for the human body. Macrobius summarizes the doctrines of "the followers of Pythagoras and later those of Plato," who

declared that there are two deaths, one of the soul, the other of the creature, affirming that the creature dies when the soul leaves the body, but that the soul itself dies when it leaves the single and individual source of its origin and is allotted to a mortal body. (*On the Dream of Scipio*: 1.11.1; actually, the closest Plato himself gets to this idea is *Phaedo*: 82e: the "soul is a helpless prisoner, chained hand and foot in the body")

As Chaucer put it, "oure present worldes lyves space / Nys but a maner deth, what wey we trace" (*Parliament of Fowls*: 53-54). This death was written of as the "descent" of the soul into the body. Macrobius writes that some Platonists thus

called the body the tomb of the soul, the vaults of Pluto, and the infernal regions....The river Lethe was to them nothing more than the error committed by the soul in forgetting its former high estate before it was thrust into a body....Similarly, they thought that Phlegethon was merely the fires of our wraths and passions, that Archeron was the chagrin we experienced over having said or done something..., that Cocytus was anything that moved us to lamentation or tears, and that Styx was anything that plunged human minds into the abyss of mutual hatred. The description of the punishments, they believe, originated in human experience. (*On the Dream of Scipio*: 1.10.10-12; for the rivers Lethe, Phlegethon, Archeron, and Styx, see **THE RIVERS OF THE UNDERWORLD**)

Guillaume de Conches (*On Boethius*), Bernardus (*On Virgil's Aeneid*: 6.pref.; see also *On Virgil's Aeneid*: 1, quoted above under **AEOLUS**), Landino (*Disputationes Camuldenses*: 213-214, 218), and Fraunce (*Countesse of Pembrokes Yvychurch*:

28r), among others, paraphrase these notions. See **GLAUCUS** for more allegory relating to the descent of the soul into the body.

Because of the frequent conflation of Plutus (the god of wealth) and Pluto (the god of the Underworld), the Underworld could also be a figure for material wealth; see **PLUTO, PLUTUS**.

URANUS (Coelus, Heaven, Sky). Uranus, the Sky or Heaven, was the son and husband of Gaia, Earth. Being, as it were, permanently in her husband's embrace, Earth brought forth many children: six male and six female Titans, the three Cyclopes, and other monsters besides. Uranus kept his children pent up in the bowels of the earth until, eventually, Gaia urged them to rebel. Saturn (one of the Titans) took up the challenge and eventually gelded his father with a scythe. The blood fell to the ground, and out of it are born the Giants and the Furies. The severed member fell into the sea, and from the resulting foam Venus was born (see Hesiod, *Theogony*: 116-210; Apollodorus, *Library*: 1.1-4).

Ross provides typical moral-allegorical commentary:

Coelus and Terra make an unequal match, therefore of them proceed strange and monstrous children. The matches of Nobles and Pesants prove for the most part unfortunate and mischievous....[Further, the] Children of Heaven and of the Light, must not (as Coelus did) joyn themselves in their affections to the Earth; for of this union shall proceed nothing but Monsters, to wit, earthly and fleshly lusts, thoughts and works which will rebel against our souls, and geld us of all spiritual grace, and of our interest in the kingdome of Heaven, and then must needs be ingendred the Furies, to wit, the torments of Conscience. (*Mystagogus Poeticus*: 76-78)

But Uranus is more often to be found in the thickets of nature allegory—territory where Ross is not usually the best guide. Here is Cicero:

A great number of gods have also been derived from scientific theories about the world of nature....For example, it was an old legend of the Greeks that the Sky-God [Uranus] was mutilated by his son Saturn and that Saturn in his turn was made captive by his son Jupiter. These impious tales are merely the picturesque disguise of a sophisticated scientific theory. Those who invented them felt that the high, aethereal and fiery nature of the Sky-God should have no use for those parts of the body which require intercourse with another to beget a child. (*Nature of the Gods*: 2.63)

And Macrobius:

Saturn, as Cronus, is identified with Time. For just as the mythographers in their fables give divergent accounts of the god, so the physicists to some extent recall a true picture of him. Thus it is said that Saturn, having cut off the privy parts of his father, Heaven, threw them into the sea and that from them Venus was born and received the name Aphrodite from the foam out of which she was formed—a myth from which we are meant to understand that, while chaos lasted, times and seasons did not exist, since time has fixed measurements and those are determined by the revolution of the heavens. Cronus then is held to be the son of Heaven, and he, as we said a moment ago, is Time. And since the seeds of all things which were to be created after the heavens flowed from the heavens and since all the elements which could comprise the complete universe drew their origin from those seeds, it followed that, when the universe had been provided with all its parts and members, then, at a fixed point in time, the process whereby seeds from the heavens caused the elements of the universe to be conceived came to an end, inasmuch as the creation of those elements had now been completed. However, the power of generating an everlasting succession of living creatures passed from the heavenly fluid to Venus, so that thereafter all things were created by the intercourse of male and female. (*Saturnalia*: 1.8.6-8; see also Vatican Mythographer II: 1)

Boccaccio (*Genealogie Deorum*: 8.1) makes use of this passage in his account of Uranus and Saturn; and Boccaccio, in turn, influenced Conti's account (*Mythologie*: 10. under *Saturn*). What follows is Lemmi's paraphrase of Conti—which I quote because it is so much clearer than Conti:

God, then, first created the heavens, or Coelum, from whose motion arose time, or Saturn. Both Coelum and Saturn were said to be castrated because neither may reproduce itself. God next created the elements, of which the ether, or pervading principle of life and reproduction is represented by Jupiter. The ether and the heavenly bodies, exclusive of the earth, were created eternal; therefore Saturn or time was said to have been cast out from among them. The earth, instead, was made the seat of mortality; therefore, it was thought of as in the power of Time. On earth, the forces of disintegration seemed leagued against those of union...therefore, the Titans were imagined to be in league with Saturn against Jove. (Lemmi 1933: 53)

Lemmi also demonstrates that Conti's interpretation largely influenced Bacon's essay on "Caelum, or Beginnings" (*Wisedome of the Ancients*: 12).

For Ficino, the story of Saturn castrating his father Uranus and then being bound in turn by his own son Jupiter is a figure for the natural principle that effects cannot equal their causes, that there is necessary diminishment as we move from God down through the scale of being in the universe:

during the reign of Necessity, the inferior gods are said...to castrate or bind their parents....[T]he gifts of God necessarily degenerate from their highest perfection in the spirit which receives them. Whence it happens that that fertility of nature, certainly whole in God, but in the Angel [i.e., the Angelic Mind] diminished and in some measure mutilated, is justly said to have been castrated...by that necessity by which the effect cannot equal its cause. For thus Saturn, that is, the Angel, seems to castrate Uranus, that is, the supreme God. Also, Jupiter, that is, the World Soul, seems to bind Saturn, that is to confine to narrower limits...the power which it has received from the Angel. (*On Plato's Symposium*: 5.12; see also *Philebus Commentary*: 136, quoted under **JUPITER**)

For more on the castration of Uranus, see **SATURN**.
Bibliography: Charles W. Lemmi, *The Classical Deities in Bacon* (1933).

V

VENUS (Acidalia, Aphrodite, Citherea, Ciprogenea, Cyprian, Cyprogones, Dione, Hespera, Lucifer, the Uranian, Vesper). There were two stories about the birth of Venus. One had it that Venus was the daughter of Jupiter and Dione (e.g., Apollodorus, *Library*: 1.3.1; Venus was sometimes referred to by her mother's name, Dione). According to the other tradition, Saturn cut off his father Uranus's testicles and threw them into the sea—or, in a later variation, Jupiter cut off his father Saturn's testicles (see **SATURN**). Organs and sea begot Venus. Hesiod wrote that she was thus called

the foam-born goddess and rich-crowned Cytherea, because she grew amid the foam, and Cytherea because she reached Cythera, and Cyprogenes because she was born in billowy Cyprus....And with her went Eros, and comely Desire...and this the portion allotted to her amongst men and undying gods,—the whisperings of maidens and smiles and deceits with sweet delight and love and graciousness. (*Theogony*: 195-206; see also Rabanus, *De Universo*: 432)

Because she was born on "billowy Cyprus," Venus was sometimes called the Cyprian—and Cyprus thus came to be associated with Venus and wantonness. Boccaccio writes for example, of the famous wantonness of the inhabitants of Cyprus (*Genealogie Deorum*: 3.23); and it is no coincidence that Shakespeare's Othello runs into love difficulties after he arrives on Cyprus: "You are welcome, sir, to Cyprus," says Othello: "Goats and monkeys!" (4.1.261)—both goats and monkeys being known for their lechery.

In recognizing the power of Venus, the ancients were, of course, recognizing the power of love. Medieval and Renaissance Christians had an even larger conception of the power and importance of love. Only with reference to love could they explain Christ's sacrifice and the possibility of their own salvation. Love was at the root of all the virtues—*and* all the vices. According to Boethius's famous formulation, love was also a force of nature:

> That the universe carries out its changing process in concord and with stable faith, that the conflicting seeds of things are held by everlasting law, that Phoebus in his golden chariot brings in the shining day, that the night...is ruled by Phoebe, that the greedy sea holds back his waves within lawful bounds...—all this harmonious order of things is achieved by love which rules the earth and the seas, and commands the heavens.
>
> But if love should slack the reins, all that is now joined in mutual love would wage continual war, and strive to tear apart the world which is now sustained in friendly concord....Love binds together people joined by a sacred bond; love binds sacred marriages by chaste affections; love makes the laws which join true friends. O how happy the human race would be, if that love which rules the heavens ruled also your souls! (*Consolation of Philosophy*: 2.mt 8; see Dronke 1984: 439-475 for a history of this conception of love, from first stirrings in the Homeric Hymns down to Chaucer)

Boethius thinks of love as *literally* the force of harmony and attraction. We think of gravity as the natural force that causes bodies to be drawn toward the mass of the earth; Boethius thought of love as the natural force that caused things to bind together in fixed relation. Love was thus taken very, very seriously throughout the Middle Ages and the Renaissance. And there was consequently a remarkable range of poetry, art, and philosophy that dealt with love. Love was so important, so pregnant with implications, that even frankly erotic poetry and pictures could support weighty allegorical/philosophical interpretations—as we see, for example, in the long tradition of sober commentary on the Song of Songs. Augustine wrote a whole volume of commentary on the Song of Songs, and Reynolds, in the seventeenth century, still regarded the Song of Songs "as the most sacred and divine" book in the Bible, because it treats of "divine and Intellectual Love" (*Mythomystes*: 150). Harington was one of many who argued for the moral benefits of properly allegorical interpretation of secular love poetry; as we see in the "Apology of Poetrie," which Harington wrote as preface to his translation of Ariosto's *Orlando Furioso*.

Given all this, it is hardly surprising that Venus and Cupid occupied the imagination of Christians more than any other pagan gods. Nor is it surprising that allegorical interpretations of Venus were as diverse as they were extensive.

The Two Venuses

Much of the Venus allegory had in some way to do with a distinction between a "good" and a "bad" Venus (see Robertson 1962: 124-127; Wetherbee 1972: 115-121; Schreiber 1975; and Hollander 1977). The idea of the two Venuses goes back at least to Prodicus and Xenophanes. But Pliny (*Natural History*: 35.36) and Plato were the best-known sources for the idea. Here is the famous passage from Plato's *Symposium*:

Now, you will all agree, gentlemen, that without Love there could be no such goddess as Aphrodite. If, then, there were only one goddess of that name, we might suppose that there was only one kind of Love, but since in fact there are two such goddesses there must also be two kinds of Love. No one, I think, will deny that there are two goddesses of that name—one, the elder, sprung from no mother's womb but from the heavens themselves, we call the Uranian, the heavenly Aphrodite, while the younger, daughter of Zeus and Dione, we call Pandemus, the earthly Aphrodite. It follows, then, that Love should be known as earthly or as heavenly according to the goddess in whose company his work is done....

Now it may be said of any kind of action that the action itself, as such, is neither good nor bad....If it is done rightly and finely, the action will be good; if it is done basely, bad. And this holds good of loving, for Love is not of himself either admirable or noble, but only when he moves us to love nobly.

Well, then, gentlemen, the earthly Aphrodite's Love is a very earthly Love indeed, and does his work entirely at random. It is he that governs the passions of the vulgar. For...whoever they may love, their desires are of the body rather than of the soul....For this is the Love of the younger Aphrodite, whose nature partakes of both male and female.

But the heavenly Love springs from a goddess whose attributes have nothing of the female, but are altogether male, and...innocent of any hint of lewdness. (180d-181c)

This distinction between Venuses of earthly and heavenly love was widely known. Some mythographers followed Plato in making the foam-born Venus the heavenly Venus. Landino, for example, in his commentary on this passage from the *Symposium* writes that the Venus born of Dione is the earthly Venus; the Venus of spiritual love is "born of heaven" (*Disputationes Camuldenses*: 61). But most poets, painters, and mythographers made the foam-born Venus into the earthly Venus. Here, for example, is Fulgentius:

They have taken Venus as...the symbol of the life of pleasure....Whereby she is called Aphrodite, for in Greek *afros* is the word for foam, either because lust rises momentarily like foam and turns to nothing, or because the ejaculation of seed is foamy....Also they depict her naked, either because she sends out her devotees naked or because the sin of lust is never cloaked or because it only suits the naked. They also considered roses as under her patronage, for roses both grow red and have thorns, as lust blushes at the outrage to modesty and pricks with the sting of sin; and as the rose gives pleasure, but is swept away by the swift movement of the seasons, so lust is pleasant for a moment, but then disappears forever. Also under her patronage they place doves, for the reason that birds of this species are fiercely lecherous in their love making....She is also depicted carrying a seashell, because an organism of this kind...is always linked in open coupling through its entire body. (*Mythologies*: 2.1; John the Scot, *Annotationes in Marcianum*: 8.8, and Guillaume de Conches, *On Macrobius*: 6, also make the foam-born Venus the earthly Venus)

Much of this was, or was to become, traditional. Boccaccio paraphrased virtually every detail of Fulgentius in his own account of Venus in the *Genealogy* (3.22-23). Bernardus's account of Venus also clearly owes a debt to Plato and Fulgentius:

We read that there are indeed two Venuses, one lawful, and the other the goddess of lust. The lawful Venus is the harmony of the world, that is, the even proportion of worldly things....This subsists in the elements, in the stars, in the seasons, in living beings. The shameless Venus, however, the goddess of lust, is carnal concupiscence which is the mother of all fornications.

...Venus sometimes designates the concupiscence of the flesh and sometimes the concord of the world....Therefore whenever you find Venus as the wife of Vulcan, the mother of Jocus and Cupid, interpret her as pleasure of the flesh, which is joined with natural heat and causes pleasure and copulation. But when you read that Venus and Anchises have a son Aeneas, interpret that Venus as the harmony of the world and Aeneas as the human spirit. (*On Virgil's Aeneid*: on book 1)

This distinction was still taken seriously in the seventeenth century. Early in his medical *Treatise on Lovesickness* Ferrand warns that "we must recognize...that just as there are two Venuses, the one called Urania or the celestial...the other called Pandemia or earthly...so there are two loves, sons of these two goddesses: divine love and common or vulgar love. Metaphysicians and theologians discourse...of the first, while physicians deal with ordinary physical love" (1).

The earthly Venus did more allegorical service than the heavenly, especially during the Middle Ages. Venus "seems to pertain to excitement and fornications of all kinds," wrote Boccaccio, "and wantonness and a multitude of sexual couplings" (*Genealogie Deorum*: 3.22; see also Petrarch, *Africa*: 3.257-266). "Venus is the goddess of lust and of carnal delight," wrote the *Chess of Love* commentator (107; see also Batman, *Batman uppon Bartholomae*: 8.26; Berchorius, *Ovidius Moralizatus*: 66). One early fifteenth-century English preacher told his congregation about a picture of Venus; this was, he said, "the Picture of Lust." In this picture, the preacher continued, Venus "was painted in the form of a nude woman floating upon the waves of the sea; and she carried roses with thorns and had a bodyguard of doves" (in Owst 1966: 53). In Mantegna's *Triumph of Wisdom over the Vices* (fig. 19) we see Venus in a pool with all the vices—Dalliance, Sloth, Hate, Avarice, Suspicion—of which Misordered Desire, or Misordered Love, is the mother. Athena, the goddess of Wisdom, advances to put them all to rout (Seznec 1961: 109). The point of Bronzino's *Allegory of Venus, Cupid, Folly, and Time* (fig. 23) would seem to be that the delights of the fleshly Venus, whom we see dallying with Cupid, are pleasures of this world only, subject to Time-Saturn and the other dark figures lurking in the background. Golding was rather more explicit: "By Venus [is meant] such as of the fleshe too filthie lust are bent" ("Preface": 68). Bodin associated Venus simply with "adulteries and lust" (*Colloquium*: 190). In seventeenth-century Amsterdam, prostitutes plied their trade in the "Venus district" (e.g., Bredero, *Spanish Brabanter*: 17), as they did in many other cities. And here is Ross: "Venus was painted of old rising out of the Sea, sitting in a shell...to signifie the nature of carnal love or lust: which is begot of the Sea-froth, for...froth is quickly gone." Ross goes on to say that "Venus was painted with fetters at her feet, so no men are tyed with such strong fetters, as they who are held with the Fetters of Love" (*Mystagogus Poeticus*: 407-408; see the fetters tying Mars to Venus in Cossa's *Venus and Her Children*, fig. 26).

The Venus of spiritual love was often referred to in contrast with the Venus of earthly love—as in the long passage from Bernardus quoted above. Erasmus, for another example, wrote that Christians should follow Christ's example "in fortifying your spirit against deadly enticements and converting it to the love of the highest good and beauty. Compare those two Venuses and Cupids of Plato: honorable love and sensual, that is, divine pleasure and lustful" (*Enchiridion*: 33).

The distinction between the heavenly and the earthly Venus was particularly important to the Renaissance Neo-Platonists. Ficino's explanation may be taken as widely typical:

That Heavenly Venus was born of Uranus, without any mother. The Vulgar Venus was born of Jupiter and Dione.

The Platonists call the supreme God Uranus....But the Mind they call by several names. For sometimes they call it Saturn, sometimes Jupiter, sometimes Venus. For that Mind exists, lives, and understands. Its being they were accustomed to call Saturn; its life, Jupiter; its intelligence, Venus. The World Soul also we call, in the same way, Saturn, Jupiter, and Venus: insofar as it understands celestial things, Saturn; insofar as it moves the heavenly things, Jupiter; insofar as it procreates lower things, Venus.

The first Venus, which is in the Mind, is said to have been born of Uranus without a mother, because *mother*, to the physicists, is *matter*. But that Mind is stranger to any association with corporeal matter. The second venus, which is located in the World Soul, was born of Jupiter and Dione....They also attribute a mother to that second Venus, for this reason, that since she is infused into the Matter of the world, she is thought to have commerce with matter.

...The soul...possesses twin powers. It certainly has the power of understanding, and it has the power of procreation. These twin powers are two Venuses in us accompanied by twin loves. When the beauty of a human body first meets our eyes, our intellect, which is the first Venus in us, worships and esteems it as an image of the divine beauty, and through this is often aroused to that. But the power of procreation, the second Venus, desires to procreate a form like this....Each love is virtuous and praiseworthy, for each follows a divine image.

What is there to censure in love? Some, Ficino continues, are so "desirous of procreation" that they "neglect contemplation or attend to procreation beyond measure with women, or against the order of nature with men, or prefer the form of the body to the beauty of the soul" (*On Plato's Symposium*: 2.7). Ficino is reluctant even to mention lust—a kind of erotic love that deals only in appearances; indeed, Neo-Platonists sometimes posited a third Venus to take care of lust, which deals with the mere appearance of beauty (see, e.g., Proclus, *Sur la République*: 6.108-109.5; and see Panofsky 1969: 117).

Titian's *Sacred and Profane Love* (fig. 27) may be understood as a working out of such ideas. Indeed, Panofsky (1969: 115-119) argues that *The Double Venus* would actually be better than the traditional title, since the painting depicts not a dichotomy but a characteristically Neo-Platonic *scale* of values associated with love and beauty. Spenser's "Foure Hymnes" depict just such a scale, moving as they do from the hymns to "Love" and "Beautie" to the hymns to "Heavenly Love" and "Heavenly Beautie." As Ficino put it, "Both Venuses are honorable and praiseworthy, for both pursue the procreation of beauty, though each in her own way" (in Panofsky 1969: 115). Merely physical love—the lust that some Neo-Platonists assigned to a third Venus—is represented in Titian's painting by the unbridled horse carved in relief on the fountain: unbridled passions, bestial love (see Appendix B, "Bestialization"). Here Titian's naked Venus could have been understood as being nude in the tradition of Heb 4:13, where we read that "all things are naked and opened" to the eye of God. The other Venus is clothed with physical adornments (Panofsky 1962: 150-151).

But more often a nude Venus suggests how very beguiling sexual love can be. This was common especially in the Middle Ages: "Venus is painted nude," Vatican Mythographer III wrote sternly, "either because the sin of lechery is least hidden, or because the naked do come together" (11.1).

Venus and Bacchus

Venus and Bacchus have been linked since ancient times—because fraternity boys were not the first to discover that wine reduces rational control. Tertullian wrote that Venus and Bacchus "are close companions. The two demons of lust and drunkenness have banded together in sworn confederacy" (*Spectacles*: 10.6). Or as Fraunce put it, "Of Venus and Bacchus, Priapus was borne: lust comes from wine and delicacie" (*Countesse of Pembrokes Yvychurch*: 51r; see also, e.g., Aristotle, *Problemata*: 953b; Terence, *Eunuch*: 732; Boccaccio, *Genealogie Deorum*: 3.22; the *Chess of Love* commentary: 107, 345, 510; Ferrand, *Treatise on Lovesickness*: 37; Sandys, *Ovid*: 199; for the proverbial association of Venus, Bacchus, and Ceres—food in plenty—see **CERES**). These ideas even supported technical explanations, such as we find in Bernardus's account of just how it came about that Aeneas forgot himself in the cave with Dido:

The abundance of humors from food and drink leads to impurity of passion in the following way. In digestion there are four humors: liquid, steam, foam, and sediment. After the humors of food and drink have been digested in the cauldron of the stomach, steam is then given off, and (as the nature of lightness demands) it ascends, and, having ascended and been collected in the arteries, it becomes less dense, moves to the brain, and produces the living powers. The liquid is condensed in the members of the body. The sediment is emitted by the lower passages through defecation, and the foam is emitted partially in sweat and partially through the sense openings. But when there is too great an abundance of foam (which happens in gluttonous eating and drinking), then it is emitted through the male member, which is nearest to and below the stomach, having first been converted into sperm, that is, the male seed, for the stomach is cleared out through the nearby and lower member. Thus one reads that Venus is born of sea foam and is therefore called *afroden*. (*On Virgil's Aeneid*: on book 4)

Venus, Bacchus, Priapus, and some other gods could thus serve as allegorical figures for license and the passions, sometimes in opposition to gods representing wisdom or rational control. Ficino, for example, wrote that the mind seeking wisdom is opposed by three earthly monsters. "The first monster is nourished by the earthly Venus and Priapus," that is, by lust; the second is nourished by "Bacchus and Ceres," that is, by gluttony; the third monster is fed by "nocturnal Hecate," that is, by witchcraft and sorcery (see **HECATE**). "Therefore," Ficino continues, "Apollo must be summoned from the heavens...in order that Apollo may pierce such monsters, enemies of Pallas, with his shafts" (*Three Books on Life*: 1.7.1-12). The same point is made by a Neo-Platonic engraving after Baccio Bandinelli, *The Fray of Cupid and Apollo* (fig. 1; for more on this picture, see **APOLLO**).

Venus and Rabbits

Rabbits were known for their sexual prowess at least as early as Aristotle, who wrote that the rabbit produces "numerous offspring...and it is abundant in semen. This is shown by its hairiness. It has an excessive amount of hair; indeed, it has hair under the feet and inside the jaws, and is the only animal which does so...and for this same reason, too, men that are hairy are more prone to sexual intercourse and have more semen than men that are smooth" (*Generation of Animals*: 774a.30-b.5). Christians also associated rabbits with matters Venerian. Shipley (1984: 129) notes that the words *coney* (rabbit), *cunt*, and *know* (in the Biblical sense) all derive from the same root. There was a medieval English pun on the French *con* (Anglo-Saxon cognate, *cunt*, Chaucer's *queynte*) and *conin*, rabbit (Robertson 1962: 113). In fact, at the time of the King James translation of the Bible, the pronunciation of the vowels in *cunt* and *coney* was so close that a pious euphemizing glossator advised: "It is familiarly pronounced cunny, but coney is proper for solemn reading" (in Shipley 1984: 129). Thus Marlowe's lusty Ithamore says to his love, "Let music rumble, / Whilst I in thy incony lap do tumble" (*Jew of Malta*: 4.6.26-27). Probably, there are thus coy sexual overtones when Shakespeare's Rosalind replies to Orlando's inquiry if she be "native of this place?" "As the cony that you see dwell where she is kindled" (*As You Like It*: 3.2.338-339). The same kinds of associations were there for *hare*—as we see in Shakespeare's virtuoso word play on hares, whores, hoar, and hair (*Romeo and Juliet*: 2.3.135-142; see Partridge 1960: 124-125). In Ariosto, the lecherous Alcyna's Isle abounds in hares and coneys (*Orlando Furioso*: 6.22).

It is not surprising, then, that rabbits should have been so often associated with Venus. On the day Christine de Pizan's youthful Duke first falls in love, he prays first to Venus, then goes off to hunt rabbits—and then falls in love (*Duke of True Lovers*: 71-243). The youthful duke was coney catching for the same reason that the rabbits are the animals closest to Cupid's throne on the title page of Jacob Cats' *Proteus, ofte Minne-beelden Verandert in Sinne-beelden* (fig. 8). We also see rabbits in front of Venus's throne in Cossa's *Venus and Her Children* (fig. 26); and in an engraving in a 1614 French translation of Philostratus's *Images* (41) a happy band of putti hunt a rabbit in front of an image of Venus.

For more on the allegory of rabbit hunting, see **ADONIS**.

Venus's Doves and Sparrows

"Doves are sacred to Venus," wrote Vatican Mythographer III, "because these birds...are supremely fervid copulators" (11.2). This avidity was well known (see also, e.g., Isidore, *Etymologiarum*: 12.7.61; Pictorius, *Apotheoseos*: 59). Alanus, for example, writes that doves labor so hard at the "sport of Cypris" that they are "drunk with the sweet Dionean evil" (*Complaint of Nature*: pr. 1.255); Dante compares the *de casibus* lovers Paolo and Francesca to doves (*Inferno*: 5.82-87); and see also the doves in Cossa's *Venus and Her Children* (fig. 26). Shakespeare's Venus has "Two strengthless doves" to draw her chariot through the sky (*Venus and Adonis*: 153).

Venus was sometimes associated with sparrows, which were also known for their sexual appetites (see, e.g., Catullus, *Carmina*: 2, 3; Pliny, *Natural History*: 10.52). Chaucer's Summoner, for example, is "lecherous as a sparwe" ("General Prologue": 626; see also Pictorius, *Theologia Mythologica*: 17v.; Lyly, *Campaspe*: 2.2.51). (But sparrows were not always figures for lust. Hugh of Fouilloy's *Aviarium*: 34 took into consideration that the sparrow nested in high inaccessible places: "He is therefore called a recluse, because he is far removed form earthly desires.")

The Red Rose as Venus's Flower

Red has been the color of the passions at least since earthy Esau emerged from Rebecca's womb "red, all over like an hairy garment" (Gen 25:25). Since red was associated with the passions, red was naturally Venus's color. Lydgate wrote that she wears "A cote y-lacyd al of Rede" (*Reson and Sensuallyte*: 1556). And her roses are red as well: the roses are red in Cossa's *Venus and Her Children* (fig. 26) and in Titian's *Sacred and Profane Love* (fig. 27); see also Boccaccio (*Genealogie Deorum*: 3.22) and the "shower of roses" that pours down upon Poliziano's Venus and Mars during their love play (*Stanze*: 1.122). Shakespeare's Venus led Mars "prisoner in a red rose chain" (*Venus and Adonis*: 110).

Van Mander explained that Venus is crowned with roses because "the rose quickly withers, meaning that the pleasure of love withers quickly" (*Wtbeeldinghen der Figuren*: 114r). But Ross's explanation may be taken as more widely typical: "for as no flower so much refresheth the spirits, & delights our smell as the Rose; nothing doth so much sweeten and delight our life as Love; but the Rose is not without prickles, nor love without cares" (*Mystagogus Poeticus*: 85; see also Vatican Mythographer III: 11.1).

Much the same point was made by associating Venus and Cupid with the sweetness of honey and the sting of the bees (see **CUPID**; see Adams 1991).

The Cestus of Venus

Statius wrote that Venus, in a vengeful mood, laid aside her "marital girdle" before she sent "Hatred and Frenzy and Discord" to roam the marriage chambers on the isle of Lemnos (*Thebaid*: 5.62-76). And so grew up a tradition that Venus's *cestus*, or girdle, suggested chaste love. Lactantius Placidus wrote that adulterers may be called "incestuous" because they have torn the bond of the marriage "cest" (On Statius: 261). "Venus's girdle is called Cestus," wrote Boccaccio (Genealogie Deorum: 4.47), but "Venus did not wear this girdle...except in honest marriage" (3.22)—that is, she laid the Cestus aside for her adulteries. Spenser explains the workings of the Cestus at some length: the "girdle gave the vertue of chast love, / And wifehood true, to all that did it beare." It is a girdle which can "bind lascivious desire"; and so, when Venus chose "To visite her beloved Paramoure, / The God of warre, she from her middle loosd" the Cestus and left it "in her secret bowre" (Faerie Queene: 4.5.2-6).

But there was another tradition, which understood the Cestus as a love charm. It was in this tradition that de Lorris's Venus is girdled (Romance of the Rose: 3435) as she incites the lover. Burton cites no fewer than seven authorities who agree that "Venus' enchanted girdle" contained "love-toys and dalliance, pleasantness, sweetness, persuasions, subtleties, gentle speeches, and all witchcraft to enforce love" (Anatomy of Melancholy: 3.2.2.5).

Venus in Nature Allegory

There were many versions of Venus's role in nature allegory, but they are all based on the idea that Venus was a figure for generation. Macrobius, for example, interpreted the story of the foam-born Venus as nature-allegory, as representing the origin of sexual procreation, "the power of generating an everlasting succession of living creatures...by the intercourse of male and female" (Saturnalia: 1.8.8).

In this tradition, Venus was essentially morally neutral—unless or until she was "corrupted." This corruption is what Dame Nature complains of in Alanus's Complaint of Nature: "I change laughter to tears, joy to sorrow, applause to lament, mirth to grief, when I behold the decrees of Nature in abeyance; when society is ruined and destroyed by the monster of sensual love; when Venus, fighting against Venus, makes men women; when with her magic art she unmans men" (mtr. 1.1-5). For Alanus—and for Bernardus in the Cosmographia—there was a group of divinities responsible for promulgating and enforcing the laws of Nature: Dame Nature was a personification of the Law of Nature; Genius was a personification of the inclinations that derive from Natural Law as these are felt by the individual (instinct, as we might say); and Venus was the personification of the inclination to procreation in particular. This is the Venus we see at the center of the fruitful garden in Botticelli's Primavera (fig. 13)—which seems to have been a marriage painting (Lightbown 1989: 122-127). She stands in front of a myrtle, a plant associated with marriage and Venus.

But alas, this Venus of procreation can be corrupted: Sexual desire can be divorced from procreation; and thus it was that lechery was thought of as unnatural, as being opposed to the Law of Nature. This Venus is destructive rather than procreative. We see this, for example, in Bruegel's engraving of Lechery (fig. 20), where the fires in the background and the blasted egg (the egg being usually a symbol of the renewal of life) in the foreground suggest the destructive potential of lechery. The Venus associated with such destructive love is, again, the "bad"

Venus. Venus can be understood in these terms in Alanus and in the long line of poems which looked to *The Complaint of Nature* for inspiration, including de Meun's *Romance of the Rose*, Gower's *Confessio Amantis*, and Chaucer's *Parliament of Fowls*. As Conti put it, "Venus is the hidden desire for coitus which nature has instilled to assure procreation" (*Mythologie*: 4.14).

For more on Venus as the inclination to procreation, see **NATURE, GENIUS**.

Other Stories Involving Venus

For allegorical interpretations of the love of Venus and Mars, see **MARS**; for Venus and Adonis, see **ADONIS**; for Paris's judgment of the contest between Venus, Juno, and Athena, see **PARIS**.

Names of Venus the Planet

Venus was the morning star (Lucifer) and the evening star (Vesper, or Hespera); see, for example, Bartholomaeus (*On the Properties of Things*: 8.14). Hesperus was the son of Atlas, swept up into the sky to become the evening star. But the evening star could also be associated with Venus; thus the feminine ending, Hespera; see, for example, Boccaccio (*Genealogie Deorum*: 3.22).

Bibliography: Alison Adams, "Cupid and the Bees," *Emblematica*, 5 (1991): 171-76; Peter Dronke, *The Medieval Poet and His World* (1984); A. C. Hamilton, *The Spenser Encyclopedia* (1990): under *Venus*; Robert Hollander, *Boccaccio's Two Venuses*, (1977); Richard Kay, *Dante's Christian Astrology* (1994): 66-97; Ronald Lightbown, *Botticelli: Life and Work* (1989); G. R. Owst, *Literature and Pulpit in Medieval England* (1966); Erwin Panofsky, *Studies in Iconology* (1962); Panofsky, *Problems in Titian, Mostly Iconographic* (1969); Eric Partridge, *Shakespeare's Bawdy* (1960); D. W. Robertson, Jr., *Preface to Chaucer* (1962); Earl G. Schreiber, "Venus in the Medieval Mythographic Tradition," *JEGP*, 74 (1975): 519-535; Jean Seznec, *The Survival of the Pagan Gods* (1961); Joseph Shipley, *The Origins of English Words* (1984); Peggy Muñoz Simonds, "Alciati's Two Venuses as Letter and Spirit of the Law," in Peter M. Daly, *Andrea Alciato and the Emblem Tradition* (1989); Winthrop Wetherbee, *Platonism and Poetry in the Twelfth Century* (1972).

VESTA (Hestia) was the daughter of Saturn and Rhea and the sister of Jupiter and Juno. She was thus one of the twelve primary Olympian deities. Courted by Apollo and Neptune, she took a vow of chastity—for which Jupiter rewarded her by making her the goddess of the hearth, so that she would be worshipped in every household. Servius mentions that Vesta, as the goddess of the hearth, was also invoked whenever sacrificial fires were lit (*In Virgilii Aeneidos*: 1.292). Janus (as the god of doorways, or openings) would thus be invoked at the beginning of religious services, and Vesta at the end.

Elsewhere Servius writes that "Vesta is the goddess of the fire which is above the earth" (*In Virgilii Aeneidos*: 2.296), the fiery ether, which was assumed to be the element of the heavens (see also Ovid, *Fasti*: 6.291-292). Eleven hundred years later we still find mythographers following Servius. Van Mander, for example: "It should be known," he wrote, that Vesta was "the fire of the heavens" (*Wtlegginghe op den Metamorphosis*: 3v; see also Pictorius, *Apotheoseos*: 65; Conti, *Mythologie*: 8.19). We see Hercules driving his chariot up into this divine, fiery ether at the top of the title page (fig. 16) of Sandys' *Ovid's Metamorphosis, Englished, Mythologiz'd, and Represented in Figures* (for more on this title page, see **APOLLO** and **MINERVA**).

But there was also a tradition which made Vesta the goddess of merely earthly fire—or even of the earth itself. Ross:

> By Vesta they meant sometimes the earth it self, and in this respect she is called the mother of Saturn, for she is the mother of all the gods; And sometimes they meant the fire within the bowles of the earth, or the natural heat by which all earthly creatures are generated and fomented; so Vesta is the daughter of Saturn and Rhea, because this fire or native heat, is begot by Time in the earth, and of the earth. (*Mystagogus Poeticus*: 410; see also van Mander, *Wtlegginghe op den Metamorphosis*: 3v)

Vesta's chastity—and the chastity of the Vestal Virgins, who were her priestesses—was proverbial. Greene, for example, has a certain wayward girl rebuked in this way: "shall now all the world wonder at thee for thy vanities, hast thou vowed thy selfe to Vesta, and wilt thou runne after Venus?" ("Perymedes": 34).

VIRGIL was considered by Medieval and Renaissance Christians to be one of the great authorities. His poetry was the backbone of Latin studies in the Medieval schools (Curtius 1963: 36). Indeed, he was considered even to be a prophet, albeit a pagan one (e.g., de Lubac 1964: 2.233-262). His standing as a prophet was largely due to his fourth *Eclogue* (6-25), which predicts the return of "the Virgin" and the birth of "the child, under whom the iron brood shall first cease, and a golden race spring up throughout the world." A "glorious age" would then begin, an age in which all "traces of our guilt shall become void," and then "The serpent, too, shall perish." Virgil, of course, was writing of Caesar Augustus, but Augustine interpreted the lines as a prophecy of Christ's coming (*City of God*: 10.27); and after Augustine, it seemed obvious to Christians that Virgil was prophesying the birth of the Christ child. Thus it was that Virgil often appears in Christian art alongside the Sibyls, who were also regarded as pagan prophets (see **SIBYLS**). Virgil appears with the Sibyls in the Miracle plays, for example in the *Mystery of the Nativity* played in the Abbey of St. Martial, Limoges (Comparetti 1908: 310).

Christians attributed a wide range of learning to Virgil; he was a philosopher, a rhetorician, a magus, even a necromancer. Small wonder, then, that early commentators on Dante interpreted the Virgil of the *Divine Comedy* as Reason or, as Pietro Allegheri put it, "rational judgement" or "reason" (*Commentarium*: 166). Caxton's *Mirrour of the World* provides a sketch of what was known about Virgil:

"Virgyl, the wyse philosophre born in Itaile, was to fore the comyng of Our Lord Jhesu Cryst. He sett not lytil by the vii sciences, ffor he travaylled and studyed in them the most part of his tyme, so moche that by astronomye he made many grete mervaylles" (*Mirrour of the World*: 12). Virgil even invented automata! Caxton's *Mirrour* mentions among other ingenious devices a mechanical fly, a brass horse, and a prophesying head, "which answerd of alle that which he was demanded of, and of that which shold happen and come in therthe." Such notions were both widespread and long lived. For example, Caxton's *Mirrour* is a 1480 translation of the *Image du Monde*, which had been widely read in France for 200 years—and there was a new London edition of Caxton's *Mirrour* as late as 1527. And Caxton was hardly alone in his estimation of Virgil. Spargo fills his book on *Virgil the Necromancer* (1934) with some 450 pages of such lore.

With all these wonders to consider, one nearly forgets that Virgil was also a poet. But he was, in fact, the model poet. Virgil wrote first his *Eclogues* (his pastoral poetry), then the *Georgics* (his farm poetry), and finally his epic, the *Aeneid*. This order was confirmed by some anonymous introductory verses that attached themselves to the *Aeneid*, lines which were long thought to have been written by Virgil himself: "I who once piped a song on a slender reed; who, quitting the woods, then caused the nearby fields to obey the ever greedy tiller of the soil—a work pleasing to farmers; I now sing the dread weapons of Mars" (in Curtius 1963: 231). Medieval readers recognized here an order rising out of the nature of things: Virgil began with the low style, progressed to the middle style, and finally wrote in the high style. (This notion of the hierarchy of styles derives ultimately from Cicero; for an account of the hierarchy of styles, see Donker and Muldrow 1982: 108-118.) This hierarchy of poetical genres confirmed and recapitulated the three social ranks: shepherd, farmer, soldier (Curtius 1963: 231). Virgil's poetic progression was still recognized as the ideal by Spenser, as we see in his Epistle to Harvey, which prefaces the *Shepheardes Calender* (for more on the Virgilian Career see Watkins 1995: 64-69).

The influence of Virgil's poetry was pervasive in the Middle Ages and the Renaissance (see, e.g., Huppé 1990). And Virgil's poetry, especially his *Aeneid*, was usually interpreted allegorically. Virgil was read in this way from Servius in the fourth century down to the seventeenth century, when Reynolds wrote that Virgil had written "golden fictions" that hid their "higher sence" from "the vulgar" (*Mythomystes*: 149; for typical allegorical interpretations of the *Aeneid*, see **AENEAS**). It was, of course, possible to interpret Virgil allegorically without assuming that Virgil was an allegorical poet. Many readers, like Dante, assumed that the poem was history; it could thus be understood allegorically for the same reason that the Bible can be so understood: God arranged the events of history in such a way as to make them meaningful (see, e.g., Hollander 1969: 57-103).

But even this philosopher/poet/prophet was not above temptation. There was a well-known apocryphal story about Virgil in the basket. Here is a thirteenth-century Latin version of the story, the earliest version known: "Virgil is enamoured of Nero's beautiful daughter and begs for her love. She invites him to appear at night at the foot of her tower, where, divested of his clothing, he enters a basket which she has lowered, is pulled up halfway and left suspended until the next day" (in Spargo 1934: 145). Hanging there in his basket, he is made fun of by the townspeople. Thus it was that Virgil—like Aristotle in the story of Aristotle and Phyllis (see **ARISTOTLE**)—could be understood as an example of a man led astray by his passions (see, e.g., Brant, *Ship of Fools*: 13). The moral was obvious: even very wise men like Virgil and Aristotle had to beware of the enticements of the flesh.

Bibliography: Domenico Comparetti, *Vergil in the Middle Ages* (1966 [1908]); Ernst Robert Curtius, *European Literature and the Latin Middle Ages* (1963); Henri de Lubac, *Exégèse Médiévale: Les Quarte Sense de L'Ecriture* (1964); Marjorie Donker and George Muldrow, *Dictionary of Literary-Rhetorical Conventions of the English Renaissance* (1982); Robert Hollander, *Allegory in Dante's Commedia* (1969); Bernard F. Huppé, "Aeneas's Journey to the New Troy," in Aldo Bernardo and Saul Levin, *The Classics in the Middle Ages* (1990); John W. Spargo, *Virgil the Necromancer: Studies in Virgilian Legends* (1934); John Watkins, *The Specter of Dido: Spenser and Virgilian Epic* (1995).

VULCAN (Hephaestus, the Lemnian, Mulciber). Vulcan was the god of fire and of the forge. He was already a standard allegorical figure for fire among the Greek Stoics and Neo-Platonics (Lamberton 1989: 51; see, e.g., Philo, *On Providence*: 2.41). But Jupiter could also represent fire, and so a distinction was sometimes made between Jupiter as a kind of celestial (or Platonic Form of) fire and Vulcan as a lower, material kind of fire. Vatican Mythographer III (10.4) mentions this. For another example, here is the *Chess of Love* commentary:

we should know that by Vulcan the poets intend fire or the god of fire. For in each of the notable things of nature they placed a god who governs the thing. Certainly the poets did not mean by Vulcan the elementary fire [figured by Jupiter] in its pure, clean, subtle species that is under the heaven of the moon, but mainly meant the material fire we use, which is here among us, made of common or foreign matter....But elementary fire is subtle, transparent, and pure, and somewhat like the sky without luminosity. But all such fires joined to foreign matter shine by nature because of their grosser nature....And the poets pretend that Vulcan is the son of Jupiter and Juno, i.e., of fire and air, because he depends on these two elements. (497-498)

Spenser also links Vulcan with the grosser form of fire (*Faerie Queene*: 7.7.26); and Ross refers to this allegorical tradition in order to explain Vulcan's traditional lameness: "Vulcan was deformed, and for this was thrust out of heaven, to shew the grosseness of our fire being compared to the Celestial fire, and therefore not fit to have any place among these sublimated celestial bodies or quintessences" (*Mystagogus Poeticus*: 416). Sometimes Vulcan-as-inferior-fire could be a figure for the sun (e.g., Sandys, *Ovid*: 202). But even in this case, he was non-celestial fire.

It is not surprising, then, that Vulcan should have been associated with the fires of the passions—"the fire of obscene cupidity," as Vatican Mythographer III puts it (10.4). Here again is the *Chess of Love* commentary: "Certainly the poets sometimes intend by Vulcan a kind of furious heat, such as the heat of nature and of concupiscence, or the fury of jealousy, or of some person strongly moved by anger. And therefore the ancient poets pretend that Venus carries a burning brand. Vulcan is sometimes taken as this brand" (499). Ficino (*Philebus Commentary*: 242) also interprets Vulcan as a figure for sexual desire.

The *Chess of Love* commentary elsewhere explains a related bit of nature allegory:

the heat that moves and inclines us to concupiscence and lust, and even to anger....For the moment, then, we can say that the poets pretended that Venus is the wife of Vulcan because she is of a feminine complexion. And especially because she is abundant in moisture, while Vulcan is abundant in heat. And these two qualities joined together are like the natural marriage of hot heat and moisture that created all things, according to ancient philosophers. And by this it appears that the marriage can be taken to refer to the planet Venus because its influence is to make moisture, which is generative of natural things when united with heat, as was said, as are the male and female who unite with each other. And this too could be well reconciled with to Venus because of the concupiscence mentioned above. For ardent and furious heat that moves and incites us to this, overcoming the moisture that nature provided, is the principal cause of the deed of generation. (350; see also Bernardus, *On Virgil's Aeneid*: 1)

This interpretation is also related to a tradition that went back to Hesiod (*Theogony*: 924-928): Hera was resentful when Zeus gave birth to Athena out of his head, without the aid of a woman. And so Hera bore Hephaestus, without the aid of a man. Berchorius interprets the tradition in this way:

I say that Jupiter signifies the intellect and Juno the will and desire. These are the two powers in the soul and even though they are joined they do not yield fruit because they are different from one another. They are never able to produce one and the same action. Nevertheless, each of these powers wants to test if it can bear fruit by itself. Jupiter from the head of his imagination produced Pallas—that is wisdom—but Juno—that is desire—generated Vulcan the god of fire—that is the ardor of concupiscence. He fell to earth because of avarice, was joined to Venus because of luxury, and is always lame because of his sinister intention and malice....In short, Vulcan's—that is concupiscence's—ugliness is so great that he is hurled from heaven with the evil angels and is received on earth—that is among sinners and earthly people. (*Ovidius Moralizatus*: 204; see also "Le Commentaire de Copenhague de l'*Ovide Moralisé*": 402-403)

Bernardus explains that we must understand Venus differently, depending on whether she is associated with Vulcan:

One must remember in this book as well as in other allegorical works that there are equivocations and multiple significations, and therefore one must interpret poetic fictions in diverse ways. For example..., Venus sometimes designates the concupiscence of the flesh and sometimes the concord of the world....Diverse names can signify the same thing....Therefore, whenever you find Venus as the wife of Vulcan, the mother of Jocus and Cupid, interpret her as pleasure of the flesh, which is joined with natural heat and causes pleasure and copulation. (*On Virgil's Aeneid*: 1)

Another myth had it that Vulcan loved Athena. Here is Fulgentius's version of the story and part of his interpretation:

When Vulcan made the thunderbolt for Jove, he accepted a promise from Jove that he might take anything he wished. He asked for Minerva in marriage; Jove ordered Minerva to defend her maidenhood by force of arms. When they were to enter the nuptial bed, Vulcan in the struggle spilt his seed upon the floor, and from it was born Erichthonius....They explained Vulcan as the fire of rage, whereby Vulcan is named as the heat of desire; he made the lightning for Jove, that is, he stirred up rage. They chose him to be the husband of Minerva because even rage is somewhat depleted for the wise. She defended her maidenhood by the force of arms, that is, all wisdom and strength of mind protects the integrity of its own habits against fury. (*Mythologies*: 2.11; see also Vatican Mythographer II: 40)

Fraunce provides what may be taken as a summary statement of much of this Vulcan allegory:

his feete are lame, and so is our earthly fire, impure, and not able to ascend upwards directly, but shaketh and limpeth, this way, and that way, by reason of the terrene corruption: Or, if you take Vulcan for the naturall heate of mans body, then he may be therefore sayd to be lame, because this vitall heate doth increase, decrease, and alter, according to the difference of mens ages, and diversity of the constitutions and complections of their bodies, and is never one and the same, or long like itself....Vulcan was maryed to Venus: for without the naturall heate, no procreation. Vulcan struggleth with Minerva, but to no purpose; for, of that aethereal fire, and subtile part of the skie, figured by Minerva, nothing is produced: But Vulcan, that is, the grosse and more earthly heate, powring himselfe on the earth, is the author of divers and sundry procreations. (*Countesse of Pembrokes Yvychurch*: 40v-41r)

Because of such associations, Vulcan could stand with Venus and Bacchus in general opposition to Apollo and Diana: the forces of license and the passions in opposition to control, reason, and temperance. We see this, for example, in a Neo-Platonic engraving after Baccio Bandinelli, *The Fray of Cupid and Apollo* (fig. 1; for more on this engraving, see **APOLLO, MINERVA**).

Because of Vulcan's association with the volcanic island of Lemnos (e.g., Homer, *Iliad*: 1.590-594), he was sometimes called the Lemnian; as the God of the Forge, he was Mulciber.

Vulcan could also be understood as an *exemplum* of the jealous old husband, usually in interpretations of the story of Vulcan trapping Venus and Mars in his net; see **MARS**.

Because winter was associated with the making of fires, Vulcan could also serve as an allegorical figure for winter (for a list of paintings that work in this way, see Reid 1993: 468-469).

Finally, I cannot resist quoting Ross's indulgence in personal allegory, the last lines of his *Mystagogus Poeticus*: "They make Vulcan lame and slow-paced: but I am sure he came too nimble upon all my Papers, Manuscripts, and Notes, which I have been gathering these forty years, and consumed them all on a sudden. I wish he had been abed with Venus, when he seized on my study...; but he was always an enemy to Minerva, and he hath shewed it by destroying my Papers" (418).

Bibliography: Robert Lamberton, *Homer the Theologian* (1989); Jane Davidson Reid, *The Oxford Guide to Classical Mythology in the Arts, 1300-1990s* (1993).

X

XANTHIPPE was the famously shrewish wife of Socrates (e.g., Plato, *Phaedrus*: 60a). Her name thus came to be attached to lists of shrewish wives. Chaucer's Jankyn includes her in his list of shrewish wives ("Wife of Bath's Tale": 727-732), and he paraphrases as well Jerome's dyspeptic remarks on Xanthippe (*Against Jovinianus*: 1.48). Gower's description of Socrates' relations with Xanthippe is in the same tradition (*Confessio Amantis*: 3:639-698). In Peele's *The Old Wives Tale*, we find a shrew named Zantippa. In some accounts Socrates bore all this so well that he became an *exemplum* of patience (Osberg 1991).

But there was at least one exception in the writing about Xanthippe: The feminist Christine de Pizan wrote about her as a loving wife to Socrates (*City of Ladies*: 2.21.1).

Socrates was not the only wise man to have woman trouble; see ARISTOTLE and VIRGIL.

Bibliography: Richard H. Osberg, "Clerkly Allusiveness: Griselda, Xanthippe, and the Woman of Samaria," *Allegorica*, 12 (1991): 17-27.

Z

ZEPHYR was the West Wind, son of Eos and Astraeus and the brother of Boreas, the North Wind. Zephyr was the wind associated with spring, the wind that blows when the green force drives, as we find in the opening lines of *The Canterbury Tales*:

> Whan that Aprill with his shoures soote
> The droghte of March hath perced to the roote,
> And bathed every veyne in swich licour
> Of which engendred is the flour;
> Whan Zephirus eek with his sweete breeth
> Inspired hath in every holt and heeth
> The tendre croppes, and the yonge sonne
> Hath in the Ram his halfe cours yronne,
> And smale foweles maken melodye,
> That slepen al the nyght with open eye—
> So priketh hem in hir corages—
> Thanne longen folk to goon on pilgrimages.
>
> ("General Prologue": 1-12)

Zephyr could thus be associated with spring, and so with renewal—physical or spiritual. Some of Chaucer's pilgrims are interested in the one, some the other. The Wife of Bath, for example, longs to be "refresshed" ("Wife of Bath's Tale": 38) in the physical sense. Hesiod would have understood. He wrote that the wine is sweetest when Zephyr blows, the flowers most fragrant, "women are most wanton, but men are feeblest" (*Works and Days*: 582-596). Zephyr was thus associated with the tenderness of love, but also with the dangers of desire (Wilhelm 1965: 8-9). Spenser writes of Zephyr in both connections. There is the "Sweete breathing Zephyrus" appropriate to such a marriage poem as the "Prothalamion"

(1); and there is the Zephyr who "lowd whisteled / His treble, a straunge kind of harmony"—harmonizing with the alluring song of the Sirens "Which Guyons senses softly tickeled" (*Faerie Queene*: 2.12.33). Boccaccio (*Genealogie Deorum*: 4.61) writes of Zephyr in much the same way.

For Zephyr's rape of Chloris—who was then transformed into Flora—and for Zephyr's role in Botticelli's *Primavera* (fig. 13), see **FLORA**.

Bibliography: Jane Chance, "Chaucer's Zephirus," in Chance, *The Mythographic Art* (1990): 177-198; James J. Wilhelm, *The Cruelest Month: Spring, Nature, and Love in Classical and Medieval Lyrics* (1965).

Appendix A: Music

After Saul fell from God's favor, his mind became diseased, full of dark imaginings: "And it came to pass, when the evil spirit from God was upon Saul, that David took an harp, and played with his hand: so Saul was refreshed, and was well, and the evil spirit departed from him" (1 Sam 16:23). This story assumes what many ancient cultures assumed, that music can cure, that music can affect human beings profoundly. The followers of Pythagoras believed in musical cures (see **MARSYAS**), for example; and Asclepiades, a physician at work in Bithynia in the first century B.C. was famous for his musical cures, especially of madness (Hoeninger 1984).

Such ideas achieved wide currency in Medieval and Renaissance Europe. In *The Consolation of Philosophy*, for example, Lady Philosophy begins her cure of Boethius by substituting her own Muses for those Muses that excite the passions "with their sweet poison" (1.pr 2). Gower, meditating upon England's social discord just a few years after the Peasants' Revolt, hoped for another Arion, a singer who would make England once again a harmonious whole (*Confessio Amantis*: pro.1053-1075). There survives an account from the fifteenth century of actual musical therapy. Hugo van der Goes, the great Flemish painter, fell victim to what we would now call a mental breakdown. Hugo's half-brother Nicholas wrote that this was a "strange disorder of his imagination. He cried out incessantly that he was doomed and condemned to eternal damnation." So distraught was Hugo that he had to be forcibly restrained. Since Hugo had taken monastic vows, he was put under the care of the Prior of his monastery. This Prior prescribed music: "Seeing this sick man and learning all that had happened he presumed that brother Hugo was suffering from the same complaint that had once afflicted King Saul, and reflecting that Saul's disorder had yielded when David plied his harp, he immediately gave orders to play music frequently in Hugo's presence." Alas, this therapy was unavailing: "his condition did not improve; he continued to talk unreasonably, and to consider himself a child of perdition" (in Wittkower 1969: 109).

Music therapy served Shakespeare's characters better than it had brother Hugo. Prospero calls up music as a part of his healing charm:

A solemn air, and the best comforter
To an unsettled fancy, cure thy brains,
Now useless, boil'd within thy skull!
                    (*Tempest*: 5.1.58-60)

Pericles is brought up out of his severe melancholia by his daughter's song (*Pericles*: 5.1.44-95). And late in *King Lear* a physician undertakes to cure the old king's ravaged mind, his "untuned and jarring sense" (4.7.16). The sleeping Lear is carried to a tent where the doctor calls for music. When Lear awakes, his jarring senses have been retuned (see Hoeniger 1984 for a brief history of musical curing as this relates to Shakespeare).

In effecting such cures, it was important of course to pick the right kind of music. Various "modes" of music were carefully described and their effects noted (for Plato on the modes, see **MARSYAS**). Music in the "Dorian mode" was slow and temperate; such music was conducive to virtue. Music in the quick-paced Phrygian mode was thought to excite the passions. Phrygian music could excite lust, for example. But since it could also excite the wrathful passions, Phrygian music was useful and appropriate on the battlefield. It could make men bolder. Music in the Lydian mode excited joy and desire. In Spenser's *Faerie Queene*, for example, Sir Guyon comes upon the Castle of Delight. This is a place of temptation, a place of easeful pleasures: "And all the while sweet Musicke did divide / Her looser notes with Lydian harmony" (*Faerie Queene*: 3.1.40). The virtuous Guyon, of course, disdained "such lascivious disport."

Medieval and Renaissance Christians recognized Pythagoras as the great originator of such ideas. Pythagoras had discovered that if two strings, one twice as long as the other, are plucked under the same conditions, the longer string will sound one octave lower than the shorter. If the strings are in a ratio of two to three—one string, for example, two feet long, the other three—they will sound a fifth. If they are in a three to four relation, they will sound a fourth. Pythagoras had thus discovered that what the ear hears as a consonance can be *measured* in space. Musical consonances can be expressed in units of measure—feet, inches, meters. An octave (or an eighth) could be expressed as a ratio: 1:2. A fifth would be 2:3. A fourth, 3:4. (Those without musical training might think of the musical scale: Do, Re, Me, Fa, Sol, La, Ti, Do. The second Do will be one octave higher than the first. An octave is thus eight notes. Or think of hitting eight consecutive white keys anywhere on a piano: The eighth key will be one octave away from the first you hit. The octave, fifth, and fourth are consonances; a seventh is a dissonance.)

This opened up a vast area of inquiry and speculation. Following Pythagoras, it came widely to be assumed that "all is number." *Every*thing in creation was thought to arise from, to be based upon, to be composed of, *number*. This dictum and its many elaborations were carried down through the Middle Ages and into the Renaissance by the Neo-Platonists and by Augustine (e.g., *On Music*) and Augustine's theological descendants (e.g., Boethius, *De Musica*). Even sins, virtues, and human relations could be explained in terms of number and ratios and so in terms of harmonies and dissonances. We find a clear statement of this in one of Cassiodorus's sixth-century letters:

Musical science, then, is diffused through all the acts of our life if we before all else obey the commands of the Creator and observe with pure hearts the rules which he has established. For whatever we say or whatever inward effect is caused by the beating of our pulse is joined by musical rhythms to the power of harmony. Music is indeed the science of proper modulation; and if we observe the good life, we are always associated with this excellent science. When we sin, however, we no longer have music. The sky and the earth and everything which is accomplished in them by the supernal stewardship are not without the science of music; for Pythagoras is witness to the fact that this world was founded through the instrumentality of music and can be governed by it. (*Introduction to Divine and Human Readings*: 190)

Cassiodorus means this literally. To live properly is to live in such a way as to preserve the proper relations—ratios—within the individual, within human communities, and with God.

Early in the twelfth century, Hugh of St. Victor elaborated upon this idea of "human music" (*Didascalicon*: 2.11-12). He explained that human beings are made up of various parts, dimensions, and characteristics. Every human being has a body and a soul, for example. The body and the soul are in a certain relationship to each other. If there is thus a relationship—what Pythagoras would recognize as a ratio—the body existing in a certain proportion, the soul in a certain proportion, one sometimes stronger, sometimes weaker, then body and soul make a kind of music. Human music. Every human body is made up of certain fluids, called "humors." These humors exist in certain measurable proportions—just so much bile, so much phlegm, so much blood. If there are proportions, there is music. Human music. And human beings possess certain virtues—but each of these virtues may be thought of, then, in terms of proportions. And so again there is music.

David playing upon his lyre for Saul, the physician prescribing music for Lear—such curing could thus be understood, literally, as a kind of "tuning," as harmonizing the individual. This kind of thinking was important to artists, ministers, poets, and architects. Because all is number, they could all think of their work in musical terms, and so they could hope to "tune" individuals and—like Gower in the *Confessio Amantis*—whole societies. Architects could design cathedrals and even private houses in such a way as to incorporate the ratios of musical consonances, the ratios of the human proportions—and the ratios that the human microcosm shares with the macrocosm (see Fludd's *Relationship of Man to the Macrocosm*, fig. 21). These ratios also corresponded to ideal human proportions, of course, and so by merely entering into a properly proportioned building, one's soul could be tuned (Wittkower 1971: 101-142).

Poetry was often said to work in the same way and according to the same assumptions. It was in these terms, for example, that Ficino explained the effects of the Fall: "the whole soul is filled with discord and dissonance." But, Ficino continues, divinely inspired poetry can reverse the effects of the Fall: "the first need is for the poetic madness, which through musical tones arouses what is sleeping, through harmonic sweetness calms what is in turmoil, and finally, through the blending of different things, quells dissonant discord and tempers the various parts of the soul" (*On Plato's Symposium*: 7.14). The devotional poets of the sixteenth and seventeenth centuries in particular liked to think of themselves as tuning their readers. "Hearken unto a Verser," Herbert exhorts his readers, "who may chance / Rhyme thee to good" ("The Church-porch": 3-4; for more on Herbert's poetry and music, see McColley 1989). The seventeenth-century writer of "The Preface to the Reader" in Crashaw's *Steps to the Temple* asserts that Herbert is like Augustine in his belief that "every foot in a high-borne verse, might helpe to measure the soule into that better world." Du Bartas, Spenser, Donne, and others would have agreed. Donne employed this allegory, for example, in his praise of Philip Sydney and his sister the Countess of Pembroke for their translation of the Psalms:

> A Brother and a Sister, made by thee
> The Organ, where thou [the Lord] art the Harmony....
> They tell us *why*, and teach us *how* to sing;
> Make all this All, three Quires, heaven, earth, and sphears;
> The first, Heaven, hath a song, but no man heares,
> The Spheares have Musick, but they have no tongue,
> Their harmony is rather danc'd than sung.

And the third choir is we fallen human beings. But this third choir can be tuned, because singers follow the organist, and "The Organist is hee / Who hath tun'd God and Man"—Christ, who reconciled man and God. It is Donne's hope that Sydney's and his sister's translation of the Psalms might "Be as our tuning, that, when hence we part / We may all fall in with them and sing our part" ("Upon the Translation of the Psalms": 16-56; for more on the tuning poets, see Malpezzi 1980).

Donne refers in his poem to the magnificent idea of the music of the spheres, the idea that the spinning of the heavenly bodies in their divinely instituted relations produces a kind of music. A great deal was written about the music of the spheres (see, e.g., Zecher 1993)—but essentially there was agreement all the way from ancient Pythagoras to John Milton in the seventeenth century. Even the great mathematician John Kepler was convinced that the spheres made music. Kepler knew that the planets moved around the sun, not the earth. In fact, it was Kepler who discovered the elliptical orbits of the planets; but this discovery delighted him precisely because it seemed to him to *confirm* the existence of the music of the spheres (Pauli 1955)! Milton described the music of the spheres as follows:

why should not the heavenly bodies produce musical vibrations?...What though no one on earth has ever heard that symphony of the stars? Is that ground for believing that everything beyond the moon's sphere is absolutely mute and numb with torpid silence? On the contrary, let us blame our own impotent ears, which cannot catch the songs or are unworthy to hear such sweet strains....

Our impotence to hear this harmony seems to be...[because] we wallow in sin and are brutalized by our animal desires....If our hearts were as pure, as chaste, as snowy as Pythagoras' was, our ears would resound and be filled with that supremely lovely music of the wheeling stars. ("Second Prolusion, On the Music of the Spheres")

Lorenzo had offered the same explanation to Jessica in Shakespeare's *Merchant of Venice*:

Here will we sit, and let the sounds of music
Creep into our ears. Soft stillness and the night
Become the touches of sweet harmony.
Sit, Jessica. Look how the floor of heaven
Is thick inlaid with patens of bright gold,
There's not the smallest orb which thou behold'st
But in his motion like an angel sings,
Still quiring to the young-eyed cherubins;
Such harmony is in immortal souls,
But whilst this muddy vesture of decay
Doth grossly close it in, we cannot hear it.
(5.1.55-65)

But it was often said that virtuous people *could* hear the music of the spheres. Milton, as we have seen, wrote that Pythagoras heard the music of the spheres. And Dante, too, heard the music of the spheres—after he had climbed the Mount of Purgatory. Once he has been purged of his sins, he sees a great light: "a sweet melody ran through the luminous air; wherefore good zeal made me reprove Eve's daring" (*Purgatorio*: 29.22-24). So keenly does Dante feel his new freedom from sin that he spontaneously reproaches Eve for first succumbing to sin and so allowing sin to enter into the world. Dante expects us to realize that the music he hears is the music of the spheres—and he expects us to understand that he can hear it only because he has been purged of sin.

The hearing the music of the spheres could thus serve as an sign of spiritual regeneration or original innocence.

For more music allegory, see **AMPHION, APOLLO, ARION, ECHO, MARSYAS, MIDAS, MUSES, ORPHEUS, SIRENS.**

For early explanations of music, see the widely influential works by Augustine (*On Music*) and Boethius (*De Musica*; and see Heninger 1985). For a brief paraphrase of Boethius, see Hugh of St. Victor (*Didascalicon*: 2.11-12); for an extended (and clear) paraphrase, see the *Chess of Love* commentary (207-305). Among the moderns: Wittkower (1971: 101-142) explains these ideas—from Pythagoras down to the Renaissance Neo-Platonists—and shows how they were closely related to conceptions of human psychology and architecture. Hollander (1961) and Heninger (1974) discuss the same ideas in relation to Renaissance poetry. Chamberlain's articles (1970a, 1970b) on Medieval music theory and allegory are useful, not least for their extensive bibliographies. Winternitz (1979) explains the allegorical meanings of the various musical instruments. Berger (1977) provides an account of music theory as it might have been understood by a Renaissance Neo-Platonist magus, all applied to Shakespeare's *Tempest*; for more on Renaissance music and Neo-Platonic magi, see Tomlinson (1993). For a wide-ranging introduction to the Renaissance understanding of music and a specific application of such ideas to Shakespeare see Simonds (1992: 334-363). Berley (1993) discusses music as it relates to Milton.

Bibliography: Karol Berger, "Prospero's Art," *ShakS*, 10 (1977): 211-239; Marc Berley, "Milton's Earthly Grossness: Music and the Condition of the Poet in *L'Allegro* and *Il Penseroso*," *MiltonS*, 30 (1993): 149-161; David S. Chamberlain, "Wolbero of Cologne (d. 1167): A Zenith of Musical Imagery," *MS*, 33 (1970a): 114-126; Chamberlain, "Philosophy and Music in the *Consolatio* of Boethius," *Speculum*, 45 (1970b): 80-97; S. K. Heninger, *Touches of Sweet Harmony: Pythagorean Cosmology and Renaissance Poetics* (1974); Heninger, "Sidney and Boethian Music," *SEL*, 25 (1985): 37-46; F. D. Hoeniger, "Musical Cures of Melancholy and Mania in Shakespeare," in J. C. Gray, *Mirror up to Shakespeare* (1984): 54-67; John Hollander, *Untuning the Sky: Ideas of Music in English Poetry, 1500-1700* (1961).

Frances Malpezzi, "Christian Poetics in Donne's 'Upon the Translation of the Psalms,'" *Renascence*, 33 (1980): 221-228; Diane McColley, "The Poem as Hierophon: Musican Configurations in George Herbert's 'The Church,'" in Mary Maleski, *A Fine Tuning: Studies in the Religious Poetry of Herbert and Milton* (1989): 116-143; W. Pauli, "The Influence of Archetypal Ideas on the Scientific Ideas of Kepler," in C. G. Jung and Pauli, *The Interpretation of Nature and the Psyche* (1955); Peggy Muñoz Simonds, *Myth, Emblem, and Music in Shakespeare's Cymbeline* (1992); Gary Tomlinson, *Music in Renaissance Magic* (1993); Emmanuel Winternitz, *Musical Instruments and Their Symbolism in Western Art* (1979); Rudolf and Margot Wittkower, *Born under Saturn: The Character and Conduct of Artists* (1969); Rudolf Wittkower, *Architectural Principles in the Age of Humanism* (1971); Carla Zecher, "Pagan Spirituality and Christian Passion: The Music of the Spheres in Sixteenth-Century French Cosmological Poetry," *FrF*, 18 (1993): 297-317.

Appendix B: Bestialization

The allegory of bestialization had its beginnings well before the age of Christianity. The Erinyes that Aeschylus put on the stage in his *Eumenides* were such terrible creatures, with their black skins and blood-red tongues, that stories were told of women in the audience having miscarriages and children convulsions. One hopes the stories were apocryphal—but they do give us a sense that Aeschylus wanted the Erinyes to look terrible in their lust for revenge. He wanted them to look inhuman.

We occasionally find the same kind of assumptions at work in the Old Testament. In the story of the twins Jacob and Esau, for example, we are told that Jacob was Yahweh's chosen one; Esau, the story suggests, was not worthy of the promise. The distinction between the two boys is apparent even at birth: when Esau was born he was "red, all over like an hairy garment" (Gen 25:25). He was so hairy, in fact, that Jacob was able to impersonate his brother simply by donning the skin of a goat. The writer wants us to see that there is something of the animal about Esau; we are not surprised to find that Esau was the forefather of the nasty Edomites (Gen 25:30; 36; Mal 1:2-3), one of the tribes with whom Israel was so often at violent odds (see Alter 1981: 42-43; *Anchor Bible Dictionary* 1992: under *Esau*). There is also the story of the creation in Genesis, which distinguishes fundamentally between human beings and the animals: "God created man in his own image, in the image of God created he him"—and these human beings, "male and female," were created to have "dominion" over all the animals (Gen 1:26-27).

Some of the transformations Ovid describes in the *Metamorphoses* work in this way. The rapist Tereus becomes a hoopoe, a filthy, dung-eating bird (see **PHILOMELA, PROCNE, AND TEREUS**); Pasiphae takes on the form of a cow in order to gratify her lust for a bull (see **PASIPHAE**); and Midas, for his stupidity, is awarded asses' ears (see **MIDAS**). Jupiter is sometimes transformed into an animal in order to achieve his amorous desires: Sexual arousal equals animal transformation (e.g., Barkan 1986: 218; see **EUROPA, LEDA**). In the case of Io, Jupiter's beloved is transformed (see **IO**).

All of this was assimilated easily by the Christians, with their characteristic insistence upon the distinction between spirit and the flesh. The New Testament interprets the human likeness to God in specifically spiritual terms. St. Paul writes that "the Lord is spirit....But we all, with open face beholding as in a glass the glory of the Lord, are changed into the same image, from glory to glory" (2 Cor 3:17-18). This is to say that human beings reflect the image of God insofar as they have been changed by Christ. Once Christians have "put off the old," Paul writes, they "put on the new man, which is renewed in knowledge after the image of him that created him" (Col 3:9-10). Augustine develops this same idea in *On the Trinity* (10.11-12; 14.16) and in the *City of God* (22.16; see also Gregory of Nyssa, *On the Image*; John the Scot, *On the Division of Nature*: 4.11). To be spiritually regenerated is to refurbish God's image in oneself. Thus it is in "Goodfriday, 1613. Riding Westward" that Donne prays:

> Burne off my rusts, and my deformity,
> Restore thine Image, so much, by thy grace,
> That thou mays't know mee.

And so a tradition developed in Western literature and art: Morally upright people are beautiful people; morally degenerate people are ugly—bestial. The outward form mirrors the inward spiritual state. Spenser explains this in Neo-Platonic terms:

> ...every spirit, as it is most pure,
> Hath in it the more of heavenly light,
> So it the fairer bodie doth procure
> To habit in.
>   ("Hymne of Beautie")

Thus it is that Spenser's chaste and virtuous Una is a "Lovely Ladie" (*Faerie Queene*: 1.1.3). The corollary is that, as Donne put it, "To wicked spirits are horrid shapes assign'd" (Holy Sonnet, "What If this Present"). Many of the creatures in Bruegel's engraving of *Lechery* (fig. 20) are grotesques—part human, part beast. Dame Lechery, there at the center of the engraving, is in lewd embrace with a lizard-like creature. Two dogs are in doggy embrace along the right margin. Those who succumb to the sin of lechery are essentially like animals; they have defaced within themselves the image of God; their wicked spirits have taken on allegorically appropriate shapes. Men even lose their virile nature—as we see in the bottom, right-hand corner, where a grotesque has just cut off his considerable member.

There were exceptions, of course. There were beautiful temptresses, for example; but good Christians were supposed to realize that this is a seeming beauty only. Temptresses can be stripped—as Spenser's Duessa is stripped (*Faerie

Queene: 1.8.46-49)—to reveal their real ugliness, their spiritual ugliness (see **SIRENS** for the stripping of temptresses). The *Lechery* engraving makes this point by showing us lechery as it appears to the worldling on the left side of the engraving. We see a flowing fountain with beguilingly bare-breasted women; everything is leafy and lovely. On the right we see the fires of destruction; we see lechery's dangerous potential—we see lechery as it really is. And when we see lechery for what it really is, Bruegel insists, we see that lechers have been bestialized.

The Centaurs, half human and half horse, were often interpreted allegorically in this way (see **CENTAUR**). As Ross put it, "Every regenerate man is in a sort a Centaur, to wit, a man in that part which is regenerate, and a beast in his unregenerate part....Where things are not ruled by Laws, Order and Civility, but carried headlong with violence & force, we may say that there is a Commonwealth of Centaurs" (*Mystagogus Poeticus*: 58).

For examples of bestialization allegory, see especially **CIRCE**; see also **ACTAEON, APULEIUS, BACCHUS, CALLISTO, IXION, MINOTAUR**, and **PHILOMELA, PROCNE, AND TEREUS**,

Bibliography: *Anchor Bible Dictionary* (1992): under *Esau*; Robert Alter, *The Art of Biblical Narrative* (1981); Leonard Barkan, *The Gods Made Flesh: Metamorphoses and the Pursuit of Paganism* (1986); David L. Jeffrey, *Dictionary of Biblical Tradition in English Literature* (1992): under *Imago Dei*.

Appendix C: Envying the Animals

Envying the animals their sexual freedoms was a traditional conceit, one which goes back at least to Ovid, who has Pasiphae envying heifers because she is in love with a bull (*Art of Love*: 289-325). Shakespeare's Romeo envies even the flies for their near proximity to Juliet:

> More validity,
> More honorable state, more courtship lives
> In carrion flies than Romeo; they may seize
> On the white wonder of dear Juliet's hand,
> And steal immortal blessings from her lips...;
> But Romeo may not, he is banished.
> > (*Romeo and Juliet*: 3.3.33-40)

There was a line of flea poems from the Middle Ages down to Donne's "The Flea" in the seventeenth century which worked in much this same way: the distraught lover envies the flea its ready access to his mistress's private parts (Brumble 1973).

Once Marlowe's Faustus begins to understand the horrors of eternal damnation, he, too, envies the animals. He envies them their soulless state:

> Ah, Pythagoras' *metempsychosis*, were that true,
> This soul should fly from me and I be changed
> Into some brutish beast. All beasts are happy,
> For, when they die
> Their souls are soon dissolved into elements,
> But mine must live still to be plagued in hell.
> > (*Doctor Faustus*: 5.2.171-176)

Donne plays with this same idea in his Holy Sonnet "If Poysonous Mineralls":

> If poysonous mineralls, and if that tree,
> Whose fruit threw death on else immortall us,
> If lecherous goats, if serpents envious
> Cannot be damn'd; Alas; why should I bee?

Bibliography: H. David Brumble, "John Donne's 'The Flea': The Implications of the Encyclopedic and Poetic Flea Traditions," *CQ*, 15 (1973): 147-54.

Annotated Bibliography of Primary Sources

Aeschylus (525-456 B.C.). *Aeschylus*, tr. H. W. Smyth. Cambridge: Loeb, 1922-1930.
A Greek tragic playwright.

Agostini (fl. 1538). *Di Ovidio Le Metamorphosi...con le sue Allegorie....* Venice, 1538.
Agostini provides an Italian translation of Ovid, with allegorical commentary.

Alanus de Insulis (1128- c. 1203). *The Anticlaudian*, tr. William Cornog. Philadelphia:
n.p., 1935.
An important figure in the twelfth-century revival of learning in France, Alanus was
best known for the two works cited here. *The Complaint of Nature*, an allegorical work
describing Dame Nature's response to fallen mankind, was particularly influential.

_____. *The Complaint of Nature*, tr. Douglas M. Moffat. New York: Holt, 1908.

Albricus of London (12th cent.). *Allegoriae Poeticae*. London, 1532; facsimile rpt.: New
York: Garland, 1976.
Albricus is perhaps a pseudonym for Alexander Neckam (1157-1217). This book
served as an iconographic and allegorical guide to the pagan gods well into the
Renaissance.

_____. *De Deorum Imaginibus Libellus*, in Thomas Munckerus, *Mythographi Latini*.
Amsterdam, 1681: 301-330.
The attribution to Albricus is not certain.

Alciati, Andrea (1492-1550). *The Latin Emblems, Indexes, and Lists*, tr. Peter M. Daly,
with Virginia Callahan and Simon Cutler. Toronto: Univ. of Toronto Press, 1985.
Alciati, an Italian lawyer, was the originator of the emblem books. His book first
appeared in 1522, but Alciati kept adding emblems in successive editions. Alciati's
emblems were heavily used by poets, painters, sculptors, and preachers well into the
seventeenth century.

Alighieri, Dante (1265-1321). *The Banquet (Il Convivio)*, tr. Christopher Ryan. Saratoga:
ANMA Libri, 1989.
The great Florentine poet is best known for his *Divine Comedy*, an account of Dante's
journey down through the Inferno, up the Mount of Purgatory, and on into Paradise.

_____. *A Translation of Dante's Eleven Letters (Epistole)*, tr. Charles S. Latham.
Boston: Houghton Mifflin, 1892.

_____. *Divine Comedy*: *Inferno, Paradiso, Purgatorio,* tr. Charles S. Singleton. Princeton: Princeton Univ. Press, 1970-1975.

Alighieri, Pietro (fl. first half 14th cent.). *Il "Commentarium" di Pietro Alighieri,* ed. R. della Vedova and M. T. Silvotti. Florence: Olschki, 1978.

This is a commentary on the *Divine Comedy* written by Dante's son.

Ambrose, St. (c. 340-397). *On the Decease of His Brother Satyrus,* in *Nicene and Post-Nicene Fathers of the Christian Church,* vol. 10, ed. Philip Schaff and Henry Wace. New York: Christian Literature Co., 1896.

Ambrose was the Bishop of Milan (374-397); he is recognized as one of the Church Fathers.

Anglicus, Bartholomaeus: see Bartholomaeus Anglicus.

Anglicus, Thomas: see Waleys, Thomas.

Apollodorus (b. c. 180 B.C.). *The Library*; *Epitome,* in *Apollodorus,* tr. J. G. Frazer. Cambridge: Loeb, 1921.

Apollodorus was a Greek scholar of wide learning. His *Library* is one of the most important sources of Greek mythology.

Apollonius Rhodius (b. c. 295 B.C.). *Argonautica,* in *Apollonius Rhodius,* tr. R. C. Seaton. Cambridge: Loeb, 1912.

This is the most important ancient source of Argonaut lore.

Apuleius (b. c. 130 A.D.). *Metamorphoses* (also known as *The Golden Ass*), tr. J. Arthur Hanson. Cambridge: Loeb, 1989.

_____. *Apologia,* ed. R. Helm. Berlin, 1905.

Apuleius was born in North Africa and educated in Carthage and Greece. The *Metamorphoses,* his best-known work, tells of one Lucius who dabbles in magic and so is transformed into an ass. In this shape he endures and sees many strange things. The novel is narrated in the first person, and so most readers identified Apuleius with Lucius (see **APULEIUS**).

Aquinas, Thomas (1225-1274). *In Aristotelis Librum De Anima Commentarium,* ed. A. M. Pirotta. Turin: Marietti, 1936.

Aquinas was one of the most important Christian theologians. He wrote several commentaries, such as this one on Aristotle; but he is best known for his great summaries of all human knowledge, the *Summa Theologiae* and the *Summa contra Gentiles.*

_____. *On Princely Government,* in *Aquinas: Selected Political Writings,* tr. J. G. Dawson. Oxford: Blackwell, 1965.

_____. *Summa Theologiae: Latin Text and English Translation.* Cambridge: Blackfriars, 1964.

Ariosto, Lodovico (1474-1533). *Orlando Furioso,* tr. with commentary, John Harington (1561-1612). London, 1591. Harington's tr. has been reprinted, without the commentary, alas. Carbondale: Southern Illinois Univ. Press, 1962.

In the *Orlando Furioso* Ariosto brought together the stories of the knights of old, the epic conventions, and allegory. This Italian poem was the most widely influential of the Renaissance epics.

Aristophanes (444?-380?). *Fragments,* in John Maxwell Edmonds, *The Fragments of Attic Comedy.* Leiden: Brill, 1957).

_____. *Plutus,* in *Aristophanes,* vol. 3, tr. B. B. Rogers. Cambridge: Loeb, 1924.

Aristophanes was a Greek comic playwright.

Aristotle (384-322 B.C.). *Generation of Animals,* tr. A. L. Peck. Cambridge: Loeb, 1942.

Aristotle was a Greek philosopher and natural historian. For Aristotle in love, see **ARISTOTLE**.

_____. *Problemata*, in *The Works of Aristotle*, vol. 7, ed. W. D. Ross. Oxford: Clarendon Press, 1927.

Arnolphe of Orléans (11th cent.). A commentary on Ovid's *Metamorphoses*, in Fausto Ghisalberti, "Arnolfo d'Orléans, un cultore di secolo XII." *Memorie del R. Instituto Lombardi di Scienze e Lettere* (1932): 157-232.

Arnolphe was a French scholar, a writer of Latin glosses.

Athenaeus (fl. c. 200). *Deipnosophistae*, tr. C. B. Gulick. Cambridge: Loeb, 1922-1949.

Deipnosophistae (*The Learned Banquet*), written in the tradition of Plato's *Symposium*, has learned guests discussing such topics as philosophy, law, medicine, and literature.

Augustine, St. (354-430). *Against the Academics*, tr. J. J. O'Meara. Westminster: Newman, 1950.

Augustine was probably the most influential of all the Church Fathers. Augustine continued to be important even to such Protestants as Luther and Calvin.

_____. *On Christian Doctrine*, tr. D. W. Robertson, Jr. Indianapolis: Bobbs-Merrill, 1958.

_____. *City of God*, tr. Marcus Dods. New York: Modern Library, 1950.

_____. *On Music*, in *Writings of St. Augustine*, vol. 2. New York: CIMA, 1947.

_____. *Of True Religion*, tr. J. H. S. Burleigh. Chicago: Regnery, 1964.

_____. *The Works of St. Augustine: A New Translation*. Edinburgh: Clark, 1872-1934.

Ausonius, Decimus Magnus (d. c. 395 A.D.). *Appendix to Ausonius* (poems by unknown authors, formerly attributed to Ausonius); *Epigrams*, in *Ausonius*, tr. H. G. Evelyn White. Cambridge: Loeb, 1919-1921.

Ausonius was a poet and a grammarian. He also served for a time as a Roman consul.

Bacon, Sir Francis (1561-1626). *The Works of Francis Bacon*, 10 vols., ed. James Spedding et al. London: Longman & Co., 1861.

Bacon was an English statesman, philosopher, scientist, essayist—and, in *On the Wisedome of the Ancients*, mythographer. *On Principles and Origins, According to the Fables of Cupid and Coelum* is precisely what the title says it is, an attempt to learn about the principles of nature by considering certain classical myths. There is nothing whimsical about his project, despite first appearances: In the same way that looking at stories allegorically can lead to fruitful ideas about morality, so allegorical contemplation can lead to fruitful thinking about matters natural and physical.

_____. *On the Wisedome of the Ancients*, tr. Arthur Gorges. London: 1619; facsimile rpt.: New York: Garland, 1976.

Bartholomaeus Anglicus (fl. 1320-1340). *On the Properties of Things*, tr. John de Trevisa (1326-1412), ed. M. C. Seymour et al. London: Oxford Univ. Press, 1975.

This is arguably the greatest of the Medieval encyclopedias. It was thought worthy of translation into English as late as 1582 (see Stephan Batman's *Batman uppon Bartholomae*).

Batman, Stephan (d. 1584). *Batman uppon Bartholomae, His Booke De Proprietatibus Rerum....* London, 1582. This is a translation of Bartholomaeus Anglicus, *De Proprietatibus Rerum*, with additions by Batman; see Bartholomaeus Anglicus.

Batman was an Anglican minister. His *Golden Booke of the Leaden Gods*, intended as a (rather ambivalent) warning against paganism, is based largely on Pictorius's *Apotheoseos*.

_____. *The Golden Booke of the Leaden Gods*. London, 1577; facsimile rpt.: New York: Garland, 1976.

Berchorius, Petrus (d. 1362). *Ovidius Moralizatus*, tr. William D. Reynolds. Univ. of Illinois: Ph.D. Dissertation, 1971.

Berchorius is one of the most influential of the allegorical interpreters of Ovid. Berchorius has a predilection for Biblical typology. This book was also known by its French title, *Ovide Moralisé*, not to be confused with the earlier, anonymous, metrical *Ovide Moralisé*.

Bernard of Utrecht (Bernard Silvester of Utrecht; late 13th c.). *Kommentar des Bernardus Ultraiectensis [über Theoduli "Ecloga"]*, in Jos. Frey, *Über das Mittelalterliches Gedicht "Theoduli ecloga"*.... Münster: Aschendorffschen, 1904.

This is a commentary on Theodulph's late ninth-century *Ecloga* (see Theodulph).

Bernardus Silvestris (fl. 1136). *The Cosmographia*, tr. Winthrop Wetherbee. New York: Columbia Univ. Press, 1973.

Bernardus was an important figure in the School of Chartres, which was in the twelfth century the preeminent center of classical learning and Platonism.

_____. *Commentary on the First Six Books of Virgil's Aeneid*, tr. Earl G. Schreiber and Thomas Maresca. Lincoln: Univ. of Nebraska Press, 1979.

_____. *The Commentary on Martianus Capella's De Nuptiis Philologiae et Mercurii*, ed. Haijo Jan Westra. Toronto: Pontifical Institute of Medieval Studies, 1986.

Bersuire, Pierre: see Berchorius, Petrus.

Boccaccio, Giovanni (1313-1375). *L'Ameto*, tr. Judith Serafini-Sauli. New York: Garland, 1985.

Boccaccio was a prolific and widely influential writer of prose and poetry. His *Genealogie Deorum* (*Genealogy of the Gods*) was one of the most important Medieval mythographies.

_____. *Amorous Fiammetta...*, tr. Bartholomew Yong (1587), ed. K. H. Josling. London: Mandrake Press, 1929.

_____. *De Casibus Virorum Illustrium*: see *The Fates of Famous Men*.

_____. *De Claris Mulieribus*: see *Concerning Famous Women*.

_____. *Concerning Famous Women* (*De Claris Mulieribus*), tr. G. A. Guarino. New Brunswick: Rutgers Univ. Press, 1963.

_____. *The Corbaccio*, tr. Anthony K. Cassell. Urbana: Univ. of Illinois Press, 1975.

_____. *Diana's Hunt*, ed. and tr. Anthony Cassell and Victoria Kirkham. Philadelphia, Univ. of Pennsylvania Press, 1991.

_____. *Eclogues* (*Buccolicom Carmen*), tr. Janet Levarie Smarr. New York: Garland, 1987.

_____. *The Elegy of Lady Fiammetta*, tr. M. Causa-Steindler and T. Mauch. Chicago: Univ. of Chicago Press, 1990. For a Renaissance tr., see *Amorous Fiammetta*, above.

_____. *Esposizioni sopra la Comedìa di Dante*, in *Tutte le opere*, vol. 1, ed. Giorgio Padoan. Milan: Mondadori, 1967.

_____. *The Fates of Famous Men* (*De Casibus Virorum Illustrium*), tr. Louis B. Hall. New York: Ungar, 1965.

_____. *Il Filocolo*, tr. Donald Cheney and T. G. Bergin. New York: Garland, 1985.

_____. *Genealogia Deorum Gentilium Libri*, ed. Vincenzo Romano. Bari, 1951.

_____. *The Book of Theseus: Teseida delle Nozze d'Emilia*, tr. Bernadette Marie McCoy. New York: Medieval Text Association, 1974.

Bodin, Jean (1529 or 1530-1596). *Colloquium of the Seven about Secrets of the Sublime*, tr. Marion L. D. Kuntz. Princeton: Princeton Univ. Press, 1975.

Bodin was a French lawyer; he wrote on legal and political subjects. He was much interested in natural law as a basis for an ethical state.

Boethius (c. 480-c. 524). *The Consolation of Philosophy*, tr. Richard H. Green. Indianapolis: Bobbs-Merrill, 1962.

Boethius was a philosopher who served as consul under Theodoric the Great. He was eventually accused of treason and put in prison, where he wrote the *Consolation*. He was regarded as one of the great authorities during the Middle Ages. His treatises on logic and music were used as textbooks throughout the Middle Ages.

_____. *De Musica. PL*, vol. 63.

Bonaventure, St. (1221-1274). *The Works of Bonaventure*, 5 vols., tr. J. de Vinck. Paterson, N.J.: St. Anthony's Guild Press, 1960.

Bonaventure was a Franciscan friar; his *The Mind's Road to God* is one of the important early guides to meditation.

Bonomii, Francis (1626-1705). *Chiron Achillis, sive Navarchus Humanae Vitae*. N.p., 1651.

Bonomii was an Italian writer in Latin and Italian and an emblematist.

Brant, Sebastian (1458-1521). *Ship of Fools*, tr. Edwin H. Zeydel, with reproductions of the original woodcuts. New York: Columbia Univ. Press, 1944.

Brant was a German didactic, satiric poet.

Bredero, Gerbrand Adriansz. (1585-1618). "Apollo...Speaks to the Netherlandish Youth"; "Den Broeders in Liefde Bloeyende"; *Lucelle*, in *De Werken van G. A. Bredero*, 3 vols., ed. J. ten Brink et al. Amsterdam: Binger, 1890.

Bredero was a poet and one of the two preeminent playwrights of the Dutch Golden Age. *The Spanish Brabanter*, a five-act social satire, is Bredero's best-known work; it fills the stage with Amsterdam's misers, beggars, whores, bankrupts, and virtuous poor.

_____. *The Spanish Brabanter*, tr. H. David Brumble. Binghamton: MRTS, 1981.

Browne, Thomas (1605-1682). *Religio Medici*, in *Sir Thomas Browne: Selected Writings*, ed. Geoffrey Keynes. Chicago: Univ. of Chicago Press, 1968.

Browne was a physician, essayist, and antiquarian scholar. His writings combine his scientific/medical knowledge with his deeply felt Christianity and his classical learning.

Bunyan, John (1628-1688). *The Pilgrim's Progress*. Harmondsworth: Penguin, 1965.

Bunyan, a Protestant preacher, prided himself on his lack of formal learning. *Pilgrim's Progress* is a heavily allegorical narrative, with Pilgrim making his difficult way through a fallen world.

Burton, Robert (1577-1639). *The Anatomy of Melancholy*. New York: Farrar, 1927.

Burton was an Oxford academic; his encyclopedic *Anatomy* was based on classical authorities and on contemporary authors. The book treats the whole range of mental disturbances then regarded as species of melancholy, but Burton is most interested in lovers' melancholy.

Calcagni, Celio (1479-1541). *Lectiones Antiquae*. Lyon, 1560.

An example of the Renaissance man, Calcagni was a soldier and a humanist scholar in Latin and Greek.

Calderón de la Barca, Don Pedro (1600-1681). *El Divino Orfeo*, in *Obras Completas*, vol. 3, ed. A. V. Prat. Madrid: Aguilar, 1967.

Calderón was a playwright and one of the great figures of Spanish literature. He was influenced by Augustine, Aquinas, and Seneca, among others.

Callimachus (c. 305- c. 240 B.C.). *Hymns and Epigrams*, tr. G. R. Mair. Cambridge: Loeb, 1955.

Callimachus was a librarian and a remarkably prolific critic and poet. He wrote the world's earliest scientific literary history.

Camões, Luis de (c. 1524-1580). *The Lusiads*, tr. Richard Fanshawe (1655), ed. Geoffrey
Bullough. Carbondale: Southern Illinois Univ. Press, 1963.
Camões is regarded as one of the greatest of the Portuguese poets. *The Lusiads*, an
epic, is his best known work.

Capella, Martianus: see Martianus Felix Capella.

Cartari, Vincenzo (b. c. 1500). *Le Imagini de i Dei de Gli Antichi*. Venice, 1571; facsimile
rpt.: New York: Garland, 1976. See also Richard Lynche.
This mythography was particularly important to artists, since it included detailed
iconographies and many illustrations. See Lynche for an early English translation.
_____. *Le Imagini....* Venice, 1647; facsimile rpt. Graz: Akademische Druk, 1963.

Cassiodorus Senator (c. 480-575). *An Introduction to Divine and Human Readings*, tr.
Leslie Webber Jones. New York: Octagon, 1966.
Cassiodorus held important political offices under four Ostrogothic rulers; he was also
a scholar, a founder of monasteries, and a Biblical commentator.

Cats, Jacob (1577-1660). *Proteus, ofte Minne-beelden Verandert in Sinne-beelden*.
Rotterdam, 1627.
Cats was a Dutch didactic poet and humorist, hardly known outside the Netherlands,
but very popular among the Dutch.

Catullus (87-54? B.C.). *Catullus*, ed. J. C. Fordyce. Oxford: Clarendon Press, 1961.
Catullus, a poet of love, was lost to the early Middle Ages; but after his rediscovery in
the fourteenth century, his poetry was widely read.

Caxton, William (1422-1491). *The Metamorphoses of Ovid*, tr. with commentary, William
Caxton. London, 1480; facsimile ed.: New York: George Braziller, 1968.
Caxton is best known as the first English printer, but he was also an important
translator. He added allegorical commentary to this translation of Ovid.
_____. *Mirrour of the World*, ed. Oliver H. Prior. London: Early English Text Society,
1913.
This is a translation, printed by Caxton, of a thirteenth-century French encyclopedia.

Cervantes, Miguel de (1547-1616). *Don Quixote*, tr. J. M. Cohen. Baltimore: Penguin,
1970.
Best known for this novel, Cervantes was also a dramatist and poet.

Chalcidius (4th cent.). *Platonis Timaeus, Interpretate Chalcidio cum Eiusdem
Commentario...*, ed. Iohannes Wrobel. Leipzig, 1876.
This partial translation of Plato's *Timaeus* (with Chalcidius's commentary) was the
only text of Plato known to the Middle Ages.

Chapman, George (?1559-1634). "A Coronet for His Mistresse"; "Hymnus in Cynthiam"
(*Shadow of the Night*), in *The Poems of George Chapman*, ed. Phyllis Brooks Bartlett.
New York: MLA, 1941.
A learned man, Chapman was a dramatist, poet, and translator.

Chaucer, Geoffrey (c. 1340-1400). *The Complete Poetry and Prose of Geoffrey Chaucer*,
ed. John H. Fisher. New York: Holt, 1989.
Clearly the greatest of the Middle English poets, Chaucer was also a translator of de
Meun's *Romance of the Rose* and Boethius's *Consolation of Philosophy*.

The Chess of Love, anonymous commentary upon, tr. Joan Jones. Univ. of Nebraska: Ph.D.
Dissertation, 1968.
This is a translation of a long commentary (1295 pp. in Jones' translation) on the
anonymous *Les Echecs Amoureuse* (late fourteenth century), which was itself written
in imitation of de Meun's *Romance of the Rose*.

Chester, Robert (fl. 1601). *Loves Martyr*, ed. A. B. Grosart. New Shakespeare Society, 1878.

Christine de Pizan (1364- c. 1430). *The Book of the City of Ladies*, tr. Earl Jeffrey Richards. New York: Persea, 1982.

Italian-born, Christine was a profeminist scholar and poet. *The Book of the City of Ladies* is an adaptation of Boccaccio's *Concerning Famous Women*.

_____. *The Book of the Duke of True Lovers*, tr. Thelma Fenster and Nadia Margolis. New York: Persea Books, 1991.

_____. *L'Epitre*, in Halina Loukopoulos, *Classical Mythology in the Works of Christine de Pisan, with an Edition of...L'Epitre Othea*.... Wayne State Univ.: Ph.D. Dissertation, 1977.

Cicero, Marcus Tullius (106-43 B.C.). *De Inventione*, tr. H. M. Hubbell. Cambridge: Loeb, 1949.

Cicero was a Roman statesman, orator, man of letters—and, in *The Nature of the Gods*, skeptical mythographer.

_____. *The Nature of the Gods*, tr. H. C. P. McGregor. London: Penguin, 1988.

_____. *The Republic*, tr. C. W. Keyes. Cambridge: Loeb, 1966.

Clanvowe, John (1341?-1391). *The Booke of Cupide*, in *The Works of Sir John Clanvowe*, ed. V. J. Scattergood. Cambridge: D. S. Brewer, 1975.

Clanvowe was active as a soldier, diplomat, administrator, and poet in the courts of Edward III and Richard II. His poetry shows Chaucer's influence.

Claudian (fl. 395-404). *Rape of Proserpine*, tr. M. Platnauer. Cambridge: Loeb, 1922.

This work by the Roman poet is an unfinished mythological epic.

Clement of Alexandria (c. 150- c. 215). *Christ the Educator* (*Paidagogos*), tr. Simon P. Wood. New York: Fathers of the Church, Inc., 1954.

This Christian writer was deeply influenced by Greek literature.

Comes, Natalus: see Conti, Natale.

"Le Commentaire de Copenhague de l'*Ovide Moralisé*" (14th cent.), ed. J. Tr. M. van 't Sant, rpt. in L. de Boer's edition of the *Ovide Moralisé* (see below): vol. 5: 387-429.

This is an anonymous commentary on the *Ovide Moralisé*.

Conti, Natale (1520?-1580?). *Mythologie, ou Explication des Fables*, tr. J. de Montlyard. Paris, 1627; facsimile rpt.: New York: Garland, 1976.

Conti was an Italian scholar, a translator, and a mythographer. This book, one of the most important Renaissance mythographies, went through many editions.

Cooper, Thomas (1517-1594). *Dictionarium Historicum & Poeticum...*, appended to Cooper's *Thesaurus Linguae Romanae & Britannicae*.... London, 1573.

Cooper's *Dictionary* and *Thesaurus* included mythological lore; Cooper was widely used by the Elizabethan poets.

Coornhert, D. V. (1522-1590). *Zedekunst, Dat is Wellevenskunste*, ed. B. Becker. Leiden: Brill, 1942.

Coornhert was a Dutch scholar, and a writer on religious and moral subjects. He also translated Boethius's *Consolation of Philosophy*.

Copernicus, Nicolas (1473-1543). *Three Copernican Treatises*, tr. Edward Rosen. New York: Dover, 1959.

Copernicus, a Polish astronomer, opened the door to modern astronomy by refuting the Ptolemaic system.

The Courte of Sapyence (anonymous, c. 1450), ed. Ruth Harvey. Toronto: Univ. of Toronto Press, 1984.

The narrator meets Sapyence (Wisdom) in a vision, and goes with her to her abode. All of this provides a narrative framework for a late Medieval encyclopedia—everything from gems to the plan of human redemption.

Crashaw, Richard (1612-1649). *The Poems, English, Latin and Greek, of Richard Crashaw*. Oxford: Clarendon Press, 1966.

Crashaw is best remembered for his meditative religious poetry. He converted to Catholicism at the age of 30.

Daniel, Samuel (c. 1562-1619). *Complete Works in Verse and Prose*, 5 vols., ed. Alexander Grosart. New York: Russell and Russell, 1963.

Dante: see Aligheri, Dante.

De Lorris, Guillaume: see de Meun, Jean.

De Meun, Jean (d. 1305), and Guillaume de Lorris (c. 1212-c. 1237). *The Romance of the Rose*, tr. Charles Dahlberg. Princeton: Princeton Univ. Press, 1986.

De Lorris wrote the first 4,000 lines of this poem; de Meun added another 18,000 lines. This is an allegorical poem about love and Nature.

De Mézières, Phillippe (c. 1327-1405). *Letter to King Richard II*, tr. C. W. Coopland. Liverpool: Liverpool Univ. Press, 1975.

De Mézières was an adviser and confidant of French kings; he was for a time Chancellor of Cyprus. In this epistle he urges peace between France and England, and so unity in Christian Europe.

De Vigenère, Blaise: see Philostratus, Flavius.

Di Bassi, Pietro Andrea (fl. mid-15th cent.) *The Labors of Hercules*, tr. W. Kenneth Thompson. Barre: Imprint Society, 1971.

Dinet, Pierre (1555-1595). *Cinq Livres des Hieroglyphiques*. Paris, 1614; facsimile rpt.: New York: Garland, 1979.

Dinet was a Doctor of Theology. This book is a working out of the common assumption that moral-allegorical significance may be discovered in the details of natural history; that is, nature is full of allegorical meaning.

Diodorus Siculus (fl. 60-30 B.C.). *Bibliotheca Historia*, in *Diodorus of Sicily*, tr. C. H. Oldfather. Cambridge: Loeb, 1933.

Diodorus was a Roman historian. This book is his history of the world; it includes an account of the Trojan War.

Diogenes Laertius (fl. c. 430 B.C.). *Lives of the Emminent Philosophers*, 2 vols., tr. R. D. Hicks. Cambridge: Loeb, 1972.

This work is for the most part a compendium of the sayings of famous philosophers.

Dolce, Lodovico (1508-1568). *Le Transformationi*. Venice, 1561.

This is an Italian translation of Ovid's *Metamorphoses*, with allegorical commentary.

Donatus, Tiberius Claudius (fl. mid. 4th cent.). *Interpretationes Virgilianae*, ed. Henricus Georgii. Lepzig: Teubner, 1905.

Donatus was an important Latin grammarian. His work was frequently published, imitated, and expanded upon down through the Renaissance.

Donne, John (1572?-1631). *The Divine Poems*, ed. Helen Gardner. Oxford: Clarendon Press, 1966.

_____. *The Elegies and the Songs and Sonnets*, ed. Helen Gardner. Oxford: Clarendon Press, 1965.

Donne was a love poet, religious poet, Dean of St. Paul's Cathedral, and a brilliant preacher.

Douglas, Gawain (1474?-1522). "Preface" to Virgil, *xii Bukes of Eneados...tr. into Scottish metir, bi...Gawain Douglas*. London, 1553.

Douglas was a Scots poet, allegorist, and bishop; the Preface to his translation of Virgil interprets the *Aeneid* allegorically.

Drayton, Michael (1563-1631). *The Works of Michael Drayton*, ed. J. William Hebel. Oxford: Shakespeare Head Press, 1961.

Drayton was a writer of diverse talents; he wrote plays, poetry, satire, pastorals, mythological poems (such as "Endimion and Phoebe"), and more.

Dryden, John (1631-1700). *The Poems and Fables of John Dryden*, ed. James Kinsley. New York: Oxford.

Dryden was an English poet, playwright, and translator.

Du Bartas, Guillaume (1544-1590). *Bartas: His Devine Weekes and Workes*, tr. Joshua Sylvester. London, 1605; facsimile rpt.: Gainesville: Scholars' Facsimiles and Reprints, 1965.

The allegorical, devotional poetry of Du Bartas, a Gascon Huguenot, was probably more admired in England (especially in Sylvester's translation) than in his native France. Spenser and Sidney, for example, were both admirers.

Edwards, Richard (1523?-1566). *Damon and Pithias*, in Joseph Quincy Adams, *Chief Pre-Shakespearean Dramas*. Cambridge: Houghton Mifflin, 1952.

Edwards was an English poet and dramatist.

Erasmus, Desiderious (1466-1536). *Adages*, tr. M. M. Phillips, vols. 31-32; *On Disclaiming the World*, tr. Erika Rummel, vol. 66, in *Collected Works of Erasmus*, ed. John W. O'Malley. Toronto: Univ. of Toronto Press, 1982-1988.

Erasmus of Amsterdam was the great humanist priest of the Renaissance. He was active in the revival and translation of ancient Greek literature; he was the most popular writer of his day. Himelick's praise is perhaps the best and most apt: Unlike Luther and other religious zealots, Erasmus "had a mind too complicated for furious certitudes, too modest to suppose that in his every insight he was realizing the final promise made to Moses that he would see God's backside."

_____. *The Enchiridion*, tr. Raymond Himelick. Bloomington: Indiana Univ. Press, 1963.

Eriugena, Johannes Scotus: see John the Scot.

Euripides (485? - 406? B.C.). *Alcestis*; *Bacchanals*; *Medea*, in *Euripides*, 4 vols., tr. A. S. Way. Cambridge: Loeb, 1912.

Euripides was a Greek tragic playwright.

Eustathius, Archbishop of Thessalonica (d. c. 1194). *Commentarii ad Homeri Iliadem et Odysseam*, 3 vols. Hildesheim: Georg Olms Verlagsbuchhandlung, 1960.

Eustathius was a widely learned man and a defender of Monasticism. His commentaries on classical authors were still consulted in the Renaissance.

Ferrand, Jaques (c. 1575-after 1625). *A Treatise on Lovesickness*, tr. and ed., Donald A. Beecher and Massimo Ciavolella. Syracuse: Syracuse Univ. Press, 1990.

Ferrand was a French medical practitioner with Neo-Platonist inclinations. This treatise is one of Burton's many sources for *The Anatomy of Melancholy*. Ferrand was translated into English as early as 1640.

Ficino, Marsilio (1433-1499). *Commentary on Plato's Symposium on Love*, tr. Sears Jayne. Dallas: Spring Pubs., 1985.

_____. *Commentum cum summis capitulorum*; *Commentarium in Phaedrum*, in Michael J. B. Allen, *Marsilio Ficino and the Phaedran Charioteer*, Los Angeles: Univ. of California Press, 1981: 131-216.

Ficino, an Italian scholar and philosopher, was the most influential of the Renaissance Neo-Platonists. His most important work was his commentaries on Plato, such as the commentaries on the *Phaedrus*, the *Symposium*, and the *Philebus* listed here.

————. *The Letters of Marsilio Ficino*, 4 vols., tr. Language Dept. of the School of Economic Science, London. London: Shepheard-Walwyn, 1978-1988.

————. *Opera Omnia*, 2 vols. Basel, 1576; facsimile rpt.: Torin: Bottega d'Erasmo, 1962.

————. *The Philebus Commentary*, tr. Michael J. B. Allen. Berkeley: Univ. of California Press, 1975.

————. *Three Books on Life*, tr. Carol Kaske and John R. Clark. Binghamton: MRTS, 1989.

Florus, Lucius Annaeus (fl. 1st half of 2nd cent. A.D.). *The Epitome*, in *Florus*, tr. E. S. Forster. Cambridge: Loeb, 1929.

Florus's *Epitome* is a history of Rome, concentrating in particular on Rome's wars.

Fraunce, Abraham (fl. 1582-1633). *Third Part of the Countesse of Pembrokes Yvychurch....* London, 1592; facsimile rpt.: New York: Garland, 1976.

This is generally regarded as the most important of the sixteenth-century English mythographies. It is packed with traditional allegory.

Fulgentius, Fabius Planciades (fl. early 6th cent.). *On the Ages of the World and of Man*; *The Exposition on the Content of Virgil*; *The Mythologies*; *Super Thebaiden*, in *Fulgentius the Mythographer*, tr. Leslie George Whitbread. Columbus: Ohio State Univ. Press, 1971.

Fulgentius was probably a North African teacher of grammar and letters; he was regarded during the Middle Ages and the Renaissance as one of the most important authorities on Virgil, the myths, and Statius.

Gallensis, Thomas: see Waleys, Thomas.

Garland, John of (d. c. 1258): see John of Garland.

Gascoigne, George (1525?-1577). "In the Commendation of the Noble Arte of Venerie," in George Turberville, *The Noble Arte of Venerie*. London, 1576; rpt. Oxford: Clarendon Press, 1908.

Gascoigne was an English writer of plays, poetry, and prose.

Geoffrey of Monmouth (c. 1100-1154). *History of the Kings of Britain*, tr. Sebastian Evans. New York: Dutton, 1958.

This history was an important influence on later writers; Geoffrey is said to be the originator of the stories of Arthur as heroic king.

Giovanni del Virgilio (fl. c. 1330). "Giovanni del Virgilio espositore delle *Metamorfosi*." *Il Giornale Dantesco*, 34, N.S. 4 (1933): 1-110.

This is an Italian allegorical commentary on Ovid's *Metamorphoses*.

Giraldi, Lilio Gregorio (1479-1552). *De deis gentium*. Basil, 1548; facsimile rpt.: New York: Garland, 1976.

Giraldi was an Italian scholar and poet. His *De deis gentium* is a deeply learned mythography.

Golding, Arthur (c. 1536 - c. 1605). "The Epistle"; "Preface (to the Reader)," in Golding's tr. of Ovid: *The XV Bookes of P. Ovidius Naso, entytuled Metamorphosis*, ed. W. H. D. Rouse. London: De la More Press, 1904.

Golding is best remembered as a translator of Ovid; Shakespeare knew Ovid in Golding's translation, for example. But Golding also translated religious treatises.

Gombauld, Jean Ogier de (c. 1570-1666). *Endimion*, tr. Richard Hurst. London, 1639.

Gombauld was a French poet and dramatist; he was one of the founders of the French Academy.

Gower, John (1325?-1408). *Confessio Amantis*, in *The English Works of John Gower*, vols. 1-2, ed. G. C. Macaulay. Oxford: Oxford Univ. Press, 1957.

Gower was a poet well known in the courts of the English kings Richard II and Henry IV. He was a friend of Chaucer.

_____. *Miroir de l'homme*, in *Complete Works of John Gower*, vol. 1, ed. G. C. Macaulay. Grosse Pointe, MI: Scholar's Press, 1968.

Greene, Robert (1560?-1592). *Robert Greene, The Life and Complete Works in Prose and Verse*, ed. A. B. Grosart. New York: Russell and Russell, 1964.

Greene was a playwright, a miscellaneous writer—and something of a scapegrace.

Gregory of Nyssa (c. 335- c. 389). *On the Image*, in *Nicene and Post-Nicene Fathers of the Christian Church*, vol. 5, ed. Philip Schaff and Henry Wace. New York: Christian Literature Co., 1893.

Gregory was Bishop of Nazianzus, but he is remembered as one of the Fathers of the Church for his mystical theological writings.

Guido da Pisa (fl. 1320-1330). *Expositiones et Glose super Comediam Dantis*, ed. Vincenzo Cioffari. Albany: State Univ. of New York, 1974.

Guido was an Italian commentator on Dante. His commentary tries to interpret Dante in keeping with the method of fourfold allegory.

Guillaume de Conches (c. 1080- c. 1150). Commentary on Boethius's *Consolation of Philosophy*, in J. M. Parent, *La Doctrine de la Creation dans l'Ecole de Chartres*. Paris: Librairie Philosophique J. Vrin, 1938: 124-136.

Guillaume was a French grammarian and classical scholar; he was interested in the astrological interpretation of ancient mythology.

_____. *Glossae super Platonem, texte critique...*, ed., Edouard Jeauneau. *Textes Philosophiques du Moyen Age*, vol. 13. Paris: Vrin, 1965.

_____. "Selections from William of Conches's Commentary on Macrobius," in Dronke, 1974: 68-78.

Hall, Thomas (1610-1665). *Wisdoms Conquest. or, An explanation and...Translation of the thirteenth Book of Ovids Metamorphoses*. London, 1651.

This is another translation of Ovid with allegorical commentary.

Harington, John (1561-1612). *An Apologie of Poetrie*, included as a preface to Harington's tr. of, and commentary on, *Orlando Furioso*: see Ariosto.

Harington was the godson of Queen Elizabeth; his translation of Ariosto's *Orlando Furioso* was undertaken at her command. One might say, then, that Harington's allegorical commentary was the reigning interpretation.

_____. *A New Discourse of a Stale Subject Called the Metamorphosis of Ajax*, ed. Elizabeth Story Donno. London: Routledge and Kegan Paul, 1962.

Heinsius, Daniel (1580-1655). *Nederduytsche Poemata*, ed. P. S. Amsterdam, 1618.

Heinsius was one of the most famous of scholars of the Dutch Golden Age. In addition to his own original poetry, he published editions of classical authors and the *Epistles* (1627) of his teacher Joseph Scaliger.

Henri d'Andeli (13th cent.). *Le lai d'Aristotle; publie d'apres tous les manuscrits par Maurice Delbouille*. Paris, Societe d'edition "Les Belles Lettres," 1951.

Henryson, Robert (1430? -1506). *The Poems and Fables of Robert Henryson*, ed. H. Harvey Wood. Edinburgh: Oliver and Boyd, 1958.

A Scots poet, one of the "Scottish Chaucerians."

Heraclitus (sometimes Heraclides, probably first cent. A.D.). *Allégories d'Homère*, tr. Félix Buffière. Paris: Budé, 1962.
Heraclitus wrote the earliest surviving allegorical commentary on Homer; he should not be confused with the better known Heraclitus, the sixth-century B.C. Ephesian philosopher.
Herodotus (c. 480- c. 425 B.C.). *History*, tr. A. D. Godley. Cambridge: Loeb, 1921.
The Greek historian Herodotus is often praised as the Father of History.
Herrick, Robert (1591-1674). *The Complete Poetry of Robert Herrick*, ed. J. Max Patrick. New York: New York Univ. Press, 1963.
Herrick was an English poet.
Hesiod (8th cent. B.C.). *Hesiod, The Homeric Hymns and Homerica*, tr. H. G. Evelyn-White. Cambridge: Loeb, 1964.
Hesiod's *Works and Days* is usually regarded as the beginning of Greek didactic poetry; his *Theogony* is an account of the origin of the gods and of the world.
Higden, Ranulph (d. 1364). *Polychronicon Ranulphi Higden*, 1381-1394, ed. J. R. Lumby. London: Rolls Series, 1886.
Higden, a Benedictine monk, was an English chronicler. This book is a history of the world from the creation down to Higden's own day.
Hippocrates (460?-377? B.C.). *Works*, tr. W. H. S. Jones. Cambridge: Loeb, 1923.
This Greek physician is remembered as the Father of Medicine. Doctors still repeat the Hippocratic oath.
Homer (9th cent. B.C.). *The Iliad*, tr. Richard Lattimore. Chicago: Univ. of Chicago Press, 1961.
Homer was a Greek epic poet. For more on Homer, see **HOMER**.
_____. *The Odyssey*, tr. Robert Fitzgerald. New York: Anchor, 1963.
Homeric Hymns (probably 6th and 7th cent. B.C.; formerly attributed to Homer). "The Homeric Hymns," in *Hesiod, The Homeric Hymns and Homerica*, tr. H. G. Evelyn-White. Cambridge: Loeb, 1964.
Horace (65 - 8 B.C.). *The Art of Poetry*; *Epistles*; *Satires*, in *Satires, Epistles, Ars Poetica*, tr. H. R Fairclough. Cambridge: Loeb, 1966.
Horace was a Roman satirist and lyric poet.
_____. *Odes*, in *Odes and Epodes*, tr. C. E. Bennett. Cambridge: Loeb, 1964.
Hugh of Fouilloy (d. 1172/3). *The Medieval Book of Birds: Hugh of Fouilloy's Aviarium*, ed. and tr. Willene B. Clark. Binghamton: MRTS, 1992.
In this illustrated monastic text, Hugh, a north French Augustinian prior, treats of birds both literally and figuratively.
Hugh of St. Victor (c. 1096-1141). *The Didascalicon*, tr. Jerome Taylor. New York: Columbia Univ. Press, 1968.
This book describes and defines all the areas of knowledge important to human beings. The book was widely influential; it survives in nearly a hundred manuscripts, dating from the twelfth to the fifteenth centuries.
Hurst, Richard: see Gombauld, Jean Ogier de.
Hyginus (fl. before 207 A.D.). *Fabulae*; *Poetica Astronomica*, in *The Myths of Hyginus*, tr. Mary Grant. Lawrence: Univ. of Kansas Press, 1960.
Virtually nothing is known about this early mythographer. His work was unknown from about the sixth century until it was published by Micyllus at Basle in 1535. Thereafter Hyginus was frequently used.
Ioannes Scottus: see John the Scot.

Isidore of Seville (c. 560-636). *Etymologiarum sive originum*, ed. W. M. Lindsay. Oxford: Oxford Univ. Press, 1985 (1911).

Isidore was a Spanish encyclopedist and historian. His *Etymologiarum* is the quintessential expression of the conviction that the names of things come from nature, not convention. This belief was general all the way from antiquity down to the Renaissance. One could discover the nature of things, then, by studying the names of things.

Jerome (c. 341-420). *Against John of Jerusalem*; *Dialogue against Jovinianus*, in *The Principal Works of St. Jerome, Nicene and Post-Nicene Fathers of the Christian Church*, vol. 6, ed. Philip Schaff and Henry Wace. New York: Christian Literature Co. 1893.

Jerome is regarded as one of the Church Fathers. He is best known for his Latin translation of the Bible, known as the Vulgate.

_____. *The Letters of St. Jerome*, vol. 1, tr. C. C. Mierow. Westminster: Newman, 1963.

_____. *Liber de viris illustribus*. *PL*, vol. 23.

_____. *Bibliorum Sacrorum*. Vatican, 1959.

John of Garland (1180-1252). *Integumenta Ovidii, poemetto inedito del secolo XIII*, ed. F. Ghisalberti. Milan, 1933.

John was an English scholar, residing in Paris.

John of Salisbury (1120? -1180?). *Policraticus: the Statesman's Book*, tr. M. F. Markland. New York: Ungar, 1979.

John was a student at Chartres when that school was preeminent in the revival of classical Latin literature and the promotion of Platonism. This book is one of the Medieval encyclopedias.

John the Scot (815? - 877?). *Iohannis Scotti annotationes in Marcianum*, ed. Cora E. Lutz. Cambridge: Medieval Academy of America, 1942.

John was best known in his own day for his translations of some of the early Greek Fathers of the Church. *On the Division of Nature* is an early example of the Medieval encyclopedia.

_____. *On the Division of Nature*, tr. Myra Uhlfelder. Indianapolis: Bobbs-Merrill, 1976.

Jonson, Ben (1573-1637). *Ben Jonson*, 11 vols., ed. C. H. Herford Percy and Evelyn Simpson. Oxford: Clarendon, 1925-1950.

Jonson was a playwright, poet, and satirist. He is generally considered to have been the most learned of the Elizabethan dramatists.

Justin Martyr (c. 100- c. 165). *The Apologies of Justin Martyr*, ed. Basil Gildersleeve. New York: American Book Co., c. 1904.

Justin Martyr converted to Christianity in Palestine, c. 130; he devoted himself to the propagation and defense of Christianity.

Justinus, Marcus Junianus (probably 3rd c. A.D.). *Epitoma historium Philippicarum*, tr. J. S. Watson. 1853.

This history was widely read in the Middle Ages.

Juvenal (60?-140?). *The Sixteen Satires*, tr. Peter Green. Baltimore: Penguin, 1967.

Juvenal was a Roman satiric poet.

Knox, John (1505-1572). *The First Blasts of the Trumpet Against the Monstrous Regiment of Women*, ed. Edward Arber. London: *The English Scholar's Library of Old and Modern Works*, no. 2, 1878.

This book by the Scots reformer and founder of Presbyterianism was aimed at Mary Queen of Scots.

Lactantius (?250-?317). *Divine Institutes*, tr. Mary Francis McDonald. Washington, D.C.: Catholic Univ. of America Press, 1964.

Born a pagan, Lactantius became an important Christian apologist. He was also the tutor for the son of the Emperor Constantine.

Lactantius Placidus (6th cent.). *Narrationes Fabularum Quae in P. Ovidii Nasonis Libris XV Metamorphoseon occurrunt*, in Thomas Munckerus, *Mythographi Latini*. Amsterdam, 1681: 185-300.

The attribution of the Statius commentary to Lactantius is difficult to establish, since it seems that some of the commentary was written as early as the fourth century. This commentary continued to enjoy accretions during the Middle Ages. The Statius commentary was important because it transmitted the Pythagorean method to the Middle Ages.

_____. *Commentarium in Statii Thebaida*, ed. Richard Jahnke. Leipzig, 1879.

Landino, Cristoforo (1424-1498). *Disputationes Camuldenses*, ed. Peter Lohe. Fierenze: Sansoni, 1980. For a tr. of bks. 3 and 4, see Peter Stahel, *Cristoforo Landino's Allegorization of the Aeneid: Books III and IV of the Camaldolese Disputations*. Johns Hopkins Univ.: Ph.D. Dissertation, 1968.

Landino was known as the "literary wing" of the Florentine Academy. With his translations and commentaries, he brought the tenets of Ficino's Neo-Platonism to bear upon the Latin classics and Dante.

_____. *La Commedia* (Dante's *Commedia*, with commentary by Cristoforo Landino). Brescia, 1487.

_____. *De Vera Nobilitate*, ed. Manfred Lentzen. Geneva: Droz, 1970.

Lavinius, Petrus (fl. 1st half of 16th c.). *Metamorphoses*. Venice, 1540.

Lavinius was an Italian priest. This book provides commentary on the first book of Ovid's *Metamorphoses*. Lavinius's commentary was widely read, and often recycled in other commentaries; see, e.g., Regius, Raphael.

LeFèvre, Raoul (fl. 1454-1467). *Le recueil des hystoires de Troyes*, ed. Marc Aeschbach. Bern: Lang, 1987.

This history of the Trojan war and related subjects was translated by William Caxton as *The Recuyell of the Historyes of Troye* (Brugge, 1464).

Livy (59 B.C.-17 A.D.). *Ab urbe condita libri*, 14 vols., tr. B. O. Foster et al. Cambridge: Loeb, 1919-1949.

Livy was a Roman historian.

Lucan (39-65). *The Civil War*, tr. J. D. Duff. Cambridge: Loeb, 1943.

Lucan was a Roman writer of prose and verse. This history of the Roman civil war is all that has come down to us.

Lucian (b. c. 120 A.D.- some time after 180). *Dialogues of the Gods*, tr. M. D. MacLeod; *Dionysus*; *Essays in Portraiture*, tr. A. M. Harmon, in *Lucian*, 8 vols. Cambridge: Loeb, 1967.

Lucian was a Greek satirist.

Lucretius (probably 94-55 B.C.). *On The Nature of Things*, in *Lucretius*, tr. W. H. D. Rouse; rev. Martin F. Smith. Cambridge: Loeb, 1975.

Lydgate, John (c. 1370-c. 1451). *Falls of Princes*, ed. Henry Bergen. London: Early English Text Society, nos. 121-124; 1924.

Lydgate was a priest and an English poet, a follower of Chaucer. This book is based upon Boccaccio's *De Casibus Virorum Illustrium*.

_____. *Reson and Sensuallyte*, 2 vols., ed. Ernst Sieper. London: Kegan Paul, 1901.

_____. *Siege of Thebes*, ed. Axel Erdmann. London: Early English Text Society, nos. 108, 125; 1911.

Lyly, John (1554?-1606). *Campaspe; Endimion; Sapho and Phao*, in *The Complete Works of John Lyly*, 3 vols., ed. R. Warwick Bond. Oxford: Clarendon Press, 1902.
Lyly was renowned for his wit; he was a poet, pamphleteer, and playwright.

Lynche, Richard (fl. 1600). *The Fountaine of Ancient Fiction*. London, 1599; facsimile rpt.: New York: Garland, 1976.
This volume is Lynche's truncated translation of Cartari's *Le imagini de i dei gli antichi*.

Machiavelli, Niccolo (1469-1527). *The Prince*, in *Machiavelli: The Chief Works and Others*, vol. 1, tr. Allan Gilbert. Durham: Duke Univ. Press, 1965.
Machiavelli is best known for his political writings, most notably *The Prince*; but he also wrote plays and history.

Macrobius (fl. c. 430). *Commentary on the Dream of Scipio*, tr. W. H. Stahl. New York; Columbia Univ. Press, 1966.
Macrobius seems to have been North African. He was certainly a Neo-Platonist and almost certainly not a Christian. This book is a commentary on the "Dream of Scipio," the closing portion of Cicero's *De re publica*. The book was a widely used encyclopedia during the Middle Ages; it was particularly important as a standard authority on dreams and visions.

_____. *The Saturnalia*, tr. Percival V. Davies. New York: Columbia Univ. Press, 1969.
This book is full of antiquarian lore about the pagan gods and their festivals. Books 3 and 4 are devoted to a commentary on Virgil.

Marlowe, Christopher (1564-1593). *The Complete Plays of Christopher Marlowe*, ed. Irving Ribner. New York: Odyssey, 1963.
Marlowe was an English playwright and poet.

Marston, John (c. 1575-1634). "The Metamorphosis of Pigmalion's Image," in *The Poems of John Marston*, ed. Arnold Davenport. Liverpool: Liverpool Univ. Press, 1961.
Marston was an English poet and playwright.

Martial (42?-102?). *Epigrams*, tr. W. C. A. Ker. Cambridge: Loeb, 1968.
Born in Spain, Martial spent most of his life in Rome. He was a writer of epigrams.

Martianus Felix Capella (fl. probably first quarter of 5th cent.). *The Marriage of Philology and Mercury*, vol. 2 of William Harris Stahl, Richard Johnson, and E. L. Burge, *Martianus Capella and the Seven Liberal Arts*. New York: Columbia Univ. Press, 1971.
This important book's description of the liberal arts was considered authoritative throughout the Middle Ages. The book also established a number of allegorical and iconographic traditions, which continued down to the seventh century.

Milton, John (1608-1674). *John Milton: Complete Poems and Major Prose*, ed. Merritt Hughes. New York: Odyssey Press, 1957.
This Puritan poet's best-known work is the epic *Paradise Lost*. Milton was deeply learned in the classics.

Mirandola, Pico della: see Pico della Mirandola, Giovanni.

The Mirour of Mans Salvacioun: A Middle English Translation of Speculum Humanae Salvationis, ed. Avril Henry. Philadelphia: Univ. of Pennsylvania Press, 1987.
This is a 1495 English translation of an anonymous fourteenth-century Latin poem. The poem is a universal history in the Biblical sense; it takes us all the way from the fall of Lucifer and his rebel angels to the end of this world, the Last Judgment. The poem was one of the most popular books of its time.

Mirror for Magistrates (1559), ed. Lily B. Campbell. New York: Barnes and Noble, 1960.
This is a compendium of didactic tragedies—*de casibus exempla.*

Montemayor, George of (c. 1520-1561). *A Critical Edition of [Bartholomew] Yong's Translation [1598] of George of Montemayor's Diana...*, ed. Judith Kennedy. Oxford: Oxford Univ. Press, 1968.
This pastoral romance is one of the masterpieces of the Golden Age of Spanish literature. The book was an important influence on Spenser's, Shakespeare's, and Sidney's sense of the pastoral mode.

Moschus (fl. 150 B.C.). *Idylls*, in *The Greek Bucolic Poets*, tr. J. M. Edmonds. Cambridge: Loeb, 1938.
The second of the three originators of Greek bucolic poetry (Theocritus, Moschus, and Bion).

Muth, Conrad: see Mutianus Rufus.

Mutianus Rufus (Conrad Muth: 1471-1526). *Der Briefwechsel des Mutianus Rufus*, ed. Krause. Cassel, 1885.
Mutianus was a German humanist.

Nashe, Thomas (1567-1601). *The Returne of the renowned Cavaliero, Pasquill of England*, in *The Works of Thomas Nashe*, 5 vols, ed. Ronald B. McKerrow. London: Bullen, 1904.
Nashe was an English dramatist, pamphleteer, and satirist.

Neckam, Alexander (c. 1157-1217). *De Naturis Rerum...with the poem of the same author...De Laudibus Divinae Sapientiae*, ed. Thomas Wright. London: Longman, 1863.
Neckam was a natural scientist, grammarian, abbot, and schoolman. This book, *On the Nature of Things*, is one of the great Medieval encyclopedias.

_____: see Albricus of London.

_____: see Vatican Mythographer III.

Nequam, Alexander: see Neckam, Alexander.

Orosius, Paulus (5th cent. A.D.). *The Seven Books of History against the Pagans*, Roy J. Deferrari. Washington, D.C.: Catholic Univ. of America Press, 1964.
Orosius was a stridently antipagan historian. He was widely read during the Middle Ages.

Ovid (43 B.C. - 17 A.D.?). *The Art of Love; The Remedies for Love*, in *The Art of Love and other Poems*, tr. J. H. Mozely. Cambridge: Loeb, 1985.
Ovid was the ancient poet best known to the Middle Ages and the Renaissance, and the *Metamorphoses* was the most widely known ancient guide to the pagan gods.

_____. *Epistulae ex Ponto*, in *Tristia, Ex Ponto*, tr. A. L. Wheeler, rev. by G. P. Gould. Cambridge: Loeb, 1987.

_____. *Ovid's Fasti*, tr. J. G. Frazer. Cambridge: Loeb, 1951.

_____. *Heroides*, in *Heroides and Amores*, tr. Grant Showerman. Cambridge: Loeb, 1958.

_____. *Metamorphoses*, tr. F. J. Miller. Cambridge: Loeb, 1960; for early translations of the *Metamorphoses*, see Agostini (Italian), Caxton (English), Dolce (Italian), Golding (English), Hall (English), Renouard (French), Sandys (English), Verburg (Dutch), and Viana (Spanish).

Ovide Moralisé (probably between 1316 and 1328), 5 vols., ed. L. de Boer. *Verhandelingen der Koninklijke Akademie van Wetenschappen*, Amsterdam, 1915-1938.

This huge poem retells the stories in Ovid's *Metamorphoses*, providing allegorical commentary along the way. It finds in Ovid many types of Biblical events and figures. This book should not be confused with Berchorius's *Ovide Moralisé*.

Pausanias (fl. c. 150 A.D.). *Description of Greece*, 5 vols., tr. W. H. S. Jones and H. A. Ormerod. Cambridge: Loeb, 1918.

Pausanius was a Greek traveller and geographer.

Peacham, Henry (1578? - 1642?). *Garden of Eloquence*. Menston: Scholar Press, 1971.

Educated at Cambridge, Peacham was a schoolmaster, college tutor, and writer. He was best known for his emblem book, *Minerva Britanna*.

_____. *Minerva Britanna, or a garden of heroical devices, furnished and adrorned with Emblemes...*. London, 1612; facsimile rpt., Leeds: Scholar Press, 1966.

Pearl Poet, the (fl. late 15th cent.). *Sir Gawain and the Green Knight*, ed. J. R. R. Tolkein and E. V. Gordon. Oxford: Clarendon Press, 1963.

The author of this allegorical romance is usually assumed also to have written *The Pearl* and some other allegorical, didactic poems.

Peele, George (1556-1596). *The Life and Works of George Peele*, ed. C. T. Prouty. New Haven: Yale Univ. Press, 1970.

Peele was a London dramatist. His *Arraignment of Paris* was staged by the Children of the Chapel Royal before Queen Elizabeth.

Petrarch, Francis (1304-1374). *Africa*, tr. Thomas Bergin and Alice Wilson. New Haven: Yale Univ. Press, 1977.

Petrarch, an Italian scholar and poet, was one of the formative figures of the Renaissance. His love poetry in particular was widely imitated.

_____. *Bucolicum Carmen*, tr. Thomas G. Bergin. New Haven: Yale Univ. Press, 1974.

_____. *Remedies for Fortune Fair and Foul*, 5 vols., tr. Conrad H. Rawski. Bloomington: Indiana Univ. Press, 1991.

_____. *Petrarch's Lyric Poems: The Rime sparse and Other Lyrics*, tr. and ed. Robert M. Durling. Cambridge: Harvard Univ. Press, 1976.

_____. *Triumphi*, ed. Marco Ariani. Milan: Mursia, 1988.

Pettie, George (c. 1548-1589). *A Petite Pallace of Pettie His Pleasure*, ed. Herbert Hartman. London: Oxford Univ. Press, 1938.

This is a collection of twelve euphuistic retellings of stories from classical sources.

Philo Judaeus (c. 30 B.C.-45 A.D.). *On Providence*, in *Philo Judaeus*, vol. 9, tr. F. H. Colson. Cambridge: Loeb, 1941.

Philo was the head of the Jewish community in Alexandria. Philo was concerned to adapt Greek philosophy and allegorical methods to Jewish scripture and traditions.

Philostratus, Flavius (c. 170-245). *Les Images*, tr. with commentary by Blaise de Vigenère. Paris, 1614; facsimile rpt.: New York: Garland, 1976.

Philostratus was a Greek sophist. Ostensibly, his *Images* describes sixty-four pictures in a Neapolitan gallery.

_____. *Life of Apollonius of Tyana*, tr. F. C. Conybeare. Cambridge: Loeb.

Pico della Mirandola, Giovanni (1463-1494). *Commentary on a Poem of Platonic Love*, tr. Douglas Carmichael. Lanham: University Press of America, 1986.

Pico was an Italian humanist philosopher; he was a part of Ficino's influential Neo-Platonist circle.

_____. *On the Dignity of Man, On Being and the One, Heptaplus*, tr. Charles Glenn Wallis et al. Indianapolis: Bobbs-Merrill, 1965.

_____. *Opera Omnia*. Basel, 1557; facsimile rpt.: Hildesheim: Georg Holms, 1969.

_____. *A Platonick Discourse upon Love*, ed. Edmund Gardner. Boston: Merrywood Press, 1914.

_____. *Conclusiones sive Theses DCCC*, ed. Bohdan Kiezkowski. Geneva: Droz, 1973.

Pictorius, Georgius (c. 1500-1569). *Apotheoseos*. Basel: 1554; facsimile rpt.: New York: Garland, 1976.

Pictorius was a German physician. This is a revised, expanded edition of *Theologia Mythologica*, including illustrations of the gods.

_____. *Theologia Mythologia*. Antwerp, 1532; facsimile rpt.: New York: Garland, 1976.

This was the first large-scale treatment of the gods after Boccaccio's *Genealogie*.

Pindar (518-438 B.C.). *Pythian Odes* and *Isthmian Odes*, in *Pindar's Victory Songs*, tr. Frank J. Nisetich. Baltimore: Johns Hopkins Univ. Press, 1980.

Pindar was a Greek poet; these odes were written in celebration of the heroes of chariot races and games.

Plato (c. 427-c. 348 B.C.). *Plato: The Collected Dialogues*, ed. Edith Hamilton and Huntington Cairns. New York: Bollingen Series, 1964.

Plato was a tremendously important influence on Christian thinking. Even during the Middle Ages, when Chalcidius's translation of a part of the *Timaeus* was the only text available, Plato was important at second hand, as he was interpreted by Augustine, for example, and Boethius.

Pliny (23/4-79). *Natural History*, 10 vols., tr. H. Rackham, W. H. S. Jones, D. E. Eichholz. Cambridge: Loeb, 1938-1968.

Pliny's work was regarded as authoritative throughout the Middle Ages and was still widely consulted during the Renaissance.

Plotinus (205-269/70). *Enneads*, in *Plotinus*, 7 vols., tr. A. H. Armstrong. Cambridge: Loeb, 1966-1988.

Plotinus was a Greek Neo-Platonic philosopher.

Plutarch (c. 46- c. 120). *Isis and Osiris*; *Of the Tranquillity of the Mind*, in *Plutarch's Moralia*, 5 vols., tr. F. C. Babbitt. Cambridge: Loeb, 1962.

Plutarch was a Greek biographer and moral philosopher.

_____. *The Lives of the Noble Grecians and Romans*, tr. John Dryden. New York: Modern Library, n.d.

Poliziano, Angelo (1454-1494). *Stanze, Fabula di Orfeo*, ed. Stefano Carrai. Milan: Mursia, 1988.

A poet and translator, Poliziano was a member of the Neo-Platonic Florentine Academy.

_____. *Opera Omnia*, 3 vols. Basle, 1553; facsimile rpt., Torino, 1971.

Pope, Alexander (1688-1744). "The Dunciad," in *The Poems of Alexander Pope*, ed. John Butt. New Haven: Yale Univ. Press, 1966.

Poet and satirist, Pope was the foremost exponent of English neoclassicism.

Proclus Diadochus (c. 410-485). *Commentaire sur la République*, 3 vols., tr. A. J. Festugière. Paris: Vrin, 1970.

Proclus was the foremost Neo-Platonist of his day. This book is a commentary on Plato's *Republic*.

Propertius (49-15 B.C.). *Elegies*, in *Propertius*, tr. H. E. Butler. Cambridge: Loeb, 1962.

This Roman poet wrote on love, the myths, and Roman history.

Prudentius (b. 438). *Psychomachia*, tr. H. J. Thomson, in *Prudentius*, vol. 1. Cambridge: Loeb, 1949.

Born in Spain, Prudentius wrote Christian poetry in Latin.

Puttenham, George (1530?-1590). *The Arte of English Poesie*. London, 1589.

Puttenham is remembered for this thorough treatment of Tudor and Elizabethan poetry, its genres and techniques.

Quarles, Francis (1592-1644). *Emblemes*. Cambridge, 1643.

Quarles was an English religious poet. This is a book of poems matched with fitting emblems.

Rabanus Maurus (c. 784-856). *De Universo*. *PL*, vol. 111.

Rabanus was the archbishop of Mainz; he was also a poet and encyclopedist.

Rabelais, Francois (1490-1553). *Gargantua and Pantagruel*, in *The Complete Works of François Rabelais*, tr. Donald M. Frame. Berkeley: Univ. of California Press, 1991.

Rabelais was, in turns, a Franciscan, a Benedictine, and a physician. He was also a humanist.

Raleigh, Sir Walter (1552?-1618). *Sir Walter Raleigh, Selected Writings*, ed., Gerald Hammond. N.p.: Fyfield, 1984.

Raleigh was a muscular embodiment of the Renaissance Man: courtier, poet, explorer, soldier, and historian.

_____. *The History of the World*. Philadelphia, Temple Univ. Press, 1972.

Raoul de Presles (fl. mid 15th cent.). Commentary on Augustine, *The City of God*. Abbeville, 1468.

Raoul added his own commentary to this edition of *The City of God*.

Regius, Raphael (fl. 1500). *Ovidii Nasonis Poete...Metamorphoseos...Raphaelis Regii luculentissime enarrationes...Necque non Lactantii & Petri Lavinii Commentarii non ante impressi*. Venice, 1540.

Regius's commentary is mainly philological; like many other editions of Regius's Ovid, however, this one includes the priest Lavinius's allegorical glosses on book 1.

Renouard, Nicolas (fl. early 17th cent.). *Les Metamorphoses d'Ovide traduittes en Prose Francoise...Avec XV Discours contenans l'explication moralé des Fables*. Paris, 1614.

This is a translation of Ovid into French, with commentary.

Reynolds, Henry (fl. 1627-1633). *Mythomystes, Wherein a Short Survay is Taken of the Nature and Value of True Poesie...*, in J. E. Spingarn, *Critical Essays of the Seventeenth Century*, vol. 1. Bloomington: Indiana Univ. Press, 1957: 144-179.

Reynolds was an English Neo-Platonist, a follower of Pico della Mirandola; this treatise was the most important early seventeenth-century Neo-Platonist account of poetics in English.

Ridewall, John (mid 14th cent.). *Fulgentius metaforalis*, ed. Hans Liebschütz. *Studien der Bibliothek Warburg*, 4. Leipzig-Berlin, 1926.

Ridewall was an English Franciscan scholar. This book purports to be a renewal of Fulgenius, but in fact its sources are quite various.

Ripa, Cesare (fl. 1600). *Iconologie*, Paris, 1644; facsimile rpt.: New York: Garland, 1976.

Ripa and Cartari were the most important Renaissance sources for the iconography of the gods. This book is a French translation of Ripa's Italian.

Le Roman de Thèbes (The Story of Thebes) (c. 1287), tr. J. S. Coley. New York: Garland, 1986.

This is a Medieval French version of the story of Thebes.

Ronsard, Pierre de (1524-1585). *Les Oeuvres de Pierre de Ronsard, Texte de 1587*, 8 vols., ed. Isidore Silver. Chicago: Univ. of Chicago Press, 1966.

Ronsard was a French humanist poet.

Ross, Alexander (1590-1654). *Mystagogus Poeticus, or The Muses Interpreter.... The second edition much enlarged*. London: 1648; facsimile rpt.: New York: Garland, 1976.

Ross was a Scottish divine. This book is a large compendium of allegorizing mythography.

Sabinus (Schuler), Georg (fl. second half 16th c.). *Fabularum Ovidii Interpretatio, Ethica, Physica, et Historica....* Canterbury, 1584.

This is a traditional guide to the allegorical meanings of Ovid's tales; much of this is derived from Conti.

Sackville, Thomas (1536-1608), and Thomas Norton (1532-1584). *Gorboduc,* in Joseph Quincy Adams, *Chief Pre-Shakespearean Dramas.* Cambridge: Houghton Mifflin, 1952.

This is the first Senecan tragedy in English. The story comes from Geoffrey of Monmouth's *History of the Kings of Britain.*

Sallustius (fl. 2nd half of 4th cent. A.D.). *Concerning the Gods and the Universe,* tr. Arthur D. Nock. Hildesheim: Olms, 1966.

Sallustius was a Neo-Platonist; this book is a fervent, allegorical defense of mythology.

Salutati, Coluccio (1331-1406). *De Laboribus Herculis,* ed. B. L. Ullman. Turici: Societatis Thesauri Mundi, n.d. (c. 1947).

Salutati was truly a Renaissance Man, determined to balance within himself the active and the contemplative lives. He was a politician, Chancellor of Florence, poet, and humanist scholar. He knew Boccaccio and corresponded with Petrarch.

Sandys, George (1578-1644). *Ovid's Metamorphosis, Englished, Mythologized, and Represented in Figures,* ed. Karl Hulley and Stanley Vandersall. Lincoln: Univ. of Nebraska Press, 1970; based on the edition of 1632.

Sandys' commentary on the *Metamorphoses* is one of the fullest of the many commentaries on Ovid. It provides in many instances what may be taken as a summary statement of 1,500 years of allegorical interpretation of classical myth and legend. Sandys was, by the way, resident treasurer of the Jamestown colony from 1621 to 1625.

Sannazaro, Jacopo (1456-1530). *Arcadia,* ed. Francesco Erspamer. Milan: Mursia, 1990.

Sannazaro was a Neapolitan poet who wrote in a number of genres, including an epic poem *On the Virgin's Parturition.* The *Arcadia* was a widely influential pastoral poem.

Schuler, George: see Sabinus, Georg.

Scotus Eriugena, Johannes: see John the Scot.

The Scourge of Venus (anonymous, 1614). In P. W. Miller, ed., *Seven Minor Epics of the English Renaissance.* Gainesville: Scholars' Facsimiles, 1967.

This epic treatment of the story of Myrrha was for a time wrongly attributed to Henry Austin.

Seneca (4 B.C. - 65 A.D.). *De Beneficiis,* in *Moral Essays,* vol. 3, tr. J. W. Basore. Cambridge: Loeb, 1964.

Seneca was a Stoic philosopher, a tragic playwright, and tutor and advisor to the emperor Nero.

_____. *Epistulae Morales,* 3 vols., tr. R. M. Gummere. Cambridge: Loeb, 1930-1943.

_____. *Medea,* in *Tragedies,* tr. Frank J. Miller. Cambridge: Loeb, 1917.

Servius, Grammarian (fl. c. 400). *In Virgilii Aeneidos; In Bucolica et Georgica commentarii,* in *In Virgilii Carmina Commentarii,* 3 vols., ed. Georg Thilo and Herman Hagen. Lipsiae, 1881-1902.

Servius was a Latin grammarian. Servius's is the earliest allegorical commentary on Virgil's *Aeneid.*

Shakespeare, William (1564-1616). *The Riverside Shakespeare*, ed. G. Blakemore Evans. Boston: Houghton Mifflin, 1974.

Shakespeare was an English poet and playwright. He was clearly aware of a wide range of allegorical interpretations of the gods.

Sidney, Sir Philip (1554-1586). *Arcadia* (1590 version); *The Defense of Poesy*, in *The Prose Works of Sir Philip Sidney*, 4 vols., ed. Albert Feuillerat. Cambridge: Cambridge Univ. Press, 1968.

Sidney was the perfect embodiment of the Renaissance Man; he was a courtier, poet, soldier, scholar, and humanist.

Sophocles (c. 497-405 B.C.). *Ajax*; *Oedipus at Colonus*, in *Sophocles*, tr. F. Storr. Cambridge: Loeb, 1912-1913.

Sophocles was a Greek tragic playwright.

Speculum Humanae Salvationis: see *The Mirour of Mans Salvacioun*, and Wilson and Wilson (1984).

Speculum Humanae Salvationis: Ein Niederländisches Blockbuch, ed. Ernst Kloss. Munich: Piper, 1925.

This is an edition of the *Speculum* (see *Mirour of Mans Salvacioune*, above) with woodcut illustrations.

Spenser, Edmund (c. 1552-1599). *Spenser: Poetical Works*, ed., J. C. Smith and E. de Selincourt. London: Oxford, 1966.

Spenser was an English poet. *The Faerie Queene* is his greatest work. It brings together Spenser's Neo-Platonism, his Protestant Christianity, the episodic form of the romances and of the Renaissance Italian epics, Arthurian legend, the epic conventions, and traditional myth-allegory.

Stampa, Gaspara (c. 1523-c. 1554). *Rime*, in *Gaspara Stampa [and] Veronica Franco: Rime*, ed. Abd-el-Kader. Bari: Laterza, 1913.

Stampa was a Venetian courtesan and poet; she wrote madrigals, elegies, and sonnets. Upon retirement, she founded an asylum for poor prostitutes.

Statius, Publius Papinius (c. 45-96). *The Achilleid*; *Silvae*; *Thebaid*, in *Statius*, 2 vols., tr. J. H. Mozley. Cambridge: Loeb, 1928.

During the Middle Ages and the Renaissance, only Homer and Virgil were held in higher esteem than the Roman epic poet Statius. Dante (wrongly) considered Statius to have been a Christian.

Stephanus, Charles (d. 1559). *Dicitionarium Historicum Geographicum, Poeticum....* London: 1595.

This dictionary includes articles on the gods and goddesses—with an occasional allegorical aside. This dictionary was widely used, not least by most of the English poets. It went through twenty editions between its first publication in 1553 and 1693.

Strabo (63/64 B.C.-probably after 23 A.D.). *Geography*, tr. H. C. Hamilton and W. Falconer. London: Bohn, 1854.

Strabo was a Greek geographer and historian. His *Geography* first appeared in Western Europe in 1469, in a Latin translation.

Tasso, Torquato (1544-1595). *Dialoghi*, ed. E. Raimondi. Florence, 1958.

The Italian poet Tasso's *Jerusalem Delivered* is one of the great Renaissance epics.

_____. *Jerusalem Delivered*, tr. Edward Fairfax (1600), ed. Roberto Weiss. Carbondale: Southern Illinois Univ. Press, 1962.

Terence (c. 195-159 B.C.). *The Eunuch*, in *Terence*, tr. John Sargeaunt. Cambridge: Loeb, 1912.

Terence was an ancient Roman comic playwright.

Tertullian (c. 155- c. 220). *An Exhortation to Chastity*, in *Tertullian: Treatises on Marriage and Remarriage*, tr. W. P. Le Saint. Westminster: Newman, 1951.
Tertullian is considered one of the Church Fathers, despite his late lapse into heretical opinions.

_____. *To the Martyrs*; *Spectacles*, in *Tertullian: Disciplinary, Moral, and Ascetical Works*, tr. Rudolph Arbesmann et al. Washington, D.C.: Catholic University of America Press, 1985.

_____. *De resurrectione mortuorum*, in *Tertulliani Opera*, pt. 2. *Corpus Christianorum, Series Latina*, vol. 2, 1954.

Theocritus (early 3rd cent. B.C.). *Idyls*, in *The Greek Bucolic Poets*, tr. J. M. Edmonds. Cambridge: Loeb, 1938.
This Greek poet is regarded as the inventor of pastoral poetry.

Theodulph, Bishop of Orléans (c. 760-821). *Carmina. PL*, vol. 105.
Appointed Bishop of Orléans by Charlemagne, Theodulf was a poet, theologian, and church reformer.

_____. *Ecloga*, with commentary by Odo Picardus. Lyons, c. 1487-1488.
This was a particularly influential book, since it was one of six elementary Latin texts in the widely used Medieval schoolbook *Liber Catonianus* (Clogan 1968: 2-3). The *Ecloga* is a "debate" between the truth of Christianity and pagan falsity. But since Theodulph proceeded by juxtaposing (false) mythic figures with corresponding (true) Biblical figures, the *Ecloga* was often read as a collection of types. Certainly this is how Bernard of Utrecht understood the *Ecloga* in his commentary on the book, *Kommentar über Theoduli "Ecloga"* (see Bernard of Utrecht).

Theodulus: see Theodulph, Bishop of Orléans.

Thibaut de Champagne (1201-1253). "A Enviz Sent Mal Qui Ne l'a Apris," in *The Lyrics of Thibaut de Champagne*, ed. and tr. Kathleen J. Brahney. New York: Garland, 1989.
Thibaut was a poet, a crusader, and king of Navarre. Dante and Petrarch both had high regard for Thibaut's poetry.

Trevisa, John de: see Bartholomaeus Anglicus.

Tritonio, M. Antonio (16th cent.). *Mythologia*. Padua, 1616; facsimile rpt.: New York: Garland, 1979.
Tritonio, an Italian mythographer, wanted to make myth allegory easily available, and so this book proceeds mainly by compiling categorized lists of gods and mythic figures. One list for "The Libidinous," one for "The Wrathful," and so forth.

Udall, Nicholas (1504?-1556). *Roister Doister*, in Joseph Quincy Adams, *Chief Pre-Shakespearean Dramas*. Cambridge: Houghton Mifflin, 1952.
Udall was a translator of Terence and Headmaster of Eton. This play is regarded as the first English comedy (1553).

Valeriano Bolzani, Giovanni Pierio (1477-1558?). *Hieroglyphica*. Lyon, 1602; facsimile rpt.: New York: Garland, 1976.
This is an important Renaissance guide to "hieroglyphics," as symbolic images came to be called in these years.

Van Mander, Carel (1548-1606). *Wtlegginghe op den Metamorphosis....* Haarlem, 1604.
The two titles by van Mander listed here were eventually made part of a large work called *Het Schilderboeck, The Painter Book* (Amsterdam, 1616). Van Mander was himself a painter, and *Het Schilderboek* has long been recognized as important for art historians in particular. I am at work on translations of the *Wtlegginghe* and the *Wtbeeldinghen.*

_____. *Wytbeeldinghen der Figuren....* Amsterdam, 1616.

Van Veen, Octavio (1560? - 1629?). *Q. Horatii Flacci Emblemata....* Antwerp, 1612.
This is a collection of emblems based on Horace's precepts.

Vatican Mythographers I (8th or 9th cent.), II (9th or 10th cent.), and III (12th cent.). In *Scriptores Rerum Mythicarum Latini Tres*, ed. G. H. Bode. Cellis: 1834.
This is an edition of three early allegorical mythographies. Vatican Mythographer III is perhaps Alexander Neckham.

Verburg, Isaak (fl. 1732). *De Gedaant-wisselingen van P. Ovidius Naso, in het Latyn en Nederduitsch....* Amsterdam, 1732.
This is a Dutch translation of Ovid's *Metamorphoses* with allegorical commentary.

Viana, Sanchez de (fl. 1589). *Las transformaciones de Ovidio.... Con el comento, y explicación de las fabulas....* Cordova, 1589.
This is a Spanish translation of Ovid with allegorical commentary.

Virgil (70-19 B.C.). *Virgil*, tr. H. R. Fairclough. Cambridge: Loeb, 1929.
Virgil's *Georgics*, *Eclogues*, and *Aeneid* came to be widely regarded as the defining examples of their genres, farm, pastoral, and epic poetry, respectively. For Virgil as providing the model of the career of the poet and for the Virgil legends, see **VIRGIL**.

Vitruvius (wrote c. 16-14 B.C.). *On Architecture*, tr. Frank Granger. Cambridge: Loeb, 1931-1934.
This book is the only classical treatise on architecture to come down to us.

Vives, Lodovico (1492-1540). *St. Augustine, of the Citie of God: with the Learned Comments of Io. Lod. Vives.* London: 1610.
Erasmus convinced Vives, a Spanish churchman, to desert Scholasticism and take up Erasmian humanism. This edition of Augustine is the most important fruit of that conversion. Vives was one of the most widely read writers of his day.

Voragine, Jacobus de (c. 1230-1298). *Golden Legend*, tr. Granger Ryan and Helmut Ripperger. New York: Arno, 1969.
Voragine was Archbishop of Genoa at the height of the city's glory. This book is a large compendium of saints' lives and other Christian lore.

Vos, Gerard (1577-1649). *De Theologia Gentili.* Amsterdam, 1641; facsimile rpt., New York: Garland, 1976.
Vos was a Dutch scholar and a canon of Canterbury. This book is a work of comparative mythography.

The Wakefield Mystery Plays (14th - 15th cent.), ed. Martial Rose. New York: Norton, 1961.
The Mystery plays were typically cycles of brief plays comprehending the whole of Biblical history, from the creation to the Last Judgment.

Waleys, Thomas (fl. 1320-1340). *Metamorophsis Ovidiana moraliter explanata.* Paris, 1515.
This is yet another of the allegorical commentaries on Ovid.

Webster, John (1580?-1625?). *The Devil's Lawcase*, in *The Complete Works of John Webster*, vol. 2, ed. F. L. Lucas. Boston: Houghton Mifflin, 1928.
Webster was a playwright best known for his revenge tragedies.

Whitney, Geffrey (1548-1603). *A Choice Book of Emblemes*, London, 1586; facsimile rpt., ed. Henry Green, New York: Benjamin Blom, 1967.
This is the first emblem book in English.

Wickram, Georg (fl. 1545). *Ovidii Nasonis des aller sinnreichten Poeten Metamorphoses....* Meinz, 1545.
This is a German allegorical commentary on Ovid.

William of Conches: see Guillaume de Conches.

Wither, George (1588-1667). *A Collection of Emblemes, Ancient and Modern.* London, 1635; facsimile rpt., ed., Charles S. Hensley. Columbia: Univ. of South Carolina Press, 1975.

Wither was an English poet and emblematist.

Yong, Bartholomew (d. c. 1621): see Boccaccio, *Amorous Fiammetta*; Montemayor.

Young, Bartholomew: see Yong, Bartholomew.

Bibliography of Secondary Sources

Works cited more than once in the *Dictionary* are listed here. Works cited only once are listed in the bibliography at the end of the article in which they appear.

Adams, Alison (1991). "Cupid and the Bees." *Emblematica*, 5: 171-76.

Aerts, W. J., and M. Gosman (1988). *Exemplum et Similitudo*. Groningen: Forsten.

Allen, Don C. (1968). *Image and Meaning*. Baltimore: Johns Hopkins Univ. Press.

_____ (1970). *Mysteriously Meant*. Baltimore: Johns Hopkins Univ. Press.

Allen, Judson B., and Patrick Gallacher (1970). "Allisoun through the Looking Glass: Or Every Man His Own Midas." *ChauR*, 4: 99-105.

Allen, Michael J. B.: see Ficino, Marsilio.

Anchor Bible Dictionary, 7 vols. (1992). New York: Doubleday.

Barkan, Leonard (1986). *The Gods Made Flesh: Metamorphosis and the Pursuit of Paganism*. New Haven: Yale Univ. Press.

Bate, Jonathan (1993). *Shakespeare and Ovid*. Oxford: Clarendon Press.

Bath, Michael (1989). "Honey and Gall or: Cupid and the Bees, a Case of Iconographic Slippage," in Daly 1989: 59-94.

Becker, J. (1991). "Amphion and Hercules in Amsterdam: Vondel's Bijschrift op Diedrick Sweelinck." *SL*, 33: 49-68.

Bernardo, Aldo S., and Anthony L. Pellegrini (1983). *Dante, Petrarch, Boccaccio: Studies in the Italian Trecento in Honor of Charles S. Singleton*. Binghamton: MRTS.

_____, and Saul Levin (1990). *The Classics in the Middle Ages*. Binghamton: MRTS.

Blankert, Albert, et al. (1980). *Gods, Saints, and Heroes: Dutch Painting in the Age of Rembrandt*. Washington, D.C.: National Gallery of Art.

Bode, G. H.: see Vatican Mythographers.

Brink, Jean, et al. (1991). *Playing with Gender: A Renaissance Pursuit*. Urbana: Univ. of Illinois Press.

Brownlee, Kevin (1993). "Dante and the Classical Poets," in Rachel Jacoff, *The Cambridge Companion to Dante*. Cambridge: Cambridge Univ. Press: 100-119.

Brumble, H. David (1973). "John Donne's 'The Flea': The Implications of the Encyclopedic and Poetic Flea Traditions." *CQ*, 15: 147-54.

_____: see Bredero, Gerbrand Adriansz.

Buffière, Félix (1956). *Les Mythes d'Homère: la Pensée Grecque*. Paris: Société d'Édition "Les Belles Lettres."

Bush, Douglas (1960). *Mythology and the Renaissance Tradition in English Poetry*. New York: Norton.

Calasso, Roberto (1993). *The Marriage of Cadmus and Harmony*, tr. Tim Parks. New York: Knopf.

Camille, Michael (1991). *The Gothic Image: Ideology and Image-Making in Medieval Art*. Cambridge: Cambridge Univ. Press.

Carpenter, Thomas H., and Christopher A. Faraone (1993). *Masks of Dionysus*. Ithaca: Cornell Univ. Press.

Chance, Jane (1985). "The Origins and Development of Medieval Mythography: From Homer to Dante," in Chance and R. O. Wells, *Mapping the Cosmos*, Houston: Rice Univ. Press.

_____ (1990). *The Mythographic Art: Classical Fable and the Rise of the Vernacular in Early France and England*. Gainesville: Univ. of Florida Press.

_____ (1994). *Medeival Mythography*. Gainesville: Univ. of Florida Press.

_____: see Nitzsche, Jane Chance.

Cheney, L. De Girolami (1993). "The Chamber of Apollo of the Casa Vasari." *SI*, 15: 135-176.

Clogan, Paul M. (1968). *The Medieval Achilleid of Statius*. Leiden: Brill.

Curtius, Ernst Robert (1963). *European Literature and the Latin Middle Ages*. New York: Harper.

Daly, Peter M. (1979). *Literature in the Light of the Emblem*. Toronto: Univ. of Toronto Press.

_____ (1988). *The English Emblem Tradition*. Toronto: Univ. of Toronto Press.

_____ (1989). *Andrea Alciato and the Emblem Tradition*. New York: AMS Press.

_____, and Mary V. Silcox (1990). *The English Emblem: Bibliography of Secondary Literature*. New York: Saur.

de Lubac, Henri (1964). *Exégèse Médiévale: Les Quarte Sense de L'Ecriture*. Paris: Aubier.

Demaray, John G. (1991). *Cosmos and Epic Representation: Dante, Spenser, Milton and the Transformation of Renaissance Heroic Poetry*. Pittsburgh: Duquesne Univ. Press.

Desmond, Marilynn (1990). "Bernard Silvestris and the *Corpus* of the *Aeneid*," in A. S. Bernardo and S. Levin, *The Classics in the Middle Ages*. Binghamton: MRTS: 129-140.

De Tervarent, Guy (1958). *Attributs et Symboles dans l'Art Profane, 1450-1600: Dictionnaire d'un Langage Perdu*, 2 vols. Geneva: Droz.

De Weever, Jacqueline (1987). *Chaucer Name Dictionary*. New York: Garland.

Donker, Marjorie, and George M. Muldrow (1982). *Dictionary of Literary-Rhetorical Conventions of the English Renaissance*. Westport: Greenwood Press.

Dozon, Marthe (1991). *Mythe et Symbole dans La Divine Comédie*. Firenze: Olschki.

Dronke, Peter (1974). *Fabula: Explorations into the Uses of Myth in Medieval Platonism*. Leiden: Brill.

_____ (1984). *The Medieval Poet and His World*. Rome: Edizioni di Storia e Letteratura.

_____ (1986). *Dante and Medieval Latin Traditions*. New York: Cambridge Univ. Press.

Economou, George D. (1972). *The Goddess Natura in Medieval Literature*. Cambridge: Harvard Univ. Press.

Edwards, Robert (1990). "The Heritage of Fulgentius," in A.S. Bernardo and S. Levin, *The Classics in the Middle Ages*. Binghamton: MRTS: 141-152.

Evett, David (1989). "Some Elizabethan Allegorical Paintings: A Preliminary Inquiry," *JWCI*, 52: 140-166.

Filedt Kok, J. P. (1985). *Livelier Than Life: The Master of the Amsterdam Cabinet..., ca. 1470-1500*. Amsterdam: Rijksprentenkabinet/Rijksmuseum.

Fleming, John V. (1969). *The Roman de la Rose: A Study in Allegory and Iconography*. Princeton: Princeton Univ. Press.

Fletcher, Anthony (1995). *Gender, Sex and Subordination in England 1500-1800*. New Haven: Yale Univ. Press.

Fraenkel, Herman (1945). *Ovid: Poet between Two Worlds*. Berkeley: Univ. of California Press.

Gombrich, E. H. (1993). *Gombrich on the Renaissance*, vol. 2: *Symbolic Images*. London: Phaidon.

Green, Richard H. (1960). "Classical Fable and English Poetry," in Dorothy Bethurum, *Critical Approaches to Medieval Literature*. New York: Columbia Univ. Press: 110-133.

Greenblatt, Stephen (1993). *New World Encounters*. Berkeley: Univ. of California Press.

Hamilton, A. C., et al. (1990). *The Spenser Encyclopedia*. Toronto: Univ. of Toronto Press.

Hanfmann, G. M. A. (1980). "The Continuity of Classical Art: Culture, Myth, and Faith," in Kurt Weitzmann, *Age of Spirituality*. New York: Metropolitan Museum of Art: 75-99.

Harding, Davis P. (1946). *Milton and the Renaissance Ovid*. Urbana: Univ. of Illinois Press.

Haskins, John E. (1971). *Source and Meaning in Spenser's Allegory*. Oxford: Clarendon.

Heinrichs, Katherine (1989). "The Denizens of Hades in the Love Poems of the Middle Ages." *Neophil*, 73: 593-604.

Henkel, Arthur, and Albrecht Schöne (1967). *Emblemata: Handbuch zur Sinnbildkunst des XVI. und XVII. Jahrhunderts*. Stuttgart: Metzlersche Verlagsbuchhandlung.

Hoeniger, F. D. (1984). "Musical Cures of Melancholy and Mania in Shakespeare," in J. C. Gray, *Mirror up to Shakespeare*. Toronto: Univ. of Toronto: 54-67.

Hoffman, Richard L. (1966). *Ovid and The Canterbury Tales*. Philadelphia: Univ. of Pennsylvania Press.

Hollander, Robert (1969). *Allegory in Dante's Commedia*. Princeton: Princeton Univ. Press.

———— (1977). *Boccaccio's Two Venuses*. New York: Columbia Univ. Press.

Höltgen, Karl Josef (1986). *Aspects of the Emblem*. Kassel: Edition Reichenberger.

Hope, Charles (1985). *Veronese and the Venetian Allegorical Tradition*. London: Proceedings of the British Academy.

Jacoff, Rachel (1993). *The Cambridge Companion to Dante*. Cambridge: Cambridge Univ. Press.

————, and Jeffrey T. Schnapp (1991). *The Poetry of Allusion: Virgil and Ovid in Dante's Commedia*. Stanford: Stanford Univ. Press.

Jeffrey, David Lyle (1992). *A Dictionary of Biblical Tradition in English Literature*. Grand Rapids: Eerdmans.

Jensen, Minna Skafte (1980). *Homeric Question and the Oral-Formulaic Theory*. Copenhagen: Museum Tusculanum.

Jones, Joan: see *Chess of Love*.

Kay, Richard (1994). *Dante's Christian Astrology*. Philadelphia: Univ. of Pennsylvania Press.

Kee, Howard C. (1983). *Miracle in the Early Christian World*. New Haven: Yale Univ. Press.

Koonce, B. G. (1966). *Chaucer and the Tradition of Fame*. Princeton: Princeton Univ. Press.

Lamberton, Robert (1989). *Homer the Theologian: Neoplatonist Allegorical Reading and the Growth of the Epic Tradition*. Berkeley: Univ. of California Press.

Lascelle, M. M. (1959). "The Rider on the Winged Horse," In *Elizabethan and Jacobean Studies Presented to F. P. Wilson*, Folcroft: Folcroft Press: 173-198.

Leesberg, Marjolein (1993/1994). "Karel van Mander as a Painter." *Simiolus*, 22: 5-57.

Lemmi, Charles W. (1933). *The Classical Deities in Bacon*. Baltimore: Johns Hopkins Univ. Press.

Lightbown, Ronald (1989). *Botticelli: Life and Work*. New York: Abbeville Press.

Lloyd-Jones, Hugh (1992). "Keeping up with Homer." *NYRB*, 39, no. 5: 52-57.

Lord, Albert B. (1981). *The Singer of Tales*. Cambridge: Harvard Univ. Press.

Lotspeich, Henry Gibbons (1932). *Classical Mythology in the Poetry of Edmund Spenser*. Princeton: Princeton Univ. Press.

MacDougall, Hugh A. (1982). *Racial Myth in English History*. Hanover, N.H.: Univ. Press of New England.

Maresca, Thomas: see Bernardus Silvestris.

Martindale, Charles (1988). *Ovid Renewed: Ovidian Influences on Literature and Art from the Middle Ages to the Twentieth Century*. Cambridge: Cambridge Univ. Press.

McCall, John P. (1955). *Classical Myth in Chaucer's Troilus and Criseyde*. Princeton: Ph.D. dissertation.

_____ (1962). "The Trojan Scene in Chaucer's Troilus." *ELH*, 29: 263-275.

_____ (1979). *Chaucer among the Gods: The Poetics of Classical Myth*. University Park: Pennsylvania State Univ. Press.

McKendrick, Scot (1991). "*The Great History of Troy*: a Reassessment of the Development of a Secular Theme in Late Medieval Art." *JWCI*, 54: 43-82.

McLane, Paul E. (1968). *Spenser's Shepheardes Calender: A Study in Elizabethan Allegory*. Notre Dame: Univ. of Notre Dame Press.

Minnis, A. J., and A. B. Scott, with David Wallace (1988). *Medieval Literary theory and Criticism, c. 1100-c. 1375*. Oxford: Clarendon Press.

Moss, Ann (1982). *Ovid in Renaissance France: A Survey of the Latin Editions of Ovid and Commentaries Printed in France before 1660*. London: Warburg Inst.

Munckerus, Thomas (1681). *Mythographi latini* (a collection of Latin mythographers including Hyginus, Fulgentius, Lactantius, and Albricus). Amsterdam.

Nees, Lawrence (1991). *A Tainted Mantle: Hercules and the Classical Tradition in the Carolingian Court*. Philadelphia: Univ. of Pennsylvania Press.

Nichols, John (1823). *The Progresses and Public Processions of Queen Elizabeth...*, 3 vols. London.

Nitzsche, Jane Chance (1975). *The Genius Figure in Antiquity and the Middle Ages*. New York: Columbia Univ. Press.

_____. See Chance, Jane.

Nohrnberg, James (1976). *The Analogy of The Faerie Queene*. Princeton: Princeton Univ. Press.

O'Daly, Gerard (1991). *The Poetry of Boethius*. Chapel Hill: Univ. of North Carolina Press.

Ohly, Friedrich (1978). "Typologische Figuren aus Natur und Mythus," in Walter Haug, ed., *Formen und Functionen der Allegorie*. Stuttgart: Metzler.

Olson, Paul A. (1957). "*A Midsummer Night's Dream* and the Meaning of Court Marriage." *ELH*, 24: 95-119.

———— (1986). *The Canterbury Tales and the Good Society*. Princeton: Princeton Univ. Press.

Olsson, Kurt (1992). *John Gower and the Structures of Conversion*. Cambridge: D. S. Brewer.

Orgel, Stephen (1975). *The Illusion of Power: Political Theater in the English Renaissance*. Berkeley: Univ. of California Press.

Ormerod, David (1978). "*A Midsummer Night's Dream*: The Monster in the Labyrinth." *ShakS*, 11: 39-52.

Owst, G. R. (1966). *Literature and Pulpit in Medieval England*. Oxford: Blackwell.

Panofsky, Erwin (n.d.). *Tomb Sculpture*. New York: Abrams.

———— (1930). *Hercules am Scheidewege. Studien der Bibliothek Warburg*, no. 18.

———— (1936). "*Et in Arcadia Ego*; on the Conception of Transience in Poussin and Watteau," in *Philosophy and History, Essays Presented to Ernst Cassirer*, ed., R. Klibansky and H. Paton. Oxford: Oxford Univ. Press.

———— (1955a). *The Life and Art of Albrecht Dürer*. Princeton: Princeton Univ. Press.

———— (1955b). "*Et in Arcadia Ego*: Poussin and the Elegiac Tradition," in *Meaning in the Visual Arts*. New York: Anchor.

———— (1962). *Studies in Iconology*. New York: Harper.

———— (1966). *Early Netherlandish Painting*. Cambridge: Harvard Univ. Press.

———— (1969). *Problems in Titian, Mostly Iconographic*. New York: New York Univ. Press.

———— (1972). *Renaissance and Renascences in Western Art*. New York: Harper.

————, and Dora Panofsky (1978). *Pandora's Box: Changing Aspects of a Mythical Symbol*. Princeton: Princeton Univ. Press.

Pantel, Pauline Schmitt (1992). *From Ancient Goddesses to Christian Saints*, vol. 1 of *A History of Women in the West*, ed. Georges Duby and Michelle Perrot. Cambridge: Harvard Univ. Press.

Parent, J. M.: see Guillaume de Conches.

Parry, Milman (1971). *The Making of Homeric Verse: The Collected Papers of Milman Parry*, ed. Adam Parry. Oxford: Oxford Univ. Press.

Patterson, Lee (1991). *Chaucer and the Subject of History*. Madison: Univ. of Wisconsin Press.

Pépin, Jean (1970). *Dante et la Tradition de l'Allégorie*. Montreal: Inst. d'Études Médiévales.

Plass, Paul (1995). *The Game of Death in Ancient Rome: Arena Sport and Political Suicide*. Madison: Univ. of Wisconsin Press.

Porteman, Karel (1977). *Inleiding tot de Nederlandse emblemataliteratuur*. Groningen: Wolters-Noordhoff.

Porter, William M. (1993). *Reading the Classics and Paradise Lost*. Lincoln: Univ. of Nebraska Press.

Quint, David (1993). "Voices of Resistance: The Epic Curse and Camões's Adamastor," in Greenblatt, 1993: 241-271.

Rahner, Hugo (1971). *Greek Myths and Christian Mystery*, tr. Brian Battershaw. New York: Biblo and Tannen.

Reid, Jane Davidson (1993). *The Oxford Guide to Classical Mythology in the Arts, 1300-1990s*, 2 vols. New York: Oxford Univ. Press.

Richardson, J. Michael (1989). *Astrological Symbolism in Spenser's The Shepheardes Calender*. Lewiston, NY: Mellen Press.

Robertson, D. W., Jr. (1962). *Preface to Chaucer*. Princeton: Princeton Univ. Press.

_____ (1968). *Chaucer's London*. New York: Wiley.

Rubin, Deborah (1990). "Sandys, Ovid, and Female Chastity," in Chance 1990: 257-280.

Russell, Daniel (1985). *Emblem and Device in France*. Lexington, KY: French Forum.

Ruud, Niall (1988). "Daedalus and Icarus, from Rome to the End of the Middle Ages," and "Daedalus and Icarus, from the Renaissance to the Present Day," in Martindale 1988: 21-54.

Saxl, Fritz (1970). *A Heritage of Images: A Selection of Lectures*. Baltimore: Penguin.

Schiller, Gertrud (1971). *Iconography of Christian Art*, 2 vols. Greenwich: New York Graphics Society.

Schlam, Carl C. (1990). "Apuleius in the Middle Ages," in A. S. Bernardo and S. Levin, *The Classics in the Middle Ages*, Binghamton: MRTS: 363-369.

Schmitz, Götz (1990). *The Fall of Women in Early English Narrative Verse*. Cambridge; Cambridge Univ. Press.

Schreiber, Earl G. (1975). "Venus in the Medieval Mythographic Tradition." *JEGP*, 74: 519-535.

_____ : see Bernardus Silvestris.

Segal, Charles (1989). *Orpheus: The Myth of the Poet*. Baltimore: Johns Hopkins Univ. Press.

Seznec, Jean (1961). *The Survival of the Pagan Gods*, tr. B. F. Sessions. New York: Harper.

Shipley, Joseph (1984). *The Origins of English Words*. Baltimore: Johns Hopkins Univ. Press.

Simonds, Peggy Muñoz (1992). *Myth, Emblem, and Music in Shakespeare's Cymbeline*. Newark: University of Delaware Press.

Singleton, Charles S. (1973). *Purgatorio*, vol. 2: *Commentary*. Princeton: Princeton Univ. Press.

South, Malcolm (1987). *Mythical and Fabulous Creatures: A Source Book and Research Guide*. New York: Greenwood.

Spargo, John W. (1934). *Virgil the Necromancer: Studies in Virgilian Legends*. Cambridge: Harvard Univ. Press.

Stahl, William Harris, and Richard Johnson and E. L. Burge (1971). *Martianus Capella and the Seven Liberal Arts*, vol. 1. New York: Columbia Univ. Press.

Starnes, DeWitt T., and Ernest William Talbert (1955). *Classical Myth and Legend in Renaissance Dictionaries*. Chapel Hill: Univ. of North Carolina Press.

Steadman, John (1984). *Milton's Biblical and Classical Imagery*. Pittsburgh: Duquesne Univ. Press.

Stock, Brian (1972). *Myth and Science in the Twelfth Century*. Princeton: Princeton Univ. Press.

Taylor, Beverly (1982). "Phyllis, Canacee, Biblis, and Dido: Keys to Understanding *The Minnegrotte* of Gottfried's Tristan." *Mediaevalia*, 8: 81-95.

Thaon, Brenda (1985). "Spenser's Neptune, Nereus and Proteus: Renaissance Mythography Made Verse." *Acta Conventus Neo-Latini Bononiensis*, 4: 630-637.

Tuve, Rosemond (1966). *Allegorical Imagery*. Princeton: Princeton Univ. Press.

Vermaseren, Maarten (1977). *Cybele and Attis: The Myth and the Cult*. London: Thames and Hudson.

Watkins, John (1995). *The Specter of Dido: Spenser and Virgilian Epic*. New Haven: Yale Univ. Press.

Welles, Elizabeth B. (1990). "Orpheus and Arion as Symbols of Music in Mantegna's *Camera degli Sposi*." *SI*, 14: 113-144.

Welter, J. T. (1927). *L'Exemplum dans la littérature religieuse et didactique du moyen age*. Paris: Guitard.

Wetherbee, Winthrop (1972). *Platonism and Poetry in the Twelfth Century*. Princeton: Princeton Univ. Press.

_____ : see Bernardus Silvestris.

Whitbred, Leslie George: see Fulgentius.

Whitman, Jon (1987). *Allegory: The Dynamics of an Ancient and Medieval Technique*. Oxford: Oxford Univ. Press.

Wilhelm, James J. (1965). *The Cruelest Month: Spring, Nature, and Love in Classical and Medieval Lyrics*. New Haven: Yale Univ. Press.

Wilson, Adrian, and Joyce Wilson (1984). *A Medieval Mirror: Speculum Humanae Salvationis 1324-1500*. Los Angeles: Univ. of California Press.

Wind, Edgar (1968). *Pagan Mysteries of the Renaissance*. New York: Norton.

Winternitz, Emanuel (1979). *Musical Instruments and Their Symbolism in Western Art*. New Haven: Yale Univ. Press.

Wittkower, Rudolf and Margot (1963). *Born under Saturn: The Character and Conduct of Artists*. New York: Norton.

_____ (1971). *Architectural Principles in the Age of Humanism*. New York: Norton.

Wood, Chauncey (1970). *Chaucer and the Country of the Stars*. Princeton: Princeton Univ. Press.

Yeager, R. F. (1990). *John Gower's Poetic: The Search for a New Arion*. Cambridge: D. S. Brewer.

Zecher, Carla (1993). "Pagan Spirituality and Christian Passion: The Music of the Spheres in Sixteenth-Century French Cosmological Poetry." *FrF*, 18: 297-313.

Index

About the Author

H. DAVID BRUMBLE is Professor of English and Associate Dean for Under-
graduate Studies at the University of Pittsburgh.

ISBN 0-313-29451-8

90000>

EAN

9 780313 294518

HARDCOVER BAR CODE